MW00849100

COMMENTARY ON
REVELATION

COMMENTARY ON
REVELATION

E.W. BULLINGER

Grand Rapids, MI 49501

Commentary on Revelation by E. W. Bullinger

Published in 1984 by Kregel Classics, an imprint of Kregel
Publications, P.O. Box 2607, Grand Rapids, MI 49501.
Kregel Classics provides trusted, time-proven publications
for Christian life and ministry. Your comments and sugges-
tions are valued.

For more information about Kregel Publications, visit our
web page at http://www.kregel.com.

Cover design: Don Ellens

Library of Congress Cataloging-in-Publication Data
Bullinger, E. W. (Ethelbert William), 1837–1913.
   Commentary on revelation / E. W. Bullinger.
     p.   cm.
Reprint. Originally published: The Apocalypse. 3rd ed., rev.
and corrected. London: Eyre and Spottiswoode, 1935. With
new preface.
   Includes indexes.
   1. Bible. N.T. Revelation. English. 1984. I. Title.
BS2825.B83   1984   228'.07   82-24917
                                          CIP
ISBN 0-8254-2289-2

Printed in the United States of America

4 5 6 / 03 02 01 00 99 98 97

ANALYTICAL CONTENTS

LIST OF ABBREVIATIONS

A.—Alford's Greek Text.

A^b.—That the reading is put by Alford in brackets; and so with the other Editors.

A^m.—That the reading is put by Alford in the margin, and so with the other Editors.

Acc.—Accusative case.

AV.—The Authorised Version of 1611.

B.—Beza's Edition of the Greek Testament, 1565-1598.

E.—The Elzevir Edition of the Greek Text, 1624.

Gen.—Genitive case.

Gr.—Griesbach's Greek Text.

I.—The pronoun I when represented by a separate pronoun in the Greek; and so with all other pronouns.

LXX.—The Septuagint or Greek Translation of the Hebrew Old Testament made in the fourth century B.C. Sometimes printed lxx. or Sept.

L.—Lachmann's Greek Text.

m. or marg.—A marginal reading.

P.B.—The Prayer Book, or Coverdale's, Version of the Psalms.

RV.—The Revised Version.

S.—Stephens's Greek Text, 1550.

Sept.—The Septuagint Version. See LXX. above.

T.—Tischendorff's Greek Text.

Text Recept.—The Received Greek Text of Stephens, which was the basis of the Authorised Version.

Tr.—The Greek Text of Tregelles.

Verses in brackets denote the number of the verses in the original when they differ from the AV.

WH.—The Greek Text of Westcott and Hort.

NOTE TO THE READER

Because of the unfamiliarity of most of us today with the Roman numeral system, used throughout this book for chapter numbers, the following conversion table may offer welcome assistance to many readers:

i	1	xxii	22
ii	2	xxiii	23
iii	3	xxiv	24
iv	4	xxv	25
v	5	xxvi	26
vi	6	xxvii	27
vii	7	xxviii	28
viii	8	xxix	29
ix	9	xxx	30
x	10	xl	40
xi	11	l	50
xii	12	lx	60
xiii	13	lxx	70
xiv	14	lxxx	80
xv	15	xc	90
xvi	16	c	100
xvii	17	cx	110
xviii	18	cxx	120
xvix	19	cxxx	130
xx	20	cxl	140
xxi	21	cl	150

PUBLISHER'S PREFACE

This is an excitingly different commentary. If you are searching for a commentary that doesn't merely state the usual viewpoint, you have found it. With a bold, solidly-scriptural style, Dr. E. W. Bullinger gives us a commentary on the Book of the Revelation that challenges the traditional views with stimulating interpretation based on a presentation of parallel scriptures and facts. This is not a book to be ignored.

Dr. E. W. Bullinger departed from writing a reiteration of other men's views. The scholarly theme of this work is that the Book of the Revelation presents "The Day of the Lord." He holds to the view that the church has been raptured before the Book of Revelation opens. He believes the seven churches of Revelation 2 and 3 are seven, literal, Jewish churches or assemblies yet to come. One will find that Bullinger very definitely believes in the pre-tribulation, premillennial rapture. However, the arrangement of the details differs somewhat from that presented by other commentators. Do not allow Dr. Bullinger's Church of England background to influence your thinking. He writes with a gifted pen and an independent opinion. His scholarly manner reveals much research, a thorough knowledge of the Scriptures, and an unusual grasp of Israel's past and prophecy.

The author will definitely, instructively challenge the reader's thinking to know what he believes concerning the time periods presented in the Revelation. Bullinger's vast knowledge of the Scriptures, scholarly grasp of history, and unusual interpretative ability will excite the reader to study and to a biblical maturity.

Dr. Bullinger's literal acceptance of "thus saith the Lord" approach is refreshing. His consistent, literary assertion to allow God's Word to be totally accepted as the verbally-inspired, inerrant truth has the ring of a holy reverence seldom found in today's commentaries. The reader will readily discern that the author believes scholars and students alike should just literally accept by faith every word as God gave it (see pages 600 and 601). His individualistic manner of outlining the various portions of the book is simple and easily grasped by a reader. The footnotes are especially valuable for their extensive research and clarity. The author's other books also add understanding to this volume.*

We are glad that once again this helpful and beneficial work can be made available. Though the reader may not concur with every interpretation of the author, as is generally true of most commentators, this is one book you will not soon forget. We send it forth with the prayer that this volume on the testimony of our Lord Jesus Christ may enrich your life and witness as you expectantly await the Blessed Hope and the glorious appearing of our Lord and Savior, Jesus Christ.

---

* *The Companion Bible*; *Great Cloud of Witnesses in Hebrews Eleven*; *Number in Scripture*; *Witness of the Stars*; and *Word Studies on the Holy Spirit* are by the same author and published by Kregel Publications.

PREFACE

IT is with a sense of devout praise to God that this exposition of the Apocalypse is now completed.

It will be found to differ in its conclusions from any other work that has been issued with the same design.

It may be permitted here to specify briefly the reason of such departure : for the reader will find that traditional teaching is set aside, and history is never appealed to to substantiate any of the events of this prophetic portion of the Holy Word.

There are numberless expositions based on historical lines ; and it must be admitted, when the different writers come to be examined, no two of them agree as to the historical events that are said to fulfil, or are put forward as fulfilling, the judgments either of seals, trumpets, or vials. Good reason, therefore, exists for attempting a more self-consistent principle of interpretation. It may be said by some that there is no authority, in any previous writer, for the views presented in the following pages ; and it is true. Very few care to be thought what is termed singular or peculiar, and therefore they like to have some names to appeal to. But this is the very reason why the mists of tradition have been allowed to take the place of independent research.

Tradition is like the tether which prevents an animal from getting a blade of grass beyond the length of that tether. We thankfully acknowledge that there are a few who have been delivered from that bondage, and have given us the results of their labours in a more or less fragmentary form.

Our own work is the result of years of study devoted to the book. During these years, notes have been gathered, and are now brought together and used as forming so many links in the chain which brings to completion the work we now send forth.

The key that unlocks the door to the understanding of this book is, we believe, that it relates to

THE DAY OF THE LORD,

and not to any tradition which limits the reception of this Vision to a particular day of the week ; and that day Sunday.

It is not a question of *when* John received this vision : but of *what* he saw in it. Whether it was a Sunday or Monday can have no real relation to the book ; nor can it have any weight in determining the interpretation of the contents of the book.

Chap. i. 10, therefore, is the key to the whole book. If that day was Sunday, then what day was chap. iv. 2 ? Surely not another Sunday, but another Vision without relation to the particular day on which it was seen.

What John saw, by the Spirit's power and agency, was "the Day of the Lord," and the whole course of future events connected with that Day.

Just as the Vision which Isaiah "saw concerning Judah and Jerusalem" was *future*; and was made known to him by the Spirit; and, therefore, seen by him "in Spirit," so it was with John.

Isaiah's Vision included "the last days" (Is. ii. 1, 2) : and John's Visions refer to "the Day of the Lord."

Thus did Abraham also see Christ's Day. He saw it, and rejoiced, and was glad. It must have been "in Spirit," whatever meaning we may put upon the expression. There was no other way of his seeing Christ's Day; and that is the way in which it says John saw "the Lord's Day."

Ezekiel, too, saw Visions of the future "by the Spirit" (Ezek. xi. 24, 25 ; xl. 2, 3) concerning the events connected with the restoration of Israel (see Ezek. xi. 16-20 ; xxxiv. 13-16 ; xxxvi. 24-38, etc.).

In precisely the same way, "by the Spirit," John saw the events as they will take place in "the Day of the Lord."

This is the foundation on which the following pages are based.

In order to get a true understanding of any passage, or book, the interpretation of the *words* must be determined by the *scope of the context*.

Before the meaning of the words can be understood, the scope of the whole book must be first ascertained. And this scope can be gathered best from the *Structure*. The *Structure* is designed and calculated to present the scope in the best, clearest, and most convincing manner.

The scope can sometimes be gathered apart from the Structure. For example, the scope of 2 Peter i. 20, 21 is clearly not what Scripture *means,* but *whence it comes.* Not what its *interpretation* is, but what is its *source.* Then, its scope furnishes the key to the words " private interpretation," and shows that they must mean *its own sending forth* or *its own unfolding.** And the statement is that no prophecy of the Scripture ever came of itself, or of its own revealment. Why ?

Because it never came by the will of man at all.

How, then, did it come ?

The Holy Spirit spake by men of God (*i.e.,* by the prophets).

This example shows us how the scope of a passage enables us to determine the meaning we are to put upon the words employed in it. The opposite course will never help us, but only lead to confusion and error. We cannot hope to get the scope of a passage from the particular words that are used.

To understand the Apocalypse, therefore, we must first regard the book as a whole, or we shall be found wrongly dividing it according to some preconceived plan ; or to some mistaken idea of the meaning of certain words or phrases.

But to get the scope of a whole book we must seek for it in the Structure.

---

* The word ἴδιος (*idios*) in 77 out of 113 places is rendered *his* or *its own* ; and " private " never in any other place but this. The word ἐπίλυσις (*epilusis*) means *an unloosing* ; and occurs nowhere else in N.T.

This Structure will, of course, be open to criticism ; and it will have to commend itself to the enlightened judgment of the spiritual mind.

On page 118 we have set forth the Structure of the Book, which seems to satisfy all requirements : and it will be found perfectly consistent with itself. The divisions appear to be so natural, and so evenly balanced, that no one part can be touched without affecting or upsetting the whole.

In the first place, the Introduction (chap. i.) and the Conclusion (chap. xxii. 6-21), are seen to correspond with each other, member for member, throughout (compare the two Structures on pages 129 and 677 respectively).

Each is composed of eight pairs of members, arranged alternately.

The person testifying and the things testified, form the first pair.

A Benediction and reference to the Advent form the second pair.

There are eight of these pairs (*i.e.,* four sets of the two pairs) in the Introduction (chap. i.) ; and eight in the Conclusion (chap. xxii. 6-21) ; four of each respectively, arranged in alternation. Thus there is a perfect harmony between the two ; and they are seen to correspond in every particular.

We detect no flaw in this Correspondence ; and are, therefore, driven to the conclusion that its perfection is Divine as to its origin : one of the LORD's glorious works which are left to be " sought out of all them that have pleasure therein."

For those who are unacquainted with our use of the capital and small letters in Roman and Italic type, we ought to explain that their adoption is arbitrary. They are used merely to mark and identify the corresponding subjects as they reappear in the text. They are useful also for purposes of reference.

The *Italic* letter shows that the subject of the member, so indicated, corresponds (in similarity or contrast) with the subject of the preceding member marked by the same letter in *Roman* type.

The plan is exceedingly simple once this fact is grasped.

Returning to the Structure of the Apocalypse, we find that the great central portion is marked off into *seven pairs of Visions.* The first of each pair is a Vision of what is seen and heard "in Heaven;" and the second of each pair is a Vision of what is seen and heard "on Earth." The Heavenly Utterances explain and show the object of what is subsequently seen on Earth; and the Judgments on Earth are the consequence and outcome of what has been previously seen and heard in Heaven.

This applies to each pair respectively.

We thus see, at once, that the Apocalypse does not consist of a few chapters of Church History, confined to one small portion of the Earth; but these great divisions show that the Book concerns the closing up of God's controversy with the Universe. It includes Satan, and the fallen Angels, as well as rebellious Man. It includes all that is "in Heaven" and "on Earth."

This is further shown by the fact that in this book the word "Heaven" is always used in the *singular* number and *not once in the plural*. This tells us that the word "Heaven" is used in contradistinction from the "Earth."

When it is used in the plural it embraces the *whole sphere* of God's rule, including the Earth. But when it is used in the *singular*, it is the Heaven, as contrasted with, and distinct from, the Earth.

When we read "Our Father which art in Heaven," it is plural (the heavens). If it had been the singular, it would have implied that our Father is in Heaven, but not on the Earth! But it is plural, and shows that He is everywhere, *including the Earth.*

On the other hand, when it goes on to say "Thy will be done on Earth as it is in Heaven;" here the word is in the *singular* number, because Heaven and Earth are set in contrast, as distinct from each other.

This is the constant usage of the singular and plural of the word "Heaven."

This is its use in the Apocalypse. It is the book which specially relates to "Heaven" and "Earth"; and to the settlement of the great controversy between the two. That controversy has been going on since Satan entered the earth and brought in Ruin and Sin and Death; and was thus the cause of man's losing and being cast out of the Paradise of God on earth.

That controversy will not be closed until Satan is first bound, and then finally cast into the lake of fire. Not until Sin and Death shall have been done away, and the curse removed, shall man see and enjoy the Glory of God in Paradise Regained and Eden Restored.

This it is that links Genesis and Revelation together with an indissoluble tie ; and shows how all that was lost in the former will be regained in the latter ; and by what judgments that controversy will be closed.

Our lot is cast in " Man's day" (1 Cor. iv. 3, marg.). Now is the time when man is judging ; and few, if any, escape from experiencing sad proofs of the fact. But, thank God, "man's day" will not go on for ever. Another day is coming, and that will be "the Lord's Day." Then, He will be the Judge. Hence, we are exhorted in view of that very fact, "therefore judge nothing before the time, until the Lord come."

Yes. He is coming. He is to be revealed from Heaven : and this book of the Apocalypse records the judgments with which He will judge the earth when His day—"the Lord's day"—shall have come.

John, in vision, and by the Spirit, saw that day, as Abraham had seen Christ's day before him.

We are now permitted to hear what John saw, and to read what John wrote.

In the Introduction to the book (ch. i.) we are at once impressed with four important facts :

The Person of the Testifier,

The Things testified,

The Blessing pronounced on those who heed that testimony, and

The Advent solemnly announced.

Four times is this enforced upon us in the Introduction as the great subject which is to be preliminary to and the foundation of all that follows. Four times also at the close of the book this is repeated, and it is done in order that we might not be diverted from the great central object of the book, which is the Apocalypse or Revelation of Christ in judgment.

His Advent is the great event to which all other events lead up. It is the central subject of the whole book. Everything said and done has its own special relation to that Advent in which all the judgments culminate.

This is the scope of the book as presented by its Structure.

After we have divided off this great central portion, consisting of the seven pairs of Visions, together with the Introduction and Conclusion, all that we have left are the two portions, chaps. ii. and iii., and chap. xxi. 1—xxii. 5.

The first of these two great members is seen at once to relate to the people who are specially addressed : who are exhorted to *faithfulness* in view of those judgments which they will witness ; to *diligence* in reading and keeping in mind what is written concerning them ; to *courage and constancy* in not yielding to the Temptation to worship the Beast, or believing the lies of his False Prophet ; to *endurance* in being faithful unto death, enduring to the end. These are reminded of the special blessing for the "over-comers" in those judgment scenes.

Hence the first portion (chaps. ii. and iii.) relates to those who will be on *the Earth* in the Day of the Lord : while the latter portion (chap. xxi. 1— xxii. 5) relates to those who will dwell on *the new Earth.*

Thus, we may well believe that these are the Divine Divisions into which the whole book falls. When we study *the Divine Plan of the Ages,* as shown on page 630, we shall be confirmed in this belief ; and feel assured that we must give up all the old interpretations which proceed on the narrow lines of a Parish Vestry, and adopt the larger and grander lines which are far above even those of worldly Empire ; and see in this book the judgments which will fill up the day of the Lord, and end Heaven's great controversy with Earth.

As to the performance of our own task, it is necessary only to add a few words with regard to the principles on which it has been carried out.

As to the Text, every departure from the Greek Textus Receptus has been noted, and the authorities given. We have judged it to be simpler to note by initials the Texts of the principal editors of the Greek Testament, and not to trouble our readers (except in a few instances) with the citations of particular Manuscripts and Versions.

As to the Translation, we assume the entire responsibility, and have endeavoured to give a rendering as accurately as possible.

Where the pronouns are emphatic (being used in addition to the pronoun already included in the verb) we have printed them in black letter or German Text.

The References, where they appear without any book being named, or simply " ch.," or " chap.," are always references to the Apocalypse itself.

The parts of verses are noted as follows :—The first part of a verse we have printed 7-, a middle part as -7-, and the last part -7.

When the number of the verses in the Hebrew or Greek differ from the number in the A.V., we have put them in brackets immediately after such references.

The Abbreviations we have presented in a separate Table.

We pray God to accept and bless our humble effort to interpret this wonderful and important Book.

We believe He has ruled it ; but where, through any infirmity, we have misused His gifts, we pray Him to over-rule it.

None are more cognisant of imperfection and failure than ourselves ; and, after all we have done, there is still much left for others to do. We do not exhaust the book ; and may, after all, have only laid out a road on which others may follow with far greater success.

We claim only one thing—an earnest desire to believe God ; and to receive what He has said, regardless alike of the praise of man or the fear of man ; and quite apart from all traditional beliefs or interpretations.

May the Lord own and use and bless our efforts for His own Glory and the good of His people.

E. W BULLINGER.

PREFACE TO SECOND EDITION.

This Second Edition has been carefully revised and corrected ; and it is published with thanksgiving to God for many tokens and testimonies of His blessing on the First Edition.

E. W. BULLINGER.

1

INTRODUCTION TO
THE BOOK OF REVELATION

MANY readers of the Bible treat it as though it were like a " puzzle-picture," where we have to "find a face," or " a man," or some other object. No matter what part of the Bible may be read, the one object seems to be to " find the Church." For, the " Word of truth " not being rightly divided, or indeed divided at all, the whole Bible is supposed to be about every one, in every part, and in every age; and the Church is supposed to be its one pervading subject.

This arises from our own natural selfishness. " *We* " belong to the Church, and therefore all " *we* " read " *we* " take to ourselves, not hesitating to rob others of what belongs to them. Here is a case in point. Open your Bibles at Isa. xxix. and xxx., and at the headings of the pages, at the same opening we read, " *Judgment upon Jerusalem*," and " *God's mercies to His Church* " ! This is a " dividing " of the word (by man) indeed ! but whether it is " rightly dividing " is another matter. The book is declared to be " The vision of Isaiah . . . which he saw concerning Judah and Jerusalem." And yet in spite of this, the blessings spoken of Judah and Jerusalem are taken away and given to the *Church*, while the curses and judgments are kindly left for " Judah and Jerusalem ! "

On this system of interpretation the Bible is useless for the purposes of Divine revelation. It is made a derision to its enemies, a ground for the attacks of infidels, while it becomes a stumbling-block to its friends. And yet it is on this same principle that the Apocalypse is usually treated.

Everywhere the Church is thrust in: John (in ch. iv. 1) re-presents the Church; the living creatures, or Cherubim (ch. iv.) are the Church; the four and twenty elders (ch. iv., v.) are the Church; the 144,000 (ch. vii.) are the Church;* the great multitude (ch. vii.) is the Church; the "woman clothed with the sun" (ch. xii.) is the Church; the man-child (ch. xii.) is the Church; the bride (ch. xix.) is the Church; the "New Jerusalem" (ch. xxi.) is the Church; the "seven churches" are the Church; and so they go on, until the humble reader of the book is bewildered and disheartened. No wonder the book is neglected. The wonder would be if it were not.

Now, it is with the object of lifting those who desire to understand this prophecy out of the quagmire of tradition that we propose to write these papers.

We believe we shall best accomplish our object by departing from the usual custom of expositors, and leaving the interpretation of words and sentences and verses until after we have learned the scope of the book, and ascer-tained the great principle on which all interpretation must be based.

Let us say at once that we believe, and must believe (1), that God means what He says; and (2), that He has a meaning for every word that He says. All His works and all His words are perfect, in their choice, order and place: so perfect, that, if one word or expression is used, there is a reason why no other would have done.

On these lines we shall proceed to put forth and explain our *theses* or propositions: begging our readers not to start at the bare statement of them, but prayerfully to test the reasons which we shall give; and to remember that, while

---

* Notwithstanding they are expressly stated to be "of all the tribes of the children of Israel." Had it been for judgment that they were sealed, we should never have heard of these being "the Church."

some are sufficient of themselves to establish our position yet, we depend on the cumulative evidence of the whole of them taken together.

Our great fundamental proposition—which we may as well state at once—is, that

The Church is not the subject of the Apocalypse

However startling this may sound and may seem to some of our readers, we implore you not to dismiss it, but to test the reasons we shall give by the Word of God itself, and to weigh them in "the balances of the sanctuary." Try to forget all that you have "received by tradition," and ask *from whom* you learned this or that. Be prepared and ready to unlearn anything that you may have received from men, and learn afresh from the Word of God itself.

The first chapter furnishes us with fifteen proofs of our fundamental proposition.

Our first point, in proof of our great proposition, is

(I.) THE FIVE-FOLD DIVISION OF THE BIBLE

The whole Bible is divided into five great divisions, each determined by its subject-matter.

1. The Old Testament has for its subject the King and His coming Kingdom, in promise and prophecy.

2. The Four Gospels the Kingdom offered and rejected. The King crucified by Israel in the Land.

3. The Acts and earlier Pauline Epistles; the King and Kingdom re-offered (iii. 19-21); and rejected, by the Dispersion in Rome (Acts xxviii. 25, 26).

4. The Later Pauline Epistles. The Kingdom in abeyance. The King made Head over all things to the Church.

5. The Apocalypse. The Kingdom set up with Divine judgment, in Power-Glory. The King enthroned.

Then, during the fourth of these, we have the Epistles relating to the Mystery—the Church of God—

during this present interval, while the King is in heaven and His Kingdom is in abeyance; and, while the preaching of "the gospel of the kingdom" is suspended, and "the gospel of the grace of God" is proclaimed. Of course, if there is no difference between these two pieces of "good-news," and the kingdom is the same thing as the Church or Body of Christ, then there is an end of the whole matter; not merely of our task, but of the Bible itself. For, if words do not mean what they say when used of a plain, literal, matter of fact like this, then words are useless for the purposes of revelation altogether. We have concealment and confusion in its place; and an Apocrypha instead of an Apocalypse.

But, believing in the perfection of God's words, and not merely of His Word, we submit that we have here a first great reason for our proposition, that the Church (the body of Christ) is not the subject of the Apocalypse.

It will be easier to receive this when we come to accumulate the evidence. We submit this first reason, simply asking our readers to believe what God says.

(II.) THE HEBREW CHARACTER OF THE BOOK

Though this may be considered by some as a minor point, it is so important that it must not be passed over.

Most critical commentators have to deal with it: because from the earliest times the enemies of the Book have made use of this undeniable fact in order to argue that it has no right to a place in a Canon of the other Greek Books of the New Testament!

The Hebrew character of the book is shown in its use of idioms, expressions, words and phrases, which cannot be called Greek; and indeed is called by many "bad Greek."

Professor Godet in his *Studies on the New Testament,* says, p. 331 : " The only serious objection that can be urged against the authenticity of the Apocalypse, lies in the difference which is observable between its style, and that of the fourth Gospel. The latter is free from Aramaic expressions, the former is saturated with them." And again (p. 351), " the Apocalypse bears, from one end of it to the other, the character of a Hebrew prophecy."

The argument based on this fact by the opponents of the Apocalypse is dealt with by scholars in various ways. But the subject is not one which would be of general interest to our readers, as it is confined entirely to questions of grammar. Those who wish to see the subject exhaustively treated are referred to the *Commentary on the Apocalypse,* by Moses Stuart, who devotes over twenty pages to it (pp. 190-210).

There is however another side to the question : and that is, that, while the enemies use the fact against the Book itself, we use it against the popular interpretations of it. Though the language is Greek, the thoughts and idioms are Hebrew; and this links it on, not to the Pauline epistles, but to the Old Testament, and shows that its great subject is God's final dealings with the Jew and the Gentile ; and not the Church of God.

Connected with this fact there is another, that emphasizes it in a remarkable manner. It is not only Hebrew in character as to its linguistic peculiarities, but especially in its use of the Old Testament. Only those who have the most intimate acquaintance with the Old Testament can properly understand the Apocalypse. But all who know anything of Old Testament history cannot fail to detect the almost constant reference to it.

All the imagery—the Temple, the Tabernacle, the Ark

of the Covenant, the Altar, the Incense, the heads of the
twenty-four courses of Priests (the pattern of which David's
was a copy, 1 Chron. xxviii. 19, see chap. xxv., and compare
Heb. ix. 23, etc.), all this belongs peculiarly to Israel.

The same may be said of the judgments, which follow on
the lines of the plagues of Egypt, and therefore are to be
just as real: indeed they are to exceed *in dread reality*
those which were executed in the Exodus from Egypt.
For it is written (Ex. xxxiv. 10)—" And he said, Behold, I
make a covenant: before all thy people I will do marvels,
such as have not been done in all the earth, nor in any
nation ; and all the people among which thou art shall see
the word of the LORD ; for it is a terrible thing that I will
do with thee." It is the fulfilment of this covenant with
Israel which is the great subject of the Apocalypse.

But it is when we come to look at the literary connection between the Old Testament and the Apocalypse that
we find evidences of the most striking kind.

If we count up the number of Old Testament passages
quoted or alluded to in the New Testament,* we find
that the gospel of Matthew has a very large number,
amounting in all to 92. The Epistle to the Hebrews
comes higher still with 102. Now both these books are
connected in a special manner with Israel. Matthew, it is
universally admitted, stands out among the four Gospels as
being specially Jewish in its character. And the Epistle
to the Hebrews was specially written to Hebrews, and they
are addressed as such.

Now, when we turn to the Apocalypse, what do we find ?
The result which to our mind is overwhelming. No less
han 285 references to the Old Testament. More than

---

* We take the lists as given in Bagster's Bible.

three times as many as Matthew, and nearly three times as many as the Epistle to the Hebrews.

We ask whether this does not give the book of Revela-tion a very special connection with the Old Testament, and with Israel? It is undoubtedly written about the people of the Old Testament who are the subjects of its history. These will understand it as Gentile Christians can never hope to do.*

We are merely stating certain important facts which must be taken into account by any who are seeking to find out what the Book of Revelation is all about. The facts exist, and the question is, What do they say to us?

Not until we discover this, and thus learn the scope of the book, can we hope to understand it.

(III.) The Church not the Subject of Old Testament Prophecy

Closely connected with this foregoing point, that the book is Hebrew in character, and intended specially for Hebrews, is another undoubted fact, that the Church of God is not the subject of the Old Testament, either in history, type, or prophecy.

Passages, &c., may be found there and used to *illustrate* what is subsequently revealed. But this can be done only

---

* It is most remarkable that at the present time, 1900, a movement has been commenced in Palestine to overcome the difficulty arising from the fact of Jews assembling in Palestine speaking different languages. *Hebrew is to be made and to become the common vernacu-lar!* It is not only to be taught in all the Jewish schools, but all other subjects are to be learnt in Hebrew. With this fact must be stated another, and that is the recent wide-spread publication of the Salkinson-Ginsburg Hebrew New Testament by the Trinitarian Bible Society and the Mildmay Mission to the Jews, amounting to some three-quarters of a million copies.

by way of *application*, and not by way of teaching or of *interpretation*.

Because, of the "Mystery" or the *secret* concerning the Church of God, we are told that it "was kept secret since the world began " (Rom. xvi. 25). That "in other ages it was not made known unto the sons of men " (Eph. iii. 5). That it, " from the beginning of the world, hath been hid in God " (Eph. iii. 9). That it " hath been hid from ages and from generations, but now is made manifest to the saints " (Col. i. 26).

These statements are " the true sayings of God," and not our own. We have no choice but to believe what He says. If any hold that, in spite of all this, the Church was not " hid in God," but was the subject of Old Testament prophecy, then we have nothing more to say to them ; for, if they will not believe God, it is not likely they will believe us.

But, believing God, we ask whether the Church is likely to be the subject of prophecy in the Apocalypse, especially when its future is clearly foretold in the Epistles which contain the revelation of the Mystery. There we learn what is to be the future and end of the Body of Christ. The members of that Body are merely waiting to be " received up in glory " (1 Tim. iii. 16). They are waiting for their "calling on high " (Phil. iii. 14). They are looking for the Saviour, the Lord Jesus Christ, who shall change their vile bodies that they may be fashioned like unto His own glorious body (Phil. iii. 20, 21).

But all this, we submit, takes place before the Apocalypse opens. There we have, not the coming of the Lord to take away His Church, but, the revelation of the events which shall take place after the Church has been " received up in glory." These events will take place during " the day of the Lord," when He shall come, not in grace, but in judgment ; not in mercy, but in wrath. But this brings us to our fourth point. What is the meaning ot " the Lord's Day," in chap. i. 9 ?

(IV.) THE LORD'S DAY

In Rev. i. 9 we are told that John saw and received this revelation on " the Lord's Day." Leaving the former part of this verse for the present, let us notice the latter expression, " the Lord's Day."*

The majority of people, being accustomed from their infancy to hear the first day of the week called the Lord's Day, conclude in their own minds that that day is thus called in Rev. i. 9 because that was the name of it. But the contrary is the fact : the day is so called by us because of this verse.

In the New Testament this day is *always* called " the first day of the week." (See Matt. xxviii. 1. Mark xvi. 2, 9. Luke xxiv. 1. John xx. 1, 19. Acts xx. 7. 1 Cor. xvi. 2). Is it not strange that in this one place a different expression is thought to refer to the same day ? And yet, so sure are the commentators that it means Sunday, that some go as far as to say it was " Easter Sunday," and it is for this reason that Rev. i. 10-19 is chosen in the New Lectionary of the Church of England as the 2nd Lesson for Easter Sunday morning.

There is no evidence of any kind that " the first day of the week" was ever called " the Lord's Day " before the Apocalypse was written. That it should be so called afterwards is easily understood, and there can be little doubt that the practice arose from the misinterpretation of these words in Rev. i. 9. It is incredible that the earliest use of a

---

* For further information on this subject see a separate pamphlet on *The Lord's Day*, by the same author and publisher, 1907.

term can have a meaning which only subsequent usage makes intelligible.

On the contrary, it ceased to be called by its Scripture name ("the First day of the week"), not because of any advance of Biblical truth or reverence, but because of declension from it. The Greek "Fathers" of the Church were converts from Paganism : and it is not yet sufficiently recognized how much of Pagan rites and ceremonies and expressions they introduced into the Church; and how far Christian ritual was elaborated from and based upon Pagan ritual by the Church of Rome. Especially is this seen in the case of baptism.*

It was these Fathers who, on their conversion, brought the title "Sunday" into the Church from the Pagan terminology which they had been accustomed to use in connection with their Sun-worship.

Justin Martyr (114-165 A.D.) in his second *Apology* (*i.e.*, his second defence of Christianity), says,† in chap. lxvii. on "The weekly worship of the Christians,"—"On the day called SUN-DAY ‡ all who live in the country gather together to one place. . . . SUN-DAY is the day on which we all hold our common assembly, because it is the first day on which God, having wrought a change in the darkness and matter, made the world ; and Jesus Christ our Saviour on the same day rose from the dead. For He was crucified on the day before that of SATURN [*i.e.*, Saturn's day] ; and on the day after that of Saturn, which is the day of the SUN, having appeared to His apostles and disciples, He

---

* See *The Buddha of Christendom*, by Dr. Robert Anderson, C.B. Hodder and Stoughton, page 68 and chap. ix.

† T. and T. Clark's edition, pages 65, 66.

‡ τῇ τοῦ Ἡλίου λεγομένῃ ἡμέρᾳ, *tee tou Heliou legomenee hecmera.*

taught them these things, which we have submitted to you also for your consideration."

It is passing strange that if John called the first day of the week " the Lord's Day," we find no trace of the use of such a title until a hundred years later. And that though we do find a change, it is to " Sunday," and not to " the Lord's Day "—a name which has become practically universal.*

Some Christians still perpetuate the name of Lord's Day for Sunday : but it is really the survival of a Pagan name, with a new meaning, derived from a misunderstanding of Rev. i. 9.

Objection has been taken to the interpretation of " the Lord's Day " here, because we have (in i. 9) the adjective " Lord's " instead of the noun (*in regimen*), " of the Lord," as in the Hebrew. But *what else could it be called in Hebrew ?* Such objectors do not seem to be aware of the fact that there is no adjective for " Lord's " in Hebrew ; and therefore the *only way of expressing* "the Lord's Day " is by using the two nouns, " the day of the Lord "—which

---

* The French, Spanish, and Italian nations have retained the Roman Pagan names. The English is tainted with Scandinavian mythology. The 1st day they call *Dies Dominica*, the Lord's Day (*i.e.*, the day of the lord, the sun). All the Oriental nations called the sun "*lord.*" The Persians called their God *Mithra* (the sun), *i.e.*, the lord *Mithra*. The Syrians called it *Adonis*, which is from the Hebrew *Adonai*, lord. The Hebrews called it *Baal* (which means lord) and *Moloch*. Porphyry, in a prayer to the sun, calls him " Dominus Sol." The Romans kept the Pagan name, *Dies Dominica* (the day of the lord sun), for the first day of the week ; but called the others by the names of the moon and planets to which they were dedicated. Thus we have *Dies Lunae* (day of the moon), *Dies Martis* (day of Mars), *Dies Mercurii* (day of Mercury), *Dies Jovis* (day of Jupiter), *Dies Veneris* (day of Venus), *Dies Saturnii* (day of Saturn).

means equally "the Lord's Day" (Jehovah's day). It is useless, therefore, to make any objection on this ground; for if a Hebrew wanted to say "the Lord's Day," he *must* say "the day of the Lord."

In the Greek there are *two* ways of expressing this (as in modern languages); either by saying literally, as in Hebrew, "the day of the Lord" (using the two nouns); or by using the adjective "Lord's" instead. It comes to exactly the same thing as to *signification ;* the difference lies only in the *emphasis.*

The *natural* way of qualifying a noun is by using an adjective, as here—κυριακῇ, (*kyriakee*) *Lord's ;* and, when this is done, the emphasis takes its natural course, and is placed on the noun thus qualified ("day"). But when the emphasis is required to be placed on the word "Lord;" then, instead of the adjective, the noun would be used in the genitive case, "of the Lord." In the former case (as in Rev. i. 9), it would be "the Lord's DAY." In the latter case it would be "THE LORD'S day." The same day is meant in each case, but with a different emphasis.

By way of illustration and proof, we may call attention to the fact that we have the corresponding expressions concerning another "day." In Luke xvii. 22 we have "the days of the Son of Man," where the emphasis must be on "THE SON OF MAN" (as shown by the context). While in 1 Cor. iv. 3 we have "man's DAY," with the emphasis on "day," marking that "day" as being actually present, as it now is. This is so clear from the context that it is actually translated "judgment," which is exactly what it means. The apostle says—"It is a very small thing, that I should be judged of you, or of man's DAY.". The emphasis is on day, because the time in which we now live is the time, or "day," when man is judging. Another day is coming, and that is the day when the Lord will be present, and He will be the judge. This is the reason why the adjective ἀνθρωπίνη (*anthrōpinee*) *man's*, is used in 1 Cor. iv. 3 ; and this is why κυριακῇ (*kyriakee*), *Lord's*, is used in Rev. i. 9. So far from the use of the adjective being an argument against our conclusion, it is an argument in favour of it. For what is the " DAY of the Lord " or " the LORD'S day " ? The first occurrence of the expression (which is the key to its meaning) is in Isa. ii. 11.* It is the day when " the lofty looks of man shall be humbled,

---

* It should be noted that the expression יוֹם יְהוָֹה (*yōm Jehovah*, the day of the LORD, occurs (in the Hebrew Bible) *sixteen* times, *viz.*, Isa. xiii. 6, 9. Ezek. xiii. 5, Joel i. 15; ii. 1, 11; iii. 14; iv. 14. Amos v. 18 (twice), 20. Obad. 16 (Heb. 15). Zeph. i. 7, 14 (twice), and Mal. iv. 5 (Heb. iii. 23).

In *four* other places where we have in the English Bible "the day of the LORD," the Hebrew has the preposition *lamed* (לְ) *for* or *to*, before the word Jehovah. In Isa. ii. 12, Ezek. xxx. 3, and Zech. xiv. 1 it means " a day for Jehovah "; and in Zech. xiv. 7 it means "a day (known) to Jehovah."

In other places where we have in English " the day of the LORD,' there is some other word between *yōm* and *Jehovah* in the Hebrew (such as " wrath " or " vengeance ; " *i.e.*, the day of the wrath of the LORD) ! and therefore these cannot be included as examples of this expression, " the day of the LORD."

In the New Testament the expression occurs *four* times; *viz.*, 1 Thess. v. 2. 2 Thess. ii. 2 (according to all the critical Greek texts and R.V., instead of " the day of Christ.") 2 Pet. iii. 10, and Rev. i. 10.

It is remarkable that all these occurrences are stamped with the number *four*, which marks that day as having special relation to *the earth*. In the New Testament four times. In the Old Testament, with the preposition, four times ; and simply *yōm Jehovah* 16 times (*i.e.*, the square of four). This is merely a note in passing, but it is most significant.

and the haughtiness of men shall be bowed down, and the
LORD alone shall be exalted."

That is the one great object of all the future events, seen
by John in vision, and recorded for us in the Apocalypse.

One other fact has to be stated, and that is the reason
why the first day of the week came to be called " Sunday."
It was called by the Pagans " *Dominus Sol,*" the Lord
Sun. Hence the Latin name " *Dies Dominica,*'
used by the early Christian Fathers for the Sunday,
and the speedy transition of its name from " the Lord
Sun " to " the Lord's Day," and then " Sunday." Bingham (*Ant.* xx., sec. 5) mentions the fact that it was the
custom in the Primitive Church to replace heathen days and
festivals by those which were Christian. We see one result
of this in our Yule-tide and Christmas. Bingham (*Ant.*
xx., sec. 2) also mentions the fact that the early Christians
were charged with being worshippers of the sun. Tertullian
also admits that Christians were only looked upon by some
as a sect of sun worshippers : * while some account for
this on other grounds : (*e.g.,* the sects of the Gnostics and
Basilideans having retained or introduced solar forms of
worship). Yet these facts are better and more fully
accounted for by the adoption of the name " the Lord's
Day" for the Sunday ; while it serves to throw light on
the transition from the original name of "the first day
of the week."

From all this evidence we feel justified in believing that
the Apocalypse consists of a series of visions, which set
forth the events connected with " the Revelation of Jesus
Christ," which will take place during " the Lord's
DAY ; " that day being so called because it is viewed as

---

* Tertullian *Ad Nationes*, Bk. i. chap. xiii., and *Apologeticus*, C. 16.
(*Latter half.*)

being *then present*; and as it had been called heretofore in prophecy, "the day of the LORD."

(V.) THE TITLES OF CHRIST

The titles used of the Lord Jesus Christ in the Revelation afford further evidence as to the Church of God not being the subject of that Book.

We propose to consider seven of these, all used in the Introduction (chap. i.).

The most important of these is that given in connection with His vision in chap. i. 13-16. In ver. 13, He is called

(1) " THE SON OF MAN "

This is a title connected with the Lord Jesus in relation to the *earth*. Its first occurrence in Psa. viii. fixes its peculiar signification. That Psalm begins and ends with a reference to the " earth," and, after speaking of " the Son of Man," it adds : "Thou madest him to have dominion over the works of Thy hands."

It will be found, therefore, that wherever this title occurs, it always refers to the Lord Jesus in connection with His *dominion in the earth*.* And, when used of His second coming, it refers to the judgment which He is then and there to exercise.

It is most remarkable, and so remarkable as to make it practically conclusive, that this title, while it occurs eighty-four times in the New Testament, is *never once used* in the Pauline epistles addressed to Churches ; thus proving that this title has nothing whatever to do with the Church. But while it has no connection with the Church, in the Epistles, it occurs no less than eighty times in the four Gospels and Acts, because there we have Christ on the *earth*, and the presentation of the King and the Kingdom.

---

* See *The Divine Names and Titles*, by Dr. Bullinger,

But, when again he reveals Himself by this title, it is in the Book of Revelation (i. 13 and xiv. 14).*

Thus we are pointed to the fact, and told (if we have ears to hear), that the Apocalypse relates to the coming of "the Son of Man" to exercise judgment in and assume dominion over the *earth.*

It is remarkable that the first use of the title in the New Testament is in Matt. viii. 20, where it is said: "The Son of Man hath not where to lay His head": and the last is in Rev. xiv. 14, where the Son of Man is seen "having on His head a golden crown." Both are connected with his "head," and with the *earth;* while in the latter there is associated both judgment and dominion.

The significance of this title is further proved by its contrast with the title "Son of God" in John v. 25-27: "Verily, I say unto you, the hour is coming, and now is, when the dead shall hear the voice of THE SON OF GOD, and they that hear shall live. For as the Father hath life in Himself, so hath He given to the Son to have life in Himself; and hath given Him authority to execute judgment also; *because* He is THE SON OF MAN."

It is thus clear that the use of this title twice in Revelation (i. 13 and xiv. 14), and not once in the Church Epistles, is a further proof that the Church is not the subject of the Apocalypse.

The Church has no more to do with Christ under the title of "The Son of Man" than the Syro-Phœnician woman had anything to do with Him as "the Son of David."

We ought to add that this fact is a key to all the passages where this title is used: and shows that Matt. xxiv. and

---

* Between the Gospels and the Revelation there are only two occurrences, one where Stephen sees Him (Acts vii. 56) in a vision, standing as though to avenge the blood of His servant, then being shed on the *earth* (anticipatory of His action in the Apocalypse); and once in Heb. ii. 6, where it is merely a quotation of Psalm viii.

xxv. have nothing whatever to do with the Church of God, because of the use of this title in xxiv. 30, and xxv. 31. Both refer to His coming in clouds to the earth in judgment, after the Church has been taken up, and after the Great Tribulation.

(2) " THE ALMIGHTY " (i. 8, etc)

This title is used *nine* times* in the Apocalypse, and only once elsewhere in the rest of the New Testament (2 Cor. vi. 18).†

It is παντοκράτωρ *(pantokrator)* and means *having dominion over all*, and is used in the Old Testament as the Septuagint translation of " LORD of Hosts " (Heb., *Jehovah, Sabaioth ;* see 2 Sam. v. 10 ; vii. 25, 27).

In Revelation the title is used in i. 8 ; iv. 8 ; xi. 17 ; xv. 3 ; xvi. 7, 14 ; xix. 6, 15, 22.

" The LORD of Hosts " means Jehovah of the hosts in heaven above, and on the earth beneath ; and especially of the hosts of Israel. Its first occurrence is (as usual) most significant (see 1 Sam. i. 3, 11 ; and iv. 4), when Israel was reduced to a low estate—oppressed by the Philistines. All had failed. The Judges had failed. The priests (witness Eli) had failed : there was " no king in Israel : " and God's sanctuary was defiled.

But the revelation of this title at this juncture, and here used for the first time, told of the blessed fact that there was going to be a king ; and a judge too ; as well as a Priest upon His throne ; that the sanctuary was going to be cleansed (Rev. xi.)., and the oppressors of Israel destroyed.

---

* *Nine* is the number of *judgment* (see *Number in Scripture* by the same Author.)

† *Ten* is the number of *ordinal perfection.*

Israel is, conversely, called "The Lord's Host" (see Exod. xii. 41), when, at the moment of the formation of the nation at the end of the 430 years of sojourning and servitude, and the birth of the new nation at the Exodus, we read these most significant words : "And it came to pass at the end of the 430 years, even the self-same day it came to pass, that all the hosts of the LORD went out of the land of Egypt."

And further, we may note that, in Joshua v. 14, 15, we have the real connection between "The LORD of Hosts" and "The Hosts of the LORD." Jehovah-Jesus announces His coming as "the Captain of the LORD'S Host," to lead them on, to fight their battles, to judge the nations, and give them rest, and settle them in their own land.

Now, we ask, Is it not most significant that this is the title used here in the Apocalypse, *nine* times ? Does not the fact speak to us and say that, when that book opens Israel is in low estate ? That Priests and people alike have failed, and there is "no king." Does it not say that "the Captain of the Lord's host" is coming down as their judge and vindicator, to deliver them from their oppressors, to fight for them, and give them rest, and to bring them into their own land ?

Surely the association of this title, *Pantokratōr*, with the LORD of Hosts in the Old Testament, and with Israel; its frequent use in Revelation, and its practical absence in the Church Epistles, shuts us up to the fact that we have in this book, not the Church, but that which concerns the Jew and the Gentile.

It is in this book we have that which the first occurrence of the title in the Book of Psalms relates to :

"Who is this King of glory (*i.e.*, this glorious King)?
The LORD of Hosts—He is the King of glory."

And it is the object of the Apocalypse to show how this comes about, and how He becomes the King of kings and Lord of lords (xix. 16). And how all " the kingdoms of the world are become the kingdoms of our Lord and of His Christ" (xi. 15).

Then, too, will Israel fulfil the forty-sixth Psalm, and say :
"The LORD of Hosts is with us;
The God of Jacob is our refuge."

(3) "LORD GOD" (i. 8)

In i. 8 the title "God" must be added to the word "Lord," according to all the Critical Greek Texts* and the R.V.

In chap. xxii. 6 we have the same title. Thus at the end of the book and at the beginning we have this peculiar title, which seems to enclose all that the book contains, and stamp it all with that which the title signifies. What it signifies is clear from the place where we first find it, viz., in the second of the twelve divisions of Genesis (chap. ii. 4—iv. 26). This division is called " the generations of the heavens and of the earth."

In the Apocalypse we have the final results of all that pertains to the heavens and the earth.

The title " LORD God " is the title used in this division, which treats of the settlement of man in Paradise, or garden of the Lord. In the New Testament it first appears in the Apocalypse; where it has reference to the undoing of the effects of the curse (described in that section of Genesis), and to the making of the earth again into the Paradise† of God—the garden of the Lord.

---

* Griesbach, Lachmann, Tischendorf, Tregelles, Alford, Westcott and Hort.

† The word Paradise occurs in the New Testament *three* times. Luke xxiii. 43, where the Lord spoke of it in promise and prophecy; in 2 Cor. xii. 9, whither Paul was caught away ; and in Rev. ii. 7.

The title implies all this : *viz.*, that God is about to do all that Jehovah has revealed. For *Elohim* is the God of *creation* and the commencement of life, while *Jehovah* is the God of *revelation* and the development and sustainer of life with regard to His covenant People. *Elohim* (God) expresses the *power* which accomplishes ; *Jehovah* (LORD) the *grace* which provides.

Hence in Gen. ii. 4—iv. 26, and in Rev. i. 8, and xxii. 6 we meet with this title ; which links the two books together in a most remarkable manner, and gives the pledge that Paradise lost will become Paradise regained ; and that the curse which drove man out shall no longer keep him out, but shall be " no more " for ever.

This use of the title " Lord God " thus assures us that He who made the promise of Gen. iii. 15, that the Serpent's head should one day be crushed, will, in His own day (the Lord's day), finally crush the Serpent's head.

The fact that this title is never used in connection with the Church of God, affords us one more great and important proof of our proposition that that Church is not the subject of the Apocalypse, but that it has to do with the Jew and the Gentile.

(4) "THE FIRST AND THE LAST" (i. 11)

This title is used in Rev. i. 11. It is used again in i. 17, ii. 8, and xxii. 13, but is never found in connection with " the Church of God." On the other hand, it is a title closely associated with " the Jew and the Gentile," as the following Scriptures will testify.

Is. xli. 4, 5 : " Who hath wrought and done it, calling the generations from the beginning? I, Jehovah, THE FIRST AND LAST; I am He. The isles saw it, and feared ; the ends of the earth were afraid."

Is. xliv. 6 : "Thus saith the LORD, the King of Israel, and his Redeemer, the LORD of hosts ; I AM THE FIRST, AND I AM THE LAST ; and beside me there is no God."

Is. xlviii. 12 : "Hearken unto me, O Jacob, and Israel, my called; I am he ; I AM THE FIRST, I ALSO AM THE LAST. Mine hand hath laid the foundation of the earth, and my right hand hath spanned the heavens: when I call unto them, they stand up together."

Is it not clear, almost to certainty, that when the Lord Jesus specially reveals Himself by this title, never using it again till He claims it in the book of Revelation four* times, He means to teach us that He is come to act on behalf of Israel and in connection with that People with which this title is thus peculiarly associated ?

The connection of Isaiah with Revelation in the use of this title is eloquent to all who have "ears to hear."

(5) "THE PRINCE OF THE KINGS OF THE EARTH"

This is a title used only in this book (i. 5). Many kings are mentioned and referred to in the book : but the Lord Jesus comes as their "Prince ;" "King of kings and Lord of lords."

The word is ἄρχων (*archōn*), and occurs in the New Testament 37 times. It is used of earthly rulers, and spirit rulers of this age; also of Christ (only of Christ) in relation to the earth; but never in relation to or in connection with the Church.

He it is of whom His God and Father has declared, "I will make Him my first-born, higher than the kings of the earth" (Ps. lxxxix. 27).

It is in connection with the earth that He comes, in Revelation, and hence this title is used. Another testimony to the truth of our proposition.

---

* *Four* being the number that relates specially to the *earth*.

(6) "WHO IS TO COME" (i. 8)

This also is a definite title of Christ; ὁ ἐρχόμενος (*ho erchomenos*), THE COMING ONE.

It is not, who is "about to come," * as though it were announcing a fact or an act, as being near at hand : but, it describes a person who has this for His special title, by which He came to be known. He has borne that title ever since the great prophecy and promise of Gen. iii. 15. From that time the coming "seed of the woman" has always been the hope of God's People, and hence He is "The Coming One."

True, he was rejected ; therefore that coming is now in abeyance. The book of Revelation is a prophecy giving further details concerning that same coming. The Church of God waits for the Saviour, not as the coming one to the earth. It is as *going* ones we wait for Him, looking to be caught up to meet Him in the air.

" The Coming One " is His special title, which connects Him with the Old Testament prophecies.

The title is never once used in any of the Church epistles. We have it variously rendered :—

"That cometh," Luke xix. 38. John xii. 13.

" He that cometh," Matt. iii. 11 ; xxi. 9 ; xxiii. 39. John i. 15 ; iii. 31 (twice).

" Who coming," John i. 27.

" He that shall come," Heb. x. 37.

" Which (or that) should come," John vi. 14 ; xi. 27.

" He that (or which) should come," Matt. xi. 3. Luke vii. 19, 20. Acts xix. 4.

---

* This would be ὁ μέλλων ἔρχεσθαι (*ho mellōn erchesthai*).

" Which is (or art) to come," Rev. i. 4, 8; iv. 8.✱

Sixteen times we have the title in the Gospels and Acts and Heb. x. 37 ; and then, not again until Revelation ; when it is used *three* times of Him who was about to fulfil the hope of His People.

This again stamps this prophecy as having to do with Christ as God, who " is " (essential being), and " was " (in eternity past), and is " the coming one " (time future).

(7) " THE LIVING ONE " (i. 18)

" I am He that liveth, and was dead " (i. 18).   ὁ ζῶν (*ho zōn*), THE LIVING ONE.   Like the previous title, it is used as a special designation of the One whose unveiling is about to be shewn to John.

Its use is peculiar to Daniel and Revelation.   The two books thus linked together by it are linked as to their character and subject matter in a very special manner.

It is used twice in Daniel :—Dan. iv. 34 (31†) and xii. 7 ; and six times in Revelation :—Rev. i. 18‡; iv. 9, 10; v. 14 ; x. 6 ; and xv. 7.‡

In Dan. iv. 34 (the first occurrence), we read of Nebuchadnezzar, " I praised and honoured HIM THAT LIVETH for ever ; whose dominion is an everlasting dominion, and his kingdom is from generation to generation ; and all the

---

✱ " Which art to come," in Rev. xi. 17, was inserted by a later scribe, thinking to make it harmonize with i. 4, 8 ; and iv. 8.   It must be omitted according to all the Critical Greek Texts (G. L. T. Tr. A. W.H.) and the R.V.   It clearly is out of place here, because the twenty-four elders say, " We give thee thanks, O Lord God Almighty, which art, and wast, because thou hast taken to thee thy great power, and reignedst " (not hast reigned).   The coming had already taken place in Rev. xi. 17 : and therefore the title of " the Coming One" is omitted in this passage.

† Verses in parentheses indicate the number of the verse in the Hebrew Bible, where it differs from that of the English Bible.

‡ It is referred to in ii. 8, but not used.

inhabitants of the earth are reputed as nothing ; and he doeth according to his will in the army of heaven, and among the inhabitants of the earth."

That exactly expresses what He who reveals Himself by the title, " He that liveth," in Rev. i. 18, has there come to do.

He is coming with the armies of heaven (Rev. xix. 14) to take the kingdom and the dominion, and to do his will among the inhabitants of the earth (not the church or the churches).

Dan. xii. 7 and Rev. x. 6 are so similar that we put them side by side. Both refer to and contrast Christ's relation to *eternity* and to *time* :

" He (the angel) held up his right hand and his left to heaven, and sware by *him that liveth for ever* that it shall be for a time, times, and a half, and . . . all these things shall be finished" (Dan. xii. 7).	" And the angel . . . lifted up his hand to heaven, and sware by *him that liveth for ever and ever* . . . that there should be time (R.V. marg., *delay*) no longer" (Rev. x. 5, 6).

Who can doubt that Daniel and Revelation are identical as to their scope ; and that they relate, not to this present church period at all, but to the time when " he that liveth," or the Living One, shall come to exercise dominion in the earth, and this in connection, not with the grace of God, but with "the wrath of God " (Rev. xv. 7)? The double testi-mony of *two* witnesses, in Daniel and Revelation, bespeak the fact that this title relates entirely to the earth, and to man.*

The church is *heavenly* in its calling, its standing, its hope, and its destiny. But here, everything relates to the execution of judgment on the *earth*, and upon *man*.

---

* For *six* is the number which marks it as relating to *man* ; while the total number, *eight* (twice *four*) connects it with the earth.

There is a related title which is also very significant, "the living God." This is used in both Testaments, and indiscriminately, because it has no special reference either to Israel or to the church ; but because of a latent reference it always has, to *idols*, and to judgment on idolaters. This is often expressed in the context; but where it is not actually expressed in words, the thought of idols and idolatry and idolaters has to be supplied mentally.

The title ("the living God") occurs 13 times in the Old Testament (Hebrew), and twice in the Chaldee (Dan. vi. 20, 26), fifteen times in all. It begins in connection with apostasy (13), but ends in grace and blessing (15 = 3 × 5).

In the New Testament it occurs *sixteen* times (4 × 4) the square of *four*, four being the number specially associated with the *earth*.

The whole matter is so important and full of interest, that we venture to give all the references.

The first, Deut. v. 26 (23) gives the key (as usual) to the whole. It is in connection with the giving of the Ten Commandments (with special reference to the *second*, iv. 19), when they "heard the voice of *the living God* (Elohim) speaking out of the midst of the fire."

We say that the title here used is in connection with idolatry ; and especially in its most ancient and universal form, *sun-worship*.

A few verses before (Deut. iv. 19), we read, "Lest thou lift up thine eyes to heaven, and when thou seest the sun, and the moon, and the stars, even all the host of heaven, shouldest be driven to worship them, and to serve them," etc.

The whole heathen world worshipped the sun and the host of heaven ; because they "associated with them certain human characters who had really performed the actions

which were thence ascribed to the celestial bodies."* The
sun had various attributes; and one was "the living one."†
The sun has a conspicuous place in freemasonry; and sun-
worship has its ramifications throughout the whole world.
We cannot impede our argument by giving further details
here. We have put them together in an Appendix, where
our readers may see the evidence for themselves.

Our point is this; that the first use of the title "the
living God" has to do with the *voice* out of the midst of
the *fire*; and the last use of it (in Rev. vii. 2) is where God's
servants are sealed with "the seal of the living God," so as
to be kept from the then coming most awful phase of
idolatry the world has ever seen, even the worship of the
Beast; and to be preserved from and through the consequent judgments which shall come on those worshippers.

In Deut. xxxii. 40, 41, we have (not the title, but) words
which connect the thought contained in it with that time
of judgment.

Deut. xxxii. contains that "Song of Moses," of which
Rev. xv. 3 speaks, and the time referred to is Apocalyptic
time. "For I lift up my hand to heaven, and say, I live
for ever. If I whet my glittering sword, and mine hand take
hold on judgment; I will render vengeance to mine enemies,
and will reward them that hate me" (De. xxxii. 40, 41).

Ps. xviii. 46 48 (47-49). ' The LORD liveth . . . It is
God that avengeth me, and subdueth the people under me.
He delivereth me from mine enemies:" etc.

The title also has to do with Israel's restoration and
deliverance. See Jer. xvi. 14, 15; xxiii. 7, 8.

The judgment on those who use this title of idols is
described in Amos viii. 14.

---

* Faber's *Mystery of Pagan Idolatry*, vol. ii. 223:
† *Adventures in New Guinea*, p. 56, Sampson, Low & Co.

If our readers will compare all the occurrences which we now give of this title, "the living God," they will see how (as a whole) they refer to Israel, to Gentiles, to the earth, to idolaters, and to idols.

Deut. v. 26 (23). Josh. iii. 10. 1 Sam. xvii. 26, 36, where David uses it against the defiance of Goliath. 2 Kings xix. 4, 16. Isa. xxxvii. 4, 17, where it is used against the reproach of Sennacherib. Ps. xlii. 2 (3); lxxxiv. 2 (3), where it is used with a latent reference to the false gods which others worship and seek. So Jer. x. 10 ; xxiii. 36, and Hos. i. 10 (ii. 1).

In the New Testament the usage is the same. Matt. xvi. 16 ; xxvi. 63. John vi. 69. Acts xiv. 15. Rom. ix. 26. 2 Cor. iii. 3 ; vi. 16. 1 Thess. i. 9 (idols). 1 Tim. iii. 15 ; iv. 10 ; vi. 17. Heb. iii. 12 ; ix. 14 ; x. 31 ; xii. 22 ; and Rev. vii. 2. Sixteen in all (4 in the Gospels and Acts, 4 in the Church Epistles, 3 in the Pastoral Epistles, 4 in Hebrews, and once in Revelation).

Enough has been said on this particular title, and upon the seven as a whole, to show that they all link on the book of Revelation to the Old Testament and the Gospels, *and not to the Church*; and that their cumulative testimony is that Christ is revealed in this book, not in the character in which He is presented to the Church of God, but in that character in which He is revealed in the Old Testament in relation to Israel and the Earth, which is again taken up in the Apocalypse.

There are other titles of Christ in this book which all add their own testimony; but these we can leave for the present, till we come to them in their own place. Enough has been said to show that these titles assumed by the Lord Jesus in the first chapter of this book shut it entirely off, by way of interpretation, from the Church, which is His Body.

(VI.) The People of the Book

"Servants"

This expression tells us who the persons are who are specially concerned in this book ; and to whom the Revelation of Jesus Christ is shown. At the very outset we are thus warned that we are no longer on, but quite off, the ground of the Pauline Epistles, which are addressed to " sons," and not to " servants."

The word is δοῦλος, *doulos*, and means *a bond servant.*

Now, without denying that the members of the Body of Christ are in a certain sense the servants of Christ, yet it is also perfectly clear that this is not their title as to their standing in Christ before God. It is distinctly declared to each of them, " Thou art no more a servant, but a son " (Gal. iv. 7). This is the one great point which is insisted on with reference to their new position in Christ.

Throughout the Old Testament, in passages too numerous to be counted, God's People Israel are constantly spoken of as His servants. This fact is too well known to need anything more than its bare statement.

Its significance will be at once seen when we come to the New Testament Scriptures. There we find the same use of the word whenever Israel is in question. It occurs 124 times ; but as in 39 of these it refers to domestic servants, or those who serve man, we have to deal only with the 85 occurrences where it is used with reference to God. Of these 85, no less than 59 are in the Gospels and Acts. Only six in the Church Epistles (Rom. i. 1 ; 1 Cor. vii. 22 ; Gal. i. 10 ; Eph. vi. 6 ; Phil. i. 1 ; Col. iv. 12), and six in the general and other Epistles (2 Tim. ii. 24 ; Tit. i. 1 ; Jas. i. 1 ; 1 Pet. ii. 16 ; 2 Pet. i. 1 ; Jude 1).

But while this is the case with the Epistles, the word "servants" occurs no less than *fourteen* times in the book of Revelation, and this, not in the exceptional manner, as in the Epistles, but as the one specific and proper title for those who are the subjects of the book.

In the Epistles the use is peculiar, as an examination of the passages will show. Out of the whole twelve, six are in the first verse of the Epistle,* describing the special character of the writer. For while all sons *serve*, and are in a sense, therefore, servants, yet "servants," as such, are not necessarily *sons*. In other words a "son" may be called a *servant*, but a "servant" can never be called a *son*.

Hence, the writers of the Epistles, being all engaged in special service, might well be called servants. And the Apocalypse, being written concerning Israel, the Israelites are, as appropriately, always spoken of as "servants."

This evidence may not seem conclusive in itself; but, taken with the other reasons given, it adds its cumulative testimony to our position that the book of Revelation has not the Church of God for its subject.

As the members of the Body of Christ, we are "in Christ." We have received a sonship-spirit, whereby we cry, Abba—*i.e.*, my Father, "... and if children, then heirs, heirs of God, and joint-heirs with Christ" (Rom. viii. 15-17).

"As many as are led by Divine-spirit (*i.e.*, the new nature) are sons of God; for we have not received a bond-service spirit" (*v.* 14, 15). This is enlarged upon in Gal. iv. 1-7, where the fact is still more clearly enforced and taught.

---

* Rom., Phil., Tit., Jas., 2 Pet., and Jude.

May we not ask why, if the Apocalypse be all about the Church of God, the people are never spoken of by this their new designation of " sons," but always by the title used of those in the Old Testament who were under the Law ? Is it not passing strange that this should be so ? And is it not the duty of those interpreters who see the Church as the subject of the book, to explain to us this striking peculiarity ?

Even in the Gospels, in speaking to the Twelve, the Lord Jesus specially calls their and our attention to such a change in the relationship, which had then taken place. Not so great a change as that revealed and contained in the Mystery. He had been showing them somewhat of the future, and He says (John xv. 15), " Henceforth I call you not servants ; for the servant knoweth not what his lord doeth : but I have called you friends." In the Apocalypse, He is about to show them things which must come to pass hereafter ; and He does not even call them " friends," still less does He speak of them as " sons," but He goes back and takes up still more distant ground, and calls them, without exception, " servants."

A careful study of the Old Testament with reference to this word " servants " will help to strengthen our position. In Lev. xxv. 42, Jehovah declares of them, "they are *my servants.*" Deut. is full of references to this great fact : and, when we pass to the Apocalypse, and read it as the continuation of God's dealings with Israel, then all is clear ; and we have no problem to solve, as to why all is turned from light to darkness, and the " sons of God " are suddenly spoken of as " servants." Neither have we any difficulty to explain as to why those who are declared to be " *no more* servants, but sons," are continually called servants, and not sons.

Even John himself, in writing by the same Spirit for the Church of God (1 John iii. 2), when speaking of them, says, " Beloved, now are we the sons of God," and he calls them this in view of their seeing Him as He is, and their becoming like Him.   But when he is writing for those who will be on the earth during the times of the Great Tribulation, he is Divinely inspired to speak of them, not as "the sons of God," but as the " servants of God."

We repeat once again, in order to make this point quite clear, that while " sons " may perform some special service, and therefore may, on that account, be called " servants : " "servants," on the contrary, whatever may be the service rendered, can never occupy the position, or have the title, of " sons."

(VII.) The Title of the Book

Our next evidence is the title given to the book by the Holy Spirit who inspired it.

It is not "the Revelation of St. John the Divine," which is man's title for it.   Indeed, among the later MSS., we find *fifteen* or *sixteen* various titles ; but the Divine title given in the text, is " The Revelation of Jesus Christ."

The word is ἀποκάλυψις (*apocalupsis*).   Hence the title of " Apocalypse " so frequently given to the book.

It is from the verb ἀποκαλύπτω (*apocaluptō*) *to unveil*, from ἀπό (*apo*) *away from*, and κάλυμμα (*kalumma*) *a veil*.   Hence *Apocalypsis* means *a taking away of a veil* (as when a statue is said to be unveiled), and thus bringing into view that which had been before hidden as by a veil.   *Unveiling* is the equivalent English word.

It is used, of course, in two senses : *viz.*, of a *bringing to knowledge* by the removing of the veil of ignorance ; or of the *visible appearance* of one who had previously been unseen, as though hidden by a veil.

Our point is that, whenever this word is used of *a visible person* or thing, it always denotes the *visible manifestation* of that person ; and it is the same in the case of all material or visible things.

This is not a matter of opinion, but it is a matter of fact, on which our readers can easily satisfy themselves by examining the passages.

The word occurs *eighteen* times ; and in the following *ten* places is used of *a person.*

Luke ii. 32.—" A light *to lighten* the Gentiles," literally " a light for a revelation to the Gentiles." What was this light ? It was a person, even the Saviour in Simeon's arms, of whom he could say, " Mine eyes have seen Thy salvation."

Rom. ii. 5.—" The day of wrath and *revelation* of the righteous judgment of God." Here it refers to the visible judgment of God, which will be manifested to all in " the day of wrath."

Rom. viii. 19.—" The *manifestation* of the sons of God : " *i e.*, the visible revelation of the sons of God when they shall appear and be manifested in glory with Christ (Col. iii. 4).

1 Cor. i. 7.—" Waiting for the *coming* of our Lord Jesus Christ." Here, without doubt, it refers to the personal appearing of Christ. This passage occurs in one of the earlier Epistles of St. Paul, written during the Dispensation of the Acts, while the offer of the Kingdom and the King was still open to Israel (iii. 19-21), before the sentence of judicial blindness was passed upon Israel (Acts xxviii. 25, 26). The words *Parousia* (1 Thes., &c.) and *Apocalypse* were suitable for that Dispensation ; and, of course, necessitated the personal presence of the Lord Jesus.

2 Cor. xii. 1.—" I will come to visions and revelations of the Lord." Here the word is joined to visions as though it meant visible manifestations of the Lord. Verse 7 may mean either a revelation of truths, or visible scenes of glory, or both.

Gal. i. 12.—" I neither received it (*i.e.*, the Gospel which he announced) from man, neither was I taught it [*by man*], but by a revelation (*i.e.*, a vision or visible appearance) of Jesus Christ." There is no reason whatever why the word should not have both meanings. Why should not the Lord have appeared to him, and made known to him that message which was given to him ? It must have been made known to him in some way; and he distinctly says it was by Jesus Christ (not by the Holy Spirit). Therefore it must have been in one of those many " visions " which he says he saw at different times; and probably during those three preparatory years which he spent in Arabia (Gal. i. 17, 18).

In verse 16 it is the *verb* that is used and not the noun, and therefore it does not come within our enquiry.

2 Thess. i. 7.—" When the Lord Jesus shall be *revealed* from heaven with His mighty angels." Here, though the English uses the verb, the Greek has the noun, and reads, " And to you who are troubled, rest with us at the revelation of the Lord Jesus from heaven, with His mighty angels." There can be no doubt about this passage. (See below, the chapter on " The scope of the book, gathered from its place in the Canon.")

1 Pet. i. 7.—" Might be found unto praise and honour and glory at (the) revelation of Jesus Christ." The context shows that the meaning here is the same as in 2 Thess. i. 10, and refers to His visible manifestation with His People in the air at His Revelation.

But, if Peter's words are taken as referring to the remnant, then the visible manifestation is to them.

So in verse 13, we have the same expression, " at (the) revelation of Jesus Christ."

Also in iv. 13 where we read of the time " when His glory shall be revealed " ; *i.e.*, visibly manifested.

Now from all these ten passages, is it not clear that the word *Apocalupsis*, when it refers to what can be seen (such as a thing or a person), always means the visible manifestation of that person or thing ?

If so, that is what we have in this book. We have an account of the various events which are to take place in heaven and on earth, connected with His visible unveiling. It is His *Apocalupsis* which God gave Him the right or authority to show, make known, or represent to his bond-servants what must shortly come to pass.

It is this thrusting of the sense of *making known a truth* into the word which, when used of a person, means the *appearance of that person*, that has led people commonly to speak of this book in the plural, " the RevelationS."

We have therefore, in the Title of this book, further evidence that the subject of this whole book is the visible appearing of Jesus Christ in power, and glory; and for judgment in the earth. It is not a series of revelations *about* Jesus Christ ; but the book which gives us the particulars about the events which are connected with His revelation or appearing. And it is made known, it says, specially, to his " servants," as we saw in our previous point.

(VIII.) THE DESCRIPTIONS OF THE BOOK

The descriptive titles given to this book mark it off as being special in its nature, distinct from the other books of the New Testament ; and in character and keeping with the prophetic books of the Old Testament.   It is called

I. "THE WORD OF GOD" (i. 2)

This is not used as a general term, of the Scriptures or
of the Bible, as such* : but in a special sense, not
uncommon in the Old Testament, of the "word which
comes from God," or which He speaks.   Hence, *a
prophetic message, e.g.,*

1 Sam. ix. 27.   Samuel said to Saul : " Stand thou still
awhile, that I may show thee *the word of God.*"

1 Kings xii. 22.   " *The word of God* came unto Shemaiah,
the Man of God (*i.e.,* the prophet), saying."   (Compare 2 Chron. xi. 2 ; xii. 15.)

1 Chron. xvii. 3.   " *The word of God* came to Nathan."
(So 2 Sam. vii. 4.)

It is difficult to distinguish between the written Word
and the Living Word.   Both make known and reveal God.

In Gen. xv. 1, we read " The Word of the LORD came
unto Abram in a vision, saying, Fear not, Abram, I am
thy shield," etc.   Here, it is evidently the Living Word,
though it may include both.

When we come to the Apocalypse, we are at once prepared for both—the Vision of the Living Word, and also
the prophetic word of the Living God ; both making
known to the servants of God the visions and words of
" this prophecy " (ver. 3).

Five times we have this expression in this book.†   Not

---

* Though, of course, as the Bible is made up of the *words* of God,
we may conveniently and very truly use "the Word of God" of the
Scriptures as a whole. See Jer. xv. 16.

† Chaps. i. 2 ; i. 9 ; vi. 9 ; xix. 13 ; xx. 4.

in the common sense, as in the Gospels and Epistles, but in this special sense of *a prophetic message.*

In i. 9 John tells us he " was in the Isle that is called Patmos, for the word of God, and for the testimony of Jesus Christ." Leaving the latter expression for a moment, we may remark that the popular interpretation of the word " for " is based on a tradition which doubtless sprang from a misunderstanding of these words. There is no idea of banishment in them. It was no accident which led to the giving of this prophecy. John went to Patmos " for " the purpose of receiving it (as Paul went into Arabia, Gal. i. 17). " On account of " is the meaning of the word here used, for " for." * If his preaching of " the Word of God " was the *cause* of his being in Patmos, another expression would have been used. See Exposition below, on i. 9.

Verse 2 tells us that " the word of God " consisted of "the things that he saw." How could John be banished to Patmos because of, or by reason of, the things which he saw in Patmos !

No, the truth here recorded is that John was there on account of (*i.e.,* to receive) "the word of God," *i.e.,* the prophetic message, even " the words of this prophecy."

There is a second descriptive title which stamps this book. It is called

2. " THIS PROPHECY " (i. 3)

Seven times we have the word *prophecy* in this book,† and prophecy is its one great subject.

---

* As in Heb. ii. 9, " *For* the suffering of death crowned with glory and honour " ; and verse 10 —" *For* whom are all things and by whom are all things." So Rom. iv. 25, " on account of."

† Chaps. i. 3 ; xi. 6 ; xix. 10 ; xxii. 7, 10, 18, 19.

It is "prophecy" for us, therefore, and not past *history*. It is prophecy concerning the events which shall take place "hereafter" during the day of the Lord, *i.e.*, during the day when the Lord will be the Judge, in contradistinction to the present day, *i.e.*, "man's day" (1 Cor. iv. 3) during which man is judging (to the painful experience of most of us). See Exposition on i. 10.

Even "Historicists" take some part of this book as prophecy.

Most "Futurists" take from iv. 1 as prophecy.

But we fall back on the first blessing in verse 3: "Blessed is he that readeth and they that hear *the words of* THIS PROPHECY."

That *reading* commences at once; that *hearing* commences with the reading. Neither is to be postponed till some future time, or to some particular part of the book: nor are we to be left in ignorance as to where our reading and our blessing commences. We believe that "this prophecy" means "this prophecy," and that we begin at once to read it and to get the blessing. It cannot be that we are to read on and wait till we come to some particular verse where the blessing commences. Our attention to what is written is not to be postponed. All the words are " the words of this prophecy." John was to bear witness of " all things that he saw " (ver. 2); and the command is "what thou seest write in A BOOK." What we have therefore is in " a book "; and that book contains all that John saw and heard; and it is called "this prophecy." The whole book, therefore, is prophecy for us. It is "those things which are written in it " which we are to keep: and it is as a whole Book that we propose to deal with it. We feel it safer to be guided by what God Himself calls it than by what man tells us as to what part is prophecy and what is not. If they who tell us this were agreed among themselves it would be something ; but when they differ, we cannot gain much by listening to them.

The evidence afforded by this title is, that, as the whole book is prophecy, the Church of God is not the subject of it : for, as we have seen, the Church is not the subject of prophecy, but of "revelation." The future of the Church is given and written for our reading and blessing in the Pauline Epistles ; especially in 1 Thess. iv., where the Apostle Paul speaks "by the word of the Lord," which means, here as well as elsewhere, *a prophetic announcement.* Further, we may add that, when John is told that he is to prophesy again (x. 11), it is not about the Church, but about "peoples and nations and tongues and kings."

But there is another title given to this book. It is

3. "THE TESTIMONY OF JESUS CHRIST" (i. 2, 9)

Now, this may mean the testimony *concerning* Him (the Gen. of the *object* or *relation*) ; or, the testimony which *comes from* Him (the Gen. of the *subject* or *origin*), *i.e.*, which he bore.

If we take it as the former, it then agrees with the whole prophetic word, which is concerning Him as "the coming One."

If we take it in the latter meaning, then it refers to the nature of the testimony which the Lord Jesus bore when on earth ; and does not go outside it. That testimony related to the kingdom and not to the Church.

The word for "testimony" is worthy of note. It is μαρτυρία, *marturia* (fem.), and not μαρτύριον, *marturion* (neuter). Now, when there are two nouns from the same root, one *feminine* and the other *neuter*, there is an unmistakable difference, which has to be carefully noted and observed : *i.e.*, if we believe that we are dealing with " the words which the Holy Ghost teacheth," as we most certainly do.

The difference here is clear and decided, and a few illustrations will be convincing.

The *neuter* noun, ending in -ιον (*-ion*), denotes something definite and substantial, while the *feminine* noun, ending in ία (*ia*), denotes the matter referred to or contained in or relating to the *neuter* noun.

For example : *Emporia* is *merchandise ;* while *Emporion* is the place or building where the merchandise (*emporia*) is stored (the *Emporium*).

Apostasia are the matters concerning which there is *defection*, *falling away*, *forsaking* or *revolt* (Acts xxi. 21, 2 Thess. ii. 3) ; while *Apostasion* is the act of falling away, or the document, etc., which contains it. Hence it is the technical term for *a bill of divorcement* (Matt. v. 31 ; xix. 7 Mark x. 4).

Geōrgia is *tillage* ; *geōrgion* is *the field* where the tillage is carried on. (1 Cor. iii. 9 only.)

Gymnasia denotes the *exercises* (1 Tim. iv. 8) ; *gymnasium*, the *place* or building where the exercises are done.

Dokimee is the examination or *proof* (Rom. v. 4. 2 Cor. ii. 9 ; viii. 2 ; ix. 13 ; xiii. 3. Phil. ii. 22) ; while *dokimion* is the *trial*, at which the examination is made and the proofs given (Jas. i. 3. 1 Pet. i. 7 only).

Mneia is *remembrance* or mention (Rom. i. 9. Eph. i. 16. Phil. i. 3. 1 Thess. i. 2 ; iii. 6. 2 Tim. i. 3. Philem. 4) ; *mneion* is the *tombstone* or sepulchre where the mention or remembrance is made.

Sōtēria is *a saving* or delivering (and is the general word tor salvation in N.T.) ; while *sōtērion* is *the act of saving*, and almost the person who delivers. See Luke ii. 30 (where it is " seen ") and iii. 6. Acts xxviii. 28. Eph. v. 17.*

Now, in the Apocalypse, we have *marturion* (the neuter), *testimony*, only once (Rev. xv. 5), where it is used of a thing, " the tabernacle of the testimony," *i.e.*, the tent and tables of stone which were placed therein. In every other place (nine times) we have *marturia, i.e.*, the *testimony given* or *witness borne* (i. 2, 9 ; vi. 9 ; xi. 7 ; xii. 11, 17 ; xix. 10, twice ; xx. 4). In all these cases therefore, it is testimony or witness borne, as a reference to them will show.

It seems, then, quite clear that, where we read in this prophecy of " the testimony of Jesus " (i. 2, 9 ; xii. 17 ; xix. 10, twice†), it means the testimony which the Lord Jesus bore or gave on earth as " Jesus " in the days of His humiliation (not as the Christ as raised from the dead).

The testimony was, as we have already said, concerning His kingdom and concerning Israel (see Rom. xv. 8) ; and it is the same testimony which the same Jesus gives in the book of this prophecy.

---

* In some cases these references support these facts ; in others they must be re-interpreted by them.

It will be noted that the accentuation of these words in -ιον intimates that they are all properly adjectives : hence the actual noun to be supplied in each case will vary with the nature of the noun from which the adjective is formed. The general distinction, however, holds good : that the words in -ια represent a *process*, or *habit*, and that, too, under its feminine, not masculine, aspect ; while the neuters represent some *special act*, or *instance* of this habit or process, or some material or instrument by which, or place in which, the habit is carried out, or the process carried on.

† In xx. 4 it is doubtless the testimony concerning Jesus for which those who gave it were beheaded. (The Gen. of relation.)

(IX.) Certain Expressions in Chaps. i.—iii

There are certain expressions used throughout the Apocalypse which are wholly unlike any expressions used in connection with the Church of God or in the Church Epistles.

Some of these are sufficient in themselves to show that the Church is not the subject of the Apocalypse, and have been already noticed. But there are others of importance which require more lengthened treatment; so we group them together under this heading, referring our reader to the Exposition which follows, where supplementary comments on them will be found.

To find these expressions we will not now travel beyond the *first* chapter, except for one expression which occurs seven times in chaps. ii. and iii.

There are sufficient in chap. i. to show us how the Holy Spirit has, at the very threshold of this book, used these expressions for our consideration and our guidance.

We find *seven* of these expressions :—

(1) " UNTO HIM THAT LOVED US " (i. 5)

Because " Christ loved His Church and gave Himself for it," we seem unable, from our natural selfishness, to rise above or beyond the thought of ourselves.

We, naturally, fill our own vision and see nothing beyond ourselves.

The thought that Jehovah said of Israel, "Yea, he loved the people," * does not enter into our minds for a moment. Gentile hatred of the Jew, added to our own natural selfishness, quite cuts out the Jew, not only from the Old Testament, but out of the Apocalypse also.

---

* חָבַב, *chavav*, a very strong word for *love*, which occurs only in Deut. xxxiii. 3, and is taken by " The Chovevi Zion " (*the lovers of Zion*) as the title of that modern Jewish society.

And yet it is strange, with the repeated assertions which Jehovah makes of His love for Israel, that not only should Israel be passed over by Bible-students, but this love actually taken from Israel and appropriated to the Church; depriving Israel of God's love and blessing, and leaving for them only the judgments and the curses.

And yet we have such passages as these concerning Israel :—

Deut. vii. 7, 8. "The LORD did not set his love upon you, nor choose you, because ye were more in number than any people; for ye were the fewest of all people. But because the LORD loved you, and because he would keep the oath which he had sworn unto your fathers, hath the LORD brought you out with a mighty hand, and redeemed you," etc. (See also Deut. v. 37; xxiii. 5, etc.)

Hos. xi. 1, 4. "When Israel was a child, then I loved him, and called my son out of Egypt. . . . I drew them with the cords of a man, with bands of love."

Isa. xliii. 4. "Since thou wast precious in my sight, thou hast been honourable, and I have loved thee."

Jer. xxxi. 3. "The LORD hath appeared of old unto me, saying, Yea, I have loved thee with an everlasting love; therefore with lovingkindness have I drawn thee."

And the LORD, the Redeemer of Israel, says (Isa. liv. 10), "For the mountains shall depart, and the hills be removed; but my kindness shall not depart from thee neither shall the covenant of my peace be removed, saith the LORD that hath mercy upon thee."

We are quite aware that these passages are all appropriated by the Church to itself; and, therefore, we can hardly expect them to be received in evidence that the words in Rev. i. 5 are not the words spoken by the Church But we must be content to leave the matter here. " These are the true sayings of God :" and if people will not believe what God says we can hardly expect them to believe what we say.

Of course we can make an *a fortiori application* of these words ; but that is quite another matter. If Israel can say, "unto Him who loveth us," how much more can we say so according to Eph. v. 25, Acts xx. 28, &c. ? But we are dealing now with *interpretation* ; and we must rest content with simply stating that, by interpretation, these Old Testament passages speak of Jehovah's love to Israel, and not to the Church. And, this being so, the words in Rev. i. 5 may well be spoken by the godly remnant of Israel, as they will afterwards be the language. of the whole People.

We would further anticipate, here, what belongs properly to our exposition of chap. ii. 4 : The first charge brought against His People in this book, *viz.*, " thou hast left thy first love."

What is this, but what Jehovah calls, in Jer. ii. 2, " the love of thine espousals," and in Ezek. xvi. 8, " the time of love." Read the whole of Ezek. xvi. and Ex. xix. 4-6, and say whether we have not here the true key to Rev. ii. 4.

But, before we leave this expression, we must give the correct rendering of the whole verse (i. 5), according to all the Critical Greek Texts and RV. (referring our readers to our further comments in the exposition below).

Unto him who loveth us (it is the present tense, ἀγαπῶντι (*agapōnti*) *loveth*, and not ἀγαπήσαντι (*agapēsanti*) *loved* ; for Jehovah's love for Israel is an ever-present love, yea, it is " everlasting ") **and loosed us** (past tense, λύσαντι (*lusanti*) *loosed*, and not λούσαντι (*lousanti*) *washed*) **from**

(ἐκ (*ek*) *from* or *out of;* not ἀπό (*apo*) *away from*) **our sins by** (not " in ") **his blood."**

(2) "KINGS AND PRIESTS" (i. 6)

The correct text and translation is as follows, and reads on from the last expression: "**And made** (not hath made) **us** (Tregelles reads ἡμῖν (*heemīn*) *for us*) **a kingdom,** (all read βασιλείαν (*basileian*) *a kingdom;* instead of βασιλεῖς καί (*basileis kai*) *kings and*) **priests to his God and Father** (or priests to God, even His Father)."

We have the same expression in chap. v. 10, where the Greek Text has to be corrected in a similar manner.

There the alteration of the text has been the parent of all the wrong translations made of it.

It is the song, the new song, sung by the four living creatures, and the twenty-four elders.* They say (ver. 9):

Worthy art thou to take the book, and to open its seals; because thou wast slain and madest a purchase for God (the word "us" must be omittèd according to Lachmann, Tischendorf, Alford, Westcott and Hort, and R.V. There is an *Ellipsis.* The R.V., having taken out "us," has supplied "*men*" in italics. We may supply "a People," or translate as we have done. All the Texts agree in altering the pronouns that follow in this and the next verse. This necessitates the omission of "us" here. If one is changed, all must be changed for the sake of consistency and sense. But this entirely does away with the supposition that these heavenly beings were them-selves redeemed, or were the subjects of their own song See below, on chap. v. 9) **by thy blood** (a purchase,

---

* The number *four* and multiple of four (4 × 6) marks these and their song as pertaining to the *earth* and to *man* as such, not the **Church.**

namely) **out of every tribe, and tongue, and people, and nation, and didst make them** (so all the Texts and oldest MSS.) **to our God** (Alford omits these words) **a kingdom** (so all the Texts and best MSS.) **and priests, and they shall reign** (so all the Texts and oldest MSS.) **over the earth** " (see further on chap. v. 9, 10 below).

Here we have again the expression "a kingdom and priests." While we have not a word like this in the Church Epistles, yet we have a passage in the Old Testament where very similar words are used, and truth declared of Israel. Ex. xix. 5, 6 : " Ye shall be a peculiar treasure unto me above all people : for all the earth is mine : and ye shall be unto me a kingdom of priests, and an holy nation."

True, these words are found in the New Testament ; but they are in the Epistle addressed to the sojourners of the *Diaspora** : *i.e.*, " the Dispersion," a believing remnant of scattered Israel. These are the People who are concerned in the promise of Ex. xix. 5, 6, and Rev. i. **6 and v. 10** : **and not the** Church of God.

(3) " HIS FATHER " (i. 6)

This is part of the expression which we have just considered : and it is important.

Twice we have it in this book, spoken of Christ (i. 6 and xiv. 1), but not once in the Pauline, or Church Epistles.

There, in every one of the Epistles addressed to Churches (seventeen times), it is always "OUR" Father. See Rom. i. 7. 1 Cor. i. 3. 2 Cor. i. 2. Gal. i. 4. Eph. i. 2. Phil. i. 2 ;

---

*Διασπορά, *scattered abroad*, came to be the technical term for the dispersed portion of Israel. It is found in LXX. Jer. xxxiv. (Sept. xli.) 17. Ps. cxlvii. 2 (Sept. cxlvi. 2). Judith v. 19. Compare Josephus, *Wars*, 7. 3. In the New Testament we have the word in John vii 35. Jas. i. 1. 1 Pet. i. 1. (We may compare the technical use, in Holland, of the term " The Beggars ").

iv. 20. Col. i. 2. 1 Thess. i. 1, 3 ; iii. 11, 13. 2 Thess.
i. 1, 2 ; ii. 16. Also in 1 Tim. i. 2. Philem. 3.

When we say that we have " His father " in Revelation,
and never in the Epistles; and " our Father" in the
Epistles and never in Revelation, we have said enough to
show that we have here a further point, affording its
cumulative evidence to our fundamental proposition that
the Church of God is not the subject of the Apocalypse.

(4) "KINGDOM AND PATIENCE" (i. 9)

John is the " brother " specially of those who were of the
seed of Abraham. The term can hardly be used here, we
submit, either of mere human brotherhood, or of Christian
brotherhood, when all else in this chapter and in the book
is so evidently stamped with a Jewish character.

John says, I "**am your brother and fellow-partaker
in the tribulation and kingdom and patience with
Jesus.**"

Here (according to all the Critical Greek Texts and
R.V.) the words "in the " before " kingdom " must be
omitted ; and the word " in " must be inserted before
" Jesus" : while the word "Christ " must also be omitted
after " Jesus." The verse then stands as we have here
given it. The R.V. inserts the italics " *which are* in Jesus."
The word ἐν (*en*), *in*, may well be rendered, *with* ; as it is
rendered 138 times in the New Testament ; and then there
is no ellipsis to be supplied.

Here is companionship in *patient waiting.* For that is
the meaning of the word rendered " patience,"* and it
always has the thought of *endurance* underlying it.

It is a patient-waiting and enduring in tribulation;
yet a patient waiting and expectation of the " kingdom " ;

---

* It occurs *seven* times in this book : i. 9; ii. 2, 3, 19 ; iii. 10;
xiii. 10 ; xiv. 12.

and all this "with Jesus," for "this man after he had offered one sacrifice for sins for ever, sat down on the right hand of God from henceforth expecting till his enemies shall have been placed as a footstool for his feet."

He is "expecting," and He is also patiently waiting (see 2 Thess. iii. 5, margin), and so are we with Him, but the waiting referred to here is a patient endurance in tribulation and for the kingdom.

We, too, as members of the Church of God have need of patience, and endurance; but we are looking, not for the *kingdom*, but for the KING Himself (not *as* King, for He is not so proclaimed till His enemies are subdued); and though we, too, exercise this patient endurance in tribulation, it is not in "*the* tribulation," but we are waiting to be taken away before that tribulation comes upon the earth.

This expression therefore is worthy of note, and its evidence has to be added to the other expressions used.

(5) " OUT OF HIS MOUTH WENT A SHARP TWO-EDGED SWORD " (i. 16)

There can be no question as to the meaning of this expression. The ῥομφαία (*rhomphaia*) *a sharp* or *two-edged sword*, is four times attributed to the Lord in this prophecy, *viz.*, i. 16; ii. 12, 16; xix. 15, 21.* And in each case it has to do with slaying and not with speaking; with deeds and not with words.

It is "the captain of the LORD's host" come with his sword (Josh. v. 13). It is the sword of Jehovah come to execute His judgments (Is. xxxiv. 6); and with which He will plead with His people (Is. lxvi. 16). It is the sword referred to under other titles (Isa. xi. 4 and 2 Thess. ii. 8),

---

* It occurs also in Luke ii. 35, making *five* times in all.

with which, at His coming in judgment, He will destroy the Man of Sin, the Lawless one.

The sword is no priestly weapon; nor can it have any relation to or connection with the Church of God in any aspect whatsoever: for grace characterises all relations between "Christ and His Church."

(6) "A GREAT VOICE" (i. 10, 12).

This expression links on the book of Revelation to the book of Deuteronomy, especially if we regard it in connection with the fire, with which it is associated in each case.

Ten times is the voice of God speaking "out of the midst of the fire" heard in Deuteronomy: *viz.*, chaps. iv. 12, 15, 33, 36; v. 4, 22 (19)*, 23 (20), 24 (21), 25 (21), 26 (23).

Here, in Rev. i. 10, John hears "a great voice," and it is connected with fire, for the eyes of the speaker were "as a flame of fire" (ver. 14) and his feet "as if they burned in a furnace" (ver. 15).

In Deut. iv. 12 (the first reference) the expression is associated with the giving of the Law, and the declaring of Jehovah's Covenant (iv. 13).

The second is a command to "take heed" to the voice (iv. 15), and keep from idolatry.

The third and fourth are connected with their turning to the Lord when scattered among the nations, seeking Him and finding Him in the "Tribulation"; and the being obedient to that voice in "the latter days" (iv. 27-36). This tells us of the latter days in Revelation, when they will be brought to hear the "Voice" (iv. 33, 36), and to attend to it.

The fifth is again associated with God's Covenant, to which He will be true (*v.* 4).

---

*The figures in a parenthesis denotes the different verse numeration in the Hebrew Text.

The sixth and seventh with the giving of the Law, *v.* 22, (19), 23 (20).

The eighth with the greatness and the glory of Jehovah (**v.** 24, Heb. 21).

The ninth and tenth are references to it by the People (**v.** 25, 26).

All these are brought together, and combined, and fulfilled in the Apocalypse, when Israel will again hear that Voice and, take heed to it, and in their Tribulation turn unto the Lord and seek His face and find Him and rejoice in the faithfulness of a covenant-keeping God.

(7) " HE THAT HATH AN EAR, LET HIM HEAR" (ii. 7).

This expression is absolutely Hebrew in its character, origin, and use. It is never used with reference to, or in connection with, the Church of God.

By *application* of course it told those who first read it of the cause of all declension—failure to hear what the Spirit had already said to the Churches by the Apostle Paul. By *application* also, it reminds us of the same cause to-day. But the *interpretation* which will exhaust the seven-fold expression is that which leaps over the present Church period, and links together the Gospels and Acts with the Apocalypse.

The expression (which is slightly varied in form) as first used in the Gospels is connected solely with, and marks, *a change of dispensation*. When used again in Revelation another great change of dispensation is about to take place. It is to be wrought by " the Son of Man," who has received authority to show it to " His servants."

Such a change could be known only to God, ruled and over-ruled by Him. None but Divine foreknowledge, therefore, could make it known.

The Son of Man alone made use of this weighty expression : and on *fourteen* separate occasions He called for the deepest attention to what was being announced.

Now, the number *fourteen* is most significant ; twice seven, denoting a special Divine revelation made by "the Son of Man."

And these *fourteen* * are divided into *six* and *eight* (just as seven is divided into *three* and *four*). For *six* of them occur in the Gospels and *eight* in the Revelation. *Six* were spoken by Him as the Son of Man on earth, and *eight* as the Son of Man from the glory. *Six* being the number pertaining to *man*, and *eight* being the number connected with resurrection.†

The *six* occasions on earth are Matt. xi. 15 ; xiii. 9, 43. Mark iv. 23 ; vii. 16, and Luke xiv. 35.

The *eight* from Heaven are Rev. ii. 7, 11, 17, 29 ; iii. 6, 13, 22 ; and xiii. 9.

These, like the *six* in the Gospels, are Dispensational, and are thus associated with the great change in God's relation to the earth, to " the Jew and the Gentile," which was about to take place.

The first use of the expression in Matt. xi. 15 is most significant, and stamps it as belonging to the setting up of the kingdom with power and glory. Elijah's presence on the holy mount characterises the scene there as representing the power and coming of that kingdom (Matt. xvi. 28. 2 Pet. i. 16, 17, 18), while Mal. iv. 5 (Heb. iii. 23) connects Elijah's ministry with the setting up of that kingdom.

---

* The *occasions* were 14, but the *actual* occurrences of this example of the Figure are *sixteen* on account of the repetition of the Parable of the Sower in the parallel Gospel records. *Sixteen* is a square number (4 × 4) marking completeness.

† For the significance of these numbers see *Number in Scripture.* Published by Kregel Publications

It had been proclaimed of John before his birth "he
shall go before Him (*i.e.*, Messiah) in the spirit and power
of Elijah" (Luke i. 17); and again, in Luke i. 76, 77, it
was announced: "And thou, child, shalt be called the
prophet of the Highest *: for thou shalt go before the face
of the Lord to prepare his ways; to give knowledge of
salvation unto his people, by (marg., *for*) the remission of
their sins," etc.

John the Baptist was therefore invested with Elijah's
"spirit and power" (*i.e.*, Elijah's spiritual power), and was
specially designated as "the prophet of the Most High."

Therefore our Lord could say in Matt. xi. 14, 15: "If
ye will receive *him*, this is (*i.e.*, represents) Elijah which
was for to come. He that hath ears to hear, let him
hear."

But "their ears were dull of hearing" (Matt. xiii. 15),
fulfilling the dispensational prophecy of Is. vi. 10: Therefore they did not "receive him"; and, consequently, "Elijah
the prophet" is still to come. Hence it is that, in the
Book which relates to the events connected with the
ministry of Elijah and his work in connection with the
restoration of the kingdom, we again meet with this dispensational admonition: which takes us back not merely to
Matt. xi. 15, but to Mal. iv. 5, "He that hath ears to
hear, let him hear."

Thus we have in this expression another proof that the
Church of God is not the subject of the Apocalypse; and
that we are reading here, not of the period belonging to
the ministry of Paul the Apostle, or of the period of present
Church history, as the historicists assert; but, of that which
belongs to the ministry of "Elijah the Prophet."

---

* This title is always connected with dominion in the earth. See
Gen. xiv. 18-22.

(X.) THE CHARACTER OF CHRIST'S ADVENT (i. 7)

Another of the points which prove that the Church of God is not the subject of the Apocalypse is the character of Christ's Coming which is there announced and described ; and with which its events are connected.

This has been already partly shown under the headings of " The Day of the Lord" and "The Son of Man." But it is now more definitely stated and distinguished.

The coming of Christ for His Church is quite a different event, and belongs to quite a different Dispensation. The end for which the Church is waiting is not judgment or tribulation, but to be " received up in glory " (1 Tim. iii. 16), to be "called on high " (Phil. iii. 14), to be changed and have glorious bodies like our Saviour's own body of glory. Their seat of government exists now in heaven, from whence they look for the Saviour (Phil. iii. 19-21).

That coming is into the air, and not unto the earth ; it is in grace, and not in judgment ; it concerns those who are " in Christ," and not either Jew or Gentile as such.

Nothing is revealed in the Old Testament or in the Gospels about this coming. Those books know nothing of it. This coming concerns the Mystery, which was kept secret from times eternal, and was " hid in God." The church of God (which is the Mystery) waits for one thing as its consummation, and that is to be " received up into glory " (1 Tim. iii. 16). But this is not the subject of the Apocalypse.

To make this more clear we must compare what we call the " second " Advent with the " first."

When the Coming of the Lord was announced in Micah v. 2, it was announced as a *coming forth ;* and in Zech.

ix. as a *coming unto*. The former speaks of the *coming forth* at Bethlehem, the latter of the *coming unto* Jerusalem.

There was nothing in those prophecies to tell the Jewish reader whether there would be any interval between these events, or what that interval would be. The Jewish Bible student might think there was a discrepancy; while the Jew with the mind of a "higher critic" might see a greater difficulty, and refuse to believe either Scripture.

But we, to-day, with our knowledge, know that there was an interval of *more than thirty years* between the two events. Both refer to one and the same Coming, but to two different stages in it; and that all the events between them go to make up what we speak of as the "first Coming."

We believe that it will be exactly the same with regard to what we call the " second Coming." There will be the same two stages, with a similar interval (or longer it may be) between them, and all the events (which are recorded in the Apocalypse and elsewhere) will go to make up what we speak of as " the second Coming."

There will be the *coming forth* (as at Bethlehem) of "the Lord Himself" and the calling of His saints on high (Phil. iii. 14), and the receiving of them in glory (1 Tim. iii. 16); and then, later on, to fulfil all the prophecies which relate to His People Israel; and, as the Son of man will " come unto " the earth, to take unto Himself His great power, and reign.

This latter coming is connected with " the Day of the Lord," and it is that which is the subject of the Book of Revelation.

Chap. i. 7 settles this for us : ' Behold, He cometh with clouds; and every eye shall see him, and they also which pierced him : and all kindreds of the earth shall wail because of him."

Only Jew and Gentile are in this verse, and not the Church of God.

This is the Coming of which the Old Testament speaks. It knows no other. See Dan. vii. 13 and Zech. xii. 9, 10, which is the Scripture referred to here.*

This is the Coming which the Lord spoke of when on earth in Matt. xxiv. 30, 31; xxvi. 64, and elsewhere (mark the "ye"). What He there said is perfectly clear, and in perfect harmony with all that had been said in the Old Testament. To read Eph., Phil., and Col. into the Gospels is only to create confusion ; and make a difficulty where none before existed : it is to use one truth for the upsetting of another truth.

The same difficulty is created when we arbitrarily introduce these later Prison Epistles of Paul into the Apocalypse.

To save us from making such a disastrous mistake, the Holy Spirit gave special instruction in 1 Thess. v., *immediately after* He had inspired the revelation of 1 Thess. iv. If we heed this and learn its great and important lesson, all will be perfectly clear.

1 Thess. v. 1. "**But of the times and the seasons, brethren, ye have no need that I write unto you.**"

Why, " no need "? Simply because the *Coming forth* into the air and our "gathering together unto Him" there, do not depend on any time or season. His "Coming unto" the earth *does;* but that is not what he had been speaking about in the chapter immediately before (Thess. iv.).

2. "**For yourselves know perfectly that the day of the Lord so cometh as a thief in the night.**"

---

* It might be rendered "the Land" better than "earth" in Rev. i. 7.

It is the " day of the Lord " which (as we have seen above) is the subject of the Apocalypse : and in Rev. iii. 3, the Lord distinctly warns as to His Coming " as a thief," which is the very opposite of what we read of in Eph., Phil., and Col., and even in 1. Thess. iv. v.   For mark the sudden change of pronouns in the latter chapters.

3. **" For when THEY shall say, ' Peace and safety,' then sudden destruction cometh upon THEM . . . and THEY shall not escape."**

It is this "destruction" which the Apocalypse describes. It is this which gives its character to "the day of the Lord."   It is " sudden," and comes " as a thief; " and it comes upon " THEM " and " THEY," not upon *us :* for, mark the change of pronouns again.

4. **" But YE, brethren, are not in darkness, that that day should overtake YOU as a thief."**

Here, our point is distinctly, emphatically, and cate gorically stated, with a precision and explicitness which leaves nothing to be added.   Can anything be more clear than the fact that the Church of God is not the subject of the Apocalypse ? and that the " Coming " which is the subject of this book is not the Coming for which the Church of God is now longing, waiting, and looking ?

If some of our points are cumulative in their evidence, this one point, by itself, is sufficient to establish our fundamental proposition that the Church of God is not the subject of the book of Revelation, either in prophecy or in history.

The book is " prophecy," as we have seen ; and therefore it awaits a future fulfilment in " the day of the Lord," when the Lord Jesus shall be unveiled as the Son of man, and every eye shall see Him.

(XI.) THE VISION OF THE SON OF MAN

This is essential, for it is directly associated with the object and purpose of the book.

The only other place in the whole Bible where we have anything like it is in Daniel x. 5, 6, where in every particular the resemblance is the same. His girdle is of *gold ;* His eyes as *fire ;* His feet as *brass ;* His voice as many *waters* (Rev.), and as a *multitude* (Dan.) ; His countenance as the *sun* (Rev.), and the appearance as *lightning* (Dan.)

In Daniel it is " a certain man " (Heb. *one—a man*). In Rev. it is " one like unto the Son of Man."

The Two Visions being identical as to the Person and as to His appearance, and also as to the effect on Daniel and John respectively, is it not more than probable that the *purpose* is also the same in each case ?

In Daniel we are expressly told why the Vision was sent. " Now I am come to make thee understand *what shall befall thy people in the latter days ;* for yet the vision is for many days . . . . I will shew thee that which is noted in the scripture of truth " (Dan. x. 14, 21).

The expression, " thy People," is most significant. It is not the Church of God which is in question, but *Daniel's People*, Israel. This People had been the subject of Daniel's prayer (Dan. ix. 4-19). He calls them (in speaking to God) " Thy People " (*vv.* 15, 19) ; and in the answer to the prayer (ix. 24), as well as here (x. 14) and in xii. 1, the angel speaks of them to Daniel as " thy people."

---

* It is beautiful to notice that when Daniel *confesses the sins* of this People he uses, throughout, the pronouns " we," " us," and " our " (see verses 5, 6, 7, 8, 9, 10, 14, 15, 16) But when he pleads with God for them on the ground of the everlasting covenant, it is always " Thy " :—" Thy People " (*vv.* 15, 19), " Thy City " (*v.* 16), " Thy Sanctuary " (*v.* 17), " Thy righteousness " (*v.* 16), " Thy great mercies " *v.* 18), " Thy Name " or " Thy Name's sake (*vv.* 18, 19).

Is it not certain that this People is the subject, and what *Is* to befall them in the latter day is precisely the import, of the Vision which John saw in Rev. i. 13-16.

It had been given to that glorious One to show unto His servants things which shall be "hereafter," and that was *what was to befall Daniel's people* (Israel) "in the latter days."

In Rev. we have "the latter days"—even "the Day of the Lord," and the time has come to show John that which is noted in the scripture of truth.

The people, therefore, who are the subjects of the Revelation, are Daniel's People, and not the Church of God.

(XII.) THE COMPLEMENT OF GENESIS

The Apocalypse is connected very closely with the Old Testament, and not as we have seen with the New; with Genesis, and not with the Church Epistles.

Indeed, the connection between Genesis and Revelation is so marked that many have noticed it.

It will be only necessary for us therefore to exhibit the likenesses and contrasts in parallel columns. No comment will be necessary.

In Genesis we have the book of the Beginning ; in Revelation the book of the End (not of the whole period which we call A.D., but the end of it).

The Apocalypse completes all that Genesis begins, and introduces the New Creation, lest we should think there is nothing beyond.

In Genesis we have therefore the primal creation and the history of the curse which came upon it : Revelation tells how that curse will be removed, and the New Creation brought in.

In Genesis we have Satan's first revolt, and in Revelation his final revolt. The parallel between the two books may be thus set forth :—

GENESIS	REVELATION
The Earth created (i. 1).	Earth passed away (xxi. 1).
Sun, moon and stars for Earth's government (i. 14-16).	Sun, moon and stars connected with Earth's judgment (vi. 12 ; viii. 12 ; xvi. 8).
Sun to govern the day (i. 16).	No need of the sun (xxi. 23).
Darkness called night (i. 5).	" No night there " (xxii. 5).
Waters called seas (i. 10).	" No more sea " (xxi. 1).
A river for Earth's blessing (ii. 10-14).	A river for the New Earth (xxii. 1, 2).
Man in God's image (i. 26).	Man headed by one in Satan's image (xiii.).
Entrance of sin (iii.).	Development and end of sin.
Curse pronounced (iii. 14, 17).	" No more curse " (xxii. 3).
Death entered (iii. 19).	" No more death " (xxi. 4).
Cherubim first mentioned in connection with man (iii. 24).	Cherubim final mention in connection with man.
Man driven out from Eden (iii. 24).	Man restored (xxii.).
Tree of life guarded (iii. 24).	" Right to the Tree of Life " (xxii. 14).
Sorrow and suffering enter (iii. 17).	No more sorrow (xxii. 4).
Man's religion, art, and science, resorted to for enjoyment apart from God (iv.).	Man's religion, luxury, art, and science, in their full glory judged and destroyed by God (xviii.).
Nimrod, a great rebel and King, and *hidden* anti-God, the founder of Babylon (x. 8-10).	The Beast, the great Rebel, a King, and *manifested* anti-God, the reviver of Babylon (xiii. xviii.)

A flood from God to destroy an evil generation (vi.-ix.).	A flood from Satan to destroy an elect generation (xii.).
The bow the token of God's covenant with the Earth (ix. 13).	The bow, betokening God's remembrance of His covenant with the Earth (iv. 3 ; x. 1).
Sodom and Egypt, the place of corruption and temptation (xiii., xix.).	Sodom and Egypt again (spiritually representing Jerusalem) (xi. 8).
A confederacy against Abraham's people overthrown (xiv.).	A confederacy against Abraham's seed overthrown (xii.).
Marriage of first Adam (ii. 18-23).	Marriage of last Adam (xix.).
A bride sought for Abraham's son (Isaac) and found (xxiv.).	A Bride made ready and brought to Abraham's Son (xix. 9). See Matt. i. 1.
Two angels acting for God on behalf of His People (xix.).	Two witnesses acting for God on behalf of His people (xi.).
A promised seed to possess the gate of his enemies (xxix. 8).	The promised seed coming into possession.
Man's dominion ceased and Satan's begun (iii. 24).	Satan's dominion ended and man's restored (xxii.).
Sun, moon and stars associated with Israel (xxxvii.).	Sun, moon and stars associated again with Israel (xii.).

Therefore

The Church not prefigured	The Church not to be looked for

It is surely impossible for us to read these solemn parallels and contrasts without coming to the conclusion that there must be the closest possible connection between the two books.

They are joined together by God in a way so that no man can put them asunder.

God has joined the Revelation to Genesis; man joins it with the Epistles.

God has joined it with Jew, Gentile and the Earth; man joins it with Christendom.

God has joined it with what He had before written in Genesis; man joins it with what man has written himself in Church history!

Can perversity go further than this? Is it any wonder that the book is misunderstood by so many, and neglected by most? For what can be made of it when such elements of confusion are introduced?

When God has placed the key to the book at the very threshold, in the first chapter, man deliberately ignores it, and makes another, which he presents to those who would fain enter; but, when it is tried, it is found that none of the wards fit the lock, and the door either has to be *forced*, or all hope of entrance abandoned!

And yet, when we look at the general scope of the book which will be given later on, how wondrous it is! How Divinely perfect! and, at the same time, how simple and easy! So simple that a child can become interested in it, and the humblest saint understand it.

(XIII.) THE SUMMARY OF ITS CONTENTS (i. 19)

In chapter i. 19 we have the summary of the contents of the whole book.

It is the misunderstanding of this verse which, we believe, has led so many astray, and turned so many into the wrong channel. This verse is usually taken as referring to three things, marking off the book into three divisions:

The things which thou sawest (past)

The things which are (present)

The things which shall be hereafter (future)

Having got these three divisions, then comes a difference of opinion as to exactly where and how these contents of the Book are to be divided.

But there is another rendering which we wish to present, suggested, in part, by Moses Stuart and Dean Alford. This removes all such difficulties, and shows that there is no such three-fold division ; and that instead of *three* subjects we have only *one*.

John was instructed to write what he had seen. It is clear, therefore, that this first chapter is the Introduction to the whole Book, and consequently, like all other Introductions, is written, or supposed to be written, last of all. For, at the very commencement (in i. 2), it is said of John that he "bare record of the Word of God (*i.e.*, as we have seen, the prophetic message), and of the testimony of Jesus Christ (which He bore) and *of all things that he saw.*"

If this chapter then be not written after John had seen these things, the words are without meaning ; for in that case John had as yet seen nothing !

Verse 19 (which we are considering) is part of this Introduction, and therefore the words " which thou sawest " are used in the same sense as in verse 2. John had seen, or is supposed to have seen, all the Visions of the Book when the command to write was given to him. This explains why the word "therefore" must be added in the Greek (according to all the Critical Greek Texts and the R.V.). Moreover, it is specially declared at the very end of the book (chap. xxii. 16), " I Jesus have sent mine angel to testify unto you THESE THINGS in the assemblies" : showing that " the things which thou sawest " refer, not as is generally supposed, only to the things in chap. i., but to the contents of the whole book.

Having seen all these things the command is—

"Write therefore the things which thou sawest, and what they are (*i.e.*, what they signify),* **even the things which shall come to pass** (*i.e., happen,* as in Acts xxvi. 22) **hereafter."**

According to this rendering, which may be rejected as an interpretation, but cannot be condemned as a translation, there is only *one* thing stated as the subject-matter of what was to be written, and not three things. It relates not to past, present, and future, but to the future alone—"hereafter," or, as it says in Dan. x. 14, "in the latter days."

Some lay a stress on the words μετὰ ταῦτα, *meta tauta,* which mean literally *after these things.* But an examination of other places where they occur will show that when used in narrative they may imply historical sequence (as in Luke v. 27 ; x. 1 ; xii. 4 ; xvii. 8 ; xviii. 4. John iii. 22 ; v. 14 ; vii. 1 ; xix. 38 ; xxi. 1. Acts xiii. 20 ; xvii . 1) ; yet when used in connection with promise or prophecy, they, as naturally, are indefinite, *hereafter.* (John xiii. 7. Acts vii. 7. 1 Peter i. 11, where it is rendered "should follow," and has not followed even yet). In any case, the A.V. and R.V. both render the expression "hereafter" where it occurs in Revelation, viz., i. 19 ; iv. 1 ; and ix. 12, in a prophetic sense.

---

* As to this rendering, "and what they ARE," the verb *to be* is constantly translated *to mean* or *signify.* See Matt. ix. 13: "But go ye and learn what that IS" (A.V. and R.V. *meaneth*). Matt. xii. 7 : "But if ye had known what that IS" (A.V. and R.V. *meaneth*). Lu. xv. 26: "He asked what these things WERE" (A.V. *meant* R.V. *might be*). Acts ii. 12: "What IS this?" (A.V. and R.V. What *meaneth* this). Acts x. 17 : "Now, while Peter doubted in himself what this vision WAS which he had seen" (A.V. What this vision *should mean* ; R.V. *might mean*). So, "and what they ARE" should be rendered "and what they mean," or **signify.**

There is no necessity therefore for anyone to regard any portion of the book as relating to the present church period. This (in which we live) is the Dispensation of the Holy Spirit; but that (which is the subject of the Revelation) is wholly the Dispensation of the Son of Man—the revelation or unveiling and manifestation of Jesus Christ.

That is still future. The book which describes it must likewise be future also, and relate only to "the things which shall be hereafter." See further the notes on chap. i. 19.

XIV.—The Seven Assemblies as a Whole (i. 11)

We must here, at the outset, remove the greatest source of all the misunderstandings which have arisen with regard to these seven "churches."

The fact of their being called "churches" has naturally led commentators and students of this book to infer that it is the Church of God, or at any rate the istoric Christian Church, which is meant.

The difficulty is thus arbitrarily created. The Bible student is at once confronted with an overwhelming difficulty. He has read the Epistles which are addressed to the churches by the Holy Spirit through the Apostle Paul; and, on turning to the Epistles in Rev. ii. and iii., he is at once conscious of a striking change. He finds himself suddenly removed from the ground of *grace* to the ground of *works*. He meets with church-officers of whom he has never before heard; and with expressions with which he is wholly unfamiliar: and he is bewildered.

Two courses are open to him: either to try and force the words into a meaning to suit both, thus lowering the standard of the Church of God, and the Christian's own standing in Christ; or, to invent some purely imaginary interpretation and baseless hypothesis by applying them to Christendom, and holding that instead of seven assemblies we have seven

stages of Church history : some going so far as to give
the very years which mark off these periods.

Those who feel this to be a very difficult task, and lack
the knowledge of history which is absolutely essential
to this system of interpretation, wonder why God gave to
Jesus Christ to show unto His servants what must come
to pass hereafter, and yet expected them to become deep
students of history in order to understand what He has
revealed !

No wonder that most Bible readers, after struggling
for a time with this fantastic idea, give it all up in
despair ; abandoning the reading of the book, and losing
the " blessing " which is pronounced upon its readers.

As a first step toward removing this great evil, let us
note at once that the word ἐκκλησία *(ecclesia)*, rendered
" church," is by no means limited to the restricted sense
which is thus forced upon it.

Ecclesia means simply an *Assembly :* any assembly of
people who are *called out* (for that is the etymological
meaning of the word) from other people.

Hence, it is used of the whole nation of Israel as
distinct from other nations.

The Greek word *Ecclesia* occurs seventy-five times in
the Septuagint Translation of the Old Testament, and is
used as the rendering of five different Hebrew words.
As it is used to represent one of these, seventy times,
we need not concern ourselves with the other four words.

This Hebrew word is קָהָל *(Cahal)*, from which we
have our English word *call.* It means *to call together, to
assemble,* or *gather together,* and is used of any *assembly*
gathered together for any purpose. This Hebrew word
Cahal occurs 123 times, and is rendered : " congregation,"
86 times; "assembly," 17 ; "company," 17 ; and " multitude," 3 times : but is never rendered " church." Its *first*

occurrence is in Gen. xxviii. 3—"that thou mayest be a *multitude* (margin, *assembly*) of people," *i.e.*, a *called-out people*. That is what Israel was, a people *called out* and *assembled* from all other peoples.

In Gen. xlix. 6 we read—

" O my soul, come not thou into their secret (*Council* or *Senate*) ;
    Unto their *assembly* (*cahal*), mine honour, be not thou united."

Here the word *cahal* is used, not of all Israel as called out from the nations, but of the *assembly* of those called out to form the Tribal *Assembly* (or Council) of the tribes of Simeon and Levi.

Then, it is used of the worshippers, or those *called out* from Israel, and assembled before the Tabernacle and Temple, and in this sense is usually rendered "congregation." This is the meaning of the word in Ps. xxii. 22 : " In the midst of the *congregation* will I praise Thee " ; and verse 25 : " My praise shall be of Thee in the great *congregation*."

This is the usage of the word in the Gospels, and even in the Acts of the Apostles before the new use, which the Holy Spirit was going to make of the word, was revealed.

When Christ said, "Upon this rock will I build my *Ecclesia*," He did not use the word in the exclusive sense in which it was *afterwards* to be used, but in the older and larger sense in which the word had been before used, which would embrace *the whole assembly* of His People, while not excluding the future *application* of the word to the Church or Body of Christ when that secret should have been in due season revealed.

When the Spirit, by Stephen, speaks of the *Ecclesia* in the wilderness (Acts vii. 38), he means the *congregation* of pious worshippers of God at the Tabernacle.

When the Lord added to the *Ecclesia* daily (Acts ii. 47), He added to the number of those 120, who first assembled themselves together in the upper room in Jerusalem.

When Saul says he persecuted the *Ecclesia* of God, he does not use the word in the limited sense, which it subsequently acquired after he had received the special revelation concerning it: but in the sense in which it had been used up to, and in which it was used at, that time. It means merely that he persecuted the People of God— the congregation of God. He is speaking of a past act in his life which took place long before the revelation of the secret, and his words must be interpretated accordingly. We must not read into any of these passages that which was the subject of a *subsequent* revelation! which passages are perfectly clear without it. The word *Ecclesia* in the Old Testament, the Gospels, and (for the most part) in the Acts, must be taken in the sense of its earlier usage as meaning simply the *congregation* or *assembly* of the Lord's people, and not in the sense which it acquired, after the later and special signification had been given to it by the Holy Spirit Himself.

As we have already abundantly shewn, in the consideration of our foregoing thirteen points, the Apocalypse is linked on to the Old Testament, the Gospels, and the Acts (and not to the later Pauline Epistles), and we ought to use the word *Ecclesia* in the sense in which it is there used; and not, surely, in the newer and special sense which it acquired, and in which it is used, in the Epistles.

In the Pauline Epistles we read nothing about an "angel" as having to do with the churches of God which Paul planted.

But we do meet with the word Angel in connection with the *Synagogue*; (though not in the Old Testament. There, there was an officer, who was called *Sheliach Tzibbūr* (שְׁלִיחַ צִבּוּר): *Tzibbūr* meaning the *Assembly*; and

Shelīach, the *Angel* or *Legate* of the Assembly, and the Leader of Divine worship, from שׁלח (*shalach*) *to send.*

The chief officer was the *Archisynagogos*, or "Ruler of the Synagogue"; and after him came the *Shelīach Tzibbūr;* or "Angel of the Assembly," who was the mouthpiece of the congregation. His duty it was to offer up public prayer to God for the whole congregation. Hence his title; because, as the messenger of the assembly, he spoke to God for them.*

When we have these facts to our hands, why arbitrarily *invent* the notion that "angel" is equivalent to Bishop, when there is not a particle of historical evidence for it?

Episcopoi, or Bishops, are clearly spoken of in other parts of the New Testament (though not in the modern sense of the term. See Acts xx. 28. Phil. i. 1. 1 Tim. iii. 2. Tit. i. 7). But the office of "Angel" in the Church of God is *never used* either inside or outside the Word of God. One might just as well argue for the popular interpretation of the word "angel," from the fact that the word has been so used and applied by the "Catholic Apostolic" Church within recent times.

Add to this the use of the word *synagogue*, which we have in Rev. ii. 9 and iii. 9. Here again translators mislead us. For, while the Greek word occurs 57 times in the New Testament, and is translated *synagogue* 55 times, it is rendered "assembly" in Jas. ii. 2, and "congregation" in Acts xiii. 43.

It should, of course, be rendered *synagogue* in these two places, as well as in all the others, as it is in the RV. (though in Jas. ii. 2 it has *assembly* in the margin. Had the AV. so rendered it in Jas. ii. it would have marked and

---

* See Jennings's *Jewish Antiquities;* and Article *Synagogue* in Kitto's *Biblical Cyclopœdia*, vol, iii, 903,

emphasised the fact that James wrote "to the Twelve Tribes which are scattered abroad," and would have shown how his epistle has a present point of appeal to the scattered people,* as well as a direct future application to them, like that of the seven epistles in Rev. ii. and iii. In any case, the use of the word "synagogue" in Rev. ii. 9 and iii. 9 stamps these Epistles as Jewish, Satan's synagogue being put in opposition to the other assemblies.

When the word *Ecclesia*, in the Apocalypse is rendered "Church," and the word "Synagogue" in Rev. ii. 9 and iii. 9, is interpreted of the church, it is playing fast and loose with the "words which the Holy Ghost speaketh," and which He has employed, not only for His revelation, but for our instruction.

We hold that the Apocalypse contains a record (by vision and prophecy) of the events which shall happen "hereafter" in the Day of the Lord; that the whole book is concerned with the Jew, the Gentile, and the Earth, but not with the Church of God, or with Christendom; or with the latter only so far as the present corruption of Christianity shall merge in the great apostasy, and form part of it, after the Church, the Body of Christ, shall have been removed.

But there will be a people for God on the earth during those eventful years. There will be the remnant of believing Israelites; the 144,000 sealed ones; the great multitude; and other bodies of faithful ones who are referred to all through the Book (see chaps. vii., xi., and xii. 17). In which latter passage we read of "the remnant of her (the woman's) seed, which keep the commandments of God, and have the testimony of Jesus Christ."

---

* As well as saved a great deal of controversy as to the anointing with oil, etc., in Jas. v. 14; and as to "faith" and "works."

Will not these need special instruction ? Have these been forgotten by Him who sees the end from the beginning ? The Pauline Epistles will of course be of use as an historical record of what will then be past, just as we have the record of Israel's history in the Old Testament now.

Our answer to these questions is that God has provided for their instruction, and warning, and encouragement, in the second and third chapters of this book.

Right at the beginning they are the first subjects of Divine remembrance, provision, and care. Their needs must be first provided for, before anything else is recorded of the things which John saw ; and there they will find what is specially written for *their* learning.

Even now; the nucleus of this Remnant is being prepared. Hundreds of Jews are believing in Christ as the Messiah, who know nothing of Him as the Saviour. And even among the unbelievers in Israel a political movement is on foot which may speedily lead up to and issue in the events of which Revelation treats.

Of course this means that we are to consider the *interpretation* of Rev. ii. and iii. as future, and belonging to the " hereafter." As to *application*, we, of course, quite understand, and readily admit that these epistles have been read by the saints of God all through the ages ; and all who have thus read them have received a blessing according to the promise. *We* may so read them now, ourselves, and *apply* them, so far as we can do so consistently with the teaching for this dispensation of grace, contained in the Pauline Epistles. *Applying* these thus we leave the full and final *interpretation* for those to whom it will specially belong hereafter.

Few are aware that the evidence as to the existence of these assemblies as churches is very scanty. Indeed, con-

cerning some, not only is evidence wanting ; but concerning
others it is quite opposed to their ever having existed at all.

Tertullian* (about 145-220) says that leaders of certain
sects, such as Cerdon and Marcion, rejected the Apocalypse
on the ground that it could not have been written by John,
inasmuch as (among other reasons) there was no Christian
Church in existence at Thyatira in the time of John.

Epiphanius (who wrote about A.D. 367) deals with the
Alogi, a sect which disputed the genuineness of the Apocalypse, and on the same grounds. He quotes their words :
" Moreover, some of them [the Alogi] again seize on this
passage in this same Apocalypse [Rev. ii. 18]. And they
allege, by way of opposition, that it is again said : ' write
to the angel of the Church which is in Thyatira,' although
there was no Christian Church in Thyatira. How then
could he write to a church which was not in existence ? "†

The answer of Epiphanius acknowledged the historical
fact : but his answer was that St. John wrote to the church
at Thyatira, not because it was then in existence, but
because it would be at some future time.

We do not see how he could have given a better answer.

In A.D. 363 was held the Council of Laodicea. It was
attended by thirty-two bishops of Asia, among whom was
the bishop of Ephesus. This Council framed a list or

---

* *Contr. Marcion* i. 1.

† The following are the words of the Alogi quoted by Epiphanius :
" εἶτά τινες ἐξ αὐτῶν πάλιν ἐπιλαμβάνονται τούτου τοῦ ῥητοῦ
ἐν τῇ Ἀποκαλύψει τῇ αὐτῇ. Καὶ φάσκουσιν ἀντιλέγοντες·
ὅτι εἶπε πάλιν· Γράψον τῷ ἀγγέλῳ τῆς Ἐκκλησίας τῷ ἐν
Θυατείροις, καὶ οὐκ ἔνι ἐκεῖ Ἐκκλησία χριστιανῶν ἐν Θυατείρῃ.
Πως ὢν ἔγραφε τῇ μὴ οὔσῃ ;" Epiphanius *Adversus Haereses*,
Book II., Vol. I. Haeres. li. Sec. xxxiii. (Migne's Ed. Vol. xli.,
p. 948).

canon of the sacred books, but the Apocalypse was not included in the catalogue.

How can we account for this as a historical fact if these seven churches were all *then existent*; and if these epistles were sent to them at that time, Laodicea being one of them ?

The facts being what they are, the enemies of the Bible draw from them an entirely false conclusion. They use them against the authenticity and genuineness of the Apocalypse, and against its claim to a place in the Canon of Scripture.

We, on the contrary, strongly hold the canonicity and inspiration of the Apocalypse, but we use the undoubted historical facts against a false system of interpretation; which is a very different thing.

An opponent of the Bible, in a large and important work, uses the common system of apocalyptic interpretation as an argument against all Scripture. Speaking of Revelation, he says, "As all parties admit that it contains the destiny of the Church, each sect has applied it to itself, frequently to the exclusion of all others."

All parties, we are thankful to say, do not admit the popular system of interpretation ; and our present object is to show that there is a "more excellent way," not of interpreting it, but of *believing it* ; a way which, while it honours it as the word of God, satisfactorily meets the erroneous conclusions drawn from facts.

If these "churches" are future assemblies of Jewish believers on the earth, after the Church has been " caught up to meet the Lord," then all is clear, consistent, and easy to be understood.

The real difficulty is created by attempting to read the Church into the book where is has no place.

As to the "seven lamp-stands," ought not this expression at once to send our thoughts back to the one golden lamp-stand of the Tabernacle (Exod. xxv. 31-39). ONE lamp-stand with seven lamps, indicative of Israel's unity in the Land and in the City? Here, the scattered condition of the nation is just as distinctly indicated by the fact that the seven lamps are no longer united in one lamp-stand. The nation is no longer in the Land, for Jerusalem is not now the centre; but the people are "scattered" in separate communities in various cities in Gentile lands. So that just as the *one* lamp-stand represents Israel in its unity, the *seven* lamp-stands represent Israel in its dispersion; and tells us that Jehovah is about to make Jerusalem again the centre of His dealings with the earth.

We must further note that John was not told to send seven separate letters to seven separate assemblies, as is generally assumed and believed. Indeed the contrary is the fact. The great Voice said, "What thou seest, write in A BOOK and send IT unto the seven assemblies."

Over three-quarters of a million copies of this Book of the Revelation have in the last few years been placed in the hands of the Jews throughout the world. We allude to the Salkinson-Ginsburg translation of the New Testament in Hebrew, published by the Trinitarian Bible Society, and distributed by the Mildmay Mission to the Jews, and by other similar agencies throughout the world.

So that "the book" has been and is being sent to those for whom it was written, and at no distant day many assemblies of Jews will hear and read the words of this prophecy, and a people be prepared who will keep "the words of this prophecy," and receive in a special manner the blessing pronounced in i. 3.

They will be able to understand what is now so inexplicable to Gentile Christian readers. We find nothing in our Pauline Church Epistles that fits into what is said to these assemblies. But those readers will be at once reminded of the various stages of their own past history, and they will find in almost every sentence some allusion to the circumstances in which they will find themselves as described in this book.

We will show this; first, from the references made to their past history ; and when we come to deal with these Epistles separately, we will, in some circumstance in the Apocalypse itself, give a reference to nearly every sentence in these seven Epistles.

It is a remarkable fact that

Seven past phases of Israel's history

are referred to in these Epistles : and the *literary* order in Revelation corresponds with, and answers to, the *historical* order in the Old Testament.

1. EPHESUS.—THE DAY OF ISRAEL'S ESPOUSALS

(Exodus)

In the Epistle to the Assembly at Ephesus, the reference is to Exodus : to God's love in choosing them out of Egypt, and then making them a nation. See Hos. xi. 1 : "When Israel was a child, then I loved him, and called my son out of Egypt." In Jer. ii. 2 we see this "first love," which Jehovah calls " the love of thine espousals." And in Ezek. xvi. we have a full description of the workings and outcome of this " first love." The whole of Ezek. xvi. must be read with Ex. xix. 4-6. It is this "first love" which Israel is here charged with having " left." This is the beginning of all the subsequent evil.

2. SMYRNA.—THE PERIOD OF ISRAEL'S WANDERINGS
(Numbers)

In Smyrna, we have a reference to a definite time of trial. In the wilderness it was *forty* years. Here it is *ten* days. If any wish to make this stand for ten years it must be on their own responsibility. We only press the point that *a corresponding time of trial* is referred to; and that it is a definite and limited time.

We are aware of the "interpretation" proposed as to there having been ten persecutions of "Christians" between A.D. 57 and 284. But unfortunately for this theory, there is nothing said here as to any *number* of separate persecutions: but only as to the *duration* of *one*! It is evident that no system of interpretation which is based on such imaginations will be of any service to us in our understanding of this book.

The year-day system, as a *principle* of prophetic interpretation, is a human invention; and as unnecessary as it is mischievous.

When God says a "day" He means a day, and when he says a year He means a year. Even in those very passages where He makes one day to stand for a year, the words are used in each case in their literal sense and natural meaning.

When the spies were gone 40 days, and Israel was made to wander 40 years ("a year for a day"), "day" means day and "year" means year (Num. xiv. 34). Because God thus orders it here, we have no authority to do this *on our own responsibility* in every other place.

When Ezekiel was told to lie on his left side 390 days, it does not mean that he was thus to lie for 390 years! And when Jehovah says, "I have laid upon thee the *years* of their iniquity according to the number of the *days*, 390 days" (Ezek. iv. 4, 5), it is clear that "days" means days, and "years" means years.

And when Ezekiel does the same with respect to Judah, 40 days, Jehovah says, "I have appointed thee each day for a year" (Ezek. iv. 6, and see margin). We have the same plain and literal statement of facts.

When human interpreters take upon themselves to "appoint" the same in other cases, whether 126 days or "ten days," or any other number, they incur a very grave responsibility. They do not adopt this "system" in other prophecies, and dare not. For when, in Gen. vii. 4, God says, "For yet seven days, and I will cause it to rain on the earth forty days and forty nights," it is said to have been so fulfilled (vers. 10, 12).

When, in Gen. xl. 12, 13, it is said "the three branches are three days," the fulfilment is given in verse 20 :—" And it came to pass on the third day," etc. (not *year*).

When God prophesied of the flesh that He would give Israel to eat, the days meant days (Num. xi. 19, 20).

So here, in Rev. ii. 9, the expression "ten days" means ten days : and many Jews in many cities already know what it is to suffer an anti-Semite tribulation for days together. Why not here and under these circumstances?

Haman had *one* day given to him to "destroy the Jews"! Why not another "Jews' enemy" be allowed ten days?

And what is this or any such period to do with the Church of God, which has nothing whatever to do with "times and seasons" (1 Thess. v. 1)?

It is quite probable that the time referred to here may be that of Matt. xxiv. 9, 10, and Isa. lxvi. 5.

3. PERGAMOS.—THE WILDERNESS PERIOD

(Numbers)

In Pergamos we have the reference to Balaam, which will have its counterpart in a yet future day.

Through "the counsel of Balaam" (Num. xxxi. 16, etc.) Israel was entrapped and led into the worst form of Midianitish idolatry, when "Israel joined himself unto Baal-peor" (Num. xxv. 3).

In the coming future day Pergamos will be in a special manner the seat (or throne) of Satan (ii. 13 ; and compare xiii. 2), and a form of idolatry more awful than that of Baal-peor will be on the earth. Peter, writing to the Dispersion, tells of this future time in 2 Peter ii., and in verse 15 he speaks specially of their "following in the way of Balaam the son of Bosor."

Jude also connects his description of a similar phase of idolatry with " the error of Balaam " (verses 10-13).

It is clear, therefore, that that special feature of idolatry connected with Balaam's "counsel" is referred to in Rev. ii. 14, and will be revived in the period described in the Apocalypse.

And, as, upon this great evil the special judgment of the " sword" was sent and executed (Num. xxxi. 1-15), so here. He who speaks to the same People of the same evil, speaks also of the same judgment, " I will fight against them with th sword of my mouth" (Rev. ii. 16), which threat will be carried out in chap. xix. 21. This is why we have that special mention of the " sharp sword," describing the speaker in ii. 12, referring to the same feature of the Vision as seen in i. 16.

4. Thyatira. — The Period of Israel's Kings

(1 and 2 Kings)

In the Epistle to Thyatira we have the reference to another and more intensified form of idolatry as developed and established in the days of Ahab, king of Israel ; another who, like Balaam, " made Israel to sin " (1 Kings xvi. 30).

Ahab was the first king who officially introduced and organised the most abominable form of heath en idolatry that the human mind ever conceived (1 Kings xvi. 33). See Revised Version, where the special significance of this abomination is conveyed and contained in the word "Asherah." To particularise on this form of idolatry would be only to defile the mind. The Lord Himself in this Epistle (Rev. ii. 20-24) gives a clue to it. We may, perhaps, add that what was introduced into Israel by Balaam (see Rev. ii. 14) became elevated into a national religious system under Ahab and Jezebel, as it had long been recognised among the heathen nations around.

What that religious system of licentious idolatry was is well known; but something may be gathered from a recently-discovered Papyrus,* containing about a sixth of the *Ascension of Isaiah*, which had before been known only in an Ethiopic Translation (except a mutilated and worthless Greek recension from a 12th century Lectionary in Paris). The origin of this Papyrus is very ancient, and its historical facts may be taken as correct, separated from its vaticinations. It says, speaking of the condition of things in the days of Israel's Kings— "And Manasseh turned aside his heart to serve Beliar [*i.e.*, Belial]; for the angel of lawlessness who ruleth this world is Beliar, whose name is Malàmbûchûs. And he delighted in Jerusalem because of Manasseh, and made him strong in his apostasy and lawlessness, for it was spread abroad in Jerusalem. And sorcery and magic increased, and divination and auguration and fornication and the persecution of the righteous at the hands of Manasseh . . . And when Isaiah the son of Amoz, saw the lawlessness which was being

---

* Now in Lord Amherst's collection, and published under the title of the *Amherst Papyri* (Oxford Press).

committed in Jerusalem, and the worship of Satan, and his triumph, he withdrew from Jerusalem, and settled in Bethlehem of Judea."

The Papyrus goes on to speak of Zedekiah, the son of Chenaanah, as being " the teacher of the four hundred prophets of Baal "; and tells how Isaiah "called Jerusalem Sodom, and the rulers of Judah and Israel he named people of Gomorrah." This was of course in reference to the special sins of Sodom and Gomorrah. See Isa. i., &c.

Many proofs abound to show that some similar system will yet be revived. None can be imagined which would more quickly and universally take hold upon the world, and unite all communities—and even the worst of characters, by making all, thus, to become *religious*, and yet able to degrade and gratify the instincts of human nature *under the guise of religion*.

Nor can we conceive any form of corruption which would mark off the people of God more effectually, and cause them to be separated from the abounding wickedness around them.

This is the best explanation which can be given of those solemn verses, Rev. ix. 20, 21 ; or rather, it is this passage which is itself the explanation of the awful character of Antichrist's great universal system of Religion, which even God's plagues, up to the point of time there referred to, will have failed to remove, and which will call down the yet greater judgments of " the seven vials."

These verses (Rev. ix. 20, 21) are so weighty that we must quote them in full.

" And the rest of the men which were not killed by these plagues yet repented not of the works of their hands, that they should not worship devils (RV. marg. *demons*), and idols of gold, and silver, and brass, and stone, and of wood : which neither can see, nor hear, nor walk : Neither repented they of their murders, nor of their sorceries, nor of their fornication, nor of their thefts."

Our point, however, must not be forgotten, which is, to draw attention to the fact, that the mention of this evil in these Epistles corresponds with the historical order in Israel's history in the Old Testament.

5. SARDIS.—THE PERIOD OF ISRAEL'S REMOVAL
(1 and 2 Chronicles)

We have had four references to Israel's history in the Old Testament, and as *four* is the number connected with the earth, so these four have been connected with Israel in the earth and the Land ; and with the culminating sin of departure from the love of God manifested to the Nation. Israel had "left her first love," forsaken God, and joined herself to idols in the most abominable form.

This is the climax of Israel's sin. All else in his history is judgment, until Israel is removed from the Land and taken away out of God's sight. His name is practically blotted out, never again to be a separate ten-tribed kingdom. So blotted out, in fact, that men speak to-day of the lost* ten tribes.

Indeed, the prophecy of Deut. xxix. 20 is fulfilled, not only as to the individual and to the Tribe ; but there is an application to the whole nation. In Deut. xxix. 18, 20 (17, 19) there is the threat to blot out the name of the " man " or " tribe " who shall introduce idolatry. As a matter of fact, the Tribes of Dan and Ephraim were the first to introduce it ; and their names *are* blotted out from the tribes of those who are to be sealed in Rev. vii.

It is in this Epistle, next in order (to the assembly at Sardis) that we have the reference to this silence, in the

---

* Not that they are "lost" in the proper sense of the word : but the proverbial expression is significant.

promise to the few names of such as have not defiled thei.
garments : "He that overcometh . . . I will not blot ou.
his name out of the book of life, but I will confess his name
before my Father and before his Angels " (Rev. iii. 5).

6. PHILADELPHIA.—THE PERIOD OF JUDAH'S KINGS
(2 Chronicles)

We have had two references to Israël's history, and now
we are to have two references to Judah's, and these refer,
not any more to failure, sin and judgment; but to the
hope of restoration and blessing.

As Ahab, king of Israel, was the first to introduce and
establish the Asherah worship, so the reference here, in the
Epistle to the assembly in Philadelphia, is to Hezekiah,
king of Judah, who did much to destroy it and cast it out.

In 2 Chron. xxxi. 1, Hezekiah "brake in pieces the
pillars (marg., *obelisks*), and hewed down the Asherim "
(RV.).

His two predecessors, like himself, are described with
special reference to their connection with the Temple and
with the Temple worship.   Indeed, these three kings
of Judah are linked together as being three of the four
reigns in which Isaiah prophesied, namely, " Jotham, Ahaz,
and Hezekiah " (Isa. i. 2).

Jotham "*entered not into* the temple of the LORD " (2
Chron. xxvii. 2).

Ahaz "*shut up* the doors of the house of the LORD "
(2 Chron. xxviii. 24).

Hezekiah, at the beginning of his reign, " in the first year,
in the first month, *opened* the doors of the house of the
LORD " (2 Chron. xxix. 3).

In Isa. xxii. 22 there is a further reference to this point.
Shebna, the Treasurer, had misused his trust for his
own glorification (see Isa. xxii. 15-19).   On this account

he was ordered to be deposed, by Divine command, and "the key of the house of David" was laid upon the shoulder of Eliakim, the son of Hilkiah (vers. 20-25): "And the key of the house of David will I lay upon his shoulder; so he shall open, and none shall shut, and he shall shut, and none shall open" (ver. 22).

Eliakim means *God will raise up*: and there can be no doubt whatever that we have here a prophetic reference to Christ, whom God would raise up. Indeed, the whole passage (vers. 20-25) reads more like prophecy than history; and points very distinctly forward to the Temple which He Himself will build, and will fill with His glory.

It is remarkable to notice how, in writing to this Assembly in Philadelphia (Rev. iii. 7), the Lord takes these very words and applies them to Himself, saying: "These things saith he . . . that hath the key of David, he that openeth, and no man shutteth; and shutteth, and no man openeth."

The reference here to Isa. xxii. 22 is unmistakable, and it is clear that we have a reference to another and subsequent, but closely connected, event in the Old Testament history.

With this reference we can understand the announcement to the Assembly of Philadelphia in Rev. iii. 8: "Behold, I have set before thee an open door, and no man can shut it."

And we can understand also the reference to the Temple in the promise, "I will make him a pillar in the temple of my God, and he shall go no more out" (Rev. iii. 12).

We are taken right on, beyond Jerusalem and its Temple, to the days of final blessing, even to the new Jerusalem and "the Temple of my God," when Is. lxii. 2 shall be fulfilled: "And the Gentiles shall see thy righteousness, and all kings thy glory: and thou shalt be called by a new name, which the mouth of the LORD shall name."

When this is exactly what is promised in Rev. iii. 12, " I will write upon him my new name," it is difficult to understand how such a promise could ever have been diverted from Israel to the Church : taken away from what it is directly associated with ; and applied to that with which it has no connection whatsoever.

7. LAODICEA.—THE PERIOD OF JUDAH'S REMOVAL
(The Minor Prophets)

We reach, in this last Epistle, the lowest point of Judah's degradation, in that long line of departure from God, from the day Israel left her " first love," even the day of her espousals, when brought forth out of Egypt, down, down through one vast scene of idolatry and judgment, until we find the nation described in the Epistle to the Assembly in Laodicea in a condition of spiritual destitution such as characterised the People in the period of the Minor Prophets.

Indeed, so complete is the correspondence, that to see it we must wait till we take the Epistle sentence by sentence, and look at the passages from the Prophets, which we shall there place side by side. We give one or two as examples :

Rev. iii. 17.	Hos. ii. 5, 8, 9.
" Because thou sayest, I am rich, and increased with goods, and have need of nothing ; and knowest not that thou art wretched, and miserable, and poor, and blind, and naked."	" For their mother hath played the harlot ; . . . for she said, I will go after my lovers that give me my bread and my water, my wool and my flax, mine oil and my drink . . . For she did not know that I gave her corn, and wine, and oil, and multiplied her silver and gold, which they prepared for Baal. Therefore will I return, and take away my corn in the

time thereof, and my wine in the season thereof, and will recover my wool and my flax given to cover her nakedness. And now will I discover her lewdness in the sight of her lovers," etc., etc.

The whole of Hosea ii.—v., xii. 8, etc., must be read to see the pointed reference to this stage of Israel's condition. Compare also Hag. i. 6. Jer. xiii. 25, 26; v. 27. Zech. xi. 5, 13-18.

Rev. iii. 18.

" I counsel thee to buy of me gold tried in the fire, that thou mayest be rich; and white raiment, that thou mayest be clothed, and that the shame of thy nakedness do not appear; and anoint thine eyes with eyesalve, that thou mayest see."

Rev. iii. 19.

" As many as I love, I rebuke and chasten: be zealous therefore, and repent."

Compare with this Is. lv. 1, 2. Hos. ii. 3. Jer. xiii. 25, 26. Isa. lix. 10; lxvi. 17. See also Mal. iii. 3.

Isa. xliii. 4.

" Since thou wast precious in my sight, thou hast been honourable, and I have loved thee."

So Deut. vii. 8; Deut. viii. 5: "Thou shalt also consider in thine heart, that as a man chasteneth his son, so the LORD thy God chasteneth thee."

Mal. iii. 7.

" Return unto Me and I will return unto you " is another form of Rev. iii. 19

In verse 16, the Lord speaks of spueing out the angel. This is the very expression used prophetically in Lev. xviii. 25-28 of Israel; where Jehovah warns that, if they adopted the abominations of heathen idolatry, the Land might spue them out (compare Jer. ix. 19. Ezek. xxxvi. 13, 17).

All this shows that the references in this last Epistle do not in any way fit the Church of God, but agree in every particular with Israel's history, and are referred to so as to enlighten them from their own past history, and thus warn them as to future evils which will then surround them.

When the Church has been removed, and Israel is again dealt with, the religious condition of the nation will exactly correspond with its condition at the Lord's first coming.

There will be, as there was then, plenty of religion. Isa. i. 10-15 minutely describes the state of things, as they were then and will be again in the future.

The truth of " this prophecy will be amply evidenced— " Thou sayest, I am rich, and increased with goods, and have need of nothing.

The Pharisee's prayer (Luke xviii. 11, 12) exemplifies it. The parables of the great supper, the wedding garment, etc., describe it. The people were blind. The answer to the question, " Are we also blind ? " (John ix. 40, 41) proves it.

The call to the wedding feast will be, as then, individual. Matthew was called, Zacchæus was called, and many others ; and those who heard that call were unable to resist its commanding and enabling power.

It is the great wedding feast of Rev. xix. 9 to which the parables pointed.

These " servants," to whom this epistle is addressed, will understand the solemn warning, " Behold, I stand at the door, and knock." " To the twelve tribes scattered abroad" it

was announced " the judge standeth before the door "
(Jas. v. 9).

The then nearness of the Judge is the thought conveyed
in this announcement. He will be then near at hand, and
ready to be revealed.

We are aware that the warning in chap. iii. 20, " Behold,
I stand at the door, and knock," has been universally
interpreted of the nearness of the *Saviour* in grace to those
living in this present Church Dispensation, and this has
been fostered by painters who have done so much to present perversions of Scripture to the eye.

It is a perversion which just suits the old nature, for it
puts man in the place of Almighty God, and turns the
Lord Jesus into a helpless suppliant.   All this is foreign to
the doctrines of grace, and makes them all of none effect.

Moreover, this popular interpretation is out of keeping
with the context.   For,   all   through   these   seven
Epistles the Lord is in the character of a Judge,
rewarding   His   " servants "   according   to   their
" works."   To those looking for Him and ready to
receive Him, He appears according to His promise in
Luke xii. 35-40 : " Let your loins be girded about and
your lights burning : and ye yourselves like unto men that
wait for their lord, when he will return from the wedding ;
that *when he cometh and knocketh*, they may open unto
him immediately. Blessed are those servants, whom the
lord, when he cometh, shall find watching : Verily I say
unto you, that he shall gird himself and *make them to sit
down to meat*, and will come forth and serve them   And if
he shall come in the second watch, or come in the third
watch, and find them so, blessed are those servants.   And
this know, that if the good-man of the house had known
what hour the thief would come, he would have watched,

and not have suffered his house to be broken through. Be ye therefore ready also : for the Son of Man cometh at an hour when ye think not." Here, we have the " Son of Man " ; the " servants " ; the illustration of the " thief " ; the " watching " ; the " knocking " ; the " opening," and the " sitting down to meat." Surely we have in Rev. iii. 20, the fulfilment of this prophecy.

How simple it all is when we look at this Epistle as relating to backsliding Israel, and read it in the light of the Prophets and the Gospels. How much more satis-factory to find these illustrations in the Old Testament Scriptures, instead of being occupied with the conflicting and fanciful references to certain phases of ecclesiastical history, *which have no Scriptural foundation whatever, and rest entirely on human imagination.* All is confusion as to interpretation, and error as to doctrine, the moment we introduce the Church or the present dispensation into these Epistles.

We have seen enough in the consideration of this fourteenth point to furnish us with further evidence that the Church is not the subject of the Apocalypse.

The same is seen when we look at our last point, viz., the order of the *promises* contained in these Epistles.

(15) The Promises to The Seven Assemblies

As we have seen that the references to the Old Testa-ment in the seven Epistles correspond with the historical order of the events, so it is with respect to the promises contained in these Epistles. The literary order follows the historical order.

They are written to a People supposed to be well-versed in the history of the Old Testament, and well-acquainted with all that had happened to their fathers and had been written for their admonition. Instructed in the past history of their nation, they will readily understand the relation between the testings and judgments in the past with which they are familiar, and those similar circumstances in which they will find themselves in a yet future day.

While the historical events connected with the rebukes are carried down from Exodus to the period of the Minor Prophets, the promises cover a different period; commencing with the period of Eden, and ending with the period of Solomon.

The subjects of the rebukes follow the order of the departure of the People from Jehovah. Their decline and apostasy is traced out in the historical references contained in these Epistles.

All blessing depended on the national adherence of the chosen nation to the conditions of the Covenant made with them from the days of the Exodus to the days of the Minor Prophets.

We see them, in the history, coming down, down, down; till we find them stripped of all blessing (nationally), poor, miserable and blind. All that seems to be hoped for, or looked for, among the People is a few individuals who will speak to one another and think upon the Coming One (Mal. iii. 16). Later, we see these in the persons of Zacharias and Elisabeth (Luke i. 5, 6), Simeon (Luke ii. 25), and Anna (Luke ii. 36-38), and others, " who were waiting for the consolation of Israel," and looking " for redemption in Jerusalem." (Compare Mark xv. 43 and Luke xxiv. 21).

We have seen that this same historical order is followed in these seven Epistles to the Assemblies.

But when we turn to the PROMISES, then all is different. They proceed in the opposite direction. The order, instead of descending—from Israel's highest ground of privilege (Exodus) to the lowest stage of spiritual destitution (Minor Prophets)—ascends, in the counsels of Jehovah, from tending a garden to sharing His throne.

This will be readily seen as we trace it out in the promises made in Rev. ii. and iii.

But first we must note that they are all intensely individual. There is no corporate existence recognised as such. Each one of the seven promises commences with the same words, "To him that overcometh." This answers to the language of the Four Gospels, and the Epistle to the Hebrews: *e.g.*: "He that endureth to the end," and resists all the flood of evil by which he will be surrounded, he shall be saved.

Such phraseology is foreign to the language of the later Pauline Church Epistles.

The whole period covered by "the day of the Lord" is called the *final meeting* of the ages, or the συντέλεια (*sunteleia*); but, the *crisis* in which it culminates is called the τέλος (*telos*), *the end* of the age.

Both are rendered "end" in the New Testament, but the use of these two words must be carefully distinguished.

Sunteleia denotes *a finishing* or *ending together*, or in conjunction with other things. *Consummation* is perhaps the best English rendering.* It implies that several things meet together, and reach their end during the same period; whereas *Telos* is the point of time at the *end of that period*.† For example, in Matt. xxiv. 3 the disciples ask,

---

* The word occurs only in Matt. xiii. 39, 40, 49; xxiv. 3; xxviii. 20, which shows that this verse refers to a yet future day. And in Heb. ix. 26, which refers to the *sunteleia* of the former dispensation. It is the Septuagint rendering of קֵץ (*keytz*) in Dan. xii. 4, 13.

† *Telos* is significant in this connection, in Matt. x. 22 and Rev. ii. 26.

" What shall be the sign of thy coming, and of the *sunteleia* of the age."

In His answer to this question the Lord speaks of the whole period, and covers the whole of the *sunteleia.* But three times He mentions the *telos* (1) to say that " the *telos* is not yet." (verse 6); (2) to give a promise to him "that shall endure unto the *telos* " (verse 13); (3) to mark the crisis in verse 14, which comes immediately after the close of the preaching of " the gospel of the kingdom." " Then shall the *telos* come." The *sign* of the *telos* is the setting up of " the abomination of desolation spoken of by Daniel the prophet." Thus the *telos*, and he who endures to this, the same shall be saved, and will be among the *overcomers* specially referred to in these seven Epistles ; to whom these promises are made, and to whom they pecu-liarly refer.

They are seven in number, as we know : but we have to note that the *seven* here, as elsewhere, is divided into *three* and *four.*

Each Epistle ends with two things : (1) an *injunction* to "hear"; (2) a *promise* to him that " overcometh." In the first three Epistles the Promise comes *after* the Injunction. In the last four it comes *before* it.

This is because the first *three* are connected, by refer-ence, to what is written of the *Divine* provisions in the books of Genesis and Exodus (the Garden and the Wilder-ness); while the latter *four* are connected with the *Land* and the thrones of David and Solomon : the number *three* marking Heavenly or Divine perfection ; and the number *four* having to do with the earth.

Let us look at these Promises in order.

I. THE FIRST (EPHESUS)

refers to Genesis ii., the promise being, " I will give to eat of the tree of life, which is in the midst of the paradise of God " (Rev. ii. 7.)

God begins from Himself. The Apocalypse relates not only to Israel, but to the earth ; and the first promise goes back to Eden and to the " tree of life."

The way to that tree was lost : but was " kept " (or preserved) by the cherubim (Gen. iii. 24). These cherubim next appear in connection with the way to the Living One, in the Tabernacle, and are thus linked on to Israel.

Only in Israel's restoration can the way to the " Tree of Life " be restored.

Sovereignty and government on the earth is the great subject of the Apocalypse; therefore the promise goes back to the point where sovereignty was ignored and government was overthrown. This becomes the starting-point. That is why the cherubim re-appear in the Apocalypse, intimately associated with this work of restoration of Divine Government on the earth. Their song is of " creation " (Rev. iv. 11). Their likeness is to creation. Their song is of the redemption of Israel (not their own. *See* the notes on them in chap iv. and v.).

2. THE SECOND (SMYRNA)

refers to Genesis iii., the promise being " Be thou faithful unto death, and I will give thee the crown of life." " He that overcometh shall not be hurt of the second death " (ii. 10, 11). The reference is to Genesis iii., where death first enters. But the promise goes beyond this ; for it relates not merely to the death which came in with sin, but to the " second death," which is revealed in Rev. xx. 14 ; xxi. 8.

3. THE THIRD (PERGAMOS)

refers to Exodus. The promise is, " I will give to eat of the hidden manna, and will give him a white stone, and in the stone a new name written, which no man knoweth, saving he that receiveth it " (ii. 17).

It is in this third Epistle, which refers to the wilderness period and Balaam's counsel, that we have special reference to the manna, the wilderness sustenance, of which Exodus contains the record. " Bread from Heaven " and " Angels' food " (Ps. lxxviii. 24, 25) are set over against the lusts of the flesh and spiritual idolatry. The manna was to be " hidden " in the Ark of the Covenant, " that they may see the bread wherewith I have fed you in the wilderness, when I brought you forth from the land of Egypt. . . . so Aaron laid it up before the Testimony to be kept " (Ex. xvi. 32-34). This " hidden " food is for remembrance ; to remind them that God can supply the remnant of His People in the coming day, when none shall be allowed to buy or sell (Rev. xiii. 16, 17), and therefore to buy food to eat, unless they consent to bear the " mark of the Beast."

God supported His People in the wilderness, where they could obtain no food : Why not here ? The false prophets will eat to the full at the table of another Jezebel : Why should not God " furnish a table " (Ps. lxxviii. 19) for His own in that coming day, in that wilderness whither they will flee (Rev. xii. 14) ? The one was literal : why not the other ? Why go out of our way to seek for a strange interpretation alien to the subject, when we have one ready to hand in the Old Testament Scriptures which are being referred to ? That manna was to be " hidden," and " kept," to remind them that God can still, and will again " furnish a table in the wilderness," that they may again be " nourished for a time, and times, and half a time " (Rev. xii. 14).

There is a further promise as to the " white stone " and the " new name." Again we ask, Why go to our own imaginations, or to Pagan customs, for interpretations, when we have in this same book of Exodus* the account of the stones on which the names of the Tribes were engraven : Two on the High Priest's shoulder, with six names on each (collective) ; and twelve on the breastplate, with one name on each (individual). The individual names being placed " upon his heart " (the place of love), and the collective names " upon his shoulders " (the place of strength) (Exod. xxviii. 8-30).

Besides these stones there were the stones of the " Urim and Thummim," of which little or nothing is known. These may have been " white " for aught we know ; but we do know that they were associated with a hearing and answering God dwelling in the midst of His People.

Here, amid their scenes of trial and tribulation, when God's people will find themselves in another wilderness, they are reminded, by this Exodus-promise, of Jehovah's presence with them ; and of the blessed fact that He has their names in remembrance ; that His love is everlasting ; that His strength is almighty, and able to nourish them when their enemies might prevail and human resources fail.

4. The Fourth (Thyatira)

refers to the books of Numbers and Samuel. The promise is, " to him will I give power over the nations : And he shall rule them with a rod of iron ; as the vessels of a potter shall they be broken to shivers; even as I received of my Father. And I will give him the morning star " (Rev. ii. 26-28).

Here again the literary order in the Apocalypse goes forward with the historical order : for it is in the book of

---

* In the Hebrew Canon Exodus is called the Book of " the Names." See *Names and Order of the Books of the Old Testament*, by Dr. BULLINGER (Eyre & Spottiswoode).

Numbers that we have the basis of this promise given to the same People, who were the subjects of it there. For "there shall come a Star out of Jacob, and a Sceptre shall rise out of Israel, and shall smite the corners (marg. *princes*) of Moab, and destroy all the children of Sheth, And Edom shall be a possession, Seir also shall be a possession for his enemies ; and Israel shall do valiantly. Out of Jacob shall come he that shall have dominion, and shall destroy him that remaineth of the city " (Numbers xxiv. 17-19).

This promise and prophecy had a first foreshadowing fulfilment in David; showing what was in store for David's Son and David's Lord : even for Him who was the "root and the offspring of David."

Luke i. 31-33 tells of His conquest, and of His reign on David's throne.

David, we have said, foreshadowed it : for he could say in the words of his song, "thou hast girded me with strength to battle ; them that rose up against me hast thou subdued under me. Thou hast also given me the necks of mine enemies, that I might destroy them that hate me. . . . Then did I beat them as small as the dust of the earth, I did stamp them as the mire of the street " (2 Sam. xxii. 40, 41, 43).

This was the theme of David's song "in the day that the LORD had delivered him out of the hand of all his enemies."

And this heralds the yet more glorious song in honour of David's Lord when the kingdoms of the world shall have become the kingdom of our Lord and of his Christ, and he shall reign for ever and ever (Rev. xi. 15).

The promise is given in this fourth Epistle, because the prophecy of Numbers xxiv. 17-19 has never yet been really fulfilled. " The day-spring (the morning star) did visit His people " (Luke i. 78); but He was rejected ; and therefore

the fulfilment remains in abeyance, as well as that of
Luke i. 31-33.

In Rev. ii. 26-28 the time is at hand for the fulfilment of
it. Hence the promise is repeated; and in chap. xx. 4
we see it accomplished; for the " morning star " shall
then have risen (Rev. xxii. 16), and the prophecy of
Psalm ii. shall be fulfilled.

5. The Fifth (Sardis)

refers again to the times of David—not to the beginning of
his reign, but to the end of it.

It is a double promise, negative and positive, and both
have to do with the names of individuals.

" I will not blot out his name out of the book of life;
but I will confess his name before my Father, and before
his angels " (iii. 5).

The reference is to " the last words of David " in 2 Sam.
xxiii. They follow " the words of this song " in the
previous chapter.

These " last words of David " were uttered as he was
about to give up the throne and the kingdom to Solomon ;
when the conflict was to end, and issue in dominion,
and in a glorious reign of peace : foreshadowing the
time when this promise of Rev. iii. 5 is about to be
fulfilled, and the Apocalyptic judgments are about to issue
in millennial glories.

" I will not blot out his name."

" I will confess his name."

So runs the double promise, and it is exactly what we
see in the history which is thus referred to.

David is confessing the names of his overcomers, and
the confessing of them begins, " These be the names of
the mighty men whom David had " (2 Sam. xxiii. 8).

They had "gathered themselves to him" in the day of his rejection. For, though he had been anointed as king, he was not as yet sitting on his own throne, but was in the cave Adullam, or the place of testimony.*

They had gone to him in their distress and debt and bitterness of soul (1 Sam. xxii. 1, 2), and David "became a captain over them." They had followed him through all his conflicts: and now, on the eve of the era of glory and peace, their names are confessed before all.

Their deeds are announced, and their exploits are recorded. But there are some who are "blotted out."

JOAB is not there, though "Abishai, the brother of Joab," is there (2 Sam. xxiii. 18); "Asahel, the brother of Joab," is there (*v.* 24); "Nahari . . . armour-bearer to Joab," is there (*v.* 37); *but not Joab himself.* He was a "mighty man." He had been the commander-in-chief of David's forces, a valiant soldier, a great statesman and wise counsellor ; but, while he was all this and more, he was not an *overcomer*, for his heart was not right with David. He remained loyal when Absalom rebelled; but he took part in the treason of Adonijah.

AHITHOPHEL is not there; though we read of "Eliam the son of Ahithophel" (*v.* 34). He was David's greatest counsellor ; so wise, that when he spoke "it was as if a man had enquired at the oracle (or word) of God" (2 Sam. xvi. 23). But he was not an *overcomer*, and he is not "confessed" even before men. He took sides with Absalom in his rebellion; and he is blotted out from this list of names.

ABIATHAR, too, is blotted out, for not even is his name here. He was David's beloved friend (see 1 Sam. xxii. 20-23), but he was not an *overcomer*. He remained loyal

---

* Adullam means *their testimony*.

in the treason of Absalom, but joined in that of Adonijah. The other names are duly confessed.

The scene is unspeakably solemn, and has, by application, a warning voice for all. But, by interpretation, it comes with special force in this promise to the Assembly at Sardis, and refers to the fulfilment of Matt. x. 32, 33 and Luke xii. 8, 9. " Whosoever therefore shall confess me before men, him will I confess also before my Father which is in heaven. But whosoever shall deny me before men, him will I also deny before my Father which is in heaven." Thus this promise refers not only to that solemn past scene in Israel's history, but is shown to be closely connected with the Four Gospels, and points on to the scenes of final judgment and glory in connection with David's Lord, and "a greater than Solomon."

6. THE SIXTH (PHILADELPHIA)

refers to Solomon, as does the seventh (Laodicea). In the former the reference is to the "Temple" and to the "City"; while, in the latter, it is to the "Throne."

The promise runs (iii. 12), " Him that overcometh will I make a pillar in the temple of my God, and he shall go no more out : and I will write upon him the name of my God, and the name of the city of my God, which is new Jerusalem, which cometh down out of heaven from my God : and my new name."

The reference here to Solomon is unmistakable.

He it was who built the temple, and put in its porch those mysterious pillars "Jachin and Boaz" (1 Kings vii. 13-22. 2 Chron. iii. 17).

"And he set up the pillars in the porch of the temple : and he set up the right pillar, and called the name thereof Jachin (*i.e., He shall establish*): and he set up the left pillar, and called the name thereof Boaz (*i.e., In it is strength*)."

Strength and permanence were thus announced to all who entered that wondrous Temple.

The Temple of God is brought in this Epistle into contrast with the Synagogue of Satan, and those were of the latter who " say they are Jews and are not." That synagogue has neither strength nor permanence. But the overcomers are endued with Divine strength, and shall have eternal inheritance, for they " shall go no more out."

Moreover, the promise refers to the name of the overcomer being written in " the city of my God."

There can be only one interpretation to this promise. Anyone acquainted with Old Testament phraseology will at once go back in memory to such Psalms as xlviii., cxxii., and lxxxvii. In this latter we read :

> "Great is Jehovah, and greatly to be praised :
> In the city of our God—His holy mount.
> Beautiful for situation,
> The joy of the whole earth, is Mount Zion,
> The sides of the north, the city of the great king.
>
> . . . .
>
> As we have heard, so have we seen ;
> In the city of the LORD of hosts,
> In the city of our God :
> God will establish it for ever " (Psa. xlviii. 1, 2, 8)

> " His foundation is in the holy mountains.
> Jehovah loveth the gates of Zion
> More than all the dwellings of Jacob.
> Glorious things are spoken of thee,
> O city of God. Selah.
> I will make mention of Rahab and Babylon to them
>   that know me :
> Behold Philistia, and Tyre, with Ethiopia,
> This one was born there.

> And of Zion it shall be said, This and that man was
> born in her.
> And He, the Most High, shall establish her.
> Jehovah shall count, when he writeth up the peoples
> 'This man was born there.' Selah.
> As well the singers, as the players on instruments
> [shall say]
> 'All my springs are in thee' " (Psa. lxxxvii.).

True, the chapter-headings of the A.V. may call this *" the nature and glory of the Church."* But we shall prefer to believe God in so plain and literal a description of " the city of God :" and those who are the subjects of the promise will have a blessed knowledge of what it will mean to be written " in the city of my God."

Ezekiel (chap. xiii.) also addresses Israel ; but as he speaks not of promises and blessings, it is not interpreted of the Church, but it is left for the persons mentioned ; though they are not more clearly defined here than in the above Psalm. In verse 9 we read of those who " shall not be in the assembly of my people, neither shall they be written in the writing of the house of Israel, neither shall they enter into the land of Israel ; and ye shall know that I am Adonai Jehovah " (Ezek. xiii. 9).

The promise in Rev. iii. 12 refers to the New Jerusalem (chap. xxi. and xxii.). If the city of David and Solomon was such that " glorious things " were spoken of it as " the city of God," what will be the glories of that city which " cometh down out of heaven from my God " ? And what will be the blessing of Zion and Jerusalem when, as written in Isa. lxii. 1, " the righteousness thereof shall go forth as brightness and the salvation thereof as a lamp that burneth"? Then it is that the promise is given, " Thou shalt be called by a new name, which the mouth of the LORD shall name."

(Compare Isa. lx. 14). In Isa. lxii. 4 and 12 we have further instruction as to this "new name" referred to in Rev. iii. 12.

7. THE SEVENTH (LAODICEA)

refers to the throne, of which Solomon's was in every respect the ideal type.

This, the highest promise, is given to the overcomers in the lowest condition of Israel's degradation, which is described as in danger of being "spued out."

What that was we have already seen (page 89), and now we have the chiefest of all the promises. The overcomers in that last terrible condition of things are the ones who most need the greatest of Divine help and encouragement. Hence the highest promise is given.

" To him that overcometh will I grant to sit with me in my throne, even as I also overcame, and am set down with my Father in his throne" (Rev. iii. 21).

To Solomon is the great promise of the throne vouchsafed through David. "When thy days be fulfilled, and thou shalt sleep with thy fathers, I will set up thy seed after thee . . . and I will establish his kingdom. He shall build me an house for my name, and I will stablish the throne of his kingdom for ever " (2 Sam. vii. 12, 13).

The defection of those who should follow Solomon on that throne was foreknown and provided for. The whole of Psalm lxxxix. should be read in this connection, as explaining how and why the throne should come to be in abeyance. After referring to this in verse 14, the promise goes on : Yet

" My mercy shall not depart away from him. . . .

" And thine house and thy kingdom shall be established for ever before thee:

" Thy throne shall be established for ever " (2 Sam. vii.
15, 16).

How and when this promise will be fulfilled, after the
period of chastening referred to in verse 14 (of 2 Sam. vii.)
shall have ended, is described in Dan. vii.   There we have
fully set forth how " the Son of Man" shall receive the kingdom and the throne, and how "the saints of the Most High "
shall share that throne with Him, as promised in this
Epistle.

The title used in Dan. vii., " The Most High" is very
significant, and shows that the whole scene relates to the
earth.   Whenever this title is used this is its meaning and
teaching. Its first occurrence, in Gen. xiv. 18-24 marks it as
belonging to the " possessor of heaven and earth."   It was
as " the Most High " that he divided to the nations " their
inheritance " in the earth (Deut. xxxii. 8), which, as its
" possessor," He alone had the right or the power to do.
In Psa. lxxxiii. 18 He is called " the Most High over all
the earth."   And so it is in all the thirty-six occurrences of
the title in the Old Testament.*

The expression, "the saints of the Most High," tells
us that the people referred to are an *earthly* people,
even those whose promise is an earthly throne and an
earthly kingdom. Not the church of God, therefore, whose
calling, standing, hope and destiny are heavenly.

Four times is the expression used in Dan. vii.   In verse 18
" *the saints of the Most High* shall take the kingdom, and
possess the kingdom for ever, even for ever and ever."

---

* Gen. xiv. 18, 19, 20, 22. Num. xxiv. 16. Deut. xxxii. 8. 2 Sam.
xxii. 14.   Ps. vii. 17 ; ix. 2 ; xviii. 13; xxi. 7 ; xlvi. 4 ; xlvii. 2 ; l. 14;
lvii. 2 ; lxxiii. 11 ; lxxvii. 10; lxxviii. 17, 35, 56 ; lxxxii. 6 ; lxxxiii.
18; lxxxvii. 5 ; lxxxix. 27 ; xci. 1, 9; xcii. 1 ; xcvii. 9; cvii. 11.
Isa. xiv. 14.   Lam. iii. 35, 38.   Dan. vii. 18, 22, 25 (twice), 27.

In verses 21, 22 the fourth Beast "made war with the saints and prevailed against them (as related in Rev. xiii. 7); until the Ancient of days came, and judgment was given to the *saints of the Most High*; and the time came that the saints possessed the kingdom."

In verse 25 the Beast "shall speak great words against the Most High," &c. (as related also in 2 Thess. ii. 4, and Rev. xiii. 5, 6).

In verse 27 we read that "the kingdom and dominion, and the greatness of the kingdom under the whole heaven, shall be given to the people of the *saints of the Most High*, whose kingdom is an everlasting kingdom, and all dominions shall serve and obey him."

These are the "elect," who shall be "gathered together from the four winds, from one end of the heaven to tae other," when the "Son of Man" shall come down on the earth (Matt. xxiv. 30, 31). Then shall His "call" go forth, "Gather my saints together unto me." This is when He will call "to the earth, that He may judge His People" (Ps. l. 4, 5; read the whole Psalm).

And when, later, in Matt. xxv. 31, we read, "When the Son of man shall come in his glory, and all the holy angels with him, then shall he sit upon the throne of his glory": then there will be a different gathering, not of his "elect" (see Matt. xxiv. 31), but "before him shall be gathered all nations,"* according to Joel iii. 1, 2 and 11, 12.

This throne of the special judgment of the "nations" leads up to and ends in the permanent throne of Divine government, according to Jer. iii. 17.

Then will this promise be fulfilled to the overcomer:

"I will grant to sit with Me in my throne, even as I also

---

* See the structure of the whole of this great prophecy of Matt. xxiv. and xxv. in *Things to Come*, vol. vi., p. 103.

overcame, and am set down with my Father in His throne (Rev. iii. 21).

This promise, therefore, like all the others is not given to the Church of God. The members of that glorious body will have already been " caught up to meet the Lord in the air," and will have had their part in the " gathering together unto him " there, before the cry of Ps. l. 5 goes forth to " the earth, that he may judge his people," and " gather his (earthly) saints together."

Thus we have traced the upward path—the ascending scale of the seven promises of these seven Epistles, and seen how are they to be interpreted of Israel, whose downward path is here also so wonderfully set forth in these same Epistles.

This concludes our *fifteen preliminary points* ; and we submit that their cumulative evidence establishes our fundamental position that, *the " Church of God "* does not form the subject of the Apocalypse. Our interpretation confines that subject to the " Jew " and the " Gentile " (1 Cor. x. 32). Whether " the word of truth " is thus " rightly " divided is for our readers to determine for themselves, according to the evidence which we shall put before them.

THE SCOPE OF REVELATION
SHOWN BY ITS PLACE
IN THE CANON

THE scope of the Apocalypse is the most important of all the preliminary subjects connected with its interpretation. Apart from its true scope, no correct interpretation is possible. This scope is best gathered from its structure; but, before considering this, we propose to look at it as shown by its place in the Canon of Scripture, and by the relation in which it stands to the other books of the New Testament. This is the first thing that must be discovered in order to get an insight as to its place, subject, object and scope.

The order of the books of the New Testament as a whole varies, both in the manuscripts, versions and catalogues* which have been preserved and have come down to us.

But while the order of the separate books may vary, they are always arranged in four groups which never vary :—
(1). The Four Gospels. (2). The Acts of the Apostles. (3). The Epistles. (4). The Apocalypse.

The four groups always follow each other in this order. We say four "groups"; but it will be observed that only the *first* and *third* are groups; the *second* and *fourth* consist of only one single book each.

The order of the separate books in these two groups varies. For example, the order of the Gospels varies.

---

*Such as the catalogues contained in the Muratorian Fragment, A.D. 160-170. Eusebius (*H.E.* iii. 25), about A.D. 340. Athanasius (Ex *Festali Epistola* (written A.D. 367) xxxix. tom. i. 767, 961. Ed. Benedict. Paris 1777. Gregorius Nazienzenus (*Carm. Sect.* i. xii. 5), A.D. 391. The Proceedings of the Council of Carthage, A.D. 397. Ruffinus, A.D. 410.

The order of the Epistles varies, for in some lists Paul's Epistles come before the general and other Epistles, and *vice versa*. But, like Paul's Epistles addressed to churches, which never vary in their order, so these four groups never vary in their order.

Their inter-relation may be set forth, in brief, in the following structure :—

The New Testament Books

GOSPELS | THE FIRST ADVENT. The coming of the "Son of Man" to present the kingdom. The rejection of the kingdom and crucifixion of the King

THE ACTS AND EARLIER PAULINE EPISTLES | H | THE KINGDOM RE-OFFERED. The Acts and earlier Pauline Epistles (Acts iii. 19, 20). The "Signs and Wonders of the Holy Ghost (Heb. ii. 3, 4). The offer rejected (Acts xxviii. 25, 26)

THE LATER PAULINE EPISTLES | H | THE KINGDOM IN ABEYANCE. The "Not Yet" of Heb. ii. 8. The Mystery revealed and consummated, Rom. xvi. 25, 26, Eph. iii. 1-4 Col. i. 5—ii. 3. 1 Tim. iii. 16. Phil. iii. 14.

(INTERVAL BETWEEN 1st AND 2nd ADVENTS.)

APOCALYPSE | THE SECOND ADVENT. The coming of "the Son of Man" to set up the kingdom in power and great glory. The establishing of the kingdom and the crowning of the King

From this structure it will be seen that the Apocalypse stands out in special relation to, and connection with *the four Gospels*, and not with the Epistles.

The Gospels record the events connected with the *First Advent,* and the Apocalypse records the events connected with the *Second Advent.*

In the Gospels we have " the days of the Son of Man " (Luke xvii. 22) ; in the Apocalypse we have " the day of the Lord " (i. 10).

The Gospels close with the great prophecy of " the Son of man in the clouds of heaven with power and great glory " (Matt. xxiv. 30 ; xxvi. 64. Mark xiii. 36. Luke xxi. 27) ; followed by the account of His sufferings, piercing and death.

The Apocalypse takes up this theme and opens by declaring the fulfilment of this prophecy, " Behold he cometh with clouds ; and every eye shall see him, and they also which pierced him " (i. 7) : followed by the account of the judgments ; the coming and the crowning.

The Gospels contain the prophecy of the Great Tribulation : the Apocalypse contains the description of it.

Between the *first* advent, which is the subject of the Gospels, and the *second* advent, which is the subject of the Apocalypse, we have the *present interval,* which is the subject of the Acts of the Apostles and the Epistles.

This interval is thus divided into two distinct periods, (1) that covered by the Acts of the Apostles and earlier Pauline Epistles, and (2) that covered by the later Pauline Epistles.

The Acts has for its subject the re-presentation of the King and the kingdom. Israel is again taken up, and Peter, using the keys of the kingdom committed to him for this special purpose, opens the kingdom to Jews and Gentiles. Through the abounding grace of God the kingdom is again offered to Israel, but this being rejected the cup of Israel's iniquity is filled up. The people not only rejected Christ Risen, but they resisted the Holy Ghost. They resisted Jehovah in the Old Testament, The Messiah in the Gospels, and the Holy Ghost in the Acts. Though the ministry of Peter partly overlaps that of Paul, yet it is clear that Israel is specially dealt with as such, until the final sentence is pronounced in Acts xxviii. 17-28, which was speedily followed by the *taking* of the People *out* of their city and their Land.

Then we have the period covered by the later Pauline Epistles, which have for their subject the Mystery, or the Church of God.

The Church has a different calling, a different standing, and a different destiny from either Jew or Gentile, and yet, composed of both, is now waiting for their calling on high (Phil. iii. 14).

It may be that these two parts of the present interval slightly overlap, as Paul's ministry in the synagogues and among the Gentiles also overlapped.

Not until shortly after the Apostle's death did God actually (as He had already begun to do judicially) cease to deal with Israel as Israel, scattering the People abroad on the earth—destroying the Temple, and effectually, for a time, breaking off the natural branches from the Olive Tree (Rom. xi.).

After this, we have set before us, in the Epistles, the calling and hope of the church, which is now being *taken out*, and is waiting to be *taken up*, to meet the Lord in the air ; waiting for " our gathering together unto Him " (1 Thes. i. 10, iv. 15—v. 4; 2 Thes. ii. 1-3 R.V.), before " the Day of the Lord " shall come.

This is fundamental to our whole position, and is necessary, we believe, to a clearer understanding of the Apocalypse.

It is well therefore that we should further establish the great scope of the Book as taught us by its position in the New Testament ; and its special relation to the Gospels.

In 1 Thes. v. 4, we are distinctly told " ye, brethren, are not in darkness, that that day ('the day of the Lord,' verse 2) should overtake you as a thief."

As the Revelation is the description of that day (i. 10, iii. 3 ; xvi. 15) and of His " coming as a thief " (compare Matt. xxiv. 43, 44), it is clear that the promise of 1 Thes. v. 4, must be fulfilled before the Lord Jesus is thus revealed. Those concerned will be already at "*rest*," with Him " when the Lord Jesus shall be revealed from Heaven with His mighty angels ; in flaming fire taking vengeance on them that know not God, and that obey not the gospel of our Lord Jesus Christ : who shall be punished with everlasting destruction, [*driven away*] from the presence of the Lord, and from the glory of His power, when HE SHALL HAVE COME to be glorified in His saints and to be admired in all them that believe . . . in that day" (2 Thes. i. 7-10).

The tense here (in verse 10) is not the simple future tense of the indicative mood, but it is the second aorist tense of the subjunctive mood, ἔλθῃ (*elthē*), and can mean only *shall have come*. In verse 7, "when the Lord Jesus shall be revealed " is not a verb at all, but a noun, ἐν τῇ ἀποκαλύψει (*en tē apokalupsei*), and means *at the revelation* (*lit.*, at the Apocalypse).

So that "at the Apocalypse" of Jesus Christ, the Raptured ones of 1 Thes. iv. will already be at rest They have their "tribulation" now (vers. 4, 5). This is the teaching of v. 7.

But when the time comes to "recompense tribulation " to the world, then Christ will already have come to be glorified in His saints. For " in that day " He "*shall have come* " to take them up to be with Himself, " for ever with the Lord." This is the teaching of verse 10.

That this is the only sense in which this tense can be taken is clear from the following examples of its use:—

Matt. xxi. 40 : " When the lord of the vineyard cometh " (*shall have come*).

Luke xvii. 10 : " So likewise ye, when ye *shall have done* all those things." (Here it is so rendered).

Mark viii. 38 : " Whosoever therefore shall be ashamed of me . . . of him also shall the Son of Man be ashamed (here we have the simple *future*) when he cometh (ὅταν ἔλθῃ, *hotan elthē*, the same as in 2 Thes. i. 10, *i.e.*, *shall have come*) in the glory of his Father."

In John iv. 25 we have the tense contrasted with another : " I know that Messias cometh (*lit.*, is coming), which is called Christ ; when He is come (ὅταν ἔλθῃ, *shall have come*) he will tell us all things."

Acts xxiii. 35 : " I will hear thee, said he, when (ὅταν) thine accusers are also come " (lit., *when thine accusers also shall have come*).

John xvi. 13 : " Howbeit, when He, the Spirit of truth, is come" (ὅταν ἔλθῃ, *shall have come*).

Rom. xi. 27 : " For this is my covenant unto them, when I shall take away (lit., *shall have taken away*) their sins."

The prophecy as to Christ's enemies' being put under His feet (Ps. cx. 1) is quoted or referred to six times in the New Testament. Christ is now at God's right hand " until His enemies *shall have been placed* (as) a footstool for His feet." (See Matt. xxii. 44. Mark xii. 36. Luke xx. 42. Acts ii. 34. Heb. i. 13 ; x. 12, 13). Then He will arise and use this footstool, treading His enemies under His feet (Ps. xviii. 37-50). This is the subject of the

Apocalypse; and result and fulfilment of it is recorded in 1 Cor. xv. 25, which speaks of Christ's after-reign, "For He must reign till He hath put (*lit., shall have put*) all enemies under His feet." So that the two acts are carefully distinguished. First, the *placing* of the footstool; and then the *using* of it. The one is at the beginning of the "day of the Lord," the other is at the end of His reign.

All this is conclusive, and tells us that the church of God will be at " rest " at the Apocalypse of Jesus Christ. And that, when He comes to take vengeance on His enemies, He "*shall have come*" already for His saints.

This enables us to see the true place of the Apocalypse in the New Testament. Chronologically it follows on the Epistles, which end with the *taking up* of (1 Thess. iv.) ; but logically, *i.e.*, in the purpose of the ages (Eph. iii. 10 R.V. marg.), it follows the Gospels; and takes up the subject of the King and the Kingdom, where it is there left.

There we see it rejected : here we see it established with judgment, and set up in Divine power and glory.

True, in order of *time* it follows on the period covered by the Epistles : and what we have to look for, now, is, not the conversion of the world, but the judgment of the world. The professing church is deceiving the world. It tells the world that its mission is to improve the world and, by improving its sanitation, housing its poor, and generally preaching the gospel of earthly citizenship, to bring on a millennium, in which no Christ is thought of or wanted !

While the majority of the Church's teachers are loudly proclaiming that "the day of the Lord" will not come till the world's conversion comes, the Spirit and truth of God are declaring that that day shall not come until the apostasy comes (2 Thes. ii. 3).

While the majority of the Church's teachers are main-taining that the world is not yet good enough for Christ, the Spirit is declaring in the Word that the world is not yet *bad* enough.

There is some difference between these two testimonies; and our labour will not be in vain, if we learn from this book of the Revelation to believe God; and, while we " wait for His son from heaven " as our blessed Hope, to warn the world of increasing apostasy (which may go on side by side with increasing morality) and of coming judgment.

Yes, coming judgment. That is the scope of the whole book. We have, here, events which cannot be limited by mere ecclesiastical history; but a wondrous unveiling of the awful scenes which shall end up God's controversy with Satan. It has as its field the whole creation, and not merely a corrupt church in Europe. All the forces of Heaven and Hell are seen in conflict, and bringing to a head the mighty issues involved.

On the one side we see,

(1). The full display of the power of God in Christ, opposed to the full energy of Satan and all his forces in the " day of battle and of war " (Job xxxviii. 23).

(2). In this final conflict, we see the full array of all the Heavenly forces which Christ can command and will command. We see spiritual beings, angels and princi-palities and powers in Heaven, and the great physical forces of creation (Zech. xii. 4-8; xiv. 1-4, etc., etc.) brought to bear on the great enemy.

(3). That mighty heavenly host will embrace all who have been delivered and redeemed from " the power of Satan " from the time of sin's beginning, as well as all the angelic beings who have not fallen.

(4). These heavenly forces are led by "the King of Kings, and Lord of Lords,"—" the Prince of the Kings of the earth "—the great "Captain of the LORD's host."

On the other side, we see

(1). The full display of Satan's power and authority (xvi. 13, 14), and that, too, from the beginning of his tyranny and usurpation as the "prince of this world" and its "god" (John xii. 31 ; xvi. 11. 2 Cor. iv. 4).

(2). To this end, all the hosts which he can and will command, from the very beginning of his power—angels and principalities and powers ; men and demons from the pit, and men on earth ; all these will be led by their captain, and all brought to bear against Him who sitteth upon the White Horse (Rev. xix. Jude 6. 2 Pet. ii. 4).

(3). This mighty host will be of far wider extent than the minds of expositors have ever yet conceived.

(4). These forces of earth and hell will have for their leader, Satan, "the prince of this world."

We have here something far beyond the ordinary interpretations put upon this Book : and, we believe that few, if any, can possibly realize all the mighty issues involved in it ; and the extent of its results as affecting creation, Israel, and the nations of the world.

To limit it to Popery, or to Christendom (so called) is, we believe, wholly to miss the scope of the Book : and, to lose the weighty lessons of its wondrous Revelation, by committing the mistake condemned by true logic—viz., of putting a part (and a small part too) for the whole.

The awful conflict is of far wider extent than this. It exceeds all the general petty views of its scope ; as affairs of State transcend those of a Parish Vestry.

" Michael and his angels " and "the Dragon and his angels " include the whole fighting forces of the heavens.

Rev. xii. reveals the HEAVENLY ARMAGEDDON, which will bring to an end the hostilities of ages by a final overthrow of the wicked (so far as the super-etherial heavens are concerned).

What the Book tells us of the conflict on earth is of the same character. The scope of it takes in the whole earth, and leads up also to an EARTHLY ARMAGEDDON (Rev. xvi. 16).

The Covenant of marvels (Ex. xxxiv. 10) refers to judgments which are cosmical in the widest sense of the term.

The scope of the book winds up all the affairs of time, and contains the end of prophecy, the end of knowledge, the end of the Secret of God (x. 7), and the dawn of the eternal ages of ages.

In short, the scope of the book, as shown by its place in, and relation to, the whole canon of Scripture, is the winding up of the affairs of the whole creation, and the fixing of the eternal states of all things in heaven and on earth.

We are thankful to feel that we are not alone in taking this serious view of the real scope of the Apocalypse.

While many fritter away its solemn scenes in the common-place history of Europe, there are others who see beyond all this, and behold the Divine interposition in the affairs of the whole creation.

We have information about the church in the Epistles : and we see, even in them, the indications of the coming corruption which has since become history. But in the Apocalypse we have something far beyond, and quite different from all this.

The Epistles prepare us for what we know as Ecclesiastical history ; and they prepare us also for the end as revealed in the Apocalypse.

Eloquent testimony is borne to this, and therefore to our view of the scope of Revelation, by Canon Bernard ;* who approaches the subject from a somewhat different standpoint. His weighty words are :—

"I know not how any man, in closing the Epistles, could expect to find the subsequent history of the Church essentially different from what it is. In those writings we seem, as it were, not to witness some passing storms which clear the air, but to feel the whole atmosphere charged with the elements of future tempest and death. Every moment the forces of evil show themselves more plainly. They are encountered, but not dissipated. Or, to change the figure, we see battles fought by leaders of our band, but no security is promised by their victories. New assaults are being prepared ; new tactics will be tried ; new enemies pour on ; the distant hills are black with gathering multitudes, and the last exhortations of those who fall at their posts call on their successors to 'endure hardness as good soldiers of Jesus Christ,'† and 'earnestly to contend for the faith which was once delivered to the saints.'‡

"The fact which I observe is not merely that these indications of the future are in the Epistles, but that they increase as we approach the close, and after the doctrines of the Gospel have been fully wrought out, and the fullness of personal salvation and the ideal character of the church have been placed in the clearest light, the shadows gather and deepen on the external history. The last words of St. Paul in the second Epistle to Timothy, and those of St.

---

* Bampton Lectures for 1864: *The Progress of Doctrine in the New Testament*, by Thomas Dehany Bernard, late Rector of Walcot, and Canon of Wells. London : Macmillan & Co., 1900 (page 189, 5th ed., 1900).

† 2 Tim. ii. 3.   ‡ Jude 3.

Peter in his second Epistle, with the Epistles of St. John and St. Jude, breathe the language of a time in which the tendencies of that history had distinctly shewn themselves ; and in this respect these writings form a prelude and a passage to the Apocalypse."

If these things be so, as we assuredly believe they are, then *the church is not the subject of the Apocalypse.*

The Apocalypse follows the Epistles in sequence of *time*, and is naturally and historically consequent upon them ; but in the Divine order and plan it is *logically* and dispensationally consequent on the Gospels and Acts.

Every previous dispensation has ended in judgment, from Satan's first rebellion (Gen. i. 1, 2) to his final rebellion (Rev. xx. 8-10) and the final judgment (verses 11-15).

That this present dispensation shall end in judgment is not only to be inferred from the uniform history of the past ; for it is clearly foretold in the Epistles. It is this judgment which is described in the Apocalypse ; and it is this book which we are now seeking to understand more clearly. This clearness, we believe, will be greater in proportion as we see the position occupied by this Book in the New Testament ; and in proportion as we believe that the Church of God has no part in the great Tribulation, and no participation in those judgments.

That it is not the subject of this book we have endeavoured to establish in our fifteen preliminary points : and this view will be further confirmed as we proceed with our consideration and study of the Apocalypse.

3

OUTLINE OF
THE BOOK OF REVELATION

HAVING seen the scope of the Apocalypse as suggested by the place of the book in the Canon of Scripture, we now propose to gather its scope from its structure.

This can be done only by looking at the book as a whole.

Most expositions of the book have proceeded on some plan formed according to the expositor's own idea. These are, for the most part, clever and ingenious; but, after all, they represent only the *opinion* of each individual writer; and are accepted or rejected according to the opinion of each individual reader. The fact that there are scarcely two alike out of the vast number of these analyses shows what a poor foundation these human opinions are to rest upon; and also that there is room for a serious attempt to search and see whether there be not some Divine plan in the structure of the book; or whether God has left us thus at sea, without chart, compass or helm.

Our answer is that God has not thus left us to interpret the book; but He has given us the book as *His own interpretation* of what " The Day of the Lord " is to be. There *is* a Divine plan in the structure of the book; and, if we follow this and proceed on its lines, believing what God says, all will be clear, simple and easy. But if, whenever God says one thing we immediately assume and assert that He means another thing, we shall, obviously, have as many different interpretations as we have interpreters! And who is to direct us in such a chaos of conflicting opinions.

Were it our aim to enumerate these opinions, and help to a choice between them, our task would be greater than we could undertake or carry out. But, as our aim is to treat the book as God's own description and explanation of the events which are to take place when the Lord Jesus shall be revealed from Heaven, our task will be a happy one; for it will be to try to understand what God *says* and not what man *thinks*.

We shall find ourselves giving little more than a translation of God's own words, first setting them forth according to His own plan.

That this plan is correct and true is not open even to question. It is so simple that a child will be able to understand it.

After the INTRODUCTION (chap. i.), which corresponds exactly with the CONCLUSION (chap. xxii. 6-21); and the Instruction for people on the earth during that Day (chap. ii., iii.), which corresponds with matters concerning people on the New Earth, in chap. xxi. 1—xxii. 5, we find that the whole body of the book is divided for us into seven pairs of connected events.

Perhaps the simplest form in which to first exhibit this will be the following* :—

𝕬 | i. Introduction

   𝕭 | ii., iii. The people on Earth

      𝕮 | iv.1—xx. 15. Visions

   𝕭 | xxi. 1—xxii. 5. The people on the New Earth.

𝕬 | xxii. 6-21. Conclusion

---

* We have marked these great divisions as well as the divisions of X, throughout the work, by using old English characters. So as to keep them quite distinct from their expansions and sub-divisions.

Now, the Holy Spirit has divided the central member, which we have marked " ✶," and which occupies the larger part of the book, into seven parts. Each of these seven parts consists of two scenes : The former of which takes place " in Heaven," and the latter " on Earth."

If we examine these more closely, we shall find that they are correlative: *i.e.*, the scene " in Heaven " is preliminary to, and explanatory of, the events which follow " on Earth." Things are seen " in Heaven," and words are there uttered which show the nature and object of what is about to take place " on Earth."

When God has described a scene as taking place " in Heaven," and caused Heavenly voices to give the key to what is to follow in another scene which immediately takes place " on earth "; and this is done *seven* consecutive times ; is it not strange that writers on the Apocalypse should overlook this exceedingly simple arrangement; and proceed to elaborate some complicated analysis of their own ; and thus wholly ignore and break up the division which God has himself made and given and marked off so clearly by the repeated expressions " in Heaven " and " upon the Earth," on purpose to guide us in understanding His book ?

How can we trust any analysis, however clever it may be, if these divisions are broken into, and the Heavenly and earthly scenes are mixed together ? All must be confusion. And any such division of the book, or any which proceeds on the lines of the chapter-divisions, as given in the authorised version, will be found useless for the purpose of gathering the real scope of the book.

Before we proceed further it may be well to set out these Divine divisions more fully.

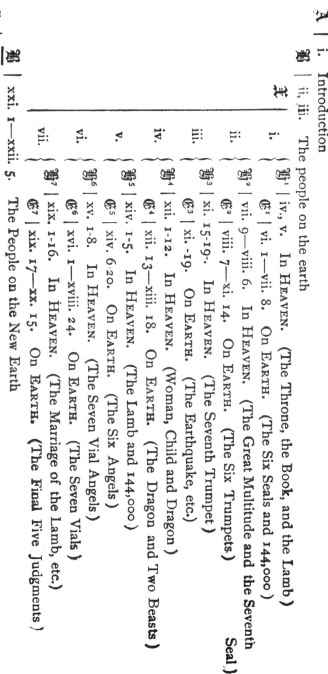

A | i. Introduction

B | ii, iii. The people on the earth

i. {
  D¹ | iv., v. In HEAVEN. (The Throne, the Book, and the Lamb.)
  C¹ | vi. 1—vii. 8. On EARTH. (The Six Seals and 144,000.)
}

ii. {
  D² | vii. 9—viii. 6. In HEAVEN. (The Great Multitude and the Seventh Seal.)
  C² | viii. 7—xi. 14. On EARTH. (The Six Trumpets.)
}

iii. {
  D³ | xi. 15-19. In HEAVEN. (The Seventh Trumpet)
  C³ | xi. -19. On EARTH. (The Earthquake, etc.)
}

iv. {
  D⁴ | xii. 1-12. In HEAVEN. (Woman, Child and Dragon)
  C⁴ | xii. 13—xiii. 18. On EARTH. (The Dragon and Two Beasts)
}

v. {
  D⁵ | xiv. 1-5. In HEAVEN. (The Lamb and 144,000.)
  C⁵ | xiv. 6-20. On EARTH. (The Six Angels)
}

vi. {
  D⁶ | xv. 1-8. In HEAVEN. (The Seven Vial Angels)
  C⁶ | xvi. 1—xviii. 24. On EARTH. (The Seven Vials)
}

vii. {
  D⁷ | xix. 1-16. In HEAVEN. (The Marriage of the Lamb, etc.)
  C⁷ | xix. 17—xx. 15. On EARTH. (The Final Five Judgments)
}

B | xxi. 1—xxii. 5. The People on the New Earth

A | xxii. 6-21. Conclusion

The more intently we look on this, and the more carefully we study it, the more shall we be struck by its beauty and simplicity. How clear, compared with man's complicated divisions made according to his own fancy! So clear that the humblest child of God cannot fail to grasp it. It requires no explanation; but it will itself explain all things to us if we have ears to hear.

It is remarkable that in each of these wondrous scenes "in Heaven" voices with utterances and songs are heard. Not one Heavenly scene is without some Heavenly voice or utterance. Indeed, there are, altogether *seventeen* of these distributed in these seven scenes "in Heaven."; and this distribution helps us to discover the order and arrangement of these seven pairs respectively.

No. iv. evidently is the great central pair; both from actual position as well as from its subject matter. As to position, it occupies, literally and actually, the central part of the book; while as to its subject matter, we shall see (when we come to consider it) that it is as important as its position declares it to be.

Then, Nos. i. and vii. are marked off as corresponding, by the fact that out of the seventeen heavenly voices ten are in these two pairs; *six* being in the first scene "in heaven," and *four* in the last. The heavenliness of Nos. i. and vii. is also more marked than in any of the others: for all heaven is engaged in either giving these utterances, or singing these songs*; and it is only in these two scenes that the four *Zōa*, or living ones, utter their voices.

In Nos. ii. and vi. we also have another pair—the former characterised by the trumpets, and the latter by the

---

* Singing is mentioned only three times in Revelation : chap. v. 9, xiv. 3, xv. 3.

vials—the two most solemn portions of all the judgments which the book contains. Moreover, it is remarkable that it is in these two that those who pass through, or come out of, the great tribulation are specially mentioned as giving these heavenly utterances.

It appears, therefore, from this that these seven pairs are arranged as an *Epanodos:* that is to say, the first corresponds with the last (the seventh); the second with the sixth; the third with the fifth; while the fourth stands out in the centre; emphasising, by its central position, its important teaching.

They may be set out formally and briefly thus:

i. | Longer and more full of heavenly voices and utterances. (Six in all.)

  ii. | The Trumpets

    iii. | Shorter and less detail

      iv. | Central in subject and position

    v. | Shorter and less detail

  vi. | The Vials

vii. | Longer and more full of heavenly voices and utterances. (Four in all.)

THE HEAVENLY VOICES

are also portioned out according to the above plan:

i. | All heaven (6). The four *Zōa*, or Living ones, and twenty-four Elders; only here and in No. vii.

  ii. | Those out of the great tribulation (2)

    iii. | Great voices (2)

      iv. | A loud voice (1)

    v. | Great voices (1)

  vi. | Those out of the great tribulation (1)

vii. | All heaven (4). The four *Zōa*, or Living ones, and twenty-four Elders; only here and in No. i

From all this it is clear that we have to do with Divine handiwork when we come to the study of this book.

We have before us not one of the many Apocalyptic writings which have been put forth at various times by men, which are for the most part unintelligible dreamings*; but we have one which differs from, and stands out amid, them all; having the Divine impress stamped upon it; thus marking it as worthy of our deepest attention and most reverent study.

It may be well to append a complete list or table of these utterances as a guide to their further study by our readers :—

A TABLE OF THE SEVENTEEN HEAVENLY UTTERANCES.
𝕳¹. Chaps. iv and v

The four *Zōa,* **or Living ones.** iv. 8. " Holy, Holy Holy," &c. (Three-fold.)

The twenty-four Elders. iv. 11. " Thou art worthy . . . to receive," &c. (Three-fold.)

The four *Zōa,* **or Living ones, and the twenty-four Elders.** v. 9, 10. (A new song.) " Thou art worthy to take the book," &c.

Many angels and the four Living ones, and the Elders and thousands of angels. v. 12. " Worthy is the Lamb," &c. (Seven-fold.)

Every creature. v. 13. " Blessing and honour and glory," &c. (Four-fold.)

The four *Zōa,* **or Living ones.** v. -14-. " Amen."

---

* Such as *The Sibyllene Oracles* (180 B.C.-350 A.D.) ; *The Testaments of the Twelve Patriarchs* (130 B.C.-10 A.D.) ; *The Psalms of Solomon* (70-40 B.C.) ; *The Book of Jubilees* (40-10 B.C.) ; *The Ascension of Isaiah* (1-100 A.D.) ; *The Assumption of Moses* (14-30 A.D.) ; *The Apocalypse of Baruch* (50-90 A.D.) ; *The Book of Enoch* (200-260 A.D.).

ℌ².   vii 9—viii 6

The great multitude out of the great tribulation.
vii. 10.   "Salvation to our God," &c.

All the angels round about the throne.   vii. 12.
" Amen : Blessing, and glory, and wisdom," &c.   (Seven-fold.)

ℌ³.   xi 15-19

Great voices.   xi. -15.   " The kingdom of the world is become," &c.

The twenty-four Elders.   xi. 17.   " We give Thee thanks, O Lord God Almighty."

ℌ⁴.   xii 1-12

A loud voice.   xii. 10-12.   " Now is come salvation, and strength," &c.

ℌ⁵.   xiv 1-5

A voice from heaven.   xiv. 3.   A new song (no words).

ℌ⁶.   xv 1-8

They that had gotten the victory over the beast, &c.   xv. -3.   " Great and marvellous are thy works, Lord God Almighty," &c.

ℌ⁷.   xix 1-16

A great voice of much people in heaven.   xix. -1-3.
" Alleluia : salvation and glory," &c.   (Four-fold.)

The twenty-four Elders and the four *Zōa,* **or Living ones.**   xix. -4-.   " Amen, Alleluia."

A voice out of the throne.   xix. 5.   " Praise our God, all ye his people," &c.

The voice of a great multitude, &c.   xix. -6, 7.
" Alleluia : for the Lord God omnipotent reigneth," &c.

We shall note, as we proceed, the relation of these Heavenly Voices to the transactions which follow on the earth.   Meanwhile, our readers may make out for themselves a more complete list of these utterances, and study the distinguishing features of each.

Before closing this chapter, we may add the following from Canon Bernard's *Progress of Doctrine in the New Testament*.* He beautifully expands the thought and the truth involved in the seven pairs of alternate visions which we have pointed out as being " in heaven " and " on earth." He says :—

" We have here . . . a doctrine of the *history* of the consummation : I mean that, besides a prophetic record of the facts of the history, we have (what is of much higher value) an exposition of the *nature* of the history. The book is a revelation of the connection between things that are seen and things that are not seen, between things *on earth*† and things *in heaven*†; a revelation which fuses both into one mighty drama; so that the movements of human action, and the course of visible fact, are half shrouded, half disclosed, amid the glory and the terror of the spiritual agencies at work around us, and of the eternal interests which we see involved. We are borne to the courts above, and the temple of God is opened *in heaven*†, and we behold the events *on earth*† as originating in what passes there. There seals are broken, trumpets are sounded, and vials are poured out, which rule the changes [of the world]. . . . While we are looking down through the rolling mists on things that pass below, we are all the time [in vision] before the throne of God and of the Lamb, and among the four-and-twenty elders, the four living beings, and the innumerable company of angels ; and we hear voices proceeding out of the throne . . . and hallelujahs that roll through the universe. We see

---

* Bampton Lectures for 1864. Macmillan. 5th Edition. 1900.
† Our italics.

further, that there is cause for this participation of the world above in the events of the world below; for it becomes more plain that the earth is the battlefield of the kingdoms of light and darkness. There is a far bolder revelation than we have had before of the presence and action of the powers of evil. The Old Serpent is on one side, as the Lamb is on the other; and the same light which shows the movements of the Head and Redeemer of our race, falls also upon those of the enemy and destroyer. In the sense of this connection between things seen and things not seen lies the secret of that awe, and elevation of mind, which we felt as children when we first turned these pages; and the assurance that it has an ever increasing value to him who has painfully sought to test the mingled form of good and ill, and to discern some plan and purpose in the confused scene around him" (pp. 193, 194).

"The book is a doctrine of the power and *coming* of our Lord Jesus Christ. 'Behold He cometh with clouds, and every eye shall see him.'‡ That is the first voice, and the key-note of the whole. The Epistles . . . [in chaps. ii. and iii.] . . . all take their tone from this thought, and are the voice of a Lord who will 'come quickly.' The visions which follow draw to the same end, and the last voices of the book respond to the first, and attest its subject and its purpose. 'He which testifieth these things saith, Surely I come quickly. Amen. Even so come, Lord Jesus.'* . . . Toward that hope our eyes have been steadily directed in the former Apostolic writings; but it is here presented, not so much in relation to our personal life as to the kingdom of God and to the world itself upon the whole. It appears here as the συντέλεια τοῦ

‡ Rev. i. 7.
* xxii. 20.

αἰῶνος (the *sunteleia* or *consummation of the age*), towards which all things tend. . . . Differences and uncertainties of interpretation as to the details . . . still leave us under the sense that it is a history of the power and coming of our Lord Jesus Christ. This assurance, enjoyed at all times, grows clearer in the days of trouble, rebuke and blasphemy : and *the darkest times which the prophecy forebodes will be those in which its fullest uses will be found*"* (pp. 194, 195).

---

* Our italics.

4

STRUCTURAL INTRODUCTION
(1:1-20)

W E now have to deal with each of these *eighteen* large members (as shown on page 118). We must expand the structure of each; and then give a translation, with such explanatory remarks as may be necessary to help us in understanding the inspired words.

We are aware that some persons consider these structures as more or less fanciful.

But we may ask, why are we to make a distinction between God's *words* and God's *works*? "All his works are perfect." Students of science never weary in examining them; and the more closely they examine them the more of this perfection do they discover in their structure, order, arrangement, beauty, etc., etc.

But God's *words* are part of His Works. Why should not students of God's Word deal with it in the same way, and expect to find the same perfection of structure, order and beauty? Why are His *words* to be treated as though they were imperfect, and His works perfect?

It is written, "The works of the LORD are great, sought out of all them that have pleasure therein" (Ps. cxi. 2).

We believe that His words also are great and perfect; and as we have, and trust our readers also have, intense "pleasure therein," we propose to seek them out and to "search" the Scriptures, so that we may all be able to say, " I rejoice at Thy word, as one that findeth great spoil " (Ps. cxix. 162).

Our readers are exhorted to study them carefully, for they are the key to the whole Book. They show us what is the *Scope* of the whole; and also of its various parts. They tell us what is emphatic; and what are the special points on which we are to fix our attention. Thus we shall have a constant and never-failing guide ever at hand to direct our studies and control our thoughts.

In the consideration of these Structures we shall get such an impression of the Divine source of the Book and of its perfections (even though we may not fully grasp them), that we shall be impelled to receive its revelation as "the Word of God," and "not as the Word of men" (1 Thess. ii. 13).

The INTRODUCTION (chap. i.) is constructed on exactly the same plan as the CONCLUSION (xxii. 6-21).

Each consists of four pairs of four members each.

It is not always, or even often, that the Introduction and Conclusion of a book thus correspond with each other.

But this book of the Revelation is peculiar. *Four* is the number symbolising that which has to do with the *earth :* and *sixteen* is the square of four. It is significant that this book should be rounded off so perfectly as to declare, thus, outwardly and symbolically, that it relates to this *earth ;* and to the putting *square* of all that concerns it.

Everything is out of course now: but all is to be put square ere long; and in this book we are told how it is going to be done.

The following is the structure of chapter i., which forms the "Introduction" to the whole book. To appreciate it more, we ought carefully to compare it with the structure of the " Conclusion," which will be given in its place.

𝔄 (page 118). THE STRUCTURE OF THE INTRODUCTION (chap i.)

E¹ | a¹ | i. 1. The angel testifying
       | b¹ | 2. The things testified
            | F¹ | c¹ | 3-. Benediction. ("Blessed")
                 | d¹ | -3. Advent. ("The time is at hand.")

E² | a² | 4-. John testifying
       | b² | -4, 5-. The things testified
            | F² | c² | -5, 6. Ascription. ("Unto Him.")
                 | d² | 7, 8. Advent. ("Behold He cometh")

E³ | a³ | 9-. John testifying
       | b³ | -9-11. The things testified
            | F³ | d³ | 12-16. Advent. (Vision of the Coming One)
                 | c³ | 17-. Salutation. ("Fear not")

E⁴ | a⁴ | -17-18. Jesus testifying (of Himself)
       | b⁴ | 19. The things testified
            | F⁴ | d⁴ | -20. Advent. (Vision (12-16, d³) referred to)
                 | c⁴ | -20. Interpretation. ("The 7 stars are," &c.)

𝔄

This Structure shows us that the emphasis is specially placed on two things :—

The Advent (F), and

Testimony concerning the Advent (E).

In each of the latter of the two pairs (F^1, F^2, F^3, and F^4) the *Advent* is alternated with four other subjects :—

Benediction,

Ascription,

Salutation, and

Interpretation.

But these are introverted. For, whereas, in the first two pairs the *Advent* follows the *Benediction* and the *Ascription* respectively, it precedes the *Salutation* and the *Interpretation* in the last two pairs.

Moreover, the *Advent* is testified in two ways. In the first two pairs (d^1 and d^2) it is testified in *words*; but in the last two pairs (d^3 and d^4) it is testified in *vision*. Our attention is called to this difference by the Introversions in F^3 and F^4.

And now, to show how perfectly, not only the introduction, as a whole, is constructed, but also, how perfect are each of its parts (or members), we must expand the first member, E^1, as an example, in full.

This makes it perfectly clear that in these first two verses we have the essence of the whole book. This first member, consisting of these two verses, is divided into two parts, which have a perfect correspondence with each other. This correspondence is hidden by the faulty human verse-division. In each division we have the same four subjects, viz., *giving* of the Book ; Its *medium, purpose,* and *subject ;* first, in Intention ; and then, in Execution.

Intention   Execution

E¹ (page 129), i. 1, 2.   *The Angel Testifying and the Things Testified*

E¹ | e | 1-. THE REVELATION GIVEN] "The Revelation of Jesus Christ, which God gave
    f | -1-. THE MEDIUM] "unto him,
    g | -1-. THE PURPOSE] "to show unto his servants
    h | -1-. THE SUBJECT] "things which must shortly come to pass;

    e | -1-. THE REVELATION GIVEN] "And he sent and signified it
    f | -1-. THE MEDIUM] "by his angel
    g | -1, 2-. THE PURPOSE] "unto his servant John: who bare record
    h | -2. THE SUBJECT] "of the word of God, and the testimony of Jesus Christ, and of all things that he saw,"

We need not proceed further with the expansions of all these members.

Our readers will have noticed that, in E¹, we have combined the full text with the outline or skeleton of the structure. But this text is from the Authorized Version. In our Exposition we propose to give our own Translation, with such explanatory notes as may serve to make it clear.

THE TRANSLATION OF E¹ (page 131), chap. i. 1, 2.

i. 1. The Revelation of Jesus Christ] This is the Divine title of the book. All other titles, whether ancient or modern, are human, and are therefore not worth discussing, or even enumerating. The book is often called the *Apocalypse*, which is the transliteration of the Greek word rendered " Revelation." 'Αποκάλυψις means literally *an unveiling*, from ἀπό *(apo) away from*, and καλύπτω *(kalupto)*, to *veil:* and may be understood either of the taking a veil from a person, and so causing him to become visible (as when a statue is said to be *unveiled*); or of taking a veil from the future, and disclosing the course of events which shall take place.* Probably both senses are

---

* We give a list of all the occurrences of the word, with its renderings, on pages 32, 33, so that our readers may be able to judge for themselves what is the sense in each passage. It is rendered *revelation* in Rom. ii. 5; xvi. 25. 1 Cor. xiv. 6, 26. 2 Cor. xii. 1, 7. Gal. i. 12; ii. 2. Eph. i. 17; iii. 3. 1 Pet. i. 13. Rev. i. 1.

With ἐν *(en) in*, *i.e.*, *When he shall be revealed*, 2 Thess. i. 7. 1 Pet. iv. 13.

Manifestation, Rom. viii. 19.

Appearing, 1 Pet. i. 7.

Coming, 1 Cor. i. 7 (marg. *revelation*).

With εἰς *(eis) into*, *To lighten*, Luke. ii. 32.

true here. And, if the latter, then is shows us that
what follows in this book is to be taken *literally ;* for,
when the Lord would not reveal, but would *hide* the
meaning of His words, He spoke in parables and used
emblems (Matt. xiii. 10-16. Mark iv. 11, 12).

which God gave to Him] Here it is not the Father
who instructs His children ; but, it is " God," as
Sovereign, who informs His " servants " through Christ,
who is (in His mediatorial character) emphatically *the*
Servant (see Is. xlii. 1, 7, &c.), where, as a " bruised
reed " and " smoking flax," He is not broken or
quenched "*till He have set judgment in the earth.*" The
time has now come for Him to execute this judgment:
and therefore God, from His throne of government,
gives to His Servant, Jehovah-Jesus, to show. (Compare John v. 19, 20 ; vii. 16 ; viii. 28 ; xii. 49 ; xiv. 10 ;
xvii. 7, 8. Matt. xi. 27. Mark xiii. 32. Acts i. 7).

to show] Here we have the same word as that
which is used in the opening of the " Conclusion " of
this book (xxii. 6). It means to *to present to view*, and
has a close connection with the visions and signs
(compare Matt. iv. 8 ; viii. 4). But it must not be
restricted to this, as is clear from Matt. xvi. 21.*

to His servants] Not " all Christians " (as such),
as Alford says, but to Israel, to whom the word
" servant " peculiarly belongs. We have already said
something on this subject (see pages 28-31), so that we
need only add that it is not used of Christians in the
Pauline Epistles, but it is in 1 Cor. vii. 22, and in
four cases where he refers to himself and others as
singled out for special service. Indeed, in one place

---

*The word occurs in this book *eight* times, viz., i. 1 ; iv. 1 ; xvii. 1 ;
xxi. 9, 10 ; xxii. 1, 6, 8.

an important argument is built on the emphatic distinction between *servants* and *sons* (Gal. iv. 7): " Wherefore thou art no more a servant, but a son." (See
2 Cor. vi. 17, 18, and compare John xv. 15).

On the other hand, it is used *fourteen* times of those
who are the subjects of the Apocalypse. In the Old
Testament it is the common word for Israel under the
covenant of works. (See Lev. xxv. 42, 55. Is. xlix. 3 ;
lxv. 15, &c., &c.).

what things must needs come to pass] by the
necessity of Divine ruling and over-ruling. That is to
say, they are not left to chance, for they must needs
come to pass. We have the exact words here from the
Septuagint of Dan. ii. 29. In other words, God will
fulfil that which He reveals.

with speed] ἐν τάχει (*en tachei*) occurs *eight* times,*
from which our readers may themselves see that it is
used in two senses : *quickly,* as to speed ; and *soon,* as to
time. Both may be true here: and, if the latter (according to Luke. xviii. 8) be relied on, then we must note that
delay is implied, " though He bear long with them "
(verse 7). Such delay is implied in Rev. x. 6: " for
there shall be no more delay." In God's speedy time
(with whom a thousand years are as one day,
2 Pet. iii. 8), He will bring them to pass ; and
when that time comes He will do it with speed, and
" make a short work of it " (Rom. ix. 28).

and He signified it] *i.e.,* God, see xxii. 6. The
word means (etymologically) *to show by signs:* but it

---

* It is rendered *quickly,* Acts xii. 7 ; xxii. 18. *Speedily,* Luke xviii.
8. *Shortly,* Acts xxv. 4. Rom. xvi. 21. Rev. i. 1 ; xxii. 16. To these
may be added 1 Tim. iii. 14, where Lachmann and Tregelles prefer it to
τάχιον (*tachion*).

must not be restricted to this meaning, as the other occurrences of the word clearly show. See John xii. 33 ; xviii. 32 ; xxi. 19. Acts xi. 28 ; xxv. 27. Rev. i. 1. The restriction referred to has caused the Apocalypse to be looked upon as a book of signs and symbols which no one can understand. The fact is that about half the symbols (14) are definitely explained (though these explanations are often again taken by expositors as being symbolical!) Being Divinely explained, they serve as a key to those which are unexplained.*

sending by His angel to His servant John] John, like Paul and others, was singled out for this special service to his own fellow-servants. Compare Is. xlix. 5. Amos iii. 7.

2. who testified] The past tense shows that the Introduction, though coming first, was necessarily written last. The word connects the Introduction with the Conclusion. Compare i. 1 with xxii. 16, 20. The only three occurrences in this book. It means here not only testified, but published and made known.

of (or, as to) the Word of God] We have seen above (pages 34, 35) that this is the common idiomatic phrase for a direct prophetic communication. This, therefore, stands first, and is used of the whole book.

and the testimony of Jesus Christ] *i.e.*, which He testified when on earth. This book or prophetic word does not go outside the scope of what Jesus bare

---

* Thus, " Lampstands " are explained for us as representing assemblies ; " Stars," angels of the assemblies ; " Torches," spirits ; " Horns " and " Eyes," spirits ; " Incense odours," prayers of saints ; " Dragon," Satan ; " Frogs," unclean spirits ; " Wild Beast," a king (xvii.) ; " Heads " of the Wild Beast, mountains and kings ; " Horns," kings ; " Waters," peoples ; " Woman," a city ; " Fine linen," righteous awards ; " City of God," Bride of the Lamb.

testimony to, in His own prophetic teaching. That is the essence of the prophecy of this book, and the "spirit" of it. See xxii. 6.

what things soever he saw] Not only what he heard as a direct prophetic message, but what he saw represented in vision. God gave the Revelation to Christ, Christ signified by His angel to John; and John hereby makes it known. He says, in xxii. 8 (where we have another connecting link between the Conclusion and the Introduction), " I John saw these things, and heard them." We have also another proof, in this past tense (i. 2), that the Introduction was written last; or, at any rate, after the seeing and the hearing referred to

The second member, F¹ (p. 129), consists of only one verse (i. 3); the subject of which is two-fold :—viz., Benediction, and The Advent.

It may be expanded as follows :—

THE EXPANSION OF F¹ (page 129), chap. i. 3

Benediction and Advent

F¹ | i | 3-. BENEDICTION] " Blessed
  | j | k | -3-. PERSONS] " be he that readeth, and they that hear
    | l | -3-. WORDS] "the words of this prophecy,
  | j | k | -3- PERSONS] " and keep
    | l | -3-. WORDS] "those things that are written therein :
| i | -3. REASON] " for the time is at hand "

THE TRANSLATION OF F¹ (page 129), chap. i. 3

3. **Blessed** (or, happy) **be he that readeth, and they who hear**] This points to one reader and

many listeners (Luke iv. 16). From the neglect of this book, one would suppose it said, " Blessed are those who do *not* read." So openly is this blessing rejected ; yea, sometimes boastfully ! If there be a reference here to *public* reading, then the neglect of this book indeed stands exposed, and the attitude so generally assumed with regard to it is tacitly condemned.

the words of this prophecy] There is a reference here to the spoken words, especially to the seventeen heavenly utterances, as distinct from the things written. The words spoken are the key to the things written, for it is added :

and keep in mind **the things** which stand **written therein**] "Keep" is a Hebrew idiom. The word שָׁמַר *(shamar)* means *to remember, to ponder upon.* See the LXX. translation of it in Gen. xvii. 9, xxxvii. 11. Num. xxviii. 2, etc. Compare also Luke i. 66, "and all they that heard them (the sayings) laid them up in their hearts"; Luke ii. 19, " But Mary kept all these things, and pondered them in her heart." So also verse 51. The word is used also of remembering so as *to obey* ; but this can hardly be appropriate here, for " prophecy " is not precept.

for the season is near] The word καιρός *(kairos)* refers to the ordained and appointed time, viz., the time occupied by what is written, *i.e.*, the Advent of the Day of the Lord. The prophecy of this book is not to be put aside as though it referred to things so remote that they have no concern for us. But they are always to be regarded as near, and kept in our minds, so that our life may be influenced by them, and that we may walk in view of the nearness of the Day when the

Lord will judge, and thus be without care as to this
present time in which man is judging, which is called
" man's day " (1 Cor. iv. 3). Paul shows us how this
prophecy may be "kept" in a practical manner in
1 Cor. iv. 1-5. Compare ἐν τάχει in verse 1.

We need not further minutely expand the various
members of this Introduction ; but proceed with the
translation, referring our readers to the Structure of
E⁹ and F² on page 129.

THE TRANSLATION OF E⁹ a⁹ (page 129), chap. i. 4

John testifying

4-. **John to the seven assemblies which are in
Asia**] We have already shown (pages 62-67) that the
word ἐκκλησία (*ecclesia*) is used in many senses. We
take it here in the neutral sense of *Assembly*, which
leaves the interpretation open. Certain assemblies are
specially addressed. They are recognised as being on
the earth at the time when the things written in this
prophecy shall be fulfilled. The continued reference in
these seven Epistles to the body or subject-matter of
the Apocalypse shows that chaps. ii. and iii. are not to
be separated from the rest of the book. We shall see
this more clearly when we come to the Epistles themselves. All are agreed that there will be, and must be,
a people on the earth during " the Day of the Lord,
such as are alluded to in xii. 17 ; xiii. 10 ; xiv. 12, etc.;
and all must agree also that they will need some special
instruction. Where is such instruction, if it be not that
which is given to them in these seven Epistles ? The
interpretation of them belongs to that day. But that
does not shut out such *application* as may have been
made by those who read them in John's day; or as

may be made by us who read them in our own day. Each read, and each get the promised blessing, in turn. But, when the Church is caught up to meet the Lord in the air, we shall not take away this book and these Epistles with us; but those who are left behind will then learn what the true *interpretation* is, as we had never done. They will see the fulfilment of what is here prophesied. They, too, will get their blessing; and we see in the Jewish Remnant, and the various companies of people in this book, what the reality of that blessing will be.

E² b² (page 129), i. -4, 5

The things testified

-4, 5-. Grace to you, and peace, from Him that is, and that was, and that is coming] Here we have an undoubted reference to, and paraphrase of, the name of Jehovah, as revealed in Ex. iii. 14.

It is not from the Father to His children, as in the Church Epistles; but it is from Jehovah as He was revealed and made known to Israel. This is in perfect keeping with what we hold to be the scope of the book. Three times we have this periphrasis of Jehovah, and yet it is varied according to the emphasis we are to place upon it.

In i. 4 and 8, it is "*is*, and *was*, and *is to come*."

In iv. 8 it is, "*was*, and *is*, and *is to come*."

In xi. 17 it is, "*art* and *wast*" (the third or future verb, being omitted according to the critical Greek Texts, L. T. Tr. W.H. A.V. and R.V).

Hence in ch. i. 4, 8, the emphasis is on "*is*."

In iv. 8, it is on "*was*."

And in xi. 17 it is on "*art*."

It is for us to learn what this emphasis teaches and we can do so as we come to the respective passages.

and from the seven spirits which are **before His throne**] This fact that they are "before," or in the presence of, God's Throne, shows that they occupy the position of *servants* (see 1 Kings x. 8), and of *created* beings (iv. 5, 10; vii. 9, 15; viii. 2; xi. 4, 16; xii. 10; xiv. 3, 5, 10; xx. 12).

This one fact ought to have precluded the idea that these seven could be one, and that one Divine! There is nothing in the whole Bible which represents the Holy Spirit in such a subordinate position. He is equal with the Father and with the Son.

On the other hand, angels are constantly represented as occupying this position. And angels are again referred to in iv. 5, under the symbol of seven lamps (to which other spiritual creatures are likened in Ezek. i. 13).

There are other references to these seven angels in the book: *e.g.*, viii. 2. "*The* seven": *i.e.*, the well-known, or before-mentioned seven.

Angels are specially called "spirits." See Heb. i. 7, 14. Ps. civ. 4. "He maketh His angels spirits." The word is used of any spiritual being, higher than men, and lower than Deity; without corporeal garb of "flesh and blood." Where there is any doubt as to the nature of these beings, they are always defined: *e.g.*, a "dumb spirit," Mark ix. 17. Compare verse 20. Luke ix. 39; x. 20; xiii. 11. Matt. viii. 16. Acts xvi. 16.*

---

* See also "unclean spirits," Matt. x. i.; xii. 43. Mark i. 23, 26, 27; iii. 11, 30; v. 2, 8, 13. Luke iv. 33, 36; vi. 18; viii. 29; xi. 24. Rev. xvi. 13; xviii. 2. "Wicked spirits"—Matt. xii. 45. Luke vii. 21; viii. 2; xi. 26.

In Acts viii. 26, " the angel of the Lord " was sent on a special mission to Philip. Immediately afterwards he is called (verse 29) "the spirit" who spake to Philip; and then, in verse 39, the same angelic messenger is called " the spirit* of the Lord," who ended his mission by catching Philip away to Azotus. In Rev. iii. 1, we have the seven spirits of God joined with the seven stars. In Rev. v. 6, we see these "seven spirits of God sent forth into all the earth." If it be objected that this interpretation opens the door to angel-worship, the answer is that the door is effectually closed in this very book, in xix. 10 ; xxii. 9 : " See thou do it not."

If it be objected that " angels " would not be mentioned in connection with God and the Lord Jesus, the answer is that they *are so mentioned* in 1 Tim. v. 21, " God and the Lord Jesus Christ and the elect angels." Are these the Holy Spirit ? The answer is No ! The thought embodied in this combination here, in Rev. i. 4, is not so much the Triune Deity, as such; but that of the supreme High Court of heaven having jurisdiction on earth ; angels being the assessors. Compare Mark viii. 38. Luke ix. 26 ; xii. 8, where we have a similar thought.

Nowhere do we find the Holy Spirit associated with the Father and the Son in any salutation. Not even in the Pauline Church Epistles. In those Epistles, He is viewed as being here on earth with the Church, and grace and peace come from Heaven; from the Father and the Son.

In this dispensation angels are our servants, see Heb. i. 14 ; ii. 1, 2, 5. In the coming Dispensation, after the Church is removed, Angels are no longer servants, they are associated with Heaven's high court, and are

---

*The AV. and RV. both have a capital " s " here.

connected with the throne. The Son Himself will act as " before the angels of God." (Luke xii. 8, 9).

All these grounds are from Scripture ; but the objections to them are only what interpreters find it " difficult to believe." It is a question of what God has said ; and not what man may think difficult or easy to believe.

5. and from Jesus Christ] The once humbled One who is now exalted and glorified.

the Faithful witness] Compare Is. lv. 4.

the First-born of the dead] See Col. i. 18.

and the Ruler of the kings of the earth] It is remarkable that all these three titles are combined in Ps. lxxxix. 27, 37. "I will make him my *first-born, higher than the kings of the earth.* . . his throne shall be as *a faithful witness* in heaven?" See also Is. lii. 15. Rev. vi. 15 ; xvii. 4 ; xix, 16. The comparison with the kings of the earth is parallel with Ps. ii. 2.

The sudden change from the genitive case (of Jesus Christ) to the Nominatives which follow it, is very remarkable ; and implies the immutability of the Divine Nature, as in " that is, and that was, and that is coming " above ; we might also compare Heb. xiii. 8, or supply, as in the A. V. "who is."

These titles have no relation to the Church of God. but to Dominion in the earth. It is the fulfilment of Luke i. 32, which is about to take place : hence these appropriate titles are here assumed. In Dan. viii. 25, Christ is spoken of as the " Prince of princes," but only in connection with Israel. That we have here an earthly rule : and that the Dominion in the Earth is about to be taken and used by the Son of Man, is clear from many Scriptures. (See Rev. xi. 17, 18; xvii. 14; xix. 16. Ps. ii., xlv., cx. Isa. ix. 6, 7).

F² c² (page 129), i. -5, 6.   *Ascription*

To Him that loveth us]   All the critical Greek Texts and R.V. read the present and not the past participle here.   We have given our reasons above, in our ninth point (page 41), for our belief that this expression is one of those which belongs peculiarly to Israel.   And the *present* participle here tells us that Jehovah's love to Israel is everlasting (Jer. xxxi. 3. Isa. liv. 10); that He who chose their fathers, and loved them, is now about to show that that love is still a present love, and what it is about to do for them.

and washed (or loosed*) us from our sins]   The reading here is somewhat doubtful.   We have given both, for both contain parts of the whole truth. " Washed," is more vivid here, and more in accordance with Hebrew idiom.   For " washed," see Ps. li. 2, 7. Isa. i. 16, 18.   Ezek. xxxvi. 25.   Heb. x. 22 : and for " loosed," compare Matt. xx. 28.   Heb. ix. 12. Rev. v. 9; xiv. 3, 4.   In either case this is the fulfilment of Ps. cxxx. 8, "He shall redeem Israel from all his iniquities," and of Isa. xl. 1, 2, where Jehovah says, " Comfort ye, comfort ye, my people, saith your God. Speak ye comfortably to Jerusalem, and cry unto her that her warfare (or appointed time) is accomplished, that her iniquity is pardoned."   And this is the object of the coming of Jehovah Jesus, as announced in

---

* Lachmann, Tischendorf, Tregelles, Westcott and Hort, and R.V. read "loosed," or "freed."   The difference is only the letter *o* (some ancient MSS. reading λύσαντι (*lusanti*), *freed*, instead of λούσαντι (*lousanti*), *washed*.

Matt. i. 21, " He shall save his people from their
sins."

by His blood]   Certainly not " in " His blood.   Such
a thing was never heard of in the Old Testament.   It
was not " in " blood that sins were purged away, but
" by " blood, for blood itself was a cause of defilement.
It was *by* the precious atoning merits of Him of whose
death the blood speaks.*   See page 153.

6. **and He made us** to be **a kingdom and priests]**
This is Hebrew in idiom and in meaning.   The
explanation will be found in Ex. xix. 6, where God says,
respecting Israel (not the Church !), " Ye shall be unto
Me a kingdom of priests"; which the Septuagint renders
" a royal priesthood."   These also are the words written
to " elect strangers," the Dispersion in 1 Peter ii. 5, 9.
It is the figure *Hendiadys*, by which the noun
" kingdom " become a superlative adjective.   Thus,
" and He made us priests—yes, and royal priests, too " ;
or, ' He made us a kingly order—the members of which
are holy and set apart for the service of God.'   We are
aware that these words are unlawfully claimed and
appropriated by the Church, and used as a poor and
weak argument against the pretensions of Rome and
Romanisers.   Where do we read one word about the
Christians being priests, in any one of the Epistles
addressed to believers by the Holy Spirit through
Paul?   The very thought is foreign to Scripture,
and contrary to fact.   But such promises were
directly and distinctly made to Israel.   See, as to
priests, Is. lxi. 6. 1 Pet. ii. 5 (and compare Rev. v. 10

---

* It is the figure *Metalepsis* (see *Figures of Speech*, page 611), by
which " blood " is first put for *death*, and then death put for Christ's
atoning *merits*.

and xx. 6). As to *kings*, see Ps. xlix. 14. Dan. vii. 22, 27. Matt. xix. 28. Luke xxii. 29, 30 (and compare Rev. ii. 26, 27, and iii. 21). There can clearly be no priests of any kind in this Dispensation. The Epistle to the Hebrews teaches that the *Aaronic* order has no longer any place; and that the *Melchizedec* order is absorbed in Jesus Christ (Heb. vi.-viii.). If Christians, to-day, are *kings*, who are their subjects? and if they are *priests*, where and for whom do they perform priestly duties? For priestly service was *on behalf of others*, "first for his own sins; and then for the people's (Heb. v. 1; vii. 27).

to His God and Father] (see John xx. 17). Not "our" Father, as in the Pauline Epistles (1 Thess. i. 3; iii. 11, etc.). In due season this ascription shall be realised, as we see from chap. xx. 4. With regard to the word "Father" introduced here, we have to remember that the Priest's office was *hereditary*. Only Aaron's sons were priests.

to Him be the glory and the dominion for ever and ever. (*Lit.*, unto the ages of the ages.) **Amen**] To Him (of course) who "loved the people" (Deut. xxxiii. 3) is this ascription given. The Greek here for "unto the ages of the ages" is merely a literal rendering of the Hebrew idiom. Such an expression for eternity was unknown to the Classical Greek writers.

F² d² (page 129), i. 7, 8. *Advent.*

7. **Behold,**] Our attention is thus called to what is the sequel to all that has been said. We are to gaze by faith on this wondrous and solemn fact.

He cometh with (or, amid the) **clouds**] This is an Old Testament reference. *Lit.*, with *the* clouds, *i.e.*, with the clouds so often mentioned in connection with His coming in glory. Believers are to be "caught up *in* clouds to meet the Lord in the air." They will accompany the Lord when "He comes *with* clouds" to the earth. Two very different scenes are described, here and in 1 Thess. iv. 17. This is the same aspect of His coming as that mentioned in Matt. xxiv. 30. "THEN (*i.e.*, "immediately" after the great tribulation) shall appear the sign of the Son of Man (Rev. i. 13) in heaven: and THEN shall all the tribes of the earth (or the Land) mourn, and they shall see the Son of man coming in (or with) the clouds of heaven with power and great glory (*i.e.*, with great and glorious power)." The clouds are mentioned as His chariot in Psalm xviii. 11; civ. 3. Compare also Ex. xix. 16; xl. 34. Is. vi. 4; xix. 1. Ezek. i. 4. The passages specially connected with Rev. i. 7 are Dan. vii. 13, 14. Matt. xxiv. 30; xxvi. 64, and Mark xiv. 62.

and every eye will see Him] "Eye" is put by *Synecdoche* for *person*, *i.e.*, everyone on the earth will see Him. So Matt. xxiv. 30. But not the Church of God, for it will be then already in heaven, and not on the earth.

even those very ones **who pierced Him]** These are specially singled out—"all those who," for His brethren, like Joseph's brethren, will then mourn for Him. Compare John xix. 34, which quotes Zech. xii. 10.*

and all the tribes of the Land] Not "kindreds," for the word is the same as in Matt. xxiv. 30. And it is the tribes "of the Land," not of the whole earth. The

---

* Here we have the correct translation of Zech. xii 10, while the Septuagint gives it incorrectly.

tribes of Israel are the subject here, as in v. 5 ; vii. 4-8 ; and xxi. 12.

will wail because of Him] *i.e.*, at (the) sight of Him ; or, over Him. This very wailing is described in Zech. xii. 10-12, and is there declared to take place "in that day," the day of the Lord. This fixes for us the sense in which "the Lord's day" is to be taken in Rev. i. 10.

How can the Church of God be brought in here ? Did the Church of God pierce Him ? Are the members of the Body of Christ members also of the " Tribes of the Land " ? And what have they to wail and beat themselves for, when they are distinctly told that " the day of the Lord " shall not come upon them as a thief (1 Thess. v. 4), but that it will come upon others " as travail upon a woman with child ; and THEY shall not escape " (1 Thess v. 3). Those who can bring the Church in here cannot possibly have any true conception of what the Church is. Even this mourning of Israel will be very different from the fear and trembling and destruction which will come upon the Gentiles. See Isa. ii. 19. Rev. vi. 16. Israel's mourning will be with that repentance which is so often spoken of as the one necessary condition of national blessing.

Yea : Amen] A double confirmation of the truth of this solemn statement. Compare the conclusion, xxii. 20. The figure is *Synonymia*, *i.e.*, the use of synonymous words in order to strengthen the certainty of this prophecy.

8. **I am Alpha and Omega***] What this means is explained in verse 17, and again in xxii. 13. This is a

---

* The words, " the beginning and the ending " are omitted by all the Critical Greek Texts and R.V.

Hebraism, in common use among the Ancient Jewish
Commentators to designate the whole of anything from
the beginning to the end; *e.g.*, "Adam transgressed the
whole law from א (*Aleph*) to ת (*Tau*)";* "Abraham
kept the whole law from א to ת."† The article is used
in the Greek, but it is not required either by
the Hebrew or English idioms. Here it means
"the first and the last," as explained in verse 17
and xxii. 12, 13. This title is not a church title, but
is specially used in connection with Israel. See Ex.
iii. 14. Isa. xli. 4; xliii. 10; xliv. 6, 8; xlviii. 12;
and Rev. xxi. 6.

saith the LORD God‡] Another Old Testament title,
used first in Gen. ii. See also remarks (pages 19, 20)
on this. The title "Jehovah" (or LORD) expresses His
covenant relation with Israel; "God" expresses His
relationship as Creator with mankind as a whole.

that is, and that was, and that is coming] See
our notes on this above, on verse 4. The emphasis is
on the word "is," as shown, by being put first.

the Almighty] We have considered this title above
(page 17) and its bearing on our conviction that it
points to relationship with Israel. Ὁ παντοκράτωρ (*ho
pantokratōr*) is rendered in the Septuagint as the equivalent for "the Lord of hosts." In Amos iv. 13 as "God
of hosts"; in Job it is used for "Shaddai." The
word is used only once in the New Testament outside the
Apocalypse, and that in a quotation from Jer. xxxi. 1, 9,
concerning Israel's future (2 Cor. vi. 18). What the

* Jalk. Reub., fol. 17. 4.
† Ibid., fol. 48. 4.
‡ The title "God" is added here according to all the Critical
Greek Texts and R.V.

combination of these titles says to us here is this : " I, the Almighty Lord of hosts, the unchangeable God, will accomplish all My will, fulfil all My word, and execute all My judgments."

We now come to the third set of four members : in which we find the same subjects repeated ; but not precisely in the same order. In the former two the *Advent* follows the *Benediction* and the *Ascription ;* while in the latter two it precedes the *Salutation* and the *Interpretation.*

E³ a³ i. 9 (page 129) *John Testifying*

9. **I John**] as in i. 4, and in the Conclusion, xxii. 8. Compare also Dan. vii. 28 ; ix. 2 ; x. 2. The word " also " must be omitted.

even (or, both) **your brother**] according to the flesh, as well as in a higher relation. (Compare Acts ix. 30 ; xi. 29. Rev. xii. 10, &c.)

and partaker with you in the tribulation and kingdom and patience] The construction and order of the Greek here is pronounced by commentators as " peculiar." Alford calls it " startling." This is because the Figure of speech is not discerned. It is *Hendiatris, i.e.,* three words are used, but only one thing is meant. The one thing is " the tribulation," and the two other words characterise it as being, not the tribulation which the world experiences, but that (for the article is emphatic here) which is specially con- nected with the " Kingdom " (Acts xiv. 22. 2 Tim. ii. 12 ; and Rev. xx. 6), and that which needs " patient waiting " (Rev. ii. 2, 3, 19 ; iii 10 ; xiii. 10 ; xiv. 12).

which are in* Jesus] Not "of Jesus," as A.V. But

---

* All the Critical Greek Texts and R.V. add the word " in."

in Him, in His Kingdom, and in His patient waiting
(2 Thess. iii. 5 marg., and R.V. Comp. Heb. x. 13).
John stood in the same relation to these things as those
to whom he wrote. Their brotherhood was "in Jesus."
But the fellowship of the Church of God is *always* said
to be "in Christ" (never "in Jesus"). The members
of His body died in Him, and are risen in Him.
Henceforth they know Him no more after the flesh*
(2 Cor. v. 15—17), but stand on new or resurrection
ground; and know Him as the great and glorious Head
in Heaven of that Body of which they are the members
here on earth.

E³ b³ i.-9-11 (page 129)   *The Things Testified*

(I) **came to be in the isle that is called Patmos**]
The verb is ἐγενόμην (*egenomēn*), not the verb *to be.*
It means *to come to be* ; and, when used of an *event*, we can
say, *it came to pass.* But how are we to render it when
it is used of a *person ?* "Came to be" is not happy
English. "Found myself" is perhaps better. The
word describes a fact, though it does not explain it.
That explanation, therefore, follows :—

**because of the Word of God, and† the testimony of
Jesus‡**] The preposition διά (*dia*), with the accusative
case following, denotes *the occasion* or *object*, rather than
the cause (which would be expressed by the Genitive
case. But chap. i. 2 settles the point for us: for there

---

* See *Things to Come* for July, 1901. Since separately published
by Eyre & Spottiswoode, Great New Street, London.

† We must omit the second "because of," according to the Critical
Greek Texts and R.V.

‡ We must omit the word "Christ" with all the Critical Texts
and the R.V.

"the word of God and the testimony of Jesus"
are other names for this Book (vi. 9 and xx. 4),
and consist of "the things which John saw in
Patmos." How could he be banished there because of the things which he saw there? No! it
was because he was to receive and see these things
that John came to be or found himself in Patmos.
He was there by Divine Spirit and power in order to
receive this Apocalypse or Revelation, just as Paul
went into Arabia to receive his revelation (Gal. i. 15-17)
(Compare Gal. ii. 1, 2). That John was banished to
Patmos on account of his witness for Christ is *tradition*.
That, probably, is the reason why it is so universally
accepted as a fact ; though not a hint is given of it
here where we should naturally expect to find it. We
prefer to accept the unanswerable evidence of verse 2,
which, to our mind, settles the matter as to the object
of John's coming to be in Patmos. Moreover, he
seems to have nothing to hinder his seeing and hearing
and writing. He had leisure to obey the seven-fold
command to write. And why does everyone take
Patmos literally here, when nearly every other place
mentioned in this book is taken as meaning some
different place? Even the places of the seven
churches are taken by some to be no places at
all, but merely periods of time! The fact that
Patmos is taken literally shows that other places mentioned in the Revelation are to be taken literally also ;
especially as we are plainly told when we are not to do
so.

But why Patmos at all? The answer is surely to be
found in the fact that it was in "the great Sea," which
is the central point of the Revelation. Rome lay to the

West.   The Land, the Euphrates, and Babylon lay on
the East.   In the Isle of Patmos then he came to be,
and, in like manner, he tells us :

10. **I came to be** (or, found myself), **by** the **Spirit,
in the day of the Lord**] *i.e.*, by the power, or
agency, of the Spirit, just as in iv. 2, xvii. 3, and
xxi. 10.

In order to see " visions of God " the prophet
Ezekiel (i. 1) was under the direct influence and power
of the Spirit.   John was transported by spiritual
instrumentality into the scenes which shall take place
in the Day of the Lord, and records what he then saw
in vision : namely : the things which shall take place
literally and actually in that Day.   How this may have
been accomplished we may learn from Ezek. viii. 3 :
" And he put forth the form of an hand, and took me by
a lock of mine head ; and the spirit lifted me up between
the earth and the heaven, and brought me in the visions
of God to Jerusalem." In chapter xl. 2, 3, he says, " In the
visions of God brought he me into the land of Israel, . . .
And he brought me thither."   Ezekiel goes on to record
what he saw of events and realities *in the far distant
future*, and describes the Temple which is then to be
built.   In Ezek. xi. 24, 25, we read, " Afterwards the
spirit took me up, and brought me in a vision by the
Spirit of God into Chaldea, to them of the captivity.
So the vision that I had seen went up from me.   Then
I spake unto them of the captivity all the things that
the LORD had shewed me."   Those things concerned the
future restoration of Israel (see verses 16-20).   In the
face of this, why should we go out of our way to put an
unmeaning sense on the phrase " in the Spirit " in
Rev. i. 10 ?   There is no article in the Greek.. It is

simply "in spirit." There is no reason why the word
ἐν (*en*) here should not have the sense of "by," denoting
in or *by the power of*. It is rendered "by" 141 times in the
New Testament. (See, for example, Matt. xxiii. 20, 21,
22. 2 Cor. vi. 6, &c., &c.) In this case it would mean
here exactly what it means in Ezekiel, *by*, or *by the
power of* the Spirit—by which power John was
transported, and thus "came to be" in future scenes
and times, and saw "visions of God," *i.e.*, visions given
by God, which he here records for our learning.
Compare similar statements, chap. iv. 2; xvii. 3;
xxi. 10.

On the phrase "the Lord's day" see our preliminary
propositions (pages 9-15).

and I heard behind me a great (*i.e.*, loud) **voice, as
of a trumpet**] This means a voice as loud as a
trumpet; the strength, not the quality, being the point
to be noted. This trumpet is specially associated in
the Old Testament with *war*, and with "the Day of the
LORD." See Zeph. i. 14-16. "The great day of the
LORD is near, and hasteth greatly, it is near, even
the voice of the day of the LORD: . . . A day of the
trumpet," &c. Compare Joel ii. 1. 15: and iii. 16, where
we have the same connection.

11. **saying :* What thou seest, write in a book**] not
in seven separate Epistles, but in this Book; so as
to be of special service for those who will be on
the earth in the future Day of the Lord. Not "what
thou at the present moment seest"; the context and the
sequel clearly show that the present tense is here used
in order to include all that he should see, and had

---

* We must omit the words "I am Alpha and Omega, the first and
the last, and" with all the Critical Greek Texts and R.V.

actually begun to see. " What thou art seeing "
carries on the action right through, so as to include all
that we now have in this Book. Hence it is that the
present tense is so often used; *e.g.*, " are proceeding "
(iv. 5); "is descending" (xvi. 21), &c.

and send it to (or, for, *i.e.*, for their use) the
seven* assemblies,† unto Ephesus, and unto
Smyrna, and unto Pergamos, and unto Thyatira,
and unto Sardis, and unto Philadelphia, and
unto Laodicea] We cannot believe that these
places are used symbolically of seven successive
stages of ecclesiastical history. If they are, what
is "Patmos" the symbol of? And how can a
Place be a symbol of Time? When one thing is used
as a symbol of another, there is always something
common to both, by which the symbol is connected
with the thing symbolised. Besides, at the best, it is
only a theory which had its origin in the mind of some
good man. We prefer to believe (1) that the book was
sent to these Assemblies at that time for them to read
and hear and keep in mind; (2) that to us also now there
is an *application*, so far as it accords with what is specially
written as to our standing in Christ in the Pauline
Epistles, and we may read and keep these words in
mind, so that we, too, may receive the promised
blessing; but (3) as there will be a People gathered in
Assemblies or Synagogues on the earth all through
the Day of the Lord and after the Church has
been caught up (this is clear from xii. 17; xiii.
10; xiv. 12), this book, therefore, will have its
final and special *interpretation* for them. They

---

* " The seven " are added by all the Critical Greek Texts and R.V.
† The same authorities omit " which are in Asia."

will receive the blessing; and these Epistles will
be exhausted by the *interpretation* they will then receive.
Thus understanding these Assemblies, we rob no one,
and deprive no one, of the blessing of verse 3. We
have already made some remarks on this point (see
pages 62, &c.), and shall have more to say when
we come to the Epistles themselves.

F³ d³ (page 129), i. 12-16   *Advent*

The Vision of the Coming One

12. **And I turned to see the Voice which was
speaking with me**] Here we have two Figures—
(1) *Metonomy* of the effect, by which the " voice " is
put for the person speaking; and (2) this, when used
with the verb " to see," produces the figure *Catachresis*
(or Incongruity), as a voice cannot be seen. These
Figures properly rendered mean, " and I turned to see
Him who spake with me."

and, on turning, I saw seven lamp-stands of gold]
They were realities that John saw, but realities
used as symbols; and what they are symbolical of
we are told in verse 20. That they were real in
Heaven is clear from Heb. viii. 2, 5 ; ix. 23. But they
are significant of things below. These seven lamp-
stands point us to the seven-fold golden lamp-stand of
the Tabernacle. Ex. xxv. 31, 32, 37 ; xxxvii. 23.
Heb. ix. 2. Then, there was but one lamp-stand:
here, there are seven. There, Israel was one, and
was gathered as one nation: here, that nation is
scattered, and in its Dispersion. The same fact
explains the absence of the table of Shew-bread.

13. **and in the midst of the seven*** **lamp-stands One like a son of man**] *i.e.*, by a Hebraism, a human being, viz., the Son of Man Himself. The title emphasizes the human nature of Him who thus appears to John. For its significance in relation to this book and its interpretation see above (pages 15, etc.), and compare Dan. vii. 31. Ezek. i. 26 ; viii. 2.

We now come to the Vision proper, and present the Expansion of the member

F³ d³ (page 129), i. 12-16

The Vision of the Son of 'Man

```
F³ d³   m | 12, 13. Accessories : Seven lamp-stands,
            | clothing, and girding

        n | o | 14-. Head        ⎫
            | p | -14. Eyes      ⎬ His Person
            |                    ⎪
            | o | 15-. Feet      ⎪
            | p | -15. Voice     ⎭

        m | 16-. Accessories : Seven stars, and sword.
            n | -16. His Person : Hand, mouth, coun-
               | tenance
```

The Vision itself, as we have seen above (page 55), is parallel with the vision Daniel saw (Dan. x.); *and its object is the same* (as there stated). " I am come to make thee understand what shall befall thy people in the latter days." Then, it was added, " for yet the

---

* L., T., W., H., and R.V. omit " seven." Tr. and A. insert it in brackets, as being doubtful.

vision is for many days." Now, the many days have passed, and "the time is at hand" (i. 3). The Day of the Lord is to be revealed to John. We need not enlarge or dwell upon the various aspects of the vision.

clothed with a robe reaching to the feet, and girt about the breasts with a girdle of gold: 14. His head and hair white, as white wool—as snow (Dan. vii. 9.) and His eyes as a flame of fire; 15. and His feet like unto polished brass (Ezek. i. 7) glowing as in a furnace; and His voice as the voice of many waters.] This is a common Old Testament simile, see Ezek. i. 24 ; xliii. 2. So Rev. xiv. 2 ; xix. 6. The comparison is, of course, the noise made by the waves of the sea upon the shore.

16. And having seven stars in His right hand; and out of His mouth a sharp two-edged sword going forth] A like Figure is used of men (Ps. lv. 21 ; lvii. 4; lix. 7). What is signified by it is clear from Isa. xi. 4; xlix. 2, and 2 Thess. ii. 8. The Divine comment on it is in Rom. xiii. 4. Compare Matt. xxiv. 50, 51. Luke xii. 46. The sword is referred to again in chap. ii. 12, 16 ; and its final purpose is shown in xix. 15, 21. Luke xix. 27.

and His countenance was as when the sun shineth in his strength.]

F C³ (page 129), i. 1   *Salutation*

17. And, when I had seen Him, I fell at His feet as dead : and He laid His right hand upon me, saying,* Fear not.]

---

*All the Critical Texts and R.V. omit "unto me."

E⁴ a⁴ (page 129), i. -17, 18.   *Jesus Testifying of Himself*

E⁴ a⁴ | q | -17, 18-.   LIFE.   " I am the First and the
Last, and the Living One

r | -18-.   DEATH.   " I was dead indeed ;

q | -18-.   LIFE.   "yet, behold! J am living for
evermore

r | 18.   DEATH.   " And I have the keys
of Death and the Grave "

-17.   **J am the First and the Last**] Compare
Is. xli. 4 ; xliii. 10 ; xliv. 6 ; xlviii. 11, 12.   The
pronoun is emphatic, marking the commencement of
a new member.

18. **and the Living One**]   See above (page 22) for
the significance of this title.   חי אל, Josh. iii, 10, the
living God.

**I was dead, indeed, yet behold! I am living for
ever and ever***]   We must keep our translation
English, otherwise the Greek is, literally, ' I came to
be (as in verses 9 and 10) dead, and behold I am
living,' &c.   The words "I live" are very emphatic,
marking the speaker as being the fountain and giver of
life.

and I have the keys of Death and the Grave†]
Greek, ᾅδης (*Hades*).   There is no occasion to introduce
any idea of "souls" or of an "intermediate state," so-
called, here.   " Death and the Grave" is a comprehensive

---

* All the Critical Texts and R. V. omit " Amen."

† The order of these words is thus reversed by the Critical Texts and
the R.V.

expression which explains itself. We translate it
" grave," as the A.V. is compelled to render it in xx. 13
(marg.) and 1 Cor. xv. 55. The R.V. transliterates in
i. 19 and xx. 13 " Hades"; and in 1 Cor. xv. 55 reads
" death " instead.

E⁴ b⁴ (page 129), i. 19   *The Things Testified*

19. **Write therefore*** **what things thou sawest
and what they are**] So Alford and Rotherham
and others: *i.e.,* " what they signify " (Stuart).
This is the sense of εἰσιν (*eisin*), *are*. It is so rendered
twice in the very next verse; and elsewhere very
frequently (*e.g.,* Matt. xiii. 37 and 39. Rev. xvii. 9, 15,
18, etc.). See pages 60-63.

even what things are about to happen hereafter]
This is not the same expression as in verse 1. There,
it was *necessity*, " must come to pass "; here, it is
sequence, " about to come to pass."

The command to write refers to *all* that John saw, and
not merely what he had seen in verses 12-16. We must
remember that the Introduction was written last, as we
have shown above.

The translation " *What they are* (or *signify*)" is so
undoubtedly good that it seems rather insecure to base
a whole system of interpretation affecting the whole
book, on the common rendering—"the things which
are." Our readers may be aware that many books on
the Apocalypse base their whole system of interpretation
on this rendering. But surely such a far-reaching system
ought to have a firmer foundation on which to rest.

---

* The word οὖν (*oun*) *therefore*, is to be added here according to
all the Critical Greek Texts and R.V.

This, in itself, is slight enough : but, when chaps. ii.
and iii. are nowhere spoken of as being "the things
which are," we have not sufficient warrant to adopt
an interpretation of the book which rests on such
hypothetical grounds.

That these Epistles are addressed to those who shall
be on the earth during the Day of the Lord, may be
seen by comparing many *expressions* contained in them
with the actual scenes and circumstances described in
various parts of the Book.

Compare	with
ii. 3.	xiii. 10 ; xiv. 12.
ii. 9, 10.	xiii. 5-8.
ii. 13.	xiii. 2 ; xvi. 10.
ii. 16.	xix. 21.
ii. 18.	xix. 15.
ii. 20-23.	xvii. 2, 4 ; xviii. 3.
iii. 3.	xvi. 15.
iii. 12.	xxi. 2.
iii. 21.	xx. 4.

Other parallels will be seen and noticed when we
come to the translation of the Epistles themselves.

F⁴ d⁴ (page 129), i. 20-.   *Advent*

The vision referred to in verses 12-16.

20-. **The mystery** (*i.e.*, the secret symbol) **of the
seven stars which thou sawest in my right hand ;
and the seven golden lamp-stands**]

F⁴ c⁴ (page 129), i. -20.   *Interpretation*

-20. **The seven stars are**]   *i.e.*, signify or represent
(as in the previous verse).   This is always the meaning
of the Figure called *Metaphor* which we have here.

the angels of the seven Assemblies; and the seven
lamp-stands are (*i.e.*, signify) the seven Assemblies]
Who shall authorize us to understand the word
" angels " as having any connection with the Church of
God ? No one ever heard (until quite recent times) of
such a title being given to any church-officer either in
Scripture, in history, or in tradition. To take the
word "angel" as meaning "bishop," in the absence
of any evidence of any kind, is one of the vagaries of
interpretation from which the Apocalypse has so long
suffered. But this brings us to the consideration of the
seven Epistles themselves.

---

*All the Critical Greek Texts and R.V. omit " which thou sawest."

5

THE PEOPLE ON THE EARTH
(2:1—3:22)

THE EPISTLES TO THE SEVEN ASSEMBLIES

W E now come to chapters ii. and iii.: which will find their true interpretation and fulfilment when used for special instruction by the people on the Earth during the Day of the Lord; by Israel, and especially by the Remnant.

We have said enough on this point already, to make this sufficiently clear. (See pages 63-99.)

We shall note, in these Epistles, constant references to the condition of things as described in this book. References which cannot be explained either by Church History or Tradition; but which are quite simple and clear when read in the light of future history, as prophetically recorded in the Apocalypse.

The difference between these Epistles and all other Epistles in the New Testament is so great, that one wonders how it was possible for them ever to be supposed as being addressed to the Church of God, the members of the Body of Christ! If it were not that we have all been brought up from earliest infancy to believe it, we could never have taken them as having anything in common with those addressed in either the earlier or later Pauline Epistles.

Everything is different: Circumstances, standpoint, references to the Old Testament, terminology, phraseology, scope, style: everything points to a different order of things altogether; yea, to a different Dispensation.

There is nothing in them about Christianity as such; nothing of our standing in Christ; nothing that can be taken, even by application, as referring to our present position as being in Christ; perfect, and complete in Him. Nothing about the " no condemnation," or no separation of Rom. viii. But all is warning or reproof Promises are made only to the " overcomer," and to those who shall " endure unto the end." It is clear that those who are "blessed with all spiritual blessings in the heavenlies in Christ" (Eph. i. 3) cannot be those to whom these seven Epistles are addressed. They are written to those who are under a covenant of works, and not to those who are under the covenant of grace. And those who interpret them of the church of God now must greatly lower that standing which He has given them in Christ, or else be altogether ignorant of it.

No! we keep our own truth as written to the churches by the Holy Spirit through Paul; and leave that which is equally *truth* written to other and different Assemblies by Christ through John. It is so very improbable that the covenant of works under which these Assemblies are addressed could co-exist, at one and the same time, with those under the covenant of grace, that we seem to be shut up to a future interpretation; when all these expressions, and references, and warnings, and threatenings, and promises (of which history knows nothing), shall find their fulfilment and reach their end.

Further comments may be left to be made as we consider the words of the Epistles themselves.

First, note the structure of the seven Epistles as a whole, and the seven lessons based on the seven stages of Israel's history. This separates them into 3 and 4; the numbers into which 7 is always divided.

In the *first three* Epistles the references are to Israel's history, as recorded in the Old Testament, and are from the period when Israel was *in the Wilderness*. All Israel is included.

In the *last four* Epistles the references are to the period when the people were *in the Land*, and Israel and Judah are mentioned alternately.

🜚 (page 118). THE SEVEN EPISTLES AS A WHOLE
(chaps. ii and iii)

The Wilderness

X | 1 | EPHESUS. Israel's Espousals
   | 2 | SMYRNA. Israel's Testing
   | 3 | PERGAMOS. Israel's Failure

The Land

Y | 4 | THYATIRA. The Day of Israel's Kings
  | 5 | SARDIS. Israel's Removal
  | 6 | PHILADELPHIA. The Day of Judah's Kings
  | 7 | LAODICEA. Judah's Removal

Failure is the great subject; and the causes which led to that failure. This is the basis of the great lesson which will be needed for another time of Trial, Testing, and Tribulation; which will end, not in failure, but in glory.

This division into *three* and *four* is further marked by the injunction and the promise with which each of the seven Epistles closes.

In the first *three*, which refer to the Wilderness, the Promise *follows* the Injunction; while in the last four which refer to the Land, the order is reversed, and the Injunction *follows* the Promise.

We now proceed to look at each of these seven Epistles separately.

i. The First Epistle —Ephesus

(ii. 1-7)

Each Epistle, though the structure itself varies, is based upon the same general plan, *viz.: The Introduction*, consisting of Christ's command to John to write, with an appropriate attribute taken from the previous vision in chap. i. The *Conclusion*, consisting of Christ's command to him that hath an ear, to hear; with His promise, fulfilled in the latter portion of the book. Between these we have the subject-matter of the Epistle proper. While this general arrangement is common to all these Epistles, yet each has its own peculiar exhibition of it.

The correspondences and contrasts between the Epistles are worthy of note, forming a useful guide to their inter-relation. They show us what are the important points which we should notice; and what are the matters on which we should place special emphasis.

In short, they give us the peculiar *scope* of and key to each Epistle respectively; and though not essential to the reader's studies, they are worthy of his close attention.

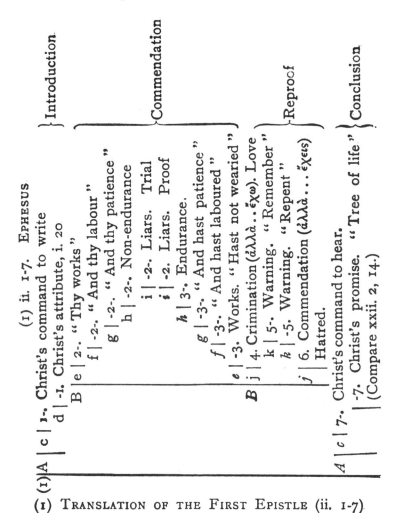

(1) TRANSLATION OF THE FIRST EPISTLE (ii. 1-7).
EPHESUS

ii. 1. **To the angel**] As we have said above, this is the *Sheliach Tzibbūr* of the Synagogue, the presiding minister. A title well understood by Jewish readers, but quite foreign to Gentile ears. (See pages 63, etc.)

of the Assembly]   As in Acts xix. 32, 39, 41.   Or
Synagogue.   The A.V. renders the Greek Synagogue in
Jas. ii. 2 " Assembly " instead of *Synagogue ;* and in
Jas. v. 14 " Church " instead of *Assembly*.   The former
passage (ii. 2) shows what the nature of the Assembly
was in chap. v. 14.   It was the congregation assembling
in the Synagogue, and there is no reason why it should
not be so taken in Rev. ii. and iii.

in* **Ephesus, write**]   No one can put this Epistle
by the side of that of Paul to the Ephesians and think
for a moment that it can be the same Assembly that
is addressed.   It is not a matter of argument or of
opinion ; it is a matter of fact.   Read the two Epistles,
one after the other, and note the standing of *grace* in
the one, and the standing of *works* in the other.   It is
true John wrote some years later than Paul ; but
though this might affect the *condition* of the Assembly,
it could not change the *ground* of God's dealings.   His
covenant had not changed.   But here, everything is
changed, as we shall see.   In Paul's Epistle to the
Church of God in Ephesus, God speaks to those who
are all of them on the highest ground of privilege and
of grace.   Here, there is no blessing at all, except to
the *overcomers*.

**These things saith He that holdeth the seven
stars in His right hand** (i. 16), **He that walketh in
the midst of the seven lamp-stands of gold** (i. 13)]
Here the reference is surely to Deut. xxiii. 14, where
this walking, and the object of it, are the same as in the
Day of the Lord.   " For the Lord thy God walketh in
the midst of thy camp to deliver thee, and to give up
thine enemies before thee ; therefore shall thy camp be

---

* So all the Critical Greek Texts and RV.

holy; that He see no unclean thing in thee, and turn away from thee." Here, Christ thus walks according to Lev. xxvi. 12. And his eye sees and exposes the unclean things in the camp of these Assemblies.

2. **I know thy works**] This is the principle on which the Lord will deal with the Remnant of Israel in the Day of the Lord. See Isa. lxvi. 18: "For I know their works and **their** thoughts: it shall come, that I will gather all nations and tongues, and they shall see **My** glory." The context in the previous verses (15-17) shows the nature of these " works " and the time of the Lord's dealing with them. Most of the seven Epistles begin with the statement of this fact, as to " works," from Isa. lxvi. 18.

and* labour, and thy endurance] or patience (ii. 3). This is the patience referred to in xiii. 10: " Here is the patience and faith of the saints "; xiv. 12: " Here is the patience of the saints; here are they that keep the commandments (the ' works' spoken of) of God, and the faith of Jesus." The statement in this Epistle refers to the then condition of things in the Day when the things written in this Book shall be fulfilled.

and that thou canst not bear wicked (or, evil) **men ; and thou didst try those who call themselves apostles, and are not, and didst find them liars** :

3. **And thou hast endurance, and didst bear,† for the sake of my name, and hast not wearied‡**

4. **Nevertheless I have this against thee, that thou hast left thy first love**] This is very emphatic.

---

* L.T.Tr.A. WH. and RV. omit "thy."

† This is the order of the words according to G.L.T.Tr.A. WH. and RV.

‡ So L.T.T.Tr.A. WH. and RV.—G. has "and didst not weary."

Lit., it is " thy love—thy first love " (see p. 51). What
have we here but a reference to Jer. ii. 1, 2, where God
commanded Jeremiah to commence his prophecy by calling this fact to their remembrance: " Go and cry in the
ears of Jerusalem, saying, Thus saith the Lord : I
remember thee, the kindness of thy youth, the love of
thine espousals, when thou wentest after me in the
wilderness." This was the day referred to in Ezek. xvi.
8-10, etc.: the day when Jehovah set His love upon
them and chose them, not because of their number,
" but because the LORD loved you" (Deut. vii. 7-9).
See above, under the expression in i. 5, " unto Him
who loveth us " (pages 41 and 143).

5. **Remember therefore whence thou hast fallen,
and repent**] This is strange language if it be
addressed to those who had been " blessed with all
spiritual blessings, in the heavenlies, in Christ "
(Eph. i. 3). Nothing could forfeit such blessings ;
because they are in the heavenlies, in Christ, whence
none can touch them or pluck them. Nor can
repentance procure them, for they are the gift of
God to His church ; and His gifts and calling are
without repentance (Rom. xi. 29). No ; the Assembly
to whom such words are addressed cannot be the
Assembly addressed by the Holy Spirit through Paul.

and do the first works; otherwise (*Lit.*, but if not)
I am coming to thee, * **and will remove thy lamp-
stand out of its place, except thou repent**] He had
come before, at His first Advent, seeking fruit. But
He found it not. Now He is coming again, and the
cry goes forth once more, " Repent "; for, He who is
coming is at hand. Repentance is '*the first work*' !

---

* Omit "quickly," L.T.Tr.A. WH. and RV.

It is .he *one condition of national blessing* for Israel. It is
the essence of the proclamation of the King and the
Kingdom. The ministries of John the Baptist (Matt. iii.
2), of Christ Himself (Matt. iv. 17), and also of Peter
(Acts ii. 38; iii. 39), were all stamped with this one
word "Repent." This is the "first work" to be done,
the first step to be taken in view of national blessing. See Lev. xxvi. 40-42. 1 Kings viii. 33, 35, 37.
Deut. xxx. 1-3. Dan. ix. 3, 4. Zech i. 3 ; etc.

6. **But this thou hast, that thou hatest the deeds
of the Nicolaitanes, which 𝕴 also hate**] The Nicolaitanes are mentioned again in verse 15. History
knows nothing definite of any people bearing such a
name during the primitive age of Christianity. Tradition has something to say; but this is so conflicting
and so uncertain, that most commentators attempt
to solve the difficulty by considering the name as
being symbolical (as they do that of Balaam (ii. 14, 15),
and Jezebel (ii. 20). They interpret it by its etymology—
νίκος (*nikos*) *conqueror* and λαός (*laos*) *people*. If there be
anything in this, it is better to leave it to "that day,"
when events will make its meaning manifest.

7. **He that hath an ear, let him hear**] None but
the Lord Jesus ever used this formula. On fourteen
occasions He used it. Always, when He was speaking
of the great change in the Dispensation which was
about to take place. It is connected therefore with
Dispensational truth. Six times (the number of man)
in the Gospels He used it as the Son of Man ; and
eight times (the Dominical Number) in Revelation, as
the risen Lord speaking from heaven : here, at the close
of each of these seven Epistles, and once in chap. xiii. 9.*

---

* See *Divine Names and Titles* by the same author and publisher.

what the Spirit saith (or is saying) **to the Assemblies**] In Rev. xix. 10 we are told that "the testimony of Jesus is the Spirit of prophecy"; *i.e.*, it is the prophetic testimony spoken by Christ Himself; or the testimony spoken by His servant John, or by angelic messengers, concerning Him who addresses these Assemblies in this Book.

To him that overcometh] This is language wholly foreign to the Epistles written to believers by Paul. The members of Christ's Body have already overcome all "in Him." They are already "more than conquerors through him that loved us" (Rom. viii. 37). The same John speaks, in his Epistle, of those who belong to the Church of God as having already overcome. (See 1 John ii. 13; iv. 4; v. 4, 5). Those who are addressed here will be living in the days of the Beast, in the midst of the great Tribulation, and there will be those who will "endure unto the end." Of some we read "the Beast . . . shall make war against them, and shall overcome them and kill them" (xi. 7). Of others it is said "they overcame him (the accuser of their brethren) by the blood of the Lamb, and by the word of their testimony; and they loved not their lives unto the death" (xii. 11). Of others again, "It was given unto him (the Beast) to make war with the saints and to overcome them" (xiii. 7). Hence the reiteration of the final promise in xxi. 7, "he that overcometh shall inherit all things." The Revelation is full of overcoming. No less than sixteen times we have the verb νικάω (*nikaō*), *to conquer*, or *overcome*. The overcomers who are addressed at the close of each of these seven Epistles will be living in the days referred to in these passages. They will be special overcomers of a specific form of evil. They are thus prophesied of in Isa. lxvi. 5 : " Hear the word of the LORD, ye that tremble at his word : Your brethren that hated you, that cast you out for my name's sake, said Let the LORD be glorified : but he shall appear to your joy, and they shall be ashamed." They are spoken of in Dan. xi. 32 as those who "do know their God, shall be strong and do exploits." In Matt. xxiv. 13, as those who " shall endure unto the end." Compare Matt. x. 22.

will I give to eat of the tree of life which is in the * **Paradise of God**] For the promises of the seven Epistles as a whole, see pages 86-99. This first promise is fulfilled in xxii. 14, where the article "*the* tree of life " is used, and refers specially to the overcomers. The Tree mentioned in verse 2 and Ezek. xlvii. 12 is another tree or trees (without the article) intended for the healing of the *nations* during the millennium.

The promise, here, refers to the New Earth, when the curse will be removed, and the whole Earth be restored as the Paradise of God. To this "Paradise" Paul was caught away (2 Cor. xii. 4); and also to this "third Heaven" (and Earth).

The *first* was overflowed with water and perished (2 Pet. iii. 6 and Gen. i. 2).

The *second* Heavens and Earth are those " which are now" (2 Pet. iii. 7), and which will be purged by fire (2 Pet. iii. 10).

The *third* are those for which we look, even the New Heavens and the New Earth (Paradise restored) (2 Pet. iii. 13 and Rev. xxi., xxii.).

---

* All the Critical Texts, with RV., omit the words " midst of."

To this third Heaven and Paradise was Paul caught away in vision. These John also saw; and was commissioned to write what Paul was unable to utter. This Paradise of the New Earth, which will characterise the Kingdom, was referred to by the Lord Jesus in His answer to the dying thief. "Lord, remember me when thou comest in thy kingdom." "Verily, I say unto thee to-day, (*i.e.*, on this day of shame and death, beyond which thou seest by the eye of faith) thou shalt be with me in Paradise." That promise will be fulfilled to him as an overcomer. His faith overcame all his circumstances; and he marvellously believed, in spite of all the awful scenes of that day, that Jesus was "Lord," and that He would yet come in His Kingdom. To him, therefore, as an overcomer, was the promise of that future Paradise given; as here it is given to all who shall overcome by the same faith.

2. THE SECOND EPISTLE —SMYRNA

(ii. 8-11.)

The Second Epistle was addressed to the angel of the Assembly in Smyrna.

It is marked by a definite period of trial being mentioned, viz., "ten days," and answers to the second stage of Israel's history, which was marked by a definite period of trial—"forty years." (See p. 87). The first Epistle (Ephesus) began with a reference to the day of Israel's Espousals, and reminds those people of their "first love." The second (Smyrna), in its definite days of trial, reminds us of the definite period of forty years in the wilderness.

Its structure is as simple and clear as it is beautiful.

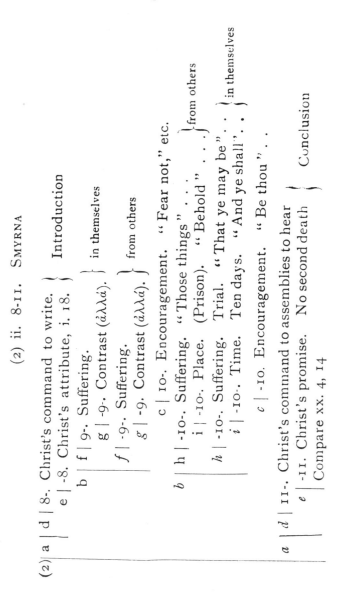

(2) ii. 8-11. SMYRNA

```
(2) a | d | 8-. Christ's command to write. ⎫ Introduction
      | e | -8. Christ's attribute, i. 18. ⎭

      b | f | 9-.  Suffering.                          ⎫
        | g | -9-. Contrast (ἀλλά).  } in themselves   ⎬
        | f | -9-. Suffering.                          ⎮
        | g | -9.  Contrast (ἀλλά).  } from others     ⎭

          c | 10-. Encouragement. "Fear not," etc.

      b | h | -10-. Suffering. "Those things" . . .            ⎫
        | i | -10-. Place. (Prison). "Behold" . . .  } from others
        | h | -10-. Suffering. Trial. "That ye may be" . . .   ⎬
        | i | -10-. Time. Ten days. "And ye shall". . . } in themselves

          c | -10. Encouragement. "Be thou" . . .

    a | d | 11-. Christ's command to assemblies to hear   ⎫
      | e | -11. Christ's promise. No second death        ⎬ Conclusion
      | Compare xx. 4, 14                                 ⎭
```

8. And unto the angel of the Assembly in Smyrna write ; These things saith the First and the Last]
This, as we have already seen, is one of the Titles
used in the Introduction (i. 18) ; as it is used in the Old
Testament, of Deity. (Isa. xli. 4 ; xliv. 6 ; xlviii. 12.)
(See page 20).

who was (*lit.*, became) **dead, and returned to life**]
(i. 17, 18) The verb ἔζησεν (*ezēsen*) means more than
merely to live or to be alive. (See Rom. xiv. 9.
Rev. xiii. 14 (where it is used of and throws light
upon the Beast being raised) ; xx. 4, 5). It means
to live again in resurrection life. See John iv. 50.
Mark xvi. 11.

9. **I know*** **thy tribulation,and** thy **poverty**] This is
the outcome of xiii. 16, 17, for when they will not be
allowed by the Beast to buy or sell, great poverty must
necessarily ensue.

nevertheless thou art rich] Poor in one sense, yet
rich in another sense.

and I know **the blasphemy** coming **from those
who say that they themselves are Jews, and they
are not, but** are **Satan's synagogue**] When have
people ever professed to be Jews in order to join a
Christian church ? Such an anomaly was never heard
of. These words alone are sufficient to prove the true
Jewish character of these assemblies. Words have no
meaning if this verse does not speak concerning those
who, for some reason or other (perhaps in order to
betray, hardly for gain or advantage), hypocritically
affirmed that they were Jews when they were not.

---

* L.T.Tr.A. WH. and RV. omit "thy works and ". The Lord
is not speaking of actions here, but of passive sufferings.

10. **Fear not the things which thou art about to suffer : lo, the devil is about to cast some of you into prison, that ye may be tried; and ye shall have tribulation ten days**] What trial and tribulation is this, if not exactly that foretold by the Lord in Matt. x. 22? "And ye shall be hated of all men for my name's sake ; but he that endureth to the end shall be saved." Compare Matt. xxiv. 9, 10, and John xvi. 1-4. In these passages the very trials are mentioned; and in Rev. xiii. 5-7 we see the very circumstances described, in which those who are thus addressed will be placed. In this special case the tribulation is limited to " ten days." And why not ? Why should we seek to make these words mean other than what they say ? In Est. iii. 13 a decree went forth that the whole nation was to be destroyed "in one day." Why should not such a decree go forth again for " ten days "? Even in our own times we read of Jews in Russia, Roumania, and elsewhere, being given over for days together to the violence of a persecuting mob. Why should not these " ten days " refer to a certain definite and limited time of trouble ? Why introduce endless difficulties into this Book by always maintaining that God means something quite different from what He says ? Moses Stuart is an example. He writes: "Let the reader mark well the *symbolic* use of number in this case ; for the exact literal one will be insisted on, I trust, by no one."

His trust is vain, for we do insist on believing that God means what He says. If we are wrong in this, then we prefer to be found wrong, hereafter, in this simplicity of faith, rather than to be reproved by God for having, in preference, believed man. When God says (Gen. vii. 4): "For yet seven days and I will cause it to

rain upon the earth forty days and forty nights," God
meant "days," not years. See verse 10: "And it came
to pass after seven days"; and see verse 12. When
Joseph said, by the prophetic spirit, "The three
branches are *three days*. Yet within *three days* shall
Pharaoh lift up thine head," he meant "days," not
years; for we read: "And it came to pass *the third
day*," etc.; see Gen. xl. 12, 13, 20. So with the
wandering in the wilderness, Num. xiv. 33; "forty
days" means forty *days*, and "forty years" means forty
years. So with Jonah; and the Lord, Matt. xii. 40. So
with Ezekiel, iv. 1-8.

be (*lit.*, become) **thou faithful unto death**] Probably
violent death is meant.

and I will give to thee the crown of life] Here
we have not the standing of the church "in Christ."
That standing does not depend on *our* faithfulness,
but on the faithfulness of Him who has already given
us life in Himself—eternal life. This life rests on no
conditions, but upon the unalterable gift of God in
Christ. Compare the Epistle addressed "to the twelve
Tribes," Jas. i. 1. The faithfulness mentioned here
refers to that which is the subject of xx. 4.

11. **He that hath an ear, let him hear what the
Spirit is saying to the Assemblies. He that overcometh shall not be hurt of the second death**] This
is mentioned again in xx. 6, 14, and xxi. 8, as the
fulfilment of this promise in those who have passed
through the great Tribulation and have not worshipped
the Beast nor received his mark. Those who are
faithful unto death, and die of a violent death, then, for
Christ's sake, are promised that they "shall not be

hurt of the second death," which shall finally destroy their enemies.

Note how the titles of Christ in verse 8 ("I am He that was dead and returned to life") agree with the exhortation of verse 10 ("be thou faithful unto death, and I will give thee the crown of life"), and the promise of verse 11 ("shall not be hurt of the second death").

3. THE THIRD EPISTLE —PERGAMOS

(ii. 12-17)

In the Epistle to the Assembly in Pergamos, the Old Testament illustrations are from a subsequent period of Israel's wilderness experiences. Balaam and Balak are used to illustrate the special circumstances of this Assembly ; the counterpart of which will be found to exist in "the day of the Lord."

It is the last of the three Epistles in which the Old Testament reference is to Israel and the Wilderness period. In the *first* we had Israel's *Espousals* ; in the *second* we had Israel's *Testing and Trial ;* now, here, in the *third*, we have Israel's *Failure.*

This failure is very marked in the Epistle to Pergamos. The predominant tone of the Epistle is that of Crimination. Two solemn warnings are given, and a call to "Repent," with a threat of being fought against by the sword of His mouth.

This will be seen in the Epistle as we proceed; and it is clearly exhibited in the Structure :—

(3) ii. 12-17. PERGAMOS

		Commendation	Reproof	

(3) a | c | 12-. Christ's command to write. ⎫
         d | -12. Christ's attribute. (i. 18.) ⎬ Introduction

b | e | 13-. Works. General
     f | -13-. Place. (ὅπου . . . τοῦ Σατανᾶ.)
   e | -13-. Works. Particular.
     f | -13. Place. (ὅπου . . . ὁ Σατανᾶς)

b | g | 14-. Crimination. "I have against thee," &c.
   h | i | -14-. Balaam. (ἔχεις.)
      k | -14. Description. "Who taught," &c.
   h | i | 15-. Nicolaitanes. (ἔχεις.)
      k | -15. Description. "In like manner," &c.
   g | 16. Warning. "Repent; or I will come," &c.

a | c | 17-. Christ's command to assemblies to hear.
   d | -17. Christ's promise. "Manna." "New Name." (Compare vii. 13-17; xix. 12) ⎬ Conclusion

ii. 12. **And unto the angel of the Assembly in Pergamos, write; These things saith he who hath the sharp two-edged sword]** This attribute of Christ is taken from i. 16. It is used here and in the closing threat of the Epistle (ii. 16), because the judgment upon "the error of Balaam" was executed with the sword. See Num. xxxi. 8, "Balaam also, the son of Beor, they slew with the sword" (So Josh. xiii. 22). Hence all the significant references to the "sword" in this epistle. In i. 16 the sword proceeds out of Christ's mouth, teaching them how, by the word which cometh out of His mouth, He can chastise and destroy. Hearken therefore to Him.

13. **I know * where thou dwellest,** even **where Satan's throne** is] Here we have a special reference to the scenes and circumstances of Rev. xiii. 2, where the Dragon gave the Beast "his power, and his throne, and great authority." In Rev. xvi. 11, "the fifth angel poured out his vial upon the throne of the Beast," &c. So that at that time, in the Day of the Lord, there will be a special place where Satan's throne will be set up in this world; and when he and the Beast will receive that worship which it is and has ever been his aim, all through, to obtain from mankind. This throne is evidently to be in Pergamos. Whatever foreshadowings there may have been of this in past history or in the history of the Roman Emperors, it only shows us the possibility of that, in which all believe when we speak of "history repeating itself." Pergamos was the seat of the ancient mysteries. That which has been, may be again. Just as the deeds of Antiochus

---

* L.T.Tr.A. WH. & RV. omit the words "thy works, and."

Epiphanes show us how another individual will yet do entirely, what he did partially.

and thou holdest fast my name] in not receiving the mark of the Beast. See Rev. xi. 18 (" which fear thy name "); and compare xiii. 13-15. 2 Thes. ii. 11, 12.

**and didst not deny my faith, [even]* in the days†
of Antipas, my witness, my faithful one, who was
killed among you, where Satan dwelleth**] Here is another allusion to Satan's future special presence on the earth in the days here referred to. History knows nothing whatever about any such person named Antipas. Later tradition has a great deal to say, but its conflicting statements will not repay us for the time and trouble involved in their consideration. There will be many martyrs in those days ; and here, one of them is mentioned by name. Compare and see Rev. vi. 9, 10; xiii. 10 ; xx. 4, when the fulfilment of the Lord's words will be understood. Matt. xxiv. 9. Mark xiii. 9. Luke xxi. 12. John xv. 20 ; xvi. 2. These are the days specially referred to in this Epistle. It is no new thing for prophecy to name a person long before his personal manifestation. (See 1 Kings xiii. 2. Isa. xliv. 28; xlv. 1). " The place where Satan dwelleth " (xiii. 2; xvi. 10) must be the place where persecution will rage most fiercely.

14. **Nevertheless I have against thee a few things,
that thou hast there those who hold the doctrine of
Balaam, who taught Balak to cast a stumbling-block
before the children of Israel, to eat things sacri-
ficed unto idols, and to commit fornication**] What " the error of Balaam " (Jude 11) was may be seen from

---

* T. omits " even." Tr. & A. put it in brackets as doubtful.
† Omit " in which."—L.T.Tr. WH. See RV. marg.

Numbers xxv. 1, &c., and xxxi. 16, &c. The whole scene has to do with idolatry of the grossest kind, where fornication will be made religion! and when religion will be turned into fornication, as it was and is in all the great heathen systems of idolatry. This was the essence of idolatry of old; and this is what is again coming on the earth. Otherwise, what mean those significant words in chap. ix. 20, 21 ? (See pages 75, 76)·

15. **So hast thou also those that hold fast the teaching of the Nicolaitanes** (*v.* 6) **in like manner*]**

16. **Repent therefore†; otherwise I will come unto thee speedily, and will fight against them with the sword** (*v.* 12) **of my mouth]** We have seen before, how foreign is such a warning and threat as addressed to the members of the Church of God to-day. On the other hand, we see the actual fulfilment of this threat in chap. xix. 11-21.

17. **He that hath an ear, let him hear what the Spirit is saying to the Assemblies: To him that overcometh will I give‡ of the hidden manna]** This promise follows in the order of Old Testament illustration. (1) To *Ephesus* it was the tree of life (Gen. ii.). (2) To *Smyrna* it was not to be hurt of the second death (Gen. iii.) Now, to *Pergamos*, it is the manna of Exod. xvi. 32-34. We have to remember how the false prophets and teachers were all fed at Jezebel's table (1 Kings xviii. 19). So all these false teachers will be supported by the State of which the Beast will be the head. The

---

* All the critical Greek Texts and R.V. read ὁμοίως (*homoiōs*), *in like manner*, instead of ὅ μισῶ (*ho misō*), *which I hate.*

† This word is added by G.L.Tr. (A). WH. and RV.

‡ All the Texts omit "to eat of."

faithful remnant of the woman's seed will be again driven into the wilderness (xii. 13-17). How beautiful therefore to be thus reminded, just here, that God can spread a table (not Jezebel's) for them in that wilderness, as He did of old (Ps. lxxviii. 19), when "man did eat angels' food, and He sent them meat to the full" (Ps. lxxviii. 24, 25). It is in this connection that the promise of the manna is given. In Ex. xvi. 34, 35 we are told that the manna was specially given " until they came to a land inhabited. Until then, God has " hidden manna " with which to support His people.

and I will give unto him a white stone, and on the stone a new name written, which none knoweth save he that receiveth it.] This new name for the new Israel is the subject of prophecy. Isa. lxii. 2 tells of the time when "Thou shalt be called by a new name, which the mouth of the Lord shall name " (see also Isa. lxv. 15). Rev. xix. 11-16 is the fulfilment of this promise. What that new name will be is not yet revealed, but its association with the " white stone " reminds us that as they will be " a kingdom of priests," so they will have the priestly signs as Aaron had (Ex. xxviii. 36, &c.). On the front of his mitre was a plate of gold " holy to the Lord." Here, instead of a plate of gold, they are to have a white stone, on which will be an inscription equivalent to Aaron's, with their new name : thus distinguishing them in a most emphatic way from those who will worship the Beast and receive his mark in their forehead.

Those who will be on the earth in those days will thus be divided into two opposing parties : the party of the Beast, and that of the Lamb ; each having its own distinctive mark or brand.

4. The Fourth Epistle —Thyatira

(ii. 18-29.)

We now come to the last *four* of these seven Epistles. In the first three the Old Testament references are to the period of the *Wilderness*. In these last four the references are to the period of *the Land* : and Israel and Judah are placed alternately.

Israel comes first; for, idolatry commenced in the Ten Tribes, and these were first removed from the Land. Judah followed, and was afterwards removed.

The first of these four Epistles, therefore, gives the illustration from the great apostasy of Israel under Ahab and Jezebel.

Few of us can realize what that apostasy was ; or what was its character and extent. Jeroboam was the first who made Israel thus to sin, but it culminated under Ahab and Jezebel. Under these two, organized idolatry of the grossest kind became the religion of the State, as opposed to the true religion established in Jerusalem. It had its own priesthood, so numerous and powerful that the prophet Elijah was specially raised up by God to do battle against them, and warn the people against the enormity of the evil. Yet again will Elijah perform a similar duty under more awful circumstances.

The structure of this Epistle is elaborate, as were the workings of that apostasy. But it is also very clear and unmistakable.

(4) ii. 18-29. THYATIRA

| | | | Commendation | Admonition. |
| | | | | The guilty | The innocent |

a | d | 18-. Christ's command to write.   } Introduction
   | e | -18. Christ's attribute. (i. 15)

  b | f¹ | 19-. Works. (General.)
     | g¹ | -19-. Particulars. (Love, Service, Faith, Service)
     | f² | -19-. Works. (General.)
     | g² | -19. Particulars. "And the last," &c.

  c | h | 20. Jezebel
     | i | 21. Her impenitence
  c | i | 22. Her punishment
     | h | 23. The Assemblies.

  b | f³ | 24-. Persons. (General.) "To you and to the rest," &c.
     | g³ | -24-. Particulars. "As many as," &c.
     | g⁴ | -24. Persons. (General.) "I will put upon you," &c.
     | f⁴ | 25. Particulars. "But that which ye have," &c.

a | *e* | 26-28. Christ's promise. Power, &c.   } Conclusion
    | (Compare xii. 4; xix. 15; xx. 4.)
    d | 29. Christ's command to assemblies to hear

11. 18. **And unto the angel of the Assembly in Thyatira, write ; These things saith the Son of God]** Here, for the first time, the speaker is directly named ; as well as distinguished by an attribute. Both speak of Divine judgment, and of the Divine power which is necessary to execute that judgment, and to perform the promises given in this Epistle.

who hath His eyes like a flame of fire] To detect all evil and alarm the evil-doers. This is the attribute of i. 14, 15 ; repeated in xix. 12.

and His feet like unto polished brass] This tells of coming judgment, when He will tread the wicked under his feet. Isa. lxiii. 1-6 ; xli. 25 ; xiv. 25. See also Mal. iv. 3 ; Dan. viii. 7, 10 ; and compare Micah iv. 13. Dan. vii. 19. Deut. xxxiii. 25. Job xl. 18. The fulfilment of all this is seen in chap. xix. 13-15.

19. **I know thy works, and thy love, and thy service, and thy faith,* and thy patient-endurance, and thy last works to be more than the first]** It is a question of " works " here, as in all these Epistles ; and also of patient endurance in the Tribulation.

20. **Nevertheless I have this against thee,† that thou lettest alone‡ the§ woman Jezebel, she who calleth herself a prophetess, and she teacheth and deceiveth my servants to commit fornication, and to eat things sacrificed to idols]** The reference here

---

* The order of these words varies in the MSS. G.L.T.A. WH. and RV. have "love, faith, and service," Tr. has "faith, love, and service."

† G.L.T.Tr.A. WH. and RV. omit " a few things."

‡ ἀφεῖς (*apheis*) instead of ἐᾷς (*eas*) *sufferest.* G.L.T.Tr.A. WH. and RV.

§ G.L. (A). WH. (marg.) RV. (marg.) read " thy wife."

is to 1 Kings xvi. 30-34. All the evil is traced up to Jezebel (1 Kings xxi. 25). The teaching is the same as that of Balaam, and of the Nicolaitanes—only it is more organized, and in the name of religion, and under the direct auspices of the State. Balaam was outside Israel; Jezebel is within. This is what it will be in the days of the Beast: and this is why these exhortations, teachings, and warnings are written in these Epistles. We do not comprehend them, because we are not living in those days; therefore, we cannot even apply them to ourselves. Three of the Assemblies are warned with regard to this evil. Ephesus (ii. 6); Pergamos (ii. 14, 15); and Thyatira (ii. 20). And there is everything in the Apocalypse to show that that will be the special form of evil in the coming days of Antichrist on earth. See also 2 Kings ix. 22, 30. Jer. iv. 30. Nah. iii. 4.

21. **And I gave her space in order that she might repent,** * **and she willeth not to repent of her fornication**] We must read the history in the book of Kings in order to understand this; and see and note how it is connected with persecution. See 1 Kings xviii. 13, 14. It may have reference to the woman of Rev. xvii. 1-4, and to the scenes then going on in the earth. Compare chap. xviii. 3 and 8-10. Also ix. 20, 21.

22. **Lo! I cast her into a bed, and those who are committing adultery with her** (xviii. 8-10) **into great tribulation** (Rom. ii. 8, 9, 16), **except they repent of her† works**] The casting into a bed, here, is in contrast with Jezebel's being cast out of a window. And it refers to a bed of anguish and of judgment. To reward and

---

* All the Texts and RV. read the verse thus.

† All the critical Texts and RV. read αὐτῆς (*autēs*) *her*, instead of αὐτῶν (*autōn*) *their*.

punish "according to works" is God's principle of dealing with Israel and the world (xviii. 6); but not with
the Church.

23. **and her children** (Ps. cxxxvii. 9) **will I kill with
death** (*i.e.*, with pestilence); **and all the assemblies
shall know** (or, *get to know*) **that ℑ am He that
searcheth reins and hearts.**] Compare Jer. xi. 20;
xvii. 10; xx. 12. 1 Kings viii. 39; and 1 Sam. xvi. 7;
and see Rev. xi. 18 and xxii. 12. This is the work of
"the Son of God" (*v.* 18). The word "death" here means
pestilence, as in chap. vi. 8; xviii. 8. 2 Sam. xxiv. 13.
**and will give unto you, each one, according to your
works**] See Jer. xi. 20; xvii. 10. Ps. vii. 9; lxii. 12.

24. **But, unto you, I say,—the rest*** **that are in
Thyatira, as many as hold not this doctrine, who
have not known** (or, come to know) **the depths of
Satan, (as they say)**] God has His Divine depths,
1 Cor. ii. 10. Rom. xi. 33. But here we have the
"depths of Satan." We see some of them in Rev. xiii.,
but the real "depths" are in turning the basest profli-
gacy into religion; and, under the pretence of worshipping idols (which is awful enough), to legalize and
patronise the lowest of vices. Read Isa. xxviii. 14-18.
I do not† **lay upon you any other burden**] or
prophetic message of judgment. See 2 Kings ix. 25, 26,
and Isa. xiii. 1.

25. **Nevertheless, what ye have hold fast till I
come** (*lit.*, shall have come). 26. **And he that overcometh and keepeth my works**] *i.e.*, keepeth in mind,

---

* Omit "and to," G.L.T.Tr.A. WH. and RV.

† L.T.Tr.A. and RV. have the present tense instead of the
future.

as to ponder over, and understand my judgments. See on the word " keep " chap. i. 3, and references there given.

unto the end,—I will give him authority over the nations; 27. **and he shall rule them with a rod of iron: as vessels of pottery are dashed in pieces : even as 𝕴 also have received of my Father]** This is an unmistakable reference to such Old Testament prophecies as Ps. ii. 7-9, and to the scenes that will be then current on the earth mentioned in chaps. xii. 10, and xix. 15-21.

To such straits are interpreters driven, who spiritualize the prophecies of the Old Testament, and thus rob them from those to whom they belong, that they hesitate not on most missionary platforms to quote Ps. ii. 7-9 of the spread of the gospel. But there is some inconsistency in this robbery, for while they quote and claim the words of verse 8, " Ask of me and I will give the heathen for thine inheritance," they always stop short, and do not go on to quote the words that follow—" Thou shalt break them with a rod of iron : and shalt dash them in pieces like a potter's vessel." Here is the asking and the giving spoken of in Ps. ii. 8, and in the verse before us : only here, the promise is to the Assembly in Thyatira. If this is the Church of God then here we have its mission. But though most commentators hold that Thyatira is a " church," they do not press this as the Church's mission, or " claim " this as its promise : This fact manifests the inconsistency of the popular principle of interpretation.

28. **And I will give unto him the morning star]** The promise is fulfilled in Rev. xxii. 16. But the prophecy is in Numbers xxiv. 17, which

connects it with Israel and with the day of the Lord's
judgment, "There shall come a *Star* out of Jacob, and
a *Sceptre* shall rise out of Israel, and shall smite the
corners of Moab, and destroy all the children of Sheth."

29. **He that hath an ear, let him hear what the
Spirit is saying to the Assemblies**] See above.

5. THE FIFTH EPISTLE —SARDIS

(iii. 1-6)

In this Epistle the Old Testament reference is to the
period of Israel's removal from the Land. Where, as
the separate kingdom of the Ten Tribes, her name is
practically blotted out, as applied to the Ten Tribes.

In Deut. xxix. God declares of those who shall turn
away from Him "to go and serve the gods of these
nations" (*v.* 18), that He will "blot out his name from
under heaven (*v.* 20).

This was fulfilled first in the case of the Ten-Tribed
Kingdom of Israel. It was Jeroboam who first "made
Israel to sin." He is known by this periphrasis. This
is his special mark by which he was best known. In
forming the Ten-Tribed Kingdom he was at once cut
off from Jerusalem and the worship which God had
established there. Religion of some kind must be the
basis of government, so Jeroboam made his own religion:
and in a yet future day the Beast will have his own
universal religion; as we shall see.

A similar warning, therefore, and a similar teaching,
will be needed by those who shall be living on the
earth in the days of which the Apocalypse treats.

Hence we have in this epistle the reference to Israel's
removal from the Land :—

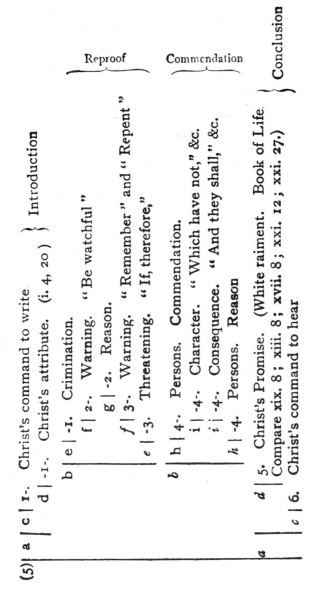

(5) iii. 1-6. SARDIS

Reproof

Commendation

(5) a | c | 1-. Christ's command to write } Introduction
d | -1-. Christ's attribute. (i. 4, 20) }

b | e | -1. Crimination.
f | 2-. Warning. "Be watchful"
g | -2. Reason.
f | 3-. Warning. "Remember" and "Repent"
e | -3. Threatening. "If, therefore,"

b | h | 4-. Persons. Commendation.
i | -4-. Character. "Which have not," &c.
i | -4-. Consequence. "And they shall," &c.
h | -4. Persons. Reason

} Conclusion

a | d | 5. Christ's Promise. (White raiment. Book of Life.
Compare xix. 8; xiii. 8; xvii. 8; xxi. 12; xxi. 27.)
c | 6. Christ's command to hear

iii. 1. **And unto the Angel of the Assembly in Sardis write; These things saith He that hath the seven spirits of God**] We submit that the Holy Spirit, as co-equal and co-eternal with the Father and the Son, could not be properly spoken of as a possession of Christ; and placed on the same footing as the seven stars, "which are the angels of the seven assemblies."

and the seven stars] These are the angels of the seven assemblies, and are spoken of as belonging to Christ (equally with the seven spirits) to cast down, punish, remove or exalt as He will. In chap. v. 6 we read that "a Lamb stood as it had been slain, having seven horns and seven eyes, which are the seven spirits of God." Indeed, these seven angels of the assemblies on earth, and the seven angels (or spirits, see under i. 4, and compare in Heb. i. 7) in heaven are connected together in the clearest possible manner. When we read in this book of "the seven angels which stood before God" (viii. 2), and of the "seven lamps of fire burning before the throne, which are (or represent) the seven spirits of God," what are we to understand beyond this? Why are we to say that they are not what it is here said they are, and explain them as being something else? When Christ speaks of "having" these, it does not mean having them in possession as *attributes*, but having them in His *power for use, disposal and command.*

I know thy works, that thou hast a name, that thou livest, and art dead.] How can such language as this be addressed to those who are in Christ to-day: they have "no name to live." *They do live* "in Christ." Their standing is not in works; neither

can it in any sense be said of them "and art dead.'
On the contrary, they were once " dead in trespasses and
sins," but they died in Christ, and are now risen in Him,
and stand on resurrection ground before God in all the
perfection of that standing which He has given them in
Christ.   No one who knows anything of the teaching of
the Church or Pauline Epistles, could ever think of
sacrificing that wondrous standing for the sake of a false
and traditional principle of interpretation.

2. **Be** (*lit.*, become) **watchful, and strengthen the
things that remain, that were* about to die: for I
have not found thy works fulfilled**] or performed.

The watchfulness required here is that of Luke xxi.
34-36.   Mark xiii. 34-37.

before my† God.]   Compare 1 Sam. xvi. 7.   Seven
times does Christ in these Epistles speak of "my"
in connection with His "Father" and His "God."

3. **Remember therefore how thou hast received
and heard, and keep** it in mind, **and repent**]   What
they heard we are told in Matt. xxiv. 14.

**If, therefore, thou shalt not watch, I will come‡ as a
thief, and thou shalt not know what hour I will come
upon thee**]   This one passage settles, for ever, the fact
that these words cannot possibly be addressed to the
members of the Church of God who have "that blessed
hope" of being caught up to meet the Lord in the air, or
of being "called on high" as in Phil. iii. 14.   We
are plainly and expressly told (in 1 Thess. v. 2), "**yourselves** know perfectly that 'the Day of the Lord' so
cometh as a thief in the night.   For when **they** shall

---

*G.L.T.Tr.A. WH. and RV., have "were" instead of "are."
†G.L.T.Tr.A. WH. and RV. add "my" here.
‡Omit "upon thee" G. L. T. Tr. A. WH. and RV.

say 'Peace and Safety'; then sudden destruction cometh upon **them**, and **they** shall not escape. But **ye**, brethren, are not in darkness that that day should over-take **you** as a thief." No language can be plainer than this, addressed to "the Church of the Thessalonians." Either Rev. iii. 3 refers to believers now, and we have a flat contradiction of 1 Thess. v. 4, or we must rightly divide the Word of truth, and say that 1 Thess. v. 4 is true of all the members of the Church of God; and that Rev. iii. 3 is equally true of those who shall be in these Assemblies (whatever they may be) in "the day of the Lord." That day will come "as a thief." See Matt. xxiv. 43. Luke xii. 39. 2 Pet. iii. 10. But it will come thus upon a world ("they" and "them") that looks not for Him. The Church of God will be "called on high;" made like Christ's own glorious body (Phil. iii. 14, 20, 21), and received up in Glory (1 Tim. iii. 16) before the thief shall come, and before the day of the Lord shall be present (2 Thess. ii. 2). Hence we are exhorted not to be moved by reports that "the day of the Lord is now present" (R.V.). If it were otherwise we have every need to be troubled, for our hope would then have been in vain. Those who have not been caught away will indeed be troubled, for they will be in the Great Tribulation. So determined, however, are many not to have this blessed hope, or even to allow others to have it, that they would rather hold that this "great and terrible day of the Lord" is our only "hope" and (!) thus be driven to interpret the "thief" or Christ coming as a friend to fetch us away as he *steals* precious jewels. And this is done in the face of the opposite statement in 1 Thess. v. 4, that that day shall "not come as a thief" on the church; and in spite

of the solemn warning to watch, so as not to suffer the
thief to break into, or to break up the house (Matt.
xxiv. 43). This thief is to be watched *against* : but
Christ is to be watched *for !*

4. Nevertheless thou hast a few names* in Sardis]
These names are evidently the distinguishing point in
this Epistle, for we read in the next verse of names
being not blotted out, and confessed.

which defiled not their garments] This is language
foreign to the Church of God. It accords with a standing in the flesh as addressed to those who can wash
their own robes (vii. 14) and establish a right to the
tree of life (xxii. 14), and make themselves ready (xix.
7). But all this is "works" and not grace. So is the
promise,

**and they shall walk with me in white :
because they are worthy**] This promise is fulfilled
in Rev. xix. 7, 8, but there is nothing like it in nature
or character promised to or hoped for by the church.
And as to worthiness, who of us can take that standing ?
No ; we are altogether unworthy in ourselves, but all-
worthy in Christ. But these are worthy because of their
own merit. The scene contemplated here is actually
described in chap. xvi. 15, and xix. 7-9. The day of the
Lord is a day when men will be treated according to
their deeds (Rom. ii. 5, 6). Those who have not defiled
their garments, and are unspotted from the flesh
(Jude 5-8) are those who have not worshipped the
Beast, or received his mark, or partaken of his idolatrous obscenities.

---

* Omit " even," G.L.T.Tr.A. WH. and RV.

5. **He that overcometh shall thus* be arrayed in white garments; and I will not blot out his name from the book of life**] How is it possible for a true believer in Christ to have his name blotted out? The teaching of Rom. viii. as to our standing in Christ is the very opposite of this. But both are true if "the word of truth" be rightly divided. Dan. xii. 1 prophesies of this "book of life," and Rev. xiii. tells us that the time for its fulfilment shall have then come.

and I will confess his name in the presence of my Father, and in the presence of His angels]. Here is the association of Christ, the Father, and the angels as in chap. i. 4, 5. See notes above; and Matt. xvi. 27. This promise, as we have seen (page 94), refers to the later scene in the life of David, when he confesses the names of his worthy ones, just before the glory of the kingdom is set up by Solomon (2 Sam. xxiii.). Some of the names are "blotted out." The others are confessed. This is the scene alluded to here; and this is what is promised by the Lord in Matt. x. 32, Luke xii. 8 and Mark viii. 38. These words refer, as the Lord Himself explains, to the time when He comes to send the sword upon the earth (Matt. x. 33-42). To interpret this of the church of God, is to utterly destroy that standing which God has given His church in Christ. There is no condemnation for those who are in Christ; and there can be no separation from the love of God in Christ. This is clear from Rom. viii.

6. **He that hath an ear, let him hear what the Spirit is saying unto the Assemblies**] see above.

---

*So L.T.Tr. WH. and RV.

(6) The Sixth Epistle —Philadelphia

(iii. 7-13)

In these last two Epistles the Old Testament illus-trations are from the period of the Kings and Kingdom of Judah; and after the removal of Israel. The one is from the days of Hezekiah ; and the other is from the days of the Minor Prophets, before and after the return from Babylon, when hope of restoration was held out to the People.

Those who will be on the earth in the days to which the Apocalypse refers, will need the instruction which such illustrations will give; for they will be days when all hope of restoration from Man has gone, and the People can hope only in God.

It will be a time of trial; but the promise of being *kept* in it is made, and the hope of being *delivered out of it* is given.

Those who have this promise fulfilled in them are seen in chap. vii. and xiv. and xv. caught up to God and His throne. They go into but come "out of" the Great Tribulation. They are afterwards seen standing before the throne, though not seated as the Church will be with Christ upon the throne. They will serve God and follow the Lamb whithersoever He goeth. (See Rev. vii. 14-17 ; xiv. 1-5 ; xv. 1-4.)

The structure exhibits these promises. The time of trial has sifted and separated the people, and there are those now who have kept the words of this book in remembrance, to whom these promises can be made.

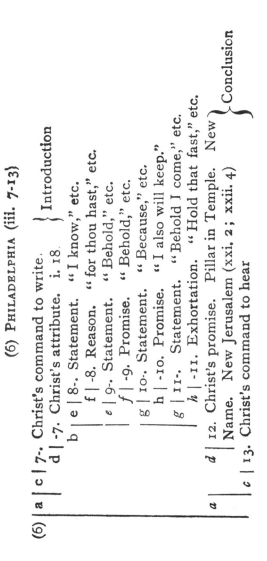

(6) PHILADELPHIA (iii. 7-13)

(6) | a | c | 7-. Christ's command to write. } Introduction
      | d | -7. Christ's attribute. i. 18.
      | b | e | 8-. Statement. "I know," etc.
      | | f | -8. Reason. "for thou hast," etc.
      | | e | 9-. Statement. "Behold," etc.
      | | f | -9. Promise. "Behold," etc.
      | | g | 10-. Statement. "Because," etc.
      | | h | -10. Promise. "I also will keep."
      | | g | 11-. Statement. "Behold I come," etc.
      | | h | -11. Exhortation. "Hold that fast," etc.
      | a | d | 12. Christ's promise. Pillar in Temple. New } Conclusion
      | | | Name. New Jerusalem (xxi. 2; xxii. 4)
      | | c | 13. Christ's command to hear

iii. 7. **Unto the angel of the Assembly in Philadelphia, write; These things saith He that is holy
and He that is true**] Seven attributes of Christ are
here given. The seven is divided, as usual, into three
and four. *Three* relate to what He *is* and *hath:*

    1. He that is holy
    2. He that is true
    3. He that hath the key of David

and *four* relate to what He *does* and *does not do:*

    4. That openeth
    5. And none shut
    6. That shutteth
    7. And none openeth

He that is holy] or the Holy One, is a title of Deity
(Hos. xi. 9. Hab. iii. 3). It is given to Christ
(Ps. xvi. 10. Acts iii. 14). The usual form of this
title in the Old Testament is "the Holy One of
Israel"; but Israel is now removed, and the illus-
tration is from Judah.

He that is true] The word here is ἀληθινός
(*alēthinos*) *real*, (not ἀληθής (*alēthēs*) *true*), and denotes
what is *real* and *genuine* in contrast to all that is merely
typical. Hence it is used of God whenever the
reference or contrast is to idols (either latent or otherwise) in the context. (See 1 Thess. i. 9. Compare
Jer. x. 10. 2 Chr. xv. 3. 1 John v. 20. Rev. xix. 11.)

He that hath the key of David] We have already
referred to this (see pages 80, 81), as specially giving its
character to this Epistle. It reminds the reader of
that period of Judah's history described in Isa. xxii.
Jerusalem was about to be taken, and instead of
repenting, they were feasting. The Treasurer of the

State "who was over the house" (Shebna), carried the key in token of his office; and he presumptuously thought he was going to retain his office and his dignity, and finally be buried in the magnificent sepulchre he had prepared for himself in the rock. But this thought was alien to the great hope given to David, which was *resurrection*, "even the sure mercies of (promised to) David." Shebna entered not into David's spirit, so he was removed, and another (Eliakim) took his office. The use of "the key of David" is explained in what follows, as denoting access to, and complete control over, the house and throne of David, and implies Regal dominion. Hence the word "house" (used in the prophecy—Isa. xxii. 22) is omitted here, for it is the *throne* that is now in question (Luke i. 32), and this could be occupied only in resurrection (Jer. xxx. 9. Ezek. xxxiv. 23, 24. Acts xiii. 34, 36). It is the Kingdom that is referred to in all this, not the church. Hence we read of "the keys of the kingdom," but never of "the keys of the church." This is left for Romanists to falsely claim, and for Protestant interpreters to weakly admit. Matt. xvi. 19 is clear as to this. This key belongs to Christ, as here stated; but the *opening* of the kingdom, *in testimony*, was committed to Peter, and Peter used those keys in his ministry in Acts i.-xii. Against that kingdom the " gates of the grave" should not prevail. If "gates" denote the entrance to the grave, then it means that *death* " shall not prevail "; and if " gates " (by *Metonymy*) denote *power*, then it means that the power of the grave will never keep and hold those who enter it. Christ holds the key (as stated in **i. 18**), and therefore He describes Himself as

He that openeth, and no one shall* shut; that
shutteth and no one shall† open.

8. **I know thy works: (behold I have set before
thee an opened door]** What this means is sufficiently
explained by what follows. It can refer only to *deliverance*, as when the opened door was set before Peter
(Acts xii. 10; and compare Isa. xlix. 9, 10). Their
enemies shall acknowledge the Lord's protecting
power. What a wrong interpretation of these words
it is, to take them as referring to an open door *for
service*, as is so universally done! Even as used by
Paul in 1 Cor. xvi. 9 it implies *deliverance* from the
"many adversaries"; and in 2 Cor. ii. 12 the reference
is clearly to *deliverance* from Satan's "devices" (*v.* 11);
in Col. iv. 3 the reference is to deliverance from his
"bonds."

**which no one can shut‡): that thou hast a little
strength, and didst keep my word]** This, the one
important injunction throughout, is obeyed by those
who are thus addressed.

and didst not deny my name] *i.e.*, by receiving
another "name"; even the name of the Beast. This,
too, refers to another special injunction so peculiarly
applicable to, and characteristic of, the coming days of
the great Tribulation. (See Rev. xiii. 17; xiv. 9, 11,
12). Here is the description of those very days referred
to, in this epistle.

9. **Behold, I make those of the synagogue of Satan,
who say that they are Jews, and are not, but do
lie]** How are these words to be explained of the

---

* L.T.Ta.Tr.A. WH. and RV. read the future tense.
† Ta.Tr.A. read the future tense.
‡ So G.L.T.Tr.A.WH. and RV.

Christian Church, either of these or of any other days?
Why should people "say they are Jews" in order to
join Christians? Why thus lie? Do we see any
fulfilment of this going on around us? No! These
claim to be Jews and meet in their assemblies (or
synagogues), but it is "the synagogue of Satan." They
claim to be "fellow-servants" (Matt. xxiv. 49). Those
who will be on the earth at that time will know what
these words mean better than we can know now. It is
for us to *believe* them.

**Behold, I will make them to come and bow down
before thy feet, and know that 𝕵 have loved 𝖙𝖍𝖊𝖊**
Is this what is prophesied of the church of God? Is
this our experience? Has it ever been the experience
of the Christian Church? No! trouble and persecution
and trial are the lot of the church; the portion plainly
foretold for it during the time of the Lord's rejection
until He shall come. To be hated because He was
hated; this is our portion now, from which no hope of
reprieve is held out to us. But this homage spoken of
here belongs to Israel *by right* in a yet future day. To
see this we have to read only such passages as Isa. xlv.
14; xlix. 22, 23; lx. 14; lxvi. 1-4, 5, 14. We can
hardly conceive it possible that, in the face of such
prophecies and promises addressed to Israel, anyone
could ever interpret their fulfilment in these Epistles
as belonging to the church of God. Look at only one
(Isa. lx. 14):

> " The sons also of them that afflicted thee shall come
> bending unto thee:
>
> And all they that despised thee shall bow themselves
> down at the soles of thy feet."

The promise made to Christ will be shared in by His people Israel. See Ps. lxxii. 9 ; cx. 1. Phil. ii. 10. Compare Exod. xi. 8. " That 𝕴 have loved 𝖙𝖍𝖊𝖊 "— both the pronouns here are very emphatic and refer to chap. i. 5. (See pages 51 and 169.)

10. **Because thou didst keep the word of my patience**], *i.e.*, the patient waiting or endurance which I didst command. See i. 9 ; ii. 2, 19. These commands as to "patience" refer particularly to the waiting during and under the tribulation. If it be asked where this is, the answer is clear from chaps. xiii. 10 ; and xiv. 12—" Here is the patience of the saints." It is the patience of those who shall be in those scenes of judgment and looking for deliverance out of them. For thus is the promise.

𝕴 also shall keep thee out of the hour of trial, which is about to come upon the whole (habitable) **world to try them that dwell on the earth**] These are the scenes foretold in Zeph. i. 14-18, and by our Lord in Luke xxi.36. This refers to a brief, definite season (xii.-xix.) ; probably " the three years and a half " closing with the manifestation of the Lord Jesus in the clouds. These earth-dwellers are repeatedly mentioned in this book (see vi. 10 ; xi. 10 ; xiii. 8, 14). For the "keeping out of the hour," etc. (see Ps. xxxii. 6. Isa. xxvi. 20, 21. John xvii. 15. Ps. xxvii. 1-5.) This deliverance may be the " wilderness," as spoken of in chap. xii.

11. " *I come quickly: Hold fast that which thou hast, that none take thy crown**] This can have no reference to the Church of God. We have no crowns to

---

* Omit " Behold," G.L.T.Tr.A. WH. and RV.

be taken and no one could take them if we had. We are in Christ ; perfect and secure in Him.

12. **Him that overcometh will I make a pillar in the Temple of my God**]   Here the promise goes on to the days of Solomon, to the "temple" and the "city" (as the next Epistle to Laodicea is associated with the throne). (See pages 209 and 210, and compare 1 Kings v. 5 ; vii. 13-22. 2 Chron. iii. 15-17.

and he shall in no wise go forth any more : and I will write upon him the name of my God, and the name of the city of my God]   The promise as to both temple and city are fulfilled in chap. xxi. 2, 3. Compare Ps. xlviii. 1, 2, 8, 9, and Ezek. xlviii. 35.

the New Jerusalem (xxi. 2, 10), **which descendeth out of heaven from my God** (xxi. 10) **and** [I will write upon him] **my new name**] Is. lxii. 2 ; lxv. 15. Inscriptions on the person are mentioned in chap. vii. 3.   The worshippers of the Beast will be marked with His name, chaps. xiii. 16 ; xiv. 11 xix. ;20 ; xx. 4.   This promise is specifically fulfilled in chaps. xiv. 1,and xxii. 4.

13. **He that hath an ear, let him hear what the Spirit is saying to the Assemblies**] See above.

7. THE SEVENTH EPISTLE —LAODICEA
(iii. 14-22)

The Epistle to the Assembly in Laodicea is the last, as it is the most solemn, of these Epistles. All the Epistles cover, in a general way, the whole period covered by the book ; but, they also mark special stages of the apostasy and of the tribulation.   Laodicea marks the last stage.   It is the final period immediately before chap. xix., when " the Judge standeth before the door " (*v.* 20. Compare James v. 9). The Old Testament illustrations are taken from the Minor Prophets, which cover the last period of the nation's history, and form the last testimony before the First Advent of Christ; because the same character will mark the period immediately preceding the Second Advent or the Day of the Lord.

The Structure is much more simple than any of the other Epistles, because the whole position at that period will be reduced to the very simple issue of allegiance to Christ or Antichrist.

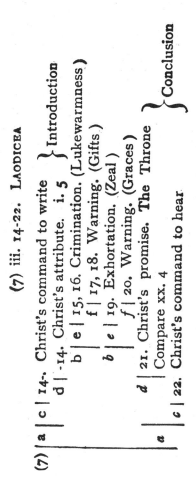

(7) iii. 14-22. LAODICEA

a | c | 14-. Christ's command to write ⎫
  | d | -14. Christ's attribute. i. 5 ⎬ Introduction
  | b | e | 15, 16. Crimination. (Lukewarmness)
  | | f | 17, 18. Warning. (Gifts)
  | b | e | 19. Exhortation. (Zeal)
  | | f | 20. Warning. (Graces)
  | d | 21. Christ's promise. The Throne ⎫
  | | Compare xx. 4   ⎬ Conclusion
a | c | 22. Christ's command to hear   ⎭

iii. 14. **And unto the Angel of the Assembly in Laodicea,* write; These things saith the Amen]** "Amen" is a Hebrew word (see 2 Cor. i. 20. Rom. xv. 8), expressing that which is immediately added, "faithful and true." Compare Isa. lxv. 16.

the faithful and true witness] See on chap. i. 5 above; and compare xix. 11 and Ps. lxxxix. 37.

the beginning of the creation of God] Reminding of the fact that by Him all things were created; and that by Him all things exist and all things consist (Col. i. 15-19). Before any created thing was formed, Elohim took created form in order to create; so that created beings might hold communion with the Creator, which they could not with God, who is "Spirit" (John iv. 24). Thus He is referred to in Prov. viii. 22-31. And thus He appeared to Adam (who was created in His image), and to the Patriarchs, and to Joshua as one who could be wrestled with and seen and spoken with. All believe that He assumed creature form specially for these appearances. It is only one step to further believe that this form was more permanent: that He took *creature* form in order to *create*, as He afterwards took *human* form in order to *redeem*. (Compare the two songs of Rev. iv. 11 and v. 9.) No other view so well enables us to understand how He could be called "the Beginning of the creation of God," or explain such passages as Prov. viii. 22-31 and Col. i. 15-17, "the firstborn of every creature" who was "before all things." This is all expressed in the words of the ancient Creed. "Begotten of His Father before the world; born of the substance of his mother in the world." He is therefore the Head of Creation, the

---

• So G.L.T.Tr.A. WH· and RV •

great subject of which this book treats, thus reminding us here of its beginning, as it afterwards tells of its end, and of the New Creation of the New Heaven and the New Earth.

15. **I know thy works, that thou art neither cold nor hot: I would that thou wert cold or hot.**

16. **Thus, because thou art luke-warm, and neither hot nor cold,* I am about to spue thee out of my mouth]** These words require no exposition. They explain with perfect clearness the condition of things among the remnant of the Jews in that day. The same result of unfaithfulness in not keeping the word and commandments of God is spoken of in Lev. xviii. 25, 28 ; xx. 22, where the people are told that for such disobedience, the very land should spue them out. Compare Zech. xi. 1-9, and Hos. iv. 6-7.

17. **Because thou sayest]** See page 82, where these verses are compared with Hosea ii. 5, 8, 9, and other passages from the minor prophets, which describe the very condition of things here referred to. We enlarged on this point in those pages (82-85), so as not to over-burden these running comments on the text itself.

I am rich and have become enriched] Compare Hos. xii. 8.

And have need of nothing; and knowest not that thou art the wretched one (Hos. ii. 11 ; v. 15), **and the miserable** (Hag. i. 6), **and poor, and blind, and naked** (Hos. ii. 3-10).

---

* So G.T.Tr.A. WH. and RV.

18. **I counsel thee to buy of me**] When are the members of the Church of God, or, indeed, anyone in this dispensation, where all is of grace and of gift, counselled "to buy" anything of God. We have "nothing to pay" and nothing to buy with; and can show no cause nor merit why we should have the slightest favour or blessing. Compare for the Dispensation of works Is. lv. 1, 2.

gold refined in the fire (Mal. iii. 3; Hos. ii. 8; Hag. ii. 8), **that thou mayest be enriched; and white garments, that thou mayest be clothed, and that the shame of thy nakedness may not be made manifest**] The reference here is to Jer. xiii. 25, 26, and Hosea ii. 3.

and eye-salve to anoint thine eyes, that thou mayest see] Compare Is. lix. 10.

19. **As many as I love**] See Is. xliii. 4, and compare context. Also Deut. vii. 8. Hos. iii. 2; xi. 4.

J rebuke and chasten] See Hos. vii. 12; Deut. viii. 5; xxviii. 20; and Prov. iii. 12.

be zealous therefore and repent.

20. **Behold, I am standing** (lit., " I have taken my station") **at the door, and am knocking**] The call is to the Wedding Feast of chap. xix. 9, to which the parables pointed, especially Luke xii. 35-38. The servants are exhorted to be "like unto men that wait for their Lord when he shall return from the wedding; that when he cometh *and knocketh* they may open to him immediately. Blessed are those servants whom the Lord when he cometh shall find watching The coming is no longer spoken of as " near "—he is already at the door.

To the twelve Tribes scattered abroad it is written in view of his coming—" The judge standeth before the door" (Jas. v. 7, 8, 9). The nearness of the Lord as the " judge" is the warning conveyed by these words in the Epistle to the Assembly in Laodicea, and not the nearness of the Saviour in grace, or an invitation to sinners in this day of grace. Can anything be clearer than this? and can language be more incongruous as applied to any in this present dispensation.

if any one hear my voice, and open the door, I will come in to him, and will sup with him, and ħe with me] It is in connection with the knocking just referred to in Luke xii. 37 that the promise is given to the " servants" spoken of (not to the church). " Verily I say unto you that he shall gird himself and make them to sit down to meat, and he will come forth and serve them" Compare Matt. xxii. 2, 3. Luke xiv. 15 ; xxii. 16-18. Mark xiv. 25, and Rev. xix. 9. This is the same watching which is spoken of in verse 39 as the watching for the coming as a thief.

21. **To him that overcometh will I give to take his seat with me on my throne, even as ℐ also overcame and took my seat with my Father on His throne]** This promise is seen fulfilled in xx. 4. The session of the Lord Jesus is spoken of here as past. He is now standing (as in the vision of ch. i.). He has " risen up from His seat" and is about to come down in judgment to avenge the blood of His martyred saints. Hence Stephen sees the same " Son of Man, standing" Acts vii. 56. Nothing proves more clearly the two thrones of which Scripture speaks. His Father's throne, on which He is now seated, and " the throne of His father David," to which Christ is the heir as David's Son and

David's Lord (Luke ii. 32). Compare Ezek. xliii. 7. Ps. cxxii. 5. It is this throne which He will occupy when He comes in His glory. Luke ii. 32. Acts ii. 30. Heb. ii. 5. Matt. xxv. 31. Ps. viii. Dan. vii. and Rev. xx. 4. There is a third throne spoken of in chap. xxii. 1, 3; but that is " the throne of God and of the Lamb," and is after the Millennium. The promise in iii. 21 refers to the throne of Solomon. (See page 99).

22. **He that hath an ear, let him hear what the Spirit is saying unto the Assemblies**] Here end these seven epistles. And we feel that no one can thus read and study them without becoming convinced that they belong to another dispensation altogether ; when " works " and not grace form the standing ; and Israel and not the Church is the subject.

6

THE FIRST VISION "IN HEAVEN"
(4:1—5:14)

The Throne and its surroundings

WE now come to the matter of the Book, which we have indicated by the letter ℨ on page 116. It consists, as we have seen, of *seven pairs of visions.*

The *first* of each pair is a Vision "in heaven"; and the *second* of each pair is a Vision "on earth."

Each Vision "in heaven" is preparatory to the Vision afterwards seen "on earth": and what is seen "on earth" is the carrying out of the Vision previously seen "in heaven." The one is mutually explanatory of the other. The heavenly Vision explains what is going to take place upon the earth; and the utterances in each heavenly Vision set forth the special object of the earthly events which are to follow. The former Vision of each pair is, therefore, the key to the latter.

These divisions are made by the Holy Spirit Himself; and the divisions, made by man into chapters, where they do not agree with the Divine divisions, are only misleading.

We shall have, therefore, wholly to ignore them, except for purposes of reference.

These heavenly and earthly Visions will form the great chapters or divisions of this part of our work. We shall take each of these fourteen Visions in order: first giving the structure, with any necessary expansions; following each with our own translation, based on a revised Greek Text, according to the authorities quoted in the notes; interspersed with such running expository remarks as may be necessary.

The structures themselves will be found full of teaching, and will give the scope of each section; showing, at a glance, what are the subjects on which our attention is to be fixed.

The following is the structure (in brief) of 𝕳¹, the first Vision " in heaven," consisting of chapters iv. and v.

𝕳¹ (page 118). THE FIRST VISION "IN HEAVEN" (chap. iv., v)

The Throne and its surroundings

𝕳¹ A | iv. 1-8-. The Throne, the Elders and the *Zōa*

B | -8-11. The utterances of the *Zōa* and the Elders. Theme : *Creation*

A | v. 1-7. The Throne and the Book : the Lion and the Lamb

B | 8-14. The New Song of the *Zōa* and the Elders. Other heavenly utterances Theme : *Redemption*

From this it will be seen that the great subjects of this Vision " in heaven " are :—

THE THRONE, THE BOOK, AND THE LAMB

That which comes first in the Book gives its importance and significance to the whole Book. It is the key to all that follows, and carries us forward by the Spirit to the future age, the coming " Day of the Lord." The first thing seen and the first mentioned (in verse 2) is

THE THRONE

" Immediately, I became in Spirit ; *and behold! a throne was set in heaven.*"

No words could be more important as fixing our minds on the great central and all-governing fact which pervades the Book of this prophecy.

It is the day spoken of in Ps. ciii. 19.

" The LORD hath prepared His throne in the heavens ;
  And His kingdom ruleth over all."

And in Pss. ix. and x., which treat of the coming great Tribulation as the " times of trouble " (ix. 9, and x. 1), it is declared : The LORD " hath prepared His throne for judgment." And in Ps. xi. 4-6 we read :

" The LORD is in his holy temple,
The LORD's throne is in heaven :
His eyes behold,
His eyelids try the children of men.
The LORD trieth the righteous :
But the wicked and him that loveth violence His soul
    hateth.
Upon the wicked he shall rain snares,
Fire and brimstone, and an horrible tempest :
This shall be the portion of their cup."

These three Psalms foretell and refer to the scenes described more fully in the Apocalypse.

Daniel (vii. 9, 10,) also speaks of this very moment when he says " I beheld till the thrones were set " (not " cast down " as in AV. but " placed " as in RV.*) " and the ancient of days did sit. . . . His throne was like the fiery flame and his wheels as burning fire. A fiery

---

* The Chaldee word רְמָה (*remah*) means *to set* or *place* by casing, putting or setting down. Eastern seats were cushions which are thus placed.

stream issued and came forth from before him; thousand thousands ministered unto him, and ten thousand times ten thousand stood before him: THE JUDGMENT WAS SET, and the books were opened."

This throne speaks of *judgment;* "the throne of grace" is no longer seen. Grace is the character of this present dispensation; while judgment, righteousness, and justice will characterise that which is coming. The heavenly voice announces it. "*Just* and true are thy ways, thou king of nations" (xv. 3 *q.v.*). "Thy *judgments* are made manifest" (*v.* 4). "Thou art *just,* who art and who wast the holy One, because thou *judgedst* thus" (xvi. 5; see also *v.* 7, and xix. 2, 11). The martyred ones are represented as crying "How long, O Sovereign Lord,* the holy and true, dost thou not *judge* and avenge our blood on the dwellers on the earth" (vi. 10). The reply is, not that this cry is out of place, but that it is only premature: they are to *wait* a little longer. Heaven itself bids all to rejoice at the execution of *judgment* (xviii. 20; xix. 2). "Fear God and give glory to him" (is the cry that will then go forth), "*for the hour of his judgment is come*" (xiv. 7). *Judgment* is also the final Vision (xx. 4); and it is given to the saints who have overcome. Psalm cxlix. 5-9 also tells of that final scene.

> " Let the saints be joyful in glory :
> Let them sing aloud upon their beds.
> Let the high praises of God (*El*) be in their mouth,
> And a two-edged sword in their hand ;
> To execute vengeance upon the heathen,
> And punishments upon the people ;

---

* Greek, δεσπότης *(despotēs)*, *Despot*, or Sovereign Lord. See below on chap. vi. 10.

To bind their kings with chains,
And their nobles with fetters of iron ;
To execute upon them the judgment written :
This honour have all His saints.   Hallelujah."

The Throne, therefore, with which this first Vision
" in heaven" commences, is the great central object.
The structure shows this; and it shows also other
prominent objects, *viz.*, the *Book* and the *Lamb*, and
their relation to two great subjects, *Creation* (chap. iv.)
and *Redemption* (chap. v.).

Before we proceed to the translation we must give the
expansion of A. (page 212) iv. 1-8-.   Its importance is
seen from the minuteness with which the Throne is
described.

> A. (page 212).   iv. 1-8   *The Throne*
> A | a | 1-3-.   On it: the Enthroned One
>   b | d | -3.   Round it : a Rainbow
>   e | 4.   Round it : 24 Thrones
>   c | 5-.   Out of it : Lightnings
>   b | d | -5.   Before it : Seven Lamps
>   e | 6-.   Before it : a Crystal Sea
>   a | -6-8-.   In the midst and round about it: the
> | four *Zōa*

We now proceed to give the translation of each
separate member, marking each with the corresponding
letters, so that its place in the general structure and
plan can be easily referred to, found and followed.

A. iv. 1-8   THE THRONE

a.   1-3-.   *On it : the Enthroned One*

iv. 1.   **After these things**]   Seven times in this
book we have this or a similar expression (iv. 1 ; vii. 1,

9 ; xv. 5 ; xviii. 1 ; xix. 1 ; xx. 3). As in the last case a thousand years intervene, it is clear that what is seen does not necessarily follow immediately. (It is a Hebrew idiom. Compare Gen. xxii. 1.)

I looked, and, behold a door set open IN HEAVEN] There are *five* openings mentioned in this Book ; and, while they do not mark special literary divisions, yet they are all of the deepest importance and significance. See xi. 19 ; xv. 5 ; xix. 11 ; and xxi. 1. This first is a " door " opened to admit John. But when the Armies of Heaven come forth, then John says : " And I saw Heaven opened " (xix. 11), and not merely a door. The same happened to Ezekiel when he saw " visions of (or from) God."

And the former voice which I heard (at the beginning, i. 10) **was as it were of a trumpet speaking with me** (i. 10), **saying,**

  " Come up hither, and I will show thee
  what things must come to pass here-
  after "]

There is no necessity for taking these words δεῖ γενέσθαι (*dei genesthai*) differently from i. 1, 19 ; xxii. 6. Matt. xxiv. 6 ; xxvi. 64. Dan ii. 28, 29. Μετὰ ταῦτα (*meta tauta*) means (literally) *after these things*, when used in historic narrative ; but when used in promise or prophecy the expression means *hereafter*. See i. 19 and ix. 12.

2. *Immediately I came to be in Spirit*] See chap. i. 10 ; xvii. 3 ; and xxi. 10. And for the further uses of ἐν πνεύματι (*en pneumati*) *in spirit*, see Rom. ix. 1 ; xiv. 17 ; xv. 16. 1 Cor. xii. 3, 9. 2 Cor. vi. 6. 1 Thess. i. 5. Jude 20 and Micah iii. 8.

---

* L.T.Tr.A. WH. and RV. omit καί (*kai*) *and*.

and, behold, a throne was set in heaven, and upon the throne was One sitting] This is evidently the Father; who henceforth, throughout the book, is spoken of as " He that sitteth upon the throne." He is distinguished from the Son in vi. 16 ; vii. 10.

3. And He that sat was, in appearance like to a jasper stone and a sardius ; and there was a rainbow round about the throne,—like, in appearance, to an emerald] It cannot be known precisely what is meant by the appearance of these stones, nor can we identify them satisfactorily. But there is no doubt as to the " rainbow." It speaks of a scene of judgment— not of water, but of fire ; and it tells also of hope and deliverance for those concerned in the covenant of which it is the " sign." The *form* tells us of the covenant of Gen. ix. 8-17 ; and the *colour*, being the opposite of that of fire, tells of mercy in the midst of judgment (Hab. iii. 3. Ps. ci. 1)

4. And round about the throne (behold) **four and twenty thrones ; and upon the four and twenty thrones*** **elders sitting, arrayed in white garments**] The word for the Elders' thrones is the same as that for " the throne " of verse **2**. Probably they were both smaller and lower; as they were also evidently subordinate.

and on their heads† crowns of gold] The common interpretation is that the Elders are symbolical of the Church of God. But why not leave them alone ? Why must they be something different from what they are ? David arranged his twenty-four courses of the Priesthood (1 Chron. xxiv. 3-5) after the heavenly order. And

---

* So L.Tr.A. WH. and RV.

† Omit "they had." G.L.T.Tr.A. WH. and RV.

he had it all " by the Spirit." "All this," said David,
" the LORD made me understand in writing by His hand
upon me "* (1 Chron. xxviii. 11-13, 19) It was the same
in the case of the Tabernacle which served "unto the
example and shadow of heavenly things, as when Moses
was admonished of God when he was about to make the
Tabernacle: for, See, saith he, that thou make all
things according to the pattern showed thee in the
mount " (Heb. viii. 5 and refs.). Hence they are
called " patterns of things in the heavens " (Heb. ix.
23). It was the same with David and the Temple, so
that what David copied on earth was a pattern of real
things "in the Heavens." The Temple worship on earth
was therefore modelled on that worship which is carried
on in heaven : and which, if we were caught up now,
we should see being carried on there by these heavenly
leaders of heaven's worship.

These elders are the heads of the heavenly priesthood ;
the chief-priests or elders of Heavenly worship and rule.
The comparative πρεσβύτερος (presbuteros) elder) has been
distinguished from πρεσβύτης (presbutes) old man), from
the most ancient times, as marking and denoting *official
position*. It is preserved in our Eng. Alderman or elder man.
In the *papyri* it is constantly used of both civil and
religious rulers. The affairs of the whole priesthood of
the Egyptian mysteries were conducted by an annual
council of 25 *presbuteroi*. The word does not mean
" priest" in any sense, for we often find the expression
" presbyter-priest " "used of a ruler among priests," so
that there were priestly-governors as well as civil-

---

* People who reject the verbal inspiration thus given by God, can
accept the " automatic writing" by means of lying spirits ! When the
Holy Spirit thus writes man will not believe it, but lying spirits are
implicitly trusted. Such is man !

governors.* The word is used in this sense in the Old Testament of "elders of the priests." (See Isa. xxxvii. 2. Jer. xix. 1 ; and passages given below.) This is the meaning of the word here also.

David distributed his twenty-four courses, *sixteen* from the sons of Eleazar ; and *eight* from the sons of Ithamar. These were "governors of the sanctuary and governors of the house of God." (1 Chron. xxiv. 5). If we ask, Why twenty-four ? the answer is because *twelve* is the number of *governmental perfection* ; and wherever we find it, or any multiple of it, it is always associated with government and rule.

It was the number (24,000) of the Levites who were to serve in the house of the Lord (1 Chron. xxiii. 3, 4).

It was the number of the prophets who were to lead the praises of God with instruments of song (1 Chron. xxv. 31).

The porters of the sons of Levi were *twenty-four* (1 Chron. xxvi. 17-19).

The same number obtained in the *Palace* as in the *Temple*.

Twelve captains presided over 24,000 (1 Chron. xxvii. 1-15).

Twelve officers were set over the Treasuries (verses 25-31).

So these four-and-twenty elders are the princely leaders, rulers, and governors of Heaven's worship. They are kings and priests. They were not, and cannot be, the Church of God. They are seen already crowned when the throne is first set up. They are crowned now. They were not, and are not redeemed, for they distinguish between themselves and those who are

---

* See Deismann *Bibelstudien*, p. 154, 433.

redeemed. See their song below (chap. v. 9, 10 and RV.). They speak of the time of "giving the reward to thy servants" (xi. 18), not to *us* thy servants. They are heavenly unfallen beings, and therefore they are "arrayed in white robes." They speak of *Creation* (iv. 8-11). And when they sing of *Redemption* (v 8-14) it is called "a new song." Redemption would be no new song to the Church of God, for it would be the old song which they had so often sung upon earth as " the old, old story." One of them speaks to John (vii. 13-17) as though separate and different from both the great multitude and from John himself. They offer " golden bowls full of odours, which are *the prayers of the saints* (v. 8). They are priests ministering for others. Is this the work of the Church? Their functions are altogether priestly. See 2 Chron. v. 11-14. And, as "elders," they were also rulers; and hence are seen seated on thrones (see Gen. xxiv. 2. Ex. iii. 16. In 1 Sam. xxx. 26, and 2 Sam. iii. 17; v. 3). They are next to the King, his councillors. (Compare 2 Sam. xvii. 4 and 1 Kings viii. 1-3). From all this we may gather the position of these four-and-twenty elders; and see that, to interpret them of the Church, is to force many passages of Scripture into a meaning which they cannot have.

5. **and out of the throne go forth lightnings and voices and thunders*; and seven torches of fire** are **burning before the throne, which are the seven spirits of God**] See above on i. 4; iii. i; and compare v. 6. These seven spirits are " before the throne " ready to obey the commands of Him who sits thereon.

---

* This is the order according to G.L.T.Tr.A. WH. and RV.; not " thunders and voices" as in AV.

The throne itself has all the accessories of judgment which inspire awe and speak of coming wrath.

6. and (behold) **before the throne, like* a glassy sea, like crystal**] It does not say what it *was*, but only what it was " like." Having been told what it was " like," it is not for us to seek for any further symbolism. Heaven, we believe, is a place of glorious realities, and not a place of unsubstantial shadows. We shall one day see what John saw, and then we shall *know*. Now, we have to *believe* what is written until faith shall be exchanged for sight.

And in the midst of the throne and around the throne, four Zōa, full of eyes before and behind.
7. **and the first Zōon was like a lion, and the second Zōon like an ox, and the third Zōon having the face as a man, and the fourth Zōon like a flying eagle.** 8. **and the four Zōa had each of them respectively, six wings; around and within they are full of eyes**] The word " beasts " is not the same as in chaps. xiii. and xvii. Here it is ζῶον (*zōon*), and means any *living creature*; but in chap. xiii. and xvii. it is θηρίον (*thērion*), *a wild, untamed beast*. It is difficult to find a term which shall exactly represent the original. " Living creature " is both vague and cumbrous ; " living beings " implies too much of humanity ; " living ones " would be better, but as the word is sometimes used in the singular number it would cause confusion to say " living one," inasmuch as " the Living One " is used in this book as one of the Divine titles of the Lord Jesus. We have judged it better therefore to leave the word untranslated, and use *Zōon* in the singular, and *Zōa*

---

* So G.L.T.Tr.A. WH. and RV.

in the plural. No difficulty will be experienced, as the word is already partly Anglicised and understood in our words, *Z*oology, *Z*oological, *Z*oophyte, *Z*ootomy, *Z*oonymy, &c., which all have to do with living things : animate as opposed to inanimate.

The first time the *Zōa* are mentioned in the Bible they are *named*, though they are not described. In Gen. iii. 24 they are called " the Cherubim," and this word has never been translated in any Version. We have, therefore, a good precedent for leaving their other names, *Zōon* and *Zōa*, also untranslated.

The *Zōa* are described in Ezekiel (chap. i. 5-14), and they are identified in Ezek. x. 20 with the cherubim. " This is the *living creature* that I saw under the God of Israel by the river of Chebar ; and I knew that they were the *cherubims*." The two terms are used interchangeably in Ezekiel. Compare i. 22 and x. 1, 15. No one can tell us anything about them beyond what God has Himself told us. Man's opinions as to what they " represent " are hardly worth controverting. Our own opinions are equally worthless ; we can only point our readers to what God has revealed about them.

Some would have it that they represent the Godhead ; but it is hardly likely that God, who commanded that no emblem of Deity should be made, should make one Himself ; especially one like unto " an ox that eateth grass." (See Deut. iv. 15, 16. Rom. i. 22, 23. Ps. cvi. 19, 20.) Moreover, they offer worship, but are never worshipped themselves (Isa. vi. Rev. iv., v.).

Some think they represent the four Gospels ; but animals can hardly represent books. Moreover, it is difficult to see the point of the four Gospels guarding the Tree of Life, or occupying such a prominent place in the Tabernacle and in the Temple.

That they cannot be the Church is clear from the following facts:

1. Three out of the four are *animals*, and there must be some sort of congruity between even a symbol and the thing signified.

2. They call for judgment (chap. vi.), and give the bowls "full of the wrath of God" to the Seven Vial Angels (chap. xv.). This is surely not the work of the Church, either now or in the future.

3. Rev. v. 9, 10, according to the correct text and translation, shows that these *Zōa* do *not* speak of themselves as redeemed, but distinguish themselves from such. See below, our exposition of those verses.

4. They cannot be any ordinary angelic beings, inasmuch, as they are distinguished from the angels in chap. v. 8, 11. Neither do they ever receive any commission, as angels always do. On the contrary, they give orders, as angels do not.

5. They are attached to the Throne of God, and are never seen apart from it.

6. They are first mentioned, as we have said, in Gen. iii. 24: "So He drove out the man; and He placed (in a Tabernacle), at the east of the garden of Eden, Cherubim, and a flaming sword which turned every way, to keep the way of the tree of life." The verb "keep," here, means to preserve and care for, and guard, as in Gen. ii. 15 and xviii. 19, etc. We first see them in connection with the Fall; and we note the fact that they are representative of *animate creation*, hence their name *Zōa*. Their number, *four*, connects them

also with the earth*; and Rom. viii. 19-21 makes the whole creation to partake of the effects of the Fall " For the earnest expectation of the creation waiteth for the revelation of the sons of God. For to vanity was the creation subjected, not willingly, but on account of Him who subjected the same : *and this was* in hope, because the creation itself also shall be freed from the bondage of corruption into the freedom of the glory of the children of God. For we know that the whole creation groaneth together and travaileth together until now " (Rom. viii. 19-21).

These words receive a new significance if we regard the Cherubim, or the *Zōa*, as being the concrete representation of this groaning creation ; and as being the pledge that its groaning shall one day cease, and its hope be fulfilled. That hope was given when they were first placed, as in a Tabernacle (as the word means), at the gate of Eden. There, at that time, was the Lord's presence manifested. Hither Cain and Abel brought their offerings ; and from this "presence of the Lord " Cain went out (Gen. iv. 14-16).

It may be that that Tabernacle of God continued up to the time of the Flood. For Shem is spoken of as the custodian of this "dwelling place." The word "placed" in Gen. iii. 24 is שָׁכַן (*shakan*), and it means *to station* or dwell *in a tabernacle*, and is commonly spoken of as God's dwelling among men and of His dwelling place.† In Gen. ix. 26, 27, we read :

" Blessed be the Lord God of Shem ;
    And Canaan shall be his servant.

---

* See *Number in Scripture*. Published by Kregel Publications

† See Exod. xxv. 8 ; xxix. 45, 46. Josh. xviii. 1 ; xxii. 19. 1 Kings vi. 13 ; viii. 12. 2 Chron. vi. 1. Ps. lxviii. 18 ; etc. It is from this verb that we have the word *Shekinah*.

God shall enlarge Japhet :
And He (*i.e.*, God) shall dwell (or place His tabernacle) in the tents of Shem."

Here, the three patriarchs are mentioned. Canaan (*i.e.*, Ham) and Japhet occupy the two central lines ; while Shem and the Lord His God occupy the two outer lines. If this be so, then, this Tabernacle of the Divine presence continued among men down to the Flood and contained the Cherubim.

After the Flood, the *Teraphim* (probably a corruption of the Cherubim) were made in imitation of them, and became objects of worship. The remembrance of them was carried away by the scattered nations (Gen. xi.), and probably the Assyrian sculptures are traditional corruptions of the Cherubim, for they consisted of a *man* with an *eagle's* head ; a *lion* or a *winged bull* with a *human* head.

When God set up the Tabernacle in Israel it was that He might " dwell among them " (Exod. xxv. 8 ; where we have the same word as that used in Gen. iii. 24 : " placed in a tabernacle "). The first thing made was not the Tabernacle itself, but the Ark of the Covenant with its mercy-seat and the Cherubim (Exod. xxv. 10-12). These were not the real cherubim, of course ; they were only copies of them on the mercy-seat. Representations of them were woven into the Vail (Exod. xxvi. 31 ; xxxvi. 35). This could only have been to show that, henceforth, the hope of *creation* was bound up with " the hope of Israel " ; and, that both were bound up in, and based on, the merits of atoning blood. From " between the Cherubim " God spoke ; and there His glory dwelt. (1 Sam. iv. 4. 2 Sam. vi. 2. Ps. lxxx. 4, 7, 14, 19.

Isa. xxxvii. 16.) The original Covenant with Adam, and with the Son of Man Himself, takes in the whole animate creation, and tells of the hope of its deliverance (Ps. viii. 6-8; cxlviii. 7-11). And millennial glory will not be complete without that hope being fulfilled (Isa. xi. 6-9).

In Rev. iv. and v. the Son of Man is about to realise this hope of *creation ;* and, therefore, creation rejoices in the blessed prospect. The *Zōa* are seen attached to the throne, and they speak of *creation.* The earth is about to be judged; and their deliverance is at hand. Hence they say, " Thou art worthy, O Lord and our God, to receive glory and honour and power ; for thou hast *created* all things, and for thy pleasure they were, and were *created* " (iv. 11). They speak, too, of the *redemption* on which the coming deliverance is based (chap. v. 9, 10 ; see below) ; and thus explain the object with which they had been associated with the blood-sprinkled mercy-seat.

In all this we are on Old Testament ground ; for when allusion is made to these momentous truths in Rom. viii., creation's hope is spoken of as being distinct from that of the Church, though bound up with it, and depending upon its manifestion in glory. In brief, then, we may say, that the cherubim are heavenly realities; living ones of whom we know nothing by experience. But, the references made to them in Scripture teach us that in some way they tell us of Creation's association with the effects of the Fall, and of the future hope of deliverance from those effects. Hence, their introduction here, now that that deliverance is at hand ; and hence their words also, which tell that it is near.

This brings us to the utterances of the *Zōa* and of the twenty-four Elders in B, iv. -8-11 (page 212).

B (page 212), chap. iv. -8-11. THE UTTERANCES OF
    THE *Zōa* AND ELDERS

The Theme—Creation

We now come to B, iv. -8-11, the subject of which is the worship and utterances of the *Zōa* and the Elders. This is part of the larger structure 🝐 on page 212, and still part of the first vision seen " in Heaven."

The following is the structure :

B ┊ f │ -8-. Worship of the *Zōa*. " And they rest not
    │   g │ -8. Their utterance (creation). "Holy, holy, holy . . .
    │ f │ 9, 10. Worship of the Elders. " And when . .
    │   g │ 11. Their new song (creation). " Thou art worthy . . .

iv. -8. **And they have no cessation day and night, saying**

"**Holy, Holy, Holy,**

Lord God Almighty,

Who was, and who is, and who is coming."

This is the first of all the seventeen Heavenly utterances. They begin with God Himself, and relate to what He is in Himself; and not to what He has, or has done, or is going to do. The emphasis is on " who *was*," because it is put first.＊ The object of the whole Book, and of all that it records, is to establish the Holiness of God, which is here, at the very outset, the

---

＊ Compare i. 8 and xi. 17, where the emphasis is on the *present.*

first thing that is proclaimed. The reign of Heaven is about to be established in the Earth, when all shall be holy, where now all is unholy. Hence we have the same thought in the great Kingdom-prayer:

" Our Father which art in heaven,
    Hallowed (or Holy) be Thy Name,
    Thy Kingdom come,
    Thy will be done on earth as it is in heaven."

Then, and not till then, we have " *us.*" " Give us." etc. It is remarkable also that there are three Psalms which proleptically speak of this coming reign. Psalms xciii., xcvii., and xcix. The three Psalms which precede these commence with the command to sing, and then these Psalms which follow each begin "the Lord reigneth." Not yet can they be sung of accomplished facts, but the day is coming when they can, and will be, sung of then present glorious realities. The point, however, we wish to notice is that, each of these three Psalms ends with a reference to God's *holiness*, because it will then be said "the Lord reigneth." But the heavenly utterances in Revelation begin with the proclamation of this holiness, because those who say " Holy, Holy, Holy," are about to call for the judgments which are to bring in that coming Holy Reign. (See Isa. xxiii. 18. Zech. xiv. 20, 21.) Those three Psalms must be carefully read in the light of the Apocalypse.

The first (xciii.) is called for by the song for the Sabbath (xcii.), which speaks of the millennial Sabbath-keeping which is to come, and tells of the destruction of the wicked, the perishing of the enemies and the scattering of the workers of iniquity, before the Lord is exalted as most High for evermore (*v.* 7-9). Then comes the answer in Psalm xciii., which begins "THE LORD REIGNETH," and tells of the Throne being established, and ends with the declaration, "*holiness* becometh thine house, O LORD, for ever."

The second (xcvii.) is called for in Psalm xcvi. 1. "O sing unto the LORD a new song; sing unto the LORD, all the *earth*"; and speaks of the millennial glory, which is summed up in verse 11:

> "Let the heavens rejoice,
> And let the earth be glad."*

This, too, is the burden of the *final* heavenly utterances in Rev. xix. 5, 7. Then comes the answer in Psalm xcvii., which begins "THE LORD REIGNETH," and tells how "righteousness and judgment are the habitation of his throne" (*v.* 2; and compare Rev. xv. 3; xvi. 7; xix. 2); and goes on to speak of the very judgments which are described in the Apocalypse, and also of the same exaltation of Jehovah high above all the earth (*v.* 9; compare xcii. 8). It ends by calling on the righteous to "rejoice in the LORD . . . . and give thanks at the remembrance of His *holiness*."

The third (xcix.) is called for in Psalm xcviii. 1-3: "O sing unto the LORD a new song: for he hath done marvellous things: his right hand and his holy arm hath gotten him the victory. . . . He hath remembered his mercy and his truth toward the house of Israel." Then comes the answer in Psalm xcix., which begins "THE LORD REIGNETH; let the people tremble:

---

* The Massorah points out a remarkable acrostic in the four Hebrew words which form this verse. The four words begin with the four letters which form the word Jehovah.

יִשְׂמְחוּ הַשָּׁמַיִם וְתָגֵל הָאָרֶץ

Thus this verse is stamped as containing the result of Jehovah's dealings.

he sitteth between the cherubim, let the earth be moved "
(marg., *stagger*). Three times in this Psalm we have
the three-fold "Holy" of the *Zōa* in Rev. iv. 8 giving
us its interpretation and significance :

Verse 3. " Let them praise thy great and terrible
name: for it is *holy*."

Verse 5. "Exalt ye the LORD our God, and worship
at his footstool, for he is *holy*." And

Verse 9. "Exalt the LORD our God, and worship at
his holy hill; for he is holy."

All this truth and teaching is embraced in this first
heavenly utterance, spoken by the four *Zōa.*

We have called attention to the fact that each Vision
seen "IN HEAVEN" is marked by heavenly voices;
and we have stated that it is in these we must look for
the key to the judgment scenes which follow on earth.
We shall have, therefore, to give more attention than is
usually done to the significance of these utterances;
weigh their words, learn their lessons, and note their
bearing on what follows "on earth."

9. **And when the *Zōa* shall give glory, honour, and
thanksgiving to Him who sitteth upon the throne,
who liveth for ever and ever,**

10. **The four and twenty elders shall fall down
before Him who sitteth upon the throne, and they
shall* worship Him who liveth for ever and ever,
and shall* cast their crowns before the throne,
saying:**

---

* B.E.G.L. T.Tr.A. WH. and RV. read the *future* tense here.

" **Worthy art thou, O Lord and our God,***
  To receive glory, and honour, and power;
  Because Thou didst create all things,
  And for thy pleasure they were,† and are
    created "]

Thus, *creation* is the subject of the first great utterance
of the *Zōa* and the Elders. Their words announce the
blessed fact that the judgments which are about to take
place, have for their great object the removal of the
curse, and of all unholiness from the earth; and the
ending of creation's groaning and travail. These
heavenly elders take part in this heavenly utterance,
and they acknowledge its truth by bowing their heads
in worship and homage.

A (page 212), chap. v. 1-7   THE THRONE AND THE
        BOOK : THE LION AND THE LAMB

Having considered the member B, iv. -8-11 (page 212),
we now come to the member *A*, v. 1-7 (page 212),
the subject of which is *The Throne, and the Book : The
Lion and the Lamb.*

Here, as in A. iv. 1-8-, we have the Throne. But,
here it is rather Him that sitteth upon the throne, than
the Throne itself.

A | h | 1-.   Right hand. " And I saw . . .
    | i | -1.   A Book
    | k | 2-5.   The Lion. " And I saw . . .
    | k | 6.   The Lamb. " And I saw . . .
    | i | 7-.   The Book. " And he came . . .
    | h | -7.   Right hand. " Out of the right hand .

---

* So L.T.Tr.A. WII. and RV.
† So G.L.T.Tr.A. WH. and RV.

232 / The First Vision "in Heaven"

v. 1. **And I saw on the right hand of Him that sitteth upon the throne, a Book** (or Roll), **written within and on** the **back, having been sealed with seven seals**]   Much ingenuity has been spent in the interpretation of this " Book," and what it represents. Some have suggested that it is the history of the Christian Church, but we trust our readers are fairly convinced by this time that the Church is not the subject of the Apocalypse.

Neither can it be " the book of the Covenant " yet to be made with Israel, because that New Covenant is in mercy (Heb. x. 16, 17), while this book has to do with judgment.   Why should we go out of our way to seek for a far-fetched meaning when we have such plain indications in the Word itself of what a sealed book denotes.   In Is. xxix. 11 we read : " And the vision of all is become unto you as the words of a book that is sealed, which men deliver to one tha is learned, saying, Read this, I pray thee : and he saith, I cannot ; for it is sealed."   In Dan. xii. 1-3, we read of the Great Tribulation, which is the central subject of the Apocalypse. But Daniel is not permitted to do much more than make known the *fact* of the great Tribulation out of which Daniel's people, the Jews, were to be delivered. The particulars, and the circumstances of that day, were not to be made known at that time by Daniel.   Hence, it is said to him (Dan. xii. 4) : "But thou, O Daniel, shut up the words, and seal the book, even to the time of the end."   And when Daniel enquired (verse 8) as to " what snould be the end of these things ? "   The answer is (verse 9), " Go thy way, Daniel, for the words are closed up and sealed till the time of the end."   The details of a former vision Daniel was told also to seal up.   " Wherefore shut thou up the vision: for it shall be for many days" (viii. 26).

What ought we to look for as the first thing, in the Apocalypse, which, as we have seen, has the end of the "many days" and "the time of the end" for its great subject, but the *unsealing* of this book, the sealing of which is so prominently spoken of in the book of Daniel? When the time comes for the fulfilment of all that is written in this book, then the seals are opened. Even then, though these seven seals be opened, there are still certain things which even John himself has to "seal up," *viz.*, "the things which the seven thunders uttered" (x. 4). We take it therefore that the opening of the seals of this book is the enlargement, development and continuation of the Book of Daniel, describing, from God's side, the judgments necessary to secure the fulfilment of all that He has foretold. The opening of each seal has a special judgment as its immediate result. The roll given to Ezekiel was of similar import. "He spread it before me, and it was written within and without; and there were written therein, lamentations and mourning and woe" (Ezek. ii. 10). In like manner, the opening of the seals of this book disclose tribulation and mourning and woe. But there is more in the "Book" than this. There is also the *object* of all this judgment. That object is the redemption of the forfeited inheritance. (See the notes on verse 2, below). The special importance of this "Book" (and all that is involved in it) is set forth by its structure, which is as follows:—

THE EXPANSION OF k. (page 231), v. 2-5. The Lion

k | | 2-. The Angel's proclamation. "And I saw . . ."

   m | -2. Question. "Who is worthy . . . ?"

      n | o | 3-. No one able. (Agent)
         p | -3. To open the book. (Action) } First consequence: Inability

      n | o | 4-. No one able. (Agent)
         φ | -4. To open the book. (Action) } Second consequence: Weeping,

   l | 5-. The Elder's consolation. "And one . . ."

   m | 5. Answer to the Question. "Behold . . ."

THE TRANSLATION OF k. (page 231), v. 2-5

v. 2. And I saw a strong angel proclaiming with a loud voice—" Who is worthy to open the Book, and to loose the seals thereof ? "] It looks as though there is something more in this 7-Sealed Book than what we have said on verse 1. There is evidently more in this book than the mere continuation of Daniel's prophecies. This is there, without doubt, but there must be that which calls for all these judgments and requires the putting forth of all this power. If the Book has to do with the whole subject of prophecy, with its causes, and not merely with its consequences and its end, then it may well take us back to the beginning, to which the cherubim already point us, when man was driven out from Paradise, when he forfeited his inheritance; and the promise of a coming Deliverer and Redeemer was given.

This First Vision "in Heaven" (iv. v.) takes up the history of man in relation to the Throne, at the point where it was left in Gen. iii. 24. The Throne is here set up; but man is outside and unable still to gain access to "The Tree of Life." Hence this proclamation " Who is worthy ? " Who has the right to redeem the forfeited inheritance, the lost Paradise? Satan is in possession of this world now. He is its " God " and " prince " (John xii. 31 ; xiv. 30 ; xvi. 11. Eph. ii. 2), and as such he was able in a peculiar way to tempt Him who had come to redeem it in the only lawful way in which it could be redeemed. (See Lev. xxv. 25 ; Deut. xxv. 5 ; and Ruth iv. 1-6). If this be so, then we understand this proclamation, which has so important a place in this heavenly vision. And the enquiry will be like that of Boaz, Who

will act the *Goel's* (or Redeemer's) part for man and for
Israel, and recover his lost estate.   Jer. xxxii. shows
that a sealed book was given in connection with such a
transaction (read verses 6-16) ; and if so, then it serves
as an illustration for a much weightier redemption, even
that of the new song which immediately follows
in this Heavenly Vision; the song whose theme is
nothing less than the Redemption of Creation, accomplished by One who was altogether worthy, both by unanswerable right and unequalled might.   For the *Goel*
was an avenger as well as a Redeemer.

3. **and no one was able, in the heaven nor upon
the earth, neither under the earth, to open the Book,
or to look at it**]   The worthiness required is so great
that no created being is able even to contemplate it.
There was not one that could make reply to the herald's
challenge.

4. **and I was weeping much because no one
worthy was found to open* the Book or to look at it**]
The scene must have been very vivid and real to
John to produce this sadness.   These tears were not
caused by disappointed inquisitiveness!   Surely, he
must have realised, somewhat, the serious nature of
the consequences involved if one worthy could not
have been found.   There must have been something,
and enough in the character or appearance of the Book,
to tell him this : for no voice had yet said anything as
to its nature or contents.   One of the Elders breaks
the silence.

5. **And one of the elders saith to me " Weep not!
Behold the Lion which is of the tribe of Judah, the**

---

* Omit "and read " G. L. T. Tr. A. WH. and RV.

Root of David, prevailed* so as **to open the Book, and
shall loose the seven seals of it**] Not one of the
Elders, or the Cherubim, or Angel, or Spirit, could
accomplish the work of the *Goel* (or Redeemer). None
of these could be " next of kin," none but the Son of
Man, who was David's Son and David's Lord.   None
but He who was at once the " Root " from whence
David sprang, and the " offspring " which sprang from
David, could be next-of-kin, and therefore entitled to
redeem the forfeited Inheritance of the Throne, the
Land, and the People.   He was " the Lion of the Tribe
of Judah " (Gen. xlix. 8-10.   Num. xxiv. 7-9.   Isa. ix.
6, 7 ; xi. 1 ; Ps. lxxxix. 20-29).

The Lord Jesus will prevail as the Lion ; and it is of
this the Book treats; but, He first prevailed as
the Lamb slain.   Hence, when John turned, he saw, not
a Lion, according to the Elder's announcement, but a
Lamb, according to the prior historical fact.

He first takes the place of man as outside the garden
and the tree of life (Gen. iii 24).   His Redemption work
commenced on earth by His coming, not into a garden,
but into a wilderness (Matt. iv. 1).   He approaches that
flaming sword and hears the words of Him who said
" Awake, O sword, against my Shepherd, and against the
MAN that is My fellow, saith the Lord of Hosts "
(Zech. xiii. 7).   This sword was sheathed in Him, and
thus He becomes entitled to enter and worthy to take the
Book.

When John first looks (*v.* 1), he sees only " the
Throne and the Book," which are separated from the
second by the structure.   For when he looks

---

* Not " hath prevailed," as though referring to some recent act, but
' did prevail," *i.e.,* at the Cross.

the second time (*v.* 6), he sees "the Lamb." The
Lamb is now seen in the midst of the Throne. He
occupies no longer the outside place. He is entitled
to enter and approach the throne, for He alone is
" worthy."

6. **And I saw * in the midst of the throne and of
the four Zoa, and in the midst of the Elders—a
Lamb, standing as having been slain, having seven
horns and seven eyes, which are the seven spirits
of God, having been sent † into the whole earth]**
The Elder spoke of a Lion: but John turns and sees
a Lamb. The Elder spoke of the consequence : John
sees the cause. The Lion is about to put forth His
power and eject the usurper from his dominion. "The
prince of this world is (already) judged " (John xvi. 11).
Sentence has been passed ; a judgment summons has
been issued (John xii. 31 ; xvi. 11) ; and execution is
about to be put in (Rev. xii). But all this is here first
shown to be in virtue of the "right " obtained by the
payment of the redemption price : that is why John sees
a Lamb as " having been slain."

Past payment is the basis of future power (Col. ii. 15.
Heb. ii. 14). This it is which established the worthiness of the true *Goël.* The horns of the Lamb speak
of His power (1 Sam. ii. 1. 2 Sam. xxii. 3. Ps. lxxv. 4 ;
cxxxii. 17 ; cxlviii. 14. Lam. ii. 3. Ezek. xxix. 21. Dan.
viii. 5, 20, 21, etc). This power is Divine and has a
spiritual and almighty agency able to carry it out.
The seven eyes, Zech. iv. 10. and iii. 9, denotes the
fact that the Lord is about to remove the iniquity of the
Land of Israel.

---

* Omit "and" G.T.Tr.A. WH. and RV. Omit " behold "
G.L.T.Tr.A. WH. and RV.
† So L.T.Tr.A. WH. and RV.

7. And He came and took it * out of the right hand of Him who sitteth upon the throne] Thus ends the member which has for its subject "The Throne and the Book; the Lion and the Lamb." It corresponds with Dan. vii. 9-14, where the Son of Man is seen coming to the Ancient of Days and receiving a kingdom, dominion, and glory ; and it is this which is immediately celebrated in the New Song which follows in chap. v. 8-14, concluding this first Vision "In Heaven."

B. (page 212), chap. v. 8-14.

THE NEW SONG OF THE *Zōa* AND ELDERS

The Theme—Redemption

The last member of Œ¹ is now reached. In the structure (on page 212) it is marked *B*, and consists of chap v. 8-14. the subject being, " The New Song of the *Zōa,* and the elders, and the heavenly utterances of other Angelic Beings.

It is arranged in orderly sequence ; the speakers and their utterances being separated and placed in five pairs, or groups.

EXPANSION OF *B.* (p. 212), chap. v. 8-14

The New Song of the Zōa, Elders and others

B | q¹ | 8, 9-. The Four *Zōa,* and 24 Elders
     r¹ | -9, 10. Their New Song
   q² | 11, 12-. Many Angels
     r² | -12. Their Utterance
   q³ | 13-. Every creature
     r³ | -13. Their Utterance
   q⁴ | 14-. The Four *Zōa*
     r⁴ | -14-. Their Utterance
   q⁵ | -14-. The 24 Elders
     r⁵ | -14. Their Utterance

*Omit "the Book," L.T.Tr.A. WH. and RV.

Here, in q¹ to q⁵ we have the heavenly speakers and singers ; while, in r¹ to r⁵ we have their song and their utterances. The latter relate to the scene which has just taken place "in heaven," and to the result of it about to be seen in the consequent judgments which follow and take place "on earth." The point at which the heavenly voices commence is the moment when the Lamb, who alone is entitled and worthy, takes the Book.

8. **And when He took the Book the four Zoa and the four and twenty elders fell down before the Lamb having each a harp*, and golden bowls full of incenses which are the prayers of the Saints]** In the Old Testament, the harp is associated with *joy and gladness* (see 1 Chron. xxv. 1, 6 ; 2 Chron. xxix. 25. Ps. lxxi. 22 ; xcii. 3 ; cxlix. 3) ; just as sadness is expressed by the absence of it: "The joy of the harp ceaseth" (Isa. xxiv. 8). Harps were also specially associated with *prophecy* (1 Sam. x. 5. 1 Chron. xxv. 3. Ps. xlix. 4).

The golden bowls were vessels belonging to the altar (Zech. xiv. 20), and the Septuagint uses the word of the vessels of the Temple (1 Kings vii. 45, 50. 2 Chron. iv. 22. Ex. xxv. 23-29 ; xxvii. 3 ; xxxvii. 10-16). The "prayers of the saints" are the prayers referred to by our Lord in the parable of the Judge, where He applies the parable Himself and asks " and shall not God avenge His own elect which cry day and night with Him though He bear long with them ? I tell you that He will avenge them speedily. Nevertheless, when the Son of Man cometh shall he find faith (Gr. the faith) on the earth ?" (Luke xviii. 7, 8). The faith here spoken

---

* So L.T.Tr.A. WH. and RV.

of is that referred to in Rev. ii. 19; xiii. 10; xiv. 12. These elect are the saints spoken of and referred to in Matt. xxiv. 31, and Dan. vii. 18, 22, 27. They are the "Saints of the Most High"; the Most High being a Divine title, always used in connection with the earth; and not with the church. The Elders perform priestly service, because it is *on behalf of others*. This, the Church cannot do. If the "Elders" are the Church, then the "Saints" cannot be, for the Church cannot offer for itself; nor can one part of it offer for another part! No! The Church is "all one in Christ Jesus," and cannot be separated or divided.

9. **and they sing a New Song, saying**] The *Zōa* speak only in this *first* Vision "in Heaven" and in the *last*, in chap. xix. 4; and *no where else*. The Elders speak in the first and last, but also a third time in xi. 17. This is significant; as showing the weight and importance of those utterances respectively. In this first vision "in Heaven" their voices are heard twice: *First*, in connection with the Throne and Him who sitteth thereupon (separately); for the *Zōa* speak first (iv. 8); and the Elders follow (iv. 11); their theme being *Creation*. The *second* time they speak it is in connection with the Lamb, and the Book, they sing *together* (chap. v. 9, 10), their theme being *Redemption*.

Six times in this first Vision "in Heaven," these Heavenly Voices are heard. All Heaven is engaged in singing the worthiness of God as the *Creator*; and the worthiness of the Lamb as the *Redeemer*. Surely these are the dominant personages of the whole Book. These are the themes which form its subject: *viz.*, the removal of the curse from creation, the redemption of the purchased inheritance, the ejection of the great usurper; and all accomplished through the payment of Redemption's *price* by the merits of the Lamb, and the putting forth of Redemption *power*. Hence, in connection with Him and with the book we have the first of four heavenly utterances :

The New Song of the Zöa and Elders. v. 9, 10.

> " **Worthy art thou**
> **To take the Book,**
> **And to open the seals thereof,**
> **Because thou wast slain**
> **And didst purchase** * a people **for God**
> **by thy blood**
> **Out of every tribe and tongue and**
> **people and nation,**
> **And didst make them** † **to our God** ‡
> **A kingdom** § **and priests,**
> **And they reign** ¶ **over the earth** "]

This is the theme of the New Song. The worthiness of the Lamb to take the Book, because of the

---

* Lachmann, Tischendorf, Alford, Wordsworth, Westcott and Hort, and the RV. omit ἡμᾶς (*hēmas*) *us*. Indeed, all the critical authorities are unanimous in substituting the 3rd person for the 1st in the next verse. But if so, then we *must* have the 3rd person here and not the 1st person. MS. authority for this is the Alexandrian MS. in the British Museum (cent. iv.). The Sinaitic MS. (cent. iv.). The Reuchlin MS. (cent. v.). The Ethiopic Version (cent. iv.). The Coptic Version (cent. v.). The Harleian MS. No. 1773 in B.M. It is quoted without the " us " by Cyprian, Bishop of Carthage, 248-258, and Fulgentius, a Bishop in Africa, 508-533, so that it was neither in the ancient MSS. from which those two versions were made; nor was it in the copies which those two Bishops had before them.

† So G.L.T.Tr.A. WH. and RV.

‡ Alford omits " to our God."

§ So L.T.Tr.A. WH. and RV.

¶ So L.Tr.A. WH. and RV. " shall reign " G.T. and Tr. marg.

Redemption He had accomplished. The People had been once redeemed from Egypt, for it is in connection with the Exodus that Redemption is first mentioned in the Bible, in the Song of Ex. xv. 13. "Thou in thy mercy hast led forth the people which thou hast *redeemed :* Thou hast guided them by thy strength unto thy holy habitation." But now the People have been scattered among "every kindred and tongue, and people and nation," and therefore they must be redeemed from these, "the second time," "like as it was to Israel in the day that he came up out of the land of Egypt" (Is. xi. 11, 16).

The importance of the various readings in verse 9 will be seen, and noted ; because upon this turns very much the interpretation of the whole Book. The true reading separates the singers from the Redeemed, and makes them heavenly beings who need no redemption, but who sing of the redemption wrought for others.

But the payment of the price is only one part of the work of redemption. If the *price* be paid and there be no power to take possession and eject the holder the payment is in vain. And if *power* be put forth and exercised in casting out the usurper, without the previous payment of the redemption price, it would not be a righteous action. So that for the redemption of the forfeited inheritance two things are absolutely necessary, *price* and *power*. The first redemption song has for its theme the payment of the *price*. The *second* celebrates the putting forth of the *power*.

We are first told by whom this second utterance is made.

11. **And I saw and heard* the voice of many angels around the throne, and of the Zoa, and of the elders, and the number of them was myriads of myriads† saying with a loud voice.**

> **"Worthy is the Lamb that was slain,**
> **To receive power**
> > **and riches**
> > **and wisdom**
> > **and strength**
> > **and honour**
> > **and glory**
> > **and blessing"]**

They give this sevenfold ascription as to the Lamb's worthiness. The words "Power" and "Strength" divide the seven into *three* and *four*. These are all marked off by the Figure *Polysyndeton* (*i.e.*, the use of "many ands") which bids us consider each of these seven features of the Lamb's worthiness separately. In doing this we are to note that the great theme is Redemption *power* and *strength*.

13. **And every creature which is in heaven and on‡ the earth and beneath the earth and such as are in the sea and all that are in them heard I saying**

> **"To Him that sitteth upon the throne**
> **And to the Lamb**
> > **Blessing**
> > **and honour**
> > **and glory**
> > **and might**
> **For ever and ever"]**

---

* T. and Tr. add "as." WH. put it in the margin. And A. puts it in brackets. † So B.E.L.G.L.T.Tr.A. WH. and R.V.
‡ So G.L.T.Tr.A. WH. and R.V.

This is the ascription of the whole *creation*. Hence it is *four-fold* because it is in connection with the earth (of which *four* is the number) and because He who sitteth upon the Throne is there in relation to the earth. Whereas the ascription to the Person of the Lamb slain is *seven*-fold because Redemption blood was offered "through the eternal Spirit" (Heb. ix. 14).

14. And the four Zoa said

"Amen"

and the four and twenty elders fell down and worshipped*]

It seems almost profane to attempt to explain, and comment on these heavenly utterances. They are Heaven's own comment on the wondrous facts seen and heard by John, and brought before us in this first vision seen "in heaven." When again He brings the First-born into the world, He saith "And let all the angels of God worship Him" (Heb. i. 6). This is the Septuagint rendering of Deut. xxxii. 43, the closing words of the Song of Moses. And why are all the nations there called on to "Rejoice," and why are all the angels of God called on to worship Him? Because He is about to fulfil the threat He there pronounced and records:

"FOR He will avenge the blood of His servants,
And will render vengeance to His adversaries,
And will be merciful to His Land,
And to His people."

These are the concluding words of "the song of Moses." Now, "the whole creation groaneth and travaileth in pain together" (Rom. viii. 22), but then,

---

* G.L.T.Tr.A. WH. and RV. omit "Him who liveth for ever and ever" as being a later addition to the Text by some scribe.

when the day to sing this song of Moses shall have
come, and the glory of the Lord shines once more upon
Israel, then the song will be in the words written:

"His way will be known upon earth
> And His saving health will be made known
> among all nations:
> Then shall the nations be glad and sing for joy.
> Then shall our land yield her increase" (Ps. lxvii.)

"The trees of the wood shall rejoice" (Ps. xcvi.)

"The floods shall clap their hands
> And the hills shall be joyful together" (Ps. xcviii.)

"The beast of the field:
> The fowl of the air:
> And the fish of the sea:
> And whatsoever passeth through the paths of
> the sea, shall say,
> 'O Jehovah Adonai, how excellent is Thy name
> in all the EARTH ' " (Ps. viii).

"And everything that hath breath" shall praise
> the Lord (Ps. cl.) and say
> > HALLELUJAH

7

THE FIRST VISION "ON EARTH"
(6:1—7:8)

the sealing of the 144,000

FROM the whole of the first Vision "in Heaven" (卷¹, iv. v.) it is clear that we have now to look (in 卷¹, vi. 1—vii. 8) for the putting forth of *power* "on Earth" in the completion of the redemption of the purchased inheritance. The *price* has been paid in the shedding of the precious blood of the Lamb; and now, the necessary *power* is to be exercised so as to secure all its wondrous results, in wresting the inheritance from the hand of the enemy by ejecting the present usurper, and forcibly taking possession. We see this *power* put forth in the Seals, Trumpets, and Vials which fill up the active judgments of God in accomplishing this: and which end with the coming of the Lord Himself (xix).

This is the great object set forth in the preceding Vision "in Heaven"; and now we are to see the result of it all as consequent on it "on Earth."

John sees it all, of course, "in Heaven," but what he saw (vi. 1—vii. 8) "in Heaven" will take place "on Earth," just as what he sees (chaps. iv. and v.) as taking place "in Heaven," does and will take place there.

This is the first Vision of what will take place "on Earth" in "the day of the Lord." The great subject is

THE OPENING OF THE SIX SEALS.

For the Six Seals are separated off from the seventh in a remarkable manner; as though to point out to us that the seventh is not immediately consecutive on the sixth, as the other seals are consecutive one on the other.

The sixth seal evidently carries us forward to the time of the end; for it speaks of the signs in the sun and moon and stars (vi. 12, 13), which the Lord associates with His personal appearance (Matt. xxiv. 29. See Joel ii. 28, 31, where it is called "the great and terrible day of the Lord," as though it were the climax of the whole period known as "the day of the Lord"). It is called in the sixth seal "the great day of His wrath" (vi. 17), and the signs in heaven are the great final scene (vi. 14) as described in 2 Pet. iii. 10.

If this be so, then these first six seals are separated, very definitely, from the seventh; and the silence in heaven which follows the opening of the seventh indicates a pause.

The six seals present us with a preliminary summary of the judgments, which cover the whole period; the sixth leading up to and ending in the actual coming of Christ; or, at any rate, to the end of chapter xviii.

There is every reason to believe that "the day of the Lord" will be a prolonged period. It must not be confined to "seven years," as is so often done. The time between the *coming forth* of the Lord into the air to meet His Church, and His *coming unto* the Earth with His Church, in power and great glory, may correspond to the thirty-three years between His *coming forth* at Bethlehem (Micah v. 2) and His *coming unto* Jerusalem (Zech. ix. 9). All the events between those two we speak of as constituting His "first coming." In like manner, all the events described in this Book, which take place between His coming "for" and His coming "with"

His Church, we may speak of as " His second coming " or "the day of the Lord." (See page 53).

These events may occupy a similar period of thirty-three years for aught we know; and if to these we add the seven years of the last week of Daniel we have a period of forty years.

We do know that in Matt. xxiv. 4-6, in answer to the first question of the disciples, " When shall these things be," *i.e.*, when the temple should be destroyed, the Lord at once adds, "*not yet is the end* (τέλος)."

He then goes on to answer the second question, "What shall be the sign of thy coming, and of the *Sunteleia* of the age ? " (*v.* 3). He describes four of these seals (*v.* 7), and adds " *all these are a beginning of sorrows.*"

This fixes these earlier seals as the " *beginning* " of the *Sunteleia* of " the day of the Lord "—this " beginning " may be spread over some years before the Great Tribulation, proper, comes on.

Thus these first six seals are again separated off from the seventh.

We now give the first vision, 𝕮¹ (page 118), vi. 1—vii. 8, showing the events *on Earth*, as a whole.

It will be seen that they are divided between two subjects—the persecutors and the persecuted: Those who are on the side of Antichrist (B¹ and B²); and those who suffer (A²), or have immunity from suffering (A³), for refusing to worship him, etc. :

It will be noted also how perfectly Matt. xxiv. corresponds with this first scene on earth—the whole summary of the *Sunteleia* and the *Telos*. (See pages 88 and 89).

𝕮¹ (page 118) vi. 1—vii. 8.   *The Six Seals and the Sealing*

𝕮"| A¹ | vi. 1, 2. The False Christ going forth to make war on the saints. (1st Seal.) Matt. xxiv. 4, 5.

B¹ | vi. 3-8. Judgments on him and his followers. (2nd, 3rd, and 4th Seals.) Matt. xxiv. 6, 7

A² | vi. 9-11. The effects of the war with the saints. Their martyrdom. (5th Seal.) Matt. xxiv. 8-28

B² | vi. 12-17. Judgments on him and his followers. (6th Seal.) Matt. xxiv. 29-30. And Question, " Who shall be able to stand ? "

A³ | vii. 1-8. Answer to Question, by the Sealing of 144,000, enabling them to stand in the judgment (Matt. xxiv. 31)

We want our readers to understand clearly our suggestion as to these Seals. We separate them off from the *Trumpets* and *Vials,* which are continuous *once they begin.* This is shown from the fact, as will be seen below, that, the last two Trumpets and the first Vial are linked together as being the "three woes." They are thus marked as *consecutive.*

The Seals, however, we feel compelled, by the events under the sixth, to regard as a summary of ALL the Divine judgments which will usher in the Day of the Lord: including the whole of the *Sunteleia,* the Tribulation," and leading up to the *Telos* or end,—the last "seven years," and "the great day of His wrath." Thus they cover the whole period in broad outline. After the last Seal there is a break, shown by the "silence in heaven," and we are turned aside to see some further details as to these judgments—beginning, may we say *de novo*, with the Trumpets. After the last Trumpet there is no such break, no "silence in heaven" or on earth, but the last Trumpet at once ushers in and contains and developes the final judgments of the seven Vials, which finish up the mystery or secret purpose of God; for, we read in Rev. x. 7 that "in the days of the seventh angel, when he shall begin to sound, the mystery of God should be finished as he hath declared to his servants the prophets." The seventh Trumpet expands into the seven Vials, and these end with the final destruction of Babylon, which closes up these earthly judgment scenes.

We will now give a summary of the first four Seals. A¹ and B¹, vi. 1-8:

A¹ and B¹ (page 250) vi. 1-8.   *The Four Seals*

A¹ & B¹

a | vi. 1, 2. The *First* Seal. White Horse. The rider with bow in hand. (Matt. xxiv. 5.)

b | vi. 3, 4. The *Second* Seal. Red Horse. War (Matt. xxiv. 6, 7-.)

a | vi. 5, 6. The *Third* Seal. Black Horse. Famine. The rider, balances in hand. (Matt. xxiv. -7-.).

b | vi. 7, 8. The *Fourth* Seal. The Livid Horse. Pestilence. (Matt. xxiv. -7-.)

A¹ (vi. 1, 2).   *The First Seal*

vi. 1. And I saw when the Lamb opened one of the seven* seals, and I heard one of the four Zōa saying, as with a voice of thunder—Go !†

* So G.L.T.Tr.A. WH. and RV.

† The words "and see" must be omitted according to G.L.T.Tr.A WH. and RV.

2. **And I saw and lo! a white horse, and he that was sitting upon it, having a bow, and there was given unto him a crown** (στέφανος (*stephanos*), *a triumphal crown*)**, and he went forth conquering, and in order that he might conquer** or overcome] If we interpret these Seals by the words of Christ in Matt. xxiv., where He is describing this very time in answer to the disciples' questions, there can be no doubt as to their meaning and reality. His very first words relate to the false Christs who shall appear as the sign when these things should be (*i.e.*, when the Temple should be destroyed). And so it was; but these were only the prelude to what should mark " the beginning of sorrows." These should begin, not by many " false **Christs**," but by one, who should give it out and say :

" **I** am the Messiah,
   and he shall deceive many "

(Matt. xxiv. 5). This first Seal, therefore, must mark the first rising of this False Christ. This is the silent secret preliminary intimation of his going forth. **Further** details of this are given in Rev. xiii., where it is expressly said that "*it was given to him* to make war **with** the saints and to overcome them, and *there was given to him* authority over every tribe and people*, and tongue and nation, and all who dwell on the earth shall do homage to him whose names have not been written (in the book of life of the Lamb slain) from the foundation of the world" (Rev. xiii. 7, 8). It seems impossible to separate this from the rider on the white horse (in vi. 1, 2), for we read of him in like manner that "*it was given to him*" to wear a crown, and to go forth and overcome. How the Lamb who opens the seal can be the

---

* So G.L.T.Tr.A. WH. and RV.

effect of the opening, and at the same time be the rider
on a white horse, we cannot understand. If, on the other
hand, we see in this rider an imitation of the "faithful and true" Messiah when He comes forth on a
white horse to really conquer, as described in Rev.
xix. 11, then, how natural for the false and deceiving
Messiah to go forth in a manner that will be most
calculated to "deceive many." It is one of the
curiosities of interpretation, first to understand the
Zōa of the Church, and then make the rider of
the first Seal to be Christ; thus making one member
of the Church give the order to Christ to go forth in
His judgment power ! How much more simple, taking
Christ's words in Matt. xxiv. as the key, to leave the *Zōa*
alone, and regard them as spiritual or heavenly beings
specially interested in the judgments about to come on
the earth, and giving the authority to the False Christ
to go forth and be "revealed in his time," just as
Christ said to Judas, "That thou doest, do quickly"
(John xiii. 27). All the other horses are judgment
horses : why inconsistently break up this uniformity
and single out one Rider as Divine and take the others
as human ? Why understand one as going forth in
grace, and the others in *judgment* ?

The descriptions of Antichrist's career in other
Scriptures coincide entirely with this. He rises
unrecognised by the dwellers on the earth. His
beginning is "Peace," but his aim is universal
dominion, which he finally acquires. When his down-
fall comes, the reflection of beholders will be :—"Is
this the man that made the earth to tremble, that did
shake kingdoms; that made the world a wilderness, and
destroyed the cities thereof" (Isa. xiv. 16, 17). In

Daniel it is said that " his power shall be mighty . . that he shall destroy wonderfully " (Dan. viii. 24) and that " he shall stretch forth his hand upon the countries " (Dan. xi. 36, 42).

As to the Command, the obedience to it " *and he went forth,*" shows that the verb ἐρχομαι *(erchomai) to come*, or *go*, must be taken in the latter sense, " Go ! " Or else the second occurrence of the verb would be " and he came forth." The commission " given to him " concerned war, as the second seal goes on to explain. Horses are specially associated with war. See Job xxxix. 19, 25. Prov. xxi. 31 (" the horse is prepared against the day of battle "). So Ps. lxxvi. 6. Zech. ix. 10 ; x. 3. Jer. vi. 23. Isa. xliii. 17. But because the rider on the white horse in Rev. xix. is Christ, that is no reason why the rider on the white horse, chap. vi., should be Christ also, especially as in this very same verse we have Him already represented as a Lamb, who opens this seal in order that the white horse may be sent forth.

We need not trouble ourselves to show that this white horse is not the Roman Empire, as some hold ; or Rome itself, as Mr. Elliott believes. Nor can we ask our readers to believe that the " Bow " in the rider's hand symbolises the island of Crete. We do not need a knowledge of the Classics or of History in order to understand this Book ; but we *do* need a knowledge of Scripture ; not to say common sense.

The Second Seal (vi. 3, 4)

vi. 3. **And when He opened the second seal I heard the second Zōon saying, Go !* 4. And there went forth another horse, fiery coloured ; and to him who**

---

* Omit " and see " G.L.T.Tr.A. WH. and RV.

sat upon it was given power to take away peace from the earth, and that men should slay one another: and there was given to him a great sword] That this relates to the whole earth, and not merely to the Land, seems to be determined by our Lord's reference to the subject of the second seal, in Matt. xxiv. 6, 7 : "And ye shall hear of wars and rumours of wars . . . and nation shall rise against nation, and kingdom against kingdom." These words, coupled with the second seal, point to a general break up of the nations in the process of their absorption into Antichrist's universal kingdom. In Ezekiel xxxviii. 21, it is written : " I will *call* for a *sword* against him throughout all my mountains, saith Jehovah Adonai : Every man's sword shall be against his brother." Jer. xxv. tells of this second seal; when God has His controversy with the nations. Read from verse 15-33, and note verse 29 : "I will *call* for a *sword* upon all the inhabitants of the earth, saith the LORD of hosts . . . for the LORD hath a controversy with the nations; He will give them that are wicked to the sword, saith the LORD (*v.* 31). Against Israel also comes the sword, " I will *bring a sword upon you* that shall avenge the quarrel of my covenant " (Lev. xxvi. 25-33). The "sword" is one of God's "four sore judgments" sent upon the earth (Ezek. xiv. 13-21).

"There was given unto him." We must note well these significant words. They are spoken of the first rider on the white horse; and similarly of all the judgments. All are initiated from the throne. It will be again, as it was in another period of Israel's history in the days of Asa, "In those times there was no peace to him that went out, nor to him that came in, but great vexations were upon all the inhabitants of the countries, and nation was destroyed of nation, and city of city; for God did vex them with all adversity " (2 Chron. xv. 5,6). Such another time is described by Josephus (*Wars*, Bk. ii. xviii. 2, 1, 5). No new thing is referred to in this second seal. The whole of Micah vii. should be read. It is too long to be quoted here. But we may quote Dan. xi. 33, "and they that under-stand among the people shall instruct many; yet they shall fall by the *sword*, and by flame, by captivity, and by spoil, *many days.*" Surely we have in these scriptures that which explains, suf-ficiently, the second seal; and shall not be likely to accept such an interpretation as Mr. Elliott offers when he says that this second rider symbolises the prœtorian prefects of Rome. Upon this it will be sufficient to remark that the sword was "given" by the Roman Emperor with the view of preserving peace in the earth and not with the object of *taking peace away from the earth*, as here stated !

It may be well to add that up to the third century this was not considered to have been fulfilled by any historical events. So Origen says in his *Commentary on St. Matthew* (Cap. xxiv.).

The Third Seal (vi. 5, 6)

vi. 5. And when he opened the third seal I heard the third Zoon saying, Go !* And I beheld, and lo ! a black horse, and he who was sitting upon it having a pair of balances in his hand. 6. And I heard as †

---

* Omit " and see," L.T.Tr.A. WH. and RV.

† So L.T.Tr.A. WH. and RV.

it were a voice in the midst of the four Zōa, saying,

> "A choenix of wheat for a denarius,
> and three choenixes of barley for a
> denarius: and see, thou mayest not
> injure the oil and the wine"]

This is the next judgment mentioned by the Lord in Matt. xxiv. -7-, "*and there shall be famines*": for this is what "black" denotes. (See Lam. iv. 4-8; v. 10. Jer. xiv. 1, 2.) In former times it was God who called for a famine. See 2 Kings viii. 1. So in prophecy. Hag. i. 11; ii. 16, 17. Jer. xvi. 4.

The "balances" some would translate "yoke"; and because yokes are generally worn by oxen, and not carried in a horseman's hand, commentators make it a spiritual yoke and a spiritual famine! though they leave us to wonder what a spiritual famine has to do with weights and measures and the prices of wheat and barley. We prefer what is so evidently the simple meaning of the words. Bread "by weight" always denotes scarcity. When God describes, through Ezekiel, the famine during the seige of Jerusalem, He says, "Thy meat which thou shalt eat shall be *by weight* . . . . and drink water *by measure*." (Read Ezek. iv. 10, 16, 17.) This is exactly what the mysterious voice (in the midst of the four Zōa) declares. Famines may occur from secondary causes, but the first cause of this Famine is from "the throne." The extent is fore-known—"A choenix of wheat for a denarius." We know from Matt. xx. 2, 9 that a *denarius* (the value of which was about 7¼d.) was a day's wage; and we know also that a *choenix* of corn (about 2 pints) was the daily ration for a slave (*Odyss.* xix. 27, 28. Athen. iii. 20. Herod. vi. 57; vii. 187, 231. Xen. *Anab.* i. 5, 6. Thucyd. iv. 16).

The usual price of a choenix was ⅛th **of a denarius;** so that corn, here, in this famine, is eight times its usual price. We are told that a denarius would buy 16 choenixes of wheat in the time of Cicero, and 20 in the time of Trajan. There will be great scarcity, therefore, when a denarius will buy only *one.*

Literal famines have been so often foretold, and have come to pass, from Genesis onward (2 Kings vi. 25; vii. 1. Acts xi. 28). Why should not this famine in Revelation be literal also? And yet interpreters seem determined to make this anything except a literal famine. Some, as we have said, make it spiritual, wrongly applying Amos viii. 11, 12. " Injure not the oil and the wine" is literal; and the Lord Himself, speaking of the beginning of these very sorrows, says, "there shall be famines." Corn, oil, and wine are three words often linked together to give the idea of plenty. (See Deut. xi. 14; xxviii. 51.)

Mr. Elliott, in his *Horae Apocalypticae,* has to make it accord with the requirements of *history,* and says " there is nothing correspondent with such era of famine" (vol. i., p. 149). One would have thought, therefore, that the best plan would be to abandon the historical interpretation. But no! history must stand, and the Scripture (the voice from the Throne) must be accommodated to it. So Mr. Elliott first insists on a larger *choenix;* but afterwards, finding this could not be sustained, he changes his ground in a third edition of his commentary, and takes refuge in a *smaller* or *"adulterated denarius"* / He actually says, " I was not aware of this adulteration when printing my two former editions; and *so resorted* to a larger and more uncommon *choenix, in order to answer the statement* of price in the prophecy." We admire the candour of this confession, but we must condemn the principle of interpretation which requires it. We prefer our Lord's own clear, but simple, words, "there shall be famines" (Matt. xxiv. 7)! This position we shall never have to relinquish in order to *resort to* another.

The Fourth Seal (vi. 7, 8)

vi. 7. **And when he opened the fourth seal I heard the voice of the fourth Zoon, saying, Go!** * (8) **And I saw, and behold, a livid horse, and he who** was **sitting upon it, his name** was **Death; and the Grave (Gr.,** *Hadēs***) followed after him: And authority was given to them over the fourth part of the earth to kill with the sword, and with famine and with pestilence, and by the wild beasts of** the **earth]** This is the result of the opening of the Fourth Seal; and it is the fourth judgment mentioned by our Lord in Matt. xxiv. 7, "pestilences."

Though the word in the Greek here is θάνατος (*thanatos*) *death*, it is put, by *Metonymy*, as the effect for the cause producing it, which is pestilence. In the O.T. it is the Septuagint rendering of דֶּבֶר (*dever*) *destruction*, *i.e.*, *plague* and *pestilence*, which causes death. It occurs some thirty times, as in I Kings viii 37. Jer. xiv. 12; xxi. 7. We call the oriental plague which raged in Europe in the 14th century the "black death" by the same *Figure*.

"Pestilence," thus personified, is followed by the grave (Gr. *Hades*), also personified The two words occur together because the latter depends on the former. See i. 18; vi. 8; xx. 13. I Cor. xv. 55; and Isa. xxviii.

---

* Omit "and see," L.T.Tr.A. WH. and RV.

15, 18.   *Hades* follows in the train of Death, because Death ends in the Grave.   Hence the authority is given to them jointly.

Tradition has thrown obscurity over what is otherwise so clear.   What is it that always follows death ? Surely it is the grave.   In chap. xx. 13 we read " Death and the grave (Gr. *Hades*) gave up the dead which were in them," *i.e.*, the dead held by them were raised to life. Hades is the place which holds the dead; and Christ, who raises the dead, is therefore said to hold the keys of *Hades*, or the grave.   The word *Hades* occurs eleven times in the New Testament, and there is no place where the rendering *grave* would not be appropriate.*   Grave being generally put (by *Metonymy*) not for one single grave ; but for all graves viewed as a whole ; or, as we might call it *Grave-dom*.   The commission of " Death " has relation to " the beginning of sorrows " in Matt. xxiv. 8, which are there, and here, said to be " wars, famines and pestilences."   These are the agencies used by " Death " (personified) ; and these are naturally followed by the common result—the grave.

" Wild beasts " are added as another agency, because they consume the wounded and dying, and seize on those who are left defenceless (Num. xxi. 6. Ez. xxxiii.

---

* Matt. xi. 23   shall be brought down to *the grave*.

      xvii. 18   The gates of *Hades* shall not prevail.

Luke xii. 5   shalt be thrust down to *the grave*.

      xvi. 23   In *the grave* he lift up his eyes.

Acts ii. 27   wilt not leave my soul (*i.e.*, me) in *the grave*.

      ii. 31   his soul (*i.e.*, he) was not left in *the grave*.

1 Cor. xv. 55   O *grave*, where is thy victory.

Rev. i. 18   have the keys of death and *the grave*.

      vi. 8   Death, and *the grave* followed

      xx. 13, 14 Death and *the grave*.

27. Lev. xxvi 22. Deut. xxxii. 24. Josh. xxiv. 12. 2 Kings xvii. 25 ; ii. 24. Ezek. xiv. 21. Jer. v. 6. Is. xxx. 6*). These three—"sword, famine and pestilence," are frequently found together (Jer. xiv. 12 ; xxi. 7 ; xxiv. 10 ; xliv. 13. Ezek. vi. 11, 12 ; v. 12, &c.) ; and joined, as here, with wild beasts, as in Ezek. xiv. 21. Three of these were offered to David in 1 Chron. xxi. 12.

The meaning of these three Seals seems to be simple and clear. They are the expansion of our Lord's own brief statement in Matt. xxiv. 7, which shows that we have here, "the beginning of sorrows." In other words, wars with their usual accompaniments, famine and plague, and ravenous beasts will be commissioned to commence the assault on the earthy portion of Satan's gathering forces.

When these three judgments fail, then the Lord will bring up others from His reserved forces. Not until the sixth seal, which, as we have seen, carries us forward to the time of the end of sorrows, do the men of the earth own these judgments as proceeding from God as their author.

We must repeat here that not one of these Seals has as yet been opened. Nor can any period of history be pointed out in which these " four sore judgments " have been in operation simultaneously over the extent here named, "the fourth part of the earth."

Gibbon's description† of the reign of Justinian, about 550 A.D., shows how possible it will be to have such a wide-spread scene of judgment.

---

* The opposite of this is promised as part of future blessing on the earth. Is. xi. 7, 9. Ezek. xxxiv. 25.

† Vol. iv. p. 331.

The Fifth Seal (vi. 9-11)

The fifth Seal is marked off and separated from all the others. It stands alone, giving us another side of the picture. The first Seal shows the mighty agency employed by Satan as the earthly leader of the earthly portion of his gathering host. The action of these Satanic forces is assumed by the next three Seals (the second, third, and fourth), inasmuch as they are directed against Satan's opposing forces.

In this earthly conflict there can be only suffering and martyrdom for those on the earth who hold and maintain the testimony of the Word of God, *i.e.*, who adhere to the special truth communicated in this book and its contents, as defined in i. 2, 9 ; xii. 17. In chap. xx. 4, this is further explained as not worshipping the Beast or receiving his mark upon their foreheads.

The two mighty forces have joined in hostilities ; the opposing hosts have met ; and those who are on the Lord's side suffer in consequence.

Hence, in the fifth Seal, we have this episode introduced to make the whole complete, and give all sides of the great conflict.

The first four Seals are connected together by each commencing with a cry from one of the four *Zōa*, and the going forth of a horseman.

The remaining three are thus marked off as a separate series.

The *first* series of four has to do with men as such. In the first of the *second* series we have the saints of the Most High.

The order of our Lord's great prophecy (Matt. xxiv.) is still closely followed. In verses 6-8 He had spoken of (1) war, (2) famine and (3) pestilence as " the beginning

of sorrows"; and then in verse 9 he immediately goes on
to say " THEN shall they deliver you up to be afflicted,
and shall kill you, and ye shall be hated of all the
Gentiles for my name's sake." These words of our
Lord (*v.* 9-28) are the key to the fifth seal.

A⁰ (page 250), vi. 9-11. *The Fifth Seal*

A⁰ | c | 9. The Martyrs under the Altar. Description.
     d | 10. Their cry.
     c | 11-. The Martyrs under the Altar. Donation.
     d | -11. The answer to their cry.

c. vi. 9. *The Martyrs under the Altar. Their
Description*

vi. 9. **And when he opened the fifth seal I saw
under the altar the persons** (souls being put by
Synecdoché for persons. See notes below) **of those who
had been slain on account of the word of God,
and on account of the testimony which they held]**
All mystery is removed if we simply take the word
" souls " here as being put, by the figure *Synecdoché* for
persons. By this figure a part is put for the whole.
This is called "*Synecdoché* of the part." By it,
the *head* is put for the man himself (2 Kings ii. 3. Ps. iii.
3; vii. 16; lxvi. 12. Prov. x. 6. Is. xxxv. 10). The
face is put for the whole person, Gen. iii. 19; xix. 21.
2 Sam. xvii. 11. 1 Kings ii. 16; x. 24, &c. The *eye* is
put for the whole person (Matt. xiii. 16. 1 Cor. ii. 9).
So the *mouth* (Prov. viii. 13). The *belly* (Rom. xvi. 18.
Phil. iii. 19). The *heart* also (Gen. xxxi. 20. Luke xxi. 34,
&c.). The *feet* (Prov. i. 16; vi. 18. Is. lii. 7. Rom.
iii. 15). In like manner the *hand;* we put the " hand '
for the whole person when we speak of so many

hands being employed. "Body " is put for person, especially in the case of slaves, Ex. xxi. 3. Rev. xviii. 13. We believe that this same figure is used here in Rev. vi. 9. "Soul" is often put for person. When we say that the population consists of so many souls, we do not mean "soul" as distinct from body, but we mean so many persons. In Gen. xii. 5 we read of "the souls that they had gotten in Haran." In Gen. xiv. 21, the King of Sodom says "give me the souls (*i.e.*, the captives), and take the goods." In Gen. xvii. 14, " that soul (*i.e.*, that person) shall be cut off from his people." And so, very frequently, we have "the soul that sinneth it shall die." The word " soul " is frequently used of *a person*,* and is so translated.

The word ψυχή (*psuche*) has no such fixed meaning as is put upon it by theology and tradition. It occurs in the New Testament 105 times, and is rendered *life*, 40 times ; *soul*, 58 times ; *mind*, 3 times ; *heart*, once ; with ἐκ, *heartily*, once (Col. iii. 23) ; with ὑμῶν (*humōn*) *you*, once (2 Cor. xii. 15 marg.) ; and with ἡμῶν (*hēmōn*) *us*, once (John x. 24).

So there is no reason whatever for adhering to the traditional rendering, " soul," in this passage as denoting a *part* of a man. The words simply mean " I saw those who had been slain." John also hears what they say. Speaking requires the organs of speech. Tongues are necessary. Vocal organs are indispensable for the utterance of words. These were the martyred saints personified and represented as waiting. They themselves were dead ; for in Rev. xx. 4, John sees them again, and

---

* See Gen. xlvi. 15, 26, 27. Ex. xii. 19 ; xvi. 16 (marg.). Lev. v. 2, 4. Josh. xx. 3 (person). Ezek. xviii. 4, 20. Luke vi. 9 (life). Acts ii. 41, 43 ; vii. 14. Rom. xiii. 1. 1 Pet. iii. 20.

it says "they lived again" in the first resurrection. "The rest of the dead lived not again until the thousand years were finished" (Rev. xx. 5). Why say "lived not again" if, all the time, they were alive in some other place. Moreover, how could "souls" wear white robes. We might as well speak of the eye, or the tongue, or the face, or any other part of the body wearing a white robe. If *souls* here are put for *persons*, then all is clear. John could see them, and hear them, and see what was given to them, and what was done to them as individuals. Even according to popular belief, "souls, " as such, cannot be *seen*. There are no such things as material souls, able to talk without the bodily organs of speech.

What John sees is a vision for the purpose of instructing him; just as Jotham's parable instructed the men of Israel when he represented trees as speaking.

Moreover, the words "of them" give a wrong emphasis. The Greek is not so definite as thàt. John sees the martyred saints at the foot of the altar of burnt offering. He sees not *animal* victims, but *human* beings. Like sacrifices, they had been slain for their testimony. Not sacrifices of atonement, but of *devotion*. These were called "drink-offerings"; and the verb σπένδομαι (*spendomai*) is used of the pouring out of a drink offering. See Phil. ii. 17; and 2 Tim. iv. 6.

Their condition here as dead is set in definite contrast to their condition when afterwards raised. Rev. xx. 4 shows that in vi. 9 they could not be reigning with Christ till they "lived again." Till then they must wait, as the answer to their cry declares. This brings us to

d. (page 263), vi. 10. *Their Cry*

vi. 10. **And they cried with a loud voice** (as Abel's blood was said to cry—Gen. iv. 10), **saying,**

" How long, O Sovereign-Lord,—
The Holy and True]

(iii. 7.   1 John v. 20).   The word here rendered " Lord " in AV. and " Master " in RV. is a remarkable word.   It is never used in the Church Epistles.   The Greek is Δεσπότης (*Despotēs*), from which we have our word *Despot*.* We could hardly use this word here; and prefer " Sovereign-Lord " as meaning more than merely " Master " of the RV., and denoting the great and sovereign disposer of the whole earth.   A careful study of the passages where the Title occurs will not only throw light upon those passages ; but will also serve to show that we have not here anything to do with the Church, or with any truly Christian martyr ; but, with a special class of martyrs, who, in the days of the great tribulation, shall give a peculiar Testimony and suffer a peculiar Martyrdom.   The other title, " Holy and True," is used in iii. 7, and belongs specially to God in relation to His covenant people. (Ps. lxxxix. 28, 35.   Isa. lv. 3.)

The Church of God in this day of grace does not, and cannot, cry for vengeance.   Indeed, it is expressly taught *not to do so* (Rom. xii. 19).   It is evident that these words are not appropriate to this present dispensation in which we are to love our neighbours as ourselves, and not to cry for vengeance

---

* It occurs *ten* times in the New Testament. *Five* times it is rendered *Master* (1 Tim. vi. 1, 2. 2 Tim. ii. 21. Tit. ii. 9. 1 Pet. ii. 18) ; and *five* times it is rendered *Lord* (Luke ii. 29. Acts iv. 24. 2 Pet. ii. 1 Jude 4   Rev. vi. 10).

upon them. But these martyrs are in quite another dispensation ; and in one to which this cry is altogether appropriate and in harmony. By the use of the title Sovereign-Lord, they own His right to dispose of them as He will, and to do whatsoever He pleases in the heaven above and on the earth beneath.

> **dost thou not judge and exact vengeance for our blood from* them that dwell upon the earth "]**

(Hos. iv. 1). This cry is, as we have said, appropriate to the coming Dispensation, as it was to the former. (See Ps. xiii. 1, 2 ; lxxix. 5, and many other Psalms). Indeed, the Song of Moses concludes with this blessed assurance on which this cry of faith is based (Deut. xxxii. 43) :—

" Rejoice, O ye nations with his people ;
  For he will avenge the blood of his servants,
  And will render vengeance to his adversaries,
  And will be merciful unto his Land and to his
      People "

just as He avenged the blood of his "servants the prophets" on Ahab and Jezebel (2 Kings ix. 7). When this present day of grace is over, then this cry will be consistent with the standing of those who utter it. We need to remember this great principle, and to rightly divide the Dispensations as to their nature and character.

In Luke xviii. 1-8 we have a prophetic parable which cannot be understood if interpreted of the Church of God ; but which is not only perfectly clear, if rightly divided as to its dispensational character, but most

---

* L.T.Tr.A. WH. and RV. read ἐκ *from* instead of ἀπό.

helpful in making us to understand better this fifth seal.

It is the cry of Israel represented as a " widow." This cannot be the Church! But is specially the title applicable to Israel in a certain condition (Is. liv. 4, 5. Lam. i. 1). The cry, " Avenge me of mine adversary," cannot be used by any child of God, now.

The break in our chapters severs the close con‑ nection between Luke xvii. and xviii. and separates the parable in Luke xviii. 1-8 from the coming of the kingdom treated of in Luke xvii. 20-end. The section commences with the question of the Pharisees as to " when the kingdom of God should come?" The Lord answers, " The kingdom of God cometh not with (hostile) watching (such as you practise. See the use of the verb, Luke vi. 7. Mark iii. 2. Luke xiv. 1. Acts ix. 24). Neither (he adds) shall they say, Lo here, or Lo there, for behold, the kingdom of God is in the midst of (RV. marg.) you (in the person of the king. It could not be within the hearts of his enemies who were seeking his life!).

The Lord goes on to speak of the coming of the Son of Man to the end of the chapter, comparing it with the judgment of Sodom and Gomorrah, and connecting it with the very end of the Tribulation, as in Matt. xxiv. 27, "as the lightning cometh out of the East and shineth even unto the West; so shall also the coming of the Son of man be. For wheresoever the carcase is, there will the eagles be gathered together." (See Job xxxix. 30.)

Then the Lord goes on, in Luke xviii. 1-8, to describe the position of His servants during those terrible days, as one of waiting and prayer. Their cry for vengeance is almost identical with that which we hear under this fifth seal. He says, with reference to those days, that " they ought always to pray and not to faint " because their desire is not at once fulfilled (Luke xvii. 22).

But now look at the Parable itself. "There was in a certain city (Jerusalem, Rev. xi. (cf. Is. i. 10). Ezek. xvi. 26, 46; xx. 7), a judge, who feared not God, neither regarded man; and there was a widow in that city." Widowhood is the condition of Israel. Though the mass of the nation may say, like Babylon, " I sit a queen, I am no widow " (Rev. xviii. 7), God speaks of her in her really desolate condition. The widow's " *Adversary* " can be none other than Antichrist, who persecutes this remnant in Jerusalem. We have the cry in Ps. lxxix. 1-3:

"O God: the heathen are come unto thine
        inheritance:
Thy holy Temple have they defiled;
They have laid Jerusalem on heaps.
The dead bodies of thy servants have they given to
        be meat unto the fowls of the heaven:
The flesh of thy saints unto the beasts of the
        earth.
Their blood have they shed like water round about
        Jerusalem;
And there was none to bury them."

This plainly refers to Rev. xi. And then comes the laintive appeal verse 5.

" How long, Lord, wilt thou be angry: for ever?
Shall thy jealousy burn like fire? "

The whole of this Psalm (lxxix.) should be read in this connection as well as other Psalms, such as x. and xi.; liv. 5; lv. 9; xciv.; cxliii. 12, &c. See also Is. lxiii. 15, &c., and lxiv. It is beautiful to notice, how, after the Lord

calls attention to the action of the unjust judge, He ex-
ultingly declares of Him that is Holy and True—" And
shall not God avenge his own elect, which cry day and
night unto him, and he is longsuffering over them ? I
say unto you that he will avenge them speedily " (RV.).

But he has to add, and to ask—" Howbeit, when the
Son of Man cometh shall he find faith (marg. *the faith*)
on the earth ?" (RV.) or, it may be in the Land, the
Jewish Land, as at the first Advent.

If we rightly divide the word of truth, as to its Dispensations, then we see that the imprecations and invo-
cations for vengeance, while entirely opposed to the
spirit of the present dispensation of grace, are quite
appropriate to the past dispensation of works, and the
future dispensation of judgment.

Romanism, not rightly dividing the Dispensations,
presses such Scriptures as these into her service now ;
using them to justify her persecutions. While
Protestant interpreters, failing also in this important
duty, have to explain such passages away, or endeavour
in vain to reconcile them with our standing in grace.

c. (page 263), vi. 11

The Martyrs under the Altar. What was given them

vi. 11-. **And there was* given to each a white
robe**] Even thus was the promise made in Rev. iii. 4,
marking them as righteous, and as the servants of God.
Robes of honour ever formed part of rewards. (See
Gen. xli. 42; xlv. 22. Est. vi. 8, 9. Isa. iii. 7. Zech. iii. 5).
The action implies that their request will be granted ;
and the words announce that there must be some delay
before their desire can be accomplished.

---

* So G.L.T.Tr.A. WH. and RV.

d. (page 263), vi. -11

The Answer to their Cry

vi, -11. **And it was said to them that they should rest** (not merely desist from their cry; but wait) **yet a little while** (*i.e.*, for a short delay, as in x. 6 and xx. 3) **until both their fellow-servants** (here we have the correlative of *Despotēs*, as well as their own standing as " servants ") **and their brethren that were about to be killed, as they also** had been, **should fill up*** the appointed number] " Fellow servants and brethren " is the Figure Hendiadys, denoting not two separate classes of persons, but one class, viz., their fellow servants even those who were their brethren. This is to define who the fellow servants were; for angels can be called such (xix. 10; xxii. 9), but not "brethren."   They will have been killed during the Tribulation for refusing to have the mark of the Beast or to worship him.   This killing is afterwards seen in xiii. 7, 15; xvii. 6 by John in vision.   Here it is revealed prophetically; for, as we have said, the Seals cover the whole period in brief, and in outline, the details being afterwards filled in by the Trumpets, and Vials.

Surely this ought to be sufficient to convince all Christians to-day that the gospel is not intended to convert the world, or to bring in universal peace and blessing. This dispensation of grace (rejected) is to be followed by a dispensation of judgment.

Not until after that shall Jerusalem be the centre of God's presence and government, and glory dwell in the

---

* G.T.Tr.A.WH.m. and RV.m. read πληρώσουσιν, should fill or fulfil it, instead of πληρωθῶσιν, should be fulfilled.   L. WH. and RV. put the latter in the text.

Land (Ps. lxxxv. 9). Then shall Judah " dwell for ever, and Jerusalem from generation to generation. *For I will cleanse their blood that I have not cleansed* : for the Lord dwelleth in Zion " (Joel iii. 20, 21. See also Isa. iv. 4 and Deut. xxxii. 43). When the appointed number is accomplished, judgment will be executed and be followed by the dispensation of glory.

The Sixth Seal (vi. 12-17)

In this sixth Seal we are carried right forward to the time of the end. The Seals, as we have said, are a summary, in brief, of the whole period of the Tribulation ; and, as the former Seals correspond exactly with the last great prophecy of Christ in Matt. xxiv., so this sixth Seal also has its place in that chapter. We may thus exhibit the parallel:

Matt. xxiv.		*The Seals.*	*Rev. vi.*
4, 5.	1st	The False Christ	1, 2
6, 7.	2nd	Wars	3, 4
-7-	3rd	Famines	5, 6
-7.	4th	Pestilences	7, 8
8-28	5th	Martyrdoms	9-11
29-30	6th	Signs in Heaven of Advent.	12-17

From this it will be seen how exactly Matt. xxiv. covers the whole period of the six Seals ; and shows that this sixth Seal takes us up to the signs immediately preceding the Advent of the Lord in Glory, as seen in Rev. xix.

This being so, it proves that any interpretation of this Seal which regards it as relating to any past historical event is condemned by this very fact.

This sixth Seal is the crucial test of all Apocalyptic interpretation.

No one can read Matt. xxiv. 30 with Rev. vi. 12-17 without seeing that they speak of the same event. The actual Advent of Christ is deferred, in Rev. vi., because it is to form a separate and special description by itself in chap. xix. The sixth Seal does not therefore include the visible appearing of the Son of man, though it is remarkable that, while (in A⁹) in Rev. vi. 13 we have the simile of a Fig Tree, and the sealing of the elect of Israel (vii. 1-8); so, in Matt. xxiv. 31 we have the gathering of the elect of Israel, and in verses 32, 33 we have the simile of the Fig Tree again. The Lord concludes this special prophecy of the Tribulation by adding " Verily, I say unto you, this generation shall not pass, till all these things begin to take place." Not " fulfilled." The word is γένηται (*genētai*) from γίνομαι (*ginomai*) *to begin to be, to come to be*,* and is quite different from πληρόω (*plēroō*), *to fulfil.* In Luke xxi. 32, which is the parallel passage, we have the former word, *begin to be*, while in verse 24 we have the latter word, *fulfilled.* What the Lord really said was " this generation shall not pass till all these things *begin to happen*." And they *did begin* to take place during that very generation; for the period immediately following the Lord's death was marked by many coming and saying " I am Christ." But in order that we might clearly understand, Christ immediately adds, " *The end is not yet* " (Matt. xxiv. 6).

But now, to turn to the sixth Seal itself; we note first, its Structure, which is as follows :—

---

* In John xiii. 2 we have the same word, which illustrates this verse :—"and supper being ended." It is quite clear from verses 26-28 that supper was not ended, but was only just beginning. The RV. renders it " during supper."

B² (page 250), vi. 12-17.   *The Sixth Seal.*

B² | e | **vi. 12-.**   The Great Convulsion
    | f | -12, 13.   Effects in Heaven
    | *e* | 14-.   The Great Convulsion
    | *f* | -14-17.   Effects on Earth

TRANSLATION OF B² vi. 12-17

vi. 12. And I saw when he opened the sixth seal, and* a great convulsion took place, and the sun became black as sackcloth of hair, and the full† moon became as blood; (13) **and the stars of heaven fell unto the earth, as the fig tree casteth her untimely** (or winter) **figs** when **shaken by a mighty wind**] Here we have the great convulsion of Nature, and its effects in the heavens. It is impossible for us to take this as symbolical; or as other than what it literally says.   The difficulties of the symbolical interpretation are insuperable, while no difficulties whatever attend the literal interpretation.   For according to some historicist interpreters‡ this Seal was fulfilled at the Conversion of Constantine.   Heaven is taken as the symbol of the invented term " Political heaven "; but it ought to be called " Religious Heaven," as the events are supposed to be Christian.   According to others § it was fulfilled in the French Revolution of 1798. As both of these cannot be right, Is it not better for us to believe what God says? In Hag. ii. 6, 7, He has foretold the events of this seal, and has connected them as

---

* Omit " behold," G.L.Tr.A. WH. and RV.

† G.L.T.Tr.A. WH. and RV. add ὅλη (*holē*) *the whole.*

‡ Mede, Newton, Elliott.

§ Cunninghame and others.

in Matt. xxiv. with the immediate Advent of the Son
of Man :—

> " Thus saith the LORD of hosts,
> Yet once, it is a little while,
> And *I will shake the heavens and the earth,*
> *And the sea and the dry land.*
> *And I will shake all nations,* and the desire of all
> nations shall come."

Here the great convulsion of the sixth Seal is clearly
foretold. We say "convulsion," because the word
σεισμός (*seismos*) means much more than a mere *earth-*
quake, as the context clearly shows. There is to be
a convulsion of the *nations*, which is spoken of as
distinct from that of the *heavens*, and is to immediately
precede the Revelation of Christ, and the glory of the
Temple. Haggai again foretells it in chap. ii. 21, 22,
and again distinguishes between the *heavens* and the
earth.

> " I will shake the *heavens* and the *earth.*
> And I will overthrow the *throne of kingdoms,*
> And I will destroy the strength of the *kingdoms of*
> *the Gentiles* :
> And I will overthrow the chariots and those that ride
> in them," etc. (See also 2 Pet. iii. 7-13, and
> compare verse 7 with 2 Thess. i. 8).

Having spoken of the great convulsion and its effects
in the heavens, the prophecy again speaks of the
convulsion and its effects on the earth.

**14. And the* heaven parted asunder as a scroll
rolling itself up; † and every mountain and island**

---

* The article is not in the Received Text, though it is in the AV. It
is added by G.L.T.Tr.A. WH. and RV.

† So L.T.Tr.A. WH. and RV.

were moved out of their places] This is referred to
in Matt. xxiv. 35, and is foretold in Isa. xxxiv. 4
(read verses 1-5 and Isa. xiii. 6-13), where we have
exactly the same phenomena described. If the sixth
Seal means the conversion of Constantine, so must these
passages in Isaiah.

15. **And the kings of the earth, and the great men**
(the civil officers of State), **and the chief captains** (the
military officers), **and the rich** men,* **and the mighty †
men, and every bondman and ‡ free** man, **hid themselves** (running for shelter) **into the caves and into
the rocks of the mountains.** (16) **And they say to
the mountains and to the rocks, "Fall on us, and
hide us from the face of Him that sitteth on the
throne, and from the wrath of the Lamb."** (17)
Because the day—the great day **of His** wrath **is
come, and who is able to stand?**] In connection
with this we must read Ps. ii. 2 ; lxviii. 4 ; xcvii. 5.
Is. xxiv. 19-23; xxxiv. 12; ii. 10-22 ; Nahum i.
5 ; Heb. xii. 26. The Lord also refers to this in
Luke xxiii. 30, quoting the very words of Hosea x. 8.
Similar phenomena are again mentioned under the
fourth Trumpet, and the seventh Vial (xvi. 20), showing that we have in the sixth Seal the preliminary
announcement of that which will take place "immediately after the tribulation of those days" (Matt. xxiv.
29) and "immediately" before the personal Advent of
Christ. To this agree the words of Joel ii. 31.

---

* G.L.T.Tr.A. WH. and RV. transpose the words, agreeing with
this order.

† G.L.T.Tr.A. WH. and RV. read ἰσχυροί (*ischuroi*) *mighty*,
instead of δυνατοί (*dunatoi*) *powerful*.

‡ L.T.Tr.A. WH. and RV. omit "every."

In Rev. xix. 19 we have the marshalling of the forces which are here detailed.

If the words describing the awful judgments of "the great day of His wrath" are to be interpreted of any past event in the history of the present dispensation, then what words are to describe the future judgments which the Old Testament foretells. Language seems useless for the purposes of revelation and instruction if, as we are told, " this Seal exhibits the overthrow of paganism " at the conversion of Constantine. Eusebius pictures that scene (lib. x.) as one of joy and gladness, and he likens it to the coming of the promised kingdom. There was no convulsion of nature in heaven or on earth; no fleeing to the mountains and the rocks; no cry of terror. The sun was bright and the sky was cloudless, instead of being " black as sackcloth of hair."

We thus come to the end of the first six Seals. It is a summary of the judgments distributed over the whole book; a brief summary of what will occur in " the day of the Lord," up to the time of His actual Apocalypse or Unveiling in chap. xix.

They are thus set here, in order to show us that these judgments do not arise from chance, but are all under Divine control. The great False Messiah of the first Seal cannot be revealed until the appointed moment shall have come and the voice from the throne gives the permissive command "Go!" The judgments cannot fall until the same command is given. Here we note the important connection between "the Throne" of chaps. iv. and v. seen "in Heaven" and the consequent summary (in the Seals) of all that takes place afterward "on earth."

They lead up to "the great day of His wrath"; and

the chapter ends with the solemn question, " **Who is able to stand ?** "

That question is answered in chap. vii. where we are shewn first the sealing of 144,000 "of all the tribes of the children of Israel," who are to pass unscathed through that great tribulation ; and the rapture of the great multitude which no man can number who are saved through it and out of it. These are not the Church of God, for they stand before the throne. They are not seated upon it. They are saved, of course, through the merits of the same precious blood of the Lamb. They are referred to in Is. xxvi. 9, " when thy judgments are in the earth, the inhabitants of the world will learn righteousness." Where are these afterwards seen if not in the great multitude of Rev. vii. ? (Read also Ps. lxiv. 7-10 ; cx.). The question, " Who shall be able to stand ? " is now to be answered

THE SEALING OF THE 144,000

(vii. 1-8)

The answer to the question of vi. 17

Few Scriptures have suffered more at the hands of Gentile Christians than this. Notwithstanding the fact that it concerns " all the tribes of the children of Israel," and that the twelve tribes are named separately, popular interpretation insists on taking them as meaning the Church of God.

Any system of interpretation which has this for its foundation may be judged and condemned at the outset as not only useless, but mischievous. Such a system has been well described by Hooker as one "which changeth the meaning of words as alchemy doth, or would do, the substance of metals, making anything of

what it listeth ; and bringeth, in the end, all truth to
nothing."

It is perfectly clear that we have here the Divine
plan and action for securing the Remnant of the nation
of Israel through all the judgments and persecutions
which shall characterise the Great Tribulation.

The Vision, though seen after the Sixth Seal, really
describes what will take place before chapter vi. and
before a Seal is broken. Their number is not left to
chance. God's declared counsels concerning this
Remnant must stand. Hence it is by Divine decree
that this purpose shall be secured at the outset.

We are told here, therefore, of the means taken to
secure this Divine purpose.

The Structure is as follows :—

A³ (page 250), vii. 1-8. *The Sealing of the 144,000*

The answer to the question of vi. 17

A³ | g | vii. 1-. Four angels
　　　h | -1-. Place. " Four corners of the earth . . .
　　　　i | -1-. Agency. " Holding the four winds . . .
　　　　　k | -1. Purpose (neg.). "Not blow on earth,
　　　　　　　sea, or tree."

　　g | 2-. Another angel
　　　h | -2-. Place. " From the rising of the sun . . .
　　　　i | -2, 3-. Agency. " Having the seal . . .
　　　　　k | -3-8. Purpose (neg.). " Hurt not the
　　　　　　　earth, sea, or tree "

All is seen to be perfect in Divine order. Nothing is
left to chance here any more than in what is described.
All is alike perfect in the words and the works of
God. And the record is as true as its structure is

perfect. It requires no explanation. It explains
Divine truth to us in a Divine form and manner.

TRANSLATION OF vii. 1-8

vii. 1. [and]* after this †] Showing that the former
vision is complete, and the two visions which follow,
commencing with similar words, come in by way of
episode: the first, anterior in time to the Seals; and the
second, during the period of the Seals, and later in time.

**I saw four angels standing at the four corners of
the earth, holding** (or, controlling) **the four winds of
the earth, that the wind should not blow on the
land, or on the sea, or upon any tree**] The
number *four* marks this vision as pertaining to the
earth. The winds are so designated in Jer. xlix. 36.
Dan. vii. 2; viii. 8; xi. 4, the four comprising all
winds; or simply marking the four points of the
compass. *Stillness* is the point to be emphasised here,
as when we say "not a leaf moves:" it tells us that
this sealing will take place before the opening events
of the great Tribulation.

2. **And I saw another angel ascending ‡ from the
rising of the sun** (*i.e.*, the East) **having the seal of the
Living God: and he cried with a loud voice to the
four angels, to whom it was given to injure the land
and the sea:** (3) **saying, " Injure not the earth, or the
sea, or the trees, till we have sealed the servants
of our God upon their foreheads"**] This is, of
course, preliminary to Matt. xxiv. 31. It precedes
the Tribulation, as shown by the reason given for

---

* L. WH. and RV. omit "and"—Tr. and A. put it in brackets.
† L.T.Tr.A. WH. and RV. read "this" singular instead of plural.

‡ G.L.T.Tr.A. WH. and RV. read ἀναβαίνοντα (*anabainonta*)
ascending, instead of ἀναβάντα (*anabanta*) *having ascended.*

the sealing. But from Matt. xxiv. 31 we learn that after the Tribulation, Angels are commissioned to gather His elect from the four winds, from one end of heaven to the other." The two passages stand in the closest connection, and show that the "elect" in Matt. xxiv. 31 belong to Israel, and not to the church. They are upon the earth during the Tribulation and this seal or sealing, whatever it is, protects and preserves them unscathed. This sealing was evidently visible, as the locusts are directed in chap. ix. 4 to injure only those "who have not the seal of God in their foreheads." The Beast has his seal, with which he will seal his followers; and this is the Divine distinguishing mark which God sets upon His servants. Just as in the days of the Patriarchs He could protect them, saying "Touch not mine anointed, and do my prophets no harm" (Ps. cv. 15): so here, with this elect Remnant. Those who have the mark of the Beast are idolators of the deepest die; but those who have the Divine mark, are sealed with "the seal of the Living God." This title here (as elsewhere) is always used with reference to idols and idolatry (See Deut. v. 26. Josh. iii. 10. Jer. x. 2-11. Dan. vi. 26. 1 Thess. i. 9, 10, and page 23). Then will Ps. xci. receive a new application of a very remarkable kind (see verses 5, 7, 8). In Ezek. ix. 3, 4 we have a similar sealing by which a devoted remnant have their lot in the corrupt city of Jerusalem. They may be part of this very number in Rev. vii. In Ex. xii. 7 the houses of the Israelites were marked for a similar purpose. In Rev. ii. 17 this mark is promised, and the promise is exhausted in xxii. 4.

The Romans marked their soldiers in the hand; and theirslaves in the forehead. Herodotus (ii. 113) speaks of the worshippers of a certain god as having his name branded upon them. In like manner the worshippers of the Beast are branded (xiii. 16-18 ; xiv. 9, 11 ; xvi. 2; xix. 20 ; xx. 4) ; and these Divinely sealed ones are marked as the worshippers of the true God.

4. And I heard the number of the sealed : an hundred and forty four thousand sealed out of every tribe of the children of Israel] Alford says of this number, " No one that I am aware of has taken it literally ! " Very likely : but we are thankful to be an exception to the rule, and to believe what God says. There is such a thing as *Figures of Speech*, but, we ask, what Figure is used here ? What is its name ? The truth is that there is here no Figure whatever ; but it is the simple statement of fact : a *definite* number in contrast with the *indefinite* number in this very chapter (verse 9). If the total number is not exact, then all the items which go to make it up are indefinite also. If this number is symbolical, then what number in the Book may we take as literal ? None, according to this principle of interpretation, which substitutes man's own vain imaginations for God's revelation. Again, we repeat, we prefer to believe God. And, believing Him, we conclude that as He had reserved 7,000 in the days of Ahab (1 Kings xix. 18. Rom. xi. 4), so He will reserve 144,000 in the Great Tribulation.

We have here, therefore, the nucleus of the new nation referred to by Christ in Matt. xxi. 43. We have also what will be the fulfilment of the prophecy of Daniel xii. 1. : " At that time shall Michael (the other angel) stand up, the great prince which standeth for the children of thy people (Israel) : and there shall be a time of trouble, such as never was since there was a nation even to that same time: and at that time *thy people shall be delivered*, every one that shall be found written in the book." Here, in Rev. vii., we have the sealing of those written names, which shall be "delivered." (Compare Joel ii. 28-32). What this seal was we learn from chap. xiv. 1.

5. **Of the tribe of Judah, twelve thousand sealed; Of the tribe of Reuben, twelve thousand;*** **Of the tribe of Gad, twelve thousand;*** (6) **Of the tribe of Aser, twelve thousand;*** **Of the tribe of Nepthalim, twelve thousand;*** **Of the tribe of Manasses, twelve thousand;*** (7) **Of the tribe of Simeon, twelve thousand;*** **Of the tribe of Levi, twelve thousand;*** **Of the tribe of Issachar, twelve thousand;*** (8) **Of the tribe of Zabulon, twelve thousand;*** **Of the tribe of Joseph,* twelve thousand;*** **Of the tribe of Benjamin, twelve thousand sealed]** In this enumeration we have to note the omission of the Tribes of Dan and Ephraim: Levi and Joseph being inserted to take their place. The reason for this seems to be quite clear. In Deut. xxix. 18-21, we read that the " man or woman or family or *tribe* " who should introduce idolatry into Israel, "all the curses that are written in this book shall lie upon him, and the LORD *shall blot out his name* from under heaven, and the LORD shall separate him unto evil out of all the tribes of Israel, according to all the curses of the covenant that are written in this law." And when it should be asked, "Wherefore hath the LORD done this? . . . then men shall say, Because they have forsaken the covenant of the LORD God of their fathers . . . for they went and served other gods and worshipped them, gods whom they knew not " (*vv.* 24-26).

---

* L. T. Tr. A. WH. and RV. omit " were sealed."

Now it was one of the tribe of Dan who first came under this curse. See Lev. xxiv. 10-16.

It is remarkable that these two tribes, Dan and Ephraim, participated in introducing idolatry later on (Judges xviii. 2, 30, 31). And afterward it was Jeroboam devised the golden calves and set them up in the tribe of Dan (1 Kings xi. 26; xii. 28-30. See also Hos. iv. 17).

True, we find Dan and Ephraim restored in the future distribution of the Land (Ezek. xlviii.), for "the gifts and calling of God, are without repentance (or change of mind)" (Rom. xi. 29). But that is a different matter, and has to do with *earthly* inheritance. Here it has to do with *heavenly* preservation. The omission in Rev. vii. is to show that these two tribes remain unprotected by the pledge of security given by this sealing. There will, of course, be thousands, besides these, of each of the other tribes on the earth; the difference will be in their not being sealed, and in their not being protected against the onslaught of the Beast. That they are on the earth is clear from Jer. iv. 5-31 (see *v.* 15); viii. 13-17 (see *v.* 16). Amos viii. 11-14.

We have a remarkable illustration of this in Num. xxxi., when in order to execute judgment on the Midianites 1,000 from each tribe were taken. And as the 144,000 here survive through all the great Tribulation, so it was with the 12,000 sent against the Midianites; for when their number was taken at the close, the officers came to Moses and said "Thy servants have taken the sum of the men of war which are under our charge, and *there lacketh not one man of us*" (*vv.* 48, 49).

Even so will it be true of these 144,000, when they stand afterwards on Mount Zion (xiv. 1-5).

8

THE SECOND VISION "IN HEAVEN"
(7:9—8:6)

𝔅² (page 118), chaps. vii. 9—viii. 6.

The Great Multitude and the Seventh Seal

We now come to the second Vision " in Heaven." It contains a yet further answer to the question of vi. 17: "Who shall be able to stand" in the judgment? while it commences the second pair of Visions: *viz.*, the opening of the seventh Seal "in heaven," and the consequent sounding of the six Trumpets "on earth."

The Structure of the Vision, as a whole, is as follows :—

𝔅² (page 118), vii. 9—viii. 6. THE SECOND VISION IN HEAVEN

The Great Multitude and the Seventh Seal

𝔅² | A | vii. 9-12. The Heavenly Voices and utterances
    B | 13, 14. The Great Multitude. Whence they came
    B | 15-17. The Great Multitude. Where they are
  A | viii. 1-6. The Heavenly Silence and Activities (Seventh seal)

Each of these four larger members may be expanded; and we give the expansions in order, with translation, as before.

A. (page 285), vii. 9-12. *The Heavenly Voices and
Utterances*

A | a | 9. The great multitude

 b | 10. Their utterance. "Salvation to our God "

 a | 11, 12-. All the angels

 b | -12. Their utterance. " Blessing and Glory "

Translation of " a," vii. 9

The Great Multitude

vii. 9. **After these things**] the expression marks a
separation from what has gone before, and introduces
the second distinct Vision " in heaven."

**I saw, and lo, a great multitude, which no one was
able to number, out of every nation, and of all tribes
and peoples, and tongues** (Gen. x. 5, 20, 31. Dan. iii.
4, 5 ; iv. 1 ; vi. 25), **standing before the throne, and
before the Lamb, arrayed with white robes, and
palm branches in their hands ;**] The definite number
of Israelites (vii. 1-8) stands in marked contrast to this
innumerable company of Gentiles. We say Gentiles,
because this Vision carries us on to the end, as the preceding Vision of the sealing carried us back to the
beginning. We are, here, beyond Matt. xxiv., and even
xxv. Two distinct companies are named, first " Jews,"
then " Gentiles." Thus both are marked off from "the
church of God," which is now composed of both Jews
and Gentiles. The twelve tribes of vii. 4-8 are distinct
from people out of " all tribes." That they are distinct
from " the church of God " is further shown, in that
they are " standing" in the position of servants (and
not seated) ; and are " before the throne" (not upon it).

True, they share the same salvation, and by the same precious merits of the blood of the Lamb. But as " star differeth from star in glory " (1 Cor. xv. 41), so do these differ in their position, dignity, and honour. They are saved, but for what? and for which one of the " many mansions " ? They are seen " in heaven," but not until after the Great Tribulation through which and out of which they will have been brought.

Not only will this elect remnant of Israel survive "through " the Tribulation, but a countless multitude from all the Gentile nations will be saved " out " of it.

Constantly do we find Gentile blessing consequent upon Israel's blessing. First, God deals with Israel, and then with mankind in general. This is stated in many passages : *e.g.*, Ps. lxvii. 1 :

  " God be merciful to *us,* and bless *us ;*
  And cause his face to shine upon *us :*
  That thy way may be known upon *earth,*
  Thy saving health among *all nations.*"

The same fact is stated in verse 7 :

  " God shall bless *us ;*
  And *all the* ends of the *earth* shall fear him."

Again in Ps. xcviii. 3, we read :

  " He hath remembered his mercy,
  And his truth toward *the house of Israel :*
  All the ends of the earth have seen the salvation of
    our God."

So in Isa. xlix. 6, Jehovah says to Messiah :

  " It is a light thing
  That thou shouldest be my servant,
  To raise up the *tribes of Jacob,*
  And to restore the preserved of *Israel ;*
  I will also give thee for a light to *the Gentiles,*

> That thou mayest be my salvation unto *the end*
> *of the earth."*

So Isa. lii. 9, 10 :

> " Break forth into joy, sing together, ye waste
> places of *Jerusalem :*
> For the LORD hath comforted *his people,*
> He hath redeemed *Jerusalem.*
> The LORD hath made bare his holy arm
> In the eyes of *all the nations,*
> And all *the ends of the earth* shall see
> The salvation of our God."

The palm-branches speak not merely of victory, as
with the heathen, but of the Feast of Tabernacles (see
Lev. xxiii. 39-43). It was not a feast for the wilderness,
but for the time " when ye be come into the Land."
(Lev. xxiii. 10). And yet it was never kept in the Land
by all Israel. Not until the return from Babylon was
it kept (See Neh. viii. 16, 17). Then "all the people
shouted with a great shout " (Ezra iii. 11, 12. 2 Chron.
xx. 19). So here, in like manner it will be again kept.

b. (page 286), vii. 10. *Their utterance.*

10. **And they cry* with a loud voice, saying,**
" Salvation to our God
That sitteth upon the Throne,
And to the Lamb."

They ascribe their salvation and their deliverance from
the Tribulation which they had passed through, to
God. A paraphrase would be, " Praise for our salvation be to our God," etc. The church calls God " my

---

* So G.L.T.Tr.A. WH. and RV., not " cried."

Father" ("Abba," Rom. viii. 15), but the Sealing Angel speaks of Him as "our God" (ch. vii. 3). The assembled angels say "our God" (ch. vii. 12), and this great multitude say "our God" (ch. vii. 10).

a. (page 286), vii. 11, 12-, *All the angels*, etc., and

b. (vii. -12), *Their utterance*

vii. 11. **And all the angels were standing*** **around the throne, and** around **the Elders and the four Zoa, and they fell before the throne on their faces, and worshipped God, (12) saying,**
" Amen!
Blessing, and glory, and wisdom, and thanksgiving, and honour, and power, and might, be unto our God, for ever and ever.
Amen!"

Such is the sevenfold ascription of the heavenly host standing around the throne, the elders and the *Zōa*. It is similar to that in chap. v. 12, but the order of the words is different, and thanksgiving is here put instead of "riches." There the ascription was to the Lamb. Here it is to "our God."

We next have the explanation of the Vision ; and the Question which one of the Elders put to John shows that we should have a like spirit of holy enquiry. It is not mere abstract wonder that God looks for in us now, but a reverential interest in what He has revealed in the Visions of this book.

The following is the Structure of B. (page 285), chap. vii. 13, 14 :

---

* So L.T.Tr. A.

B. (page 285), vii. 13, 14.   *The Great Multitude :*
  Whence they came

B | c | vii. 13-. The Elder
       d | f | -13-. Persons } Question
            g | 13. Place)
         e | 14-. John
     c | -14-. The Elder
       d | g | -14-. State } Answer
         | f | -14. Persons)

TRANSLATION of B, vii. 13, 14

vii. 13.   **And one of the Elders answered, say-**
ing (*i.e.*, by the Figure, *Idiom* "asked me, saying")
unto me,

> " **These who are arrayed in white**
> **robes, Who are they? and Whence**
> **came they?** "

(14) **and I said, my* lord, thou knowest. And he said**
to me,

> " **These are they who come out of**
> **the Great Tribulation, and they**
> **washed their robes, and made them**
> **white through the blood of the**
> **Lamb.**]

Not " in the blood"; nothing under the Law was ever
washed " in blood," nothing can be made white
" washed in " blood.   It is through a forced literal
meaning of the preposition ἐν (*en*) which has led to this
false notion.   This preposition constantly means *by*, or
through: and is translated "by" 142 times and "through"
37 times.   (See Matt. ix. 34 ; v. 34, 35.   Gal. iii. 11.

---

* G.[L.]T.Tr.A. WH. and RV. add " my."

2 Tim. ii. 10.) In this very book (v. 9) it is rendered "by." So here and in i. 5 this must be the meaning. This is the standing of " works"; and not our standing in "grace," as in the present dispensation We are " washed, justified, and sanctified in the name of the Lord Jesus, and by the Spirit of our God " (1 Cor. vi. 11). These have washed their own robes, and made them white. This is followed by the consequence :—

   B. (page 285), vii. 15-17. *The great multitude :*
                       Where they are

B| h | i | 15-. The Multitude. Position before the throne
   | | j | -15. God upon the throne
   h | *i* | 16. The multitude. Their Blessing
   | | *j* | 17. God. The Lamb the Blesser

15. " For this cause are they before the throne of God, and serve him day and night in his temple : and he who sitteth upon the throne shall spread his tabernacle over them.]

This is exactly what we read in Isa. iv. 5, 6.
" And the Lord will create
  Upon every dwelling place of Mount Zion,
  And upon her assemblies,
  A cloud and smoke by day,
  And the shining of a flaming fire by night ;
  For above all the glory shall be a covering (marg.,
    Heb. חֻפָּה, (*chuppah*), *the marriage canopy*, for the
    marriage of the Lamb will have come)
  And there shall be a tabernacle
  For a shadow in the day time from the heat
  And a place of refuge, and for a covert
  From storm and from rain."

They perform priestly service day and night, and fulfil the duties of " servants," for they "serve before the throne."   Other Old Testament passages referred to here are Lev. xxvi. 11. Ezek. xxxvii. 27.

And then, alluding to the privations and trials they have undergone, we have further earthly blessings :—

h. (page 291), vii. 16, 17.   *The Blessing and the Blesser*

h | k | 16-. No hunger
　　 l | -16-. No thirst 　　　　　　} The Blessing　Negative
　　　 m | -16. No suffering

　　 k | 17-. Hunger satisfied
　　　 l | -17-. Thirst assuaged 　　} The Blesser　Positive
　　　　 m | -17. Sorrow banished

16. **" They shall not hunger any more, nor yet thirst any more; neither shall the sun in any wise fall upon them ; no, nor any burning heat. (17) Because the Lamb that is in the midst of the Throne shall tend them** (as a shepherd), **and shall lead them unto the fountains of the waters of life :* and God shall wipe away every tear from their eyes"**]

Thus ends the Elder's description of the great multitude and their ultimate blessings.   The blessings of the Church are heavenly.   We have the same blessing prophesied in Isa. xlix. 8-10; xxv. 8; and lxv. 19. Jer. xxxi. 16.   Thus are Israel's blessings extended to Gentiles.   The fulfilment is seen in Rev. xxi. 3, 4; xxii. i. and Ezek. xlvii.

---

* So G.L.T.Tr. WH. and RV.

The Seventh Seal (viii. 1-6)

From the Structure of this Second Vision "in Heaven" (page 285) we saw that this last great member *A* (viii. 1-6) is set in contrast and corresponds with A (vii. 9-12), the Heavenly voices and utterances.

We have shown that the six Seals cover not only the whole period of the Great Tribulation, but that the sixth bring us right up to the great day of wrath; co-terminous, apparently, with chap. xi. 17, 18 (the seventh Trumpet), and chap. xx. (the final Judgment).

But that, whereas the seventh Trumpet expands into the seven Vials—which are consecutive—the sixth Seal is followed by silence in heaven, as though to break off all continuity, and to show us that we have to go back and learn how the details of the judgments of the Seals are to be filled in.

The following is the Structure of viii. 1-6, describing the close of this second Vision "in Heaven":

A. (page 285), viii. 1-6. *The Heavenly Silence and Activities*

(The Seventh Seal)

A | n | p | 1. Silence in heaven.
        q | 2. The 7 angels and the 7 Trumpets.
             o | r | 3. Another angel with censer and prayers.
                  s | 4. Result. Smoke ascended up to heaven.
            o | *r* | 5-. The angel with censer and fire.
                  s | -5-. Result. Fire descended to the earth.
    n | *p* | -5. Sounds on the earth.
        q | 6. The 7 angels and the 7 Trumpets.

The breaking of the seventh Seal, instead of producing one single result, as the other six had done, is closed by this "silence," which seemed to John to last half an hour; after which, John is shown how the prayers of the saints under the fifth Seal are presented (*vv.* 3, 4), and answered (*v.* 5), by the commencement of a series of judgments ushered in by the sounding of seven Trumpets. But we will first give the translation of viii. 1-6.

viii. 1. **And when he opened the seventh seal, there was** (*i.e.*, became, came on, or followed) **silence in heaven about half an hour.**] At the sounding of the seventh Trumpet there are "great voices in heaven" (xi. 5). And at the pouring out of the seventh Vial, a great voice came out of the throne (xvi. 17).

But this "silence" means more than that. It marks very solemnly the pause between the *prayer* and the answer, which shall turn the prayer into *praise*. On earth, the cry of the saints has been incessant. They "cry day and night." In heaven the cry is now about to be answered, and there is a solemn pause—the silence of expectation.

The Heb. דּוּמִיָה (*dūmĕyyah*) *silence* (fem. adj.), which occurs four times, exactly expresses the position.

(1) "O my God, I cry in the daytime, but thou hearest not ;
   And in the night season, there is no *silence* to me.
   But thou art holy,
   O thou that inhabitest the praises of Israel" (Ps. xxii. 2, 3 (3, 4).

(2) "I was dumb with *silence*" (Ps. xxxix. 2 (3)).

(3) "Truly my soul is *silence* toward God :
   From him cometh my salvation" (Ps. lxii. 1 (2)).

(4)   " There shall be *silence* before thee,
 And praise, O God, in Zion.
 O thou that hearest prayer,
 Unto thee shall all flesh come " (Ps. lxv. 1 (2). RV.
  marg.).

In all these four passages the word denotes a period
of waiting between the offering of the prayer, and the
giving of the answer which shall call forth praise.   The
adverb in Lam. iii. 26 exactly expresses it: " It is good
when one doth wait even *in silence* for the salvation of
Jehovah."

That goodness is here seen, for the prayers offered on
earth are, during this period of *silence*, formally presented
before God, and the answer is formally announced in
the preparation of the seven angels to sound their
Trumpets and declare war against Satan and all his
hosts.   This is what is now seen by John.

2. and I saw the seven angels]   *i.e.*, at the expiration of the half-hour.   Not merely seven angels, but
THE seven, because well known, and before referred
to as "the seven spirits which are before the throne"
(i. 4; iii. 1; iv. 5; v. 6), for " he maketh his angels
spirits" (Heb. i. 7).

At the breaking of the seventh Seal there is silence.
This shows that here we have a pause with a view of a
return, to fill up details.   While in the other two (the
Trumpets and Vials) we have continuous and consecu-
tive and consequent action arising from the seventh
Trumpet.

who stand in the presence of God ;]   In chap iv. 5,
they are called THE seven spirits of God (So. iii. 1)
for it is said of the angels: He "maketh His angels
spirits " (Heb. i. 14).   The word πνεύματα (*pneumata*)

spirits, is used of any spiritual being. In chap. **v. 6** also we again read of "THE seven spirits sent forth into all the earth."

There seems to be no doubt but that all these passages relate to the same seven "Presence-Angels."

In Dan. iv. 13 (10), 17 (14), 23 (20), they are called עִירִין (*īrīn*) *watchers* (Greek, ἐγρήγοροι (*egrēgoroi*), lxx. Lam. iv. 14). This term is from Ps. ciii. 20, *i.e.*, those who watch and wait for the Divine commands. That GABRIEL is one of these is clear from Luke i. 19. MICHAEL may be another.

and there was given unto them seven trumpets.] By whom they were given is not stated. But they were given by direction from the Throne; the action of which is now renewed, though it is changed. The Lamb opened the Seals, but Angels sound the Trumpets. The Seals were opened in secret; the Trumpets publicly proclaim war. (See Num. x. 9. Judges vi. 34; iii. 27; vii. 8, 16, 18. 1 Sam. xiii. 3. Jer. iv. 5. Job xxxix. 25. Rev. xiv. 14). They notify also the presence of the great and terrible day of the Lord. See Zeph. i. 14-16.

3. **And another angel came and took his stand at the altar, having a golden censer** ;] We are not told who this other angel was, and therefore it is simple speculation to assert, as many do, that he was the Lord Jesus Himself. The golden censer belonged to the Holy Place (Heb. ix. 4), and it was the golden altar on which the incense was offered.

And there was given unto him much incense, that he should offer it with the prayers of all the saints upon the golden altar that was before the throne. (4) And the smoke of the incense went up before God, with the prayers of the saints,

out of the hand of the angel.] We have here
a Vision of events in Heaven, from which we learn
that Heaven is a place of great and grand realities; the dwelling-place of God, in which Heavenly
worship is carried on. The Tabernacle on earth and
its worship; and afterward the Temple with its
ordinances, were only copies of the realities in heaven;
" figures of the true," and " patterns of things in the
heavens." "Moses was admonished of God when he
was about to make the Tabernacle : for, see, saith he,
that thou make all things according to the pattern
showed to thee in the mount" (Heb. viii. 5 ; ix. 23, 24).
In like manner was David admonished, when he
received the plan and pattern of the Temple "in
writing" from God (1 Chron. xxviii. 11-13, 19).

The prayers of the martyred saints were over, but
the cry of their blood from the ground is voiced in
words (vi. 10). These prayers are the living saints, the
people of the book; the 144,000, and the great multitude before they are taken out of the great Tribulation,
who " cry day and night unto Him " (Luke xviii. 7). We
have specimens of these prayers, given (proleptically)
in the Psalms :

" Give them according to their deeds,
 And according to the wickedness of their
  endeavours :
 Give them after the work of their hands;
 Render to them their desert " (Ps. xxviii. 4).
" Do unto them as unto the Midianites;
 As to Sisera, as to Jabin, at the brook of Kishon "
                                (Ps. lxxxiii. 9).
And the very Psalm which likens prayer to incense,
also contains similar prayers (Ps. cxli. 1, 2, 7, 10).

" LORD, I cry unto thee :
Make haste unto me :
Give ear unto my voice, when I cry unto thee.
Let my prayer be set forth before thee as incense ;
And the lifting up of my hands as the evening
  sacrifice. . .
Our bones are scattered at the grave's mouth,
As when one cutteth and cleaveth wood upon the
  earth. . .
Let the wicked fall into their own nets,
Whilst that I withal escape (marg. Heb. *pass over*)."

The Golden altar " is before the throne."   So it was
in the earthly copy of the heavenly pattern.   It was
" *before the vail* that is by the ark of the testimony,
before the mercy-seat that is over the testimony " (Ex.
xxx. 6 ; xl. 5, 26.)

5. **And the angel took the censer, and filled it
from the fire of the altar** (Lev. xvi. 12), **and he cast
the fire unto the earth: and there were thunderings,
and voices, and lightnings,* and an earthquake.**]
We have a similar scene in Ezek. x. 2, &c., where the
fire is taken from between the cherubim under the
throne, and scattered over the city of Jerusalem in
token of its destruction.   So here: that on which the
fire falls is to be consumed and destroyed.   This is the
answer to the prayers which had been so solemnly
offered.   In other places " fire " is mentioned as one of
the judgments which He will send on the earth.   (See
Ezek. xxxix. 6 ; xxxviii. 22.   Hos. viii. 14.   Amos i.
4, 7, 10, 12 ; ii. 5).   Compare Deut. xxxii. 22.

---

* This is the order according to T.Tr.A. WH. and RV.   L. and
WHm. read " thunderings and lightnings and voices."

This very scene is prophesied in similar words in Ps. xviii. 4, 6-8 :

" The floods of ungodly (marg. *Belial*) men made me afraid . . .

In my distress I called upon the LORD,
And cried unto my God:
He heard my voice out of his Temple,
And my cry came before him, even into his ears.
Then the earth shook and trembled ;
The foundations also of the hills moved
And were shaken, because he was wroth,
There went up a smoke out of (marg. *by*) his nostrils,
And fire out of his mouth devoured :
Coals were kindled by it."

The fulfilment of the next verse, which speaks of this actual descent, is deferred here by the description of other events which are also to take place.

6. **And the seven angels who had the seven Trumpets made themselves ready that they might sound them.**] The prohibition of vii. 1 is now about to be removed. Twice the sevenfold enunciation is given, and the reproach of Ps. lxxix. 11, 12 is about to be rewarded " sevenfold," in answer to the prayers which had been offered.

This heavenly vision is a vision showing what will one day literally take place. If they are Symbols, they are symbols of solemn realities. If they are Figures, they are figures, not of speech, but of facts. Just as the judgments of God at the time of the Exodus were real and literal ; and the announcements of them were literally fulfilled, so will these be. For they are exactly what is foretold. " According to the days of thy coming out of the land of Egypt will I show him marvellous things " (Mic. vii. 15).

Indeed, we are distinctly told that the physical marvels of that day shall be " like as it was to Israel in the day that he came up out of the land of Egypt " (Is. xi. 15, 16).

We are even told in Jer. xxiii. 7, 8, that the coming judgments (for which preparation is now made, Rev. viii. 1-6) shall exceed those which God performed in Egypt, and the covenant of marvels we must once more quote as being conclusive on this point:

" Behold I make a covenant: before all thy people I WILL DO MARVELS, such as have not been done in all the earth, nor in any nation: and all the people among which thou art shall see the work of the LORD: for it is a TERRIBLE THING that I will do with thee " (Ex. xxxiv. 10, and compare Deut. xxviii. 10).

9

THE SECOND VISION "ON EARTH"
(8:7—11:14)

A. (page 118), *The First Four Trumpets*
(viii. 7-12)

Before we give the Structure of this section we must again call attention to the fact that the *sixth* Seal takes us on to the time of the end; and the *seventh* Seal takes us back and commences a new series of judgments initiated by the seven Trumpets and followed by the seven Vials. So that the whole of the rest of the Apocalypse comes under the seventh Seal. Whereas the seventh Trumpet issues in and contains the seven Vials.

First of all we have (as we have seen) the six Seals (chaps. vi., vii.)

Then the seventh Seal expands into and contains both the seven Trumpets (viii. 7—xi. 14) and the seven Vials (xvi. 1—xviii. 24).

Finally, the seventh Trumpet expands into and contains the seven Vials (xvi. 1—xviii. 24).

Thus the seventh Seal embraces the whole of the great Judgment period of the Trumpets and Vials (from viii. 7—xviii. 24) and is immediately followed by the Apocalypse of the Son of Man in power and great glory.

A careful study of the following Presentation will explain our meaning; and set forth the order of the general contents of these judgment Visions, viii. 1—xviii. 24:

The Seventh Seal, viii. 1—xviii. **24**

THE SEVENTH SEAL consisting of The Seven Trumpets and the Seven Vials		
	viii. 7. The 1st TRUMPET. Fire mingled with blood. Third part of Trees and grass burnt up.	
	viii. 8, 9. The 2nd TRUMPET. Burning mountain cast into sea. Third of sea becomes blood.	
	viii. 10, 11. The 3rd TRUMPET. Burning star falls on third part of Rivers ("Wormwood").	
	viii. 12, 13. The 4th TRUMPET. Third part of Sun smitten. Moon and stars darkened.	
	ix. 1-12. The 5th TRUMPET. (THE FIRST WOE). Pit opened. Locusts.	
	ix. 13—xi. 14. The 6th TRUMPET. (THE SECOND WOE). The 4 Euphratean Angels loosed. Horsemen.	
	xi. 15. THE SEVENTH TRUMPET (x. 7). The 3rd WOE (Rev. xi. 14). Consisting of the Seven Vials.	xvi. 1, 2. VIAL I. (THE THIRD WOE). On the earth. Sores on Worshippers of Beast.
		xvi. 3. VIAL II. On the Sea. Sea became blood.
		xvi. 4-7. VIAL III. On the Rivers. Rivers became blood.
		xvi. 8, 9. VIAL IV. On the Sun. Men scorched with fire.
		xvi. 10, 11. VIAL V. On the Throne of the Beast. Kingdom full of darkness.
		xvi. 12-16. VIAL VI. On the River Euphrates. Euphrates dried up. 3 spirits like Frogs. Armageddon.
		xvi. 17—xviii. 24. VIAL VII. "It is done." The judgment of Great Babylon.

The whole of this great judgment period, covered by the Trumpets and Vials, is given in two pairs of alternate Visions of events " in Heaven " and " on Earth."

The 2nd Vision " in Heaven" (viii. 1-6) consists of *the opening of the seventh Seal*
The 2nd Vision " on Earth " (viii. 7—xi. 14) consists of the effects of this opening (the first six Trumpets)

The 3rd Vision "in Heaven" (xi. 15-19-.) consists of *the Sounding of the seventh Trumpet*
The 3rd Vision " on Earth " (xi. -19) consists of the effects of this sounding

We are then (in chap. xii.) taken back to a time prior to chap iv.; while the sequence of the Trumpet and Vial judgments is broken in order to admit of this parenthetical break.

The Trumpet and Vial judgments are *continuous once they begin.* It is only the description of them (not the *course* of them) which is interrupted, in order to allow of the necessary information being given which shows the necessity for them.

This digression commences at chap. xii. 1 and is carried on to xv. 8. Then the description of the Vial Judgments is taken up and continued, giving the results "on Earth" of the sounding of the seventh Trumpet ; an epitome of which had been given in a few words in xi. -19. These Vial Judgments are then continuous from xvi. 1—xviii. 24, which ends their mission, accomplishes their object, and issues in the Revelation of Christ from Heaven in power and great glory (chap. xix.).

But we must return now to the second Vision " on Earth," runs from viii. 7—xi. 14.

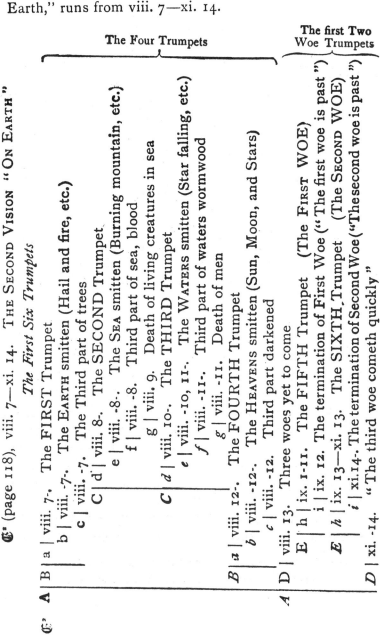

The Four Trumpets | The first Two Woe Trumpets

𝕮³ (page 118), viii. 7—xi. 14. THE SECOND VISION "ON EARTH"
The First Six Trumpets

𝕮³ **A** | B | a | viii. 7. The FIRST Trumpet
     b | viii. -7. The EARTH smitten (Hail and fire, etc.)
     c | viii. -7. The Third part of trees
      C | d | viii. 8. The SECOND Trumpet
       e | viii. -8. The SEA smitten (Burning mountain, etc.)
       f | viii. -8. Third part of sea, blood
        g | viii. 9. Death of living creatures in sea
      C | d | viii. 10. The THIRD Trumpet
       e | viii. -10, 11. The WATERS smitten (Star falling, etc.)
       f | viii. -11. Third part of waters wormwood
        g | viii. -11. Death of men
  B | a | viii. 12. The FOURTH Trumpet
     b | viii. -12-. The HEAVENS smitten (Sun, Moon, and Stars)
     c | viii. -12. Third part darkened
  D | viii. 13. Three woes yet to come
   E | h | ix. 1-11. The FIFTH Trumpet (The FIRST WOE)
     i | ix. 12. The termination of First Woe ("The first woe is past ")
   E | h | ix. 13—xi. 13. The SIXTH Trumpet (The SECOND WOE)
     i | xi.14. The termination of Second Woe ("The second woe is past ")
  D | xi. -14. "The third woe cometh quickly"

Here we have the whole of the *six* Trumpets. The six refer to the earth ; the *seventh* consists of the *third* Vision "in heaven." So with the Seals : *six* referred to the earth, and the *seventh* was opened "in heaven." It is the same with the seven Trumpets ; *six* Trumpets refer to the earth, the *seventh* refers to heaven. Moreover, they are divided into four and three : the four (A. viii. 7-12, page 304) being grouped together, and the last three (*A.* viii. 13—xi. 14, etc., page 304) being the three " Woe " Trumpets.

The first *four* Trumpets and their results are recorded with brevity ; while the last *three* are set forth in more detail. The *four* occupy only seven verses ; the last *three* occupy some fifty verses.

The first of the four affects the earth ; the fourth affects the heavens ; while the second and third affect the waters of the earth. Thus all is recorded in perfect order.

THE FIRST TRUMPET (viii. 7)

viii. 7. **And the first* sounded** his **trumpet,]** The verb σαλπίζω (*salpizō*) means to sound a trumpet ; the noun σάλπιγξ, (*salpingx*) being included in the verb.

and there followed hail and fire mingled with blood, and they were cast upon the earth : and the third of the earth was burned up,† and the third of the trees was burned up, and all green grass was burned up] In the plagues of Egypt, to which these judgments were to be like, the seventh plague was " hail, and fire mingled with the hail " (Ex. ix. 22-28), and plants of the earth were smitten (*vv.* 31, 32). Here blood was

---

*G.L.T.Tr.A. WH. and RV. omit the word "angel."

† This sentence is added by G. L.T.Tr.A. WH. and RV.

mingled with the fire and hail. We are aware that a majority of interpreters maintain that the results of this first Trumpet are not literal. They seem as anxious to get rid of the miraculous and the supernatural from Interpretation, as the Rationalists are to eliminate it from Inspiration. But why, unless the plagues of Egypt also were not literal plagues, we cannot understand. Again we ask, Why should not these be literal judgments which are to come on the earth ? What is the difficulty ? God has said concerning the events of the day of the Lord, "I will show wonders in heaven above and signs in the earth beneath, *blood and fire*" (Joel ii. 30). How He will do this we are here told.

To explain this away is to manifest a want of faith in the power of God, and in the Word of God. Such things have taken place on earth. Why should they not take place again ?

Cicero* tells us that word was brought to the Roman Senate, on one occasion, that it had *rained blood*, and that the river Atratus had flowed with blood.

On August 17, 1819, Dr. Seiss tells us that " Captain Ross saw the mountains at Baffin's Bay covered for eight miles with *blood-red* snow many feet in depth." Also that Saussare found it on Mount St. Bernard, in 1778 ; that Ramond found it on the Pyrenees ; and Summerfield in Norway.

Why may it not be seen again ?

The historical interpreters differ so much among themselves that we may well ask, Which one of them are we to believe ? It is this very diversity which has caused so many earnest students to put the Apocalypse aside in despair. Our object in writing is that they may

---

* *De Div.*, ii. 27.

take up the book again with hope; asking them only to believe God. It will be better to err in such simplicity of faith in the Word of God, than to adopt the most plausible scheme based upon the opinion of man; and which differs not only from God, but from every other human interpretation.

For example, Elliott says that this first Trumpet denotes the wars of Alaric the Goth and Rhadagaisus the Vandal against the Western Roman Empire. We should never have guessed this ourselves. There is nothing about this or even like it in this Scripture. John saw *one* result, Mr. Elliott gives two. John saw the blood-red rain of hail and fire from heaven; this gives human blood on earth!

One says "trees" mean princes and great men; and "grass" means men's power and glory (Wordsworth).

J. N. Darby says "that which is elevated, eminent, lofty is intended by the trees; the young, feeble and aged are meant by the green grass."

Wetstein says "Trees mean fortified cities; grass, unwalled villages."

Others say "by trees are signified apostles and great doctors; by grass, common Christians" (Paralus).

Alford holds that "it appears rather to indicate a general character of the judgments, than to require any special interpretation in each particular case."

To all this we have one simple remark to make—We prefer to believe God's own special interpretation of His own judgments, in the plain literal sense of the words.

THE SECOND TRUMPET (viii. 8, 9)

viii. 8. **And the second angel sounded his trumpet, and as it were a great mountain burning with fire** was cast into the sea: and the third of the sea became blood; (9) and there died the third of the creatures which were in the sea, which had life; and the third of the ships were destroyed.] It does not say it was a mountain, but that it was *like* one. This shows us what is not to be taken literally, as well as what is. It was something which resembled a mountain. John does not say he saw a volcano (as some assert). What John saw was a fiery mass like a mountain cast into the sea, and turning it into blood. "This cannot be literal" exclaim the interpreters. But again we ask, Why not? In one of the plagues of Egypt it is written that Moses "lifted up his rod, and smote the waters that were in the river, in the sight of Pharaoh, and in the sight of his servants, and all the waters that were in the river were turned to blood" (Ex. vii. 20). In Ps. cv. 29 it is written, "He turned their waters into blood"; so Ps. lxxviii. 44. The poorest and humblest reader can understand this. It does not require education in order to believe God. All it needs is a spiritual understanding, and a childlike mind. (1 John v. 20 and 1 Cor. ii. 14.) It does not require wide reading to understand God. It requires faith.

To follow what man says it requires only credulity. Which are we to believe of the following interpretations?

One interpretation asks us to believe that

The fiery *mountain* means Satan.

The *sea* means the nations.

The dying of the *fish* denotes the persecution and slaughter of Christians.

The wreck of the *ships* denotes the extinction of congregations.

(2.)   Another system (E. B. Elliott's) tells us that

The *mountain* was Genseric with his Vandals, forced by the Huns from their native seat.

The *sea* was their plunging through France and Spain into Africa, settling themselves in the conquered territory.

The *destruction of fish*, etc., was their depredations on the neighbouring islands and shores of the Mediterranean.

(3.)   A third system tells us that

The *sea* is the church with its baptismal waters.

The *mountain* is some great heresy.

The *blood* is the corruption by deadly error.

The *destruction of fish* is the destruction of souls.

The *wreck of ships* is the overturning of churches

(4.)   Another system is that

The *sea* is the sea of Galilee, put for Palestine.

The *mountain* is Vespasian.

The *fishes* are the Jews.

The *ships* are the cities of Palestine.

(5.)   A fifth scheme is that

The *sea* is pure doctrine.

The *mountain* is prelacy.

The *fire* Episcopal ambition.

The *blood*-red waters means the introduction of false doctrine.

The *fishes* are Ecclesiastics, monks.

The *ships* the bearers of the Gospel.

(6.)   A sixth system is that

The *mountain* is Rome.

Its *burning* the burning of Rome by Alaric.

The wreck of its *ships* is the sack of Rome.

(7.) William Kelly would have us believe him. He says

> " The second blow supposes a great change : it falls on the sea, and so refers not to that sphere which is under special and settled government, but to that which is, or will then be, in a state of confusion and anarchy." And again " the mountain burning with fire, represents a system of power, itself under the judgment of God and the occasion of judgment to others " (*Apoc.*, p. 141).

Again, we ask, *Is it not better to believe God ?* Is it not easier to understand what *He* says ?

It is perfectly clear that *all* the above systems cannot be right. Which of them, then, are we to accept ? Why is there this universal effort to have us believe that God always means something different from what He says ? Whence comes this spirit ? Dr. Seiss well asks, " What do we want with Vespasian and Alaric and Rhadagaisus, Attila, Genseric, Romans, Goths, Vandals, Arians, Prelates, or the Devil," when God tells us that it was a fiery mass like a mountain cast into the sea ? That God's coming judgments will affect the fishes and the ships we are distinctly told in Hosea iv. 1-3. Zeph i. 3. Isa. ii. 16, &c.

All Bible readers and commentators believe that waters were turned to blood in the plagues of Egypt. Why not believe that they will be so turned again ? If God had said ink instead of blood, we would believe Him. All things are possible with Him.

Indeed, it is quite recently that we were told that this had happened ; or something like it. *The Daily Express* (London, May 19, 1900) says : " Great consternation has been caused at Santa Cruz, by the sea turning suddenly black," and given an extract from the *San Francisco Examiner*, which says :

" There are many theories as to the cause of this remarkable change. One man thinks it is due to the tides. Another says the turbid waters are the result of a submarine upheaval in the blue mud of the channel. A third believes the water is full of animalculæ—the whale food.

" Still another states that a storm from the ocean has muddled the water, and talks wisely, too, of marine earthquakes and the like. They all agree that the whole bay was never before like *the sea of ink* it is at present."

If, in our day, the sea can be turned *black*, Why cannot it be as easily turned *red* ? And when it is, when these words of " the book of this prophecy " shall be fulfilled, men will doubtless speculate about the cause of it, just as they speculate about the sea at Santa Cruz: and remain just as ignorant as before, because " God is not in all their thoughts."

In like manner, the cleaving in two of the Mount of Olives in Zech. xiv. 4 is regarded by most commentators as being quite beyond a literal interpretation : and yet, a few years ago, *The Illustrated London News* gave some interesting drawings of the scene of the great volcanic eruption in the North Island, New Zealand. It will be remembered that the outburst of volcanic energy began by the explosion of MOUNT TARAWERA, a mountain which had no crater upon it, and showed no signs of recent activity. TARAWERA *was split in two* by the sudden opening of a great chasm or line of craters four miles long, about 500 feet wide, and, in many places, 400 feet deep.

What happened in that case may easily happen again ; not that we require, or ought to require, any such aid to our faith ; for we believe that God means exactly what He says, in this and in other prophecies.

THE THIRD TRUMPET (viii. 10, 11)

viii. 10. **And the third angel sounded** his **trumpet, and there fell from heaven a great star, burning as it were a torch** (λαμπάς (*lampas*) *a torch*; not λύχνος (*luchnos*) *a lamp*), **and it fell upon the third of the rivers, and upon the fountains of waters;** (11) **and the name of the star is called Wormwood** ("Αψινθος (*apsinthos*) *Absinthe*): **and the third of the waters became wormwood; and many men died of the waters, because they were made bitter**] That stars should fall from heaven is a subject of prophecy (vi. 13). Here is one special star, smaller, evidently, than the burning mountain. When we are distinctly told it was "like a torch" there is no occasion to introduce the idea of a comet (as Dr. Seiss does), or a meteor, or anything else. As a torch it was burning only at one end, and not burning all over as the mountain was. All this is quite clear as it stands. It requires no explanation if we believe what is written.

On the other hand, the ideas of historical interpreters are in wild confusion and mutual opposition. As to the "Star," the interpretations include Mahomet, Simon Magus, Montanus, Arius, Cerinthus, Pelagius, among ecclesiastics. Those who hold it to be a military personage say it was some Jewish leader, as Eleazar, Josephus, etc. Others bring in poor Genseric again, or Attila, and a long series of wholesale murderers.

But a few questions will dispose of them all: What was the heaven out of which they fell? What was their fall? How did they burn? How did they embitter the fountains and rivers and make them bitter like themselves? When were they called by the name "Wormwood?" or "Absinthe?"

There is no reasonable answer to these questions. It is a very sad reflection to think that, with so many, these definite and particular revelations of the Holy Ghost may mean anything.

We ourselves might add another interpretation ; and however extravagant it might be, men would not mind. Some would probably receive it. But, we dare to commit the unpardonable sin of adopting a principle of interpretation which requires us to believe that these things " mean " exactly what God says, and are consequently looked on as " cranks " for so doing.

And yet events somewhat similar have happened. In the *Annual Register* for 1823, p. 683, we read that, as the result of a volcanic explosion, showers of sand darkened the sky and "the sea water became thick, and river water assumed the colour of beer, and was so extremely bitter as to be unfit for use. This was in the Aleutian Islands, and it is quoted by Mr. Govett in his *Apocalypse Expounded.* Something like this was foretold as God's punishment of His People (Jer. ix. 13-15) : " Behold I will feed them, even this people, with wormwood; and give them water of gall to drink." So Jer. xxiii. 15. Lam. iii. 15. Jer. viii. 14 ; ix. 15.

The result of one of the plagues of Egypt was that "the Egyptians could not drink of the water of the river" (Ex. vii. 18-24). That was real and literal. So will this be.

THE FOURTH TRUMPET (viii. 12)

viii. 12. **And the fourth angel sounded his trumpet, and the third of the sun was smitten, and the third of the moon, and the third of the stars; in order that the third part of them might be** darkened, and the day might not shine for a third of it, and the night in like manner] " Signs in the sun and in the moon and in the stars " are what the Lord foretold as part of the wonders to be looked for. (Luke xxi. 25. So Matt. xxiv. 29 and Mark xiii. 24). Here, some of those signs are seen by John. Others are foretold in Isaiah, " Behold darkness and sorrow : and *the light is darkened in the heavens thereof* (Isaiah v. 30). " I will cause the sun to go down at noon, *and I will darken the earth in the clear day** (Amos viii. 9). Read Jer. iv. 23, 28. Ezek. xxxii. 7, 8. Joel ii. 10, 30, 31 ; iii. 15. Amos v. 20. Zeph. i. 14-16.

The interpretations of this, differ, as usual ; and it seems hardly worth our time to name them. We read about the " imperial sun " and the " political day " and " political noon " and " political stars," whatever they may be. Is it any wonder that teachers and students are alike confused and bewildered ? They first assume that it is past ; and are then at their wits' end to find something or anything, however irrelevant, that can be forced into any connection with the word.

Ask a little child what are the sun, moon and stars ? and he will experience no difficulty. Neither shall we, if we, with childlike minds, believe what God says.

D. and E. (page 304), The Fifth Trumpet (*or First Woe*)
(viii. 13—ix. 12)

The fifth and sixth Trumpets are the first and second of the three " Woe " Trumpets. These three are introduced in a special manner, *viz.,* by an Eagle and its cry (viii. 13), which marks off the last *three* of the whole seven, from the first *four*.

---

* On the other hand, millennial light is to be increased. Isaiah xxx. 26 ; lx. 19, 20.

The Eagle and its cry separates the four from the three.

viii. 13. **And I looked, and I heard an** (Greek, *one, single,* or *solitary*) **eagle* flying in mid-heaven, saying with a loud voice,**

> **"Woe, woe, woe, to those that dwell upon the earth by reason of the remaining voices of the trumpet of the three angels, who are about to sound!"]**

(ix. 1, 12, and xi. 14). We believe it to be what it says—a veritable eagle. All the critical Greek texts, and all the ancient manuscripts read "eagle." Bengel, 150 years ago, said that the "most ancient authorities, widely separated from each other in age and clime, and in very great numbers, clearly vindicate the reading of ἀετοῦ (*aëtou*), *eagle,* from all suspicion of gloss." Eagles are often connected with judgment. (See Deut. xxviii. 49. 2 Sam. i. 23. Is. xl. 31. Jer. iv. 13. Hos. viii. 1. Hab. i. 8). It was flying in mid-heaven, *i.e.,* the meridian, or the highest point reached by the sun at noon. The word rendered "mid-heaven" occurs only here, and in xiv. 6 and xix. 17. The fifth day saw the creation of birds which "fly above the earth *in the open firmament of heaven*" (Gen. i. 20); and it is an eagle that announces this fifth Trumpet.

This eagle speaks. So did Balaam's ass. If God could "open the mouth" of the one, so He can of the other. Thus it is written, and thus we believe.

---

* G.L.T.Tr.A. WH. and RV. read ἀετοῦ (*aetou*) *eagle,* instead of ἀγγέλου (*angelou*) *angel.* In xvi. 7 we have the *altar* speaking; so here an *eagle* is represented as speaking.

The Structure of the member containing the description of this Trumpet is as follows :—

h. (page 304), ix. 1-11. *The Fifth Trumpet.* (1st WOE)

h | k | 1-. The Star fallen to the earth.
    l | -1, 2-. The Abyss. (The key and the opening).
    l | -2. The Abyss. (The result of the opening).
    k | 3-11. The Locusts coming upon the earth.

This structure shows that three things form the subject of this Fifth Trumpet:

> The fallen Star,
> The Pit of the Abyss, and
> The Locusts.

ix. 1. **And the fifth angel sounded his trumpet, and I saw a star from heaven fallen** (So RV. Not "fall" as in AV.) **to the earth : and there was given to him the key of the pit of the abyss.]** The star (or angel) had fallen from heaven before John saw it. (Compare Isa. xiv. 12. Luke x. 18).

Angels are called stars in Job xxxviii. 7, and often in the Old Testament, the phrase " host of heaven " means the *angels*, as in 1 Kings xxii. 19. 2 Chron. xviii. 18. Ps. cxlviii. 2. Josh. v. 14. It sometimes means the literal stars, as in Is. xxxiv. 4 ; xl. 26; xlv. 12. Jer. xxxiii. 22. That the word " star," here, is used for "angel" seems clear from the personal actions ascribed to it.

" The pit of the abyss " appears to be the abode of demons. See Rev. xx. 1-3. Luke viii. 28, 31.

2. **And he opened the pit of the abyss ; and there went up smoke out of the abyss, as the smoke of a**

great furnace; and the sun and the air were
darkened by the smoke of the pit.] We are not to
confuse this pit with Hades, or Sheol, or Tartarus. It is
called the Abyss, and is shown by the smoke to be a
place of fire. (Compare xviii. 9, 18; xix. 3, and Gen. xix.
24-28).

In Jeremiah iv. 23-28, we read:

" I beheld the earth, and lo, it was without form, and
    void :
And the heavens, and they had no light.
I beheld the mountains, and lo, they trembled,
And all the hills moved lightly.
I beheld, and lo, there was no man,
And all the birds of the heavens were fled.
I beheld, and lo, the fruitful place was a wilderness,
And all the cities thereof were broken down
At the presence of the LORD,
And by His fierce anger.
For thus hath the LORD said,
The whole land shall be desolate;
Yet will I not make a full end.
For this shall the earth mourn,
And the heavens above be black:
Because I have spoken it, I have purposed it,
And will not repent, nor will I turn back from it."

This refers, of course, to Judah and the Land. What
John sees, refers to the earth in general. This judgment corresponds with the eighth and ninth plagues of
Egypt (Ex. x. 5), when Moses threatened that the
locusts should "cover the face of the earth, that one
cannot be able to see the earth."

This judgment is now to be more particularly described in verses -3-11.

The Structure is as follows:—

k. (page 316), ix. -3-11.   *The Locusts coming on the Earth*

k |m | o | ix. -3. Their power
　　　　　p | ix. 4, 5-.   Their commission
　　　　　　　q | ix. -5-. Their continuance. ("5 months ")
　　　　　　　　　n | ix. -5-10-.   Description of locusts
　　　m | *o* | ix. -10-.   Their power
　　　　　　p | ix. -10-.   Their commission
　　　　　　　q | ix.-10. Their continuance. ("5 months ")
　　　　　　　　n | ix. 11.   Description of their king

Here we have the symmetrical statement which distinguishes their Power, Commission, Continuance, and
Description; and shows the points which are important;
and on which we are to dwell.

ix. 3.   **And out of the smoke there came forth
locusts into the earth: and there was given** to them
power, as the scorpions of the earth have power.]
These were no ordinary locusts.   Those that came in
the plagues of Egypt were no common locusts either,
for we are told "before them there were no such locusts
as they, neither after them shall be such" (Ex. x. 14).
Ordinary locusts have " no king" (Prov. xxx. 27); but
these have; and his name is given (*v.* 11).   They seem,
from their description, to be a kind of *Infernal Cherubim.*
The horse, the man, the lion, and the scorpion are combined in them.   They are called locusts, though they
are supernatural and, apparently, incapable of being
killed.   But of this we shall see more as we proceed.

4.   **And it was said to them that they should
not injure the grass of the earth, nor any green**

thing, nor any tree; but should injure **the men* who have not the seal of God on their foreheads.]** Common locusts eat up and destroy only vegetation (Ex. x. 5, 12, 15): beyond this they are not injurious. But these, from the bottomless pit, are designed for a very different purpose. Human beings are the objects of their assaults. Though released from the pit, they cannot go beyond the power "given" to them. A similar limitation is seen in Ezek. ix. 4-6.

5. **And it was given to them that they should not kill them, but that they should be tormented five months: and their torment was as the torment of a scorpion, when it striketh a man]** Here is another limitation. Under the second Seal there is no such limit. "Torment" applies in a special manner to demons (Matt. viii. 29; Rev. xiv. 10, 11; xx. 10). The duration of this plague is fixed. It is to last "five months." A similar fixed date is given in Num. xi. 19, 20: "a whole month." In 2 Sam. xxiv. 13, also we have "seven years," "three months," and "three days," as the fixed limit of certain judgments. These periods are always taken literally. Why not this? The time limit of these infernal locusts corresponds with that of ordinary· locusts, which is five months (from May to September).

6. **And in those days shall men seek death, and shall in no wise† find it; and shall desire to die, and death fleeth‡ from them.]** "In those

---

* Omit "only," G.L.T.Tr.A. WH. and RV.

† G.L.T.Tr.A. WH. and RV. read οὐ μή (*ou me*) *by no means,* instead of οὐχ (*ouk*) *not.*

‡ L.T.Tr.A. WH. and RV. read φύγει (*fleeth*) instead of φεύξται (*shall flee*).

days" refers to the period of "five months" mentioned in the previous verse. The result of the
plague is not the producing of repentance; but only a
desire for death. A similar state of things is foretold in
Jer. viii. 3 : "Death shall be chosen rather than life by
all the residue that remains of this evil family." How
this desire is to be thwarted we are not told; it may be
part of the result of the torment. This one feature of
the plague proves that it must be future and literal :
for no period in history is known where such a condition
of things lasted for " five months." There have always
been isolated cases where men have sought death
(1 Kings xix. 4); but this is to be universal.

**7. And the likenesses of the locusts were like
to horses prepared for war: and there were upon
their heads as it were crowns like unto gold, and
their faces were as the faces of men.**] Four verses
are given to this description, so that the matter
is evidently important. Their *size* is not given. The
words "like" and "as" occur nine times. In
verses 7 and 8 we have the fore-part described ; in verse 9
the middle part; and in verse 10 their hind part. Joel
has a description of similar beings (See Joel ii.).

**8. And they had hair, like women's hair, and
their teeth were like lions'** teeth. (9) **and they had
breastplates like iron breastplates; and the sound
of their wings** was **as the sound of chariots of many
horses rushing into battle.**] Some ordinary locusts
have hair. See Jer. li. 27, "locusts bristling with
hair."* Joel i. 6 has two references to the lions' teeth.

---

* The AV. has "the rough caterpillars"; RV. has "the rough
cankerworm."

10. **And they have tails like scorpions, and stings were in their tails: and their power** (or licence) **is to injure men five months.**] Here is developed what was only alluded to in verse 5. This discloses their origin, from the bottomless pit. The *action*, commenced in verse 5, is suspended so that their description might be completed.

11. **And they have over them a king, the angel of the abyss, whose name in Hebrew is Abaddon, and in the Greek he hath his name Apollyon.**] It is a special characteristic of ordinary earth-born locusts that they have " no king " (Prov. xxx. 27), but these awful beings from the Abyss have a king. It is beside the point to say this king is Satan, for his special name is given. The Wild-Beast is twice described as coming up " out of the bottomless pit " (xi. 7 and xvii. 8). The name is evidently important, as it is given in two languages. They are equivalent as to their meaning, which is *Destruction*. It is literally the name of the bottomless pit, in Hebrew. It is distinguished from *Sheōl* (See Job xxvi. 6; xxviii. **22.** Ps. lxxxviii. 11. Prov. xv. 11; xxvii. 20). The name of the pit is given to the angel of the pit,* and means *Destroyer*. Hence his name in Jer. iv. 7; vi. 26. Isa. xvi. 4. Dan. viii. 24, 25; ix. 26; xi. 44.

12. **The first woe is past; behold, there are coming yet two woes after these things.**] The awful character of these three Woe - Trumpets is seen from what we are told of the first. The mighty forces of heaven and hell are gathering for the final conflict. We have here some of the outpost work,

---

* By the figure called *Metonymy* (of the adjunct), by which the abstract is put for the concrete.

which gives an indication of what is to follow. From Joel ii. 11 we learn that Almighty God Himself will lead on His own great army.

> " Jehovah shall utter his voice before his army ;
> For his camp is very great :
> For he is strong that executeth his word :
> For the day of the LORD is great and very terrible ;
> And who can abide it ? "

On the other hand, one of Satan's superior officers, "the angel of the abyss," Abaddon, leads forth this great division, and forms part of the Satanic forces to be brought against the King of kings. All is clear and simple and plain if we read this as one of a series of literal judgments which is to take place in the "day of the Lord." As literal and real as were the plagues of Egypt. But the moment we turn to the opinions of men, we are landed, as Alford himself says, "in an endless Babel of allegorical and historical interpretation."

It seems a terrible descent from these awful and sublime realities to come down to the petty and trivial views of man with regard to them. We must, however, give our readers an idea of some of the interpretations, so that they may thankfully return to, and rest on, the simple statements of God's Word.

The most common interpretation sees the fulfilment of this judgment in the Invasion of Europe by the Turks. In that case the "*star*" is said to be Mahomet. His "fall from heaven" means that his family was once high and wealthy ; he being an orphan and poor. "To him was given the key of the bottomless pit :" *i.e.*, "he *professed* to receive a key from God." So that in his case profession was evidently possession! How he opened the pit the interpreters do not tell us, but the "smoke" was his false teaching. Out of the pit came the *locusts*. *Arbah* in Hebrew means a locust. That is quite near enough with them for *Arabians*, though there could hardly be Mahommedans before Mahomet. The locusts were forbidden to destroy men; but the Arabians killed off just a few :—50,000 in one battle, 150,000 in another, etc. Indeed Mahomet commanded slaughter (See *Koran* xlvii. 409).* Elliott gets over this command "not to kill" by saying it means "not to annihilate them as a political body"!

The *crowns* like gold" were the turbans of linen. "*Faces* as men" means *courage*. "They had *hair* as women:" this refers to the *horse tail* decorations worn by the Pashas on their heads ; one, two, or three, to distinguish their respective rank and dignity. Here, the Scripture says *all* the locusts had them, not merely certain leaders !

Dr. Cumming held that their breast-plates as of iron "denotes their invulnerability." The trouble with this interpretation is that thousands of the Mahommedans were slain in battle. The tails and stings, however, baffle the interpreters! The sparing of the sealed also is difficult with the Protestant interpretation, because Rome and the Pope were untouched by the Saracens. Their *duration* also, "five months," is another difficulty. This, according to "the year-day theory," becomes 150 years, whereas the Saracenic invasion lasted over 400 years, and has continued to this day. Twice the Holy Spirit mentions

---

* "When ye encounter the unbelievers, strike off their heads, until ye have made a great slaughter of them : as for the infidels, let them perish."

the period, "five months," as though to emphasize it and impress us with the fact.

Others tell us that the star was Luther. Let our readers try the puzzle, and see how it works out, in view of the Reformation blessings which Luther was the means of conferring on the world.

No wonder Alford gives it up. Moses Stuart gives it up. Hengstenberg and others give it up. No wonder that most Bible-students have given the whole book up, in despair of ever understanding it.

What God says is plain enough. He does not ask us to understand it. He asks us to *believe* it; and this, by God's help, we mean to do.

He has promised us a blessing if we do this. But man asks us to choose from his Babel of interpretations; and gives us, instead of a blessing, only the curse of confusion.

E. (page 304), THE SIXTH TRUMPET (*or Second Woe*)

(ix. 13—xi. 14)

The Sixth, or "second Woe" Trumpet is set forth with more detail than any of the others: no less than *thirty-three* verses being devoted to its description. Like the fifth Trumpet (or first Woe) it is distinguished from the first four by being introduced by a "voice." In the former it was the voice of "an eagle flying in mid-heaven;" in this latter, it is the voice "from the four horns of the golden altar which is before God." Coming from this altar it seems to say that we have here the continuation of the answer to the prayers of vi. 10.

Coming from the "*four* horns," the direction goes forth to the *four* quarters of the earth.

But the Structure will give us the scope of the whole. The literal fulfilment of this judgment, interpreters will not have at any price. It is altogether too much to ask them to believe it. Stuart says it is symbol "excessive and unnatural." Of course it is "unnatural," simply because it is *supernatural.* So we believe is the Structure :—

h. (page 304), ix. 13—xi. 14. *The Sixth Trumpet* (2nd WOE)

```
h  r  t | ix. 13-.   The SIXTH Angel (2nd WOE Trumpet)
         u | -13-.    His sounding
         v | -13.     The Voice from the altar
         w | 14.      Its Command: Loose the 4 angels . . .
         x | 15.      Execution of command
         y | 16-21.   Result: The Horsemen
              s | z | a | x. 1, 2.  "Another" mighty angel
                      b | 3, 4-.    His cry and the seven thunders
                  z | a | -4-.      The "Voice from heaven"
                      b | -4.       Its command.  "Seal up"

   t | x. 5.    The Angel
         u | 6, 7.    His oath
         v | 8-.      The Voice from heaven
         w | -8.      His Command: "Go and take . . .
         x | 9-11.    Execution of command.
         y | xi. 1-14. Result:  The Two Witnesses
```

ix. 13. **And the sixth angel sounded** his **trumpet, and I heard a voice from the four horns of the golden altar which is before God.**] In the earthly Tabernacle and Temple the golden altar is described as standing " before the vail that is by the ark of the testimony, where I will meet with thee " (Ex. xxx. 6; xl. 3). Here, there is no veil; and the voice comes from " before God."

The sixth angel is not only to blow his trumpet, but is also to obey the command. The utterance of this voice from the Altar is important enough to have its own Structure, and the members w. and x. may be expanded thus :—

w. and x. (page 325), ix. 14, 15

The Command and its execution

w | a | ix. 14-. " Loose the four angels "
    | b | -14-. Bound
       | c | -14. Place. Euphrates . . .

x | a | ix. 15-. The four angels loosed
    | b | -15-. Prepared
       | c | -15. Time. " An hour and . . .

ix. 14. **Saying to the sixth angel who had the trumpet,**

" Loose the four angels which are
bound at the river Euphrates."

15. **And the four angels were loosed, who had been prepared for the hour, and day, and month, and year, that they should kill the third part of men.**] These four angels cannot be identified with any

others ; for they are " bound." There can be no doubt
about their being of the number of those who are
described as being " delivered into chains of darkness,
to be reserved unto (or for) judgment " (2 Peter ii. 4).
This is the judgment for which they (four of them at
least) are " reserved " and " prepared " or ready.   In
Jude 6 we are again told of the angels which are
"reserved in everlasting chains under darkness, unto
(or for) the judgment of the great day." Not only
that they should be then judged, but that they should
be the executors of God's judgments also in that great
day which we are now studying and learning about in the
Apocalypse. There are other " in-prison spirits " (1 Pet.
iii. 19), to whom the Saviour's triumph was proclaimed
at His resurrection ; not for their comfort or blessing,
but for the proclamation that the price of Redemption
had been paid, and the work done which should hereafter be celebrated in Rev. v., when the worthiness of
the Lamb that was slain should be proclaimed, not only
to Tartarus, but to all Creation.*

These angels are at present " bound."   Satan will be
bound by-and-by (xx. 2-7). But before that day a
further division of the Satanic forces is to be let loose
upon the earth.

Why " at the river Euphrates " we are not told.
What connection there may be between Babel and the
Abyss we do not know. Seeing that Satan's earlier
activities were connected with that region, there must
be some appropriate reason.   The Euphrates is asso-

---

* Why, when we read of angels (who are spirits) being "bound"
and "in chains," we should think of *men* (who are never called
"spirits") as being the "in-prison spirits," we cannot understand.
It only shows the power of tradition. See *The spirits in prison*, by
the same author and publisher.

ciated with the coming judgments of the great day. See
Jer. xlvi. 4-10 (RV.)

> " Harness the horses ; and get up, ye horsemen,
> And stand forth with your helmets ;
> Furbish the spears, and put on coats of mail.
> Wherefore have I seen it ? They are dismayed
> And are turned backward ;
> And their mighty ones are beaten down,
> And are fled apace, and look not back :
> Terror is on every side, saith the LORD
> Let not the swift flee away, nor the mighty man
>   escape ;
> In the north, *by the river Euphrates*, have they
>   stumbled and fallen.
> Who is this that riseth up like the Nile,
> Whose waters toss themselves like the rivers ?
> Egypt riseth up like the Nile,
> And his waters toss themselves like the rivers :
> And he saith, I will rise up, I will cover the
>   earth :
> I will destroy the city, and the inhabitants thereof,
> Go up, ye horses ; and rage, ye chariots ;
> And let the mighty men go forth :
> Cush and Put, that handle the shield ;
> And the Ludim, that handle and bend the bow.
> For that day is a day of the LORD, the LORD of
>   hosts,
> A day of vengeance
> That he may avenge him of his adversaries ;
> And the sword shall devour and be satiate,
> And shall drink its fill of their blood :
> For the LORD, the LORD of hosts, hath a sacrifice
> In the north country *by the river Euphrates*."

From the same quarter will come these future and greater judgments.

For greater transgressions (*v.* 20, 21) shall a greater army, not of men, but of evil spirits, come forth. See Jer. iv. 13, 29 (RV.)

"Behold he shall come up as clouds,
  And his chariots shall be as the whirlwind.
  His horses are swifter than eagles.
  Woe unto us! for we are spoiled . . .
  The whole city fleeth *from the noise of the horsemen*
     and bowmen;
  They go into the thickets, and climb up upon the
     rocks:
  Every city is forsaken,
  And not a man dwelleth therein."

These four angels, now bound, we are distinctly told are "reserved unto judgment." The word is εἰς (*eis*) *unto, with a view to* judgment (not merely to being judged); and this judgment is that of "the great day." They are reserved for the particular appointed moment; the moment of this their loosing. There seems to be little doubt as to the meaning of the period of time. It does not imply the duration of the judgment, but the preparation for the particular moment which has been appointed by God. The one article and one preposition before the four times, unites them: whereas had the article and preposition been repeated it would have implied the separation of the four which, added together, would make a period of more than thirteen months. As it is, it denotes the appointed hour of the appointed day of the appointed month of the appointed year. The emphasis on the words "pre-pared" or "reserved" supports this interpretation.

Finally, the general object is stated, to be particularised below.

We now come to the description of these "horsemen"; and from this it is to be seen that they were not human beings of any kind. Difficulties have been made on account of the vast number of these horsemen, and had they been human beings, we could well understand it. But spirits are "legion," and no difficulties can arise from their number.

First we give the Structure of **y.** (page 325).

y. (page 325), ix. 16-21. *The Horsemen*

```
y | d | f | ix. 16, 17-. Description. Number. Heads and
  |   |   | breastplates
  |   |     g | ix. -17-. Mouths
  |   |       h | ix. -17. Agency : "Fire"
  |   |
  |   |       e | ix. -18-. Result : Men killed
  |   |
  |   d |       h | ix. -18-. Agency : "Fire."
  |   |     g | ix. -18, 19. Mouths
  |   | f | ix. -19. Description. Power. Heads and tails
  |   |
  |   |         e | ix. 20, 21. Result : Men not killed
```

ix. 16. **And the number of the* armies of the horsemen** was **two myriads of myriads:** †(**I heard the number of them).** (17) **And thus I saw the horses in the vision, and those sitting on them, having breastplates fiery, and hyacinthine, and sulphureous : and the heads of the horses were as the heads of lions; and out of their mouths goeth forth**

---

* G.L.T.Tr.A. WH. and RV. have the article.

† G.L.T.Tr.A. WH. and RV. omit "and."

fire, and smoke, and brimstone. (18) **By these three plagues* were the third part of men killed, by the fire, and the smoke, and the brimstone, which goeth forth out of their mouths, (19) for the power of the horses is in their mouth, and in their tails†: for their tails are like serpents, having heads, and with them they do injure.**] This is the description of these supernatural beings. They are not human. They come from below. We know of nothing like them. When God thus describes them nothing ought to be easier than to believe what He says. They need no explanation. This description is given to explain them to us. Is it not easier to believe they are what God says they and their spirit riders are, than to believe what Dr. Adam Clarke says they are? He says they are brass cannon, ornamented with lions' heads cast at their mouth and at their breach. He adds that nothing could better describe "gunpowder" than "the fiery sulphurous smoke which goeth forth out of their mouths." We find this much more difficult to believe. And our difficulties are not less when, again, we are asked to believe that this was fulfilled in the taking of Constantinople by the Turks! Mr. Elliott says that the horses and tails refer to the horse-tails worn by the Pashas! Dean Alford says: "I will venture to say, that a more self-condemnatory interpretation was never broached, than this of the horse-tails of the Pachas." But the Turks still rule in Asia. Are they like these horsemen? Cannon were used *on both sides* of that war. Why is it, that one side is so different from the other?

---

* G.L.T.Tr.A. WH. and RV. add πληγῶν (*plēgōn*) *plagues.*

† G.L.T.Tr.A. WH. and RV. add " and in their tails."

It is not as though we had anything here unheard of before. It is *wonderful*, truly ; but that is just what God said the future plagues were to be. " *The LORD will make thy plagues wonderful* " (Deut. xxviii. 59). " I will do *marvels* which have *not been done in all the earth, nor in any nation*" (Ex. xxxiv. 10).

When Israel would trust in the horses of Egypt they were warned that their riders and horses were " flesh and not spirit " (Is. xxxi. 3). Here we have horses that are *spirit, and not flesh*. In Jer. viii. 17, Jehovah says " Behold, I will send serpents, cockatrices, among you, which will not be charmed, and they shall bite you, saith the LORD " (read 13-17).

The number of these infernal horsemen is also wonderful, *two hundred millions* ! John says " I heard the number of them " (*v.* 16). Twice he refers to it. And why not ? What is it that makes man hesitate to believe God ? These, as we have said, are no mere human beings : they are wicked spirits ; and Are not these legion and innumerable ?

The results of this plague which follow the sounding of the sixth Trumpet are given in the concluding portion of this chapter.

20. **And the rest of the men who were not killed by these plagues neither repented of the works of their hands,**] And we know not what these may be ; nor the awful form of idolatry hinted at in these verses. The expression " works of their hands," always points to idolatry (Deut. iv. 28. Psalm cxxxv. 15). And here, it is idolatry of the grossest kind.

that they should not worship the demons, nor the* idols which are golden, and silver, and brazen, and

---

* G.L.T.Tr.A. WH. & RV. add the article.

stone, and wooden : which are neither able to see, nor to hear, nor to walk :] This cannot possibly refer to the Church. No Christian of any kind worships demons ; for these are always *evil*. (See Matt. x. 1-8 ; xii. 43-45. 1 Cor. x. 20. 1 Tim. iv. 1. Compare Deut. xxxii. 17). This evil is spoken of in Deut. xxxi. 29, as recurring "in the latter days."

Spiritism, which is now making rapid strides, is the forerunner of all this ; and will surely develope into what is referred to in these verses. *Planchette* is becoming a household god with many, and is openly advertised in the Spiritist magazines and newspapers. Thousands are being "guided" by "Crystals," *Planchette*, and evil spirits at the present moment. They are "lying spirits," as the scripture calls them. (1 Kings xxii. 22, 23. 2 Chron. xviii. 21, 22). "Deceiving spirits" they are called in 1 Tim. iv. 1, pretending to be whom they are not, and thus gaining a hearing with many. They do speak ; and hence speaking is specially excluded here. It says only that they are not able to *see*, or *hear*, or *walk*. It is the final and full develop-ment of what is called "Spiritualism" which is here referred to, and which calls for the plague of this sixth Trumpet. It Spiritists could see the end to which they are rapidly approaching, some might be alarmed ; and many ministers and religious professors would be prevented from dabbling in the Bible-forbidden "mystery of iniquity." And if Christians, at large, could realize, in only a small degree, the awful nature of these coming judgments and plagues, they would welcome and be thankful for any evidence which exposed their real character and end.

21. **And they repented not of their murders,**

nor of their soceries (or spiritualism), **nor of their fornication** (which will be a great feature of the coming religious apostasy), **nor of their thefts.**] These "sorceries" are the dealings of men with spirit-agencies; accepting the teaching of evil angels and deceiving spirits (1 Tim. iv. 1). The word occurs only here, xviii. 23, and Gal. v. 20, where it is rendered "witchcraft." It is used of the Egyptian sorceries * (Exod. vii. 22) and of the Babylonian (Is. xlvii. 9, 12).

No wonder God has so solemnly warned us against these things, and no wonder such awful judgments are to be visited upon them. (See Lev. xix. 31; xx. 6, 27. Ex. xxii. 18. Deut. xviii. 10. 1 Sam. xxviii. 7. 1 Chron. x. 13. Isa. viii. 19. Acts xvi. 16; &c., &c.)

z. (page 325), x. 1, 2 " *Another Angel* "

We have considered the sounding of the sixth Angel and its results as described in "r" (ix. 13-21) page 325, we now have "Another Angel" in "s" (x. 1-4); and then to complete the whole scene, we have, in "*r*" (x. 5—xi. 14), his actions and their results set forth on exactly the same lines as those of the sixth Angel, in six particulars. The description and activities of this— "another angel" (x. 1-4), differ from that of the sixth Angel, and his own subsequent activities (x. 5—xi. 14). While the sixth Angel's has six members, this, "another angel," has only *four* ("s," page 325). The following is the Structure of the first of these four members :

---

* The word "sorcery" is the old French *sorcerie*, and includes all such things as divination, enchantment, incantation, magic, necromancy, witchcraft, and all things connected with what is called "the black art," culminating in the worship of Satan himself, as prophesied in Rev. xiii., and already known as "the black mass."

a. (page 325), x. 1, 2   *"Another Angel"*

a | i | x. 1-.   His descension from heaven
    k | -1-.   His accessories.   (Cloud ; Rainbow.)
       l | -1-.   His person : (face as the sun)
       l | -1.   His person : (feet as pillars of fire)
    k | 2-.   His accessories.   (The little book)
  i | -2.   His station on the earth

TRANSLATION OF "a " (x. 1, 2)

x. 1.   **And I saw another mighty angel coming
down out of heaven, arrayed with a cloud: and
the * rainbow** was **upon his head, and his face**
was **as the sun, and his feet as pillars of fire:** (2)
and he was **holding† in his hand a little scroll
opened‡: and he set his right foot upon the sea,
and his left upon the earth,]** We are here still
under the effects and consequences of the sounding of the sixth Trumpet.   It is not till xi. 14, that
we have the announcement of this "second woe"
trumpet as being "past."   As chap. vii. was Episodal
to the sixth Seal, so chaps. x.—xi. 14 are Episodal
to the sixth Trumpet.   It continues the same
prophecy of judgment, but introduces new details connected with that judgment ; and new subjects and phases
of it.

It is not one of the Trumpet Angels, but " Another "
and a " mighty " one.   His descent is with great
majesty ; and the cloud betokens his high dignity ; for

---

* G.L.T.Tr.A. WH. and RV. have the article.

† G.L.T.Tr.A. WH. and RV. read the particle.

‡G.L.T.Tr.A. and WH. read ἠνεῳγμένον (ēneōgmenon) *opened*, or
had been opened; instead of ἀνεῳγμένον (aneōgmenon) *open.*

the cloud is generally associated with Divine movements (Ps. xviii. 11 ; civ. 3. Is. xix. 1. Ezek. i. 4. Matt. xxiv. 30. Rev. i. 7).

He comes "down from heaven," as the great antagonist of the "angel of the abyss," who comes up from below, and is enveloped in the cloud of the smoke of the pit.

The book *opened*, or which *had been opened* (according to the revised reading, noted above) points us to chap. v., and seems to show that nothing now remains but to sound the seventh and last Trumpet. This, the angel says (in verse 6), shall take place without further delay. The sealed book has been opened ; and now the little book, not sealed, discloses new directions. John devours its contents and continues his prophetic duty ; while the judgments take different forms and have different subjects. Its contents must surely refer to the future, and begin where the other book (chap. v.) ends. Moreover, it relates specially to Israel and Israel's ancient enemy, Babylon. Michael is the mighty angel that "standeth" for the children of Israel (Dan. xii. 1). He is called with reference to Israel, "Michael your prince" (Dan. x. 21 ; compare verse 13, Jude 9, and Rev. xii. 7). There is no reason why we should take this Angel to be Christ. True, Christ is sometimes called "the Angel of the Covenant," but He is not "another" angel (*i.e.*, another of the same kind, as the word ἄλλος implies). It says "another angel." Let us leave the words as meaning what they say.

Everywhere else in this book Angels mean Angels, and are always distinct from Divine Persons. They are, throughout, the ministers of the Divine will. They are invested with such delegated glory and attributes as befits their special missions respectively. It may

well be the " strong angel " of chap. v. 2 or viii. 3; but
there is no need to identify him, as he is not identified
here in this scripture.

The setting or planting of his feet on sea and land is
the formal taking possession of both; or the formal
expression of the purpose to do so. In Deut. xi. 24 it
was said to Israel, "every place whereon the soles of
your feet shall tread shall be yours." Judgment has
long since been pronounced (John xii. 31; xvi. 11). A
judgment-summons has been issued (Rev. v.), and now,
at length, execution is to be put in. The right to
execute this judgment has been established in the fifth
chapter; and here we have the assertion of that right,
and the expressed determination to enforce it.

In verses 3 and 4 we have His cry. The following
is the Structure:

b. (page 325), x. 3, 4. *His cry*

b | m | x. 3-. Occasion. ὅτε, " and when . . .
      n | -3. Action. " Seven thunders uttered . . .
   m | x. 4-. Occasion. ὅτε, " and when . . .
      n | -4. Action. " I was about to write . . .

x. 3. **And he cried with a loud voice, even as** when
**a lion roareth : and when he cried, the seven thun-
ders uttered their voices.** (4) **And when the seven
thunders had *spoken, I was about to write: and I
heard a voice from heaven, saying,†**
> **" Seal up the things which the seven
> thunders spoke, And do not write
> them."**]

---

* G.L.T.Tr.A. WH. and RV. read "spoken" instead of "uttered
their voices."

† Omit " to me," G. L.T.Tr.A. WH. and RV.

It was not a cry of distress or fear; but a shout of power, telling of the coming execution of judgment. The prophets have foretold of this roaring cry, which the LORD, by His agents and messengers, will cause to be heard. (See Joel iii. 16. Jer. xxv. 29-31.) This cry is at once answered by a "voice from heaven" (v. ·4·).

The definite article here marks these seven thunders. In chap. iv. 5 they are spoken of generally; here the seven are particularised. They may have been consecutive, and heard by John "in heaven" as thunder, just as when a voice from heaven spoke to the Lord Jesus on earth some of the people "said that it thundered; others said, an angel spake to him" (John xii. 29). These may have been angel-voices, the effect (thunder) being put, by *Metonymy*, for the cause.

John heard what the thunders said, and understood; for he was about to write. But God, in order to conceal them, ordered John not to write. Some would have us believe that these seven thunders are the Papal Bulls issued against Luther and the Reformation.* If this be so, then God sealed the book in vain! for all know what those thunders uttered. No, God's purpose in this book is very different from man's ideas of it. God has caused it to be written in order to make things known to us. Man treats it as though what is written is to conceal what is said, and make it incomprehensible.

In chap. xxii. 10, John was told "*Seal not* the words of the prophecy of this book." But there were certain things sealed up, as there were with Daniel (see Dan. viii. 26, 27; xii. 9). A whole dispensation was to pass

---

* Elliott, vol. ii., p. 100, etc.

before Daniel's words could be known. But her э, " the season is near."

The actions of this angel and their results are then set forth in exactly the same form as were those of the sixth angel in ix. 13-21. They correspond in the same six particulars. See "*r*," page 325, where, in x. 5—xi. 14, we have them duly displayed.

r (page 325). x. 5-11. *Another Angel—(continued)*

x. 5. **And the angel whom I saw standing upon the sea and on the earth lifted up his right hand towards heaven (6) and sware by Him that liveth for ever and ever, who created the heaven, and the things that are therein, and the earth, and the things that are therein, and the sea, and the things that are therein,* that " there shall be no longer delay: "]** *i.e.*, time should no longer intervene. The allusion is still to the martyrs' cry for vengeance in vi. 10, 11. Indeed, the whole series of these Trumpet-judgments (the seventh of which expands into the seven Vials) is the answer to those prayers (the formal offering of which takes place under the seventh Seal). It was said to them " that they should rest yet for a little season until their fellow-servants also and their brethren that should be killed as they were should be fulfilled."

That time is now about to be fulfilled; and the execution of final vengeance, should no longer be delayed. That this is the meaning is clear from the words which immediately follow.

7. **But, in the days of the sound of the seventh angel, when he is about to sound his trumpet,** then

---

* Lachmann omits this sentence.

shall have been completed also the secret of God, as he announced the good news to His servants the prophets] The oath seems fatal to the theory that makes this angel to be the Lord Jesus Christ; especially in the face of Matt. v. 33-37. Jas. v. 12. But here, "another angel" is commissioned by God to make a formal announcement which only He Himself could know. "In the days" is a remarkable expression; and denotes that the days commence with his sounding, which develops into the seven final plagues of the seven Vials. These will complete the judgments which God had hitherto kept secret. It is quite unnecessary to take the word "mystery" or secret, here, in the Pauline sense. In the Ephesian Epistle it is used with reference to "the Body of Christ." Though before this (Rom. xi. 25) we have the secret of the *duration* of Israel's blindness spoken of; and in 1 Cor. xv. 51, the "secret" that all should not die. In Matt. xiii. 10, 11, and 34, 35 we have secrets concerning the kingdom. When we have these other secrets connected with Israel and the Kingdom, why should we go to Ephesians and Colossians and fix on the "great" secret, and confine it to that? All are God's secrets, and each may be so called; but to introduce the Church of God here, is wholly unnecessary, because it tends only to create confusion where all is perfectly clear without it. The secret, here, refers to what had already been made known by God to his servants the prophets. The word "servants" identifies these with the Old Testament prophets. The great secret "concerning Christ and the Church" was made known only to the New Testament prophets; the prophets given to and for the Church. (See Eph. iv. 11. 1 Cor. xii. 28. Rom. xvi. 25, 26.

So Eph. ii 20 and iii. 5). God has revealed the secret
of coming judgment to " his servants the prophets," as
it is written : " Surely, Adonai Jehovah will do nothing,
but he revealeth his secret unto his servants the
prophets " (Amos iii. 7). It is then in the Old Testament that we are to look for the announcements of these
secrets ; and we have done so in our many and constant references to the prophecies of the Old Testament
which will receive their fulfilment in " the Day of the
Lord." And in the days when the seventh angel shall
sound they will be completed, for his sounding calls
for the pouring forth of the seven Vials which will fill
up the cup of Divine Vengeance, and answer the cry
of the martyrs' blood.

8. **And the voice which I heard out of heaven**
I heard **again speaking with me, and saying, " Go,
take the scroll*** **which lieth open in the hand of the
angel that standeth upon the sea and upon the
earth."** (9) **And I went up to the angel, saying unto
him, " Give me the little scroll." And he saith unto
me, " Take, and eat it up; and it shall make thy
belly bitter, but in thy mouth shall be sweet as
honey."** (10) **And I took the little scroll out of the
hand of the angel, and ate it up; and it was in my
mouth sweet as honey : and when I had eaten it my
belly was made bitter.** (11) **And they say**† **to me,
" Thou must again prophecy against peoples,
and nations, and tongues, and many kings "**] The
eating of the book has its counterpart in Ezek. ii. 9
and iii. 3. Ezekiel ate the roll of the book given to

---

* L. Tr. A. WH. and RV. read βιβλίον (*biblion*) *book*, instead of
βιβλαριδιον (*biblaridion*) *little book.*

† So L.T.Tr.A. WH. and RV.

him, and it was in his mouth as honey for sweetness. The bitterness he describes in verse 14, saying, " I went in bitterness and in the heat of my spirit." " Eating " is a Hebrew idiom for *receiving knowledge*; just as we idiomatically use the word *digesting* of considering what we have learnt. Ezekiel ate that he might speak with God's words (Ezek. iii. 4). So in John vi., the eating and drinking of Christ is explained as believing on Him; compare verses 47 and 48 with 53 and 54. See also 1 Cor. xii. 13 compared with Luke xiii. 15. In Ezek. iii. 10 it is explained as receiving in the heart; compare Deut. xxxi. 26. Jer. xxxi. 33. If any prefer to take it literally, there is no reason why they should not do so. It is better to err on that side, than to have the responsibility of erring on the other. In either case, the result is the same. There was *sweetness* in the assurance that the prayers of God's Israel, who had "cried day and night unto Him," were about to be answered. There was *bitterness* in the solemn announcements of the awful judgments which were to form that answer.

The last sentence is peculiar and important. " They say unto me," *i.e.*, the Angel and the other voices which had before spoken, "thou must prophecy again *against* peoples," etc. ἐπί (*epi*), with the Dative following, means, literally, *upon*. It is never rendered " before," except in this place. Six times it is rendered "against"; in Luke xii. 52, 53.* In the RV. it is " over." Margin *concerning*.

---

* Like the Hebrew עַל (*al*). See Judges xvi. 12. Job xvi. 4, 9 10 ; xix. 12 ; xxi. 27 ; xxx. 12 ; xxxiii. 10. Isa. ix. 20. Ezek. iv. 7 ; v. 8 ; xi. 4 ; xiii. 17 ; xxv. 2 ; xxviii. 21, etc.

In the chapters immediately following (chaps. **xi.**—xviii.) these prophecies are clearly seen. The contrast between "kings" and "nations" and "peoples" prove to us that we cannot take these kings as referring to *systems* religious or political.

The contrast also with the historical interpretation is very clear. The angel here *descends*. This, we are asked to believe, is the "sun of righteousness *rising* over Europe." The cry like a lion is, we are told, "the preaching of Luther." But others tell us it was the Papal Bulls: others, that it was the "shout of the Wittenbergers when Luther burnt the Pope's Bull." But these voices and thunders came from *heaven*. They do not come from Rome, nor were they made in Germany. John was commanded to "seal up" what he heard; Luther made it known. We need not go further. The bare statement of such wild extravagancies are their own, sufficient and best, refutation.

THE TWO WITNESSES

y. (page 325), xi. 1-14. *The Two Witnesses*

o�ʳ. (page 346), xi. 1,2. *The Measuring of the Temple*

The second Vision "on Earth," which consists of the six Trumpets, is given to us in three parts.

(1) The Immediate judgments or plagues which follow its sounding: (r. page 325. Ch. ix. 13-21)

(2) The Episode of "another mighty Angel;" His oath and the little book: (s. and *r.* page 325 Chap. x. 1-11)

(3) The Two Witnesses: (*y.* pages 325 and 346 Chap. xi. 1-14)

The connection of the three is continuous and close. It is the same angel who addresses John throughout:

and the command "Rise, and measure" is only a sequel to "Seal up" (x. 4), and "Take, and eat" (x. 9).

Chap. xi., etc., is the fulfilment of the command "Thou shalt prophesy": taking prophesying as being witnessing in its widest sense.

The descent of "another mighty angel" (x. 1) is, as we have seen, the formal taking possession of the earth in the name of the King of Kings, before actual occupation takes place (which is not till chap. xix.), though it is celebrated by anticipation in the next Vision "in heaven" (xi. 15). Two earthly Witnesses are added to the making of the claim as the accredited agents of the throne. They are the link between the judgments and men's sins which are the cause of them. Their witness is a comfirmation of the faith of God's people then on the earth, and a witness to the "dwellers on the earth" that the end is near, and the interval of delay will last "no longer."

(1) The angel takes possession by planting his feet on the sea and on the earth;

(2) John takes possession by measuring out part of the territory occupied; and

(3) The Two Witnesses take possession by prophesying in Divine and miraculous power.

Just as after the sixth Seal there was an Episode relating the protection and deliverance of God's people then to be on the earth: so here, after or at the end of the sixth Trumpet, there is a similar Episode with a similar object, viz., to show that with all the external destruction that shall go on, there shall be the preservation of all that is essential to God's purposes, and to God's People.

This third Episode of the sixth Trumpet is one whole, and is recorded in chap. xi. 1-14, completing at once the sixth Trumpet and the second Woe. The seventh Trumpet, which follows, is expanded into, and consists of, the seven Vials of wrath, which speedily prove that there is no more delay, and bring on the consummation in chap. xix.

We do not propose, here, to trouble our readers with all the conflicting interpretations of this chapter. Some are half symbolical and half literal. Others are wholly ridiculous. Of course, the " The *Temple* is said to mean the church ; the *altar*, Christ ; the *porch without* means heretics and pseudo-Christians." Others hold that John was " not only ignorant of the future, but that he designed nothing more than to express his *hopes*, and give vent to his remaining Jewish sympathies for the literal temple and its ritual" (Stuart, Heinrichs, Ewald, Bleek, &c).

The Structure of the whole passage tells us that we are dealing with something far more important than all this ; even with what shall yet take place in connection with future judgment-scenes preparatory to the final ejection of the great usurper from God's Earth, over which he has so long held sway.

Let us therefore approach this scene, not with the view, merely, of interpreting it ; but of receiving it and *believing* it as God's own interpretation of real events which are yet to take place. God is telling us of some of the " marvels " and of the "terrible things " which He will do in the Day of the Lord. Let us not bring it down to " man's day " and treat it as mere Ecclesiastical or Roman history. This it is which causes all the difficulty, combined with the yet greater difficulty which man ever finds in believing God.

The Structure of the whole passage is as follows :—

```
y.  (page 325). xi. 1-14.   The Two Witnesses.

y | o¹ | p¹ | xi. 1-. | Person.  John
  |    | q¹ | -1-.    | What he was to do.  To measure
  |    |    | r¹ | -1, 2-.  | Commencement
  | o² | p² | -2-.    | Persons.  The Gentiles
  |    | q² | -2-.    | What they were to do.  To trample
  |    |    | r² | -2.      | Continuance : 42 months
  | o³ | p³ | 3-.     | Persons.  The two Witnesses
  |    | q³ | -3-.    | What they were to do.  To prophesy
  |    |    | r³ | -3.      | Continuance : 1260 days
  | o⁴ | p⁴ | 4.      | Persons.  The two olive trees
  |    | q⁴ | 5, 6.   | What they were to do.  To inflict judgments
  |    |    | r⁴ | 7-14.    | Conclusion : " After three days and a half "
  |    |    |    |          | " The second woe is past "
```

xi. 1. And there was given to me a reed] by whom, it is not said.   It is indefinite, as in vi. 11 ; viii, 2, &c

like a measuring rod: and he* (*i.e.*, the angel who continued speaking with him) **said**] Bishop Wordsworth imagines that it is the *reed* that speaks. He says, " The reed speaks: it is inspired ; the Spirit is in it; it is the word of God, and it measures the church : that is, the Canon of Scripture is the Rule of Faith."†

Rise, and measure the Naos (or Temple) **of God,**] Observe the word is ναός (*naos*), the holy place; not ἱερόν (*hieron*), the temple-building as a whole.   The two words must always be carefully distinguished.   It is a pity that the AV. confuses both by rendering them " temple" indiscriminately.

This reed was a light measuring rod.   The Heb. שֵׁבֶט (*shevet*), *staff*, also means a measuring-rod (Ps· lxxiv. 2. Jer. x. 16; li. 19).   In Ezek. xl. 3, etc., the object was for the building of a new Temple.   Here (*v.* 2) it is for destruction, as in Lam. ii. 8. 2 Kings xxi. 13. Isa. xxxiv. 11. Amos vii. 8, 9.   It is also (*v.* 1) for protection, as in Zech. ii. 1-5.   Part was holy and part profane.   There is no difficulty whatever if we leave the Temple alone.   But if we say (with Alford and others) that it means " the church of the elect servants of God, everywhere in this book symbolized by Jews in deed and truth," then we create difficulties which are insurmountable ; for how John was to measure the Church we are at a loss to understand.

That there is to be a " Temple of God " in Jerusalem is clear from 2 Thess. ii. 4, for Antichrist is to sit as

---

*G.L.T.Tr.A. WH. and RV. omit "and the angel stood," which are only in the Elzivir edition (1624) of the Received Text ; and not in Stephens's edition, 1550.

† *Lectures on the Apocalypse*, in loco.

God there ; and " the abomination of desolation" is to be there set up (Matt. xxiv. 15).

One would have thought that the words employed here would have effectually shut out the church from the interpretation. We read of the Temple, the Altar, and the Court of the Gentiles, which surely have nothing to do with the church of God. Even Dr. Adam Clarke admits that " this must refer to the temple of Jerusalem," though he confesses he does not know what to do with it ! We confess that we have no wish to do anything with it. We know that it will be re-built, and once we recognise that, there is no need to fix the period at seven years after the church is caught up ; but to understand that these seven years may be the *Telos* or last seven of some thirty or forty years of the *Sunteleia*. See pages 88, 89 and 249, where it is shown that there is ample time for all this and much more to be done in bringing about the fulfilment of all that is written in this book. God has not yet done with His people Israel. They are already, though in partial blindness (Rom. xi. 25), feeling their way back to their land, and to a restoration of their national Polity. Since the year 1896, the Zionist movement has been at work to this end. We regard this as leading directly up to this longer period, the *Sunteleia* (ending with the seven years of Daniel's last week, the *Telos*), and after the church has been caught up, the movement will rapidly develop and issue in the re-settlement of the Jews in their Land and City in partial independence, but in unbelief. It may be at first under the suzerainty of Turkey, or the protection of the Great Powers ; until *he* arises who will make a covenant with them,

and bring on such events as will be the crisis or end of
" the Great Tribulation."

and the altar,] By being mentioned separately from
the *Naos* (in which was the golden altar of incense) it
looks as though the brazen altar of sacrifice· was
intended. The word will suit either.

and take account of **those who worship therein.**]
Although the Zionist movement does not openly profess
to act under Divine authority, that is no reason why it
should not be most *religious.* Hence there will be
worshippers : and among the worshippers the 144,000
sealed for Divine protection ; beside those who
suffer martyrdom at the hands of the Beast, and those
with whom he makes war.

Such a condition of things will need a re-survey when
God is going to take action. He will separate the
chaff from the wheat, Israel from the Gentiles, and His
" servants " from the " dwellers on the earth."

In this command with regard to the worshippers, we
must recognise the figure called *Zeugma,* by which one
verb is used of two things, and is strictly appropriate
only to the former. A second verb must be supplied
for the second noun, properly related to it. We have
here supplied the verb " take account of " (λόγισαι); for
measuring, while quite appropriate to building, is incongruous when used of persons.

2. But the court that is without the Naos (or
Temple) **cast without, and measure it not ; because
it is given up to the Gentiles : and the holy city
shall they tread under foot forty and two months.**]
The *Court* of the Temple is thus distinguished from
the *Naos.* The former is owned by God ; the latter is

rejected and delivered over to the Gentiles. These are distinguished in Luke i. 22.

We must again remind ourselves that we have here what relates to the *Earth*. Had expositors noticed that this was the second Vision of what takes place " on earth," they could never have supposed that the Temple, etc., here was the Temple in heaven. To apply this measuring and treading down by the Gentiles to heaven betokens confusion of mind, and brings hopeless confusion into the Sciptures, besides showing a very poor idea of what heaven is.

The outer court of this Temple is ordered to be rejected ; and the reason is given. It is given over to the Gentiles. This, of itself, is sufficient to establish the fact that we are here in another Dispensation. During this present Dispensation Jews and Gentiles stand on the same level. There is " no difference " (Rom. iii. 22 ; both are equally sinners before God, and both need the same Saviour. The Church of God cannot be here, for in Col. iii. 11 we are distinctly told that now there is " neither Greek (*i.e.*, Gentile) nor Jew, circumcision nor uncircumcision, Barbarism, Scythian, bond nor free ; but Christ is all and in all." But here (in chap. xi.) the Jews are again in remembrance for the father's sake, and the Gentiles are put back to the place which they occupied in the former Dispensation. This measurement of the Temple, etc., is the formal acknowledgment of the Jew again, and the re-grafting him on his own olive-tree ; and it is the formal putting back of the Gentiles from the privilege and position which they hold under the present Dispensation. The " middle wall of partition," which is now " broken

down " (Eph. ii, 14), is to be again built up, and this
measurement is the proof of it.

The " court " of the Temple and the city is given
over to be " trodden under foot " by the Gentiles. It
is given over to the Gentiles for a special treading
down, and for a definite period. The period of 42
months is connected with the measuring. It closely
follows it in order of time. We dare not reverse
the two events. This proves, again, that the
Church cannot be here, because it could not be
at one and the same time delivered from Papal
oppression, and yet still be under that oppression. In
other words the treading down of the true Church by
Rome, preceeded the Reformation (which is said by the
Historicists to be denoted by the measuring) ; whereas,
here, the order is opposite. This, at once, effectually
disposes of the historical interpretation.

As to the period of " forty and two months " Alford
truly says "no solution at all approaching to a satis-
factory one has ever yet been given of any one of these
periods. This being so, my principle is to regard them
as still among the things unknown to the Church."*
But why ? Why does this period require any " solution " at all ? When it makes known a fact to us as to
the duration of a certain period, Why regard that
period as " among the things unknown " ? "Secret things
(we read) belong unto the LORD our God, but those things
which are revealed belong to us and to our children for
ever " (Deut. xxix. 29). Surely this period of " forty
two months " is among the things that are " revealed."
It is not a " secret" thing ; and therefore, being revealed,
we are not to regard it as " unknown," but as among

---

* Comm. *in loco.*

the things which we assuredly know; and that, upon Divine authority. The great "solution" of this (and similar difficulties) is to believe that the words mean what they say: that "months" mean "months"; and "forty-two" mean forty-two. There is no difficulty then. All is natural, simple and easy. The "city" is literal. The treading down is literal. The Gentiles are literal. Why is not the duration of their oppression of the holy city literal also? And when this duration is given to us as "forty and two months" (or 3½ years), why should it need any so called "solution"? It matters not how great or learned the men may be who offer us these solutions. They are all vain imaginations; and mere fancy-work, which only obscures instead of elucidating the word of God.

Something more than learning is needed when we come to His book. Faith is the great thing needed, and if we possess this we shall have to unlearn much that man has taught us.

  y. (page 325), xi. 3-14. *The Two Witnesses*
 o³ (page 346), xi. 3. *Their Endowment and Testimony*

In xi. 3-14 we have the account of the Two Witnesses, one of the most solemn and mysterious scenes of the whole Apocalypse. It is the test of all interpretations, and one over which many make shipwreck. The particulars of the mission of these Two Witnesses are given with great detail.

In verses 3 and 4 we have, first, their Equipment and endowment; *vv.* 5, 6, their Judgments on their enemies and the elements; *vv.* 7-10, their Sufferings; *vv.* 11-12, their Reward; and *v.* 13, their Avengement. These divisions will be seen to be marked off by the Structures given below (see pages 357 and 359).

xi. 3. **And I will endow my two witnesses, and they shall prophesy a thousand two hundred and sixty days, clothed in sackcloth.**] Literally, it is " I will give," but as there is the *Ellipsis* of the object, it does not say what is given. The AV. supplies the word "*power*." The RV. supplies nothing, but renders it baldly : " I will give to my two witnesses and they shall prophecy," etc. We have (with Tregelles) avoided both by rendering the word " endow," which includes "*power*," and whatever other gifts were necessary for their mission. The duration of their prophecy covers an exactly similar period as the 42 months : for it is 1260 days. We are not told that it is the same period as the treading down, but it reads as though the two periods were synchronous. The computation is given in *months*, for these seem to have a special relation to judgments. The beginning and duration of the Flood is given in months. The Plague of Locusts is to be "five months." The blasphemies and persecutions of the Beast are reckoned by months. But when it comes to *man*, the duration of his years are reckoned by " days" (Gen. xlvii. 9, 28 ; Ps. xc. 10, 12 ; cxix. 84, &c.). Our life is lived by days. And the testimony of these Two Witnesses is to be given by days, day by day.

The period is given in three forms in the Apocalypse.

> Forty-two months—xi. 2 ; xiii. 5
> 1260 days—xi. 3 ; xii. 6
> A time, times, and a half (3½ years), xii. 14 ;
> and see Dan. vii. 25 ; xii. 7

The duration of the period in which Elijah's prayer shut up the heaven corresponds with this, and is given as "three years and six months" (Luke iv. 25, Jas. v. 17).

p⁴ (page 346), xi. 4. *The Two Olive Trees*

xi. 4. These are (or represent) **the two olive trees, and the two lampstands which stand before the Lord* of the earth.**] The Divine title here used tells us that the events here recorded refer to the *Earth*; for this is the special title which the Holy Spirit uses when right to dominion and authority in the Earth is asserted. The title is first used in Joshua iii. 11, 13 where Jehovah claims the right to give the Earth to whom He will (Ps. cxv. 16). But the reference is to Zech. iv., where, in verse 14, the title is again used. Now, while Israel is *Lo-Ammi* ("not my People"), the title used with respect to Israel is "the God of Heaven" (See Ezra, Neh., and Dan. ii. 18, 28, 37, 44, &c.); *i.e.,* the God who no longer dwells between the Cherubim, in the midst of His People; but who has withdrawn Himself from them and removed to a distance; God who is now known to Israel as "the God of Heaven." Hence, in Rev. xi. when He again assumes direct relationship with Israel and the Earth; it is as "the Lord of the Earth" that He will be known. The two Olive Trees in Zech. iv. are there explained as denoting Zerubbabel the prince, and Jeshua the high priest. And when it says here in Rev. xi. 4: "These (two Witnesses) are the two Olive trees, the Figure is *Metaphor*, and the verb "are" means *represents*. "These represent the two Olive trees," etc. This is the Spirit's own explanation of these two Witnesses. Just as Zerubbabel and Jeshua were raised up, and gifted, and Divinely endowed, and protected against Satan's assaults, so in the coming day of Israel's acknowledgment by

---

*G.L.T.Tr.A. WH. and RV. read κυρίου (*kyriou*) *Lord,* instead of θεοῦ (*theou*) *God.*

God, two other great Witnesses from God will be raised up, corresponding to them, occupying a similar position as the depositories of Heavenly power and wisdom, and exercising a similar ministry.

The two Olive Trees represented two individuals *then* ; and they represent two individuals here in this Scripture. They will be the " two Olive Trees " for their day, as Zerubbabel and Jeshua were in a former day.

The Angel gave the essence of the meaning to Zechariah ; and the same is the meaning here. The secret Divine supply of oil to these two Trees and Lamp-stands illustrates the great reality—" This is the word of the Lord unto Zerubbabel, saying, Not by might (marg. *armies*), nor by power, but by my Spirit, saith the Lord of hosts" (Zech. iv. 6). That is to say, it was a material representation of mighty spiritual potencies which were coming forth from the Spirit of God to give success and power to Zerubbabel and Jeshua for the completion of the work in which they were then engaged. That work was the restoration of Jerusalem, its temple, and its worship. In like manner shall these Two Witnesses be spiritually endowed with still greater power for a greater work, which will be carried out in face of the opposition of more formidable enemies. In that day Satan was present to " resist " (Zech. iii. 1, etc.) : and the Lord, who had " chosen Jerusalem," was present to " rebuke " him. So here, Satan will be indeed present ; and his resistance will reach its highest point : hence these Two Witnesses must needs be equipped as witnesses never were before, in order to carry out and fulfil their testimony.

Expositors have exhausted their ingenuity in endeavouring to answer the question, which they all ask,

" Who are the two witnesses?" We do not ask the question, and therefore we have nothing to answer. Why cannot we leave them alone? If God wished us to know He could have told us. The fact that He has not done so ought to stop our mouths. The wildest extravagances have been indulged in from the earliest times, and it would fill very many pages if we were merely to name them. They would require no refutation, for they are all mutually destructive of one another. Alford says: " No solution has ever been given of this portion of the prophecy." He means, of course, no satisfactory solution, for the interpretations themselves are innumerable.

Malachi (iii. iv.) speaks of Elijah as coming to restore all things; and the Lord Himself endorses it in Matt. xi. 14; xvii. 11-13. In one sense (He explains) *he had come* in the person of John the Baptist who ministered in the "spirit and power " of Elijah (Luke i. 17). But this was conditional: " If ye will receive it." They did not receive it; and, therefore, in another sense *he was yet to come.* This undoubted prophetic truth has led some expositors to add another witness to Elijah, so as to make the " two " Witnesses here foretold. They are not agreed whether it should be Moses (as on the Mount of Transfiguration) or Enoch. So we must perforce wait. What is *certain* is, that in the coming day of Israel's recognition and in the days of the Beast, God will raise up two individual men, whom he will call " MY two witnesses," and will endow them with wondrous powers to enable them to carry out the commission which He will then give them. Beyond this it is neither necessary nor desirable for us to go.

We now come to their power to inflict judgments,

which is given us in verses 5, 6.   It is important, for the Structure of these two verses is as follows :—

Judgments on their enemies   Judgments on the elements

q⁴ (page 346), xi. 5, 6.   *The Infliction of Judgments*

q⁴ | s

t¹ | 5-. Injury. " And if any man will hurt them
u¹ | -5-. Retribution. "fire proceedeth out of their mouth ...

t² | -5-. Injury. " And if any man will hurt them,
u² | -5. Retribution. "he must in this manner be killed

t³ | 6-. Power. " These have power
  u³ | w¹ | -6-. Object. "to shut heaven
      x¹ | -6-. Drought. "that it rain not
      v¹ | -6-. Time (total) "in the days of their prophecy

t⁴ | -6-. Power. " And have power
  u⁴ | w² | -6-. Object. "over waters,
      x² | -6-. Effect. "to turn them to blood,
      w³ | -6-. Object. "and to smite the earth
      x³ | -6-. Effect. "with all plagues,
      v² | -6. Time (occasional) "as often as they will"

We have included the translation of the AV. in the Structure, but we give our own here, for the sake of uniformity :

xi. 5. **And if any one desireth to injure them, fire goeth forth out of their mouth** (2 Kings i. 10 ; Jer. v. 14), **and devoureth their enemies : and if any-one desireth to injure them, thus must he be killed.** (6) **These have authority to shut the heaven** (1 Kings xvii. 1), **so that no rain may fall during the days** (the 1260 days) **of their prophecy : and they have authority over the waters to turn them into blood,** (Ex. vii. 19), **and to smite** (xix. 15) **the earth with every plague, as often as they will]** It is impossible to make this harmonise with the powers and functions of any Ministry during this present Dispensation of "the gospel of the grace of God." Its ministers are to be " harmless " (Phil. ii. 15. Rom. xvi. 19). This is their characteristic. But this Vision refers to Judgment-times and Kingdom-scenes, affecting the Jew and the Gentile, but not the church of God. Alford's weighty comment on this is worthy of attention. He says * " this whole description is most difficult to apply, on the allegorical interpretation ; as is that which follows. ʿAnd, as might have been expected, the allegorists halt, and are perplexed exceedingly. The double announcement here seems to stamp the literal sense, and the εἰ τις [if any one] and δεῖ αὐτὸν ἀποκτανθῆναι [he must be killed] are decisive against any mere *national* application of the words (as Elliott). Individuality could not be more strongly indicated."

---

* Comm. *in loco.*

Interpreters talk about the "political heaven"! We may well ask what is political rain? We can only say that Scripture knows nothing of either.

r⁴ (p. 346), xi. 7-13. *The Completion of their Testimony*

The *completion* of their testimony (xi. 7-14) marks a distinct portion of their history and description here given. It is as strongly emphasised as is the *nature* of it. This is shown by the beautiful Structure which sets it forth.

Three things are shown to characterise the completion of their testimony:

1. *vv.* 7-10.   Their Sufferings
2. *vv.* 11, 12.   Their Reward
3. *v.* 13.   Their Avengement

r⁴ (p. 346), xi. 7-13. *The Completion of their Testimony*

r⁴ | a | c | 7-. Time. "And when . . . ⎫
            d | -7. Death. "The beast . . .   ⎪ Their
              e | 8, 9. The City. Bodies lie in its street ⎬ Sufferings
                f | 10. Enemies rejoice   ⎭

        b | g | 11-. The spirit from heaven ⎫
              h | -11-. Resurrection   ⎪ Their
                i | -11. Enemies see   ⎬ Reward
          b | *g* | 12-. The Voice from heaven ⎪
                 h | -12-. Ascension   ⎪
                   i | -12. Enemies see   ⎭

   a | c | 13-. Time. "And the same hour . . . ⎫
            d | -13-. Earthquake   ⎪ Their
              e | -13-. The City. Tenth part falls ⎬ Avengement
                f | -13. Enemies slain   ⎭

No harm can come to them during their witness. Not till their testimony is completed can they be injured or overcome. Till then they are invulnerable. As with "the Faithful Witness" Himself, so with them. Not till His hour had come could His enemies lay their hands on Him. (See John vii. 6, 8, 30; viii. 20; xii. 23; xiii. 1; xvii. 1, 11).

xi. 7. **And when they shall have finished their testimony, the Beast that cometh up out of the abyss shall make war upon them** (xii. 17; xiii. 7; xix. 19. Dan. vii. 21), **and shall overcome them, and kill them.**] This shows that these Witnesses are upon the earth during the thirteenth chapter; and that the Beast is on the Earth during the eleventh chapter. The account of the *rise* of the Beast is postponed till ch. xiii., but his actual revelation must already have taken place a long time before. The events recorded in the twelfth chapter must also have then taken place. We must remember, therefore, that when we come to chap. xii., we are, chronologically, taken back and told what will have previously happened. Just as an author to-day takes us by one line of events up to a certain point, and then goes back, and by another line of events reaches the same point again. All through these judgment scenes, or, at any rate, the greater part of them, the Beast is on the earth, and it is against him and his forces that the plagues of the Seals and the Trumpets are directed. This fact is often overlooked in the interpretation of chaps. vi.-xi., but it must be allowed its full weight in our present consideration of the Apocalypse. It is clear from this verse that the whole period of their testimony will be at an end when that which is here said shall take place. The allegorists attempt to escape this by assuming that it means any one complete delivery of it which other witnesses might have continued. But this is impossible; as is the interpretation of the Two Witnesses, as being the Old and New Testaments (as Bishop Wordsworth does). How these can become a corpse passes our understanding. For see the next verse.

8. **And their dead body*** (or corpse) **shall lie on the street of the great city, which is called spiritually Sodom, and Egypt,]**

Here, then, in the street of "the great city" Jerusalem, these two witnesses will be slain, and Ps. lxxix. will receive its fulfilment, for it is to this very time that it refers.

"O God, the heathen are come into thine inheritance;
Thy holy temple have they defiled;
They have laid Jerusalem on heaps.
The *dead bodies of thy servants* have they given to be meat unto the fowls of the heaven,
The flesh of thy saints unto the beasts of the earth,
Their blood have they shed like water on every side of Jerusalem,
And *there was none to bury them.*"

The whole Psalm should be read in this connection, as well as Psalms ix. and x., which relate to these very "times of trouble" (ix. 9; x. 1) when the "wicked

---

*All the Critical Texts read the singular instead of the plural. Wordsworth thinks this is mystical, and means "the two Testaments are one." But the *plural* is used in verse 9, which disposes of this conceit.

man," or "the man of the earth" oppresses and slays the saints of God.

where their* Lord also, was crucified] So jealous is the Holy Spirit over His words, that He effectually prevents any allegorical interpretation here. Lest any-one should for a moment think He meant " Sodom " and " Egypt," He not only says it is only " spiritually " called by these names, but also immediately adds " where their Lord also was crucified "; and yet, in spite of this, interpreters—for example, Alford—say, " not Jerusalem, which is never called by this name "; *i.e.*, " the great city." But it is so called in Neh. vii. 3, 4. Jer. xxii. 5, 7-9. (Compare Jer. v. 1. 2 Chron. xxxii. 6.) One would think " where their Lord was crucified" would settle the matter. But, no! he says, " It is true, He was crucified at Jerusalem ; but it is also true that He was crucified, not in, but outside, the city." Was ever such interpretation heard of ? It is sufficient to notice that it does not say " in," but " where." (ὅπου, *hopou*). A Sunday-school child could tell us where the Lord was crucified; but these learned men cannot. They say "the great city " here means " the church of God"! Well, what is gained by this ? Was "the church of God " the place where the Lord was crucified ? And is "the church of God" spiritually called "Sodom" and "Egypt"? The fact is, that these proper names are used to describe the character and condition in a spiritual and moral sense. What the character of " Sodom " was, we know from Gen. xviii.; xix. ; and 2 Pet. ii. 6. What that of " Egypt " was, we know from Ex. i.-xv.

---

* G.L.T.Tr.A. WH. and RV. read αὐτῶν (*autōn*) *their*, instead of ἡμῶν (*hemōn*) *our*.

Jerusalem is compared to "Sodom" in Isa. i. 9, 10; iii. 8, 9. Jer. xxiii. 14; and in the Song of Moses, which refers to these very times, Deut. xxxii. 30-33. It is also spiritually likened to "Egypt" in Ezek. xxiii. 3, 4, 8, 19, because of the adoption of the customs and vices of Egypt. There is another reason why they may be spiritually so called; and that is, because both were visited with judgments and plagues similar to those described in this prophecy. But, beyond this, lest there should be any doubt left in the reader's mind, or any danger of being misled by the use of these names, it is added, " where their Lord also was crucified."

9. **And the peoples** (*lit.,* by Hebrew idiom, "some of the peoples") **and tribes and tongues and nations, look upon their corpse* three days and a half, and do not suffer their† corpses to be put into a tomb.‡]** The "year-day" theory surely breaks down here, for corpses could hardly lie exposed for three years and a half! But to avoid this difficulty, we are told that these are not corpses! According to Elliott, the period is that which elapsed between the ninth session of the Lateran Council, and the posting up of his Theses by Luther at Wittenberg. This fulfils the prophecy, he says, "precisely to a day." But, unfortunately, he has to take the three years (from May 5th, 1514, to May 5th, 1517) as years of 365 days, and the half year (from May 5th, 1517 to October 31st of the same year) as a year of 360 days; *i.e.,* two days and a half short of the "precisely to a day." And yet in the face of this he

---

* See above.

† So L.T.Tr.A. WH. and RV.

‡ So G.L.T.Tr.A. WH. and RV.

exclaims " O wonderful prophecy ! O the depth of the riches of the wisdom and of the foreknowledge of God !"

Bishop Wordsworth is equally unfortunate, for he builds on the amended reading " tomb," or sepulchre (which he takes to mean *monument*), this fantastic inter-pretation, that Papal Rome (the Wild Beast) " has laboured that the two witnesses [*i.e.*, the Old and New Testaments] may not be committed to the immortal *monuments* of Editions, Translations, and Expositions.' It is fatal to this theory, (1) that μνῆμα (*mnēma*) never means anything but grave, tomb, or sepulchre,* and (2) that we are indebted to Papal Rome for the only edition of the oldest published Codex, of the Old and New Testament know as the Vatican Codex (B). But such interpretations need no serious disproof.

The tenth verse, in which their enemies look upon their dead bodies, is thus constructed :

f. (page 359), xi. 10. *Enemies rejoice*

f | k | 10-. Dwellers on the earth
        l | -10-. Rejoicings
        l | -10-. Torments
        | -10. Dwellers on the earth

xi. 10. **And they that dwell on the earth** (the earth-dwellers) **rejoice** † **over them, and make merry,**‡ **and**

---

* See Mark v. 5. Luke viii. 27 ; xxiii. 53 ; xxiv. 1. Acts ii. 29 ; vii. 16, and so in all its twenty occurrences in the Septuagint : Ex. xiv. 11. Num. xi. 34, 35 ; xix. 16, 18 ; xxxiii. 16, 17. Deut. ix. 22. Josh. xxiv. 31. 2 Chron. xvi. 14 ; xxxiv. 4, 28. Job x. 19. Is. lxv. 4. Jer. xxvi. 23. Ezek. xxxii. 22, 24, 26 ; xxxvii. 12 (twice).

† So G.L.T.Tr.A. WH. and RV. reading *present* tense instead of *future*.

‡ So L.T Tr.A. WH. and RV.

shall send * gifts one to another: because these two
prophets tormented them that dwell on the earth.]
The older commentators might have felt a difficulty in
understanding how the whole earth could rejoice at an
event happening at Jerusalem. But in these days of
electric inventions, telephones, and wireless telegraphy,
we all know how the next day the whole world
sympathises and rejoices together.†

But "the triumphing of the wicked is short"
(Job xx. 5).

11. **And after three days and a half the breath
of life** (or life-spirit) **from God entered into them, and
they stood upon their feet; and great fear fell upon
those who beheld them.**] The Two Witnesses are
raised from the dead by the power of God (Gen. ii. 7.
Job xxxiii. 4. Compare Ezek. xxxvii. 10). The rejoicing is soon turned into fear—great fear. Their Lord
was raised to life in Jerusalem after three days, and
they after a somewhat similar period. Like Him, too,
they ascend up into heaven; but, unlike Him, this
follows immediately on their resurrection.

The twelfth verse is constructed as follows:

b. (page 359), xi. 12. *Ascension*

b | m | 12-. Hearing
     n | -12-. Invitation
     n | -12-. Reception
   m | -12. Seeing

xi. 12. **And they heard a loud voice out of heaven,
saying to them,**
              "Come up hither."

---

* T. reads "send."

† Witness the death of Queen Victoria; the murder of President
M'Kinley; or the American Yacht Race—all the stages of the latter
were known the world over within a few moments of the passing events.

**And they ascended up to heaven in the cloud
(Acts i. 9) ; and their enemies beheld them]** The word
they hear is "with power;" for immediately they
ascend; and are for ever delivered out of the hand of
their enemies. Their death, resurrection and ascension
are all literal. This shows that the words, "first
resurrection," in chap. xx., refer to the contrast between
that and the second ; it is the first (or former) of
those two, and not the first that ever took place. Nor
is this the only ascension. The Church shall have
ascended long before these judgment scenes commence ;
and during those times we have the ascension of the
great multitude of chap. vii., and the 144,000 of chap.
xv., besides that of the Two Witnesses here recorded.
The "great fear" of their enemies is completely
justified ; for judgment speedily follows, and the death
of the Lord's Two Witnesses is avenged.

This is recorded in verse 13 :

f. (page 359), xi. -13. *Enemies Slain*

```
o | 13-.  Killed
   p | -13-.  Number
   p | -13-.  Remainder
o | -13.  Affrighted
```

xi. 13. **And in that same hour there was a great
earthquake, and a tenth part of the city fell,]** *i.e.,* of
the great city mentioned above. But how can this be
if this great city is "the Church of God"? Why
should a tenth part of "the Church of God" be thus
judged because of sins of "the peoples, and tribes,
and tongues and nations"?

and there were killed in the earthquake seven thousand men :] "Names of men " is an Idiomatic expression for persons. Both in Scripture and in the Papyri, ὄνομα (*onoma*), *name,* is used of *a person.* The word χιλιάς always means the number 1,000, and yet Elliott interprets this of the seven Dutch republics which were lost to the Papacy by the Reformation ! so he takes these " names of men " literally, and says they mean " titles of dignity and command," such as Duchies and Lordships. Hence, perforce, the smiting down of these by the earthquake must denote the setting of them up, and establishing them in a better and independent position !

and the rest became affrighted and gave glory to the God of heaven] This giving glory to God is not equivalent to praising or blessing God. It is extorted, not by penitence, but by terror. The idiom is well known. See Luke iv. 15, where those referred to in the words " glorified of all," soon attempted to take the life of the Lord Jesus (*v.* 29). See also Josh. vii. 19 (Sept.). Ps. cvi. 12-15. Mark vi. 20. Luke v. 26 ; xvii. 12-18 ; xviii. 43 ; xxiii. 47. John ix. 24. Acts xii. 23 ; xxiv. 25. Rom. iv. 20). The context here clearly shows the sense in which this is to be taken. God is said to be glorified when His power is acknowledged in an emergency ; just as the magicians said to Pharaoh, " this is the finger of God " (Ex. viii. 19). And just as the ungodly admit the same thing every day. Even the demons acknowledged the Lord Jesus, and confessed His Deity.

Here, it is only " the God of Heaven " who is acknowledged ; not a covenant God (Jehovah) known and loved. Only a God at a distance, unknown and feared. We have already spoken of the title, " God of heaven," and its significance as occurring only here, and in chap. xvi. 11. Ezra i. 2. Neh. i. 4. Dan. ii. 18, 19, etc.

Thus ends the sixth Trumpet or "second Woe." Hence it is added :

14. **The second woe is past : behold, the third woe cometh quickly.**] The second Woe consists of two parts : The Horsemen, and the Two Witnesses.

The third Woe, which is the result of the sounding of the seventh Trumpet, occupies four chapters (xv.— xviii.); and after the sounding of the seventh Trumpet three chapters are interposed (xii.—xiv.), taking us back (probably) to a time prior to ch. iv.; conducting us by a different route to the same point ; describing to us how it is the Wild Beast is to be revealed ; and telling us the causes and consequences of his revelation. Then the seventh Trumpet is taken up again in chap. xv.

The second Woe ends with the earthquake following on the ascension of the Two Witnesses. Theirs is a marvellous history. It comes upon us suddenly, as does the history of Elijah in 1 Kings xvii. 1 ; and the description of their course is soon told. In spite of all unbelief, misapplied learning, and fanciful interpretation, they will one day appear on the earth and fulfil their mission. Then this Scripture will be understood in all its simplicity and clearness.

10

THE THIRD VISION "IN HEAVEN"
(11:15-19)

The Seventh Trumpet brings us back to Heaven and to the Third Vision seen there by John. For it is " in heaven " that the Trumpet is sounded.

After it is sounded, we again hear the heavenly utterances which tell us of the *design* of this sounding. In xix. 1-16, heavenly voices again tell us of the completion of its *effect*. After it is sounded, and its object unfolded, there is a break; and an episode occupying chaps. xii., xiii. and xiv.; the effects of the sounding not being resumed till chap. xvi. 1, and occupying chaps. xvi., xvii., xviii.

The Seventh Trumpet thus embraces the whole of the seven Vials, or last seven plagues, which make up the " Third Woe."

The Seventh Trumpet, therefore, really reaches from chap. xi. 15 to xviii. 24, or even to xx. 5, for it takes in the whole of the remaining judgments, and consists of the remaining five pairs of Visions "in heaven" and "on earth," and occupies about one half of the whole Apocalypse. This shows us the importance of the Scripture on which we are now about to enter. It tells us also why the heavenly utterances, which follow on its sounding, anticipate the end, including the setting up of the throne of earthly dominion, the raising of the dead, " small and great," and the final judgment. All is anticipated by these heavenly voices, which are answered by the concluding utterances of chap. xix. in the seventh and final Heavenly Vision.

In chap. x. 7, the mighty angel declared that " in the days of the voice of the seventh angel, when he shall sound, the secret of God should be finished": *i.e.*, that it will be finished during the days covered by his sounding (embracing, as we have seen, the whole of the seven Vials, and bringing us down to xx. 15). The whole of God's secret purposes, the details of which were known only to Himself, will be accomplished.

The whole of this great division, therefore, opens with the small section (xi. 15-19-), concerning the act of sounding the Seventh Trumpet. The structure is as follows :—

𝕳³ (page 118), chap. **xi. 15-19-.** THE THIRD VISION

" IN HEAVEN "

The Sounding of the Seventh Trumpet. (3rd WOE)

𝕳³ A | xi. 15-. The sounding of the Seventh Trumpet in heaven
 B | a | -15-. Loud voices in heaven
   | b | -15. Their utterance
 B | *a* | 16. The 24 Elders
   | *b* | 17, 18. Their utterance
A | 19-. The opening of God's Temple in heaven

xi. 15. And the seventh angel sounded his trumpet; and there were loud voices in heaven ;] Each seventh Seal, Trumpet and Vial is marked off from the preceding six by unmistakable signs, sufficient to show us that they are resumptive rather than continuous.

Each going over the same ground to give particulars not contained in the others, bringing us up to a crisis; and giving the other events in the corresponding period, but from a different point of view.

This is called the "seventh" Trumpet, and it is the "last" of this special series. But it does not follow there will be none after: or, that a trumpet sounding before it may not also be called the "last," relatively to another subject. In 1 Cor. xv. 51, 52, we read of "the last trumpet: for a trumpet shall sound." In 1 Thess. iv. 16, we read that the Lord "shall descend from heaven with a shout, with the archangel's voice, and with the trump of God." This is the "last" Trumpet as regards the church of God, but not the last absolutely. It will be sounded long before these judgments begin, in order to raise His sleeping saints, and take them up with the living saints, to be with Himself for ever. There will be another great Trumpet after the great Tribulation, immediately connected with the Lord's Apocalypse. See Matt. xxiv. 31. This is subsequent to this "seventh Trumpet," for that Apocalypse is recorded in Rev. xix. So that the seventh Trumpet in Rev. xi. 15 is not the "last Trump," absolutely, but only relatively; for it is only *the last of this series of seven*. Moreover, this is neither called "the last": nor is it necessary for us so to call it. The Trump in 1 Cor. xv. 51, 52, is called the "last" with reference to the church of God. It is the Trump which shall close our connection with the earth; it will end up all longing expectation, and therefore there is a true sense in which it is our last Trump.

The Trump of 1 Cor. xv. 51, 52, is the same that is mentioned in 1 Thess. iv. 16. We have had so many

positive proofs that these " Seven Trumpets " belong to
another Dispensation altogether, that we cannot read
this into our " calling on high " (Phil. iii. 14), where no
trump at all is even mentioned, and confuse it with the
trumpet which shall bring on the last of God's plagues
and end up His judgment of the earth.

The sounding of this Trumpet produces great activity
and stir in Heaven, where it is sounded. It is nothing less
than the proclamation of the coming Coronation of earth's
rightful king (compare 2 Sam. xv. 10, 1 Kings i. 39).
It is the signal that, at length, the hour has come to
herald the glorious news of the setting up and establishing of God's kingdom on earth. It is the announcement that the prayer of the ages—" Thy kingdom come "
—is about to receive its wondrous answer. For this is
the subject of the loud voices in heaven.

saying

> **"The sovereignty* of the world is
> become the sovereignty† of our
> Lord, and of His Christ; and He
> shall reign for ever and ever."**
> (Ex. xv. 18.   Ps. x. 16.   Dan. ii. 44;
> vii. 14.)

The whole subject is one of sovereignty. This is the
whole matter which has been in question. And this
question is now about to be settled by these final
judgments of the seven Vials. The result is celebrated
in this Vision " in heaven " by anticipation. It looks
forward to the close of the whole book of Revelation.
It is not till the events of chap. xx. have taken place

---

* G.L.T.Tr.A. WH. and RV. read the *singular* instead of the
plural.

† or " is become our Lord's and His Anointed's."

that this change of sovereignty is consummated. "The kingdoms of the world" are represented as *wild beasts*, knowing no master and having no owner. This is God's view of all earthly governments. Government in the world, committed, for the present, to man, has never yet been exercised for God. Not only is His sovereignty not recognised, but even His suzerainty is rejected. It is folly to talk about " Christian kingdoms " or " Christian nations ; " and it is worse than folly for ministers of the Gospel to occupy themselves with the taming of these wild beasts, instead of warning all of the coming judgments, which will destroy them altogether ; and meantime witnessing of the " grace of God " to lost and helpless sinners. We are not referring to any lawful acts which we may do (as it were, in passing) to improve the condition of things, or to remove crying evils ; but we are speaking of laying ourselves out for these things and of making them our great aim ; and especially of ministers of the Gospel so doing. What is wanted is, not a " Citizen Sunday," but a Sunday for God, when men will be told of what God's verdict is on all these things ; of what His remedy for them is ; and of what means He is going to take to set right all that is so wrong. A Sunday when men will be told that there can be no Millennium without Christ ; and that there is no hope for the world until it comes under the direct sovereignty of God and of His Anointed.

The very laws which God gave on Sinai, and the Divine Ritual of the Tabernacle and the Temple did not keep Israel from Religious Apostasy and political ruin. It ought therefore to be perfectly clear that there is no hope for the world in human laws or religions.

Righteous government is the one great want of the whole world. The obtaining of this is the mighty spring of all political movements for Reform ; and of all national conspiracies, and revolutions. It is this that gives Anarchists the motive for their crimes. But man does not know or see (and there are so few to tell him) that there can be no righteous government for the world until the Righteous one shall come " whose right it is " (Ezek. xxi. 27) to rule in righteousness : and no peace for the earth until the Prince of Peace, whom man hath foully murdered, shall return to establish it. When he came, His object was angelically heralded as " Peace on earth " (Luke ii. 14); but when He had been rejected, His disciples knew there could be no " peace on earth " while the blood of the Prince of Peace cried for vengeance, and hence they sang of " peace in heaven " (Luke xix. 38). That is where our peace now is (Eph. ii. 14-17); and peace is now preached to sinners and rebels.

All this, and more, is involved in this heavenly utterance. The coming kingdom is not "from this world " (John xviii. 36). It is not " from hence." It comes from heaven, and from thence we look for the coming King. Here will be the fulfilment of the second Psalm and many other similar scriptures.

To the general utterance of the loud voices is added the special utterance of the twenty-four elders, which fills out the former with the details embraced in it

16. **And the twenty-four elders, who, in the presence of God sit upon their thrones, fell upon their faces, and worshipped God, (17) saying,**
"We give thanks to thee, O Lord
God, the Almighty, who art, and

who wast,* because thou hast taken
thy great power and hast reigned.
(18) **And the nations were wroth
(Ps. ii. 1; xlvi. 6), and thy wrath is
come, and the time of the dead, to
be judged, and to give the reward
to thy servants the prophets, and
to the saints, and to those who fear
thy name (*i.e.*, Thee), the small and
the great; and to destroy those who
destroy the earth"]**

There are seven things here celebrated by anticipation. And the seven is divided into *four* and *three*. The
last *three* are marked off by their belonging to the
special appointed season in which they are to take place.
The first *four* relate to four actions on the part of God,
and their effects.

The first act of taking His power is seen in the seven
Vials (chap. xv. 8), where the temple is filled with
smoke from the glory of God and from *His power*. The
wrath of the nations, and of God, are both mentioned in
Ps. ii. 1, 5. In connection with this we may read many
of the Psalms, which are proleptic, and therefore in like
manner celebrate by anticipation: *e.g.*, Ps. xciii.—xcix.,
Ps. lvii., and others, which ought all to be read carefully
through with reference to the particular time referred
to in this utterance of the twenty-four elders. There
are other Scriptures which refer to this time of wrath.
Read Isa. xxvi. 20, 21 (RV.):—

* G.L.T.Tr.A. WH. and RV. omit "and art to come." The Text
was altered here by some later scribe to make it agree with i. 4, 8 and
iv. 8. But here the actual coming is celebrated, and therefore it
forms no part of the original Text.

" Come, my People, enter thou into thy inner
    chambers,
And shut thy doors about thee,
Hide thyself for a little moment, until the indig-
    nation be overpast :
For behold, the LORD cometh forth out of His
    place
To punish the inhabitants of the earth for their
    iniquity :
The earth also shall disclose her blood,
And shall no more cover her slain."

(So, Isa. xxiv. 17-21 ; xxx. 27, 28, 30-33. Ezek. xxxviii.
16-23. Zeph. i. 2, 3, 14-16 ; iii. 8).

In these judgments, under the seventh Trumpet,
amendment or repentance is no longer looked for. All
is wrath and vengeance. Jehovah at length replies to
the reiterated cry of his people : " Arise, O God "
Ps. iii. 7 ; vii. 6 ; xliv. 26. The time has come when
the appeal of Ps. lxviii. 1-3, &c., shall be answered :

" Let God arise, let His enemies be scattered :
Let them also that hate him, flee before him,
As smoke is driven away, so drive them away :
As wax melteth before the fire,
So let the wicked perish at the presence of God.
But let the righteous be glad ; let them rejoice
    before God :
Yea, let them exceedingly rejoice."

The last two greatWitnesses of God will have finished
their testimony, attested by miraculous evidences.
Now, all further testimony is to be withdrawn, and
vengeance is to take its course.

The last three statements of the Elders' utterance relate to the appointed season (καιρός, *kairos*), which has come for their fulfilment.

(1) " *The time of the dead to be judged.*"

This connects, therefore, the events of chapter xx. with the sounding of this Trumpet (see xx. 12, 13). Resurrection also is included, for the dead, " small and great," stand then before God for this judgment. Here we have more than mere avengement of the martyrs; or, righteous government.

(2) To give the Reward (a) "*to thy servants the prophets,*" as stated in chap. x. 7 (compare 2 Kings ix. 7). We have the same phrase in Dan. ix. 6, 10, as well as in 2 Kings xvii. 13, 23 ; xxi. 10; xxiv. 2, &c. The Old Testament prophets have a pre-eminent place in the coming kingdom (not in the Church of God). See Luke xiii. 28. Matt. v. 10-12.

(3) "*And to the saints.*" This is a special term for the Old Testament saints, and is not to be confused with the usage of the word in the Pauline sense, where it is applied to the members of the Body of Christ ; or with angels, of whom the word is also used in such passages as Deut. xxxiii. 2. In Ex. xxii. 31 it is used of holy men under the Law, as also in Ps. xvi. 3; xxx. 4; xxxi. 23 ; xxxiv. 9; l. 5.

The " saints " here are those spoken of in Daniel vii. 18 : " the saints shall take the kingdom " (see verses 22, 27). These are the " saints " against whom the Wild Beast will "make war" (Dan. vii. 21, 25). These are the " elect " of Matt. xxiv. 31 ; Luke xviii. 7 ; and the " saints " elsewhere spoken of in the Apocalypse. (See xiii. 7, 10 ; xiv. 12 ; xv. 3 ; xvi. 6; xvii. 6; xviii. 24 ; xix. 8; xx. 9). These have their reward under this seventh Trumpet, and we see it actually bestowed on them in chap. xx. 4. This is the reward referred to in the Gospels, in such passages as Matt. x. 41, 42 ; xvi. 27 ; xxv. 34. Rev. ii. 23 ; xxii. 12.

(c) "*Them that fear Thy name, the small and the great.*"

Note, that the Elders do not say " us." They again distinguish themselves from human beings. It was the special character of saints under the Law, to fear the Lord. See Josh xxiv. 14. 1 Sam. xii. 24. Ps. xxxiv. 9. But the words here probably include Gentiles (as distinct from Israel, who, as the "holy nation," are called "saints ").

They are so distinguished in **Ps. cxv.**, where we have first " Israel " (*v.* 9) ; then the " house of Aaron " (*v.* 10) ; then "ye that fear the Lord " (*v.* 11). Then in verse 13 : " He will bless them that fear the Lord, both small and great."

The seventh Trumpet includes as its last object :

(3) "*to destroy them that destroy the earth.*"

This involves the destruction of Babylon, and of those who worship the Beast and receive his mark. It would also include the great destruction of the armies of Satan and the rebels who join it, in Rev. xx. 9. (Compare Isa. xxiv. 21.)

With the destruction of these God's judgments end, and the " mystery (or secret) of God is finished " (x. 7), as well as " the mystery of Iniquity."

This third vision " in heaven " closes with the words :

xi. 19. **and the temple** (Naos) **of God which is in heaven was opened,*** **and there was seen the ark of his covenant in his temple :**] We have already seen

---

* So L.T.Tr. WH. RV. add ὁ (*ho*), which makes the Text read as above, and not as in the AV.

that heaven is a place of grand and glorious realities ; and not a place of airy nothings, as popular theology pictures it. There is a heavenly Temple, and heavenly worship, and a heavenly priesthood, on the pattern of which the earthly was modelled (See Ex. xxv. 40. Heb. ix. 23).

The Apocalypse is the book of unveiling and of opening. Seven great openings characterise it.

In iv. 1 : A *Door* is opened in heaven

In vi. 1-9 : The *Seals* are opened

In ix. 2 : The *Abyss* is opened. Here,

In xi. 19 : The *Temple* of God is opened

In xv. 5 : The *Tabernacle* of Testimony is opened

In xix. 11. The *Heaven* is opened

In xx. 12. The *Books* of judgment are opened

The opening of the Heavenly Temple discloses the Ark of the Covenant, and speaks of the Covenant-keeping God redeeming His pledges of blessing to His People ; and tells of judgment on His enemies.

It is from this Temple that the judgments which follow, proceed forth (xiv. 15, 17 ; xv. 5, &c. ; xvi. 17).

This tells us that those judgments have respect to the restoration of His People Israel, and of the fulfil-ment of all His covenant promises, concerning the Land (Gen. xv.) and the throne (2 Sam. vii.), which were unconditional and therefore certain and sure. The Ark of the Old Covenant was concealed : this is revealed, and it is displayed as a token of Israel's sal-vation and of their enemies' destruction. The "secret" of God is finished (x. 7) because the Temple is laid open, and the Ark revealed.

The Ark of the Old Covenant had stood closely con-nected with the *Tabernacle* and Moses ; with the *Land*

and Joshua; with the *Kingdom* and David; and with the *Temple* and Solomon.   All are united here in connection with this Heavenly Ark of which the Earthly Ark was only a copy and a figure.

Under this covenant is at length to be fulfilled all that was announced in the Song of Zacharias (Luke i. 68-79); but which, owing to Christ's rejection, has been since in abeyance:

A | "Blessed be the Lord the God of Israel;
   | For He hath **visited** and redeemed His people,

   B | And hath raised up a horn of **salvation** for us
      | In the house of His servant David;

      C | As he spake by the mouth of his holy **prophets,**
         | Which have been since the world began:

         D | That we should be saved from our **enemies,**
            | And from the hand of all that hate us;

            E | To perform the mercy promised to our fathers,
               | And to remember his holy **covenant;**

         B | The **oath** which he sware to our father Abraham,

         D | That he would grant unto us, that we being delivered out of
            | the hand of our **enemies**
            | Might serve him without fear,
            | In holiness and righteousness before him, all the days of our
            | life,

      C | And thou, child, shalt be called the **prophet** of the Highest;
         | For thou shalt go before the face of the Lord to prepare his ways;

   B | To give knowledge of **salvation** unto his people
      | By the remission of their sins,

A | Through the tender mercy of our God;
   | Whereby the Day-spring from on high hath **visited** us,
   | To give light to them that sit in darkness and in the shadow of death
   | To guide our feet into the way of peace."

The words printed in thicker type show us the great subject of each member. They may be more clearly seen if presented thus:

A | 68.   The visitation of God

    B | 69.   Its subject : Salvation raised up

        C | 70.   Foretold : by all His Prophets

            D | 71.   Its result :   Destruction of Enemies

                E | 72.   Its basis : The Covenant

                E | 73.   Its basis : The Oath

            D | 74, 75.   Its result :   Worship of Delivered Ones

        C | 76.   Fulfilled : The Fore-running prophet

    B | 77.   Its object : Salvation known

A | 78, 79.   The Visitation of Christ

Thus, beautifully, has God the Holy Ghost emphasised for us what is included in His Covenant, of which the manifestation of the Ark of His Covenant, seen in His opened Temple in heaven, is at once the token and assurance. The revelation of the Ark of the Covenant is at once answered on earth by signs which betoken its meaning for the earth.

That we reach a great crisis here, is evident. It anticipates the end, including the judgment of the great white throne in chap. xx. This Third Vision in heaven is followed by a Third Vision on earth, which fitly answers it. Before all that it involves and includes is fulfilled, we are taken back to the foundation of the world, in order to have various matters explained to us; and we are shown how the End is connected with the Beginning; and what the great Crisis really means.

This is why the Third Vision in Heaven is so solemn in its anticipation; and this is why the Third Vision on Earth is so brief in its response.

11

THE THIRD VISION "ON EARTH"
(11:19)

This is very brief; the briefest of all. But, in reality it is the longest of all, for it anticipates the end of the Book. Before entering upon the judgment of the seven Vials, an Episode is to be given (as we have already shown) in chaps. xii., xiii., xiv., xv. Hence, before giving this Episode, the sounding of the Trumpet and the Heavenly utterances are briefly acknowledged by signs which betoken the coming judgments, which are to be taken up later and fully described in chaps. xvi. to xx.

xi. -19. **And there were lightnings, and voices, and thunderings, and earthquake, and great hail.**] That we have here a Vision relating to the earth is clear; though it is not, and need not be, so stated; for it is manifest that the *earth*quake must refer to the *earth*, as must the hail also. Similar phenomena are mentioned as the consequences of heavenly visions and announcements. (See viii. 5; x. 3; xvi. 18; xix. 6.)

The concluding words of the Elders closely connect the seven Vials as being the fulfilment of their prophetic utterance in xi. 18, 19.

The Temple is opened; so the opening of the Tabernacle in xv. 5 is the initiatory act of the seven Vials.

"*Thy wrath is come*," the Elders say. "Pour out the seven Vials of the *wrath of God*," cries the voice from the Throne, in xv. 7; xvi. 1.

The voices and hail, also, of xi. -19, correspond with the " voices " and " hail " which accompany the pouring forth of the seventh and last Vial in xvi. 17-21.

But before the account of this seventh Trumpet is resumed and its details set forth, we have three more visions "in heaven" interposed by way of parenthesis (viz., the *fourth, fifth,* and *sixth,* together with the *fourth* and *fifth* Visions " on earth "). The sixth Vision " on earth " takes up this third Vision, which, till then, is held over to allow of other information being given, which is necessary to the understanding of it.

Chapters xii. 1 to xv. 8 are, therefore, parenthetical as regards the actual sequence of the Judgment scenes.

12

THE FOURTH VISION "IN HEAVEN"
(12:1-12)

𝕭⁴ (page 118), chap. xii. 1-12. *A Great Sign*

We now come, not only to the great central subject of the whole Book, but to the central pair of the seven Visions, and to the actual *literary* centre of the Book.

All this shows us that we are on the threshold of an important part of Scripture which relates to the actual Revelation or Unveiling of the glorious Person of the Lord Jesus Christ.

The whole section (chaps. xii.—xv.) is not only Episodal in subject and Parenthetical in form, but is a good example of historical, or, rather, prophetic *Hysterologia,** by which the events, though written down later, took place earlier than those which immediately precede in historical narration.   That is to say, we have in chaps. xii.—xv. a prophetic record of events which will take place before chap. vi., and will lead up to, and run parallel with, what is recorded in chaps. vi.—xi.

Chaps. vi.—xi. thus give the *exoteric* (or *outer*) view of that portion of prophetic history ; for the Beast and the False Prophet are on the earth all that time, as is clear from xi. 7, where the Beast that ascendeth out of the abyss made war against Two Witnesses.   But how he came to be on the earth we have not yet been told. The course of the prophetic record is therefore sus-

---

* See *Figures of Speech,* by Dr. Bullinger, page 708.

pended, while we are taken back to a point prior to chap. vi., and in chap. xii. are given the *esoteric* (or inner) view of the same period, and told of the causes which shall lead up to the revelation of the Beast and the False Prophet. Chap. xii. occupies much the same position with regard to chaps. xiii. to end; as chaps. iv. and v. do to chaps. vi.—xi.

First, the war takes place in heaven, and the Devil is cast out into the earth. Then "he" stands on the sand of the sea (xiii. 1 RV.), and John sees these two awful beings coming up—the one from the sea, and the other from the earth. There is no record of their doings except in chap. xiii., and what may be gathered from the judgments directed against them and their followers recorded in chaps. vi. —xi. and other Scriptures of the Old and New Testaments.

The Structure shows that the Woman and the Dragon are the two great subjects of the Vision, the " Man-child" occupying only one verse (the sixth).

𝕳⁴ (page 118), xii. 1-12. THE FOURTH VISION "IN HEAVEN"

A Great Sign

𝕳⁴ A | xii. 1-. A great Sign in heaven

B | a | -1-5. The Woman and the Dragon
    b | 6. The Woman's flight
    c | 7-9. The War in heaven

A | 10-12. A loud Voice in heaven

*** With this structure should be compared that of the following scene "on Earth" (ℭ⁴), with which the part marked "W" (xii. 13—xiii. 1-) exactly corresponds. See page 414.

xii. 1-. **And a great sign was seen in heaven:**]
Here, at length, for the first time in this Book, we have
a "Sign." The word is σημεῖον (*sēmeion*) *a sign*; not τέρας
(*teras*) *wonder*.* We are thus warned at the outset that
we are not to take this literally, but to see in it a
"sign" of something else. Thus does the Holy Spirit
guide us as to what is *literal* and what is not. What it
is that is signified by the Sign we must learn from the
Scripture itself. If we are thus warned that we are to
treat this as a "sign," we may assuredly gather that,
when we are not so cautioned, we are not to treat the
things in this Book as symbols, but as literal facts and
events.

It is not only a Sign, but it is "a great sign," as
important in its significance as it was vast in its appearance. It represented something remarkable in itself
and momentous in its teaching.

The Sign itself is described in "a" (page 386), verses
-1-5. The following is the structure :—

    a (page 386), xii. 1-5.   *The Woman and the Dragon*

  a | d | e | xii. 1-. A great sign in heaven
            f | -1. The Woman
               g | 2. The travail of the Woman
      d | e | 3-. Another sign in heaven
           f | -3, 4-. The Dragon
              g | 5. The travail of the Woman

---

* We are to distinguish these two words because they are often
joined together; Matt. xxiv. 24. Mark xiii. 22. John iv. 48. Acts
ii. 19, 43; iv. 30; v. 12; vi. 8; vii. 36; xiv. 3; xv. 12. Rom. xv.
19. 2 Thess. ii. 9. So in the Old Test., Deut. xxviii. 46; xxxiv. 11.
Neh. ix. 10. Isa. viii. 18; xx. 3. Jer. xxxii. (xxxix.) 20, &c.

xii. -1. **A woman arrayed with the sun, and the moon under her feet, and upon her head a crown of twelve stars :]** This at once takes us back to Gen. xxxvii. It is the *only* scripture in the whole Bible where we have any thing corresponding to this sign. There we read of Joseph (*v.* 9): "he dreamed yet another dream, and told it to his brethren, and said, Behold! I have dreamed a dream more; behold, *the sun,* and *the moon, and the eleven stars* made obeisance to me. And he told it to his father, and to his brethren; and his father rebuked him, and said unto him, what is this dream that thou hast dreamed? Shall *I, and thy mother, and thy brethren* indeed come to bow ourselves to thee, to the earth" (Gen. xxxvii. 9, 10). Joseph thus saw a similar "Sign," and both he and his father Jacob understood it at once, and interpreted it correctly, as the sequel shows.

Now, when we have such a scripture as this, why go out of our way to seek for another explanation outside scripture altogether. That the same twelve stars are referred to in Genesis is clear, because Joseph himself made the twelfth. Here we have the earliest reference to the twelve signs of the Zodiac. These are the only "twelve stars," or asterisms, in the heavens. There are the "seven stars" meaning the seven planets; but the twelve stars can mean only the twelve signs (or stars) of the Zodiac, thus embracing the whole heavens.

The heathen nations, being ignorant of the written word of God, did not know the primitive truth preserved by the Antideluvian Patriarchs in the signs and constellations of the heavens before it was written down by God through Moses in "the scriptures of truth." Hence, the nations preverted it, and overlaid it with their own vain imaginations.   This was the origin of the old Greek mythology; and before that, of the various ancient mythologies of Babylon and other nations.   Those mythologies were not *invented* by those nations, but they were the corruption of primitive truth after that truth had been forgotten.

As Rom. i. 20, 21 declares, they were " without excuse," for the invisible things of God were clearly seen and understood by the things that are made.   The heavens declared His glory and spoke of His purposes. This is what Rom. i. 19-23 refers to.

The Patriarchs had, long before the times of Jacob and Joseph, so mapped out the heavens, as to preserve the great foundation promise and prophecy of Gen. iii. 15, by making arbitrary configurations of the stars.

That this is no mere conjecture is shown by an important article in *The Nineteenth Century* magazine (for Sept., 1900), by Mr. E. W. Maunder, of the Greenwich Observatory, on " The Oldest Picture Book of all."   He says : "There are some indications, which seem to have escaped notice hitherto, by which we may fix, roughly at least, the date of certain other constellations than those of the extreme South.   These are the twelve commonly known as the Signs of the Zodiac, and which, beyond all controversy, were planned in order to mark out the Ecliptic.   The division of the Zodiac into *twelve* signs is one of very great significance. . . . .   Now this perhaps was the most difficult discovery which up to the present date has yet been made in Astronomy."

" The interdependence of so many of the designs, and the fact that the sphere is thus manifestly the work of a single authority, furnish reasons for thinking that it was *intended to be of the nature of a document.*   An exami-

nation of the individual forms supports this conclusion." · · · Again, he says: "We are sure that the
Zodiac is not later than 1800 B.C., and does not date
further back than to 4400 B.C."

He sums up the article by saying that "this oldest
picture book of all was designed nearly 5,000 years
ago" and that "Many of the constellations, then, were
mapped out to *express the religious belief of their designers.*
No doubt the others, of which at present we have no
explanation, had *just the same purpose.*"

Mr. Maunder says also that the *religion* of those who
designed the Zodiac and mapped out the Constellations
"involved the erection of altars and the rite of sacrifice.
They were acquainted with the stories of the Fall and
the Deluge, substantially the same as those preserved
to us in the early chapters of Geneses, and *they devised
many of the constellations to give appropriate and permanent
record of them.*"

The italics are our own, and the parts thus marked confirm our conclusions, on the highest authority ; while the
date assigned places its origin far beyond the domain of
heathen mythology, and throws great light on Psalm xix.

All readers of that Psalm are struck with the fact
that the first part is about the Heavens, and that then,
in *v.* 7, there is a sudden and abrupt transition to the
written Word.

This is explained by the fact that the reference is, in the
first part, to the primitive truth witnessed to by the Sun
and Stars in the heavens (an expansion of Gen. i. 14, 15);
and in the second part the reference is to the written
Word of God recorded in " the Scriptures of Truth."

For some 2,000 years before Moses, the heavens
declared the glory of God ; and not only showed His

handiwork, but from day to day *uttered speech*, and from night to night *showed knowledge*.

True, there was no speech nor language; their voice was not heard; and yet, their " line " (*i.e.*, their inherit-ance,* or sphere of teaching) is gone out through all the earth, and *their words* to the end of the world. In them (*i.e.*, in the heavens) hath He set a Tabernacle (or dwelling) for the Sun (*i.e.*, the path of the sun through the signs of the Zodiac, called the " Ecliptic") which the sun never leaves, but goes forth from one end of the heaven to the other, preforming his annual circuit. See the whole of Ps. xix.† But these " words," and this " knowledge," after they were written down in Scripture, naturally fell into disuse, and in time were forgotten ; and afterwards were overlaid by the traditions of men. If Moses wrote by the time of the Exodus, this would give about 1491 B.C., for the date of the books of the Pentateuch, and thus leave mankind for some 2500 years without the Word of God *written*. Thus, for all that long period, the Heavens would be showing their knowledge, and sending forth their words to the ends of the earth, and preserving the great primeval promise and prophecy of Gen. iii. 15 alive in the hearts of God's people ; making known the Coming one who, though bruised in the heel, should finally crush the serpent's head.

These twelve stars, therefore, were the Zodiacal signs, which are thus associated with Israel in the persons of Jacob, and the twelve Patriarchs. These constituted and represented *the whole nation in embryo*. Their

*See *Figures of Speech*, and *The witness of the Stars*, by Dr. Bullinger. Published by Kregel Publications

† Where, after speaking of the teaching of the Heavens (*vv.* 1-6), it goes on to speak of the teaching in the written word of God (*vv.* 7-14).

presence here in Rev. xii. tells us that God is about to reveal His own truth, write folly on all devices of the heathen, expose their false use of His own handiwork; and, as He smote "the gods of Egypt" when He delivered Israel from thence (Jer. xliii. 12, 13 ; xlvi. 20), so, when He is about to deliver Israel again, He will execute His judgment on the gods of the heathen, by showing that their perversions of His primal promise will not affect its fulfilment; but all their mythological gods shall be helpless and useless to deliver them out of His hand.*

Again we ask, Why introduce the Church here? Alford says "the whole symbolism points to it." On the contrary, the only like symbol in the whole Bible connects this woman, thus arrayed, with Israel. What has the Church got to do with Gen. xxxvii. ? Are we to look for the Church there? If not, then why look for it here, in Rev. xii. Jacob, his wife and his twelve sons, may well be taken as a most fitting interpretation of the sign of the sun, moon and twelve stars : but the Church has no connection whatsoever with these.

Further, Israel is again and again compared to a woman, and a married woman, in the Old Testament (Is. liv., etc.). Also, in her time of rejection, to a widow (Is. xlvii. Lam. i. 1. Luke xviiii.); and a divorced woman (Is. l. Jer. iii.); but not so the Church. Nor can what follows be anywhere properly understood of the Church.

xii. 2. **And being with child she crieth out,†
being in travail, and being in pain to bring forth]**

---

* See Appendix for the whole question of the relation of the Apoca-lypse to the ancient Astro-theology.

† Was crying, L.

When could this ever be spoken of the Church? What is the Church's travail? And what is the man-child which the Church brings forth?

On the other hand, this "sign" exactly expresses the position and condition of the true Israel all through the history of the nation.

The promise of Gen. iii. 15, as to the coming "seed" of the woman to crush the head of the great Dragon, was fundamental to the ground of Israel's faith.

This chapter, therefore, takes us back to the beginning of evil wrought by Satan, and carries us right forward to the great crisis of human history. It shows how "the mystery of God" and "the mystery of Iniquity" will be finished; and take some 6,000 years to work out.

The birth of that "seed" became, therefore, the object of Israel's hope; the subject of Israel's prophets; and the "joy" of Israel's mothers when a man was born into the world (John xvi. 21).

The "sign" of the travailing woman, and her being in pain to be delivered, signifies the expectant attitude of Israel—*de jure*, if not *de facto*. The promised seed was meant to be the one great hope of the nation; to which everything pointed and of which everything testified.

The first sign of the Zodiac was a permanent and constant reminder of this great primeval promise and prophecy.

VIRGO is always represented, in all the ancient Zodiacs, with a branch in her right hand. That branch has come down to us, with the name of the star, which is of the *first* magnitude, *Tzemech*. This is the Hebrew צֶמַח, which means "branch," and is used of Christ, the promised seed, in Jer. xxiii. 5, 6 (signifying the " King," of Matthew) ; in Zech. iii. 8 (signifying the "Servant," of Mark) ; in Zech. vi. 12 (signifying the " Man," of Luke) ; and in Isa. iv. 2 (signifying the " Lord," or Jehovah, of John). As these prophecies of the coming seed, under the name of "the Branch," were read in the Scripture, it would be impossible not to connect them with this first great " sign " of the Zodiac. And until those Scriptures were written, this sign in the heavens told of the coming seed, " the Branch of Jehovah."

Of the great Creator it is written (Ps. cxlvii. 4, RV.) :

" HE telleth the number of the stars,
HE giveth them all their names."

And this name *Tzemech* is inseparably connected with the Divine omniscience of Him who created and named the stars; and gave and fulfilled the promise.

In like manner the constellation of

"The Woman and Child."

was set as the first of the three constellations which are assigned to the sign " Virgo." * It is found in the most ancient Zodiacs, notably that from the Temple of Denderah, in Egypt. It dates from at least 2,000 B.C., and may be seen to-day at the Louvre, in Paris (whither it was taken in 1821). The Hebrew name of this constellation of " the woman and child " was called *Komah*, which means *the desired* or *longed for*. It is from the Hebrew כָּמַה (*kahmah*) *to desire*, which occurs only in Ps. lxiii. 1 : " My flesh *longeth for* Thee." It is akin to חָמַד (*chamad*) *to desire* (Ps. xix. 10. Isa. liii. 2. Hag. ii. 7, &c). We have the word *komah* used by the Holy

---

* Each sign had three constellations assigned to it, which further developed the central truth signified by the respective signs of the Zodiac.

Spirit in this very connection in Hag. ii. 7 : " The DESIRE of all nations shall come."

" The woman and child " was, therefore, part of the primeval truth revealed to man as a sign of Him who was to be the object of this desire.

That it was ancient is testified by Albumazar (or Abu Masher), an Arabian astronomer, who wrote in the eighth century.* He says : " There arises in the first Decan† (as the Persians, Chaldeans, and Egyptians, and the two Hermes and Ascalius teach), *a young woman,* whose Persian name is ADRENEDEFA, a pure and immaculate virgin, holding in the hand two ears of corn, sitting on a throne, nourishing an infant in the act of feeding him, who has a Hebrew name (the boy, I say), by some nations called IHESU, with the signification IEZA, which we in Greek call CHRISTOS."

This is, as we have said, the testimony of the ancient Zodiacs ; otherwise this constellation was altered and corrupted in the third century B.C. by Conon, an astronomer of Alexandria (B.C. 283—222).‡ Even

---

* A Latin translation of his Arabic work is in the British Museum Library.

† The constellations were called *Decans.* The word means *a part,* and is used of the (three) parts into which each sign is divided ; each of which parts, or Decans, is occupied by a constellation.

‡ It appears that Berenice, the wife of Euergetes (Ptolemy III.), king of Egypt, made a vow that, if her husband returned in safety from a dangerous expedition on which he had gone, she would conse-crate her wonderful head of hair to Venus. He did return in safety, and her hair was deposited in the Temple of Venus. Subsequently it was stolen, and Conon, to console her, gave it out that Jupiter had taken it and made a constellation of it. The similarity of the Greek word κόμη (*komē*) *hair,* and the Hebrew *koma* facilitated the change (if it did not suggest [it). And so it came to pass that in our Plani-spheres to-day *Coma Berenice* (*the hair of Berenice*) figures in the place of the woman and child—" the *Desire* of all nations."

Shakespeare refers to " the good boy in Virgo's lap."*
So that the fact has not been lost, though the name
of the constellation has been changed.

But long before the constellation had been changed,
its real signification had been lost and perverted.

Naturally, when the promises and prophecies had
been written down in the Scriptures of Truth, the meaning of the signs and constellations, and the very names
by which God had called the stars, would fall into
disuetude and became gradually forgotten. This would
lead to the easy perversion of their meaning by those
nations who did not possess the Word of God. Hence
this constellation of the " woman and child" passed
into the Babylonian and Egyptian mysteries under the
names of " Isis and Horus"; and thence, from the
pagan mysteries, the picture passed into Romanism,
with many other symbols and doctrines.†

Indeed, so closely is Romanism allied to Paganism,
of which it is the outcome, that those who do not see
the difference between Paganized Christianity and
Bible Christianity, draw the false conclusion that
Romanism is merely a corruption of Christianity,
whereas it is little more than Christianised Paganism.

Hence it was that, the real meaning of " the woman
and child" having been lost, the symbol was Paganized,

---

* *Titus Andronicus.* Act vi. Scene 3.

† Whatever modern meanings of such symbols as I.H.S. may be
given, the fact remains that it was part of the name of Bacchus : and, the
letters I.N.R.I., which were changed by Rome into Iesus Nazarenus
Rex Judæorum (Jesus of Nazareth King of the Jews), originally formed
the pagan symbol that by fire nature will be renewed in its entirety
(*Igne Natura Renovetur Integra*). See *The Rosicrucians : their Rites
and Mysteries*, by Hargrave Jennings (Vol. ii. 1887), quoted by the
authors of *The Computation of 666* (p. 70, published by James Nisbet).

and we are told that representations of it as being " Isis and Horus " were so common (long prior to Christianity), that "there was not a house or a crossway where it was not found."

Many of these Pagan symbols, rites, and ceremonies were brought into " Christianity " by the Greek Fathers, who were converts from Paganism, and had not lost their earlier teaching and training.

What we have here, therefore, in Rev. xii. is the fact that God is going right back to the beginning, and in spite of all the opposition of Satan and the perversion of Primitive Truth by Paganism, He is showing us His purpose in this closing book of Inspiration, which is to take us back to the causes of the great Apostacy, and onward through the great Apostacy, which is close upon us, to its final confusion and destruction.

This is why we have, here, His vindication of those " Signs " by which He first promulgated His great primeval promise, and His own Revelation as to its final accomplishment in the crushing of the serpent's head.

It is clear, so far, that the woman is the " sign " of Israel, viewed as representing the nation as a whole. Israel is thus personified, with the marks which characterise the nation in its constitution and in its hope.

Having thus given the great " sign " of the " woman," we next have " another sign in heaven"—the woman's enemy.

xii. 3. **And another sign was seen in heaven; and behold a great red dragon, having seven heads and ten horns, and upon his heads seven diadems.**] This "sign " also is seen " in heaven," and we are not left in any doubt as to what it signifies. Verse 9 explains to us that "the great red dragon " is

"that old serpent called the Devil (Slanderer) and
Satan (Adversary)." He has seven heads and ten
horns, and upon his heads seven diadems. These
are the "signs" of the universality of earthly
dominion : for Satan is the "prince of the power
of the air" (Eph. ii. 2), "the prince of this world"
(John xii. 31; xiv. 30; xvi. 11). As such, the
Lord did not dispute his claim (Luke iv. 5-7). His
colour is the colour of fire, and of blood. This is a
"sign" of his cruelty and blood-thirstiness (John viii.
44. 1 John iii. 12), and of the war which he makes "in
heaven" and "on earth." The heads and horns and
crowns are manifestly the "sign" of earthly power,
gathered up in himself : for to whomsoever he will he
gives or delegates it (Luke iv. 6, 7; chap. xiii. 2). Thus
briefly is the authority and power of the woman's
enemy set before us.

xii. 4. **And his tail draggeth down the third part
of the stars of heaven, and he cast them to the
earth :**] Here we have further details concerning this
"sign." The "woman," as we have seen, is the "sign"
of the Jewish nation as a whole; and the object and
action of the Devil could not be more clearly stated.

We are again taken back to the beginning of things ;
even to Satan's first rebellion, and to the angels who
fell with him. This is surely the "sign" of Satan's
power among the angels; as the heads and horns are
a "sign" of his power among men on the earth. It
seems clear from this that the third part of angels
followed him in his great rebellion.

**and the dragon standeth before the woman
that is about to bring forth, that when she
should bring forth he might devour her child**]

Here we have a sign indeed; far beyond any mere passing event; or, even far beyond what Alford suggests, " the whole course of hostility against the Lord during His humiliation."

We believe it goes much further back than this. These two Signs take us back to events which date " from the foundation of the world";* and do not go beyond the question of the Government of the Earth, which the Dragon has usurped since the creation of man.

The verb is " stands," not " stood." It refers to a continuous act, and not to a mere passing event.

The moment the word went forth that the seed of the woman should one day finally crush the serpent's head, that old serpent, the Devil and Satan, took his stand before the woman in order to destroy her seed as soon as it should be brought forth.

Satan's object, from the going forth of that prophecy, was to prevent that " seed of the woman " from ever coming into the world. He does not mean to be crushed if he can prevent it, and hence it is that, just as we are about to be told of the serpent's doom and how it is brought about, we are thus reminded of the fact, and told how he took his stand so as to prevent His coming at all ; or to bruise His heel, if He should come.

He has used, of course, various instruments and agents, and while these have had their own respective

---

* This phrase occurs *seven* times : Matt. xiii. 35; xxv. 34. Luke xi. 50. Heb. iv. 3 ; ix. 26. Rev. xiii. 8 ; xvii. 8. On the other hand, the phrase " BEFORE the foundation of the world " is very different, and concerns the church of God in its Head and members, and occurs *three* times (John xvii. 24. Eph. i. 4. 1 Peter i. 20), because it is an act of Deity, and flows from uninfluenced grace.

objects and motives, Satan's object has been one—and one only—and this has formed

THE GREAT CONFLICT OF THE AGES

We see the first great attempt in Gen. vi. 1, when Satan strove to corrupt the whole of mankind. He succeeded so far, that only one family was uncon. taminated. That is the meaning of the " perfect in his generation " in Gen. vi. 9. תָּמִים (*tahmīm*) means *without blemish*, especially as to pure descent, or blood (Ex. xii. 5 ; xxix. 1, etc.). It refers to genital perfection.*
So vast was the corruption from the irruption of evil angels (2 Pet. ii. 4-7. Jude 6-8), that the whole race had to be destroyed. Noah and his three sons were alone pure from the awful defilement.†

Nothing but Divine interposition saved the race and preserved mankind from a total overthrow. In Shem, the line of " the seed of the woman " was continued, and the promise of Eden was preserved.

The second great attempt was made in Exod. i. to destroy the male children of Israel at their birth. Pharaoh's object was to prevent the increase of the people, so that they might not get up out of Egypt. Satan's object was to destroy the male line altogether, and thus make the birth of " the seed of the woman " impossible.

Again Divine interposition defeated Satan's plans. It was a spiritual conflict in which Heaven and Hell

---

* " generation " is not the same word rendered "generations " in the former part of the verse. Here it means *contemporaries;* there it means *family history.*

† If so, and his sons married the fearful progeny, we have a side light on the diversity of the great races, though originally descended from a single pair.

were taking part all along. It is the same conflict
which we see here in Rev. xii. But it is written, "He
taketh the wise in their own craftiness" (Job v. 13),
and what Pharaoh had said with Egypt's "wisdom"
(Ex. i. 10) was frustrated by a baby's tear (Ex. ii. 6):
for when Pharaoh's daughter opened the ark of bul-
rushes, "she saw the child, and behold *the babe wept.
And she had compassion on him.*" Thus, Pharaoh's wisdom
was made to end in having to board, lodge, bring up,
and educate the very man who accomplished the very
object Pharaoh had striven to prevent; for Moses
delivered the nation out of his hand, and God overthrew his armies in the Red Sea.

We see another very special and determined attempt
of Satan to break up the Royal Line, by which the seed
of the woman was to come, in 2 Chron. xxi., xxii.

On the death of Jehoshaphat, his son Jehoram,
made a beginning (to serve his own purposes, of course).
He "slew all his brethren with the sword" (2 Ch. xxi. 4).
So the Royal Line was reduced to himself—one life.

But he had children; and of these, we read that the
Arabians came up against Judah, and slew all his sons,
"so that there was never a son left him, save Ahaziah,
the youngest of his sons" (2 Chron. xxi. 17). Mark the
emphasis put by the Holy Spirit on this solemn fact.
That they were slain, is clear from 2 Chron. xxii. 1.

Ahaziah was then the only lineal descendant of the
Royal Line of the seed of the woman, through David,
Abraham, and Shem. But Ahaziah had children. These,
in their turn, were slain by Athaliah. She evidently
left them all for dead, for it says (2 Chron. xxii. 10) she
"destroyed all the seed royal of the house of Judah."
That is what she meant to do, and would have done

had not God again Divinely interposed and rescued the infant "from among the king's sons that were slain" (2 Chron. xxii. 11). For six years all the hopes of God's people rested on that one life. All the faithfulness of God depended on the life of that one babe. While Jehosheba, the wife of the high priest, was hidden, with the child, in one of the chambers of the House of God, her husband, Jehoiada, was going about among the people testifying and saying, "Behold, the king's son shall reign, as the LORD hath said, of the sons of David." That was the burden of the testimony—the faithfulness of Jehovah. And nothing but the Divine interposition frustrated the designs of Satan (and the plans of Athaliah) from succeeding in cutting off the Line by which the seed of the woman was eventually to come into the world.

In the book of Esther we see another attempt on the part of Satan to destroy the whole nation; and not merely the males, or the seed royal. He used Haman's pride as the secondary cause. But again a small thing was used to frustrate the design of "the Jews' enemy." A sleepless night: that was all; but it was enough (Est. vi. 1). And again Satan was defeated.

But he still " stood before the woman ready to devour her child as soon as it should be born." And at length the hour came when the seed of the woman entered into the world.

Herod was used this time; and having ascertained the *place* (Bethlehem) from the Scribes (Matt. ii. 4), and the *time* when the star appeared from the wise men (Matt. ii. 7), he slew all the babes in Bethlehem under two years of age, and thought he had devoured the seed of the woman. But again Heaven interfered and defeated his plans.

The suggestion of Satan that Christ should throw Himself down from the pinnacle of the Temple (Matt. iv. 6) ; the attempt of the people of Nazareth to cast Him down from the brow of the hill (Luke iv. 29) ; the two storms on the Lake (Matt. viii. 24 and Mark iv. 37 ; Luke viii. 23), were all so many attempts of Satan to devour this man-child.   And when he saw Him on the cross, and laid in the sepulchre, and the stone sealed, and the watch set, he thought he had his prey within his grasp.   But again Heaven interfered.   " God raised Him from the dead,'' and the child was " caught up to God and His throne '' (Rev. iii. 21).   But we are anticipating.

xii. 5.   **And she brought forth a son, a male** (*i.e.*, a man-child), **who is about to rule all the nations with a rod of iron** :] The word rendered male is ἄρσεν* (*arsen*), and is of the *neuter* gender.   It is therefore of no sex, and is most appropriate here.   It is He of whom it is specially prophesied that He should rule the nations with a rod of iron.   Ps. ii. 9.

And her child was caught away to God, and to†‎ his throne.] This, again, is emphatically true of Christ (see Rev. iii. 21).   But it is not true of the Church of God.   We are to be " called on high " by a special calling ; and our bodies made " like unto His most glorious body " (Phil. iii. 14, 20, 21).

Moreover, this calling will be all at once ; and not " born." Each member of the Body of Christ is *created*, and is " a new creation in Christ Jesus."

It seems a pity, almost, to have our minds disturbed

---

* According to L.T.Tr.A. WH. and RV.

† G.L.T.Tr.A. WH. and RV. repeat the word πρός (*pros*) *to.*

by alluding to other common interpretations; but it is well for our readers to have the opportunity of judging for themselves, and of seeing the vagaries of expositors. We are asked to believe, for example, that the man-child is "a baptized Emperor, the son of Christ's faithful [!] church, elevated to the whole Empire, to an avowedly Christian throne" (Elliott).

Adam Clarke affirms that it is "the dynasty of Christian Emperors, beginning with Constantine." Some see "the Valenses and Albigenses as sequestered from the pure worshippers generally." Others believe it is "the Nicene Creed"!

We thus see what comes of not "rightly dividing the word of truth"; and of interpreting of one dispensation that which properly relates to quite another

This is the end of the second sign, and there is a break in the continuity.

xii. 6. **And the woman fled into the wilderness, where she hath a place prepared* there† by God, that there they should nourish her a thousand two hundred and sixty days.**] This is said by way of anticipation: for the war in heaven occurs before the flight of the woman, and, indeed, leads to that flight. This flight, therefore, is consequent on the war, and not on the catching up of the child to God and His throne. This is clear from verse 14.

c. (page 386), xii. 7-9. *The War in Heaven*

xii. 7. **And there was war in heaven: Michael and his angels** going forth **to war with‡ the dragon; and**

---

* The verb ἐτοιμάζω (*hetoimazō*) *to prepare*, occurs seven times in the Apocalypse (viii. 6; ix. 7, 15; xii. 6; xvi. 12; xix. 7; xxi. 2).

† G.T.Tr. (marg.) A. WH. and RV. add ἐκεῖ (*ekei*) *there*.

‡ So, G.L.T.Tr.A. WH. and RV.

the dragon warred and his angels,] The various reading here is abundantly attested by the best codices, and cannot be rendered as in the AV. Tregelles renders it baldly, " Michael and his angels to war." We have supplied the word " going forth," as in RV. This is absolutely necessary to make English. This reveals the fact that the initiative will be taken by Michael, and not by the Dragon : a very important point in the interpretation. The time has come in the Divine counsels for this great event of the ages. Satan, who has hitherto had access to the heavens is at length to be cast out.

We are not to think of Heaven as consisting of one place. The word is so often used in the plural, that, though we are not free to adopt the teachings of Jewish tradition, yet we are to think of many (it may be) different spheres. As the heavens are " higher than the earth," so we may look on them as being larger than the earth. And as the earth is divided into various countries and states, so may heaven have its various divisions. In one of them these mighty spiritual forces set themselves in battle array.

On the one side we have Michael, who is elsewhere described as "one of the chief princes" (Dan. x. 13) ; "your prince," *i.e.*, of Israel (Dan. x. 21) ; "the great prince which standeth for thy (Daniel's) people " (Dan. xii. 1) ; "the archangel " (Jude 9). He it is, with his heavenly hosts, who makes war against the dragon, and not the dragon who makes war against the man-child (as is so often stated). He does not do this at all, but makes war against the woman (verse 13) ; and that war is made on earth and not in heaven. So that the interpretation of this, as meaning Satan's opposing the rapture of the church, falls to the ground. The church will be removed long before these judgment scenes commence; and is therefore not to be looked for in any place in this chapter.

On the other side we have the Beast of chaps. xiii. and xvii. In Daniel ii. we have these powers in their earthly, human, mortal, successive and historical form. But in Daniel vii. and in the Apocalypse, we have the superhuman revival and contemporaneous concentration of them in the Beast.

The Dragon's dominion covers all the powers and governments of the world, and are here seen included in and controlled by one being—the Dragon. The sovereignty of the world is about to become the sovereignty of our Lord and of His Christ, as we have just heard it announced " in heaven " (xi. 15). We are here shown the source and the embodiment of this sovereignty. This is why the prophecy is suspended just at this point. It is in order to explain to us what this sovereignty is, whence it comes, and whither it goes. All is here gathered up into one head.

In 2 Thess. ii we find further information as to the rise of this final embodiment of Satanic power. There we are clearly told that the revelation of that awful being has an appointed season. He cannot arise before his time. We are told why and how this is. In Rev. xii. we have the events which lead up to that revelation, and in Rev. xiii. we have the actual manifestation of the Beast himself.

2 Thess. ii. therefore forms an important link when studied in connection with Rev. xii. There we learn that the Beast could not be manifested on earth as long

as he (*masculine*) now holdeth fast∗ [to his place in the heavenlies, Rev. xii. 7]. He will hold it fast until he be cast out.† This casting out is described in Rev. xii., and we are here told exactly how it will take place, and what will be its causes and consequences. When Paul wrote, worldly power was then being used, and has all along been used by Satan for the accomplishment of his secret purposes ; and it is still thus working, but here (in Rev. xii.) we see it come to a head, and Satan is about to openly manifest it. Meantime, "Ye know what (*neut.*) holdeth‡ him (the lawless one) fast, that he (the lawless one) may be revealed in his time." Paul could write thus to the church of the Thessalonians, for he had previously told them and they knew ; but *we* do not know. All we know is that it cannot be a *person* who holds the lawless one fast, for the word is in the neuter gender. It can only be

---

∗ This is the meaning of the word, as is clear from its use in the other epistle : 1 Thess. v. 21 (" prove all things, *hold fast* that which is good "). Here are all the occurrences of the word, so that our readers may judge for themselves :— Matt. xxi. 38 (G.L.T.Tr.A. WH. and RV. have a different verb here). Luke iv. 42 ; viii. 15 ; xiv. 9. John v. 4. Acts xxvii. 40. Rom. i. 18 ; vii. 6. 1 Cor. vii. 30 ; xi. 2 ; xv. 2. 2 Cor. vi. 10. 1 Thess. v. 21. Philem. 13. Heb. iii. 6, 14 ; x. 23.

† This is the meaning of the idiomatic expression "$\dot{\epsilon}\kappa$ $\tau o\hat{v}$ $\mu\acute{\epsilon}\sigma ov$ $\gamma\acute{\epsilon}\nu\eta\tau\alpha\iota$ (*ek tou mesou genetai*). See Matt. xiii. 49. Acts xvii. 33 ; xxiii. 10. 1 Cor. v. 2. 2 Cor. vi. 17. Col. ii. 14. So in the Septuagint of Isa. lii. 11 ; lvii. 1. The same usage is seen in the classics : Plutarch. (*Timol.* p. 238, 3) ; Herodotus (3, 83 ; and 8, 22) ; Terence (*Phorm.* v. 8, 30) ; and Xenophon (*Cyr.* 5, 2, 26). It is absurd therefore to take this idiomatic phrase literally (as B. W. Newton does) and render it : "until he (Antichrist) arises (or is revealed) *out of the midst* " !

‡ See Note (∗) above. The verb is transitive, and *must* have an *object*.

a place, and we suggest that it is τὸ φρέαρ (*to phrear*) *the pit of the Abyss*, Rev. ix. 2, out of which he is to ascend. In any case, the popular view cannot be correct, which takes it of the Holy Spirit. What does the Holy Spirit " hold fast " (1 Thess. v. 21) in order that the lawless one may be revealed in his appointed time ? This idea arose from a wrong translation of the verb κατέχω (*katechō*), which means *to hold something fast*.

We have given all the occurrences of this word in a note on the previous page, so that our readers can judge for themselves. That wrong translation of both the AV. and RV. arises from ignoring the fact that the verb is *transitive*, and must have an *object*. Something must be held fast. Further confusion is also introduced by not preserving the important difference between the *genders*, which is *neuter* in verse 6 (" THAT which holds him fast "), *i.e.*, the Pit of the Abyss ; and *masculine* in verse 7 (" HE who holds something fast," *i.e.*, his position in the heavenlies, etc.

Having regard to these four facts—

(1) The *meaning* and usage of the verb ;

(2) The fact that it is *transitive* ;

(3) The distinction between the two genders in verses 6, 7 ; and

(4) The undoubted idiom in *v.* 7—*cast out*,

it is clear that 2 Thess. ii. 6, 7 has suffered much at the hands of translators, and needs to be entirely recast.

At the first advent the announcement was made " on earth, peace." But now, at the time of the Second Advent, it is " in heaven, war " ; for the Dispensations have changed.

At the return of the remnant from Babylon, Satan was present to resist the restoration of the Nation (Zech. iii. 2), and was rebuked. So it will be again when the great restoration is about to take place : but war will be declared against him.

The mystery connected with this conflict is easy to faith, though hard for reason. A little insight is given into these spiritual realities in such passages as Job i. and ii. 1 Kings xxii. 19-22. Eph. vi. 11, 12. Jude 6.

Milton has described this war, but he only drew on his imagination, which was limited by earthly battle-fields. This war is wholly different in its occasion, its scenes, its combatants, and its weapons. This war has its foreknown and therefore its foretold ending.

xii. 8. **And they prevailed not; nor was even their place found any more in heaven.**] The great object with which that war is waged will be accomplished.

9. **And the great dragon was cast down, the old serpent; who is called the Devil, and Satan, he who deceiveth the whole world: he was cast down unto the earth, and his angels were cast down with him.**] There can be no doubt as to whom this " sign " refers. By four names is he defined, so that we might make no mistake. And yet, it will hardly be believed that, in spite of this, there are interpreters who maintain that it means the " Pagan Roman Empire," and Michael is the " Christian Roman Empire." There are others who understand it of no real war at all, but only a pro-longed antagonism between good and evil. How refreshing to come back to the Word of God, and believe that we have here the climax which the Lord Jesus, looking forward to the result of His " sufferings," in " the glory " that should follow, already foresaw with

His spiritual prophetic vision in Luke x. 18, and said:
" I beheld Satan as lightning fall from heaven."

A. (page 386), xii. 10-12.   *The Loud Voice in Heaven*

Each of these visions seen in heaven are marked by
heavenly voices and utterances. We have one in this
Vision. The Structure is as beautiful as it is simple.
The subjects of the utterance are two :

>   (1) Rejoicing in heaven ;
>   (2) Woe to the earth ;

and between them there is a call for universal rejoicing.

A. (page 386), xii. 10-12.   *The Loud Voice in Heaven*

```
A | h | k | 10-.  Rejoicing in heaven
  |   | l | -10, 11.  Reasons
  |
  |   | i | 12-.  Call to rejoice
  |
  | h | k | -12-.  Woe to the earth
  |   | l | -12.  Reason
```

xii. 10.   **And I heard a loud voice in heaven, saying,***

> **"Now is come the salvation, and the
> power, and the kingdom of our God,
> and the authority of His Christ:
> because the accuser of our brethren
> is cast down, who accused them be-
> fore our God day and night.   (11)
> And they overcame him because**

---

* This is the order of the words according to G.L.T.Tr.A. WH. and
RV.

of the blood of the Lamb, and
because of the word of their testimony ; and they loved not their life
even unto death. (12) Therefore
Rejoice, ye heavens, and ye who
dwell in them. Woe to* the earth
and to the sea ! because the devil
is come down to you, having great
fury, knowing that he hath but
a short season."]

This is the song of victory sung in heaven. It
will be sung by those who will have been caught
up to heaven out of "the great Tribulation."
(Ch. vii., xiv., xv.) For they speak of "our brethren."
"*Now* is come" is the shout of triumph which celebrates, by anticipation, the results of Satan's being
cast out of heaven. This is the first step arising out of
Heaven's declaration of war. The emphasis is on the
pronoun "they," in verse 11, for they who overcame on
earth now call on all heaven to rejoice over the wondrous victory. When the fruits of this heavenly victory
are fully reaped on earth, then there will be others to
call for the new songs, which are already written down
for the singers in Ps. xciii.—xcix., xcviii., cxlix. This
call to rejoice finds its echo in the final song of triumph
in Rev. xix. But all is traced up to and grounded on
the infinite merits of "the blood of the Lamb": and
the wondrous efficacy of His atonement.

Again, we see that the Church cannot be here,
for no one can accuse the Church before God. See
Rom. viii. 33.

We shall be indeed surprised if our readers are able

---

* G.L.T.Tr.A. WH. and RV. omit " *the inhabiters of.*"

to see, as the cause of that heavenly outburst of joy, the mere " casting down of paganism from the throne of the Roman Empire."

The result of that was blessing to the world.

The result of this is " woe to the earth " (*v.* 12) !

But such a difference as this does not count with the expositors of this Book. Nor does the fact that the result of that conflict has gone on for centuries, in which the whole Reformation period is included ; while this is to last for a very brief period—one of many great events occurring in the last 3½ years.

When Satan is cast down, "he hath but a short time," which is definitely stated to be 3½ years, during which he is wroth with the woman, and makes war with the remnant of her seed (xii. 14-17).

This " Woe " is the last of a series of three (viii. 13); and must, therefore, be *subsequent to the first two*, which at this stage will have passed (xi. 14). The third is proclaimed in chap. xii. 12, and consists of the casting out of Satan.

This conclusively shows that, though the *Vision* of ch. xii. is anticipative, the actual casting out cannot take place till the middle of the last of the seventy weeks (Dan. ix. 27). The Beast will be reigning on the earth during the first half of this week (Rev. vi.—xi.) ; but, in his human and *mortal* form ; and acting "peaceably"(Dan. xi. 21). But now, in the middle of the week, the crisis or " Third Woe " comes (xii. 12). Satan is cast out. The Beast, having received his "deadly wound," reappears in his *superhuman* form, and " makes war with the saints" (xiii. 7). This last half of the week is " the great and terrible day of the Lord." But this brings us to the next, the Fourth Vision " on Earth " (xii. 13—xiii. 18).

13

THE FOURTH VISION "ON EARTH"
(12:13—13:8)

This Vision, as a whole, is occupied with the Result " on Earth " of the " war in heaven " (chap. xii.). It is two-fold: First, the effect is given as it concerns Israel, and then, the effect as it concerns the Earth as a whole; and all forming part of this parenthesis or Episode, which takes us back to the period before xi. 13, and shows us how the Beast came to be on the earth. It is he who makes war against the " Two Witnesses " (ch. xi.); and it is against him and his armies that the judgments and plagues of chaps. vi.-xi. are directed.

Now, we are taken back to have these prior events further made known and explained to us. The Episode does not end till chap. xv. 8.

The Structure of this fourth Vision "on Earth" is presented in two separate parts, because they concern two separate Peoples (Jew and Gentile), which are never "reckoned" together (Num. xxiii. 9). The two divisions are as follows:—

𝕮⁴ (page 118), xii. 13-xiii. 18. THE FOURTH VISION "ON EARTH"

The Result " on Earth " of the " War in Heaven "

𝕮⁴ | W | xii. 13—xiii. 1-. The effect as regards ISRAEL
| X | xiii. -1-18. The effect as regards the EARTH

Dealing first with the former of these two divisions, we have to give its expansion. It will be seen, by a reference to page 386, that its Structure exactly corresponds with the preceding Vision "in heaven," (chap. xii. 1-12); the correspondence showing that both parts of chap. xii. refer to the same subject, viz., Israel. The following is the expansion of W (page 413):

W (page 413), xii. 13—xiii. 1-. *The Result of the War "in Heaven" as regards Israel*

W | A | xii. 13-.   The Dragon cast unto the earth
    | B | a | -13.   The Dragon and the Woman
          | b | 14-16.   The Woman's flight
          | c | 17.   War on the earth
  | *A* | xiii. 1-.   The Dragon standing on the sand of the sea

The Dragon, as soon as he is cast down into the earth, at once proceeds to make war with the Woman, and the remnant of her seed. He does this by bringing up the Beast in his *superhuman* form.

xii. 13. **And when the dragon saw that he was cast** down **to the earth, he pursued** (or persecuted) **the woman which brought forth the man-child** * (14) **And there was given to the woman the† two wings of the great eagle, that she might fly into the wilderness, unto her place, where she** is nourished there a **time, and times, and half a time, from the face of the serpent.**] Thus the wilderness will, as of old, afford a refuge for Israel; for the coming Exodus is to be like the

---

* ἄρσεν *(arsen)* T.Tr.A. WH., not ἄρρην *(arrhēn)*.

† L.T.Tr.Aᵇ. WH. and RV. add the article, here.

first. (See Isa. xi. 16. Ezek. xx. 35-38.) "*There will I plead with you face to face, like as I pleaded with your fathers in the wilderness of the land of Egypt.*" These are significant words. And we have like words in Hosea ii. 14, 15, where we read that the valley of Achor (which was the first place on the road from the wilderness to Canaan, Josh. vii. 26) shall prove "a door of hope."

"Therefore, behold, I allure her,
And bring her into the wilderness,
And speak comfortably unto her.
And I will give her her vineyards from thence,
And the valley of Achor for a door of hope :
And she shall sing there, as in the days of her youth,
And as in the day when she came up out of the
land of Egypt " (Hos. ii. 14, 15, and see Ex. xv.).

"The woman *fled* into the wilderness." So of old " it was told to the king of Egypt that the people *fled*" (Ex. xiv. 5. Josh. xxiv. 6). That flight was literal. So will this be. And at that time such passages as Ps. xxxv. 1-5 and Lam. iv. 19, etc., will find their exhaustive fulfilment. They "shall be hid in the day of the Lord's anger" (Zeph. ii. 3). The Lord Jesus spoke of this "flight" in Matt. xxiv. 15-28 and Mark xiii. 14-23. This flight is not the same as that which He spoke of in Luke xxi. 20-24, for that took place at the destruction of Jerusalem, long "before all these things" (Luke xxi. 12) which the Lord spoke of in Matthew and Mark.

This "flight" is from Jerusalem and Judea, for this is the central point where the two witnesses had been slain ; and the final testimony borne to the doings of the Beast. The woman (*i.e.,* the nation) flies because of the persecution of the Dragon. If none might buy or sell save those who have the mark of the Beast, some miraculous sustinence must be provided. And God Himself will again "furnish a table in the wilderness." Of old, He fed them there. In Ex. xix. 4, He appeals to them and says: "Ye have seen . . . how I bare **you** on eagles' wings and brought you unto myself." And so again, in Deut. xxxii. 11, 12, in the song of Moses, he mentions the same form of Divine help. The eagles' wings are "a sign " which signifies the miraculous swiftness, by which the Divinely given help will come to them. They are no " Roman eagles "! It does not say eagles, but eagles' *wings*. The Roman eagles possessed no wings, and had themselves to be carried !

Fleeing, first to the " mountains" and then on to the " wilderness," there the people will be fed for three years and a half. The period is expressed exactly as in Dan. vii. **25** and xii. 7. And it has already been mentioned in this book in different forms (see chap. xi. **2**, 3, and page 412)

xii. 15. **And the serpent cast out of his mouth after the woman, water as a river, that he might cause her to be carried away of the flood.**] At the first Exodus it was the sea through which she went into the wilderness with its forty-two stations. It is " a flood " which drives her into the wilderness for forty-two months. ⁋ The delivering from the sea was miraculous ; so will be the deliverance from this " flood." Why should not one be as literal as the other ? Where is the difficulty ? Observe, it does not say " like a flood," as in Jer. xlvi. 7, 8. Nor does it say an army like water ; but " water like a river." The first is literal, and its likeness is given. It does not expand into a lake, but rushes forward like a " flood."

16. **And the earth helped the woman, and the earth opened her mouth, and swallowed up the flood which the dragon cast out of his mouth.**] And why not ? The sea helped the same woman when it swallowed up the armies of Pharaoh, and why should not the earth help the woman again by swallowing up the forces of Satan. It is to be again as it was at the Exodus. And it will be a time of earthquakes and great physical disturbances. (See Is. xi. 15, 16.)

In Isa. lix. 19, we read of the enemy coming in like " a flood," just before " the Redeemer shall come to Zion," and when Gentile times shall come to the full.

The earth once opened to swallow the host of Dathan and Abiram (Num. xvi.) ; and so it is written : "*According to the days of the coming up out of the land of Egypt, I will show unto him marvellous things*" (Mic. vii. 15).

17. **And the dragon was wroth with the woman, and went to make war with the rest of her seed, who keep the commandments of God, and have** (or keep) **the testimony of Jesus.***] Being baffled in his attempts to destroy the seed of the woman, who has been, ere this, " caught away to God and His throne," ! he turns his forces against the remnant of her seed. The description of this remnant is given, and agrees with that spoken of in other parts of this book; and while the bulk of the nation is safe and nourished, a faithful remnant on earth is having war made against it. We have these two seeds in chap. vii. First, the 144,000 sealed for testimony in the earth ; and, afterwards, the great multitude caught away to heaven. In the next

---

* G.L.T.Tr.A.WH. and RV. omit " Christ," which keeps this passage in harmony with the expression in other parts of this Book.

chapter they are called "saints"; and we nave the two bodies again, the former in xiii. 15 and the latter in vi. 9.

In the *Textus Receptus* the first sentence of the first verse of chap xiii. is the concluding sentence of the twelfth chapter, but the AV. wrongly transposes it, and puts it as the first sentence in chap. xiii. The transla'tors were doubtless misled by the wrong reading of the *Textus Receptus*, which has ἐστάθην (*estathēn*) *I stood*, instead of ἐστάθη (*estathē*) *he stood* (*i.e.*, the dragon). The RV. (agreeing with L.T.Tr.A. and WH.) has restored the sentence to its proper place, at the close of chap. xii. 17 ; and given the correct reading, "he stood," in accordance with all the critical Greek texts and oldest and best manuscripts.

The structure (on page 414) shows that this must be right; as that sentence is necessary in order to balance the first sentence of xii. 13.

It is the dragon who has been cast into the earth (A. xii. 13-); and it is the same dragon who stands on the sand of the sea (*A.* xiii. 1-). Foiled in his attempts to destroy the woman's seed, as he had been foiled in his assault on the woman herself, he is now seen by John standing on the sand of the sea, and from thence, as it were, calling up the first of the two Beasts from the Abyss to carry out his final plans. So this section ends with the words :

And he stood upon the sand of the sea.] *i.e.*, upon the shore. Daniel saw this same "great sea" and the four winds of heaven striving upon it (Dan. vii. 2).

Before proceeding to the second great division of this fourth Vision "on Earth," it may be well to read and study carefully Dan. vii. 7, 8, 19-27, which treats of the manifestation of Satan's power in the two powers of chap. xiii. in their final superhuman form, and in their obsessed spirit characters.

X. (page 413), xiii. -1-18

The Result of the " War in Heaven" as regards the Earth at large

We have seen and considered the result of the "War in Heaven" as it concerns *Israel*. (W. (page 414), xii. 13-17.) We have now to consider its further effect as it concerns the *Earth* at large.

This effect is twofold, inasmuch as it results in the rise of the Two Beasts:

The one from the Sea (verses -1-10)
The other from the Earth (verses 11-18)

The description of these two—the Beast and the False Prophet—occupies the whole of chap. xiii. The chapter is divided thus:—

X. (page 413), xiii. -1-18. *The Twofold Result as regards the Earth at large*

X | Y | xiii. -1-10.   The Beast from the Sea
  | Z | xiii. 11-18.   The Beast from the Earth

Y and Z are now to be expanded. They concern the last mighty form of Satanic re-incarnation.

The one is *Anti-Christ*
Another is *Anti-Spirit*
The other is *Anti-God*

Thus completing the Infernal Trinity.

These two (the Beast and the False Prophet) are described in seven particulars, and the two members marked Y and Z are arranged precisely in the same order. They are given in a corresponding *Extended*

Parallelism, of which the last members of each are divided into two; these two being arranged as an *Introversion*—h, i ; i, h.

The following is the Structure:—

X. (pages 413, 419), xiii. -1-18. *The Effect of the "War in Heaven"*

```
X | Y | a | -1-.  The Vision.  "And I saw" (καὶ εἶδον)
    |   b | -1-.  The first Beast
    |       c | -1-.  His origin.  The Sea (ἀναβαῖνον)
    |       d | -1, 2-.  His description.
    |           e | -2-.  His power (δύναμις) derived from the Dragon
    |           f | 3-8.  His deeds
    |               g | h | 9.  The call to hear.  "Let him hear"
    |                   i | 10.  The lesson.  "Here is patience and faith"
  |
  | Z | a | 11-.  The Vision.  "And I saw" (καὶ εἶδον)
    |   b | -11-.  The second Beast.  The false prophet (xvi. 13; xix. 20)
    |       c | -11-.  His origin.  The Earth (ἀναβαῖνον)
    |       d | -11.  His description
    |           e | 12-.  His authority (ἐξουσία) derived from first Beast
    |           f | -12-17.  His deeds
    |               g | i | 18-.  The lesson.  "Here is wisdom"
    |                   h | -18.  The call to count.  "Let him count"
```

This Structure is already so minute and exhaustive, that none of its members have (or need) any expansion. It completes the effect of the "war in heaven" so far as it regards the earth at large as distinct from Israel; and concludes the fourth Vision " on Earth."

After the failure of Satan's attempt to destroy Israel (the woman's seed), John sees him standing on the sand, or shore of the sea, as though pondering over, weighing, and forming his future plans. And while thus occupied, John sees the outcome, in the Beast which rises (as though at Satan's call) out of the sea.

The beasts of chap. iv. are (as we have seen) ζῷα (*zōa*), and are rendered by us as *Zōa*, and in the singular *Zōon*. This, is θηρίον (*thērion*), *a wild beast*, or *a beast of prey*.

The text supplies us with the Divine information given on this great subject.

xiii. 1. **And I saw a beast rising up out of the sea, having ten horns and seven heads,* and upon his horns** (gen.) **ten diadems, and upon his heads** (acc.) **blasphemous names.**] This is the Beast in his *superhuman* stage. Already he has been on the Earth for 3½ years, in his mortal stage. He then receives his death-wound mentioned below, in verse 3 (as the seventh head), and comes up out of the Abyss as the *eighth* king, comprising all the seven heads and the ten horns. These are, in their now *superhuman* form, *crowned*. In their *mortal* form they were not crowned. (See xvii. 12.)

It will be better to defer the interpretation of the heads and horns of this Beast until we come

---

* This is the order here according to G.L.T.Tr.A. WH. and RV., and not as in AV., where the "heads" are put before the " horns."

to chap. xvii., where we can consider it with greater advantage. The Holy Spirit has confined Himself here to an outline description, or brief statement, as to the general characteristics of these two Beasts; while in chap. xvii. He has explained them more fully.

It will be well, therefore, for us to follow on these lines, and content ourselves now by the general state-ment that we have here something far beyond Rome, papal or pagan; something far beyond the "fourth Beast," or Roman Empire, as it is called. We have all the world powers, and all dominion in the earth, gathered up and concentrated in this one sign. We see them in their *superhuman* form, here in the Apoca-lypse, as we see them in their human or *mortal* form in Daniel. It is the whole Image of Dan. ii. in its superhuman form which we see here, rather than one of its mortal parts. IT IS THE IMAGE REVIVED AS A WHOLE. It reaches to " wheresoever the children of men dwell " (Dan. ii. 38); it affects " all that dwell upon the earth " (Rev. xiii. 8; xi. 10; xiv. 6). When the time for these final judgments arrives the great stone falls. It smites the image upon the feet, it is true (Dan. ii. 34); but it is immediately added, "Then was the iron, the clay, the brass, and the gold BROKEN TO PIECES TOGETHER " (Dan. ii. 35).* This is far more extended than the Roman Empire.

It takes in the whole earth; in fact, **all earthly power, and** all worldly dominion, in its final consum-

---

* The Figure of *Asyndeton*, or "no ands," hurries us on to the great final catastrophe, which affects all "the kingdoms of this world"; and bids us dwell, not on any one of them, but upon the whole of them as one. (See *Figures of Speech*, page 137.)

mation. Hence, all the heads and horns of the various successive powers are here combined and united in one, forming the embodiment of all political sovereignty on earth. There is to be no other during its existence; and there will be none but our Lord's and His Christ's after it is gone. In chap. xvii. we have them separately, and can so consider them when we come to that chapter.

2. **And the Beast which I saw was like unto a leopard, and his feet as** the feet **of a bear, and his mouth as the mouth of a lion: and the dragon gave him his power, and his throne, and great authority.**] We are at a loss to understand how this can be the Roman Empire revived! For the Beast itself is like a *leopard* (Greece) (Dan. vii. 6). Its feet are those of the *bear* (Medo-Persia); and its mouth is like a *lion's* mouth (Babylon). Where is the Roman Empire here in any form? If the Beast be the Roman Empire, does he have himself, intact, for one of his own heads? The notion is only a venerable, but vain, imagination. Rome cannot be at the same time one of the heads, and yet the whole Beast himself. " One is " (xvii. 10). That is said to be the Roman Empire. But it is added, "the other is NOT." Is this the Roman Empire, too? Clearly, Not! What we have here is the embodiment and personification of the sovereignty of the world under Satanic power, for "the whole world lieth (in the power of) the wicked one."

When we say personification, we must recognise the spirit-being from the Abyss (xvii. 8), *i.e.*, the superhuman agent, through whom he works. As Satan delegates this special mission to the Beast (a superhuman-being), so does the Beast act through a human being by obsession, or in some other way. God, here, takes us behind the scenes and shows us the Satanic machinery by which the whole thing is operated. While the people on earth see only a man,—" the Man "—they may know nothing of the power of the Abyss behind him, and out of which he comes.

This is exactly what is foretold by our Lord, in the parable of the strong man (Matt. xii. 43-45), when He tells how the unclean spirit returns to his house whence he came out, and " taketh with himself seven other spirits more wicked than himself, and they enter in and dwell there : and the last state of that man is worse than the first. EVEN SO SHALL IT BE ALSO UNTO THIS WICKED GENERATION."

This shows that the Lord is speaking a parable with regard to the nation of Israel ; and what does it teach if it does not show us that there will be obsession by evil spirits acting through human agency; not only with regard to Israel, but with regard to the whole world. Doubtless, the human agent will have already been alive some time on earth, working up to this point, when Satan takes him in hand and uses him henceforth for his own purposes ; by rapid strides raising him to the pinnacle of earthly pride and power.

The moment will come when a human being will be found who is willing to accept that which the Lord Jesus rejected in Luke iv. 6, 7, when the devil, having shown Him " *all the kingdoms of the world*," said unto Him : " All this power will I give Thee, and the glory of them : for that is delivered unto me ; and to whomsoever I will, I give it. If, therefore, thou wilt *worship* me, all shall be thine." The Lord refused it, but he did not deny the truth of the words, or dispute Satan's

authority or power. He merely says: "Get thee
behind me, Satan : for it is written, Thou shalt worship
the Lord thy God, and him only shalt thou serve."
The whole question is one of worship, and it will never
be settled till at last Satan finds one to worship him.
In return, Satan will get for him, and give to him, the
worship of the world.

xiii. 3. **And I saw*** **one of** (*lit.*, from among) **his
heads as it were slain to death; and his death-
wound was healed: and the whole earth wondered**
and followed **after the Beast.**] What is said of the
Lamb in chap. v. 6, is here said of the Beast.

It does not say *which* of the seven heads is thus
characterised; or *when* the sword wound was given :
but the Beast is repeatedly spoken of as "he whose
stroke of death was healed." It is this last or seventh
head, this man himself who is killed and restored to
life. The whole world wonders at him and follows
after him, on account of this great satanic miracle
worked on his behalf.

This is the hour spoken of in iii. 10, "which is to
come upon the world, to try them that dwell upon the
earth." "Satan's throne" will then be set up in the
earth (ii. 13 ; xvi. 10), and a man, "the lawless one,"
will occupy it, and take the sovereignty of the world,
obsessed and energised by satanic power.

xiii. 4. **And they worshipped the dragon because†
he gave the‡** (*i.e.*, his) **authority to the Beast: and**

* G.L.T.Tr.A. WH. and RV. omit this verb, but nevertheless the
Ellipsis has to be supplied and repeated from the previous verse.

† G.L.T.Tr.A. WH. and RV. read ὅτι (*hoti*) *because*, instead of ὅς
(*hos*) *who.*

‡ They also add the article here.

they worshipped the beast, saying,
   " **Who is like unto the Beast?**
   And* **who is able to make war with**
      him? "]

It is clear from this that everything is combined in this man to make him not only acceptable to the world, but to call forth their wonder, admiration and praise. He is not in any way a terror to men, but full of blandishments, attractions, allurements, and activities which will be all put forth in the interests of human greatness and happiness. It will be Satan's brief millennium, in which mankind will, by every art and artifice, be made happy. It will be a time of peace and progress for the whole world. Great secrets of nature will be discovered; evil angels will be the teachers, and deceiving demons the guides of mankind. Great inventions and discoveries will be made, and turned to the utmost possible account. Philanthropy will be the governing principle of the world. It is fast becoming the dominant principle of the world and of the "Church." The great ethical revival is at our doors. Its advent is announced by the foremost preachers of the day. All this is preparing the way for the man of sin, and the lawless one, who shall be a law unto himself and unto the whole world. Men will delight in him, and regard him as the greatest benefactor the world has ever known. Kings will gladly owe him suzerainty; and behind all will be Satan himself, swaying the hearts, tongues and energies of thousands of willing agents.

   xiii. 5. **And there was given to him a mouth speaking great blasphemous things** (*lit.*, "great things and blasphemies." The Figure is *Hendiadys*; for the great

---

*G.L.T.Tr.A. WH. and RV. add "and."

things are his blasphemies); **and authority was given to him to act** thus **forty** and **two months.** (6) **And he opened his mouth in blasphemies* against God, to blaspheme his name, and his tabernacle, and those who dwell in heaven**] This is the one great distinguishing mark of this wild Beast (see Dan. vii. 8, 11, 20; xi. 36. Ps. lii.), and it identifies him with the former of the two described in 2 Thess. ii. If we place the words side by side, this will be at once seen :—

Rev. xiii. 5, 6.	2 Thess. ii. 4.
"There was given to him a mouth speaking great blasphemous things . . . and he opened his mouth in blasphemies against God, to blaspheme His name, and His tabernacle, and those who dwell in heaven."	"Who opposeth and exalteth himself above all that is called God, or that is worshipped; so that he as God sitteth in the temple of God, shewing himself that he is God."

Is it not clear from this comparison that the same person is the subject of both? and that 2 Thess. ii. 4 relates to the same judgment scenes as Rev. xiii. 5, 6? Indeed, the connection is closer than this; for in each of these Scriptures the same two beings are referred to. This will be more clearly seen if we notice

THE STRUCTURE OF 2 Thess. ii. 1-12 (in brief)

A | ii. 1-3-. EXHORTATION *not* to believe what the Apostle did *not* say

    B | -3, 4. REASON. "For . . .

A | ii. 5, 6. EXHORTATION to believe what the Apostle *did* say

    B | 7-12. REASON. "For . . .

* L.T.Tr.A. read this as *plural.*

This may be set forth more fully as follows:

THE STRUCTURE OF 2 Thess. ii. 1-12 (expanded)

A | ii. 1-3-. Exhortation, etc. Negative
  B | a | -3-. The Apostacy: (open)
       b | -3. The revelation of "the man of sin." The Beast from the *sea*, of Rev. xiii. 1-10
          c | 4. The character of his acts (Compare with Rev. xiii. 6-8)   } REASON

A | ii. 5, 6. Exhortation, etc. Positive
  B | *a* | 7. The Mystery or secret purposes of lawlessness
       b | 8. The Revelation of "the lawless one." The Beast from the *earth*, of Rev. xiii. 11-18
          c | 9-12. The character of his acts (Compare Rev. xiii. 13-15)   } REASON

The two Beasts thus stand out very clearly. We have compared the character of the first, and may leave that of the second till we come to consider it in its place, below, in this chapter.

We are told, of this first wild beast, that his course will be limited in its duration. It will be as brief as it will be brilliant. Only for 42 months will be the duration of his superhuman career. "In the midst of the week" (Dan. ix. 27) will he break his covenant which he will have made with Israel, and make war against the saints (commencing, as we have seen, with the Two Witnesses, xi. 7), and persecute the woman (xii. 13-17).

It is during this time that the martyrs will be slain
(vi. 9 ; xx. 4).

xiii. 7. **And it was given to him to make war with
the saints** (Dan. vii. 21 ; viii. 12, 24 ; xi. 31. Rev. xi. 7),
**and overcome them : and there was given unto him
authority over every tribe, and people,* and tongue,
and nation.**] What do the great bulk of interpreters
do with this when they teach that this is the Roman
Empire revived within its old limits ? It surely agrees
with what we have said above as to this being the
sovereignty of the world gathered into one head for
"a little season" (x. 6 ; xii. 12 ; xvii. 10), and soon
to become the sovereignty of our Lord and of His
Christ (xi. 15).

But although authority was given him over all, all
will not at once submit to it. Hence this war is to
compel men to worship him and receive his mark.

8. **And all who dwell upon the earth will
worship him,** each one **whose† name‡ hath not been
written from the foundation of the world in the
book of life of the Lamb slain.**] There is nothing to
show whether the sentence, " from the foundation of the
world," should be connected with the verb " **written,**"
or " **slain.**" We have rendered the words in the same
order as the Greek, which looks as though it should
be read with the word " **written.**" Moses knew of this
book (Ex. xxxii. 32), and Daniel (xii. 1). Compare
Is. iv. 3. But the latter connection is the mos
natural, and agrees with 1 Pet. i. 19, 20. The death

---

* G.L.T.Tr.A. WH. and RV. add " and people."

† So L.T.Tr.A.WH. and RV. who read οὗ (*hou*) *of him*, instead of
ὧν (*hōn*) *of them* ; *i.e.*, singular, instead of plural.

‡ They also read singular instead of plural here.

of the Lamb was thus "foreordained before the foundation of the world"; while the names are written "from" the foundation of the world.

"All who dwell upon the earth will worship him." Is this worship given to the superhuman individual who will thus exalt himself, or to the Roman Empire revived? Few, if any, will be so bold as to maintain the latter; and in this case the revival of that Empire, as such, so confidently taught, cannot be looked for.

This worship of the Beast will be well-nigh universal. Even in the plain of Dura, only three out of all the Jews there present stood out true to God. But these days will be more terrible than those. See Matt. xxiv. 9-27. Flight is the only resource of the faithful (chap. xii.).

xiii. 9. **If any one hath an ear let him hear**] For the last time this appeal of the Son of Man goes forth. Assemblies are no longer in question. It has come down to individuals. The last of the Dispensations is about to end, hence this admonition is given for the last time.

10. **If any one is for captivity,* into captivity he goeth: if any one is to be killed with the sword, with the sword he is killed.**] The Greek Text of this verse is very confused, and there are many various readings. But the sense is perfectly clear. The Hebrew idiom was not understood by the transcribers of the MSS. and hence they tried to correct it. It is a Hebraism expressing destiny, and denoting a certainty of approaching judgment, from which-

---

* L.T.Tr.A. WH. and RV.

ever side it comes. See Jer. xliii. 11 : " And
when he (Nebuchadnezzar) cometh, he shall smite the
land of Egypt, and deliver such as are for death, to
death ; and such as are for captivity, to captivity ; and
such as are for the sword, to the sword." And Jer. xv.
2 : " And if they say to thee, Whither shall we go forth ?
then thou shalt tell them, Thus saith the LORD, such as
are for death, to death ; and such as are for the sword,
to the sword ; and such as are for the famine, to the
famine ; and such as are for captivity, to captivity."
See also Ezek. v. 2, 12 and Zech. xi. 9. From these
passages it is abundantly clear that Rev. xiii. 10 means
that so sure and certain will these judgments be which
are executed by the Beast, that none will escape them.
Hence the need for the admonition of verse 9 and the
words which follow.

Here is the patience (*i.e.*, patient endurance) **and the
faith of the saints**.] These will be the three great
requisites for those " times of trouble."

Flight (Matt. xxiv. 15-28. Mk. xiii. 14-23. Rev. xii. 14) ;
Patience (chap. i. 9 ; ii. 2, 19 ; iii. 3, 10 ; xiv. 9-12); and
Faith (chap. ii. 10, 13, 19 ; xvii. 14).

Z. (page 419), chap. xiii. 11-18

The Second Beast : from the earth

The Second Wild Beast is distinguished from the
first, twice in the twelfth verse, and elsewhere. As
soon as he is mentioned, " *the* Beast " always means the
first Beast, as being pre-eminent and predominant.

xiii. 11. **And I saw another Beast coming up out of
the earth ; and he had two horns like a lamb, and he
spake as a dragon**.] The second Beast, like the first, is

superhuman, obsessed and energized by Satanic power. Three times he is called "the False Prophet" (xvi. 13 ; xix. 20 ; and xx. 10). He is also the great coadjutor of the first Beast, and his mission is to aid the first Beast by deceiving mankind. The Lord Jesus, in speaking of this great Tribulation, warned against False Prophets as well as against False Christs, and spoke of their great work and power to deceive (Matt. xxiv. 5, 11, 24. Mark xiii. 22). Here is " *the* False Prophet," and this is his proper title.

He has two horns, and not ten, as the first Beast. The ten denote dominion ; the two speak of testimony ; in this case *false* testimony. He spake as a dragon, *i.e.*, subtilely, craftily and deceitfully. (Compare Gen. iii. 1 ; xlix. 17. 2 Cor. xi. 3).

And all these are used in behalf of the first Beast. The former is Political, the latter is Religious. The Dragon, the Beast and the False Prophet form the Devil's travesty of the Holy Trinity.

It is infernal, as the other is Divine. The Dragon is the anti-God ; the Beast is the anti-Christ ; the False Prophet is the anti-Holy Ghost.

The majority of interpreters know nothing between " the Church " on the one hand, and " Popery " on the other. The Jew is cut out of the Apocalypse and almost out of all prophecy. All that is good refers to the Church, and all that is evil to Papal Rome. So contracted is man's vision that his conceptions savour of a Village Club instead of the mighty crisis of the struggle for universal Sovereignty. Others see only the Greek Church, the French Republic, or the heathen priesthood. Most interpreters view the two Beasts as two aspects of the same thing. All seem to be agreed that they are not individuals; which is the very thing that the ordinary reader would at once take them to be. Little help, therefore, can be expected from such guides.

All the Scriptures which refer to these Beasts speak of them, without exception, as individuals. There is no hint as to their being anything else.

But because we believe this False Prophet to be an individual, there is no necessity for singling out some dead man, such as Judas Iscariot! His sin was surely great enough, without adding all this on to it. The second Beast is a spirit-being, but it is a man who is obsessed by it. The *man* will not have two horns. To the world he will be seen *as a man*. To us, now and here, he is shown to be superhuman; and as immediately led, influenced and energized by special spirit-agency. Already, there are many who are tampering with Spiritism, and who have their "familiar spirits" and guides. Spiritists, themselves, are well aware of the dangers and evils of obsession. But presently there will be one who will be obsessed by this mighty spirit-agent of Satan. Acts xvi. 16-18, and xix. 15, 16 throw a little light upon it.

Eight times is the expression "he causeth" used of this False Prophet*; so that he is an efficient agent. What "he causeth" we are told in the verses which follow:

xiii. 12. **And he exerciseth all the authority of the first Beast before him** (*i.e.*, in his presence), **causeth the earth and those who dwell therein that they shall worship† the first Beast, who**

---

* The characteristic word used of the first Beast is "It was given."
† So L.T.Tr.A.WH. and RV.

was healed of his deadly wound.] "The earth and they that dwell therein" is a figure of speech called *Pleonasm*, or redundancy ; a Hebrew figure characteristic of this book. The sphere of activity of the first Beast will be *Political* ; of the second it will be *Ecclesiastical.* The basis of the worship will be his miraculous resurrection. People are induced to pay him divine homage. The False Prophet reduces it to a system. There is nothing in all this that is beyond our faith. Such things have happened before ; why not again ? Herod received Divine homage and took it as his right (Acts xii. 21-23). History is full of similar examples, and can easily repeat itself. "New" Religions are in the air in our own day ; and in each there is less and less of God. In the new religion that is coming, God will be entirely left out, and man exalted. It will be a combination of wisdom, science, progress, and philanthropy, combined with all that panders to the lowest instincts of fallen humanity. Given all this, *plus* Satanic and spirit-agency, and what is here described is easily possible, and what is more— it is *revealed* as positively certain.

xiii. 13. **And he worketh great signs** (*i.e.*, miracles), **so that he causeth even fire to come down out of heaven to the earth before men,**] That these are real miracles there can be no doubt, since that very same word is constantly used of the miracles wrought by Christ. And these miracles are "great." This again is no new thing. Jannes and Jambres withstood Moses (Ex. vii. 11. 2 Tim. iii. 8), and up to a certain point worked the same miracles. Elijah caused fire to come down out of heaven more than once (1 Kings xviii. 38. 2 Kings i. 10, 12), and in

this Book it is used by God as one of His judgments
(xx. 9). The two witnesses deal in like manner with
their enemies (xi. 5).

xiii. 14. **And he deceiveth those who dwell
on the earth by reason of the signs** (miracles)
which it was given him to work before the Beast :]
Here we have the very words, almost, used of this
same second Beast in 2 Thess. ii. 9. We will place the
two descriptions side by side (as we did with the first
Beast, page 427) to show that the same person and
work and time are referred to in both scriptures :—

<table>
<tr><td>Rev. xiii. 13, 14.</td><td>2 Thess. ii. 9-11.</td></tr>
<tr><td>"And he worketh great signs, so that he causeth even fire to come down out of heaven to the earth before men. And he deceiveth them that dwell on the earth by reason of the signs which it was given him to work before the Beast."</td><td>"Whose coming is according to the working of Satan with all power and signs and lying wonders ; and with all deceivableness of unrighteousness in them that perish . . . For this cause God shall send them strong delusion, that they should believe the lie."</td></tr>
</table>

Here we have two accounts of the same being and
his work. In 1 Tim. iv. 1-3 we are told of the times
coming on the earth when "deceiving spirits" (*i.e.,*
evil angels) should be teachers, and "teachings of
demons" should be taught and received. We are in
those days already, and these lying spirit-teachers are
at their awful work. Demoniacal teachings are being
received on every hand. Many professing Christians
are dabbling with Spiritism; and even ministers are
presiding at lectures where this abomination is being

advocated. What it will come to ere long, we are told in these scriptures.

Miracles are becoming common-place. And, strange as it may sound, they are, in themselves, no evidence whatever as to proof of a Divine Mission. We are aware that theology teaches the opposite; adopting the false premisses of Paley and his successors.

Christ's miracles, as miracles, were no evidence of His Divine mission. The real evidence was that the miracles which He wrought were the very miracles which the Prophetic Word had declared He should work, and which were *on that account* the sign and seal of His ministry, and formed His credentials from on high. This is clear from Matt. xi. 1-6. It was not that they were mere miraculous acts, but that they were what God had foretold, and the essence of their testimony was *to the truth of God's word*, rather than the power of Christ. Hence it is that they are so generally called " signs," and not merely " wonders." They are not for the crowd to gape at, but for Bible students to study and learn their Divine lessons and teaching as to the truth of God's word and the Divine mission of the Lord Jesus.

Miracles and wonders, as such, have always been wrought; and will be wrought again by the Dragon, the Beast, and the False Prophet. And while the evidence furnished to the people by their miracles will be to the establishment of *their false claims*: to those who will keep the faith in those days, the evidence will be to the truth of *God's Word*, which has foretold these very miracles. Their miracles will establish their infernal origin and Satanic power, and not their Divine mission.

Ordering those who dwell on the earth, to make an image to the Beast, who hath the sword-wound, and lived. (15) **And it was given to him to give breath to the image of the Beast, that the image of the Beast should speak, and cause also** that as many as **would not worship the image of the Beast should be killed.**] Again we ask, Why not ? What has been can be again. On the plain of Dura (Dan. iii.) a similar scene was witnessed and a similar law enacted, so far as the worship and the penalty are concerned. How the speaking will be effected we do not know, but we know enough to see how easy the task is becoming.

Nikola Tesla, the Hungarian-American electrician, boldly declares (in *The Century* magazine for June, 1900), that he has a plan for the construction of an automaton which shall have its " own mind," and be able, " independent of any operator, to perform a great variety of acts and operations *as if it had* intelligence." He speaks of it, not as a miracle, of course, but only as an invention which he " has now perfected."* But again we say we care not how it is going to be done. God's word declares that it will be done, and we believe it. " Human energy " is getting on, and it will, ere long, be superhuman when developed by the Satanic agency of the second Beast, exercised through the human

---

* The only clue he gives to it is by comparing it to a blindfolded person obeying directions received through the ear. Astounding photographs are given of the power of these electrical currents which act on the " ear " tuned to receive the vibrations. In one of these photographs a volcano of devouring flame, sixty-five feet across, is shown, blazing from the centre of the " oscillator." Tesla himself, the coolest of men, described this as " a marvellous electrical phenomenon."

This, and Tesla's idea for the " increase of human energy," is further described in *The Daily Express* (London) for June 12, 1900.

False Prophet. We already hear of talking machines; with "a little" Satanic power thrown in, it will be a miracle very easily worked.

In seven passages we read of "the image of the Beast" (xiii. 15 ; xiv. 9, 11 ; xv. 2 ; xvi. 2; xix. 20; xx. 4).

Psalm lxxiii. refers to those troublous and perplexing times, when the faithful are at their wits' ends, and desolation and destruction of the ungodly are described. In verse 20 it is added :

" As a dream when one awaketh,
So, O Lord, in the city (בָּעִיר, *bāïr*), thou shalt tread down their Image."

בָּעִיר (*bāïr*) means *in the city*, as in the P.B. version (Coverdale) and RV. margin ; and בָּזָה (*bāzāh*) means *to tread down, tread under foot*, as in Ps. xliv. 5. Isa. xiv. 19 ; lxiii. 18. So, when God awakes to judgment, He will tread down this Image, and cause it to vanish from the city as a dream vanisheth on awaking. The city is, of course, Jerusalem, where this abomination will be set up.

xiii. 16. And he (*i.e*, the Second Beast) **causeth all, even the small and the great, and the rich and the poor, and the free and the bond, to receive* a mark on their right hands, or upon their foreheads :**] Thus, out of Democracy comes Despotism : out of Liberalism comes " Boycotting " on a large scale : out of Reason comes Idolatry ; out of Socialism comes the abrogation of the rights of " Free labour." What was thought impossible in this direction a few years ago is now seen to be an accomplished fact in all directions. In whole districts it is often forbidden to buy or sell either their merchandise or their labour ; and none are

---

* G.L.T.Tr.A. WH. and RV. read the *plural* thus.

exempted from this new enslavement. The False Prophet will bring " Boycotting " to perfection, and employ it as a political power and a religious agency. The object is

xiii. 17. * **That no one should be able to buy or sell, except he who has the mark, or the name of the Beast, or the number of his name.**] The plan is truly Satanic in its wisdom : for each one becomes a spy on the other. Living will be made next to impossible : even money will be useless. The rich will be as the poor if they have not this mark. It will be far worse than famine.

The word for " mark " is χάραγμα (*charagma*) *brand*. In the *Papyri*, χάραγμα is always connected with the Emperor, and sometimes contains his name and effigy, with the year of his reign. It was necessary for buying and selling. It is found on all sorts of documents, making them valid ; and there are many on " bills of sale." *Charagma* is therefore the *official seal* ; and this brand will be received by the great majority rather than suffer the torture of death from violence or privation.

xiii. 18. **Here is wisdom. He who hath understanding let him calculate the number of the Beast : for it is man's number ; and its number is Six hundred and sixty-six.**] The words imply that the calculation is possible but difficult. The task is generally undertaken on the assumption that the problem is to be solved by *Gematria* ; *i.e.*, by reckoning (after the manner of the Hebrews and Greeks, who had no Arabic numerals) a *letter* as being put for the corresponding *number* for which it stood. But this is *enumeration*, not *computa-*

---

* L.T.Aᵇ. WHᵇ. omit καί (*kai*) *and*.

tion ; and the vast number of names which have been thus formed forbid us either to increase the number, or to select from it. We believe the clue is to be found in the statement that it is "man's number."

Now *three* is the Divine number. *Seven* is the number of the Spirit. *Eight* is the Dominical number, and so on. But *Six* (with its multiples) is peculiarly *man's number*. It is first mentioned in connection with *man* (for man was created on the *sixth* day). Six, therefore, is to man what the " hall-mark " is to silver. It is *man's hall-mark* ; stamping everything which it is used in connection with as pertaining to man. The great defiers of God have been so stamped. Goliath was *six* cubits in height, his spear's head weighed *six* shekels, and he had *six* pieces of armour.

Nebuchadnezzar's Image was *sixty* cubits in height, and *six* cubits wide ; and *six* instruments of music summoned its worshippers.

The number 666 has, moreover, another remarkable property. It is marked by the triple concentration or essence of six, being the *sum* of all the numbers which make up the *square of six*. The square of six is 36 ; and, $1 + 2 + 3 + 4 + 5 + 6 + 7 + 8 + 9 + 10 + 11 + 12 + 13 + 14 + 15 + 16 + 17 + 18 + 19 + 20 + 21 + 22 + 23 + 24 + 25 + 26 + 27 + 28 + 29 + 30 + 31 + 32 + 33 + 34 + 35 + 36 = 666$.

But the great significance of this number is seen when we remember that the secret symbol of the great ancient Pagan mysteries was SSS or 666; and that to-day it is the secret connecting link between them and their revival in Spiritism and Theosophy which aim at the union of all religions in one.

The number 666 is expressed in the Greek by the

letters χξs, The first (χ) stands for 600, the second (ξ) for 60, and the third (s) for 6. The last is not a real letter, but was a mark invented by the Greeks to repre. sent 6. They called it στίγμα (*stigma**), and it is not without significance that, as associated with *man*, the word has come to be used in a bad sense.

The first and last of these three letters are the abbreviation of the word "Christ," being the first and last letters of the word *Christos*. So that, when we have the ξ, like a crooked serpent, put between them, we see a fitting symbol of Satan's Messiah—the Anti-Christ.

---

* *Stigma* is a sign usually made on the body (especially on the forehead and hands) by branding or puncturing, on slaves, soldiers, &c. It was especially used as a symbol of the god whom they served (Lev. xix. 28 ; xxi. 5. Deut. xiv. 1. 3 Macc. ii. 29), and supposed to be *protective*. This explains the use of the word in Gal. vi. 17. Paul regarded his wounds and scars received in the service of his Lord and God as not only being marks of his servitude, but marks implying that he was under God's protection. (Compare Isa. xlix. 16. Ezek. ix. 4 Ex. xiii. 9, 16.) Therefore he says, beware how you trouble me ! (this explains the word "for.") See also Rev. xiv. 1 ; vii. 2 ; ix. 4.

14

THE FIFTH VISION "IN HEAVEN"
(14:1-5)

The Lamb and the 144,000

The Fifth Vision in heaven is very brief. It is another Episode, telling us of those who will have come through the great Tribulation, and have been caught up to Heaven.

It is part of the larger Episode, and is parenthetical. The previous vision on Earth has told us of those who were slain because they refused to worship the Beast or receive his mark. Those who were for death, had been killed; and those who were to be kept alive, have been kept alive (xiii. 10). The worshippers of the Beast received his mark; and these received the mark of the Lamb (Christ) and of His Father in their foreheads. This seems to point to the 144,000 sealed ones, of whose sealing we read in chap. vii. They had passed unscathed through the judgments of God, and through the persecutions of the Beast.

The Vision occupies only five verses, and their Structure is as follows :—

H⁵ (p. 118), xiv. 1-5. THE FIFTH VISION "IN HEAVEN"

The Lamb and the 144,000

H⁵ | A | xiv. 1.   Description

     B | 2.   The heavenly Voices.   The **Singers**

     B | 3.   The heavenly Voices.   The Song

   A | 4, 5.   Description

xiv. 1. **And I saw, and behold the* Lamb standing upon Mount Zion, and with him an hundred and forty-four thousand, having his name and His Father's name† written upon their foreheads.**] This was the promise made to the overcomers in iii. 12 ; and this was the seal of chap. vii. 3. At least this seems to be the case, though some regard this as another body. It seems, however, more natural to take them as the same ; no other such number being mentioned, and nothing being said to prevent us making the mistake of identifying them.

In chap. vii. we have the sealing; here, we have the end for which they were to be sealed. In chap. vii. the object of their sealing is that they might pass through the Tribulation unscathed; here we see the object attained. The result of their testimony will be seen in the formation of that body which will be the nucleus of the new nation.

The Vision is in heaven; for the singers stand before the Throne, and they are with the Lamb. He is not yet descended to the Earth. This decides the point that it is the heavenly Zion which is here referred to. The Temple on Earth was close to Mount Zion ; so the Temple in heaven is correspondingly near to the heavenly Zion.

They are comparatively a small body, but these are the firstfruits to God and the Lamb; and the firstfruits are necessarily a small proportion compared with the harvest. In Rev. vii. 1-8 and xiv. we have " firstfruits," and in Rev. vii. 9-17 and xv. the whole harvest, or the larger number.

---

* G.L.T.Tr.A. WH. and RV. add the article.

† So L.T.T.Tr.A. WH. and RV.

In the second verse we have the Heavenly voices and the singers. This again shows the Vision to be in Heaven; for none of these Heavenly Visions are without the utterances of Heavenly voices.

xiv. 2. **And I heard a voice out of heaven, as** the **voice of many waters, and as a voice of great thunder: and the voice which*** **I heard** was as that **of harpers, harping with their harps :**] The word rendered " harpers," κιθαρῳδῶν (*kith_arōdōn*), denotes those who accompany the voice with the harp.

The next verse is constructed as follows, showing the importance of its statements :—

B (p. 442), xiv. **3.** *The Heavenly Voices. The Song*

B | a | 3-.   The New Song. (pos.)

    b | -3-.   The Place : before the Throne

   a | -3-.   The New Song. (neg.)

    b | -3.   The Number

xiv. 3. **And they sung,** as it were, **a new song before the Throne, and before the four Zōa, and the Elders: and no one was able to learn the song except the hundred and forty-four thousand, who have been purchased from the earth**] Here we have the reference to their song. This is the only instance where the actual words of the song are not given. It is called "a New Song"; that is, it had a new subject or theme. As only the 144,000 could learn it or sing it, it probably concerned only themselves, and the wonderful miracles God had wrought in saving them from and through and out of the great and awful temp·

---

* So G.L.T.Tr.A. WH. and RV.

tations and dangers hinted at in the concluding description in the 4th and 5th verses. Only those who
had gone through that Tribulation could understand the
song which celebrated it. It is not a general statement
that the wicked cannot participate in the joys of the
church! but a far more important fact which is stated.
The song is "new" because it is sung by a new company, and has a new theme for its subject.

> They sing it before the Throne,
> before the *Zōa*, and
> before the Elders.

They can all understand and appreciate it, for they
are participants in these judgment scenes.

Its new theme can be gathered from the next two
verses; the structure of which is as follows:—

> *A* (p. 442), xiv. 4, 5. *The Second Description*

A | c | e | 4-. Character. Undefiled. (neg.)
        f | -4-. Reason
        d | -4-. Employment. Followers. (active)
        d | -4. State. Redeemed. (passive)
   c | *e* | 5-. Character. Faultless
        f | -5. Reason

The character of the singers is twice given; and the
two are separated by the active and passive employment
and condition of the singers.

xiv. 4 . **These are they who were not defiled with
women, for they are virgins.**] These words are
generally taken as "figurative." But figures of speech
are known, and can be named and defined. What is

meant is that they are taken as symbolical, or as meaning something different from what is said. But this
comes from not seeing the scope of the book as a whole,
and from not discerning the real character of the days
and of the religious condition of things. We have
more than once, in the Epistles to the Assemblies, and
on chap. ix. 20, 21, said that Fornication will be part of
the great religious system of Anti-Christ in the coming
time of trouble and temptation; as it formed an obligatory
part of the great pagan systems of idolatry. Idolatry
was not a mere sin into which people gradually sunk;
but it was a Satanic device into which people rose in
order to gratify the lusts of the flesh under the cloak
of religion.

Hence the references to Balaam (ii. 14) and Jezebel
(ii. 20). Hence, too, the description of these 144,000
here, who had been kept from all these abominations.
It is not merely that only one single virtue (chastity) is
predicated of the redeemed in general, as some put it;
but, it is a special feature of the evils from which this
special company will be preserved, and for refusal to
partake of it multitudes (vii. 9-17; and xv. 1-4) will
have suffered martyrdom. Only those who know what
those evils will be can understand the import of their
wonderful deliverance, or sing their song. It is not because of any moral difference between us and them; or
between the ungodly and the righteous, but because of
the different experience through which they will have
passed. That is why none can learn that song; and
that is the explanation of the words we are here considering; and that is why the pronoun "They" is so
emphatic.

-4. These are they who follow the Lamb whithersoever he goeth. **These were purchased from among men, a first-fruit to God and to the Lamb.** (5) **And in their mouth was not found** the lie,* for† **they are blameless‡**] *i.e.*, blameless as to the matter above referred to ; and have not received " the Lie " which all others will have believed. See 2 Thess. ii. 11, where the definite article is used, "*the* Lie," *viz.*, the Lie that it is right to set God's laws at defiance by adopting the practices of the new Religion framed by the infernal Trinity of Satan, the Beast, and the False Prophet. The three explanatory statements, each commencing " these are they," are to be taken literally, and as meaning just what they say. The teaching of demons in 1 Tim. iv. 3 in "forbidding to marry and commanding to abstain from meats," goes far deeper than Popish celibacy of the clergy, and Fasting. This teaching " forbidding to marry " comes from the Abyss, and is connected with Anti-christ's Religion ; while the " abstaining from meats" is only to weaken people's will-power, and to make them more susceptible to the influences of these evil angels and demons.

---

* G.L.T.Tr.A. WH. RV. read ψεῦδος (*pseudos*) *a lie*, instead of δόλος (*dolos*) *quite*.

† L.R. (marg). A. WH. and RV. omit γάρ (*gar*) *for*.

‡ G.L.T.Tr.A. WH. and RV. omit the last clause " before the throne of God."

15

THE FIFTH VISION "ON EARTH"
(14:6-20)

The Six Angels and the Son of Man

The next vision which follows " on earth," follows closely on the last, and is preliminary to the pouring out of the seven Vials. No angel has been seen or heard since the seventh angel sounded the seventh trumpet in xi. 15. This shows us that the passage xii. 1—xv. 8 is parenthetical, and constitutes one series or episode.

This fifth vision on earth consists of the appearance of six angels consecutively, each having his separate mission, and all but one (the fifth) having his own proclamation. They are distinct from each other, and continue the Episode by giving us God's side of what is going to happen ; and telling us of what He is doing during the time that the Beast and False Prophet are running their course in chap. xiii. They form also a compendium of all the remaining judgments contained in the rest of the Book.

The six angels with the Son of Man make *seven* heavenly appearances and utterances. These are divided, as shown in the Structure (page 449), into *three* and *four*. The first three stand out clearly by themselves. The last four form two pairs, in which the first of each has a sharp sickle, and the second of each gives the command to use it. The first of these pairs is the Harvest, and the second is the Vintage.

The following is the structure of this Vision as a whole :—

C⁵ (p. 118) xiv. 6-20. THE FIFTH VISION "ON EARTH"

The Six Angels and the Son of Man

C⁵ | A | i. | a¹ | 6. The *First* Angel
   | | | b¹ | 7. His Proclamation
   | | ii. | a² | 8-. The *Second* Angel
   | | | b² | -8. His Declaration
   | | iii. | a³ | 9-. The *Third* Angel
   | | | b³ | -9-13. His Denunciation (-9-11). His Consolation (12, 13)
   | B | iv. | a⁴ | 14-. THE SON OF MAN
   | | | b⁴ | -14. What he had. A sharp sickle
   | | v. | a⁵ | 15-. The *Fourth* Angel
   | | | b⁵ | -15, 16. His Command to the Son of Man (-15). Its Execution (16) — The Harvest
   | B | vi. | a⁶ | 17-. The *Fifth* Angel
   | | | b⁶ | -17. What he had. A sharp sickle
   | | vii. | a⁷ | 18-. The *Sixth* Angel
   | | | b⁷ | -18-20. His Command to the Fifth Angel (-18). Its Execution (19, 20) — The Vintage

The First Angel (xiv. 6, 7)

xiv. 6. **And I saw another* angel flying in mid-heaven, having the everlasting gospel to announce unto those that dwell on the earth, and unto† every nation and tribe, and tongue, and people, (7) saying with a loud voice,**

> **"Fear God, and give glory to Him; because the hour of His judgment is come: and worship him that made the heaven, and the earth, and the sea, and the fountains of waters."]**

We have to remember that though the Gospel is often used in a technical sense, the word itself means *glad tidings* or *good news*. It is clear that this news may vary and yet be good. As a matter of fact there are several subjects connected with this good news. It will be sufficient to mention the " gospel of the kingdom," and " the gospel of the grace of God." All are preached, and are to be preached, according to the dispensations to which they belong. For example, in the present dispensation it is only " the gospel of the grace of God " which is to be preached (Acts xx. 24), and he is accursed who now preaches a different gospel (Gal. i. 8). " The gospel of the Kingdom " was preached by John the Baptist, by Christ, and by Peter, &c. (Matt. iv. 23; ix. 35). And it will yet be preached again in the Great Tribulation, after the Church of God has been taken away (Matt. xxiv. 14), up to this point; and then it will be replaced by " The Eternal Gospel," as it is rendered in the RV. It is so called

---

* Tr. and A. put " ἄλλον " (*allon*), *another*, in brackets.

† G.L.T.Tr.A. WH. and RV. repeat the ἐπί (*epi*), *upon* or *unto*.

because it takes us back to the beginning, and tells of the earliest good news, or gospel, preached from God as Creator, and consists of the one great truth which was preached from the beginning. It is manifest that it cannot be "everlasting" in the strict sense of the word, because when "the hour of his judgment is come," and gone, it will not be possible to preach it any longer. This settles the matter for us. If it did not, it is equally clear that God's gospel of grace which is preached now consists of something more than the fact that men are to "fear God"! And who would dare to preach now that "the hour of His judgment (or crisis) has come." No, this "everlasting gospel" cannot be preached now. The moment has not yet arrived when these words can be proclaimed. We can tell of "judgment to come" (Acts xxiv. 25, μέλλοντος (*mellontos*), coming), but not of the "hour" having actually arrived. If "grace" and "judgment" are the same thing, then again we may say that words are useless for the purposes of revelation. "Now is the day of salvation" not of judgment (2 Cor. vi. 2).

It is therefore eternal in the sense that it belongs to the first and the last of the dispensations in which God deals with men. It goes back to the beginning, before the Law. It tells of God's claim as Creator; and not of Christ's work as Saviour. "Now I know that thou fearest God" was God's word to Abraham (Gen. xxii. 12). "This do and live, for I fear God," said Joseph (Gen. xlii. 18). So with Job (i. 1); and the Egyptian midwives (Ex. i. 17-21). The "fearers of God" was a title specially given to proselytes from the Gentiles (Acts xiii. 16, 26).

The time will have then come to add the sentence

in Isa. lxi. 2, which the Lord omitted when He read Isa. lxi. 1, 2-, in the Synagogue at Nazareth (Luke iv. 18-20): "The Spirit of the Lord is upon me," &c., down to and including the first sentence of verse 2, " to preach the acceptable year of the Lord." Then it is significantly added that "he closed the book and sat down." Why? Because that was not yet the time to preach what follows in Isa. lxi. 2, *viz.,* "the day of vengeance of our God." But here, when this first angel preaches in mid-heaven to all on earth, the time will have come to preach this "day of vengeance," as having then come. It was through falling into the mistake of not "rightly dividing the word of truth," and distinguishing its times and seasons and Dispensation, that the church of the Thessalonians was so upset. A forged letter had been sent to them, in which Paul is represented as having taught that "the Day of the Lord had set in " (2 Thess. ii. 2). Of course, if that had been the case, they saw they had not been "caught up to meet the Lord in the air " before that great and terrible Day, and they had every need to be "troubled "; for their faith and their hope were alike "in vain." Indeed, though faith remained, "hope" seems to have gone, for while in 1 Thess. i. 3 it was mentioned, in 2 Thess. i. 3 it is omitted. So Paul proceeds to undeceive them and give them further revelations as to the Lord's Coming.

And, observe here, it is not the "day of his judgment is come," but "*the hour.*" This refers of course to the last and final crisis of the judgment—the seven Vials—which closes everything up. "Fear God and give glory to him . . . worship him (not the Beast) who made the heaven and the earth," &c. It is God as *creator* who is proclaimed, and that by an angel, not by men. The heavenly utterances proclaim the Father and the Son, but here it is the Creator. That is the basis on which worship is demanded. What a state the earth must then be in, when only this one part of the primeval gospel can be proclaimed. This takes place probably before Rev. xiii.

And yet, in spite of all this, Commentators take it as "the inauguration of Christian missions," or "the operations of the Bible Society"! These words could never have been read with their context by those who thus misinterpret them! No! this is the first step in these angelic announcements. A solemn note of warning is loudly sounded.

The Second Angel (xiv. 8)

xiv. 8. **And another, a second* angel followed, saying,**

> **"Fallen, fallen, is Babylon the great, †**
> **which‡ hath given all the nations to**
> **drink of the exciting wine of her**
> **fornication."]**

This is the first mention of Babylon in the Apocalypse, and it gathers up in this brief preliminary announcement the whole of chapters xvii. and xviii. The words of this angel are prophetic, and look forward to the pouring out of the last Vial. The judgment on Babylon, therefore, closes up the whole series of God's judgments. Chap. xvii. 1-3 and xviii. 2, 3 are identified by the announcement of this *second* angel.

---

* L.Tr.A. WHb. and RV. add " second."

† G.L.T.Tr.A. WH. and RV. omit " *city*."

‡ L.T.Tr.A. WH. and RV. read ἥ (*hē*), *which*, instead of ὅτι (*hoti*), *because*.

While the action of the *first* angel goes back to a time prior to chap. xiii., the words of the *second* angel take us on to beyond the end of that chapter. If we take the word θυμός (*thumos*) as meaning *inflammatory* or *exciting*, as it does when used of wine, all difficulty is taken away. Her "fornications" refer us back to the prevailing religion of that time, as we have seen in xiv. 4, 5, above; and this is the cause of her judgment. What this Babylon is we shall see when we come to consider chapter xvii.

The Third Angel (xiv. 9-13)

Five verses are devoted to the third Angel and his announcement. The Structure on page 449 shows that this member " b³ " is two-fold ; viz. :

b³ | His Denunciation : *vv.* -9-11; and
   | His Consolation : *vv.* 12, 13.

These two are of such importance that each has its own separate structure.

The Denunciation is twice announced : at the beginning, " c," and at the end, "*c.*" From this we see the special nature of the *sin* which is to be punished : It is the worship of the Beast, and the receiving of his mark (*charagma*). Between these mentions of ·the sin, we have the *punishment* which is threatened. First positive ; then negative. The Structure is designed to call our attention to the solemnity and importance of the mission of this Third Angel. We give the structure of His Denunciation first :—

b³ (page 449), xiv. -9-11. *The Denunciation of the Third Angel*

c | -9. The Crime denounced. { x | -9-. Worship of Beast
                                      { y | -9. Receiving his mark

d | 10-. The punishment (positive). Drink

  e | -10-. Torment
     g | -10. Its nature (fire)

  e | 11-. Torment
     g | -11-. Its duration (eternal)

d | -11-. The punishment (negative). No rest

c | -11. The Crime denounced. { x | -11-. Worship of Beast
                                        { *y* | -11. Receiving his mark

b³

This proclamation again takes us back to a time prior to chap. xiii. It is a solemn warning as though directed against an opposite proclamation which the Beast will then have made or be about to make.

This warning naturally follows the designation of the sins for which the judgment is announced.

xiv. 9. **And another,* a third Angel followed them, saying with a loud voice:**

> **"If anyone worshippeth the Beast and his image, and receiveth his mark on his forehead, or on his hand, (10) even һҽ shall drink of the wine of God's fury, which is mingled undiluted in the cup of his wrath; and he shall be tormented with fire and brimstone in the presence of the angels, and in the presence of the Lamb; (11) And the smoke of their torment ascendeth up for ever and ever: and they have no rest day and night, who worship the Beast and his image, and whosoever receiveth the mark (or brand) of his name."]**

Here we have one of the most solemn warnings given in the whole of the Bible. It must not be toned down in the slightest degree, but taken in all the fulness of its awful meaning. It ought to be sufficient to warn thousands from yielding to the temptations or submitting to the threats of the Beast and the False Prophet. Their threats and enticements will be serious enough. But God's threat here is intended to outweigh them, and enable many to "endure unto the end." Here will be the "patient endurance of the saints." Here they will be strengthened and encouraged to "keep the commandments of God," and not the commandments of the

---

* G.L.T.Tr.A. WH. and RV. add ἄλλος (*allos*) *another.*

Beast; to keep "the faith of Jesus," and not believe the Religion of the False Prophet. If this warning will not keep them, nothing will.

The consolation given affirms that it will be better to die than to yield : better to have the blessing connected with death, even the martyr's death, than to live and come under God's curse and suffer the vengeance of eternal fire. If we take the first part of this threat of the future and everlasting state, we may take the latter part as referring to their previous condition on the earth, as "day and night" can hardly be spoken of the eternal state. "And they have no rest who are worshipping," etc. It is the *present* participle, and cannot mean who have worshipped or did worship; "receiveth" is also in the *present* tense, implying that on earth they will have no rest day and night while they are engaged in worshipping the Beast; and as to eternity, "the smoke of their torment ascendeth up for ever and ever."

This prepares us for the consolation which follows, which is also intended as an encouragement.

Its structure is as follows :

b (page 449), xiv. 12, 13. *The Consolation of the Third*

Angel

b |h | k | 12-. The "Patience" of the saints
  | | l | -12. The "Obedience" of the saints
  | | i | m | 13-. The Voice from heaven
  | | | n | -13-. Benediction
  | *h* | *k* | -13-. The "Rest" of the Saints
  | | *l* | -13. The "Works" of the Saints

458 / The Fifth Vision "on Earth"

12. **Here is the patient endurance of the saints :
who keep the commandments of God, and the faith
of Jesus. (13) And I heard a voice from heaven
saying :** *

> **"Write, Blessed are the dead who die
> in the Lord from henceforth : "**]

This is another voice : not that of the third angel.
The connection is clear, " from henceforth " refers to
death from that time. It is persecution, ending in
certain death. Hence the special Benediction here
pronounced upon all such as die rather than yield to
the temptations and threats of the Beast and the False
Prophet. " Worship, or be slain " is their cry. " Be
slain, and be blessed " is God's encouraging reply to
them. That blessing is seen in xiv. 1-5, and xv. 1-4,
and the words refer to those Scriptures.

> **" Yea, saith the Spirit, that they may
> rest from their troubles, for † their
> works follow them."**]

The word κόπων (*kopōn*), which we have rendered
"troubles," is from κόπτω (*koptō*) *to beat; to beat* the
breast; hence, *to lament.* (See Matt. xi. 17; xxi. 8;
xxiv. 30. Luke viii. 52; xxiii. 27. Rev. i. 7; xviii. 9.)
The noun may well, therefore, denote *troubles.* See Matt.
xxvi. 10 : " Why do ye give *trouble* to the woman ? "
So Mark xiv. 6. Luke xi. 7; xviii. 5. Gal. vi. 17.

It is violent death that is in question here; not the
" falling asleep " of saints in this dispensation. The
words have no reference to the present state of things.
They cannot be interpreted of the Church of God;

---

* G.L.T.Tr.A. WH. and RV. omit μοι (*moi*) *to me.*

† L.T.Tr.A. WH. and RV. read γάρ (*gar*) *for*, instead of δέ (*de*) *and.*

though, of course, by way of general application, it is always better to die than worship any idol, or have fellowship with idolators. Their " works " which follow them consist of their " testimony," their "obedience," and their " patient endurance," so frequently mentioned in this book. These works do not go before them to procure their reward, but they follow after as the evidence of their obedience.

The Son of Man, and the Last Three Angels

A. (page 449), xiv. 14-20

The *Six* Angelic Appearances of this fifth Vision on Earth are made into *seven* by the Vision of the Son of Man in the centre. These seven are divided in *four* and *three*, as usual.

We have considered the first *three*. The last *four* go together, and are closely connected; the first two with the HARVEST, and the last two with the VINTAGE.

The Son of Man stands out as the centre of the whole seven, thus dividing the six angels into two threes. This is seen from the Structure of the whole of this Vision on page 449.

The last four form two pairs. The first of each pair is seen with a sharp sickle in his hand; while the second of each pair gives forth the command for it to be used. In the first pair the Harvest of the earth is reaped. In the second pair the Vintage of the earth is gathered.

We now have to present the last four together, and give the Structure, which is as follows :—

A (page 449), xiv. 14·20. *The Son of Man, and the Fourth, Fifth, and Six Angels*

The Fourth Angel and the Harvest

The Sixth Angel and the Vintage

A | B | iv. | 14. THE SON OF MAN and His sharp sickle

v. | o | 15. The FOURTH Angel, and whence he comes (Temple)

p | -15-. His cry to the Son of Man

q | -15. Command to reap

r | 16-. Reasons

s | -16. Compliance

t | -16. The HARVEST reaped

B | vi. | 17. The FIFTH Angel and his sharp sickle

vii. | o | 18. The SIXTH Angel, and whence he comes (Altar)

p | -18-. His cry to the Fifth angel

q | -18-. Command to reap

r | -18. Reason

s | 19-. Compliance

t | -19, 20. The VINTAGE gathered

The Harvest and the Vintage are reaped and gathered respectively by the Son of Man, and the Fifth Angel, though they are *recorded* under the Fourth and Sixth Angels, as shown in the Structure.

xiv. 14. **And I looked, and behold a white cloud, and upon the cloud I saw one sitting like unto the Son of Man, having upon His head a golden crown** (*stephanos*), **and in His hand a sharp sickle.**] The Son of Man was the *sower* (Matt. xiii. 37); and the Son of Man is the *reaper*. This is the last time the title is used in the Bible. It connects the Lord Jesus with the earth, and is therefore used of this "harvest of the earth."

When the title was first used in the day of His humiliation (Matt. viii. 20), He had not where, on the earth, to lay His head. But now, in the day of His judgment, He has on that head a crown of gold. (See pages 15, 16.) He is on the cloud, and invisible on earth ; but though unseen, the effects of the sharp sickle in His hand will soon be manifest. This crown is associated with Ps. xxi. 3 : "Thou settest a crown of pure gold upon his head"; for it is a token of His incoming of Dominion; and "Thou settest" is put in strong contrast with the "crown of thorns" which others set upon His head at His first coming.

The Fourth Angel and the Harvest (xiv. 15, 16).

xiv. 15. **And another Angel came out of the Temple** (Naos), **crying with a loud voice to Him that sat on the cloud,**

> **"Put in Thy sickle, and reap ; because the hour is come *to reap ; because the harvest of the earth is ripe."**]

---

* G.L.T.Tr.A. WH. and RV. omit σοι (*soi*) *for thee.*

There can be no doubt that this is a judgment scene.
The title "Son of Man" betokens it; for God hath
" committed all judgment unto the Son, because He is
the Son of Man " (John v. 27). The Old Testament connects this harvest with judgment ; for a precisely
similar command is given in Joel iii. 13 : " put ye in the
sickle, for the harvest is ripe," and this is mentioned in
close connection with the vintage : " come you down ;
for the press is full, the fats overflow; for their wickedness is great." This is the scene in which " the sun
and moon shall be darkened " (v. 15).

Most Commentators allow that the Vintage is judicial;
then, why not the Harvest. The one is " the vine of
the earth," and the other is "the harvest of the earth."
It is the *earth* that is ripe, and what can this be ripe for,
but for judgment ? The Vine is "the Vine of the Earth ";
the Harvest is "the Harvest of the *Earth*." We thus
have the two great spheres in which judgment will be
carried out, most clearly and explicitly put before us.

What is seen here is one of the six brief announcements connected with and filling up that which goes
before; heralding and explaining in a few words
certain judgments yet to follow.

xiv. 16. **And He that sat upon the cloud put forth
His sickle upon the earth ; and the earth was reaped.**]
The word " earth " is repeated so as to impress our
minds with the fact that it is with the earth, as the
earth, that we have to do here. It is " the hour of His
judgment " which has come. How this can be interpreted of the " church," or be taken in the good sense
of reward, we are at a loss to understand. The first of
these six angels used precisely the same words (v. 7).
It is 2 Thess. i. 6-8 that we have here. When the time

has come for Him to "gather out of His kingdom all
things that offend" (Matt. xiii. 41), "immediately He
putteth in the sickle, because the harvest is come" (Mark
iv. 29). Matt. xxiv. 37-42 must be read in connection
with the scene here referred to. The good may be
gathered into barns: these barns are seen in the next
chapter ; but the thought connected with the harvest
is judgment. And why a "*sharp*" sickle. The vintage
is admittedly judicial (*vv.* 18-20), and that is gathered
with a *sharp* sickle. That the harvest is judicial also is
confirmed by a reference to Jer. li. 33 : "Thus saith
the Lord of hosts, the God of Israel ; The daughter of
Babylon is like a threshing-floor, it is time to thresh
her : yet a little while and the time of her harvest shall
come." Babylon is mentioned in the verses immediately preceding this harvest (chap. xiv. 8) ; and chap.
xvii. and xviii. identify it with Jer. li. 33, for "the
harvest is the end of the age."

After the harvest comes the vintage, in the order of
nature ; so here it is the same in the order of judgment.

This brings us to

The Fifth Angel (xiv. 17)

xiv. 17. **And another angel came out of the Temple**
(Naos) **which is in heaven, he also having a sharp
sickle.**] And it is to him that the Sixth Angel calls
upon to gather the vintage.

The Sixth Angel and the Vintage (xiv. 18-20)

xiv. 18. **And another angel came out of the altar,
who * hath authority over its fire: and he cried**

---

* G.L.T.Tr.A. WH. and RV. add ὁ (*ho*) *who.*

with a loud voice to him that had the sharp sickle, saying,

> "Thrust in thy sharp sickle, and gather
> the clusters of the vine of the earth,
> for her grapes are fully ripened."

(19) **And the angel thrust in his sickle into the earth, and gathered the vine of the earth, and cast it into the great winepress of the wrath of God.** (20) **And the winepress was trodden without the city, and blood came out of the winepress, even up to the bits of the horses, to the distance of a thousand and six hundred furlongs.**] This, too, takes in the final judgments of this book. Both of these angels are the servants of "the Lord *of the earth*" (xi. 4). Three times are we reminded that the sickle was "sharp," and therefore would do its business without difficulty. The vine is "the vine of the earth" (See Deut. xxxii. 32, 33).

We have here a fore-announcement of the sixth Vial (xvi. 12-16) and of the great battle of Armageddon. It is to this scene that Joel iii. 12-15 refers, where we read "the press is full, the fats overflow." And this is closely connected with the "harvest" in the same verse. (Compare Zeph. iii. 8. Isa. xxxiv. 1-8.) Rev. xix. 15 tells us of this treading of the Wine-press. And Isaiah records it in chap. lxiii. 1-4. Nothing can equal the awful nature of those final judgments of the seven Vials, which are here epitomized in the few words describing this harvest and this vintage. "Threshing" is the end of the one, and "treading" is the end of the other; and it is Palestine and not Italy; Jerusalem and not Rome, which is in question here.

16

THE SIXTH VISION "IN HEAVEN"
(15:1-8)

The Seven Vial Angels.

This Sixth Vision in Heaven is very briefly described. It occupies this fifteenth chapter, which consists of only eight verses.

The structure of the Vision is as follows :—

B^6 (p. 118), xv. 1-8. THE SIXTH VISION "IN HEAVEN"

The Seven Vial Angels

B^6 A | xv. 1. The Seven Angels

    B | 2-4. Worship offered

  A | 5-7. The Seven Angels

    B | 8. Worship no longer possible

It is the Vision which introduces us to the most terrible of all the Visions which affect the earth ; for, it is followed by the Seven Vials, the seven great and final judgments which close up the whole series set forth in chapters—

    xvi. The Great Judgments
    xvii. The Great Whore
    xviii. The Great City

The next, and last, Vision in Heaven is immediately followed by the Apocalypse of the Son of Man Himself.

Short as this *sixth* Vision is, it is full of significance, and points to the decisive results to be obtained in the next Vision on Earth, to which it introduces us.

This is clearly set out in the first member:

xv. 1. **And I saw another sign in Heaven, great and marvellous: seven angels having the last seven plagues** (or, seven plagues, which are the last); **because in them was completed the wrath** (or fury) **of God :]** The word "because" is connected with the word "last," as shown in the alternative rendering, above. This sign is "great and wonderful," *i.e.*, *wonderfully* great in its nature and extent and importance and results. It is the completion of the "covenant of marvels" which the Lord made with Israel in Ex. xxxiv. 10. The plagues themselves are not yet. They do not actually follow till the next chapter; and then they follow on from the sounding of the seventh Trumpet. That Trumpet contains, and consists of, and expands into, the seven Vials, and is "the third Woe" Trumpet. The results of that sounding are about to take place: and they are heralded by the Heavenly utterance, which sets forth their object. The sign itself is given in the first verse.

xv. 2. **And I saw, as it were, a glassy sea]** It does not say it was glass, or even glassy, but that it looked *as if it were* glassy or smooth. It was

mingled with fire :] In iv. 6 it was "like crystal." Here it looks as though fire were mingled with it, betokening the heat and fierceness of the coming judgments which were then about to be announced; for wrath was at its height.

and those that had gotten the victory from the

Beast, and from his image, and from* the number
of his name standing upon the glassy sea, having
harps of God (*i.e.*, Divine or Sacred harps).] The
worshippers here are particularly defined as those who
had come out of and through the great Tribulation.
Their numbers are not given, so that they appear to
be distinct from, or to include the 144,000 mentioned
in the previous chapter and in chap. vii. They may be
"the remnant of the woman's seed" (xii. 17), for they,
by Divine protection, were "overcomers." If so, this
glassy sea is in contrast with the Red Sea; while the
harps tell of the Kingdom at length come; for we do
not read of harps in the earthly temple till the Kingdom was set up on earth.

In the previous Vision in Heaven (the Fifth), singing
is mentioned, but no words are given, for the song was
"new," and no one but the singers themselves could
learn or understand it.

The song which is sung in this *Sixth* Vision is both
old and new, for it is the song of Moses and of the Lamb:

xv. 3. **And they sing the song of Moses the servant
of God, and the song of the Lamb,**] Why these two
songs are always regarded as one, and referred to
Exodus xv., we do not understand. Alford says "it is
not meant that there are two distinct songs; the song is
one and the same," and it is "similar to that song of
triumph" in Exodus xv. The simple question is, Whom
are we to believe. If words are of any use, it says two
songs, as plainly as words can say it. The word
"song" is twice repeated. "The song of Moses the
servant of the Lord" is one song, and "The song of
the Lamb" is another song. There is nothing about

---

* G.L.T,Tr.A. WH. and RV. omit "and from his mark."

the former being "similar" to Exodus xv. Such an interpretation as that robs the whole statement of all accuracy, deprives it of its beauty, and takes from us the instruction which is intended to be conveyed to us. In Exodus xv. 1 it merely says, "Then sang Moses and the children of Israel this song," and it is as much connected with Miriam as with Moses, as to human agency in authorship.

But there is a song, particularly and definitely described as "the song of Moses," in Deut. xxxii. And a most wonderful song it is.

This we believe to be "the song of Moses" which is sung here; while the words given in Rev. xv., in verses -3 and 4, are "the song of the Lamb."

"The song of Moses" in Deut. xxxii. 1-43, is a rehearsal of God's dealing with Israel from the beginning to the end. It is an epitome of the history of the whole nation in its relation to God. It is introduced to us in Deut. xxxi. 19: "Now, therefore, write ye this song for you, and teach it the children of Israel; put it in their mouths, *that this song may be a witness for me* against the children of Israel. (20) For when I shall have brought them into the land which I sware unto their fathers, that floweth with milk and honey; and they shall have eaten and filled themselves, and waxen fat; then will they turn unto other gods, and serve them, and provoke me, and break my covenant. (21) And it shall come to pass, when many evils and troubles have befallen them, that *this song shall testify against them as a witness*; for it shall not be forgotten out of the mouths of their seed: for I know their imagination which they go about, even now, *before I have brought them into the land* which I sware. (22) *Moses therefore wrote this song the same day,* and taught it the children of Israel." Then in verse 28 we read that Moses said " Gather unto me all the chiefs of your tribes, and your officers, that I may speak these words in their ears, and call heaven and earth to record against them: (29) For I know that after my death ye will utterly corrupt yourselves, and turn aside from the way which I have commanded you; and evil will befall you IN THE LATTER DAY, because ye will do evil in the sight of the Lord, to provoke him to anger through the work of your hands. And Moses spake in the ears of all the congregation of Israel the words of THIS SONG until they were ended."

Introduced with such solemnity, we expect to find something most wonderful and significant in "the words of this song"; and we are not disappointed.

It is divided into *ten* members (*ten*, the number of *ordinal perfection,* marking its completeness), and these members are arranged as an *Introversion:* the first corresponding, in its subject, with the *tenth;* the *second* corresponding with the *ninth;* the *third* with the *eighth;* the *fourth* with the *seventh;* and the *fifth* with the *sixth.*

All the stages of Israel's history receive the Divine description and verdict; and the Scriptures recording that history are marshalled in their order.

It will not be necessary for us to give all the words of this song; but our readers will turn to the place where it is written, and read it with the key to it which we now give. They will at once see the wonders of this song, and understand why it should be heaven's theme at this particular juncture in this Sixth Vision in heaven, immediately before those judgments which shall fulfil all its words :—

"THE SONG OF MOSES" (Deut. xxxii. 1-43)

A | 1-6.   God's call to Hear: and the reason.   The publishing of Jehovah's name: His perfect work and righteous ways.

　B | 7-14.   The goodness and bounty of Jehovah to Israel.   (Period of the Pentateuch).

　　C | 15-19.   Israel's evil return for that goodness. Their pride: forsaking of God; despising the Rock of their Salvation; moving Him to anger. (Period, past history.   The Historical books).

　　　D | 20.   Divine reflections on the period while Israel is "*Lo Ammi*" (not my people). (Period of Minor Prophets, esp. Hosea).

　　　　E | 21.   Jehovah's provocation of Israel. (Period of Acts and present Dispensation).

　　　　E | 22-25.   Jehovah's threatening of judgment on Israel in the great Tribulation.

　　　D | 26-33.   Divine reflections on the period while Israel is scattered.   (Hosea).

　　C | 34-38.   Israel's evil return for Jehovah's goodness.   Their helpless condition moving Him to pity.   He not forsaking them.   Their Rock useless.   (Period of present history).

　B | 39-42.   The Judgments of Jehovah.   (The period of the Apocalypse).

A | 43.   God's call to Rejoice: and the reason.   The publishing of Jehovah's Kingdom.   Vengeance on Israel's enemies.   Mercy for His Land and for His People.   (Fulfilment of all Prophecy).

How fitting that now, and here, at this stage of the Apocalyptic visions and judgments, the witness and testimony of this Song should be rehearsed, as intimated in Deut. xxxi. 19, and that another Song should be associated with it, adding and combining such phrases of Ex. xv. as will be appropriate for that particular season which shall then have arrived.

The words of "the Song of Moses" are given in Deut. xxxii : and the words of "the Song of the Lamb" (*i.e.*, given by Him and relating to Him), are now recorded, as follows :

-3. saying,
"Great and marvellous are **Thy works,**
O Lord God, the Almighty :
Righteous and true are **Thy ways,**
Thou King of the nations.*
(4) **Who should not fear,**† **O Lord,**
And glorify Thy name ?

Because thou **only** art **holy :**
Because all the nations shall come and
worship before Thee :
Because Thy righteous judgments were
manifested."]

These are the words of " the Song of the Lamb," and. they tell us that, in spite of the awful character of these coming judgments, God is " Holy " and " Righteous '• and " True." The Old Testament Titles are heaped together here. " The Lord God," pointing us back to Gen. ii. iii., and the setting right of all that was then put wrong. " Almighty," or the Lord God of Hosts

---

* G.L.·Tr.A. WH. and RV. read ἐθνῶν (*ethnōn*) *nations*, instead of ἁγίων (*hagiōn*) *saints.* † L.T.Tr.A. omit " thee."

(see Preliminary Points, pages 18, 16, &c.). He is the God of the hosts of Israel (Ex. xii. 41, 51). "The Song of the Lamb" looks forward to the completion of all that "the Song of Moses" foretells.

Many passages in the Prophets and Psalms speak of the same glorious result of God's judgments.

The first of the Six Angels (xiv. 6, 7), had proclaimed that Gospel which is from everlasting, which calls on all to " Fear God : " and now the heavenly singers ask, " Who shall not fear Thee ? " They take up the very words of Jer. x. 7; and to this time Ps. cii. 13-22 and Micah vii. 16, 17 refer.

But Ps. lxxxvi. 9-12 is specially to the point :

" All nations whom Thou hast made shall come
and worship before Thee, O Lord :
And shall glorify Thy name,
For Thou art great, and doest wondrous things.
Thou art God alone.
Teach me Thy way, O Lord : I will walk in Thy
truth :
Unite my heart to fear Thy name.
I will praise Thee, O Lord my God, with all my
heart :
And *I will glorify Thy name* for evermore."

" The Song of the Lamb," it will be seen, is made up of *nine* lines, nine being the number associated with *judgment.**

The second of the three reasons, " Because all the nations shall come and worship before Thee," points to one of the results of completed judgments, realised in Millennial days. (See Is. lxvi. 15, 16, 23. Zech. xiv. 16, 17. Ps. lxvi. 1-7; lxxii. 1-4; lxxxvi. 8, 9. Zeph. ii. 11.

---

* See *Number in Scripture.* Published by Kregel Publications

The third reason is the "righteous judgments" of
God, which will then be made manifest. This is the
meaning of δικαιώματά (*dikaiōmata*). Lit. it is *righteousnesses*, but the form of the word denotes the *outcome* of
the righteous act, the righteous thing done ; * and the
thing done, must be added, according to what the context requires. Here, it is "righteous judgments." That
they are, and always will be righteous is testified
again and again. (See Isa. lix. 18, 19).

With this agree the closing words of "the Song of
Moses" (Deut. xxxii. 41—43).

" Rejoice, O ye nations, with His People :
For He will avenge the blood of His servants,
And will render vengeance to His adversaries,
And will be merciful unto His Land,
And to His People."

Compare also Ps. lxxvi. 8, 9. Is. xxvi. 5, 8, 9. Ezek.
xxxix. 17, 21.

xv. 5. **And after these things I looked, and†
the Temple (***Naos***) of the tabernacle of the testimony
was opened in heaven : (6) and the seven angels who‡
had the seven plagues, came forth out of the temple**

---

* Thus, in Rom. v. 16 it means *righteous acquittal*. In Luke i. 6 and
Heb. ix. 1, 10 it means *righteous ordinances*. In Rom. i. 32 and Rev. xxi.
4 it means *righteous judgments*. In Rom. ii. 26 ; viii. 4 it means
righteous requirements. In Rev. xix. 8 it means *righteous awards*.
It never means the attribute of righteousness as such, for that
is either δικαιοσύνη (*dikaiosunē*), which is the attribute of righteousness, or δικαίωσις (*dikaiōsis*), which is the act of the judge in
justifying.

† G.L.T.Tr.A. WH. and RV. omit "behold."

‡ G.L.T.Tr.Ab. WH. and RV. add οἱ (*hoi*) *those* or *who*.

(*Naos*), **arrayed with precious*** **brilliant stone,†** **and girt about their breasts with golden girdles.** (7) **And one of the four Zōa gave to the seven angels seven golden Vials** (or Bowls) **full of the fury of God, who liveth for ever and ever]** We have already noticed above that both the Tabernacle of Moses and the Temple of Solomon were only copies of the Tabernacle and Temple in Heaven. The Realities were there, the copies were on earth. It was the *Naos* or Holy of Holies which was opened, *i.e.*, the *Naos* of the Tabernacle. Opened to give exit for the seven angels from the presence of God, as it was in chap. xi. 19. Again the *Zōa* are introduced as initiating judgments. The *Zōa* are related to Creation and to the earth, as we have seen, and these judgments are to clear the earth of all that causes creation's groanings. We have retained the word "Vials" because its usage is so fixed and associated with these judgments, though all know that the φιάλη (*phiale*) was a shallow *bowl*. The bowls were golden, and belonged to the altar.

xv. 8. **And the Naos** (or Holiest) **was filled with smoke from the glory of God, and from His power; and no one was able to enter into the Naos, until the seven plagues of the seven angels should be finished.]** When the Tabernacle was opened by Moses and the Temple by Solomon, there was cloud, but not smoke (Ex. xl. 34-36. 1 Kings viii. 10, 11). Here it is "smoke," for this is the hour of God's judgment (xiv. 7). No intercession can now be

---

* G.L.T.Tr.A. WH. and RV. omit "and."

† L.Tr. WH. and RV. read λιθον (*lithon*) *stone*, instead of λίνον (*linon*) *linen*. Compare Ezek. xxviii. 13 and Dan. x. 6.

made. No worship can be offered while it lasts. It will be again as it was in the days of Lam. iii. 44 :—

" Thou hast covered thyself with a cloud,
    That our prayer should not pass through."

Five of the ten plagues of Egypt are the same as five of these Bowls, as we shall see below. We would only add here, that as they were literal, so will these be.

We have now come to the end of the long parenthesis and series of Episodes which are given in chap. xii. 1—xv. 8. We now take up again the results of the sounding of the *seventh* Trumpet in the chronological order of events. Chap. xi. -19, gave us the general but very brief summary of those results, in the third Vision on Earth. The full detailed account of these results would have postponed too long several things necessary for us to know, had they been given in exact chronological sequence. We have now had that necessary knowledge interposed, and are ready to take up the events in their proper order.

17

THE SIXTH VISION "ON EARTH"
(16:1—18:24)

V. Chap. xvi. *The Seven Vials*

This is by far the most important of all the Visions seen by John, in relation to the earth.

It has also the largest space apportioned to its description.

It consists of the great judgments introduced by the sounding of the seventh Trumpet, which completes " The Mystery of God," by the pouring out of the seven Vials. The next Vision is the last seen in Heaven, and it introduces the actual Revelation or *Apocalupsis* of the Lord Jesus, personally, to the earth ; and thus brings on the conclusion of the whole prophecy.

This Sixth Vision on Earth consists of three divisions, which are so marked and distinct that those who divided the chapters found no difficulty in making a right division here.

The following brief structure of this Vision as a whole, is shown to consist of these three. Their many and various expansions will follow in their respective places. The reader will find no difficulty in following and connecting them, if the references to the back pages and letters be carefully noted :—

℟⁶ (page 118), chap. xvi.—xviii. THE SIXTH VISION
" ON EARTH "
The Seven Vials

℟⁶ | V | xvi. The Great Judgments. (The Seven Vials)
    | W | xvii. The Great Whore. (Mystery. Babylon)
    | X | xviii. The Great City. (Great Babylon)

Of these three we commence with the first, which we have marked " V," and which consists of the whole ot chap. xvi., describing

V. (page 476) chap. xvi. *The Great Judgments.*

Eleven times we have the word " great " in this chapter; more often than in any other chapter in the New Testament, the next being chap. xviii., where it occurs *nine* times.

We are justified, therefore, in entitling the judgments and subjects of these chapters as " great."

All is now ready to begin this final assault on the kingdom of the Infernal Trinity—the Dragon, the Beast, and the False Prophet, which will mark " the great and terrible day of the Lord."

Since we were told of the sounding of the seventh Trumpet (xi. 15), we have been taken back and enlightened as to several important particulars, so that we might understand more clearly the relation of these Visions to each other; we have been informed, by the last heavenly utterances, what we are to look for as the result of these judgments.

The Dragon is to be attacked in his capital and on his throne. The Beasts are to be attacked in their seats of authority; and their followers and worshippers are to " have no rest day and night " upon the earth (xiv. 11.)

There is some similarity between the Vial-judgments and those of the Trumpets; but there are some variations also. (See the diagram on page 302.)

The structure of this first division " V," shows that these seven Vials are divided into five groups: each consisting of cause and effect. The third and sixth are marked off by an additional characteristic: the third by " things *heard*," the sixth by " things *seen*." The Structure is as follows :—

V. (p. 476), chap. xvi. *The Great Judgments.* (The 7 Vials)

V
- A¹
  - a¹ | xvi. 1, 2-. The FIRST Vial
    - b¹ | -2. Effect. Sore on worshippers of Beast
  - a² | 3-. The SECOND Vial
    - b² | -3. Effect. Sea, blood
  - B¹
    - c | 4-. The THIRD Vial
    - d | -4. Effect. Rivers, blood
    - e | 5-7. Things heard. (Angelic voices)
- A²
  - a³ | 8-. The FOURTH Vial
    - b³ | -8, 9. Effect. Scorching. Worshippers of Beast impenitent
  - a⁴ | 10-. The FIFTH Vial
    - b⁴ | -10-11. Effect. Seat of Beast darkness. Men impenitent
  - B²
    - c | 12-. The SIXTH Vial
    - d | -12. Effect. Euphrates dried up
    - e | 13-16. Things seen. (Three demons like frogs)
- A³
  - a⁵ | 17-. The SEVENTH Vial
    - b⁵ | -17-21. Effect. Earthquake, and Great Babylon comes into remembrance (19)

We have observed above that the 1st and 2nd Vials form a pair, also the 4th and 5th; and, like the 7th, consist of two parts, *viz.*, the pouring out of the Vial and its effect. These three groups are separated by the 3rd and 6th Vial, which have each three parts. To the pouring out of the Vial and its effect is added, in the former case, *Things heard*; and in the latter case, *Things seen*. The effect of the last (or seventh) Vial is to bring up "great Babylon into remembrance"; and this leads on naturally and consecutively to the judgment on Babylon in chapters xvii. and xviii.

We now come to the translation.

The First Vial, and its Effect (xvi. 1, 2).

The first verse is general and introduces the whole seven.

xvi. 1. **And I heard a loud voice out of the Temple** (Naos), **saying to the Seven Angels,**

> **"Go forth, and pour out the seven***
> **Vials of the fury of God into the**
> **earth."**]

These seven Vials and their effects we take to be literal; *i.e.*, to be exactly what is said of them. They belong to no figures of speech. The language is clear and precise. There is nothing beyond our faith, though there may be beyond our reason. True, they are supernatural, but not unnatural. In the plagues of Egypt, which all take to be literal, we have many judgments exactly similar. Indeed, six out of the seven Vials are just the same as the plagues of Egypt, and God has again and again declared that their final judgments

---

* G.L.T.Tr.A. WH. and RV. add ἐπτά (*hepta*) *seven.*

should be like, yea, should be worse than those (Ex. xxxiv. 10).

The first Vial is like the sixth plague, which was of Boils, etc.

The second and third Vials are like the first plague, when the waters became blood.

The fifth Vial is like the ninth plague, when darkness overspread the land.

The sixth Vial is like the second plague, of frogs.

The seventh Vial is like the 7th plague, of hail, &c.

The fourth is the only Vial which has no counterpart in the Egyptian plagues; and that is the great " heat." Now, if six out of these seven judgments have already been *once* seen and experienced, why should not like plagues be sent again, when it is expressly said that the supernatural events connected with Israel's return shall be " like as it was . . . in the day that he came up out of the land of Egypt " (Is. xi. 16) ?

In the face of this, Is it not strange that these Vials should ever be taken to mean :

The first, the French Revolution ; and the " sores " its infidelity, &c. ;

The second, the naval wars of the French Revolution ;

The third, Napoleon's campaign in Italy ;

The fourth, Napoleon's military tyranny, &c., &c. ?

It is a waste of precious time and space even to chronicle such interpretations, which make the Word of God of none effect.

Does any one believe that we have passed through the greater part of the " great and terrible Day of the Lord " without knowing it; and yet all the time preaching the Gospel of God's Grace, instead of proclaiming that " the hour of his judgment is come "? Is this really "the day of vengeance of our God," and yet Ministers on every hand are telling us how the Millennium is actually dawning; and some that it has already come — a Millennium without Christ? No! Bible students, who believe what God says; and whose one desire is to understand what He has said, can never be satisfied with such confusion as that, which only perplexes the mind, instead of enlightening it.

xvi. 2. And the first went forth, and poured out his Vial into* the earth; and there broke out a noisome and grievous sore upon† the men who had the mark (or brand) **of the Beast, and** upon **those who were worshipping his image.**] The words "poured out" are more than hinted at in Ps. lxxix. 1-6. Lam. iv. 11; and a similar plague had been more than once seen before. Ex. ix. 8-12. Job ii. 7, 8. 1 Sam. v. 6. Num. xii. 10.

Moreover it was one of the judgments threatened to Israel. Deut. xxviii. 15, 27, 35. Lev. xxvi. 16.

The first to suffer on account of this plague are the worshippers of the Beast and his Image. These had been warned (xiv. 9-11) that those who are engaged in worshipping the Beast (it is the present participle both there and here) should have no rest day and night." Here we see how this is to be brought about: none can rest who are afflicted with these "noisome and grievous sores."

The Second Vial (xvi. 3)

<u>**xvi. 3. And the second‡ poured out his Vial into the**</u>

* L.T.Tr.A. WH. and RV. read εἰς (*eis*), *into*, instead of ἐπί (*epi*), *upon*.

† L.T.Tr.A. WH. and RV. read ἐπί (*epi*), *upon*, instead of εἰς (*eis*), *in* or *into*.

‡ L.T.Tr.A. WH. and RV. omit "angel."

sea : and it became blood, as of one dead ; and every living soul died that was in the sea.] We may compare this with the second Trumpet (viii. 8) and the first Egyptian plague (Ex. vii. 20-25. Compare Ps. cv. 29. Isa. l. 2. Nahum i. 2-4). The literal understanding of these plagues makes things so clear, that little or no further explanation is necessary. They explain to us the nature and effect of these judgments.

The Third Vial (xvi. 4-7).

xvi. 4. **And the third* poured out his Vial into the rivers, and† the fountains of waters; and they became blood.** (5) **And I heard the angel of the waters saying,**

> **"Righteous art Thou,‡ who art, and wast, §**
>
> **Holy ‖ art Thou, because Thou didst judge these things.**
>
> (6) **For they shed the blood of saints and prophets,**
>
> **And Thou hast given them blood to drink;**
>
> —— ¶ **They deserve it ! "**

7. **And I heard** (the angel of)** **the altar saying,**

---

* G.L.T.Tr.A. WH. and RV. omit " angel."

† L.T.Tr.A. WH. and RV. omit εἰς (*us*) *into.*

‡ G.L.T.Tr.A. WH. and RV. omit κύριε (*kyrie*) *O Lord.*

§ The AV. seems to have added " and shalt be " on its own authority It must, however, be omitted (with the RV.), as in xi. 17, because He will have then already come.

‖ G.L.T.Tr.A. WH. and RV. substitute ὅσιος (*hosios*) *holy*, instead of καὶ ὁ (*kai o*) *and who* [wast].

¶ G.L.T.Tr.A. WH. and RV. omit γάρ (*gar*) *for.*

** G.L.T.Tr.A. WH. and RV. omit ἄλλου ἐκ (*allou ek*) *another out of.*

"Even so, Lord God, the Almighty,
True and righteous are Thy judgments."]

This is Divine comment from heaven on the judgment
of the third Vial. The expression, "angel of the
waters," shows that angels have their spheres and
offices ; that the operations of nature are not left to
blind chance, but that He who made what men call
"the laws of nature" has a mighty and capable
executive to see that those laws, and God's will, are
carried out.

The Altar is either personified (for the prayers of the
saints are upon it ; and the martyrs are beneath it) ; or
the words "[*the angel of*] the Altar" must be supplied.
In either case, the emphasis is on "the Altar."

The Angel's words, here, show that they are uttered
in another dispensation, altogether different from the
present dispensation of grace ; even in the dispensation of
retribution and judgment.   That dispensation to which
such passages as Ezek. xxxv. 6 and xvi. 38 refer.

Just as Matt. xxiii. 34, 35, and Luke xi. 47-51, refer
to a day of judgment and not of grace.   God is "not
imputing their trespasses" unto His people now, having
imputed them all to Christ.   This shows that unless we
rightly divide the Word according to its dispensation,
our reading of it must be in hopeless confusion.

The reference of verse 6 (" They have shed the blood
of thy prophets," etc.) is evidently to chap. xvii. 6;
xiii. 15 ; xi. 18 ; and xviii. 20. Pss. lxxix. and lxxiv.
should be read in this connection.

The Fourth Vial (xvi. 8, 9)

xvi. 8.   **And the fourth** [angel *] **poured out his**

---

* G.L.T.Tr.A. WH. and RV. omit "angel," though the *Ellipsis*
may well be thus supplied.

**Vial upon the Sun ; and it was given to him to scorch
men with fire.** (9) **And men were scorched with
vehement heat, and they blasphemed the name of
God** (*i.e.,* God Himself), **who hath authority over
these plagues: and they repented not, to give Him
glory.**] At the sounding of the fourth Trumpet the
Sun was smitten, but only one third of it. There are
to be "signs in the sun" (Luke xxi. 25). Isaiah tells
of a time when " the inhabitants of the earth are *burned*
and few men left" (Isa. xxiv. 6; xlii. 25). Compare
Mal. iv. 1, which says : " Behold, the day cometh that
shall burn as an oven; and the proud, yea, and all that
do wickedly, shall be as stubble." The moral effects,
here, are a defiance of the demands of the angel in
xiv. 6, 7. They refuse to " give glory to God." They
cry not for quarter, nor will quarter be given. Yet men
tell us that all we have here is the tyranny and oppression of Napoleon !

The Fifth Vial (xvi. 10, 11)

xvi. 10. **And the fifth** [angel *] **poured out his Vial
upon the throne of the Beast: and his kingdom
became darkened ; and they gnawed their tongues
from their pain,** (11) **and they blasphemed the God of
heaven because of their pains and their sores** (*v.* 2),
and repented not and turned not **from their works.**]
This proves that the Seven Assemblies belong, by *interpretation* to that dispensation of judgment. For to the
Assembly at Pergamos Christ says: "I know thy works
and where thou dwellest ; where the throne of Satan is ;
and thou holdest fast my name, and didst not deny my
faith, even in the days of Antipas, my faithful martyr,

---

* G.L.T.Tr.A. WH. and RV. omit "angel." But we must supply
the *Ellipsis*, nevertheless.

who was killed among you, where **Satan** dwelleth "
ii. 13; xiii. 2). So that not only is it clear
that those Assemblies are on the earth at this time, but
that chap. xii. records events prior to chap. ii., and that
the persecution and martyrdom of chap. xiii. have
already commenced in the days to which chap. ii. 13
refers. This Vial initiates a direct attack on the throne
of the Beast, the vice-gerent of Satan. He is no more
able to defend himself against this plague of darkness
than Pharaoh was (Ex. x. 21-23). The darkness here
referred to will be as real as the darkness was in Egypt.
Joel prophesied of this when he said (ii. 1, 2, 31) :
   " The Day of the Lord cometh. . . .
   A day of darkness and of gloominess ;
   A day of clouds and thick darkness.
   The sun shall be turned into *darkness*," etc.
In Mark xiii. 24, 25, the Saviour said "the sun shall be
darkened, and the moon shall not give her light."
   Great is the vexation caused by this awful darkness.
And yet we are asked to believe that this is nothing
more than the Suppression of the Monasteries, etc., in
France, in 1789, by Napoleon.
   Is this what all the prophets have been occupied
with ? Even symbols must symbolise something that
is congruous. But, here, the bringing on of gross darkness is made to symbolise the suppression of what is
the cause of darkness ! If it were taken to symbolise the
setting up of monasteries, it would be more relevant. No
wonder that darkness has come over this book—when
imagination is substituted for faith.

The Sixth Vial (xvi. 12-16)

The sixth Vial, like the third (xvi. 4, 5), has **three**
divisions (whereas all the others have only two). These

three are (1) the pouring out, (2) the effect, and (3) things seen. The third Vial was the same, except that there we had things *heard*: and here we have things *seen*.

xvi. 12. **And the sixth** [angel*] **poured out his Vial upon the great river** the† **Euphrates ; and the water thereof was dried up, that the way of the kings** that come **from the East might be prepared.**] We take this to refer to the actual river Euphrates. All else in the chapter is literal ; and so is this. There is no reason why it should not be so. Those who assert that this means the wane of the Turkish Empire say so on their own responsibility. There is not a word about it here, and there is nothing to lead us to imagine it ; especially when we think of the object for which the river is to be dried up. The sixth Trumpet has to do with the river Euphrates also. The context here, and the " things seen " in connection with this Vial, tell us that the kings of the earth are about to be gathered to-gether to the great battle in which the Heavenly and Satanic and earthly forces are about to be engaged. With the view of preparing for this gathering, the way of those kings which are to come from the East, is to be prepared. The Vial is connected with judgment, and not with mercy ; and therefore to interpret these kings of the Ten Tribes, or of " Christian princes," or of any propitious or auspicious event, is out of all harmony with the whole scope of the context. At the sounding of the sixth Trumpet a vast supernatural army is let loose to slay a third part of men. Here, under the sixth Vial, a vast human army is gathered

---

* G.L.T.Tr.A. WH. and RV. omit "angel," though we have **to** supply the *Ellipsis* as before.

† G.T. omit " the." Tr. and WH. put it in brackets.

together, the whole of which is destroyed by God. Moreover, a similar effect on the river Euphrates is the subject of another prophecy: "And the LORD shall utterly destroy the tongue of the Egyptian sea ; and with His mighty wind shall he shake his hand over the river [Euphrates] and shall smite it in the seven streams, and make men go over dry-shod" (Isa. xi. 15).

Again, "I will bring them also out of the land of Egypt, and gather them out of *Assyria ;* and . . . *the deeps of the river shall dry up* ; and the pride of *Assyria* shall be brought down, and the sceptre of Egypt shall depart away" (Zech. x. 10, 11).

The kings from the East journey Westward to Palestine. East and West are to be reckoned from the standpoint of the prophecy, and not from that of the reader. Here, that standpoint is God's Land and City.

The Euphrates is indeed a great river, as here stated. It is 1,800 miles long, and from Mohammarah to the sea it is 3,600 feet wide and 30 feet deep.* This river is to be dried up for the more easy gathering of this infernal Crusade against the Lamb and His host. They gather to a scene of slaughter, from which they never return. It is this gathering which the Scripture now proceeds to describe to us.

xvi. 13. **And I saw** going forth **out of the mouth of the Dragon, and out of the mouth of the Beast, and out of the mouth of the False Prophet, three unclean spirits, as it were† frogs.** (14) **(For they are demon**

---

* See Col. Chesney's *Euphratean Expedition.*

† G.L.T.Tr.A. WII. and RV. read ὡς (*hōs*), *as it were*, instead of ὅμοια (*homoia*), *like.*

spirits working miracles), which go forth to the kings*
of the whole world to gather them together to the†
battle of that great day of God, the Almighty.]   The
Holy Spirit does not say they were frogs, but that they
seemed to look like frogs.   But He actually says they
were *not* frogs, and thus not like the plague of frogs in
Egypt (Ex. viii. 1-14), but "spirits," *i.e.*, demon spirits
They work miracles, as does the false prophet (xiii. 13-
15. 2 Thess. ii. 9).

They give apparently convincing evidence of their
reality and mission : and if thousands could be gathered
to the Crusades by a man (like Peter the hermit), tens
of thousands will be gathered by these wonder-working
demons, and persuaded to join the advancing hosts
against God and His saints.   We see a similar and
real persuasion in 1 Kings xxii. 19-38.   See Joel iii.
9-11. Ps. ii. 1-3.

Then we have this interjectional clause, which must
be read as a parenthesis ; for it does not interfere with
the course of the prophetic events.‡

While the demon spirits are gathering the kings and
their armies, John hears the Voice of Christ, saying :

[15. "Behold I come as a thief.   Blessed
     is he that watcheth, and keepeth his
     garments, lest he walk naked, and
     they see his shame."]

These words are addressed to those in the other host
who have not worshipped the Beast or his image, and

---

* G.L.T.Tr.A. WH. and R.V. omit τῆs γῆs, καί (*tēs gēs, kai*), *of
the earth, and.*

† G.L.T.Tr.A. WH. and RV. add the article.

‡ When a parenthesis is complete in itself, and is independent of the
context, it is called *Parembole*.   See *Figures of Speech*, p. 476.

have not received his mark or the number of his name.
They receive this encouraging Benediction. True, it is
"as a thief" He is now coming. This proves that the
Church of God is not in the judgment scene here
described, for the Thessalonian believers were positively assured that that day shall NOT come on
them as a thief (1 Thess. v. 4. Compare Matt. xxiv.
38-44. Luke xii. 35-40). This blessing is not for
us now, in this dispensation of grace, even as the
assurance is not for us. The Lord is then about to
come as a thief. Hence this announcement; and
hence this blessing. Those who will need it will be
on the earth at that time, as we learn from chap. iii. 3
(compare Mark xiii. 34-37).

   After this *Parembole* the prophecy proceeds as though
it had not been interrupted.

   xvi. 16. **And they** (*i.e.*, the demon spirits of *v.* 14)
gathered them (*i.e.*, the kings and their armies)
**together unto the place which is called in Hebrew
Har-mageddon***] This mention of Hebrew connects
the Apocalypse with the Gospels (See John v. 2; xix
13, 17. So Rev. ix. 11). And in this we have also a
reference to the Old Testament. The name הַר־מְגִדּוֹן
(*har-megiddō*) means *the mount of Megiddo;* and the name
is ominous as to what the result of this battle will be.
For there Deborah and Barak destroyed Sisera and his
host (Judg. v. 19); there King Josiah was overthrown
by Pharaoh-Necho, king of Egypt (2 Kings xxiii. 29.
2 Chron. xxxv. 22-25). Slaughter and lamentation are
associated with Megiddo (Zech. xii. 11). In Isa. x. 28,
which describes the invasion of Anti-Christ, the Septuagint version reads Megiddo.

---

* So spelt by G.L.T.Tr.A. WH. and RV.

Megiddo probably means a *place of troops* (from גָד, *gad*), *a troop* (Gen. xlix. 19) ; and the verb גָדַד (*gādad*), *to cut to pieces*. See Deut. xiv. 1. 1 Kings xviii. 28. Jer. xvi. 6 ; xli. 5. Mic. v. 1). It is part of the great plain of Esdraelon. It is a real locality, and the transactions yet to take place there will be real also.

Having gathered the hosts of the enemy thither, the sixth Vial ends. The description of the events which took place there is delayed until the events of the seventh Vial bring on the final catastrophe in chap. xix. There we have the battle itself (xix. 11-18). The sixth vial brings us up to the point where everything is seen to be in readiness, and then abruptly breaks off so as to allow of our coming up to the same point through another course of events, which are brought on by the pouring forth of

The Seventh Vial. (xvi. 17-21)

xvi. 17. **And the seventh [angel*] poured his Vial upon† the air ; and there came forth a loud voice out of‡ the Temple** (Naos),§ **from the throne, saying,**

"It is done."]

i.e., the last Vial has been, at length, poured out; the last judgment entered upon ; the last plague begun. This will end all up and fulfil and accomplish all the Divine counsels as to these judgments. Therefore

---

* G.L.T.Tr.A. WH. and RV. omit " angel," but the *Ellipsis* must be supplied as before.

† G.L.T.Tr.A. WH. and RV. read ἐπί (*epi*) *upon*, instead of εἰς (*eis*) *into*.

‡ L.T.Tr.A. WH. and RV. read ἐκ (*ek*) *out of*, instead of ἀπό (*apo*) *from*, or *away from*.

§ L.T.Tr.A. WH. and RV. omit "of heaven."

this voice comes forth; and this solemn announcement is made, " It is done." The Temple is seen at the close of each of the three series of judgments. This is the last. In the New Heaven and New Earth there will be no Temple (ch. xxi. 22). This is the final act, which chronologically brings on the opening of heaven and the coming forth of the Son of God Himself to the battle in xix. 11.

But before that happens we are detained and told of the destruction of Babylon and the Empire of the Beast (xvii. and xviii.); and the marshalling of the heavenly forces (chap. xix). We are, however, told of the commotions in heaven and on earth, which are given in a general statement or summary.

xvi. 18. **And there were lightnings, and voices, and thunders;** * **and there was a great earthquake, such as was not since man was on the earth, so mighty an earthquake, or so great.**] Similar results take place at the opening of the seventh Seal (viii. 5); and at the sounding of the seventh Trumpet (xi. 19). This is the great earthquake spoken of by the prophets (Ezek. xxxviii. 20. Isa. ii. 19, 21 Hag. ii. 21, 22).

xvi. 19 **And the great city became divided** (or split) **into three parts, and the cities of the nations fell; and great Babylon came into remembrance before God, to give to her the cup of the wine of the fierceness of his wrath.**] Not only is great Babylon split up into three parts by this earthquake, but the capital cities also of the confederated nations, the allies of the Beast (*v.* 14; xvii. 13-17) were destroyed. Some say that "Great Babylon" means " Rome "; others hold that it

---

* This is the order according to G. L.T.Tr.A. WH. and RV.

means " Jerusalem "; while others, like ourselves, believe what is written. Babel or Babylon was the scene of the first apostasy from God after the Flood. Always the enemy of God's people, she became in later days the metropolis of the first great Gentile Empire as seen in the image and dream of Nebuchadnezzar. God promised to remember His covenant with Israel ; and when He did so He promised also to remember Babylon in the day of His wrath. Hence His people cry concerning it, " Remember, O Lord." Ps. cxxxvii.; xcviii. 3 ; cv. 8, 42.

Babylon is only partly destroyed now in token of its total destruction soon to follow. One tenth of the city will have fallen, as we are told in xi. 12, 13. And chapters xvii. and xviii. are going to tell us of the causes, and of the manner, and the consequences of that judgment.

xvi. 20. **And every island fled away, and** certain **mountains were not found.** (21) **And a great hail, as of a talent's weight, falleth out of heaven upon men; and men blasphemed God because of the plague of the hail; because the plague thereof is exceedingly great**.] The judgments increase in their severity. In chap. vi. 14, the mountains and islands were moved. Here, they flee. By and by the whole earth and heaven will flee away, and no place be found for them. There is no article before mountains, so we have supplied its absence by the word " certain." Had every mountain been meant the article would have been used. Mountains will exist during the millennium. (See Ps. lxxii. 3, 16; cxlviii. 9. Isa. ii. 2; xliv. 23. Ezek. xxxvi. 8). The plague of hail in Egypt was real (Ex. ix. 18-21). So is this. Why not? The stones are indeed great in size. A Jewish talent was 114 lbs. troy weight. Josephus says that stones of a talent's weight were thrown by the Romans against Jerusalem (*Wars* iii. vii. 9). Surely God can send from heaven what man could send on earth.

M. Huc says, in his *Travels in Tartary* * : " Hail is of frequent occurrence in these unhappy districts, and the dimensions of the hailstones are generally enormous. We have seen some that weighed twelve pounds. One moment sometimes suffices to exterminate whole flocks. In 1843, during one of these storms, there was heard in the air a sound as of a rushing wind, and therewith fell in a field near a house, a mass of ice larger than an ordinary millstone. It was broken to pieces with hatchets ; yet though the sun burned fiercely, three days elapsed before these pieces entirely melted."

Hail had been before one of God's engines of war, beyond the use or defence of man. (See chap. xi. 19. Ex. ix. 22-26. Ps. lxxviii. 47 ; cv. 32. Josh. x. 11). And they are the tokens of Divine wrath. (See Isa. xxx. 30. Ezek. xiii. 11).

No wonder the blasphemy that follows from the worshippers of the Beast, impenitent to the end, will also be exceeding great.

This concludes the great Judgments of the Seven Vials recorded in chap. xvi. We come now to chap. xvii., the Judgment of the great Harlot.

---

* See *Travels in Tartary*, by M. Huc, vol. i., p. 12. " National Illustrated Library."

494 / *The Sixth Vision "on Earth"*

W. (page 476). Chap. xvii. *The Great Harlot.*

This is the second of the three great divisions of the sixth Vision " on Earth." On page 476 we have shown them as follows :—

The 1st (chap. xvi.). The great Judgments (p. 477)
The 2nd (chap. xvii.). The great Harlot (p. 494)
The 3rd (chap. xviii.). The great City (p. 550)

It is the first of these which we have just completed ; and we pass on to the second—in chap. xvii.— which, perhaps more than any other, has caused the widest gulf between the various schools of expositors. It is one of the most prominent of all the subjects of which the Apocalypse treats. Indeed, taken with the eighteenth chapter, which is part of the same Vision (the 6th " on Earth "), it is the most conspicuous prophecy of this book. None of the current expositions are sufficiently consistent or satisfying. Preterist Expositors differ among themselves as to whether " great Babylon " means the City of Rome, or the Church of Rome : Rome Pagan or Rome Papal. But, if this is all that these solemn chapters mean, we may well say with Dr. Seiss, " If we cannot find more solid ground than that on which the Rome theory rests, we must needs consign the whole subject to the department of doubt and uncertainty ; and let all these tremendous foreshadowings pass for nothing."*

But we shall best accomplish our object by keeping to the Text of the Word itself; learning its scope from its structure ; and giving its translation.

No current theory takes in the *whole* scope. One or two points are seized upon, and treated quite out of all proportion to the rest ; while others, quite as essential,

* *Lectures on the Apocalypse*, vol. iii., p. 109.

are passed over slightly, or ignored altogether. Any
satisfying interpretation must take in the *whole* of what
is written; and must treat each part, not as though it
were in the way, or inconvenient, but as though it
were indispensable.

The chapter itself is divided into two parts; (i.) the
Vision, and (ii.) its *Interpretation*.

> W. (page 476). Chap. xvii. *The great Harlot*
>
> W | Y | xvii. 1-6. The Vision
> | Z | xvii. 7-18. The Interpretation

And first expanding " W," *The Vision* (xvii. 1-6), we
find it is constructed as follows :—

> Y. (above), xvii. 1-6. *The Vision*

Y | C | f | xvii. 1-.   Place: " Hither "   ⎫
  | | g | -1-.   The great harlot   ⎬ Promise
  | | h | -1.   Her seat |
  | | i | 2.   Her accomplices   ⎭

  | C | f | 3-.   Place: " Wilderness "   ⎫
  | | g | -3-.   The woman   ⎬ Performance
  | | h | -3.   Her seat |
  | | i | 4-6.   Herself   ⎭

xvii. 1. **And there came one of the seven angels
who had the seven Vials,**] Which of the seven we
are not told; but it was probably the last; inasmuch as
it was the pouring forth of his Vial that brought Great
Babylon into remembrance before God.

and talked with me, saying*
>   "**Come hither; I will show to thee the
>   judgment of the great harlot, that**

---
* G.L.T.Tr.A. WH. and RV. omit μοι (*moi*) *unto me.*

> sitteth upon many waters: (2) **With whom the kings of the earth committed fornication, and those who dwell on the earth were made drunk with the wine of her fornication.**"]

We have before observed, that when symbols are used in this book they are generally explained by the Holy Spirit Himself. When this is not the case, we must, of course, use our best judgment and compare other Scriptures, so as to see, as far as we can, what the symbol means. But, when He does tell us what the symbols mean, we are not left in any doubt or uncertainty. We cannot go wrong if we keep to the interpretation which the Spirit Himself gives. *We are not to re-interpret His interpretation;* or to further explain His explanation. If so, we should be treating the Divine interpretation as though it were *another symbol.* This, therefore, we may not do; but we are to accept it, and believe it, and rest on it.

Now, in this chapter, the Spirit has been pleased to give us *His own interpretation* of the Vision. We have seen how this is emphasised in the structure, which is expressly divided into these two parts. We have marked them

" Y " (*v.* 1-6), which is the *Vision,* and
" Z " (*v.* 7-18), which is the *Interpretation.*

These two are again subdivided in a similar and corresponding manner. Each is introduced by a *Promise* (" C " *vv.* 1, 2 and " D," " E " *v.* 7); and is followed by the *Performance* of that promise (" C ' *vv.* 3-6 and " E," " D " *vv.* 8-18). See the structure of " Y," page 495, and " Z," page 497.

In this manner has the Holy Spirit called our attention to His interpretation, and impressed its importance upon us.

If we follow this, all will be easy and plain.

Indeed, it will be better to give the structure of the Interpretation (*vv.* 7-18) here, and now, and incorporate the two together, in order that the one may elucidate the other; and, that we may thus use both to greater profit.

Z. (page 495). xvii. 7-18. *The Interpretation of the Vision*

$$Z \left| \begin{array}{l} D\ |\ 7\text{-}.\quad \text{The Woman} \\ \quad E\ |\ \text{-}7.\quad \text{The Beast} \end{array} \right\} \text{Promise}$$

$$\left| \begin{array}{l} \quad E\ |\ 8\text{-}17.\quad \text{The Beast} \\ D\ |\ 18.\quad \text{The Woman} \end{array} \right\} \text{Performance}$$

The member *E* (*vv.* 8-17) will require expansion later on; together with the special consideration for which the structure of that member calls.

Now, there is a well-known principle which is often practised in algebra with great advantage in the solution of a problem; and that is, where one thing represents another, to *express that one in the terms of the other.*

The same principle may be followed here, where we have the Vision and the Divinely-given interpretation. We will re-write the Vision *in the terms of the interpretation*: *i.e.*, instead of putting what John saw, we will put the explanation at once, and thus bring the whole more clearly before our minds.

We will, therefore, do this, using two different kinds of type to make the matter more clear and enable us to distinguish what is the symbolic prophecy, and what is the Divine interpretation. Thus we shall introduce the *interpretation* given in the latter part of the chapter, and substitute it (in italic type) for the *symbols* used in the former part of the chapter, thus :

> *v.* 1. "**Come hither : I will show to thee the judgment of** *that great City that reigneth over the kings of the earth* (*v. 18*), *and over peoples and multitudes and nations and tongues* (*v. 15*), **with whom the kings of the earth have** *practised idolatry,** *and the inhabitants of the earth have been made to partake of* HER *idolatrous worship.*"

This, of course, characterised the worship of Pagan Rome, but cannot truly be said of Papal Rome, or of which this chapter is commonly interpreted. But inasmuch as this was the mark of *all* the heathen nations, it does not, of itself, identify this city with Pagan Rome : for it is a city, the Spirit says (*v.* 18).

3. **And he** (*i.e.*, the angel) **carried me away by the spirit**] as in chap. i. 10, upon which passage it throws great light. ἐν πνεύματι (*en pneumati*) means *by the spirit*, or by spiritual power, as in i. 10 ; iv. 2 ; xxi. 10. Acts viii. 26, 29, 39.

---

* Fornication is everywhere in the Bible the common term for the sin of *idolatry*, not only because it is unfaithfulness to God in forsaking Him, the true God, for the worship of false gods ; but because it literally formed an essential part of all heathen idolatry. See Lev. xx. 5. Num. xxv. 1. 2 Chron. xxi. 11. Isa. i. 21 ; xxiii. 17. Jer. ii. 20 ; iii. 1, 6, 8. Ezek. xvi. 15-17, 28, 29, 31, 34, 35, 41 ; xx. 30 ; xxiii. 5, 9, 43, 44. Hos. ii. 5 ; iii. 3 ; iv. 5, 10, 13-15. Mic. i. 7.

into the* **wilderness; and I saw a woman**] *i.e.,* that great city (*v.* 18).

sitting upon a scarlet beast] *i.e.,* supported by that being who is described in verses 8-11.

full of blasphemous names, having seven heads and ten horns] Now we must treat this verse as we have treated verses 1, 2 above, and *express the vision in the terms of the interpretation:*

-3. "**And I saw** *that great city which reigneth over the kings of the earth* (*v. 18*), *supported by* **the Beast full of blasphemous names** *which was, and is not, and shall ascend out of the bottomless pit, and go into perdition* (*v. 8*), *even he who is the eighth king,* **and** *is of the seven* (*v. 11*), **having seven kings** (*v. 10*), *which support that great city which reigneth over the kings of the earth* (*v. 9, 18*) ; **and ten** *kings which are contemporaneous and which have received no kingdom as yet ; but receive power as kings at one and the same time with the Beast* (*v. 12*), *who is the eighth king* (*v. 11*), *that was, and is not, and shall be present*"(*v. 8*).

Now, from this, Is it not clear that we are dealing, not with world-powers in their successive or mortal

---

* The article is often omitted after a preposition; and nothing can therefore be built upon its omission here.

stage, but with individuals in their contemporaneous and superhuman form ?

It is very important for us to note this important fact, which is vital to the understanding of the whole Vision and its Divinely-given interpretation.

Our business is not to interpret the Vision. That is done for us. What we have to do is first *to believe* what God says, and then to try and understand it.

The world-powers of Dan. ii. are there seen in their mortal stage, and hence are seen in their *successive* existence, in which they were *rival* powers. In Rev. xiii. and xvii. they are seen in their superhuman stage, and they then form one vast colossal Power, having absolute dominion in the world. In Dan. vii. 26, this Power is seen judged as a whole, and goes down into perdition. Dan. vii. 26 treats of the superhuman stage as do chapters xiii., xvii., here.

The Beast receives his deadly wound in his mortal stage, previous to going down into the Abyss. He comes up with the other heads and ten horns. All come together and are seen together in their super-human form.

Chapter xii. when compared with chap. xiii. and xvii. shows that there are two great confederacies treated of —the Heavenly and the Earthly—and they are not identical.

There is the Dragon Confederacy of seven heavenly dominions with their ten armies. This is a Confederacy of evil angels with Satan at their head (chap. xii.)

The other Confederacy is of mortals who went down into the Abyss, and come up a superhuman Confederacy on the earth (chaps. xiii. and xvii.).

Angels form the Confederacy under Satan in the heavens.

Superhuman men form the Confederacy under the Beast on earth.

These Confederacies are distinct from each other.

What we are told of the Beast in xvii. 4, concerns his relation to Babylon.

xvii. 4. **And the woman** (*i.e.* the great city, *v.* 18) **was arrayed in purple** (Judg. viii. 26. Est. i. 6), **and scarlet, and bedecked with gold and precious stone and pearls, having a golden cup** (Jer. li. 7) **in her hand full of abominations and** having **the unclean things of her fornication :**]

Again we must present the vision of this verse in terms of the interpretation :

4. **And** *that great city which reigneth over the kings of the earth* (*v. 18*) **was beautified with purple and scarlet, and adorned with gold and precious stone, and pearls, having** *a wondrous and attractive idolatrous system* **full of abominations, and having the unclean** *provisions for her idolatrous practices.*"

That great city is described as having all luxuries, combined with her idolatrous worship. The word " Abomination " is used of an idol (see 2 Kings xxiii. 13. Is. xliv. 19) ; and in the plural, of idolatry (see Deut. xviii. 9 ; xxix. 17 ; xxxii. 16. 1 Kings xiv. 24. 2 Kings xvi. 3 ; xxi. 2 ; xxiii. 24. So Ezek. viii. 6, 9, 13, 15, 17 ; xi. 18 ; xiv. 6 ; xvi. 2 ; xx. 7, 8). Doubtless the idols and idolatry were so called, because of the uncleanness practised in their worship. Can we doubt that when we meet with the word here in Rev. xvii.

4, 5, we have the same idolatrous uncleanliness referred to?

5. **And upon her forehead a name written,—a secret sign.**] By printing (on its own authority) the word "mystery" in large capital letters, the AV. has made it appear as part of the name. The Revisers have followed this example, printing the name in small capitals instead of large. But they have, in the margin, said "*or*, a mystery, *BABYLON THE GREAT*," as though the word "mystery" did not form part of the title. We believe this to be the case, and we further believe that what follows the word "great" does not form any part of this "name," but is the Divine meaning and description of it.

So we read it, that she had **a name written on her forehead—a secret symbol—**

"BABYLON THE GREAT,"

the mother of the harlots and of the abominations of the earth.] Written on the woman's forehead, it was a secret sign or symbol. It does not mean that she or any woman could be so described. But that, as the explanation of what the woman represented is deferred till the very last verse of the chapter, the meaning of the name was a secret, till it was then and there revealed that it referred to "that great city" (*v.* 18), and not to an individual woman, or to any human being.

The word μυστήριον (*mustērion*) means simply *a secret*. It occurs in the Septuagint (280 B.C.) only nine times, of the king's secret which had gone from him (Dan. ii. 18, 19, 27, 28, 29, 30, 47 (twice), and iv. 9) See also its usage in the Apocryphal books in the same sense.* But

---

* Ecclus. xxii. 22, "If thou hast opened thy mouth against a friend, fear not ; for there may be a reconciling ; excepting it be for upbraid-

the Greek Christian fathers used the word of any such
sign, whether of words or actions.   They spoke of the
offering of Isaac as a *mustērion*: *i.e.*, a *sign* or symbol of
the *secret purpose* of God concerning His Son, Jesus
Christ.   And they used it interchangeably with the
words τύπος (*tupos*) *type*; σύμβολον (*sumbolon*), *symbol*, and
παραβολή (*parabolē*) *parable.*

The meaning of the word *mystery*, therefore, here in
Rev. xvii. 5, 7, must have this later signification which
the word had acquired.   We give a few examples in a

---

ing, and arrogance, and disclosing of a *secret*, and a treacherous blow :
for these things every friend will flee.''

Ecclus. xxvii. 16, '' He that revealeth *secrets* destroyeth credit : and
shall never find a friend to his mind.''

Ecclus. xxvii. 17, '' Love thy friend, and keep faith with him; but
if thou reveal his *secrets* thou shalt not pursue after him.''

Ecclus. xxvii. 21, '' A wound may be bound up; and after reviling
there may be a reconcilement; but he that revealeth *secrets* hath lost
hope.''

2 Maccabees xiii. 21, '' But Rhodocus, from the Jewish ranks, made
known to the enemy the *secrets* of his countrymen.''

Wisdom ii. 22, '' And they (*i.e.*, the wicked) knew not the *secrets*
of God.''

Wisdom xiv. 23, '' Slaughtering their children . . . or celebrating
secret rites.''

Tobit xii. 7, 11, '' It is good to keep close *the secret* of a king, but
to reveal gloriously together the works of God.''

Judith ii. 2, '' Nebuchadonosor called together all his servants, and
all his great men, and communicated with them his *secret* counsel (*lit.*,
the secret of his will) ''; *i.e.*, his plan as to the campaign on which they
were about to set out.   This expression is remarkable : *to mustērion
tēs boulēs*.   In Eph. i. 9 we have a similar expression : *to mustērion
tou thelēmatos, the mystery of his will.*   The words for '' will '' are
different.   With Nebuchadonosor it means that which he willed
because he had *determined* to do it.   With God (Eph. i. 9) it means
that which He willed because He *desired* to do it—*i.e.*, His secret
purpose, counsel, or plan.

note.* And others might be cited, but these will be sufficient to show us how the word *mystery* had, at that time, come to be practically synonymous with *symbol.* Perhaps *secret sign* would best express it ; and this was the usage of the word when this Revelation was given to John. Hence, in this book, we must give the word this signification.

In Rev. i. 20, the seven stars are used as a *secret sign* for something which they signified (So also Eph. v. 32).

So here, in xvii. 5, 6, the woman's name is a *secret sign*; and refers to something much deeper than the name itself would convey. The name was the name, not of a woman, but of a city, "that great city," even Babylon. But it signified not merely the material city as such, but the vast system of idolatry connected with it. That is why the explanation of the secret sign follows "the mother of the harlots and of the abominations of the earth." Not merely of Rome, or even Babylon (as a city), but "of the earth" : *i.e.,* the mother, or fountain-head of all the systems of idolatry which

---

* Justin Martyr (A.D. 148) says that in all false religions the serpent was represented as "a great *symbol* and *mystērion*" (*Apol.* i. 27).

So in his reference to the Paschal Lamb he says, "the *mystērion* therefore of the Lamb . . . was a *type* of Christ."

Speaking of Isaiah vii. 14, "Behold a virgin shall conceive and bear a son," he says, "since this refers to the house of David, Isaiah has explained how that which was spoken by God to David, ἐν μυστηρίῳ (*in a mystery*), would actually come to pass. Perhaps," he adds, "you are not aware, my friends, of this—that there were many sayings written ἐπικεκαλυμένως (*epikekalumenōs*) *obscurely;* or ἐν παραβολαῖς (*en parabolais*), *in parables;* μυστηρίοις (*mustēriois*), *for secret signs;* or ἐν συμβόλοις (*en sumbolois*), *in symbols*, which the prophets who lived after the persons who said or did them expounded" (*Trypho*, c. 68).

have since flooded "the earth" from that one great source; and of which Romanism is only a part.

This is the *secret* or "mystery of iniquity" referred to in 2 Thess. ii. 7.

Babylon was the fountain-head of all idolatry.

We have here two things, (1) the reality, which is that "great city," which will be seen by the uninitiated; and (2) the woman, which is the "secret sign" of what it means.

The picture of the woman, as described, may be regarded as the "drop-curtain." But the initiated are those who will be admitted behind it, and learn "the depths of Satan:" and, behind the scenes in his own great theatre, will learn what Satan's religion means as they "worship the Dragon."

The *un*initiated will see only the curtain—the wonderful city. Compare Prov. ix. 13-18, where both are shown and may well be applied to the passage here.

Idolatry was no mere sin into which people gradually sunk; but it was the creation, by Satanic wisdom, of a mighty system, which he intended to use, and to lead up to his own worship.

Nimrod was used as the great founder of this marvellous scheme of Satan. Babylon was his city (Gen. x. 10). Would not Cain's city before the flood answer to the people of that day, the same end as Babylon did afterwards (Gen. iv. 17)? Each would be the capital of their respective idolatrous systems. The words "Cain went out from the presence of the Lord" are very significant. So is the name of Cain's city. He called it "Enoch," which means *initiated.** The corruption of mankind spoken of in Gen. vi. (see page 400) must have

---

* From the root חָנַךְ (*chahnak*), *to initiate, to dedicate.*

led to abnormal forms, which would account for the half-human, or super-human beings, which became the Nephelim, the Rephaim, and Anakim of Scripture ; the Titans of the Greeks. It would account for the worship of Ishtar, Isis, Ashtaroth, and all the abominations of spiritual harlotry.

We thus see how " that great city," Babylon, founded by Nimrod, was the source of all idolatry.

This is not true of Rome. Pagan Rome itself was only one system ; one of the polluted streams from that corrupt source. Papal Rome is only another single stream. It is not possible that *a part can be the whole !* It is not possible that one of many streams can be the fountain-head of all streams. Was there no idolatry before Pagan Rome ? Whence then came the worship of " Moloch " and " Remphan," and "Chiun," in the wilderness (Acts vii. 43. Amos v. 25, 26); and the worship of Ashtoreth, the abomination (*i.e.*, *idol*) of the Zidonians, and Chemosh, the abomination of the Moabites, and Milcom, the abomination of the children of Ammon, which were introduced by Solomon (1 Kings xi. 5. 2 Kings xxiii. 11)? Was Rome the mother of these ? The description here goes back to the origin of all the abominations of heathen idolatry. Rome's place in history makes this an absolute impossibility. It would be just as absurd to say that the Zionist move ment of to-day was the source or the mother of the Jewish nation !

Just as impossible was it for the Babylon of Nebu-chadnezzar's day ; and for the same reason. It does not date back far enough. We must go farther back, and find it in Gen. x. 8-10 and xi. 9. There we find it in the land of Shinar. Under Nimrod began the work

in the spirit of Anti-christ; his object being to build a
city, and make for his People a name, so that they
might not be scattered. Babylon was founded in
rebellion against God. Nimrod was " a mighty one on
the earth " (Gen. x. 8). He called his city Bab-El.*
Some take this to mean *the court or gate of God*; for he,
like his antitype, would fain thus exalt himself (2 Thess.
ii. 4).

Others derive it from *Belus*, the name of the principal
idol of the Babylonians. Sometimes written Bel בָּל.
If so, Babel would mean—*for Bel* or *of Bel.*

In any case we are taken back to the fountain-head,
and shown the source and origin of all idolatry.
Nimrod is called a mighty hunter.† The Targum of
Jonathan (an ancient Jewish commentary) interprets
this to mean that he was *a mighty rebel before the Lord.*
The Jerusalem Targum reads it as meaning *mighty in sin,
lying in wait* to catch and overthrow men; drawing
them away from the worship of the true God, as taught
by Shem, to join that taught by Nimrod. Hence, his
name became a proverb for any great rebel or Apostate.
(Read Gen. x. 9).

It is equally impossible to interpret the words of
Rome — and to say that this woman made "the
inhabitants of the earth drunk with the wine of her
fornication," *i.e.*, made the whole earth partake of her
idolatrous system. Neither of Rome, papal or pagan,
can this be said. They both drank of her cup; but it
is a perversion of all known history, to say that either

---

* From בָּבָה (*babah*), *a gate*, and אֵל (*El*), *God;* in contrast with
Bethel, the house of God.

† From צוּד (*tzud*) *to lie in wait.*

of them was the tutor of all the nations; and an insult
to common sense to apply this to " the inhabitants of
the earth for more that 3,000 years before Rome was
dreamt of." As Dr. Seiss well puts it, this wine " was
already bottled and labelled before the first dispersion.
[Gen. xi.]. It went with that dispersion into every
country and nation under heaven. As a matter of fact
we find it to this day among all the nations of the
earth; affecting, if not controlling their thinking, their
politics, their faith, and their worship. Not less than
two-thirds of the population of the earth at this hour are
Pagan idolators, drivilling under the same old intoxica-
tion which came forth from Nimrod and Babylon;
whilst the great body of the other third is either
Mohammedan, Catholic, Jewish, Infidel, or adherents
of some tainted and anti-christian faith and worship.
Nor is there a kingdom or government on the face of the
whole earth at this hour which does not embody and
exhibit more of the spirit of Nimrod than of the spirit,
commandments, and inculcations of God. All the kings
of the earth, and all the governments under heaven, have
more or less joined in the uncleanness of that same old
Babylonian Harlot who has defiled every spot and
nook of the whole inhabited world, notwithstanding that
God from the beginning set His seal of wrath upon it.
The Jewish whoredoms, and the Papal whoredoms, and
the Mohammedan whoredoms, and the whoredoms of
all perverted Christian religionists, though not entirely
letting go the confession of one only God, are still, in
essence, the same old harlotry which first found place
and embodiment on the banks of the Euphrates. It is
the same old Babylon, and her harlot daughters, bearing rule or kingdom upon the dominions of the earth,

and intoxicating the inhabitants thereof out of the wine of her fornication." *

It is indeed surprising how any mistake could have been made in the identification of this woman. For the Holy Spirit first shows us her very name upon her forehead. Then, in verse 18, He tells us as plainly as words can tell anything, that "the woman which thou sawest is that great city, which reigneth over the kings of the earth "; and chap. xvi. 19, as well as xvii. 5, identifies this city with Babylon. God says it is a "city." He does not say *a system* or *a religion*, but a " CITY."

Now, when the Vision is a " Woman "; and God tells us that He means by the woman "that great city," Is it legitimate for us to treat this again *as another symbol*, and say it is not the city He says it is, but another ?

There is no limit to such a process as that. We may go on to say that Rome means London, and that London means some other place. Why not be content with the explanation which God has Himself given? instead of taking the solemn responsibility of saying that His explanation is no explanation at all; and that it means something else. We are not saying there are no symbols : We are not saying that Jerusalem is not called Sodom. It is; but God leaves us in no doubt as to what He says and what He means. That is one thing : but it is quite another thing when we treat His own interpretation of a symbol, as though it were only *another symbol* which is left for *us* to interpret.

It is not that we wish in any degree to minimise the awful abominations of Romanism. None can have a greater abhorrence of them than we have. We

---

* Dr. Seiss's *Lectures on The Apocalypse*, vol. iii., pp. 121-2.

see in it one of the most filthy of all the streams that have flowed from Babylon; but we do try to rise above the level of "a Local Board" when we are dealing with God's account of how He is going to close His great controversy with Jew and Gentile, with Earth and Hell. Our survey must extend beyond the Tiber. We must see something beyond Protestantism and Romanism. These do not make up the whole history of the Universe, either in time or extent.

There are many other absurdities connected with the current interpretations, which we shall notice as we proceed further into this chapter, and consider the Divine interpretation there given of the Vision as a whole. There is one point, however, to be referred to here, and that is "the cup." It is "golden"; and hence, beautiful and attractive in appearance. The cup is *one*. This tells us that the corrupt streams which flow from this one fountain-head are all one in essence, and character, and effect. It is the religion originally instituted at Babylon, by Nimrod, at the instigation of Satan. (See Appendix.)

It is seen in all the great religions of the world. They are all alike in substituting another God for the God of the Bible: a God, made either with the *hands* or with the *imagination*; but equally *made*. And a religion consisting of human merit. These things are common to all systems of false Religion, and unite them in *one*. True, some of the rivers from this corrupt source are great and mighty; others are in smaller streams, but their waters are *one*, and the cup is *one*. Those who say that this "cup" means the cup used in *the Mass*, furnish us with a good example of the value of all such interpretations. We have only to remember concerning this "cup," here, that all nations are *made to drink of it*; while the one great characteristic of the Romish "cup" in the Mass is that it is *withheld from the people* !

6. **And I saw the woman** (*i.e.*, the great city, *v.* 18) **drunken with the blood of the saints, and with the blood of the martyrs of Jesus : and I wondered when I saw her, with great wonder.**]

Here again we must express the Vision in the terms of the Divine Interpretation.

6. **And I saw** *that great city which reigneth over the kings of the earth (v. 18)* **drenched with the blood of the saints, and with the blood of the Martyrs of Jesus: and I wondered when I saw** *the city*, **with great wonder.**

Here we have another reference to the martyrdoms which will take place during the time covered by the Apocalypse.

They are referred to also in chap. xiii. 7. Dan. **vii.** 21 ; xi. 7 ; xii. 1, 7.

The Psalms, also, connect these martyrdoms with the future "times of trouble" under the rule of the Beast:

" O God, keep not thou silence :
  Hold not thy peace, and be not still, O God.
  For, lo, thine enemies make a tumult :
  And they that hate thee have lifted up the head.
  They take crafty counsel against thy people,
  And consult together against thy hidden ones.
  They have said, Come, and let us cut them off
    from being a nation ;
  That the name of Israel may be no more in
    remembrance.

> For they have consulted together with one con-
> sent ;
> Against thee do they make a covenant. (Ps.
> lxxxiii. 1-5, RV.)

The Psalm then goes on to speak of a ten-kingdom
confederacy similar to that which we have in Rev. xvii.

Psalm lxxix. also speaks of that same time.

> " O God, the heathen (or nations) are come into thine
> inheritance ;
> Thy holy temple have they defiled ;
> They have laid Jerusalem in heaps.
> The dead bodies of thy servants have they given
> to be meat unto the fowls of the heaven,
> The flesh of thy saints unto the beasts of the earth.
> Their blood have they shed like water round about
> Jerusalem ;
> And there was none to bury them. (*vv.* 1-3, RV.)

That many martyrs—very many—have been killed at
the hands of the Church of Rome, if not in the city of
Rome itself, none can deny.

But these are not " ALL that have been slain on the
earth" as martyrs. Myriads of martyrs for God and
His truth were slain, as such, hundreds of years before
Rome ever had a Pope. The " prophets" of the Old
Testament were dead, and many had been slain as
martyrs centuries before Rome existed, whether Papal
or Pagan.

Rome, whatever may be her guilt in this matter,
cannot be charged with "all" the martyrdom of the
ages. All persecution can be traced up to false religion.
False religion has ever been possessed of a persecuting
spirit from the day that Cain slew his brother Abel;
and Rome, as one of the largest streams from the

Babylonian fountain of corruption, has slain her full quota, for which she is verily guilty, and will share in the judgment when " the cities of the nations fall." But not all the martyrs have yet been slain. Many passages in this book show us that the days of the coming Great Tribulation will fill up the measure of Babylon's bloodguiltiness. (See chap. vi. 9-11 ; xi. 7, 8 ; xii. 13, 17 ; xiii. 7 ; xviii. 24 ; xx. 4.) The same future period of martyrdoms is prophesied of or referred to in the Psalms. (See Ps. ix. ; x. ; lxxix., 2, 3 ; xliv. 22 ; xciv. 5. Also in Dan. vii. 25, 28 ; viii. 27 ; xi. 33, 35.) All these passages should be carefully read and noted. If these Old Testament passages do not speak of the same future time spoken of in the Apocalypse, to what period can they be referred ? When they are read together they form one harmonious whole ; but, if they are not rightly divided according to their respective dispensations, all will be, and cannot but be, confusion.

We come, now, to the Interpretation of this Vision (seen by John in xvii. 1-6) which is given to us by Divine inspiration.

We have seen (on pages 495 and 497) the structure of both the *Vision* and the *Interpretation*. As the latter is very brief we may repeat it here.

Z. (page 497). xvii. 7-18. *The Interpretation of the Vision.*

Z | D | 7-. The Woman.   } Promise.
       E | -7.   The Beast.   }

       E | 8-17. The Beast.   } Performance.
     D | 18. The Woman.   }

We are struck with the gracious words of the Interpreting Angel. " I will tell thee the secret sign of the woman and the wild Beast " (*v.* 7). This being so, we

are made independent of human interpreters, for God
has sent and signified it to us by His special angelic
messenger. In fact, we are, here, really placed on the
same level as the Apostle John himself.   No further
explanation than this was given to him by the angelic
interpreter. Therefore, we, in reading his words, have
exactly what John had himself : no less and no more.
Oh for grace and wisdom to understand his words !

7. **And the angel said to me, Wherefore didst
thou wonder ? I will tell thee the secret** (*i.e.*, the meaning of the secret sign) **of the woman, and of the Beast
that carrieth her, that hath the seven heads and the
ten horns**] We have the *promise*, as shown by the
structure (*v.* 7) ; and in the rest of the chapter (*v.* 8-18)
we have the *performance* of the promise. The woman
and the Beast are first mentioned in brief ; and then the
explanation is given in full, the order being inverted.
First the *Beast* is explained, and then the *Woman*.
Ten verses (8-17) are given to the former, and only *one*
(*v.* 18) to the latter : so that the Beast is now,
evidently, the more important of the two subjects.

We shall have to expand the member consisting of
this longer structure concerning "the Beast," marked
E. in the above structure.

E. (page 513). xvii. 8-17. *The Beast*

E | F¹ | k¹ | xvii. 8. The Beast (His origin and history).
| | | l¹ | 9, 10.   His confederates (the seven heads or kings)
| F² | k² | 11.   The Beast (further history)
| | | l² | 12.   His confederates (the ten horns ; their hour " with the Beast ")
| F³ | k³ | 13.   The Beast (power of horns given to him)
| | | l³ | 14-17.   His confederates (their war " with the Lamb ")

It will be seen from this Structure that the Inter-pretation of the Vision concerning the Beast (*E.* xvii. 8-17) consists of three pairs, the Beast alternating with his Confederates :—

> F¹ (8-10) gives the *first* pair. (p. 514)
> F² (11, 12) gives the *second* pair. (p. 541)
> F³ (13-17) gives the *third* pair. (p. 544)

In order to understand the words of the Interpretation here given, it would be well if we could forget all that we have ever heard from man on this subject. We find even ourselves hampered at every turn by what we have learned from tradition. Not until we can divest ourselves of all traditional interpretations can we hope to understand the interpretation given us in these verses.

The Structure shows us that "the *Beast*" and his *confederates* are the two subjects with which we have to do. They are arranged in the form of a *repeated alterna- tion*; and are given in three pairs.

If we keep these before us we shall be able to dis-tinguish them as we proceed.

F¹. (p. 514). xvii. 8-10. *The first pair*

8. **The Beast which thou sawest was, and is not; and is about to ascend out of the Abyss, and to go* into perdition: and those who dwell on the earth shall wonder, whose name† is not written in the book of life from the foundation of the world, when they behold the Beast; because he was, and is**

---

* L.A. WH. and RV. marg. read ὑπάγει (*hupagei*), *goeth*, instead of ὑπάγειν (*hupagein*), *to go*.

† L.T.Tr.A. WH. and RV. read the singular number here.

not, and shall be present.*] These three notes as to time (twice given in this verse), mark off for us, as clearly as possible, most important and significant points necessary to the interpretation.

The Beast is he who "hath the seven heads and the ten horns" (*v.* 7). The word "hath" refers to the ten horns equally with the seven heads. The *seven* are therefore contemporary with the *ten.*

In their *mortal* stage of being, the seven kings were successive. But that *mortal* stage is referred to in Daniel, not in Revelation.

In chap. xiii., the Beast comes up out of the Abyss, and is therefore, clearly, *superhuman.* During the first half of the week he is in his mortal stage. In the last half he is in his *superhuman* stage; for in chap. xiii. 3, he is seen as having been "wounded to death." But, here, in chap. xvii., we are taken back, and are further informed as to the past, present, and future of the Beast,

(1) He "WAS," in his mortal stage.

(2) He "IS NOT," for he (at the point of time to which the vision refers) had been assassinated: *i.e.,* had "received his deadly wound," by which he was "wounded to death," and died (xiii. 3).

(3) He "SHALL BE PRESENT," for he "is about to ascend out of the Abyss."

This eighth verse therefore refers to the mid-career of the Beast; and the point of the vision is the moment between the mortal and the superhuman stages: *i.e.,* between chaps. xii. and xiii.

---

* The reading of the AV. ("and yet is") arises from a different division of the two words in this place. All the best MSS. and Critical Texts read καὶ παρέσται (*kai parestai*), *and shall be present,* instead of καίπερ ἐστίν (*kaiper estin*), *and yet is.*

In the ninth verse the previous *mortal* stage of the seven heads are spoken of. In that stage they were successive; but in their *superhuman* stage they will be contemporary.

We have already seen that the seven heads or kings are individuals; and that the Beast himself, when revived from the dead, will be "the eighth" king. We believe that all the confusion, and all the divergent opinions on this chapter arise from ignoring this simple fact, and from looking at these as kingdoms instead of "kings"; and as world-powers instead of individuals.

Moreover, further confusion has been introduced by taking the words of the interpreting angel (in verse 10) as referring to the time of his speaking to John; instead of, as in all other cases, as referring to the time of or stage in the fulfilment of the vision. In other words, the expressions " was and is not" (*v.* 8, 11), and " one is and the other is not yet come" (*v.* 10), are taken as referring to the moment when the angel was actually speaking to John.

But why not take it, as in all the other cases, as referring to the time when the vision shall be accomplished?

The words of the souls under the altar (chap. vi. 9-11), are regarded as spoken at the time when the fifth seal shall be opened. The cry to the rocks " Fall on us " will be uttered under the sixth seal. The angel himself states (verse 1) that the vision is the future judgment of that great city. When the present time is thus used in prophetic language it refers to the future time which is spoken of as being present, and not to the time when the prophecy was written or spoken.

We have seen, throughout, that this whole book refers to "the Day of the Lord." It is in that day that the Beast will be manifested in his superhuman form with his seven heads and ten kings. At the future point of time spoken of in verse 10, *five* of these kings will, as to their mortal stage, at that moment " have fallen " (*i.e.*, have been removed by violent death *) ; *one* of the kings (the sixth) will be reigning ; and the *seventh* will not at that juncture have yet come. When he shall have come (ἐλθη, *elthe*) he will first overthrow the last three of the seven (Dan. vii. 8) ; but will remain only for the first half of the seven years, or thereabouts, in his *mortal* stage (xvii. 10) ; for he will then receive a deadly wound (by assassination probably), xiii. 3 and afterwards be brought to life by Satanic power, have his deadly wound healed, and become the " eighth " king. In his *mortal* stage he is the *seventh* head ; but in his *superhuman* stage he is the *eighth* king.

All is thus intensely individual. Who the *five* kings will be, as to their *mortal* stage ; or who the *sixth* will be, we know not ; nor is it necessary for our understanding of the Vision. Who the *seventh* will be, we *do* know ; for it is the Beast in his mortal stage, "the little horn" of Daniel's Visions. He will be in his superhuman stage, " the *eighth* " king—the final embodiment of Satanic power, whose doings are described in chap. xiii.

The ten kings of verses 12-17 are not successive in their mortal stage ; they will be contemporary when they form an integrant part of the

---

* The word, in the case of individuals, is always used of violent death. See Judg. iii. 25 ; v. 27. 2 Sam. i. 19, 25. Violence is also true of kingdoms. Isa. xxi. 9. Jer. l. 15 ; li. 8. Ezek. xxix. 5 ; xxx. 6.

Beast. The seven heads and the ten horns, with the necessary members which go to make up the leopard, the bear, and the lion parts of the beast as an organised body, as shown in chap. xiii. 2, are all superhuman, all contemporary, have all passed through the mortal stage, and have all suffered the first death, so that afterwards they can altogether be " cast alive into a lake of fire," which is the second death (see chap. xix. 20).

It is well to remember that "the time of the end" (Dan. vii.) takes in the full extent of Gentile Dominion. " The end time " (Dan. viii. 23) is the end of this " time of the end"; the *Sunteleia* or Consummation. While " The last days " (xi. 21) is the *Telos*, the crisis of " the end time."

The *Sunteleia* or " End-time," commencing immediately on the removal of the Church of God, may run into thirty or forty years ; and of these, the last " week" of Daniel (ix. 27) will be the *last seven.*

This allows all the prophetic periods marked off in 42 months, 1,260 days, and $3\frac{1}{2}$ years, to be taken as literal months, days, and years, if we understand them as falling within these last seven years which form the crisis, and end up with the final judgment.

If the period referred to under the word " hour " (one and the same hour, or time) of xvii. 12 and of iii. 10 be the same as the 42 months, then this " day of vengeance " of Isa. lxi. 2 may be these 42 months.

The term kings and kingdoms are used interchangeably in Daniel. The kingdoms of Dan. ii. 37, 39, 40, 42, are spoken of as "these kings " in verse 44, and so elsewhere.

But in looking for them we must note four very great and important governing principles which will be a sure and certain guide in our understanding of this matter. They are these :—

(1) *Israel* and *Israel's Messiah* : in other words, God's Anointed, God's Land, God's City, God's People, form the great centre around which all prophecy circles.

(2) Jerusalem is also the centre of the points of the compass. East and West, North and South, are to be reckoned from Jerusalem, or from the standpoint of the writer : and not from that of the reader ; or from any other astronomical or geographical arbitrary position.

(3) The "Heads" denote headship over the People, the City, and the Land of Israel.

(4) The world-powers or kingdoms of prophecy are reckoned only as they come into connection with, or into possession of, Israel's Land, and City.

In these four simple propositions we shall find the key to the understanding of the Vision and its interpretation.

The nations were originally formed with reference to Israel; for we are expressly told, in the wondrous "Song of Moses," that "when the Most High (the title that relates to dominion in the Earth) divided to the nations their inheritance, when he separated the sons of Adam, he set the bounds of the people according to the number of the children of Israel" (Deut. xxxii. 8). The nations were not divided by chance ; neither were the stars of heaven; for in Deut. iv. 19 it says "the Lord thy God divided them unto all the nations under the heaven."

Many nations are mentioned in the Bible ; but only those are the subject of Divine history and prophecy which have relation to Israel ; and even these, in proportion to the closeness and extent of that relation. For example, the monuments show us the large numbers of Dynasties and Kings, etc., there were in Egypt. But only those come into the Word of God which had to do with Israel. Many have been, and are, perplexed because of this Biblical silence as to the ancient kingdoms of Egypt and Assyria, etc.; but this great principle explains it. The Pharaohs of the Oppression and the Exodus would never have been more than mere names but for their connection with Moses and Israel. " Pharaoh, king of Egypt, is but a noise " (Jer. xlvi. 17) —a noise that is heard for a moment and then passes away. Such would Pharaoh (Ramases II. and Meneptah) have been but for Moses and Israel.

There were many kings of Egypt before Pharaoh; and many kings of Babylon all through the centuries; but they are mentioned only as they come into touch with Israel. The Bible ignores them all except on this ground. That is why it could be said to Nebuchad-nezzar, "THOU art this head of gold" (Dan. ii. 38). This was said of him only in connection with the Counsels of God, and the People of God; for Nebuchad-nezzar was not the head or first king of Babylon. It is of Nimrod that it is written, "the beginning of his kingdom was Babel" (Gen. x. 10). Nimrod was, historically and chronologically, the first king of Babylon, and there was a long list of Babylon's kings from that time before Nebuchadnezzar possessed its throne.

Why, then, after all that lapse of time, is Nebuchad-nezzar singled out and spoken of definitely as the "head"? It can be accounted for only on the great principle which we seek to enforce, viz., that all Gentile history is ignored in the Bible, both as to kings and kingdoms, except as they stand and come into the Divine Counsels concerning Israel, and became "heads" over God's Land, and City, and People.

This being so, we have a limit set to our interpretation of the great Kingdoms or Heads in the prophecies given in Daniel and in the Apocalypse. These prophecies are concerned with them only within those limits.

Nebuchadnezzar and his father came into power, and made Babylon the new capital of Assyria in B.C. 625.[*] On this account, and because he was the first of the Gentile powers into whose hands dominion and headship over God's Land and City and People were given, it could be said of him, "Thou art this head of gold" (Dan. ii. 38). There is not a word here as to when he became the "head"; but the fact is declared as to his person that he, as the head of Babylon, was also the head of the Image, and, therefore, the head of Gentile supremacy.

The earlier history of Babylon is not taken into account. A new departure is made in reckoning when, in the Counsels of God, Nebuchadnezzar becomes the king of Babylon.

God sends him notification of the fact in that wonderful dream, where the great outline of this Gentile dominion over Israel's People, City, and Land is made known.

The Image in Dan. ii. is clearly marked as consisting of *five* parts:—

1. *v.* 32. "This image's head was fine gold, (*one*)
2. *v.* 32. his breast and his arms of silver, (*two*)

---

* See *Babylonian Life and History*, by Dr. Budge, of the British Museum. Published by the R.T.S., 1885.

3. *v.* 32. his belly and his thighs of brass, (*three*)

4. *v.* 33. his legs of iron, (*four*)

5. *v.* 33. his feet part of iron and part of clay." (*five*)

This seems to be clear enough; only we have always been so accustomed to hear the *fifth* spoken of as part of the *fourth*, or the fourth revived, that we read the Scripture in the light of our tradition.

It is not any answer to say that Dan. ii. mentions *only four* Gentile Powers. Dan. ii. says nothing of the kind. It mentions "the fourth." That is not "four." The Original is not אַרְבַּע *arbag* (*four**); but it is רְבִיעִי *rebēgahē* (*fourth†*). It is most important to note the difference between the *ordinal* number and the *cardinal* number. It nowhere says there were *only four*. On the contrary, the *five* are twice distinctly enumerated as being perfectly separate and independent. In verses 35 and 45 we have two separate enumerations of these five :

Verse 35.	*Verse* 45.
1. the iron,	1. the iron,
2. the clay,	2. the brass,
3. the brass,	3. the clay,
4. the silver, and	4. the silver, and
5. the gold.	5. the gold.

Here, the *five* are not only mentioned separately, as to their material; but diversely, as to their order; so as to distinguish "the clay" as being one of five, and not as part of the iron (the "fourth") as is usually done.

---

* As in Dan. i. 17 ; viii. 8, 22 ; x. 4 ; xi. 4.

† As in Dan. iii. 25 ; vii. 7, 19, 23. These are all the occurrences of both words in the book of Daniel.

The same *five* kingdoms are equally clear in the interpretation :

1. *v.* 38. " Thou art this head of gold " (*one*)

2. *v.* 39. "**And** after thee shall arise another kingdom. . . ." (*two*)

3. *v.* 39. "**And** another, third kingdom. . . ." (*three*)

4. *v.* 40. " **And** the fourth kingdom. . . ." (*four*)

5. *v.* 41. "**And** whereas thou sawest the feet and toes. . . ." (*five*)

We need not dwell long on the details of the fulfilment of this Image. They are well known, and belong rather to the book of Daniel than to the Apocalypse. We content ourselves with their enumeration :

1. The first of these Gentile Dominions was given by the God of Heaven to Nebuchadnezzar. It was formally taken from Israel and " given " to the Gentiles. *Headship over Jerusalem* (as well as over the Gentile powers) was that which specially marked that Gentile Power from all the other Gentile Powers that were, or might be, in the world at that time.

The Powers that followed Babylon successively held Jerusalem in possession ; and each succeeded the other, by conquest, in obtaining and holding that possession.

2. The second was Medo-Persia.

3. The third was Greece.

4. The fourth was Rome.

5. The fifth was, either the present power, which succeeded Rome in 636-7, and is still treading down Jerusalem, thus fulfilling the Lord's prophecy in Luke

xxi. 24; or, it is a yet future power, which is to be manifested in the *Sunteleia* after the Church shall have been removed: in which case the Lord's prophecy in Luke xxi. 24 would refer to some future treading down *e.g.*, that mentioned in Rev. xi. 1, 2.

The common interpretation reckons the "feet and toes" as part of the "legs," and divides the fourth power into two manifestations: one past, and the other future. But, even in this case, the future manifestation of the fourth could still be called the fifth as to numerical order.

Surely, the mixture of "clay and iron" can no more be left out of our calculations than any of the other four metals.

But what this fifth power is remains to be seen. It is partly strong and partly fragile*; *i.e.*, there is in it "the strength of the iron," and the weakness of "potters' clay." There can be no real union between the two characteristics of this fifth kingdom. It can be merely a mechanical mingling like that of iron and potters' clay; for, it truly says, "iron is not mixed with clay" (verse 43).

On the one hand we have a *fifth* power which did actually succeed the fourth power, as the *fourth* succeeded the third, as the *third* succeeded the second, and the *second* succeeded the first.

Neither of these, so far as we know, ever *exercised* the universal dominion which was given at the first; but what marked the true succession was *Headship over God's Land and God's City*, while Israel was excluded

---

* This is the meaning of the Chaldee תְּבַר (*tevar*). The word occurs nowhere else, though there are some sixty other words rendered *break*.

from the place and power which had been transferred, and committed to the Gentiles.

When the Lord (in Luke xxi. 24) uttered that prophecy of the treading down of Jerusalem by the Gentiles (not "the nations"), the *fourth* Gentile power was exercising headship over the Land. To what *treading down* did He refer? Did He refer to the power which did actually succeed the fourth in 636-7? or Was He referring to a treading down that is still future? and Did He ignore and pass over the present *treading down*, which has lasted as long as all the other four put together?

Whatever answer we may give to these questions, all must agree that after the Church shall have been removed; and the time shall have come for steps to be taken to reinstate Israel in its own Land, *there must necessarily be some Gentile power in possession.*

The beginning of the *Sunteleia* must find some Gentile power exercising sovereignty over the City and the Land; and it cannot be denied that the present power now in possession *may be* the power found there when Israel comes into connection again with the Land.

Rapid and sudden national changes, of course, may take place any day in the near East. But whatever may happen, the power then in possession will be the *fifth*, referred to in Dan. ii. and in the angel's words, uttered at the particular point of the Day of the Lord referred to in Rev. xvii. 10, which will be true of the Gentile powers as well as of the individual "heads," or kings, which may arise in the new Jewish State, after its resettlement; and immediately prior to the covenant which Antichrist will make with Israel at the beginning of the *Telos*, or seventieth week of Dan. ix.

The Zionist Movement commenced with the first National Congress in 1896, and has made great strides since then. Other changes in the Balkan States, and in the Constitution of Turkey, which took place so unexpectedly in 1908, show us how suddenly a change may take place which will lead up to the re-settlement of the Jews in their own land, perhaps, at first, under the suzerainty of the Sultan; and prepare the way for the rise of the Beast, first, in his *mortal* stage as the *seventh* head, and then in his *superhuman* stage as the *eighth* king.

The dream was not given to Nebuchadnezzar until after his portion of it had been accomplished. The words, "Thou art this head of gold," were not uttered until some years after he had actually become the "head"; and many years after he acted as the "head," when he first came against Jerusalem.

It is clear, therefore, that the date of the dream and its interpretation is not the date from which our reckoning of the times of Gentile dominions is to commence; for they had already commenced, and that dominion was an accomplished fact at the time the dream was given.

It is also clear that the date of the taking of Jerusalem and burning of the Temple is not the commencement of "the times of the Gentiles," or of Gentile dominion; inasmuch as Nebuchadnezzar besieged Jerusalem in the nineteenth year of his reign, and exercised a Suzerain power for many years before. For he first came against Jerusalem in the eighth year of Jehoiakim, and Jehoiakim served him three years (2 Kings xxiv. 1). Then his son Jehoiachin reigned three months—reckon it one year (2 Kings xxiv. 8), when Nebuchadnezzar came again against Jerusalem, and sent him a prisoner to Babylon in the eighth year of the reign of Nebuchadnezzar (2 Kings xxiv. 12).

Then Nebuchadnezzar set up Zedekiah as king in the place of Jehoiachin (his uncle), and for eleven years he reigned in Jerusalem (2 Kings xxv. 2); but having rebelled and sought to regain his independence (2 Kings xxiv. 20), Nebuchadnezzar came against Jerusalem, and finally took it in his nineteenth year (being the eleventh of Zedekiah, 2 Kings xxv. 8). Not until the twenty-third year of his reign did Nebuchadnezzar complete the carrying away of the people (Jer. lii. 30).

Now, if the Holy Spirit reckons the actions of Nebuchadnezzar, not by date of the year, but by *the year of his reign*, we have a clear indication that we are to reckon the years in the same way, and say that " the times of the Gentiles " began with *the first year* of the reign of him of whom it was afterwards said, " Thou art this head of gold."

If so, then we have a period of *at least* twenty-three years cut off from, and marking the commencement of, these times of Gentile headship over the Land, the City, and the People.

Why may not the closing period of these Gentile times (called the *Sunteleia*) be marked by a corresponding or similar number of years (23 or more)?

We believe there is a double fulfilment ; first in *Kingdoms*, then in *Kings*. There have been, up to the present, four kingdoms, as enumerated above (Babylon, Medo-Persia, Greece, Rome), then the *fifth*, present or yet future. The Kingdom of the Beast will be the *sixth*, and the *seventh* will be " the Kingdom of our Lord, and of His Christ." The Kingdoms being reckoned distinct from the Kings on p. 518.

So likewise, will there be at the time of the end (in the *Sunteleia*), five individuals who will briefly and successively contend for independence, and then the sixth (the " one is " referred to at the point of time of the Vision); he will be followed by the Beast, who will be " the seventh head" in his *mortal* stage for 3½ years, and then "the eighth" king in his *superhuman* stage for the other 3½ years (the last half of the seven years referred to in Dan. ix. 27).

There were three kings in Jerusalem who struggled for independence, and whom Nebuchadnezzar put down and punished. Why may not there be five individuals in the *Sunteleia* who will lead the Jews to struggle likewise for independence against the Mohammedan Suzerain power ?

We read of "five kings" and the "sixth" in Rev. xvii. 10. Under these the Jews may rebel against the Suzerain power and finally "make a covenant" with the *seventh*, the Beast (Dan. ix. 27), in order to regain their complete independence.

This would of course be in the *mortal* stage of these five kings, and of the sixth as well as the seventh. The duration of the *mortal* stage of the Beast, as the seventh head, will be, we know, only 3½ years.* The rise and fall of the other kings may also be of very short duration. A few years would suffice for the fulfilment of Rev. xvii. 10.

Dan. xi. shows how the Jews will be affected by him who in his mortal career is the first king of Syria : and then, on the rooting up of three of the kings, becomes the seventh head of Gentile power.

At the point contemplated in the Vision (Rev. xvii. 10)

---

* And his *superhuman* stage will be for a similar period.

this fifth head will have fallen: The fifth head of Gentile dominion over Jerusalem; as well as the fifth of these last individual kings in their mortal stage. Thus a co-terminous point may mark an important epoch, for it is of the " sixth " king that it is said, at this juncture " one is." Of the " seventh," at that moment, it is said he " is not " but is then *about to arise* and " be present."

During the years of the *Sunteleia,* or consummation, there will be ample time for the Euphrates valley to be developed and Babylon to be rebuilt. That it will be rebuilt is necessitated by the fact that it has never yet been destroyed in the manner prophesied. The further evidence of this must be reserved till we come to chap. xviii.

One thing we know, and that is, that God will accomplish all that He has foretold; and, if we refer to present movements, it will be only to show how easily and simply all may come about; and so naturally too, as to be almost unnoticed except to those who " know the times."

With regard to the Beast, proper, we are further told in this verse, 8, that the Beast spoken of " **shall ascend out of the Abyss and go into perdition.**" We see this ascending in chap. xiii. 1. This is the Beast in his *superhuman* stage. For John saw the mark of the wound on him. And John wondered. All shall wonder at this manifestation, and the object of that wonder is this Beast who " **was, and is not, and shall be present.**" The world-powers are, when represented as " the Beast," always viewed as *one.* The Beast is never seen apart from his seven heads and ten horns; if so, they must be contemporary.

In chap. xvii. the Beast is seen as *one* individual, as

well as collectively. The Dragon in heaven comprises seven heads and ten horns; but, when the *one* individual who directs all the movements of the Dragon Power is spoken of, Satan is referred to (chap. xi. 7; xiii. 5. Comp. Dan. vii. 11; xi. 36). The same is true when the *one* who is the executive head of the seven, and all the parts comprising the Beast is referred to.

At the close of his mortal stage, *i.e.*, the first 3½ years, he receives his death wound; and therefore at this stage, before he comes up out of the Abyss in his superhuman form, it can be truly said that he **"was"** and **"shall be present."** It could also, at the moment of time referred to by the Angel, be *as truly said* **"and is not."***

The "is not" does not mean that he never had an existence, for the very expression implies it; as it could not be used of one who never had any existence at all. Just as with Christ Himself, relatively, as regards the earth, it can at this present moment be truly said He *was* and *is not*, and yet *shall be present* here again.* But of course as regards Himself absolutely, "He was, and is, and is to come."

The following verse connects this Beast directly with the Beast of chap. xiii., for it is added

9-. **Here is the mind which hath wisdom.**] This repetition of xiii. 18 identifies and connects these two chapters "Here is wisdom. Let him that hath understanding count the number of the Beast, for it is man's number" (See above, on xiii. 18). The word rendered

---

*See Gen. v. 24, which explains this. As Enoch "was not" on the earth, but in heaven, whither he had been caught up: so it will be said of the Beast, he "is not" on the earth, because he will then have been cast down into the Abyss.

" mind " in xvii. 9, and " understanding " in xiii. 18, is the same, *viz.* νοῦς *(nous)*. And this " wisdom " is, to understand that, though a " Beast " is seen in the vision, it is not a wild Beast that is meant, but one great final superhuman personality ; viz., "a man" energized by Satanic power.

-9. **The seven heads are** (or represent) **seven mountains on which the woman sitteth,** (-10-) **and they are** (or represent) **seven kings :**] We translate the last clause thus, with Alford, V., and others. The punctuation of the AV. in this verse is very faulty. Verse 9 should end with the word "wisdom," and the remainder of the verse should form part of the tenth verse.

The explanation of the angel would not then have been cut in two, and interpreted separately as is commonly the case ; and the " seven mountains " would not have been treated independently of the clause which goes on to further explain what they signify. The " seven mountains " are, according to this, " seven kings." It does not say that " there are seven kings " over and above, and beside the " seven mountains ; " but that the "seven mountains are (*i.e.*, represent) seven kings." The seven heads belong to the *Beast* on which the woman sitteth. According to the structure of " *E.*, lᵗ." (page 514), *vv.* 9, 10 have for their subject the confederates of the Beast. Now " mountains " cannot be confederates, but kings can. Hence, though the word " mountains " is used, it is at once explained that " kings " are meant, so as to keep us from making a mistake. Compare Zech. iv. 7.

These mountains, then, are no mere heaps of earth or rocks, but " kings." The word " mountain " is often used as a Figure (*Symbol*, or *Metaphor*, or *Metonymy*) for a kingdom. It is used of Babylon itself in Jer. li. 25, and of Messiah's kingdom in Dan. ii. 35.

For interpreters to take these *literally* as "mountains," in the midst of a context which the same interpreters take to be *symbolic*; and in the face of the *interpretation* actually given by the angel that "they are seven kings," is to play fast and loose with the word of prophecy. It says here that "they are seven kings," and we believe what is said.

The seven heads do not belong to any one of the world-Powers; for each kingdom had many such "heads" or kings.

They necessarily belong to *all* of them, and are viewed as *one* Beast, so that they may be seen as belonging to, and forming part of, the whole. That is why this Beast in chap. xiii. 2 is like unto a "*leopard*" (the third, Greece), and his feet as the feet of a "*bear*" (the second, Persia), and his mouth as a "*lion*" (the first, Babylon). He combines in himself the symbolic marks of the others.

The woman (*i.e.*, that great city, *v.* 18) sitteth on many waters (*i.e.*, reigneth over peoples, and multitudes, and nations, and tongues, *v.* 15), and is seen seated on a scarlet coloured beast (*i.e*, carried and supported by all the kings and all the members which make up the body of the Beast. This will be the condition of things at the point of view referred to in the Vision. In this 9th verse we have a description of what will be at an early part of the first 3½ years. It is the present tense, "IS SITTING," and is prophetic of what is now still future. It does not say *has sat* or *did sit*, but *is now sitting*, *i.e.*, not at the moment when the Angel was interpreting it to John, but the moment when it will be actually taking place in " the day of the Lord." It is the woman (*i.e.*, that great city, *v.* 18), upon which our attention is concentrated in this verse, and the support afforded to her at that time. All are contemporary with each other; joined together as the metals are joined to make up the figure of a man).

If in *vv.* 9, 10, literal mountains be meant, then commentators are divided between Constantinople, Brussels, Jerusalem, and Rome.

The late Albert Barnes says, " All respectable interpreters agree that it refers to Rome; either Pagan, Christian, or Papal."

If this be so, then we must be content to be reckoned, with many others, among those who are not " respectable." Rome *Papal* cannot be meant, as it never had seven regal powers. Rome *Christian* cannot be meant, as it never had any regal powers at all. Rome *Pagan* cannot be meant, as no *seven kings* can be agreed upon by commentators; and it is to be destroyed by the stone of Dan. ii. 35, 45. See also Dan vii. 26, 27.

Of these seven heads, or kings, it is added, that

-10-. **Five are fallen, the*** **one** (the sixth) **is** (at this stage of the Vision), **the other** (the seventh), **is not yet come.**] If this be interpreted of Gentile Dominion at the future point of the Vision referred to by the Angel; then, as to the dominions, the five will have fallen : (1) Babylon, (2) Medo-Persia, (3) Greece, (4) Rome, (5) Mohammedan. The sixth will be the Kingdom of the Beast, (7) the seventh will be the Kingdom of our Lord and of His Christ.

---

* The AV. does not translate the article, which forms part of the *Textus Receptus*, and G.L.T.Tr.A.WH. and RV. omit the και (*kai*), *and.*

And as to the individuals, five of the seven (and the sixth) will have obtained sovereignty or independence for the Jews, and the way will be clear for the seventb to come in his mortal stage.

The seven are all of one series. How can the sixth be Rome, and thus be the Beast, and contain the whole seven, including the eighth !

If we interpret these kingdoms and kings in any other way, and on any other principle than that given above, we are at once landed in a mass of conflicting opinions and speculations that are perfectly appalling.

Alford gives us (1) Egypt, (2) Nineveh, (3) Babylon, (4) Persia, (5) Greece (with, of course, Rome for the sixth), and the seventh the Christian Empire under Constantine !

Others give us (1) Assyria, (2) Egypt, (3) Babylon, (4) Persia, (5) Greece, (6) Rome, (7) Future.

Others (Moses Stuart among them) give (1) Julius Cæsar, (2) Augustus, (3) Tiberius, (4) Caligula, (5) Claudius, (6) Nero, (7) Galba. He also suggests beginning with Augustus, so as to make Nero the sixth ; but in this case he defies all history, which makes Domitian the Emperor in John's day.

Others make (1) Romulus, (2) Numa Pompilius, (3) Tullus Hostilius, (4) Ancus Martius, (5) Tarquinius Priscus, (6) Servius Tullius, (7) Tarquinius Superbus.

Others, confining the list to those who died violent deaths, make it (1) Julius Cæsar, (2) Tiberius, (3) Caligula, (4) Claudius, (5) Nero, (6) Galba, (7) Otho

Another suggests (1) Pharaoh, (2) Sennacherib, (3) Belshazzar, (4) Antiochus Epiphanes, (5) Herod Agrippa, (6) Nero Cæsar, and (7) Napoleon.

These are all by " respectable " interpreters. But is not the confusion such as to make us regard this book with anything but *respect* ?   Which of these and many others are we to take as the meaning of the angel's words, " five are fallen, the one is, the other is not yet come " ?

With regard to Gentile power, why, we may ask, go back behind the beginning God has Himself set and given when it was said to Nebuchadnezzar, " thou art this head of gold " ? (Dan. ii. 38).

Why go back to Egypt, Assyria, and Nineveh; or begin with Rome, when God makes the beginning at Babylon ?

And with regard to individuals, Why make all the seven kings belong to *one* of the four world-powers, when the Beast represents the whole ? If we confine ourselves to one—the fourth—it had many more than seven heads. And if we include all the " heads " or " kings " which the whole contained, then we have so many that it is quite impossible to do anything with them in connec-tion with the interpretation of these prophecies.

The great error has always been in making anything, rather than Israel, the pivot of the prophecies : and reckoning the points of the compass from any centre except Jerusalem, or the place where the Vision was seen, or the prophecy written.

There are other difficulties connected with the com-·non interpretations of the fourth World Power, which makes Rome the whole Beast, and yet one of its heads at the same time.   " Respectable inter-preters " who make the *whole* Beast, Rome ; make also *one* of its heads or kings to be Rome ; and this one head atterwards comprises the ten kingdoms into which it is subdivided !   Whereas the ten kings of Daniel are not identical with the ten of the Apocalypse, for the ten of Rev. xvii. never were kings in their *mortal* stage, for it expressly says in verse 12 that they "have received no kingdom as yet."

How anyone can hold that this one "head" afterwards comprises the ten kingdoms, it is difficult to understand. Territory may be divided into ten kingdoms, but the "head" cannot be.

The image of Daniel ii. was seen complete as it will be in "the end time," while as yet only the first of these powers was then existing, and all the others were future. So, in like manner, the image is to be viewed also as complete when the whole shall be combined in the Beast (and the seventh and eighth heads), though all the others will then be past. The stone falls on the feet of the image and destroys the whole image at one blow. The Beast as seen in Rev. xiii. and xvii. combines the whole, and is destroyed at one stroke at the Apocalypse of the King of kings in Rev. xix.

It is important to observe that the Beast is never seen in the Apocalypse without the seven heads and ten horns, because they are then seen as being contemporary and in their superhuman form. But they were successive in their mortal form.

The Beast in Daniel has not got seven heads. He could not have unless they were contemporary, which is against the prophecy in Daniel. He has ten horns during the time when the seventh head becomes supreme.

The only solution of all these difficulties seems to be in the "eighth" king, who is regarded as "of the seven," and yet fulfils all that is said of "the fourth Beast" and of "the little horn" of Dan. vii. and viii.

We have to note (1) that Dan. ii. and vii. show the full length of duration from Nebuchadnezzar to the coming of the Son of man in Rev. xix.

(2) that within that duration the whole of unfulfilled prophecy concerning Gentile Dominion must find its place.

(3) that Dan. viii. gives the "end time" of that duration linked on to the earlier period in order to show its connection with the whole.   And

(4) that Dan. xi. gives the "last days" of that "end time," but linked on to the earlier verses (xi. 1-4).

Thus we have the whole period of "the times of the Gentiles;" then, "the end time" of Gentile rule; and, finally, "the last days" of that rule.

What is said in Dan. vii. and viii. is for the most part still future.   It is seen in immediate connection with the setting of the throne of the Ancient of Days (Dan. vii. 9-27). " At the time of the end shall be the Vision " (Dan. viii. 17).   It relates to "what shall be in the last end of the indignation, for at the time appointed the end shall be " (Dan. viii. 19).   The prophecy relates to "the latter end of their kingdom, when the transgressors are come to the full" (Dan. viii. 23; marg., *are accomplished*).

In Dan. vii. 17, 18, we are expressly told that "these great Beasts, which are four, are four kings which shall arise out of the earth, but the saints of the most High shall take the kingdom."   Their rising, therefore, is at the time of the end, and they are " kings."

When it was said to Nebuchadnezzar, "Thou art this head of gold" (Dan. ii. 38), did he realise all that it meant?   Did the sons of Abraham realise all the promises to Israel as to the complete possession of the whole Land? Just so with the Beasts of Daniel. In their *mortal* stage they failed (especially the fourth) to realise all the prophecies of it. But as Israel will realise all its prophecies in its second manifestation, so will it be with the Beast in its superhuman stage.

Rev. xvii. 10 fixes the point of the Vision, there referred to, as being just between the *mortal* and the *superhuman* stages.

"Five are fallen, the one is, the other is not yet come:

-10. **and when he shall have come, he must remain a short time.**] *i.e.*, a short time compared with the others. We have a similar statement in xii. 12; where, when Satan is cast down, he had "great wrath, because he knoweth that he hath but a short time."

Seven years will be "a short time." Three-and-a-half will be still shorter.

Six "heads" will then have already appeared, both as dominions, and as individuals in their *mortal* stage. They will have gone down into the Abyss. At that point in the Vision the rise of the "seventh" head will be imminent as to his mortal stage. Then after three-and-a-half years will come his death; and then (after three to four days' public exposure), his re-incarnation.

The *seventh* head can be no person or king that has ever yet existed on the earth. We have no kingdom here, but a mighty and terrible king. He "falls" like the preceding six. He will be slain with the sword (chap. xiii. 3, 14), but he comes to life again; and then the last great superhuman ruler of "the kingdoms of this world" will stand revealed until he is destroyed by "the King of Kings." Everything will then have been prepared, and events will move with unparalleled rapidity.

The " Kingdoms " and the " Kings," in Dan. and Apoc. :

" KINGDOMS "	" HEADS " or " KINGS "
" The times of the Gentiles "	
1. Gold	
2. Silver	
3. Brass	
4. Iron	
5. Clay (or Iron and Clay)	
	The Sunteleia, or *" Day of the Lord "*
	1. The 1st Head
	2. The 2nd Head
	3. The 3rd Head
	4. The 4th Head
	5. The 5th Head (" Five are fallen ")
	6. The 6th Head, (" one is "; " the other is not yet come ")

" The Great Day of the Lord " (*The last " week "*)

The making of the Covenant (Dan. ix. 27)

6. The Kingdom of the Beast	7. The 7th Head (Mortal Stage) (" who was, and is not, and shall be present " as the 8th King)

" The Great and Terrible Day of the Lord"
(the last half of the " week ")

The breaking of the Covenant (Dan. ix. 27)

	8. The 8th King. The Beast. (His super-human stage)

7. " The Kingdom of our Lord and of His Christ "

The above refers to Headship over God's City, People, and Land. It does not, therefore, include the "Ten Kings" or "Kingdoms," either of Daniel or Revelation, which are outside the Land.

The eleventh verse brings us to the second pair of members which interpret the Beast and his Confederates. Chap. xvii.

> verses 8-10 give the *first* pair ;
> „ 11, 12 give the *second* pair ;
> „ 13-17 give the *third* pair ;

See the Structure, above, on pages 514, 515.

F². (page 514). xvii. 11, 12.   *The second pair of members*

11. **And the beast that was, and is not, even 𝖍𝖊** himself **is an eighth, and** is **of the seven, and goeth into perdition.**] We must carefully note that while he is commonly spoken of as " the eighth head," he is not so called in Scripture. There, he is known only as "an eighth" *king*. We have in this verse (according to the Structure on page 514) the further history of the Beast.

In verses 8 and 11 we have the two stages of the Beast's career clearly distinguished. In chap. xiii. ͡ John saw what had already happened before xiii. 1, ii the mortal stage of the Beast, before he came up out of the Abyss. John saw what had *caused* the Beast to go down into the Abyss. And when John saw him "*coming up*," he observed (xiii. 3) one from among his heads as having been slain.

In his mortal form he runs his career during the first part of the week (Dan. ix. 27 ; the " forty and two months " of Rev. xiii. 5). During this period God's two witnesses (xi. 3) are the Divine testimony on earth.

When they shall have finished their testimony, or immediately before the fulfilment of their mission, the Beast (in his mortal form) is killed. He receives his deadly sword-wound (xiii. 3), and comes to life again : he comes up out of the Abyss (xi. 7), makes war on the Two Witnesses, and runs the rest of his career in his superhuman form (xiii.—xix.).

He is first called "the Beast" in this book, in Rev. xi. 7.

He is "of the seven." That is to say, he is the 7th in another (his 8th, or superhuman) form. And though he is "an eighth" king, there are not really eight, but only seven, for the *seventh* and *eighth* are the same personage ; therefore, it is said that the eighth is "of the seven."

As the mortal *seventh* Head, he is the "little horn" of Dan. vii.; the King of Dan. xi. 21.

Roughly speaking, the *mortal* stage would fill the first half of the last of "the seventy weeks" (*i.e.*, the first 3½ years of Dan. ix. 27) ; and the *superhuman* stage would occupy the last half. But there is nothing to show us what length of time will run between his *rise* and his *assassination.* Neither can we say exactly how long the time will be between his death-stroke and his reappearance. We suppose the latter would not exceed four days.

Then, immediately upon his resurrection, he kills (crucifies ?) the Two Witnesses (ch. xi.). Consequently, *their* 1,260 days must just overlap into *his* 42 months. They must have witnessed, therefore, for nearly 1,260 days during his mortal stage, before his assassination.

It would appear that he is on the scene, entering into various political affairs, before he is actually manifested

as the 7th head, *i.e.*, the Anti-Christ. The " League "
of Dan. xi. 23 appears to be made before the " Covenant"
of Dan. ix. 27. The " League " is one of the first
steps he takes to mix himself up in the Jews' affairs.

The " Covenant " of Dan. ix. 27 seems to be a subsequent advance upon that. The Covenant would mark
the beginning of the seven years.

During the first half of the week (in which the
seventh head runs and completes his mortal career),
God's Two Witnesses (ch. xi. 3) are the proclaimers of
the special Divine Testimony on the Earth. Just before
the completion of their Testimony the Beast is killed.
His mortal stage is thus ended. When he comes to
life again, he comes up from the Abyss and makes war
upon them, and upon all who will not worship him.

As to the heads : In their mortal stage they are only
seven, and are successive. But in their superhuman
stage they are still seven (xiii. 1 and xvii. 7), and they
are collective in the one—the wild Beast.

This verse thus contains further particulars about the
Beast already mentioned in verse 8. And now, in
verse 12 we have the confederates again.

12. **And the ten horns which thou sawest are**
(*i.e.*, represent) **ten kings, who have not yet received
a kingdom ; but they receive authority as kings at
one** and the same **hour with the Beast]** (*i.e.*, at the same
time or season. See chap. xiv. 7, 15 ; xviii. 10, 17, 19.
Matt. xiv. 15 ; xviii. 1. Mark vi. 35. Luke i. 10 ; xiv. 17.
1 John ii. 18. John v. 35. 2 Cor. vii. 8. Philem. 15).
These ten kings, in their mortal stage, were not
actually kings ; but now, in their superhuman form, they
are contemporary, and receive power at one and the
same time with the Beast. Popular phraseology always

speaks of them as "ten kingdoms." No wonder they cannot be identified or prognosticated, for the Scripture says nothing about "ten kingdoms," but always "ten kings." The substitution of "kingdoms" only introduces confusion. The verse would then read "They are ten kingdoms, which have received no kingdom as yet, but receive authority as kingdoms." This is absurd as well as confusing.

They are seen as kings only in connection and company with the last or *eighth* king. We know not who or what these ten kings may be. They are not the "kings of the earth" mentioned in verse 18; for these are subordinate to the ten of which this verse speaks.

On the first emergence of the corporate wild-beast out of the Abyss, the woman (*i.e.*, the great city, Babylon) is supported by it (or as it is expressed, "she sits upon it"). But *she is not true to this new and superhuman power.* She intrigues with "the kings of the earth" (mortals) while the Beast out of the Abyss is supporting her. Then it is that he and the ten kings turn against her. As Henry VIII. dealt partially with the Roman Church in England, so will the Beast deal with Babylon universally. He will confiscate her revenues, appropriate her real estate as well as personality. The city, thus "stripped" will be wholly in the hands of this superhuman power (chap. xviii.), and filled with evil spirits, until a mighty angel from heaven completes the destruction.

F². (page 514). xvii. 13, 14. *The third pair of members*

13. **These have one mind** (*i.e.*, the same view, intent, and consent), **and give up their power and authority unto the beast.**] Not only are they contemporaneous

as to time, but they are of one accord as to purpose. This will be something very different from a so-called "concert" of Europe. Never were any ten kings found of one accord. It is a powerful spirit-influence that brings about this unanimity (ch. xvi. 14).

14. **These shall make war with the Lamb, and the Lamb will overcome them: because he is Lord of lords and King of kings : and they that** are **with** him are **called, and chosen, and faithful.**] Here is the wa₁ for which the demons go forth to gather the kings of the eaɪ̠h together. Two reasons are assigned for the result of this war. The glory of the King, and His own chosen forces. The battle is prophesied in xvii. 14, but not fought till chap. xix.

15. **And he saith to me, The waters which thou sawest, where the harlot** (*i.e.*, "the great city") **sit-teth, are** (*i.e.*, represent) **peoples, and multitudes, and nations, and tongues.**] This commences the second division of the Angel's interpretation of the Vision. It is indicated by the words, "And he saith to me," repeated from the commencement of the first division in verse 7. The woman represents "that great city." Babylon is thus addressed (Jer. li. 13) : "O thou that *dwellest upon many waters*, abundant in treasures, thine *end is come*." How this can be interpreted of Rome we know not; for it is not the vision we have here, but the *interpretation* of it.

We ask our readers to compare the following passages as here arranged in parallel columns. The first column contains the passages from the Old Testament, and the other from the Apocalypse. Both are distinctly said to concern Babylon. We recognise no authority, however "respectable," which assures us that these passages all refer to Rome :

Jer. li. 13.	Rev. xvii. 1.
„ li. 7.	„ xvii. 4.
„ li. 7.	„ xvii. 2.
Isa. xlvii. 5, 7.	„ xvii. 18 & xviii. 7, 8.
Jer. li. 25.	„ xviii. 8.
„ li. 6, 45 ; l. 8.	„ xviii. 4.
„ li. 9.	„ xviii. 5.
„ l. 15 ; li. 24-49.	„ xviii. 6.
„ l. 29.	„ xviii. 6.
„ li. 8 (Isa. xxi. 9).	„ xviii. 2.
„ li. 63, 64.	„ xviii. 21.
Isa. xiii. 21.	„ xviii. 2.
„ xxiv. 10, 8.	„ xviii. 23.

16. **And the ten horns which thou sawest, and** *
the beast, these shall hate the harlot (*i.e.*, that great
city), **and shall make her desolate and naked** (*i.e.*,
shall loot the city and strip it), **and shall eat her flesh**
(*i.e.*, take possession of her treasures), **and shall burn
her** (*i.e.*, the city) **with fire.**] How a false system of
religion, Papal or any other, can be thus treated we
cannot understand. The reading " and," instead of
" upon," is very important. It associates the hatred
of the eighth king with that of the ten, instead of
making him distinct in this hatred, and separate from
this war. The word " these " links them all together.
The words " these " is masculine, while " the horns "
and " the beast " are neuter. It is the figure called
Syllepsis, by which the concord of the pronoun is logical
rather than grammatical.

The Beast himself will be at the time in occupation of
the City, while the Ten Kings are exercising their author-

* G.L.T.Tr.A. WH. and RV. read καί (*kai*) *and*, instead of ἐπί
(*ebi*) *upon*.

ity each in his own part of the world; and that, just as the Papacy exercises its authority in many lands—so the woman's agents do the same, with this difference : that in all the kingdoms of the world the (mortal) "kings of the earth" are committing fornication with this woman *i.e.*, are one in religious intrigue and confederacy. Babylon sits upon many waters : *i.e.*, "peoples, multitudes, nations, tongues : " among all these Babylon is religiously a-whoreing.

Above "the Kings of the Earth," (mortals), reign "the Ten Kings." The whole earth is divided to them. For a little while (till they shall have secured a firm position) they will support the woman. As soon as they feel themselves to be secure, then, in all these "peoples, multitudes, nations, and tongues" they begin to make war with her simultaneously : the Beast (the last king of Babel in Babylon) and the Ten Kings in their respective parts of the world. So that, in every nation, people, tongue, and multitude, the merchants of the earth can stand afar off and bewail the destruction of the woman. For there will be an *auto-de-fe* among all the peoples by whom the woman has been supported.

For this destruction compare the passages from Jeremiah given above ; and compare them with its execution in Rev. xviii. 8. The reason of this is given in the next verse.

17. **For God put it** (*lit.*, gave it) **into their hearts to carry out** (*lit.*, to do) **His mind, and to carry out their own mind, and to give their kingdom to the beast until the words of God shall be accomplished.**] Apparently it is Satan's work, but God is over all, and He "shall send them strong delusion" (2 Thes. ii. 11.

Compare Is. x. 7). They carry out their own wilful desires, but blindly fulfil the counsel of God.

They give their kingdom, not kingdoms. They transfer no territory, for all the kingdoms are one under the Beast which shall "devour the whole earth."

Just as the Beast is *one*, though composed of many individual superhuman beings; so will the kingdom of the Lord Jesus Christ be one, though there will be in it many kings and principalities and powers.

These "ten kings" give their royal power. But there is a limit to it all, and that limit is expressed in the words "the true sayings of God," to these all must come: beyond these none can go.

We now come to the end; to the interpretation concerning the woman: the final statement which sets the whole matter at rest. See the structure on page 513.

D. (page 513). xvii. 18. *The Woman*

18. **And the woman whom thou sawest is that great city, which exerciseth sovereignty over the kings of the earth**] viz., those who have been so called in xvi. 14.

Babylon is the city named in verse 5, but its destruction, as prophesied in chap. xviii., is very different from that of which Jeremiah speaks. Other cities have been suggested, and even England has been added to the interpretations, because of its union of Church and State. Though how it can be a city we know not.

The revival of Babylon is prophesied in *Zech.* v. 1-11, 500 years before the Christian Era. The lawless woman there, answers to the great harlot here, and the angel says it was intended "to build it an house in the land of Shinar; and it shall be established and set

there upon her own base." " The land of Shinar"
carries us back, not to Italy, England, or Palestine, but
to Babylon and to Gen. xi. 2-9 and Dan. i. 1, 2. That
prophecy has never yet been fulfilled. Babylon is to
be the last of the powers of the earth to drink the cup
of Divine wrath in the day of the Lord (Jer. xxv. 17-26).
" All the kings of the earth, far and near, one with
another, and all the kingdoms of the world which are
upon the face of the earth : and the king of Sheshac
(*i.e.*, Babylon) shall drink after them."

The common interpretation of Zech. v. will hardly
bear examination : and it is certainly an error to suppose that Rev. xviii. is commercial. Babylon in Rev.
xviii. is a *buyer* and *not a seller*. It is not an exchange of
merchandise. And with respect to Zech., commentators
seize upon the measure and weight.

The Ephah is a measure of capacity, dry measure,
say for grain. As grain is put into a measure, so the
sinners will be collected in a heap. Are not these the
thieves and perjurers of the previous vision ? When the
leaden lid is lifted up there is seen a woman sitting in
the measure. The woman, it says, is " wickedness,"
not " commerce." *She is not permitted to get out of the
measure.* The lead is put back again. It seems to have
been lifted just to let the prophet see what was inside.
The Ephah, with its contents, is not suffered to remain
in the Land : it is carried into the land of Shinar.
This looks more like the expulsion from Palestine of
" wickedness " or reprobates, thieves and perjurers,
possibly at the time when the Two Witnesses are on
the earth.

It suggests, not commerce, but rather the worst kind
of financing maintained by thieving and perjury

(Zech. v. 1). So intense is the "wickedness" that a "flying roll," of the same dimensions as the porch of the Temple, goes forth as a curse, showing that the wicked will be judged by Temple measurements.

This is hardly the place to go into the prophecies of Zechariah. But all are too ready to follow a plausible tradition, without independent study of God's Word.

We are all agreed that Zech. v. is future; and that it concerns Babylon. But the question is, Does "lead" (no matter of what weight) ever represent money ? And does not a "woman" represent a religious system, rather than commerce ?

Jerusalem, we know, is to become a great city, the joy of the whole earth. But, before that comes to pass, Babylon also will become a great city ; the astonishment, but the curse, of the whole earth.

We have more than once referred to and spoken of the revival and rebuilding of Babylon. Many laugh at the very idea. But if they will not listen to the clear teachings of the word of God, will they listen to what man says ? If they deem this revival as unlikely or impossible, judging by the standard of their own imagination, what will they say to the following, from *The Daily Express* (London), Jan. 28, 1902 ? It is not speculation, but news, which is given us under the heading of "Germany's Great Railroad" : and the sub-title "Some facts about the grand Mesopotamian railway scheme," by William Durban. He says,

"An immense revolution is likely to be brought about in the Near East within the next decade. The shriek of the locomotive will in a few years be heard echoing over the salt marshes, bituminous plains, and magnificent higher and more fertile tracts, which make the vast Mesopotamian plain between the Euphrates and the Tigris the most curious mosaic of landscape in the world.

" It is startling to think of this coming raid of the engineers into the cradle of the world's most ancient civilisation. Abraham's native country is to be invaded by hordes of navvies, and all along the western bank of the mighty historic Tigris will gleam the twin steel riband which will bring the whole length of the effete Empire within the grip of European influence.

" A RESURRECTION OF BABYLON "

"The Kaiser has undoubtedly scored. When in December, 1899, it was announced that the German Anatolian Railway Company had received a concession from Abdul Hamid for the construction of a railway from Konieh to Bagdad, it was generally felt that the scheme would hang in the air for at least a generation. But the German Emperor is a model man of business, who has posed of late as the Sultan's ' only friend.' He did not for nothing organize, by means of a splendid squad of his military officers, that Turkish army which crumpled up the Greek legions at Domoko and everywhere on the Thessalian plains. The new *Iradé* settles the affair.

" It is a favourite thesis with the people who ponder over prophetic mysteries that *both Babylon and Nineveh are to be resuscitated in more than the ancient glories of Nebuchadnezzar and Sennacherib*. Who can tell? It is certain that the Kaiser entertains the dream of founding a magnificent empire in the Near East. He is going to work in the way which is like to follow up his sermon at Jerusalem by practical results. . .

" Few people realise the magnitude of the Sultan's Asiatic dominions. They form the most important section of the earth's surface in connection with the international political situation of the near future. The Eastern Question only sleeps, and its slumbers are very uneasy."

With this comes the news that this Railway is to be begun at once (1902), in five different places: and that Edison has invented a new cement which will enable houses to be built in three or four days!

For ourselves, we need no evidence of this kind; but it clearly shows that what we regard as certain, from God's Word, is not altogether impossible from man's point of view.

X. (page 476). chap. xviii. *The Judgment of the Great City*

This is the third and last of the three great divisions of the Sixth Vision " on earth" (chap. xvi.—xviii).

The *first* (on page 476) we lettered V. chap. xvi., The Great Judgments.

The *second* (page 494), we lettered W. chap. xvii., The Great Harlot.

The *third* we are now to consider is X chap. xviii., The Great City.

The last verse of chap. xvii. closed it by giving the interpretation of the woman as being " that great city." Though the woman is the first thing mentioned in that chapter, yet her interpretation is left till the end, so that the mention of the city may lead on to the account of its destruction, which is the subject of chap. xviii. In chap. xvii. we have the conflict about that great city in which the seven heads, and ten kings, and "the kings of the earth," and the Beast ("the eighth " king), all take part. But now, the city itself is to be judged *as a city.*

Its fall had already been prophetically *fore-announced* in preliminary and general terms (xiv. 8). But the seventh Vial has since been poured out, and the city has already been shaken to its foundation (xvi. 17-21). Its final judgment and utter extinction, however, yet remain to be accomplished. And the description of this is now to be given in chap. xviii.

Many who see Rome in some form in chap. xvii., yet find Babylon, literal, in chap. xviii. But where is the authority for making such a vital separation between the subjects of the two chapters? There is no indication of such a marked distinction, either in the Text, or in the context.

It is perfectly well known that Rome was never either " great" or commercial. It is no Port ; and no "ship-master " goes thither. Babylon itself was never "*suddenly*" destroyed, as this city will be. The suddenness of its destruction is the one dominant feature of this chapter. True, Babylon has come under judgment, but has never yet experienced this *sudden* judgment which is the subject of this and other prophecies concerning her (Is. xlvii. 11. Jer. li. 8). Nothing in history is known to have thus happened to Babylon. And besides, it is prophecy, and not history, which is given to us in this chapter : something that was to happen *after* this Revelation was given to John. But nothing like this has happened, before or since. So that if Rome be the city, Rome must yet become the great political and religious centre ; with port and harbour. And it is quite as difficult to believe in this revival of Rome, as to believe in the revival of Babylon. In either case it is a question of *revival.* Babylon was not suddenly destroyed. She has gone down in *gradual* decay, but her history is known, and her ruins stand to-day. Arabs pitch their tents there. It is not the "abode of dragons," as it is yet to be after its sudden destruction (See Is. xiii. 9, 12. Jer. l. 3). There was a church there in Peter's day (1 Peter v. 13). There is to this day a governor of the land, who collects the taxes and customs for the Turkish government.

It does not fulfil the conditions described in Jer. l. 1-4, 28, 40, 41, 46; xxv. 12; li. 3, 6, 26, 27, 29, 43. Is. xiii. 20, where it is said that it is to be "perpetual desolations," "where no man dwelleth," "empty without inhabitant." The above references need not be quoted in full. They have only to be read to convince the reader that they have never yet been fulfilled: This being so, we have the fulfilment of them described in this chap. xviii.

The Structure of the chapter, as a whole, is exquisite; and its symmetry is perfect.

It is composed of a Repeated Alternation of six members; three concerning Babylon and its people (F); and three concerning God and His people (G).

The three concerning Babylon's judgment are (1) The Proclamation of it, (2) The Reasons for it, and (3) The Manner of it.

The three concerning Babylon's people are (1) Their Sin, (2) Their Lamentation, (3) Their Silence.

The three concerning God's people are (1) Their call to come out of her, (2) Their call to Rejoice over her, (3) Their blood found in her.

We shall have little to do or say regarding this chapter, beyond giving the Structure, and the Translation.

The Structure of chap. xviii. is as follows :—

X. (page 476). chap. xviii. *The Judgment of the Great City*

X
F'	m¹	1, 2.	Babylon's judgment.	Announcement of it
	n¹	3.	Babylon's associates.	Their sin
	G¹	4.	God's people.	Their call to "Come *out of* her"
F²	m²	5-8.	Babylon's judgment.	Reasons for it
	n²	9-19.	Babylon's inhabitants.	Their lamentation
	G²	20.	God's people.	Their call to "Rejoice *over* her"
F³	m³	21.	Babylon's judgment.	Manner of it
	n³	22, 23.	Babylon's inhabitants.	Their silence
	G³	24.	God's people.	Their blood "found *in* her"

This is the manner in which this solemn chapter is constructed for us, and presented to us.

Every part brings out its perfection, and apprises us of the Divine source of Babylon's judgment; and of the Divine authority and truth of its prophetic declaration.

m'. (page 555). xviii. 1-3. *Babylon's judgment announced.*

1. ***After these things I saw another†angel coming down from heaven, having great authority; and the earth was lighted up with his glory.**] This was another angel, and not the one who had been speaking to John in chap xvii. The Vision is still "on Earth"; hence, John sees this angel coming down out of heaven. Interpreters seem as anxious to make this, and other of the angels, to be the Lord Jesus, as they are to make all else to be the church. There is no occasion to go beyond the simple understanding of the words. This was no ordinary angel; for he was invested with great power and glory.

2. **And he cried with a mighty voice,† saying,
Fallen, fallen§ is Babylon the great,
and is become a habitation of demons**
(see Isa. xxxiv. 14, especially in lxx),
**and a hold of every unclean spirit,
and a hold of every unclean and hateful bird.**

---

* L.T.Tr. A. WH. and RV. omit καί (*kai*) *and.*

† G.L.T.Tr. A. WH. and RV. add ἄλλον (*allon*) *another.*

‡ So G.L.T.Tr. A. WH. and RV.

§ Tr. omits the second "fallen;" A. includes it in the text, but puts it in brackets.

n¹ (page 555). xviii. 3.   *Babylon's Associates.*

3. because all the nations have
   drunk of the exciting wine* of her
   fornication, and the kings of the
   earth committed fornication with
   her, and the merchants of the earth
   waxed rich through the power (or
   abundance) of her luxury."]

This identifies this city with that of chap. xvii. We
have the same wine and the same idolatries and the
same " kings of the earth."   But, in addition to these,
we have the announcement which implies that Babylon
will become the headquarters of Spiritism, the habitation of demons, and the hold and home of every unclean
spirit. As a cage is full of birds, so will Babylon be full
of evil spirits and demons, controlling the great
apostasy at its fountain head.

It seems impossible to miss the clear marks of identification which are given in verse 3.

If we look at these two chapters carefully, we fail to
find the distinction so persistently affirmed. Some one
states a thing as a fact ; and then others think they see it.
There is no such thing as " Mystic Babylon." The
Babylon mentioned in chap. xvii. is the same as that in
chap. xviii. It is the " Woman " which is a secret
symbol or sign. But that means only that we are not
to take it literally as a woman, but as " that great city,"
as is explained in verse 18. Her name is clearly
written on her forehead " Babylon the great." What is
there " mystical " about this, in the sense of *mysterious ?*
Nothing. It means, as we have seen, a *secret sign.* but

---

* L. and A. omit " the wine ; " Tr. and WH. put it in brackets;
the RV. puts it in the margin.

that refers to the "Woman" as being the sign or symbo of the "city."

The war which is waged concerning that city in chap. xvii. tells us of its necessary revival. (See page 550). Chicago was once burnt, but in a very few years was entirely rebuilt. The difficulty arises from supposing that all these wonderful events are to be crowded into *seven* years, and no more. Whereas, after the "calling on high" of Phil. iii. 14, and the *Parousia* of 1 Thess. iv. and the "meeting of the Lord in the air," and the "gathering unto Him" there, there is practically, so far as we are concerned, no limit to the time which shall elapse before the actual Apocalypse of the Lord as "the King of Kings" (chap. xix.). Several events have to take place *before* the first half of the last seven years (Dan. ix. 27).

The "end time" of Daniel is longer than this first half of the week, and commences before it.

It begins with the appearance of the *four* Greek kings of Dan. vii. 17, 23.

According to Dan. xi. 5 (RV.), the King of Egypt precedes the king of the North. So that until *this* king of the North appears we have not reached the "end time."

There are three kings of the north. First, the one who, before his accession, was one of the princes of the king of the South. This first king is engaged in many wars, which must occupy some considerable time. Upon his death he is succeeded by the one (Dan. xi. 20) who becomes "the seventh head," referred to in the Apocalypse as having been slain to death.

From the rise of the *first* king of the North to the assassination of the one who is the *seventh* Head, appears to be the "end time"; and this includes the first-half of the last seven years.

Upon the coming up of this seventh head from the Abyss as the eighth king, he immediately stops "the daily sacrifice."

From this point to the end is the 42 months of Rev. and the "last days" of chap. x. 14, which belong to Dan. xi. 31 to end.

The *Sunteleia* (consult the Index) corresponds to the "end time" of Daniel.

But the removal of the Church will take place before it commences.

If the length of this *Sunteleia* should be, say, 33 years, then the *Telos* would be the last seven years, making 40 in all.

Nothing whatever is said as to the length of this interval. But the analogy of the two Advents (see pages 52-55) leads us to the belief that there will be a considerable period; and the end of "the times of the Gentiles" may be similar to their commencement.

When Nebuchadnezzar first took Jerusalem, it remained for some twenty to thirty years, during which he set up and put down kings there (see 2 Kings xxiv., xxv. Jer. xxxiv.—xl). It was not till the close of that long period that he finally burnt the City and Temple and deported the people to Babylon. So it may easily be again. There may be thirty years or more from the rise of the Zionist movement, which will bring the Jews into a *quasi* national existence, before the last seven years which shall fulfil the prophecies of Dan. ix. 27.

So that, from this point of view, *time* is no difficulty to our believing that the ten kings may burn the city

(xvii. 16), and yet that it may revive and be destroyed suddenly, as in chap. xviii. The difficulty is not removed by the other interpretation ; for how can anything " mystical " be burnt with fire ?

The Babylon, then, of this chap. xviii. is the Babylon of chap. xvii. and of all the other chapters which speak of her origin, her character, and her destiny. The " Kings of the Earth " did not thus become partakers of the idolatries of Pagan Rome : neither did the merchants of the earth wax rich through the merchandise of Papal Rome : nor were her adherents and votaries confined to " merchants " and " kings."

This is literal Babylon ; and before the Lord's advent (or Apocalypse), as described in chap. xix., takes place, she will have arrived at this height of idolatry and luxury.

It is strange that, in spite of all this, commentators still cling to the traditional interpretation that Babylon means Rome. Even Alford, after saying " Rome never has been, and from its very position never could be, a great commercial city," adds " I leave the difficulty unsolved." So there *is* a " difficulty " ; but we submit that it is of the commentators' own creation. There is no difficulty if we believe what God says. But so loth are expositors to do this, that Alford says again " the details of this mercantile lamentation far more nearly suit London, than Rome, at any assignable period of her history."

We believe that it is Babylon revived and restored (as other cities have been), and that this state of magnificence will characterise her in the day of the Lord's Apocalypse.

Hence, the final announcement of her then impend-

ing judgment is followed by God's call to His people to
come out of her.

G'. (page 555), xviii. 4. *God's people. Their call
to come out of her*

**4. And I heard another voice from heaven, saying
"Come out of her, My people,
That ye may not partake of her sins,
And that ye receive not of her plagues.]**

There is no need for us to take this angel as being
Christ. He speaks in the name of God, as in chap. xi. 3.
His cry is a warning summons to God's people who
will then be on the earth. The church will have been
taken up some years before. And there will be others
also who will have been safely caught up, and will give
forth the rejoicing cry foretold in Rev. xii. 10. We
have seen them in chaps. vii., xiv., and xv., " standing
before the throne," and upon mount Zion. But the
" remnant of her seed " *i.e.*, Israel's seed (chap. xii. 17)
will have been taken to Babylon (Micah iv. 8-10); and
to them, this warning cry is given. We need not wonder
at many of them being found in Babylon ; for, where
merchandise is to be sold there will these be gathered
together. It would be strange were it otherwise.

And this is exactly what is foretold in Jer. l. There
the destruction of Babylon is foretold; for it is " the
word that the LORD spake against Babylon " (Jer. l. 1).
We have not yet heard of any commentator who
thought Jeremiah prophesied this of Rome, or of any
city except the literal Babylon.

Then, immediately after the announcement " Babylon
is taken," we read " In those days, and in that time,
saith the LORD, the children of Israel shall come ; they,
and the children of Judah together, going and weeping :

they shall go and seek the Lord their God" (*v.* 4).
" MY PEOPLE hath been lost sheep " (*v.*6). To these
the call will go forth, " Remove out of the midst of
Babylon, and go forth out of the land of the Chaldean,"
(*v.*8). And again, " Flee out of the midst of Babylon,
and deliver every man his soul (*i.e.,* let every man save
his life) : be not cut off in her iniquity : for this is the
time of the LORD's vengeance "; he will render unto
her a recompense (Jer. li. 6, and compare Rev. xviii. 6).
And again, " MY PEOPLE, go ye out of her, and
deliver every man his soul from the fierce anger of the
LORD" (Jer. li. 45).

Israel, as a nation, now repents (Jer. l. 4, 5). There-
fore she is no longer "*Lo-Ammi*," "not my people."
Hence this call is made " Come out of her, MY
PEOPLE."

This cannot refer to any but to the literal Israel, and
to the literal Babylon. No such heavenly call ever
went forth to any Christians in Rome. Nor did they
come forth as a body. They have been slaughtered
there; but that is a very different thing.

It is Israel that is thus warned, as in Isa. xlviii. 20,
and in Jer. li. 50, as we shall see below.

In the sentence, " have no fellowship with her sins,"
the word " sins " is put by *Metonymy* for the *judgment*
brought about by her sins. (Compare Jer. li. 9.) It
is because God's People will not have fellowship in
her sins that this gracious call to " Come out " from
her judgments is given.

The cause of this judgment and of these plagues is
now to be stated.

m². (page 555), xviii. 5-8. *Babylon's judgment. Reasons for it.*

5. **"Because her sins reached* up to heaven, and God remembered her iniquities.**]

This is a Hebraism. (Compare Gen. iv. 10 ; xix. 29. 2 Chron. xxviii. 9. Jer. li. 9. Jonah i. 2.) The length of time during which Babylon's sins have been accumulating is implied in this " remembrance." Compare chap. xvi. 19, "and great Babylon came into remembrance before God." This " remembrance " implies a former rebellion : a rebellion which was repressed by dispersion, but is at the time of the end to find in *re-union*, another opportunity for outbreak. Thus, in the very same place and under the same circumstances, defiance of God meets with its final judgment. This effectually shuts out Rome (Papal or Pagan) ; for Rome, though one of the daughters, is certainly not " the mother."

6. **Render to her**
    As she also rendered † to others,
And render double punishment ‡
    According to her works :
In the cup which she mixed,
    Mix for her double.

---

* G.L.T.Tr.A. WH. and RV. read ἐκολλήθησαν (*ekollē.hēsan*) *were joined* or *builded together ;* hence, *reached*, as buildings rise higher and higher ; instead of ἠκολούθησαν (*ēkolouthēsan*) *followed.*

† G.L.T.Tr.A. WH. and RV. omit ὑμῖν (*humin*) *to you*, so we must fill up the *Ellipsis* by supplying " to others."

‡ *Lit.*, " Double the double to her." This is the figure of *Metonymy*, by which the word " double " is put for completeness or full compensation. Compare Ex. xxii. 7, 9. Isa. xl. 2. Jer. xvi. 18. ; xvii. 18.

7. **In proportion as she glorified herself,**
         [and waxed wanton,
       So much torment and mourning
           [give to her :

Is this call for vengeance given to the church? Certainly not! Nor does it belong to any period of history since the Lord's death ; for the present is the day of grace, when God " maketh his sun to rise on the evil and on the good, and sendeth rain on the just, and on the unjust " (Matt. v. 45). This proves that Rev. xviii. belongs to a future *dispensation of judgment* which has not yet come. Of that day, Ps. cxxxvii. 8, 9 may be applied, even though the interpretation may refer to past history :

" O daughter of Babylon,
   Who art to be destroyed.
   Happy shall he be that rewardeth thee as thou
      hast served us.
   Happy shall he be that taketh and dasheth thy
      little ones against the rock " (RV.).

These words, so contrary to Christian sentiment, will be perfectly correct in the next dispensation, which will be one of judgment.

The mingled cup refers us back to xvii. 4, and further identifies the two chapters. Babylon is now to drink another cup, herself. Compare Jer. li. 7, and especially chap. xxv., where the cup of God's wrath is sent to the nations (*vv.* 15, 16), and Babylon drinks last (*v.* 26).

7. **" Because, in her heart, she saith,**
      'I sit a Queen, and a widow I am not ;
      and mourning I shall in no wise see ']

These words are spoken of the same Babylon (not Rome) in Isa. xlvii. 8, 9. The whole of that chapter is about Babylon "the daughter of the Chaldeans" (*vv.* 1, 5).

> 8. " For this cause, in one day, shall come her plagues—death, and mourning, and famine (Isa. xlvii. 9); and with fire shall she be utterly burned up; because strong is the Lord God who judged * her.]

This is the burning which has already been mentioned in chap. xvii. 16; but is now, in this chapter, more fully described. Isa. xlvii. 9 declares that this judgment shall come suddenly, "in a moment."

This suddenness and completeness of Babylon's judgment and *disappearance from the face of the earth* is the one prominent feature of this prophecy : and it effectually proves that it has not yet taken place. For Jehovah's prophecies are far too accurate and particular for this suddenness and completeness to be fulfilled by the gradual decay of old Babylon, the site and ruins and remains of which are still to be seen in the land of Shinar.

We now come to the Lamentation over her, and the member n² above (page 555) must be expanded.

It consists of eleven verses (xviii. 9-19); and these are elaborately constructed of four members, arranged as an Introversion. Each of the four larger members consists of three smaller ones, each perfect in its correspondence with the others.

---

*G.L.T.Tr.A. WH. and RV. read κρίνας (*krinas*) *judged*, instead of κρίνων (*krinōn*) *judgeth*.

	Their Merchandise	Their Loss

n². (page 555), xviii. 9-19. *Lamentation of the Inhabitants of Babylon*

```
n²
H | r | 9. Kings of the earth.  (Earth )
  | s | 10-. Their Lamentation.  " Alas, alas '
  | t | -10. Reason.  " For in one hour "

J | u | 11-. Merchants
  | v | -11-. Their Lamentation
  | w | -11-14. Reason.  "For"

J | u | 15-. Merchants
  | v | -15, 16. Their Lamentation
  | w | 17-. Reason.  "For"

H | r | -17. The Shipmasters.  (Sea )
  | s | 18, 19-. Their Lamentation.  "Alas, alas "
  | t | -19. Reason.  "For in one hour"
```

H. (see above). xviii. 9-10. *The Lamentation of the Kings of the Earth over Babylon's fall.*

9. "And the kings of the earth, who committed fornication and waxed wanton with her, shall weep, and wail over her, as soon as they see the smoke of her burning, (10) standing afar off on

account of the fear of her torment,
saying,
     '**Alas, alas, the great city Baby-
lon, the mighty city! for in one
hour has thy judgment come.'**]

These are "the kings of the earth" mentioned in
xvii. 2 ; the confederates and associates of Babylon.
In xviii. 3 the mourners over Babylon are first enumerated, and afterwards described more fully.*

We have before noted that "the ten kings" are
never seen apart from the Beast ; and "the kings of the
earth" are never seen apart from Babylon. It is the
former who hate and burn Babylon; it is the latter
who weep and wail over her. In both chapters (xvii.
and xviii.) the city is called "Babylon the great." God
and man both so call her.

This great city cannot be separated from her own
corrupt religion. They must be connected together,
just as chapters xvii. and xviii. are connected; and yet
distinguished as they are there distinguished.

Idolatry of the grossest kind is Babylon's sin ; and
not commerce. Whoredom points to, and means,
idolatry. That is Babylon's chief end.

In commerce, goods of many are exchanged for the
goods of others. But Babylon will not do *that*. She is
only a *buyer*. What she gives to "the kings of the
earth" and their peoples comes out of her "cup," and
that stands for something having to do with religion:
just as our Lord's Cup does. So Babylon's cup stands
for corrupt religion, which has woman for its central
object.

---

* This is the figure of *Prosapodosis.* See *Figures of Speech*, p. 394.

We do not deny that the Church of Rome to-day is preparing for this *Womanolatry*; and, in all Roman Catholic countries, is fostering (not intentionally, it may be) a Womanolatry of a different kind, which is leading on to that moral corruption which will end in a religious corruption of a similar kind.

At the first, Babylon had male Gods. Later on, each male God was given a female partner, with the result that *Ishtar* became pre-eminent.

This it is that makes the sin of Babylon; and it is this religion of Womanolatry which will be perfected in Babylon. It will be received by "the kings of the earth"; and the peoples of the kings of the earth will be taught it by an order of priests, just as were the people of Ephesus. But Babylon will be the great goddess. She will have her Temples the world over: "Mother of all the harlots." And this is the religion which is being prepared for even now.

In any case, the common view of the chapter as relating *only* to "Commerce" must be modified. Babylon is a buyer. As a buyer, she cannot be regarded as engaged in Commerce, because that implies manufacture and selling as well as buying; and certainly buying with a view to selling again. But *that* is not Babylon. She sits, a woman, who buys to satisfy her lusts, and to furnish her allurements.

Surely if Commerce were the point, Babylon would be represented as masculine, as Tyre is (Ezek. xxvi.— xxviii} A woman is not the ideal to represent Commerce in the ordinary acceptance of the word.

But Mariolatry is increasing more and more, and is not now confined to Rome. And *this* is preparing the way for the revival of *Ishtar*.* It puts woman, as woman, at the head of the universe, teaching that which is a perversion of "the mother of all living."   Is not *this* the only logical reason for the hatred of the Beast? Commerce does not furnish any adequate reason for this hatred.

The great Question will be Supremacy.   Who is to be supreme, *Woman* or *Man;* Babylon or the Beast? THAT is an all-sufficient reason for their hatred; and as the supremacy involved in Babylon is contrary to God's ordinance, He will "put it into their heart to destroy the woman."

This view makes things much clearer than commerce can do.   And if the sin of Babylon be as we have suggested, viz., a system which makes drunk with this false religious excitement the kings of the earth, the Priests and Priestesses, and Temple servers, then it is these who will be stripped of all their possessions and burnt with fire in every land where they are found. This will take place pre-eminently in Babylon.   But before this takes place, the call will go forth to God's people to come out of her, that they be not partakers in her judgments.

---

* Already, Commentators are fulfilling 2 Tim. iv. 4; and, turning away their ears from "the truth," are turned into "myths" (for that is the Greek word rendered "fables"). Winkler is quoted by Canon Cheyne with apparent approval, for he says, if scholars accept Winkler's teaching, he will accept their verdict. The latest theological "Myth" which commentators are turning to is this: *viz.,* that Abraham, Isaac, and Jacob are *lunar* heroes. Sarah is at once Abraham's sister and his wife; because Sarah, being the counterpart of ISTAR, has a double *rôle.* She is the daughter of the *Moon-god,* and, therefore, Abraham's sister; and she is the wife of TAMMUZ, and, therefore, Abraham's wife. See Canon Cheyne in *The Nineteenth Century* Magazine for January, 1902.

As this will take place in every land, the kings of the earth can stand afar off and wail; for, the superhuman Ten Kings and the Beast will dominate the world.

The final judgment of Babylon will be sudden and complete. The conflagration will be so great that, from the first, total destruction will be seen to be inevitable.

Three times this lament is made, " Alas! Alas!" More literally, " Woe, woe," as elsewhere rendered in this book. But the AV. rendering is very expressive. The *Kings* of the earth make this lament. The *Merchants* make it (*v.* 16) : and the *Mariners* make it (*v.* 19). In the first, the verbs introducing it are in the *Future* tense (*v.* 9) : in the second, in the *Present* (*v.* 11), and in the third, the *Past* tense (*v.* 17). It is as though a moving scene is passing before the eyes, while the interpreting angel explains it.

The lamentation of the merchants is divided into two parts. In J. (xviii. 11-14) the merchandise and its varieties are the subject; while in *J.*(xviii. 15-17-) it is the merchants' irretrievable loss.

J. (page 566), xviii. 11-14. *The Merchants' Lamentation*

11. "**And the merchants of the earth weep and mourn over her ; because no one any longer buyeth their cargo** (Acts xxi. 3. Ex. xxiii. 5): (12) **the cargo of gold, and of silver, and of precious stones, and of pearls, and of fine linen, and of purple, and of silk, and of scarlet, and all thyine wood, and every article of ivory, and every**

article of most costly wood, and of
brass, and of iron and of marble, (13)
and cinnamon, and spice,* and odours
(for incense), and frankincense, and
wine, and oil, and finest flour, and
wheat, and cattle, and sheep, and of
horses, and of chariots, and of slaves†
and men.‡ (14) **And the harvest of thy
soul's desire departed from thee,
and all the things that were dainty
and brilliant have perished§ from
thee, and they** (men) **shall never more
at all find them.**]

This list of the merchandise is most significant and
instructive. We see at once that it consists entirely of
luxuries (see verse 3). If Babylon be the Religious
system, which we suggest, then her priests and
priestesses in every land—the harlot daughters of this
harlot mother—will deal in the same luxuries.

It is not commerce that we see in this list. It is no
exchange of produce against produce. There is no sin
in that. That is a good thing, and not an evil thing. It
is in her *imports* that the city is great; and these
imports are *luxuries* (see *v.* 3).

---

* G.L.Tr.A. WH. and RV. add καί ἄμωμον (*kai amōmum*) *and
amōmum*, i.e., *and spice.*

† Greek, "bodies," put by *Metonymy* for slaves: just as we put
"hands," for workmen.

‡ Lit., "souls of men," a Hebraism for *persons of men*, or simply
men (see Ezek. xxvii. 13. 1 Chron. v. 21, and Num. xxxi. 35, the
Hebrew being נֶפֶשׁ אָדָם (*nephesh adam*). So Gen. xxxvi. 6, where,
of course, the Hebrew is somewhat different.

§ G.L.T.Tr.A. WH. and RV. read ἀπώλετο (*apōleto*) *perished*
instead of ἀπῆλθεν (*apēlthen*) *departed.*

The articles of merchandise here are not enumerated in any hap-hazard way, but are arranged so as to impress us with the vast range and character of the commodities.

They are arranged in four groups, and these are sub-divided as follows :—

Natural { Adornment (12-) Jewellery
{ Apparel (-12-) Drapery

Artificial { All ↑
{ All |
{ All } Vessels (-12) of { Ivory
{ All | { Wood
{ All ↓   { Brass
                          { Iron
                          { Marble

Vegetable { Aromatic (13-)
{ Nutritive (-13-)

Animal { Cattle (-13-)
{ Human kind (-13)

These call for no comment beyond the great fact that they have no relation whatever to Rome, Pagan or Papal. Even Alford, who holds that Babylon in chap. xvii. means Rome, and is to be identified with chap. xviii., says, " It must not for a moment be denied that the character of this lamentation throws a shade of obscurity over the interpretation, otherwise so plain, from the explanation given in chap. xvii." We admit that, if we start with the assumption that in chap. xvii. we have Rome Papal, and in chap. xviii. Rome Pagan, there is a difficulty ; for of neither could this lamentation ever be used. But the difficulty is *created* by an assumption. It is not in the Word. If we allow God to mean what He says, it is all clear. It is only when we assume that He means something quite different from what He says that we get into difficulties.

Rome's merchants were never " the great men of the earth." Rome's religion is not based on astrology and sorcery. Well may Alford sum it up by saying, "I leave the difficulty unsolved : " and " the details of this mercantile lamentation far more nearly suit London than Rome at any assignable period of her history."

" Babylon the Great " includes more than the city proper on the Euphrates. She sits upon many waters, and includes all the many peoples among whom her " Cup " passes.

In verses 15-17- we have the merchants and their loss ; rather than the merchants and the particulars of their merchandise.

J. (page 566). xviii. 15-17-. *The Merchants and their loss*

15. **The merchants of these things** viz., in *vv.* 12, 13), **who were made rich by her, shall stand afar off on account of the fear of her torment, wailing and mourning, (16)* saying,**

> **" Alas ! alas ! the great city, which was arrayed in fine linens, and purple, and scarlet, and bedecked with gold, and precious stones, and pearls ! (17-) for in one hour is so great riches come to naught.]**

The ruin is complete. It is even as was foretold of this very Babylon, " the beauty of the Chaldee's excellency shall be *as when God overthrew Sodom and Gomorrah* " (Isa. xiii. 19. Jer. xlix. 18 ; l. 40).

We now come to the third great category of mourners. (1) the kings of the earth ; (2) the merchants of the

* G.T.Tr.A.WH. and RV. omit καί (*kai*) *and.*

earth ; and now (3) those upon the sea. The mercantile world includes both land and sea. The sea is indeed the chief factor in carriage and freights. Hence, those who have to do with the sea now make their lamentation

H. (page 566). xviii. -17-19. *The Lamentation of the Shipmasters*

-17. **And every shipmaster, and everyone that saileth any whither,* and mariners, and as many as trade by sea, stood afar off, (18) and cried out as they looked upon the smoke of her burning, saying,**

> **" What city is like unto this great city ? "**

(19) And they cast dust on their heads, and cried, wailing and mourning, saying,

> **" Alas ! alas ! the great city, wherein were made rich all that had their ships in the sea, by reason of her costliness !† for in one hour is she made desolate."]**

The mention of passengers shows the nature and extent of the traffic ; embracing travellers as well as merchants and traders. Rawlinson‡ speaks of the Euphrates as being navigable for ships for some 500 miles from its mouth. And with little effort could be made available for ships of large size.

---

* *i.e.*, the passengers. So G.L.T.Tr.A. WH. and RV.

† *i.e.*, costliness including more than costly treasures ; costly living as shown in extravagance.

‡ *Herodotus*, i. 512.

The "dwellers of the earth" judge by earthly size and grandeur; but God has a different standard, and sees that which shall bring down this tremendous judgment. These again are impressed with its suddenness; and remind us that no such *sudden* judgment has ever overtaken Babylon.

God's people are again introduced; and the cry goes forth to " Rejoice over " Babylon in this hour of their avengement upon her (Ps. cxxxvii.)

G². (page 555), xviii. 20.   *God's people.   Their call to*
"*Rejoice over her*"

20. **Rejoice over her, thou heaven. and ye saints,* and ye apostles, and ye prophets: for God hath executed your judgment** (or avenged† you) **upon her.**"]

The command here given is obeyed in the next (the seventh and last) Vision " in heaven," and the words are given in chap. xix. 1-5. At length the waiting of the Martyrs is about to end (vi. 10-12), and they are to rejoice that God has avenged them.   That avengement has now come (Luke xviii. 7, 8).   This again shows that the dispensation of grace has ended, and that the coming dispensation of judgment has been entered on in this eighteenth chapter; yea, is about to close.

Some commentators apologise for this rejoicing in vengeance; and endeavour to tone it down, as being inconsistent with the Gospel. Of course it is incon-

---

* So G.L.T.Tr.A. WH. and RV.

† Lit. judged your judgment." This is the figure of *Polyptoton*, and is used for emphasis. It means *hath fully avenged* you.

sistent with the Gospel; but this is because the dispensations are not the same. Once rightly divide the word of truth, and all difficulty is removed.

Saints and apostles and prophets have been martyred in and by Babylon: both there, at its fountain head, as well as in some of its many streams by her daughters; for she is a " mother " and has daughters (xviii. 5).

We now come to the final mention of this judgment, and are informed as to the manner of it, and the result of it.

F³. (page 555). xviii. 21-23. *Babylon's Judgment.*
The manner of it

21-23. And a mighty angel took up a stone as it were a great millstone, and cast it into the sea saying,

> " **Thus, with violence** (or, with a rush)
> **shall Babylon, that great city, be
> cast down, and**
>> **Shall be found no more at all** (Jer.
>> li. 63. Ezek. xxvi. 21).
> **And sound of harpers, and musicians,
> and flute players, and trumpeters.**
>> **Shall never be heard in thee any**
>>> [**more;**
> **And no craftsman, of any craft**
>> **Shall ever be found in thee any**
>>> [**more;**
> **And sound of millstone**
>> **Shall never be heard in thee any**
>>> [**more.**
> **And the light of a lamp**
>> **Shall never shine in thee any**
>>> [**more:**

> And the voice of bridegroom or bride
> Shall never be heard in thee any
> more :
> Because thy merchants were the great
> ones of the earth : because by thy
> sorcery were all the nations deceived."
> (Is. xlvii. 8, 9).]

Sorcery, corrupt religion, and idolatry are the great means by which Babylon will ensnare the nations. And these are the two things which are rising up and advancing before our eyes.

The great stone represents the great city; and the symbolic act gives, with great vividness, the suddenness of Babylon's final destruction. Four times we have this suddenness emphasised :—" in one day " (*v.* 8), " in one hour " (*vv.* 10, 17, 19). Every word is employed to impress us with its suddenness and completeness. And inasmuch as all other fulfilled prophecies have been fulfilled *to the very letter ;* and Babylon, though fallen gradually, and very low, has never suffered such a destruction. There is only one conclusion, that in the interval of, say some 30 or more years between the removal of the church and the last " week " of Daniel's prophecy, it will be revived, and exceed all its former magnificence (see page 555-1).

Similar desolation was prophesied against Jerusalem, and the cities of Judah (Jer. vii. 34), but this was not to be like Babylon's. They were to be restored again Jer. xxxiii. 10, 11). But no such restoration follows on the destruction of Babylon here described.

And now we come to the last mention of God's People in connection with Babylon; and the whole scene closes with the one all embracing reason for this judgment.

G³. (p. 555), xviii. 24. *God's people. Their blood found in her*

24. **And in her was found the blood of prophets, and of saints, and of all the slain upon the earth.**]

With this we must read Jer. li. 49. "As Babylon hath caused the slain of ISRAEL to fall, so at Babylon shall fall the slain of all the earth." This decides for us who the saints, apostles, and prophets are. They are "of Israel" (see verses 47, 48). But their blood is at length avenged, and that "speedily," with a mighty, and sudden, and complete avengement.

18

THE SEVENTH VISION
"IN HEAVEN"
(19:1-16)

The final heavenly Utterances and Actions

We now come to the last of the seven Visions seen " in Heaven," which is the subject of chap. xix. 1-16, giving us the final heavenly *Utterances* and *Actions* which lead up to, explain, and introduce the five concluding judgments which close up the things of *Time*, and pass on to what we call the Eternal State.

This last Vision "in Heaven " is divided into two parts, each having its own independent construction. The first contains the *words* of the heavenly voices ; and the second describes the *actions* of the heavenly beings.

𝕭⁷. (page 118), xix. 1-16. *The Seventh (and last) Vision " In Heaven "*

𝕭⁷ | P | xix. 1-10.   The Final Heavenly *Utterances*
‎ | Q | xix. 11-16.   The Final Heavenly *Actions*

These must be expanded in turn, in order to see the beauty and the scope of each.

We have already called attention (pages 119-122) to the *seventeen* Heavenly Utterances in these *seven* Visions " in Heaven " ; and pointed out that *ten* of them occur in the first and last together, viz., *six* in the first (chaps. iv. and v.), and *four* in the last (chap. xix. 1-10). All heaven seems to be moved at the first announcement and opening of these final judgments, which end in the ejection of the Usurper from the earth : and all heaven is stirred when we come to the final scenes of these judgments.

It is only in the first and last of these Visions " in Heaven," that we have the utterances of the four *Zōa*. Only in the first announcement do they praise God that the time has at length come for Him to interfere in the affairs of this world, and wind up His great controversy with it and Satan. And again in chap. xix., when that great controversy shall have closed.

Only on these two occasions, and in these two Visions do we hear their voices and listen to their significant utterances. In all the other Visions in Heaven they are silent.

This shows us that we are approaching the end; and prepares us for the final Heavenly actions (xix. 11-16).

The structure does not appear to be governed here by the utterances themselves. The heavenly excitement is not reduced to the order of literary form. Yet the structure, as a whole, is perfect, and the utterances are significantly marked by being alternated with prostration and worship : first, of the Elders; and then of John. This seems very marked, as does also the voice of the " great multitude." (See the Structure below, on page 582).

In A and *A* we have the first and fourth utterances, while in B and *B* we have the Harlot and the Wife set in strong and severe contrast ; the smoke of the one in B, and the array and blessedness of the other in *B*.

In C and *C* we have the prostration of the worshippers. In C that of the Elders; and in *C* that of John. This is combined with an exhortation in each case : addressed in C to the servants; and in *C* to John the fellow-servant.

The four utterances themselves are arranged so that in the 1st and 4th we have the voices of many concerning the two symbolic women—the harlot and the wife; while in the 2nd and 3rd we have the voices from the Throne concerning God.

x | Much people (concerning the harlot). (*v.* -1-3-)
    y | Elders and *Zōa* (worship of God). (*v.* 4)
    y | Voice from the Throne (praise of God). (*v.* 5)
x | Great multitude (concerning the wife). (*v.* -6-7)

It will be seen that in the two centre members we have the Throne and God for their subject. In the former we have the worship of God (*v.* 4); and in the latter the praise of God (*v.* 5). In the former, the Elders and *Zōa* fall down before the Throne; in the latter, the Voice comes out of the Throne.

In the first and fourth members (for these last four utterances are arranged as an Introversion) we have the correspondence of the " much people " of *v.* 1; and the " great multitude " of *v.* 6. We have also the vivid contrast between the destruction of the Harlot and the Blessedness of the Wife.

This beautiful Structure shows us the importance of the subject which is to be set before us in this chapter; and the final Heavenly Utterances we are about to hear reveal to us the solemnity of the final judgments which are afterwards to be described.

All is perfect; for all is Divine. The utterances close up the Divine communications; and the five concluding judgments close up the great Conflict, which began in Gen. iii. 15, and ends in Rev. xx.

The following is the structure of the whole of the member P. (page 579), xix. 1-10, containing the last four Heavenly Utterances :—

P. (page 579), xix. 1-10.   *The Final Heavenly Utterances*

P | A | a | xix. 1-.   The Voice of the great multitude
    b | d | -1.   Hallelujah. } (1st Utterance)
       e | 2, 3-.   Reason.
      B | -3.   The smoke and destruction of the Harlot
        C | f | 4.   Prostration of the Elders (2nd Utterance)
           g | 5.   Exhortation from the Throne (3rd Utterance)
             to the servants of God (Pos.)

A | *a* | xix. 6-.   The Voice of the great multitude
    b | *d* | -6-7. Hallelujah. } (4th Utterance)
       e | 7.   Reason.
      B | 8, 9-.   The array and blessedness of the Wife
        C | *f* | -9, 10-.   Prostration of John
           g | -10.   Exhortation of Angel to John, his fellow
             servant (Neg.)

a. (page 582). xix. 1-.   *The Voice of the great Multitude*

1-. *After these things I heard as it were† a loud
voice of a great multitude in heaven, saying,]   This
puts us on sure ground by notifying us that the Vision
has returned again to, and is seen for the seventh and
last time, " in Heaven."   The voices which we are to
listen to, and the words which we are to hear will prepare us for, and explain to us, all that is about to take
place.   Babylon had been destroyed, and the injunction
had just gone forth, " Rejoice over her, O heaven "
(xviii. 20).   Here we have the obedience to the command, and all heaven rejoices.   Babylon's inhabitants
had   cried   " Alas!   alas! "   " Woe!   woe! "   Her
merchants wailed and mourned because their market
was gone.   Now all heaven rejoices because deliverance
had come ; and they cry " Hallelujah . . . Hallelujah."

b. (page 582). xix. -1.   *The First Utterance*

" Hallelujah ! the Salvation, and‡ the
glory, and the power of§ our God are
come "].

The ascription is threefold, and not fourfold, if we
omit " and the honour " with all the best and oldest
manuscripts.   The utterance is elliptical, for there is no
verb.   A verb, therefore, must be supplied.   The RV. and
Alford supply " belong to." but this hardly agrees with

* G.L.T.Tr.A. WH. and RV. omit καί (*kai*) *and.*

† The same authorities add ὡς (*hōs*) *as it were.*

‡ G.L.T.Tr.A. WH. and RV. omit καὶ ἡ τιμή (*kai hē timē*) *and the
honour.*

§ G.L.T.Tr.A. WH. & RV. read τοῦ θεοῦ ἡμῶν (*tou theou hēmōn*).
at our God, instead of κυρίῳ τῷ θεῷ ἡμῶν (*kyriō tō theō hēmōn*) *tὸ
the Lord our God.*

their revised reading; otherwise we might supply *be ascribed to.* It seems almost better to leave the words as they stand above, and add, at the end, " are come." For this is what the utterance of the great multitude celebrates, in the *reason*, which is immediately added.

This is the first occurrence of the word Hallelujah in the New Testament. It is a compound Hebrew word הַלְלוּ־יָהּ (*hallelu-jah*) *praise-ye Jah.* It occurs altogether *twenty-eight* times in the Old and New Testaments,* viz., 24 in the Old Testament, and *four* in the New Testament.

The Greek spelling in the New Testament is ἀλληλούϊα *allēlouia*; and the word is left untranslated. In the Old Testament the word is always translated " praise ye the LORD" Six times it is given in the margin, as in the Hebrew, *Hallelujah* (Ps. cxi. 1; cxii. 1; cxiii. 1; cxlvi. 1; cxlviii. 1; cl. 1). In the RV. it is translated " praise ye the LORD," and given always as *Hallelujah* in the margin, except once (cxxxv. 3). In the New Testament the Revisers do not translate it, but give it in the Text with the Hebrew spelling, "Hallelujah."

The first occurrence of the word Hallelujah in the Old Testament corresponds in a marked manner with its first occurrence in the New Testament. We first find it in Ps. civ. 35.

---

* Viz. : in seven Psalms, once each : civ. 35; cv. 45; cxi. 1; cxii. 1; cxv. 18; cxvi. 19; cxvii. 2. In seven Psalms, twice each ; cvi. 1, 48; cxiii. 1, 9; cxlvi. 1, 10; cxlvii. 1, 20; cxlviii. 1, 14; cxlix. 1, 9; cl. 1, 6. In one Psalm three times, cxxxv. 1, 3, 21. Making *twenty-four* times in all, or twice *twelve*, the double of divine *government* in the earth. If we add the *four* in Revelation (xix. 1, 3, 4, 6) we have 28 times, or *four* times *seven* : *i.e.*, spiritual perfection with regard to the earth.

" Let the sinners be consumed out of the earth,
And let the wicked be no more.
Bless thou the Lord, O my soul.
Hallelujah."

So here, in Rev. xix. 1. The utterance begins and ends with the word " Hallelujah " ; and Jah is praised for a similar reason, for at length is come the salvation and the glory and the power of God, manifested in the judgment of chap. xviii., and in xix. 11-16, when the sinners will be consumed out of the earth, and the wicked will be no more and when God's People will be avenged.

The utterance, beginning (*v.* 1) and ending (*v.* 3) with the same word, is the Figure *Epanadiplosis*, which emphasises the statement, marking it off as being as complete as it is important.

Yes ! it will have at length come. Salvation, with complete and final deliverance from Satan's usurpation in the earth.

What the people of the earth *lament* over, the great multitude in heaven *rejoice* over. While they said " Alas ! alas ! " or " Woe ! woe ! " these say " Hallelujah ! . . . Hallelujah ! " So opposite is Heaven's estimate of the things of this world. It is thanksgiving for vengeance and avengement. It belongs, therefore, to the coming dispensation of judgment, and not to the present dispensation of grace.

The church says " Hallelujah " now on earth (though, alas ! it has become a common, not to say an almost unmeaning expletive, just as we say " hear, hear," to the words of mere mortals). Here, and in the Bible the word is associated with the most terrible judgments of

God on the enemies of Himself and His people ; and it is the shout of praise for complete avengement.

e. (page 582). xix. 2, 3-.   *The Reason*

2. **"for true and righteous are His judgments ; for He hath judged the great
harlot, which did corrupt the earth
with her fornication, and He hath
avenged the blood of His servants at
her hand."**

3-. **And a second time they say** (*Greek*, have said),
" Hallelujah."]

So that the special subject which moves all heaven to praise is that, judgment on Babylon is at length accomplished, and the blood of all the saints of God avenged.

The reference here is to the " song of Moses " (Deut. xxxii. 43).

> " Rejoice, oh ye nations, with His people ;
> For he will avenge the blood of his servants,
> And will render vengeance to His adversaries,
> And will be merciful to His land,
> And to His people."

The cry had been (Rev. vi. 10) : " How long, dost thou not, O Sovereign Lord, holy and true, judge and avenge our blood on the dwellers on the earth ? "

The Songs, and Praises, and Rejoicings are all uttered because at length this cry has been answered, and this judgment has come.

B. (page 582), xix. -3.   *The Smoke, and Destruction of the
Great Harlot*

-3. **And her smoke goeth up for ever and ever.**] The destruction of the Great Harlot is set in contrast (by the structure) with verses 8 and 9 (see page 582), where (in

B) we have the array and blessedness of the wife).   It
is like the destruction of Sodom and Gomorrah, which
suffered "the vengeance of eternal fire."   There are
eternal fires which are unquenchable.   This is the fire
which will destroy Babylon at last.   It is indicated in
chap. xiv. 11 (see xviii. 9).

f. (page 582). xix. 4.   *The Prostration of the Elders : and
Second Utterance*

**4. And the four and twenty elders and the four
Zōa fell down and worshipped God, who sitteth upon
the throne, saying,**

"Amen: Hallelujah ! "]

The elders now appear again.   We have seen, above (on
chap. v. 9, 10), that they are not the church nor are
they men, nor are they redeemed ; though they speak
of redemption. This is the last time they are mentioned.   They come before us when the Throne is set for
judgment.   They appear no more after that judgment
has been accomplished.   They merely but significantly
say "Amen,"—acquiescing in all that has been done ;
" Hallelujah "—praising Jehovah that avengement is at
length completed.   Their prostration is set in correspondence with the prostration of John in "*f*," verse 10 ;
and, as an exhortation is there given to John the fellow-
servant, so here, to the servants of God, is given the

g. (page 582), xix. 5.   *Exhortation to Praise*

**5. And a voice came forth from the throne, say-
ing,**

**"Give praise to our God, all ye His
servants** (Ps. cxxxiv. 1) ;
**And ye that fear Him, both small and
great** (Ps. cxv. 13).]

Here we have two distinct references to the Psalms, which show that the interpretation to be put on these words must be in connection with God's earthly People; for this is the People and the Time to which the Psalm refers. God's judgments are still the subjects of praise. We are not told from whom the Voice comes; only that it comes from the place of authority. Of the coming King, when in His humiliation, it was prophesied (Ps. xxii. 22, 23, 25) :—

> "I will declare thy name unto my brethren:
>> In the midst of the congregation will I praise thee.
> Ye that fear the LORD, praise him;
> All ye of the seed of Jaccb, glorify him;
> And fear him, all ye of the seed of Israel."

The reason is given in verses 27, 28 :

> "For the kingdom is the LORD's;
> And He is the governor among the nations."

Now will have come the moment of the fulfilment of Matt. v. 10, 12. "Blessed are those which are persecuted for righteousness' sake; for *theirs is the kingdom of heaven.*" "*Rejoice and be exceeding glad,* for great is your reward in heaven."

It can hardly be the voice of Christ, for He does not thus associate Himself with us in this relationship. On the contrary, He distinguishes Himself from His people, and says, "*My* Father and *your* Father; *my* God and *your* God" (John xx. 17). See Heb. ii. 11.

a. (page 582), xix. 6, 7. *The Voice of the great Multitude and the Fourth Utterance*

6, 7. And I heard as it were the voice of a great multitude, and as it were the voice of many waters,

and as it were the voice of many thunders, saying,
  "Hallelujah !
  For the Lord our* God, the omnipotent,
     reigneth.
  Let us rejoice and be exceeding glad,
  And give the glory unto Him :
  For the marriage of the Lamb is come.
  And his wife hath made herself ready."]

We can never have a clear understanding of this heavenly utterance if we introduce the Church of the Pauline Epistles, *i.e.*, the Great Mystery, here.

One would have thought it quite unnecessary to make this statement, considering that we have so many references to Israel, or Israel's elect remnant, in the Old Testament. And these, quite irrespective of the Church of God which is the subject of subsequent revelation.

As to the relationship of God with Israel, it is the *resumption* of a former relationship. The Old Testament Scriptures speak of the marriage between the Lord and His People again and again. As to the Church of God, the New Testament Scriptures state, as clearly as possible, that it was "hid in God." Mark, it does not say, hid in the Scriptures, but "hid in God," Himself. It is impossible, therefore, that the Mystery, or the Church of God, can be spoken of or revealed in the Old Testament.

Did pious Jews think of the Church of God when they read in Isa. liv. 5-8 ?

  " Thy Maker is thy husband ;
    The LORD of hosts is his name,
    And thy Redeemer the Holy One of Israel.

---

* G.T.Tr. WHb. and RV. add ὑμῶν (*hēmōn*) *our*.

The God of the whole earth shall he be called.
For the Lord hath called thee as a woman for-
saken and grieved in spirit,
And a wife of youth, when thou was refused, saith
thy God.
For a small moment have I forsaken thee :
But with great mercies will I gather thee.
In a little wrath I hid my face from thee,
But with everlasting kindness will I have mercy on
thee, saith the Lord, thy Redeemer."

(Isa. liv. 5-8).

Did they understand the Church when they read in
Isa. lxii. 4, 5 ?

" Thou shalt no more be termed Forsaken,
Neither shall thy land be any more termed Deso-
late :
But thou shalt be called Hephzibah (i.e., *my delight
is in her*),
And thy land Beulah (i.e., *married*).
For the Lord delighteth in thee,
And thy land shall be married.
For as a young man marrieth a virgin,
So shall thy sons possess* thee ;
And as the bridegroom rejoiceth over the bride,
So shall thy God rejoice over thee."

(Isa. lxii. 4, 5).

What did they understand, as they read Hosea ii. 16,
and Jer. iii. 14 ?

" It shall be at that day, saith the Lord, that thou
shalt call me Ishi (i.e., *my husband*).
And shalt no more call me Baali (i.e., *my lord*) . . .

---

* This is the meaning of the word. " Marry " is only a secondary
or derivative meaning, as expressive of the fact.

And I will betroth thee unto me for ever ; . . .
I will betroth thee unto me in faithfulness,
And thou shalt know the Lord."

(Hosea ii. 16, 19).

" Turn, O backsliding children, saith the LORD,
For I am married unto you."

(Jeremiah iii. 14).

This marriage is referred to in Isa. iv. 5.   When
Jehovah shall have purged away the filth of the
daughters of Zion, it is added : ·"beyond all this glory
there shall be the *Chuppah*" : *i.e.*, the marriage or bridal
canopy mentioned elsewhere only in Ps. xix. 5, and
Joel ii. 16 ; and referring to Isa. lxii. (quoted above).
The *chuppah* is the *bridal canopy* beneath which Jewish
nuptial ceremonies are performed to this day.

Why are we to do away with all these references by
interpreting them in a way in which *the original readers
could never have understood them ?*   Either they must have
been wrong in understanding them of Israel, or we must
be wrong in interpreting them of the Church of God.
Both cannot be right.

The." wife " is earthly (xix.) : the " Bride " is heavenly
(xxi.).

The marriage of the one is on earth (though rejoiced
over in heaven beforehand), and is consummated on
earth for 1,000 years.   All earthly or mortal relationships must run out by expiration along with the earth,
before the other, the heavenly relationships, are entered
upon.   Thus, understanding Rev. xix. of Israel, and
xxi. of the Elect Remnant, there is neither Polygamy
on the one hand, nor Divorce on the other.

It is important to observe the various callings.
(1) There is the " earthly calling," which all Israel

shares—the Wife, γυνή (gunē), Rev. xix. (" The sand," of Gen. xiii. 16) ;

(2) there is the "heavenly calling" of an elect remnant of Israel—the Bride, νύμφη (numphē), Rev. xxi. 9 (" The stars," of Gen. xv. 5) ; and

(3) there is the distinct calling of the Church of God —which is " The Christ " (i.e., the Mystery).

These *three* distinct callings have their separate standings; their different hopes, different promises, and different destinies.

We must rightly divide these " callings," or we shall get only confusion.

How, for example, can it be said of the Church that she "hath made herself ready." As members of the Body of Christ we are already "made meet" (Col. i. 12); God Himself hath made us meet : and even now we are "complete in Him" (Col. ii. 10); and are "perfect in Christ Jesus" (Col. i. 28) ; "accepted in the Beloved" (Eph. i. 6).

We can never be more "ready" than He Himself hath made us. The language in Rev. xix. 7 is wholly foreign to the perfect standing of the church, which is in grace.

The next verse also shows this very clearly, where we have

B. (page 582), xix. 8, 9. *The array and Blessedness of the Wife.*

8. **And it was given to her that she should be arrayed in fine linen raiment, bright and pure : for the fine linen raiment is the righteous** awards **of the saints.**] The word rendered " righteousness " is not δικαιοσύνη (dikaiosunē), the state or quality or condition of righteousness; but it is δικαίωμα (dikaiōma), a *righteous act.*

It is in the plural here, and denotes the righteousness of the things indicated by the context.

In Luke i. 6 it is righteous *ordinance*.
Rom. i. 32, righteous *sentence*.
 ii. 26, righteous *requirement* of the Law.
 v. 16, righteous *acquittal*.
 v. 18, righteous *work*.
 viii. 4, righteous *requirement*.
Heb. ix. 1, 10, righteous *ordinances*.
Rev. xv. 4, righteous *sentence*,

and *here* in Rev. xix. 8, it denotes the righteous *awards*, The RV. and Rotherham put "righteous acts." But "acts" are not "given." Whatever the word refers to, here, is said to be "given to her." And what was given was given by way of reward, or better, as *awards*. Alford and Tregellis render it "righteousness," as in the AV. Alford says "it is *their own*,* inherent, not imputed." The Scripture here declares it was theirs because it was "given." They would say, we are sure in the words of Isa. lxiv. 6: "All our righteousnesses are as filthy rags." This is, and ever will be, the common confession of all justified ones. It cannot be, as many hold, that it is their own inherent righteousness in men of any dispensation; for the universal verdict was, and is, "there is none righteous, no not one."

The same angel goes on to describe, not merely the array of the Bride, but the blessedness of those who shall be called to the marriage.

9-. **And he saith to me, Write, " Blessed are they that are called unto the marriage supper of the**

---

* Alford's italics.

Lamb."] Thus we not only have the Wife; but as in Ps. xlv. 14, "the virgins, her companions"; and also those who are the invited guests. As "star differeth from another star in glory" (1 Cor. xv. 41), so the people in glory differ in ranks and orders and degrees; but all, all-glorious, in the "many mansions."

Just as in an earthly family there are the Husband, the Wife, the Children, the Relatives, the Friends, the Visitors, and the Servants, yet all in the same mansion and all one household; so in the glory there will be the Christ and the Church which is His Body; the Lamb and the Lamb's wife; the "friends of the Bridegroom" (John iii. 29); the "virgins" that be the Bride's "companions" (Ps. xlv.14); those who are "called" to the marriage supper; the "servants"; the great multitude of Rev. vii.; the 144,000 of sealed ones; and of all, it is true, that they are "blessed." For the angel goes on at once to announce this in the most solemn and formal manner, which calls forth the adoration of John.

f. (page 582), xix. -9, 10-. *The Prostration of John*

-9. **And he saith to me, " These are the true words of God."**] The angel is the speaker of xvii. 1. Thrice is the assurance given (xix. 10; xxi. 5; xxii. 6), showing that it refers to the immediate context.

10-. **And I fell down before his feet to worship him.**] Twenty-four times is the word προσκυνέω (*proskuneō*) used in the Apocalypse, and we ought, before this, to have pointed out that when followed by the *Accusative* case it means merely *to do homage* or *obeisance* to another, as from man to man. When used with the

Dative case it means to *worship with Divine honour.**
This shows that John, here, was going to give the
angel Divine worship, which was, of course, at once
forbidden, as it is also in xxii. 8.

g. (page 582), xix. -10. *Exhortation of the Angel to John*

-10. **And he saith to me " See** thou do it **not: I am a
fellow-servant with thee, and with thy brethren that
hold the testimony of Jesus: Worship God: for the
testimony of Jesus is the spirit of prophecy."**] What
the angel says is, *I am a servant as well as thou*, and
therefore I cannot receive the worship which is due only
to God.   Both the angel and John are sent on the same
business, are engaged in the same matters, and are
witnesses of the same truth: the one, therefore, cannot
worship the other.   Both were fellow-servants of John's
brethren.   Both were engaged in the same work.   The
angel was explaining and John was writing, so that
John's brethren might learn and know these true
sayings of God.   We cannot determine whether " the
testimony of Jesus " should be taken *objectively* as testimony *concerning* Jesus; or *subjectively* of testimony borne
or sent by Him: as in i. 1.   Probably both are true,
and it is often better to take the inclusive meaning
All prophecy concerns in some way the Lord Jesus

* When Divine worship is offered to God it is always followed by
the *Dative* case: iv. 10; v. 14; vii. 11; xi. 16; xiv. 7; xix. 4, 10
(twice); xxii. 9.

This shows that Divine worship will be actually offered to the
Beast (xiii. 4 twice, 15; xvi. 2; xix. 20): though the *Accusative* case is
also used of the worship of the Beast (ix. 20; xiii. 8, 12; xiv. 9, 11;
xx. 4).

In the other passages where *proskuneō* occurs the case is not shown
on account of some other part of speech being used with the verb.

Christ. He is the spirit of it : yea, the sum and the substance of it. He Himself is *the* prophet. He bore His prophetic testimony concerning these things when on earth, in the Parables of the Kingdom, the Marriage Supper, and in the last great Prophetic discourse concerning the Great Tribulation : and now it is given to Him to show unto His servants the things which are yet to come to pass.

Q. (page 579). xix. 11-16.   *The Final Heavenly Actions*

The Seventh (and last) Vision in heaven is divided, as we have seen (page 579) into two parts, the former consisting of *Utterances* only ; and the latter of *Actions.* In xix. 1-16 we have the *Utterances*, which we have been considering.   In xix. 11-16 we have the *Actions* described.   They are arranged as follows :—

Q. (page 579), xix. 11-16.   *The Final Heavenly Actions*

Q | C | 11.   The Rider on the white horse
     D | 12, 13.   His description
  C | 14.   His followers : " the armies of heaven "
     D | 15, 16.   His further description

C. (see above), xix. 11.   *The White Horse and his Rider*

11.   **And I saw the heaven opened, and behold a white horse ; and he that sat thereon was called Faithful and True ; and in righteousness He doth judge and make war**]   Here, at length, we have the actual Apocalypse of the Messiah. We see him coming forth in all His power and glory. He is not named, but He is described by those attributes which suit His action.   He is " Faithful " to all the promises He has

made; " True " to execute all the judgments He has threatened. The " war " which He will make is righteous. The similarity of this white horse and his rider has led many interpreters to identify him with the one mentioned in chap. vi. 2. But there is no necessity for this. There is a likeness ; but there is a *contrast,* also. That was the false Christ ; this is the true Christ. The former was neither faithful nor true ; the latter is both. The one will go forth in order to conquer and subdue all to himself ; the other will go forth to judge and make war upon the former in righteousness. There is neither judgment nor making war in the rider of vi. 2 : his object is simply to overcome, conquer and subdue. But here it is judgment ; and an aggressive war which shall accomplish that judgment.

Many stumble at the White Horse and his rider here : and ask, in amazement, whether we really believe it ? We answer, Yes ! We believe it, just as we believe the prophecy in Zechariah ix. 9, about the coming of that same Blessed One riding upon an ass, and the fulfilment of that prophecy in Matt. xxi. 4-11.

The Jews probably stumbled at the Prophecy of Zechariah in the same manner, as being improbable. But all is easy to faith.

It is as easy to believe one prophecy as the other, and we believe both.

Then, He came in humiliation. Now, He will come in glory, even as Psalm xlv. 3-6 testifies.

" Gird thy sword upon thy thigh, O most mighty,
   [*And gird thyself*] with glory and majesty,
   And in thy majesty ride prosperously because of
      truth and meekness and righteousness ;

And thy right hand shall teach thee terrible things..
Thy throne, O God, is for ever and ever;
The sceptre of thy kingdom is a right sceptre."

All this stands in connection with His marriage
with His wife as it does here, in Rev. xix.

The prophecy in Zechariah ix. takes in both Comings.
The coming to Jerusalem in humility (*v.* 9), and the
judgment which he will execute at His second Coming;
for, the next (the 10th) verse goes on to say :—

" And I will cut off the chariot from Ephraim,
And the horse from Jerusalem,
And the battle bow shall be cut off:
And He shall speak peace unto the heathen;
And his dominion shall be from sea even to sea,
And from the river even unto the ends of the earth."

D. (page 596). xix. 12, 13. *His Description*

12. **And His eyes** were **as a flame of fire, and upon
His head** were **many diadems: and He had a name
written, that no one knew, but** He **Himself.** (13) **And
He was arrayed with a garment dyed***(or stained) **with
blood; and his name is called " The Word of God "**].
The reference to blood here is clearly to Isa. lxiii. 1-6,
where this same mighty conqueror is seen coming up
from Edom : his garments being stained with the blood
of his enemies. We have two Questions with their
Answers :

Qu.—" Who is this that cometh from Edom
With dyed garments from Bozrah?
This that is glorious in his apparel,
Travelling in the greatness of his strength?

---

* T. WH. and RV. read *sprinkled.* But the reading is doubtful and
the authorities are divided.

Ans.—I that speak in righteousness,
    [*I that am*] mighty to save.
Qu.—Wherefore art thou red in thine apparel,
    And thy garments like him that treadeth in the
        winefat ?
Ans.—I have trodden the wine-press alone ;
    And of the people there was none with me :
    For I will tread them in mine anger,
    And trample them with my fury ;
    And their blood shall be sprinkled on my
        garments,
    And I will stain all my raiment.
    For the day of vengeance s in mine heart,
    And the year of my redeemed is come.
    And I looked, and there was none to help ;
    And I wondered that there was none to uphold :
    Therefore mine own arm brought salvation
        unto me ;
    And my fury, it upheld me.
    And I will tread down the people in mine
        anger,
    And make them drunk with my fury,
    And I will bring down their strength to the
        earth."

The whole scene is one of judgment and of vengeance (compare Is. ix. 5). How any could ever understand this as referring to, or foretelling, the Redeemer's sufferings in grace, we cannot imagine. No! This is the language of the Gospels, where the Lord, referring to this very judgment scene, exclaims, "Those mine enemies, who would not that I should reign over them, bring them hither and slay them before me " (Luke xix. 27). The Rider on the white horse is not the Gracious

Saviour in His work of saving His people from their sins ; but the Righteous Judge who avenges them on their enemies.

His name is called " the Word of God." This connects Him with His attribute of Creator (Ps. xxxiii. 6) ; with the Eternal One (John i. 1, 2) ; and with the Incarnate One (John i. 14).

He leads the Armies of Heaven, and these, in the Structure above, are set in correspondence with Himself as coming forth from Heaven. (Compare C. and *C.*, page 596).

C. (page 596), xix. 14. *His followers. The Armies of Heaven*

14. **And the armies which*** are **in heaven followed him upon white horses, clothed in fine linen, white** and **pure**] " Behold, the Lord cometh with ten thousands of His saints (or holy ones) to execute judgment upon all " (Jude 14, 15). This was the primitive subject of prophecy ; and this is the spirit of its testimony concerning Jesus. There is no need to introduce the Church here. It will be with Christ. For ever united to its glorious Head, not separated from Him into " Armies." These are angelic hosts who are accustomed to " make war " (see chap. xii.), and fight against Satan and his hosts.

All here is a grand reality. These armies are **no** mere symbols. Horses and chariots of fire were seen by Elisha's servant at Dothan when his eyes were " opened." Horses of fire took Elijah into heaven. These were real ; and what they accomplished was real also. It is neither necessary nor wise to explain away any portion of God's Word. Neither is it safe : **for**

---

* So G.L.Tr. Ab. WH. and RV.

there are many things in heaven and earth which have never entered into man's imagination; and it is childish and absurd to measure and judge of everything by our own limited experience. Things are not unreal, unlikely, or impossible merely because we have never seen them. It is both wiser and safer to believe God. If any ask, "Do you then believe that these are real armies and real horses?" we answer, Most certainly! The Word of God declares it in language that does not admit of Figures of Speech.

For our part, we find it easier and happier to accept those statements in all simplicity; assured that it is much more pleasing in God's sight, than to explain away His revelation merely because some things are different from anything we happen to have heard of before.

These Angelic armies take their place as opposed to the Satanic armies.

We have

Anti-Christ against Christ.

Angels against angels.

Superhuman beings against glorified saints.

Mortals against mortals.

The whole kingdom of God opposed to the whole kingdom of Satan.

D. (page 596), xix. 15, 16. *Further Description of Messiah*

15. **And out of His mouth proceedeth a sharp sword** (see i. 16; ii. 12, 16), **that with it** (as invested with it) **He should smite the nations: and He shall rule them with a rod of iron: and He treadeth the winepress of the fierceness** * **of the wrath of God the**

---

* G.L.T.Tr.A. WH. and RV. omit "and."

Almighty. (16) **And He hath upon His vesture and on His thigh a name written, "KING OF KINGS AND LORD OF LORDS."**] All judgment is committed unto Him; and "by the breath of His lips He shall slay the Wicked One." Chap. xvi. has already prepared us for the conflict. Chap. xvii. has shown us the enemy and his allies. Chap. xviii. gave us details of the judgment as regards "Babylon the great." But now we have, at length, the final fulfilment of the second Psalm. The nations rage and are smitten. The treading of this winepress had been foreshown in chap. xiv. 19, 20. The Gentiles at last have all power taken from them. "The times of the Gentiles" will have reached their end. For, all government will then be at length centred, and settled for ever, in "the Prince of the Kings of the Earth," "the King of Kings and Lord of Lords."

19

THE SEVENTH VISION "ON EARTH"
(19:17—20:15)

The Final Five Judgments

We must get a complete view of these in order to embrace them all and view them as a whole.

The Structure shows their true sequence :*

ℭ⁷. (page 118), xix. 17—xx. 15. The Seventh (and last) Vision "On Earth"

The Final Five Judgments

ℭ⁷ | A¹ | xix. 17-21. MEN. The Judgment of the Beast and the False Prophet

B¹ | xx. 1-3. SATAN. The Judgment of Satan (Before the Millennium)

A² | xx. 4-6. MEN. The Judgment of the over-comers. The "rest of the dead" left for Judgment

B² | xx. 7-10. SATAN. The Judgment of Satan (After the Millennium)

A³ | xx. 11-15. MEN. The Judgment of the Great White Throne

From this Structure, we see that these judgments are arranged alternately, as they affect *Men* and *Satan*: thus completing the 7th Seal, the 7th Trumpet, and

---

*For another Structure of this Vision, see page 644. Both are equally correct.

the 7th Vial, finishing the " mystery " or secret purpose of God concerning Satan and Man; Jew and Gentile; Heaven and Earth.

These judgments embrace the setting right of what is wrong; the setting up of what is good; and the putting down and final destruction of all that is evil.

Each of these five Scriptures has its own peculiar Structure, which we propose to give in their due order.

The following is the Structure of

THE FIRST JUDGMENT

A¹. (page 603), xix. 17-21. *The Judgment of the Beast and the False Prophet*

A¹ | C | 17-. The Angel in the Sun
    | D | -17, 18. The Angel's proclamation
    | C | 19. The Beast and his Confederacy on Earth
    | D | 20, 21. Fulfilment of the Angel's cry

C. (see above), xix. 17-. *The Angel in the Sun*

17-. **And I saw one—an angel—standing in the Sun;**] An angel proclaimed the fall of Babylon, and now an angel proclaims the destruction of the Beast and his confederacy. From this grand and exalted position, unreachable by any earth-born being, goes forth the proclamation, and reaches all the earth.

D. (see above), xix. -17, 18. *The Angel's Proclamation*

-17. **And he cried with a loud voice, saying to all the fowls that fly in mid-heaven,**
    " Come, be gathered* together unto

---

* G.L.T.Tr. WH. and RV. read $\sigma\upsilon\nu\acute{\alpha}\chi\theta\eta\tau\epsilon$ (*sunachthēte*) *be gathered together*, instead of $\kappa\alpha\grave{\iota}$ $\sigma\upsilon\nu\acute{\alpha}\gamma\epsilon\sigma\theta\epsilon$ (*sunagesthe*) *and gather yourselves together*.

God's great supper ;* (18) **that ye may
eat** the **flesh of kings, and** the **flesh of
chief-captains, and** the **flesh of mighty
men, and** the **flesh of horses, and
of them that sit thereon, and the
flesh of all, both free and bond,
both small and great."**]

So Ezekiel had been told to cry, chap. xxxix. 17-22,
where the cry is made concerning this or a subsequent†
period, when the Prince of Rosh (Russia) and Meshech
(Moscow) and Tubal (Tobolsk) will come against Israel
in the days of the Antichrist.

The scene in Rev. xix. -17,18 is occupied with the Beast
and the False Prophet and their confederacy. Beasts of
the earth are not summoned here, as they are in Ezekiel;
for this cry goes forth from the sun, and is to be immediately and universally obeyed. This could be done only
by flying creatures. The feast in Ezekiel is more local,
and hence the beasts of the earth are summoned.

The issue of this battle is never in any doubt. It is
fore-announced. The description is yet to be recorded.
The call to devour the carcases of the slain is given
before the battle has begun. The marriage supper of
the Lamb has just been celebrated in heaven, and now

---

* G.L.T.Tr.A. WH. and RV. read τὸ μέγα τοῦ (*to mega tou*),
the great supper of, instead of τοῦ μεγάλου (*tou magalou*) *of the great.*

† We say "subsequent" to this, for (1) it comes on a Land and
people brought back (Ezek. xxxviii. 8). (2) It finds them dwelling
safely. (3) They dwell in unwalled Towns (*v.* 11). (4) They have
been gathered out, and have got cattle and goods (*v.* 12). (5) God
calls it "My Land" (*v.* 16). (6) They get no nearer than "the
Mountains of Israel" (xxxix. 4). (7) It will take seven months to
destroy their *debris* (*v.* 12).

the great supper of God is furnished for the fowls of heaven and the beasts of prey on the earth.

C. (page 604), xix. 19.   *The Beast and his Confederacy*

19. **And I saw the Beast, and the kings of the earth, and their armies, gathered together to make war with Him that sitteth on the horse, and with His army.**] Unclean spirits gather the kings of the earth to fight in xvi. 12-16.   A holy angel summons the birds to devour them.   "The kings of the earth," who opposed the Beast, now unite with him to fight against God.   "Strong delusion" is upon them now, "that they should believe the lie, that they all might be damned. . ." (2 Thess. ii. 9-12).   Hence : with one accord, this vast confederacy, having subdued the earth, now prepares to resist all heaven.   " The heathen rage, and the people imagine a vain thing.   The kings of the earth set themselves, and the rulers take counsel to-gether against the LORD and against His anointed." (Ps. ii. 1-3).   Here we see them gathered together to complete their subjugation of the earth and shut out its rightful owner.

But the issue is not kept long in suspense.

D. (page 604), xix. 20, 21. *The fulfilment of the angel's cry*

20. **And the Beast was taken, and with him the False Prophet who wrought the miracles before him** (xiii. 11-17), **with which he deceived those that had received the mark of the Beast, and those who wor-shipped his image. These two were cast alive into the lake of fire which burneth with brimstone. (21) And the rest were killed with the sword of him that**

sitteth upon the horse, which sword proceedeth out
of his mouth: And all the birds were satiated with
their flesh.] The Beast and the False prophet therefore are no mere systems, no mere companies of men.
They are superhuman, but they are as truly men as Judas
and Mahomet were men. They will be cast "alive"
into the lake of fire. If these be not individual beings,
then language is useless for the purposes of revelation.

They are real persons, as are those who will receive
the mark of the Beast, and worship his image. They
receive their punishment together. They cannot be
slain, now, as mortals.

They will have come up from the Abyss; and they
are still found alive in the lake of fire at the close of the
thousand years (xx. 10). The armies being mortals are
slain; and their dead bodies are eaten by the fowls of
the air. There are none to bury them.

Thus ends the first of these final five judgments.

THE SECOND JUDGMENT

The outcome of the first of these final five judgments
is the binding of Satan. The judgment of the Beast
and the False Prophet and their Confederacy is not
enough. He who has planned all, and used all for the
accomplishment of his purposes, must now be dealt with.
The chief instigator of all the evil must now be de-
prived of all further opportunity of attempting to
frustrate the counsels and purposes of God. He has
been cast out of heaven: he must now be cast out of
the earth.

The structure of the passage which describes his
judgment is as follows:—

B¹. (page 603), xx. 1-3. *The Judgment of Satan.*

(*Before the Millennium*)

```
B¹ │ E¹ │ a¹ │ xx. 1, 2-.   The binding of Satan.  (The
   │    │    │ Key and the Chain )
   │    │ b¹ │ xx. -2.   Time.  (1,000 years )
   │    │
   │ E² │ a² │ xx. 3-.   Satan bound.  (The Abyss and
   │    │    │ the Sealing )
   │    │ b² │ xx.- 3-.   Time.  (1,000 years )
   │    │
   │ E³ │ a³ │ xx. -3-.   The loosing of Satan.
   │    │ b³ │ xx. -3.   Time.  (" a little season ")
```

This Structure consists of three pairs. The first of each pair has to do with Satan and his binding ; and the second with its duration.

xx. 1. **And I saw an angel descending out of heaven, having the key of the Abyss, and a great chain in his hand. (2) And he laid hold of the dragon,—the old serpent, which is the Devil, and Satan, and bound him a thousand years, (3) and cast him into the Abyss, and shut him up, and set a seal upon him, that he should not deceive the nations any longer, until the thousand years be completed : Afterward he must be loosed a little season.]** Who this angel is does not concern us. If it did, we should have been told. Speculation here is worse than useless. It is enough for us to know that it will indeed be a mighty angel to accomplish this business. Satan is a personality ; a spirit-being. He can be seized, and will be bound ; just as his subordinate angels have already been, and are now reserved for future judgment under " chains of darkness " and " everlasting chains " (2 Pet.

ii. 4. Jude 6). There are chains that can bind flesh and blood; and there are chains that can bind spirits. We are asked, with a triumphant air: " Do you really believe Satan will be bound with an iron chain ? " Our answer is, that there is not a word said about an " iron chain " ! Our imagination and knowledge are so limited, that when God says " a great chain," we can think only of an "iron " chain, because the chains that we know of are mostly iron. But we are having great and wondrous facts and realities revealed to us here; and it behoves us to believe, where we cannot understand. It becomes us, as the recipients of such a revelation, to humbly receive it, and not to criticise it.

The grand reality is, that Satan will one day be "bound"; and he will be bound with something that can bind him. He will be cast into the Abyss; and, in spite of his being a spirit-being, he will not be able to get out, or " walk about " (1 Pet. v. 8) as before. When this blessed fact is revealed to us, it is for us, not to reason about it, but to praise God for the wondrous news, and sing:

> " O what a bright and blessed world
> This groaning earth of ours will be,
> When, from its throne, the Tempter hurled,
> Shall leave it all, O Lord, for Thee ? "

That is to be our attitude. We believe that the War is literal; the taking of the Beast and the False Prophet is literal; Satan is literal, and his binding is literal. It does not say he will be bound with a steel chain, or an iron chain; but it says " a great chain." It will be a chain of Divine make, and it will be suitable for—and will effectually accomplish—its great object.

How all this can be done we do not know; nor are

we called upon to show. There are such things as Figures of Speech ; but this is not one, nor is it what commentators call " figurative language," that cannot bind anyone, except themselves and others, to their false system of interpretation. In Rev. xiv. 14, 15 we read of a "Sickle"; but Matt. xiii. 30, 39-42 shows that it denotes a grand and dread reality. So the "great chain " does here.

The Abyss is literal; as is the lake of fire. Satan is to be cast into the Abyss (from whence the Beast came, xvii. 8), for 1,000 years, when he will join the Beast and the False Prophet in the lake of fire (xx. 10).

There is another place called "*Tartarus*" (2 Pet. ii. 4) —unless Tartarus is another name for the Abyss. This is where the fallen Angels are bound (1 Pet. iii. 18, 19. 2 Pet. ii. 4. Jude 6).*

In the face of all these great, solemn, and grand realities, it is sad to notice the fanciful interpretations put upon them.

Some maintain that this binding took place at the beginning of the Christian Dispensation. In that case the Millennium was over nearly 1,000 years ago, and we call that very period " the dark ages." In that case

---

* 1 Pet. iii. 18, 19 becomes quite clear when we remember (1) that men are *never* called " spirits," and (2) that " He maketh His angels spirits." (3) That these " disobedient " spirits in verse 20 are contrasted with obedient " angels . . . made subject unto Him " in verse 22. (4) That in 2 Pet. ii. 4 we read of the " angels that sinned being cast down to *Tartarus*, and delivered . . . unto chains of darkness to be reserved unto judgment." (5) That in Jude 6 we read of the " angels which kept not their first estate," being "reserved in everlasting chains under darkness unto the judgment of the great day."

With all these Scriptures about *Angels* being bound with chains, etc., it is strange, indeed, that, in spite of the words " in prison," 1 Pet. iii. 19, "spirits" should be interpreted of *dead men*, instead of fallen angels.

also Peter was inspired to say that Satan "walketh about" (1 Pet. v. 8) on earth, while he was bound in the Abyss!

Some assert that the binding took place at the conversion of Constantine. But that was the beginning of all that has led to the corruption and apostasy of the Church.

Others hold that whenever the binding took place, Satan is bound now. Such can never read the newspapers, which teem with little else than the most awful evidences to the contrary, both of crimes in the world and of corruption in the Church.

Others maintain that the 1,000 years are not literal, but mean any prolonged period.

If the year-day theory is to be consistently held, then we have a period of at least 360,000 years during which Satan is bound.

We believe what Scripture says, and hold that Satan will be bound for 1,000 years; and that the Millennium is the period during which he is to be bound.

After the 1,000 years Satan "must be loosed a little season." The consideration of why this "must be" we will defer till we come to verse 7 (see pages 626-635). Meantime, the Structure bids us consider first the blessedness of the Millennial state on earth.

THE THIRD JUDGMENT

The third, or central judgment of the last five differs from the two that precede and follow it, in that it is a judgment of vindication and award, and not of condemnation and punishment.

Its subjects are the Overcomers: and by its Structure it is divided into six members, grouped in three pairs:

Persons alternating with the duration of *Time*, as in the previous Structure concerning Satan :—

> A⁹. (page 603), xx. 4-6. *Judgment given to the Overcomers*

A⁹ | F¹ | 4-. Persons. "And I saw thrones . . .

G¹ | -4. Time. "And they lived again .. 1,000 years

F² | 5-. Persons. "But the rest of the dead . . .

G² | -5-. Time. "Until the 1,000 years were finished"

F³ | -5, 6-. Persons. "This is the first resurrection Blessed and holy is he," etc.

G₃ | -6. Time. "And shall reign with Him 1,000 years"

> F¹. (see above), xx. 4-. *Persons*

4-. **And I saw thrones, and they sat upon them, and judgment was given unto them:]** If this refers to "the souls" mentioned in the second pair, then we have certain statements quite out of the natural order. Acts and actions are attributed to them *before* they are said to be risen again! Thrones, judges, and sentence are the subjects of this first pair; while martyrs, resurrection, and reigning are the subjects of the second pair. It seems, therefore, that we have, here, the setting-up of the tribunal to judge or vindicate those who shall have had part in the "first resurrection;" and to righteously and formally give them their position in glory. Dan. vii. is the key to this scene. In the 9th verse the word rendered "cast down" means *to set* or *place.* We see the one throne thus placed, in verse 22; while here (Rev. xx. 4) we have the placing of the other thrones, and we see those who will sit "upon them." The war of the Beast against the saints is said to prevail (Dan. vii. 21, 22) "until the Ancient of days came, and judgment was given to the saints of the Most High, and the time came that the saints possessed the kingdom." The words, "judgment was given them," must be compared with Rev. xviii. 20: "God hath judged your judgment upon her (Babylon)." So the RV.: and the AV. renders this, "God hath avenged you on her." The "judgment" here, therefore, means the right or power to exercise judgment which at length shall righteously, not only avenge the saints on their enemies, but vindicate them and award them their position in glory.

The plural, "*they* sat," must be taken as including God and Christ, and the seven angelic assessors (see Rev. i. 4 and 1 Tim. v. 21, where they are thus united, as well as in Matt. xxv. 31). "When the Son of Man shall come in his glory and all his holy angels with him, THEN shall he sit upon the throne of his glory." That throne is here seen placed for judgment immediately before the Millennium, and in connection with the "first resurrection." That throne is referred to in Joel iii. 12, Jer. iii. 17, Dan. vii. 18, 22. Then will take place, not merely the judgment and vindication of the martyred saints of the Tribulation, but that of the living nations (or Gentiles), as described in the above Scriptures.

That throne, as well as the thrones of the twelve apostles, are seen here placed for judgment according to Matt. xix. 28. Luke xxii. 30. Compare Ps. cxxii. 5. Ezek. xliii. 7. Zech. vi. 13. Isa. xxxi. 8, 9; xxxii. 1-4.

Christ will have come, not only to " make war," but to
"judge"; for, "in righteousness He doth judge and
make war" (xix. 11). If this be not the judgment of
saints and living nations, then there is no place for it at
all; for the only other judgment mentioned is that of
the great white throne after the Millennium, at the end
of this chapter. Of these final five judgments, one
is that of living nations before the Millennium, and is
connected with the first resurrection; while the other
is after the Millennium, and is connected with the
second resurrection.

The thrones are seen here placed. A tribunal is set
up, and power and authority to execute judgment, and
pronounce the sentence of vindication, and award "is
given." Upon whom? That question is now to be
answered. The words, "the souls," &c., are in the
accusative case, and the AV. and RV. supply in
italics, " I saw." But the *Ellipsis* is arbitrarily supplied.
After the giving of authority to exercise judgment,
the natural sequence of thought would be *the exercise of
it* ! So we supply

-4-. **and** [they judged, *i e.*, vindicated, xviii. 20]
those that were beheaded (*lit.*, the souls of those
who were beheaded, but see below) **on account of
the testimony of Jesus, and for the word of God,**]

" The souls of those who were beheaded " are clearly
those who had been mentioned in chap. vi. 9. They at
length enjoy their resurrection and receive their vindication there promised to them.

The expression " souls " in vi. 9 is clearly the ante-
cedent of verse 11, where we read " it was given to
them." As in chap. vi. 11, so here in xx. 4 we must
note that the word " them " is masculine, αὐτοῖς

(*autois*), and not feminine, αὐταῖς (*autais*), which is the gender of ψυχάς (*psuchas*), *souls*. This proves that the expression, which consists of four words, "the souls of those who were beheaded," is a Pleonasm, and is to be treated as a figure, and not to be translated literally; but, being in the masculine gender, should be rendered without circumlocution "those who were beheaded" (compare Jer. ii. 34; xlvi. 15, &c.). The promise made to them in chap. vi. 11 is at length seen fulfilled in chap. xx. 4.

But now another statement is made, and it begins with the words καὶ οἵτινες (*kai hoitines*), which are rendered "and which" (AV.), "and such as" (RV.), "and those who" (Tregelles), as though the pronoun were in the accusative case and depended on the same verb as "souls": *i.e.*, as though it read, "I saw the souls . . . and I saw those which," &c. But the fact is that this pronoun, οἵτινες (*hoitines*) is in the nominative case, and therefore does not depend on any verb, but is the subject of a new sentence altogether, of which the verb is "lived again." This is a grammatical fact that scientifically determines the matter for us, and prevents us from introducing our own opinions. Of one class of persons, viz., the beheaded martyrs, it is said that they were righteously judged and vindicated. The next statement of verse 4 goes on to say that not only these (who were beheaded), but all, including these who refused to worship the Beast, "lived again": *i.e.*, had part in the first resurrection, which is presently described.

-4-. And whosoever* did not worship (*i.e.*, had not

* For so οἵτινες (*hoitines*) is rendered in Matt. v. 39, 41; vii. 24; x. 32, 33; xiii. 12; xviii. 4; xxiii. 12. Mark viii. 34. Luke xiv. 27. Gal. v. 4. Jas. ii. 10.

worshipped) **the Beast, nor yet his image, and did not
receive the** (his) **mark** (xiii. 16) **on their foreheads,
and on their hands, both lived again and reigned
with Christ**] Here the point is resurrection. They
" lived again." The verb means *to come to life* (see Luke
xv. 32. John xi. 25. Rom. xiv. 9. Rev. i. 18; ii. 8).
Here we have the fulfilment of that repeated statement
of the Lord Jesus. " He that findeth his life shall
lose it; and he that loseth his life for my sake shall
find it " (Matt. x. 39; xvi. 25, 26. Mark viii. 35-37.
Luke ix. 24; xvii. 33. John xii. 25).

If these refer to and include all who had lost their
lives for faithful testimony, then the next clause
includes those who had specially done so during the
Tribulation; for all these " live again," in the first
resurrection. It is not the *extent* of the first resurrection
which is here in question, but a statement concerning
some of those who shall have part in it. That there are
and will be others is implied in verse 6. All these
" both lived again and reigned with Christ."

G¹. (page 612), xx. -4. *Time*

-4. A thousand years.] This is the duration of the
millennial reign of the Lord Jesus; and this is the throne
spoken of in Luke i. 32, 33 : " He shall be great, and the
Lord God shall give unto Him the throne of his father
David, and he shall reign over the house of Jacob for
ever." This is the throne the Lord refers to in Matt.
xxv. 31. " When the Son of man shall come in his
glory, and all his holy angels with him, THEN shall
he sit upon the throne of his glory." In Rev. xix, we
have that *coming*; and in chap. xx. 4, we have the
session upon that *throne*.

Psalm ii. points to the same throne, and Matt. xix. 28 distinctly promises to the Twelve Apostles "a kingdom as the Father appointed" Him, that they may "eat and drink at his table in his kingdom, and sit on thrones judging the twelve Tribes of Israel" (Luke xxii. 29, 30). This "judgment" consists in *ruling*; for "at that time shall they call Jerusalem the throne of the LORD, and all nations shall be gathered into it" (Jer. iii. 17). This is explained in Matt. xxv. as the judging of the "nations." "I saw thrones." Hence there is not only "the throne of his glory," but the other thrones on which "they" also (who are mentioned in other scriptures) shall sit.

This is the day when "the Lord shall be king over all the earth" (Zech. xiv. 9); when "the Lord of hosts shall reign in Mount Zion, and in Jerusalem, and before his ancients gloriously" (Isa. xxiv. 23; ix. 7). See also Jer. iii. 17; xxiii. 5. Micah iv. 7. Ezek. xliii. 7.

Many scriptures tell of the glories of that thousand years. We can only sum them up, and that briefly:— Those years will be characterised by (1) the absence of Satan; (2) the restoration of the earth (Ps. lxvii. 6): many physical marvels, converting its deserts into gardens, and causing its wildernesses to blossom as the rose; (3) changes in the sun, moon, and stars, which shall affect the climates and fruitfulness of the earth; (4) changes in the nature and habits of the wild animals; (5) righteous government, which is to-day the world's greatest need (Is. xxxii. 1; xxix. 18, 19; xxxiii. 6). (6) life prolonged and health improved (Is. xxxiii. 24; lxv. 20-23).

When the thousand years end, their blessedness does not end, but increases with the glory of the new heavens and the new earth (Rev. xxi., xxii.). Men will not cease to live. The nations of the new Earth will "consist" and be upheld by the eternal power of the great Creator.

F². (page 612), xx. 5-. Persons

5-. * **The rest of the dead lived not again**] The verb means *to live again* in the sense of resurrection (see Rom. xiv. 9. Rev. ii. 8). These words require no explanation. They are written to explain a great and solemn fact to us. "The rest of the dead" include all who have no part in the "first resurrection."

If they "lived not again" until they rise from the dead, in what sense can they be said to "live" now while they are dead? The one is the antithesis of the other. In like manner, if they are suffering punishment in purgatory or elsewhere, in what way does this differ from the punishment which is awarded to them when they shall have been judged (xx. 14, 15). Another question raised is, In what sense is the "second death" different from the first? The questions are easily asked; and, if we believe God and His Word instead of tradition or theology, they are easily answered. This Scripture is part of a Book where future, unseen, and otherwise unknown facts and truths are made known to us. Apart from revelation no one knows anything about death and judgment. But, thank God, the humblest student of His word, if he knows all that God has told us on these subjects, knows all that can be known, and is as wise as the wisest of his teachers.

But, alas, these teachers too often give heed to the teachings of lying spirits, through Spiritists and mediums who are themselves deceived; and, in conse-

---

* L.T.Tr.A. WH. and RV. omit "but."

quence, find a difficulty in receiving and believing the simple but true revelations of the Word of God.

G². (page 612), xx. -5-. *Time*

-5-. **Until* the thousand years should be finished**.] or completed : so that their condition, whatever it may be, runs on during the whole period of the reign of those who " have part in the first resurrection."

F³. (page 612), xx. -5, 6-. *Persons*

-5. **This is the first resurrection.** (6-) **Blessed and holy is he who hath part in the first resurrection ; over these the second death hath not power** (or authority), **but they shall be** (and continue) **priests of God and of Christ, and shall reign with Him**]

G³. (page 612), xx. 6. *Time*

-6. **a† thousand years**.] " This is the first resurrection "; or, this *completes* the first resurrection. There is an *Ellipsis* of the verb in this sentence ; and we may supply *completes*, having in mind the several resurrections which shall before then have taken place. It is also a fact that, when two ordinal numbers are used in such a connection as this, they are used *relatively*. The one is *first* in relation to the *second*, which follows ; and not to what may have occurred before. In like manner the *second* stands in relation to the first. Hence, in English we always say, in such cases, *former* and *latter*, where we have only two things thus related ; and not *first* and

---

* G.L.T.Tr.A. WH. and RV. read ἔζησαν ἄχρι *(ezēsan achri)*, instead of ἀνέζησαν ἕως *(anezēsan heōs).*

† T.Tr.Ab. WHb. and RVm. read " the."

second, unless there are more to follow in the series. It is the same in chap. xxi. 1, where we read of the new heavens and the new earth ; "for the first heaven and the first earth were passed away."

Here, again, we have *two* things standing in related contrast, the " first " and the " new ": *i.e.*, the new, and the one that immediately precedes it; the *former*, and not the " first." For, the present " heavens and the earth which are now " (2 Pet. iii. 7) are not the first. For Scripture tells us of *three*, of which the present is the *second*. In 2 Pet. iii. 6, 7, 13, we read of the *first*— the world that "*then was*" (Gen. i. 1); of the *second*— " the heavens and the earth which *are now* "; and of the *third*—" a new heavens and a new earth," for which we now look. This (second of three) is what is called in Rev. xxi. 1 the " first " of the latter two.

Hence this " first resurrection " is the *former* of the two mentioned in this verse: and not the calling on high of Phil. iii. 14, or the resurrection of 1 Thess. iv. 16, 17. This special resurrection (1 Thess. iv. 16) must be carefully distinguished from that which is called the " first resurrection " in Rev. xx. 6. The word " first " in 1 Thess. iv. 16 does not refer to " the first resurrection " so called in Rev. xx. 6, but merely records the order of events, and simply states that " the dead in Christ" will " rise first "; *i.e.*, before the taking up of either them or the living saints.

The resurrection of 1 Thess. iv. 16 is not the resurrection of Rev. xx. 6. It was never revealed in the Old Testament ; but was a special revelation made " by the word of the Lord " to Paul ; and by Paul to the Thessalonian saints and to the Church of God.

The resurrection of Rev. xx. 6 is the well-known

" former " of two resurrections which had both been long the subject of revelation, and was the hope of Israel. The Holy Spirit spoke, by the Psalmist, of the righteous dead who should " have dominion " over the rest of the dead " in the morning " of this resurrection (Ps. xlix. 14). The Lord spoke of it when He called it " the resurrection of the just " (Luke xiv. 14); " the resurrection from (among) the dead " (Luke xx 34-36); " the resurrection of life " (John v. 29). Paul spoke of it as " the resurrection of the just " (Acts xxiv. 15), for which the twelve tribes hoped, according to " the promise made of God unto the fathers " (Acts xxvi. 6-8). In Dan. xii. 2 it is spoken of as a resurrection " to everlasting life," in which " many " (not all) have part, and " awake."

Martha expressed her belief in " the resurrection at the last day " (John xi. 24); *i.e.*, the last day, at the end of the present age, and immediately before the introduction of the new age of the thousand years. " Jesus said unto her, I am the resurrection and the life." By this figure of *Hendiadys* the Lord distinguishes the resurrection for which Martha hoped, as the resurrection " to everlasting life " (Dan. xii. 2). He refers not to two things, but to one. It is as though He had said, " I am the resurrection—yea, the one that is to eternal life; he that believeth on me, though he die, he shall live again ; and everyone who thus liveth again in resurrection and believeth (again *Hendiadys*, every believer who lives again in resurrection), shall in no wise die again for ever " (John xi. 25, 26). No ! he shall rise again in the first resurrection, and shall by no means die " the second death." That shall have no power over such.

It was for this " first (or former resurrection " that

the Old Testament Saints looked. It was the "better resurrection" of Heb. xi. 35. It was God's revealed promise to them. It was no secret. Its revelation was given quite irrespective of the Church of God; and it will take place as though the Church had never existed at all.

But the Church of God, as the Body of Christ, was a " secret." All that concerned it was " hid in God " : its calling, its standing, its hope, and its destiny. All were subjects of special revelation.

It was " by revelation " that it was made known to the apostle Paul, and to us through him (Eph. iii. 3).

It was by a special and subsequent revelation that we know what God has made Christ to be unto His Church ; and what He has made the Church to be in Christ (Eph. i. 17.   Col. ii. 2, 3, etc.).

It was by special revelation we know that all will not die ; that there is to be an exception to the Appointment of Heb. ix. 27, " For this we say unto you by the word of the Lord." This special prophetic revelation* was necessary in order to make known the fact that a distinct company of believers should be " alive and remain," and not die at all, but be caught up to be for ever with the Lord, together with the dead in Christ, who shall first (*i.e.*, before this) have been raised (1 Thess. iv. 15-17). The living saints will not precede or get before " the dead in Christ."

Tradition, as represented in our Hymn-books and on our Tomb-stones, reverses all this, and assures us that " the dead in Christ " have already preceded or got there before those who are " alive and remain." But we believe God ; and are assured that the Truth is exactly

*See page 35.

the opposite of Tradition; *viz.*, that those who are "alive and remain" shall not precede "the dead in Christ," or be caught up to "be with the Lord," before "the dead in Christ" shall have been raised. These shall "rise first," and then be caught up, together with the living saints, "to be with the Lord."

To teach otherwise is to fall into the heresy of Hymenæus and Philetus; to "overturn the faith"; and to say that "the resurrection is passed already" (2 Tim. ii. 17, 18).

This secret is again mentioned in 1 Cor. xv. 51: "Behold I show you a mystery": *i.e.*, "behold I tell you a secret: we shall not all sleep, but we shall all be changed."

The great secret in 1 Tim. iii. 16, to the still greater secret of Eph. and Phil. and Col., includes a special "calling on high," and being "received up into glory."

All this is quite independent of "the first resurrection" of Rev. xx. 6. That was never a secret, but was revealed of old as the hope of Israel (Acts xxvi. 6, 7).

The hope of Israel is one thing, and is quite distinct from the hope of the Church, which is another thing. The Gentiles are "without hope." The Scriptures of truth which treat of "the Jew, the Gentile, and the Church of God" must be rightly divided, or we shall not get the truth. These resurrections must be divided according to the dispensations to which they respectively belong.

The resurrection in 1 Thess. iv. belongs to this present dispensation of grace; while the two in Rev. xx. belong to the time of the end, in the future dispensation of judgment.

We know not how long a time will elapse between

the resurrection of believers (1 Thess. iv.), and the
" first," or former of the two resurrections of Rev. xx :
but we are told, and therefore know, that there will be
a thousand years between these latter two.

1 Cor. xv. treats of the subject of Resurrection. This
was the subject in dispute, and this is the scope of
the chapter. It is the "gospel" (*v.* 1), not the
"mystery." It is the "Kingdom" (*v.* 24), and not the
Church of God. It is the fulfilment of the Old Testament promise of Isa. xxv. 8, and not the revelation of
the Rapture of 1 Thess. iv. It is "them" and "they"
(*vv.* 20, 23, 29) ; and not "we." The moment it comes
to "we" in verse 49, he proceeds, briefly, in a few words,
to speak of the "mystery" in verses 51, 52*, but immediately returns, in verse 53 to the end, to speak of THE
Resurrection. It is "the second man" (*v.* 47), "the
last Adam" (*v.* 45), not the "Head" of the Body. It
is the "firstfruits" in connection with the Harvest
(Rev. xiv. 4) ; and not the "Head" in relation to the
members. It is "all" in connection with mankind
vv. 22), and not the elect members of the Body of Christ.
It is of various "ranks," not of "one Body."

The *ranks* or *corps*† of the different bodies referred to
shut out the thought of the "one body." The Church
is a *corps* by itself, which will be caught away long
before the "first resurrection." Christ is not the
"firstfruits" of the Body, but its "Head." The first
τάγμα (*tagma*) is Christ (Personal and Mystical). The

---

* All shall not sleep (or, die) but all shall be changed. The
thought in *vv.* 51, 52 is parenthetical.

† The word τάγμα (*tagma*) means a body, or *troop* or *corps* of
soldiers. See 2 Sam. xxiii. 13. Xen., *Mem.*, 3, 1, 11. Often in
Polybius. Diod. Sic. 27, 18. Josephus, *Wars*, 1, 9, 1 ; 3, 4, 2.

Second *Tagma* is the first Resurrection at His Apocalypse or Revelation in glory. The Third *Tagma* is the
last *corps* (τὸ τέλος, *to telos*) at the end of the Millennium.
The church will, necessarily, have risen before these, so
as to be able to " appear with Him in glory." When
His Apocalypse or Revelation takes place, He will
already have come for His Church and have been
" glorified in His saints " (2 Thess. i. 10*). This
really settles the whole question, and proves that
the resurrection and ascension of the Church in
1 Thess. iv. are quite distinct in time, and order,
and character, from the " first " resurrection of
Rev. xx.

The latter is the subject we have before us now, and
the first resurrection has special reference to the overcomers, according to the promise made to them in
chap. ii. 11: " he that overcometh shall not be hurt of
the second death." In contrast with this is set the
fact that they shall be priests of God and of Christ."
This also is the realization of what is stated in chap. i.
6 and chap. v. 10, where the *Zōa* and the Elders say
of those who were redeemed, Thou " hast made them
kings and priests : and they shall reign on the earth."
This is what was prophesied in Is. lxi. 6: " Ye shall
be named the Priests of the LORD, and men shall
call you the Ministers of our God " (compare Ex.
xix. 6).

It is again affirmed that those who have part in the
" first resurrection " will have this blessedness for the
thousand years. During that time they live and reign

---

* See *The Church Epistles*, by the same author and publisher,
pages 241-243.

with Christ. How "principles" can do this (as some
teach) we are at a loss to understand! How the
"memory" and the "character" of the saints can
reign over the Gentiles is a still greater mystery, and
we must leave the difficulty with those who create it,
and "give it up." Man may say they reign "*as if
they were martyrs raised from the dead.*" The Word
says that they will be actually raised, and will actually
reign. They do not "live again" "spiritually," or
"in their successors." Those who were beheaded are
the same as those who reign; and how "principles"
or "character" can be beheaded we have yet to learn.

The Fourth Judgment

We come now to the fourth of these final five judgments. The third—the *central* one—differs (as we have
seen) in character from the others. It is a judgment
which vindicates and rewards those who are the subjects of it. The others are all for condemnation and
judgment.

B². (page 603), xx. 7-10. *The Judgment of Satan
(After the Millennium.)*

B² | H | 7. Satan "loosed out of his prison "
    | J | 8. The Nations deceived
    | *J* | 9. The Nations devoured
    | H | 10. Satan "cast into the lake of fire "

H. (see above), xx. 7. *Satan loosed out of his prison*

7. **And when the thousand years are completed,
Satan shall be loosed out of his prison,**] In verse 3
it was stated that "he should deceive the nations no
more until the thousand years should be finished;
after this he MUST be loosed a little season." Here,

In verse 7, we have the fact, the necessity of which is there declared.

But why "MUST" Satan be loosed, even for "a little season"? Wherein lies the reason for this mysterious necessity?

To understand the word "must" of verse 3, we shall have to discover something of the Divine purposes and counsels in ruling and overruling the course of this world. "Known unto God are all His works from the beginning of the world" (Acts xv. 18).

"The LORD of hosts hath sworn, saying,

Surely, as I have thought, so shall it come to pass;

And as I have purposed, so shall it stand"

(Isa. xiv. 24).

At the beginning there was Satan's *first* rebellion; and now, at the end, we have his *final* rebellion. In Gen. i. 1, we have the primal creation of the heavens and the earth, in perfect order and beauty. In verse 2 we are told that they became a ruin—empty, waste, and desolate. How, or why, or when, they thus became, we are not told. We believe that it was on account of Satan's first rebellion. That he did rebel, we know. And we know also that it was through *pride* (1 Tim. iii. 6, 7). It must have happened at that time, between the first and second verses of Gen i., for in Gen. iii. he is introduced as a fallen angel, the enemy of God and man.

We know, also, that God did not originally *create* the world as it is described in Gen. i. 2. It is there described as תֹהוּ (*tohū*) וָבֹהוּ (*vabohü*) *i.e., empty, waste, and desolate.** Now, it does not matter what תֹהוּ (*tohū*) means, because it is expressly declared by the Creator in Isa. xlv. 18, that He did *not* create it *tohū*. And the

---

* The expression occurs in Isa. xxiv. 10; xxxiv. 11, and Jer. iv. 23.

expressions describing the Divine Creator are heaped together to impress us with the fact that He who made it ought to know. He says :—

> " Thus saith the LORD that created the heavens :
> God himself that formed the earth and made it :
> He hath established it,

HE CREATED IT NOT *TOHU*."

Therefore it must have *become* so at some time, and in some manner, and for some reason, which are not. revealed. This is the very meaning of the Hebrew verb הָיָה (*hayah*) *to come to be.** " And (or but) the earth BECAME wasteness and emptiness."

We submit that this catastrophe was brought about by the first rebellion of Satan.† Of no other than Satan could it be said at that time that he was the author of evil, and of " the lie."

---

* See Gen. ii. 7, " Man *became* a living soul "; xix. 26, " She *became* a pillar of salt "; xxiv. 60, " Be thou (*i.e., become* thou) the mother of thousands of millions." Ex. xix. 15, " Be ready (*i.e., become* or *get ready*) against the third day." Isa. i. 9, " We should have been (*i.e., become*) as Sodom." Jer. xlviii. 6, " Be (*i.e., become*) like the heath in the wilderness."

† In reference to Satan's first interference with the earth, see Matt. xiii. 24. " *His* field " seems to disprove the notion of some that this earth was once apportioned to Satan (especially in connection with Job xxxviii. 4). Was it not Satan who caused the waters to gush out of the earth and drown it—just as when a man stabs another, and leaves him weltering in his blood (Ps. vii. 15). Job xxxviii. 8 suggests the thought that the earth had been violated, and the Lord acted the part of a healer (*vv.* 9-12). Yet, as if the wound were not perfectly healed, the seas are witnesses of the violence done to the earth. But perhaps Ez. xxviii., especially *v.* 15, takes us to the origin of his sin. Satan never would acknowledge the authority of *law* ; would never acknowledge *authority.* All who are of him, say, " Our mouths are our own." ' Who is lord over us ? " expresses his conduct as well as man's.

If this be so, then we are able to see the order of all
the various dispensations; and learn how all the evil is
to be overcome; how the new heavens and the new
earth are to be brought about; and how the curse is to
be removed.

The following Structure of the Divine Plan of the
Ages sets forth the correspondence between the steps
of the Ruin and the Restoration; and shows that
the Restoration is to be brought about in an *inverse*
order to that of the Ruin. The eight steps roll back
upon themselves, until the Primal blessedness is at
length seen restored. In this Structure, which is seen
to be an Introversion, the first member (A) corresponds
with the last (*A*); the second (B) with the next to
the last (*B*); and so throughout: that is to say, the
Primal Creation (A) is placed in contrast with the New
Heavens and the New Earth (*A*). Satan's first rebellion (B) stands in connection with his final rebellion (*B*).
The Restored Earth of Gen. i. ii. (C) stands in correspondence with the Millennial Earth (*C*). Satan loose
in Gen. iii. (D) is put in contrast with Satan bound in
Rev. xx. 1-3 (*D*). The dealing with mankind as a
whole in Gen. iv.—xi. (E) is set in correspondence with
similar dealing foretold in prophecy (*E*). The Calling
of Israel in Gen. xi. (F) is placed in contrast with their
Re-calling and promised blessing (*F*). The first Advent
(G) is seen to stand in contrast with the second Advent
(*G*), and to be quite a separate and distinct event from
the " Calling on high of Phil. iii. 14, or the *Parousia* of
1 Thess. iv. The second Advent was the subject of
Old Testament prophecy, but the Pre-taking up of the
Church was a special revelation given to Paul " by the
Word of the Lord " in 1 Thess. iv. 13—v. 11.

630 / The Seventh Vision "on Earth"

The Dispensational Plan of the Bible

A | THE PRIMAL CREATION. The first heaven and the first earth. Gen. i. 1. ("The world that then was," 2 Pet. iii. 6)

  B | SATAN'S FIRST REBELLION. Gen. i. 2-

    C | THE EARTH RESTORED AND BLESSED. Gen. i. 2- —ii. 25 2 Pet. iii. 7. " The heavens and the earth which are now."

      D | SATAN ENTERS, AND THE CONSEQUENCE. Gen. iii.

        E | MANKIND DEALT WITH AS A WHOLE. Gen. iv.—xi. 30.

          F | THE CHOSEN NATION CALLED, AND BLESSED. Gen. xi. 31 to Malachi

            G | THE FIRST ADVENT. The Four Gospels. Rom. xv. 8. The Kingdom rejected, and King crucified

              H | THE KINGDOM RE-OFFERED. The Acts and earlier Pauline Epistles. (Acts iii. 19, 20). The " Signs and wonders of the Holy Ghost." (Heb ii. 3, 4). The offer rejected. (Acts xxviii. 25, 26)

              H | THE KINGDOM IN ABEYANCE. The " Not yet " of Heb. ii. 8. The mystery revealed and consummated. Rom. xvi. 25, 26. Eph. iii. 1-4. Col. i. 5—ii. 3. 1 Tim. iii. 16. Phil. iii. 14

            G | THE SECOND ADVENT. Rev. " The Day of the Lord." Isa. ii. 11-17. Joel. ii. Matt. xxiv

          F | THE CHOSEN NATION RE-CALLED, AND A BLESSING. Rom. xi. 11-36. Acts xv. 16. Jer. xxx. ; xxxi. Isa. lxi. ; lxii. Zech. xii.—xiv

        E | MANKIND DEALT WITH AS A WHOLE. Joel. iii. 2. Matt. xxv. 31-46. Rom. xv. 8-12. Acts xv. 17

      D | SATAN BOUND, AND THE CONSEQUENCE. Rev. xx. 1-3

    C | THE EARTH RESTORED AND BLESSED. Rev. xx. 4-6 Is. xxxv. The Millennium

  B | SATAN'S FINAL REBELLION. Rev. xx. 7-10

A | THE NEW HEAVENS AND THE NEW EARTH. Rev. xxi. ; xxii. (2 Pet. iii. 12, 13. " The Day of God." The " Third Heaven " and "Paradise," 2 Cor. xii. 2, 4. Compare 2 Pet. iii. 6, 7, and 13)

A careful study of this Structure will show that the several dispensations which form the great subject of the Word of God could not be otherwise divided. Jew, Gentile, and the Church of God are distinguished ; and each has its own proper place. The two Advents are separated, and the second is distinguished from the *Parousia* and the "blessed hope" which are quite distinct and separate events. The Church occupies the central position ; and its present standing is separated from its future destiny and hope. The two rebellions of Satan are also seen to be in direct correspondence, so that now we can see the necessity for this " must be " of verse 3 ; and for this loosing in Rev. xx. 7-10.

But there is a deeper reason than that which appears on the surface of this Structure of the Divine Plan of the Ages.

All the counsels and purposes of God have Christ for their centre, their subject, and their object. Not only " by him were all things created " (Col. i. 16, &c.), but " by him all things consist " (Col. i. 17).

From this it follows that no created being, heavenly or earthly, can stand ("upright"), or "consist," apart from Him. He is "upholding all things by the word of His power " (Heb. i. 3).

In Eph. iii. 10 we are told that God is using the Mystery, *i.e.*, the Church, as an object-lesson ; and through (RV., *i.e.*, *by means of*) it He is making known, NOW, unto the principalities and powers in heavenly places, something of His manifold wisdom.

What is the lesson that God is now teaching these heavenly beings ?

It is simply this :—that *no created being can stand apart*

from Christ the Creator. It is this that is brought out by the Structure of the Dispensations.

B. Satan could not stand, though blessed with untold powers and dignities.

D. Man could not stand, though placed in the most favourable circumstances.

E. The Nations could not stand. They soon rebelled against God's commands; and set up Babel as the monument of their defiance.

F. The chosen nation (Israel) could not stand, though placed in a position as favourable (nationally) as man had been in Adam (individually). The nations having all failed : then, a new nation, a chosen nation, is formed out of one man, Abraham ; and placed in a country which was as another Garden of the Lord ; and blessed with national blessings such as no nation ever enjoyed before or since. But Israel failed, and instead of being a blessing became a curse. They forsook the Covenant of the Lord ; despised His Law ; threw down His altars, and slew His prophets with the sword (1 Kings xix. 10). Then came

G. The First Advent. "Having yet one Son, his well-beloved, he sent him also last unto them." But those wicked husbandmen "took him and slew him, and cast him out" (Mark xii. 6-8). Those husband-men were "miserably destroyed." Their city was razed to the ground, their temple burnt, and their people scattered to the four winds of heaven. The Gospels and Acts set forth the terrible story. And now

H. After the rejection of the King and the Kingdom (Acts iii. 19, 20 (RV.), compared with xxviii. 25, 26). We have in

H. The Kingdom in Abeyance ? NOT YET " do we see all things put under His feet" (Heb. ii. 8) ; but we

have " the mystery of Christ and His Church " revealed
(Eph. v. 32), and not until this has been " received up
in glory " (1 Tim. iii. 16) will the time have come for
Christ to sit upon His own throne.

It is not God's counsel to use the Church as the
means by which He will bring in the New Heavens and
the New Earth. That new creation will be full of
physical marvels, which cannot be brought about by
spiritual agencies. Cause must have some relation to
effect. And God has appointed other means to remove
the curse from the earth, and make an end of sin and of
death. Physical means will be used to bring about
physical changes and bring in physical blessings.

The Church is now waiting—not for the world's
conversion, because it knows that its apostasy is foretold (2 Thess. ii. 3). The Pauline Epistles tell of the
Church's calling, and standing, and object, and hope
The members of the Church of God WILL STAND
and stand for ever ; because they are " in Christ," and
are the members of that Body of which He is the
glorious Head in heaven, and they the members of that
Body on earth. In Him they will know "no condemnation." From Him there will be no separation
(Rom. viii. 1, 39). They will stand, for their standing is
Christ's own standing. They stand for ever in Him.*

F. And Israel. What of Israel ? Will Israel stand?
Yes, for Jehovah has said :

" I will take you from among the heathen,
    And gather you out of all countries.

---

* This, of course, refers to *individual* standing here. Not to
corporate standing. That has totally failed, as the Epistles testify.
Corporate standing, now, is only " IN CHRIST," which includes all
the members of His Body.

And will bring you into your own land,
THEN will I sprinkle clean water upon you
And ye shall be clean ;
From all your filthiness, and from all your idols,
  will I cleanse you.
A new heart also will I give you,
And a new spirit will I put within you ;
And I will take away the stony heart out of your
  flesh,
And I will give you a heart of flesh,
And I will put my Spirit within you,
And cause you to walk in my statutes ;
And ye shall keep my judgments and do them,
And ye shall dwell in the land that I gave to your
  fathers,
And ye shall be my People, and I will be your
  God . .
I, the LORD have spoken it, and I will do it "
(Ezek. xxxvi. 24-28, 36).

Then shall be seen the only indefectible nation the
world has ever known. Israel shall "no more go
astray " (Ez. xiv. 11). "Thy people shall be all righteous, they shall inherit the land for ever " (Isa. lx. 21).
Their sins and their iniquities will be remembered no
more (Jer. xxxi. 33, 34. Zech. xiii. 2. Isa. xliii. 25).
" I will no more make you a reproach " (Joel ii. 19).
" Neither will I hide my face any more from them:
for I have poured out my Spirit upon the house of
Israel, saith Adonai Jehovah " (Ezek. xxxix. 29).

Yes, Israel WILL STAND then, because, and only
because, Israel shall be holden up by the infinite power
of Jehovah— their Almighty Creator and Covenant God.

E. And the Nations. What of them? They will

have beheld and enjoyed for a thousand years the goodness of Jehovah. The knowledge of His glory shall have
flooded the earth.   All shall be taught of God.   For a
thousand years they shall have known a righteous and
holy government, and enjoyed peace, prosperity and
plenty.   What of this?   Will these things give a new
heart ?   Will they be able to undo the enmity of the
natural heart to God ? (Rom. viii. 7.   Jas. iv. 4).   No !
"The carnal mind is enmity against God : for it is not
subject to the Law of God, neither indeed can be."
"That which is born of the flesh, is flesh," and remains
flesh.   And only "that which is born of the Spirit is
spirit," and remains spirit (John iii. 6).   The only
safety for any Gentile will be Ex. xii. 48.

The Nations did not stand in the midst of all the
corruptions with which they corrupted their way in
Gen. iv.—xi.   Neither will they stand in spite of all the
manifestation of God's glory in the earth.   Even in the
midst of Millennial glory many will render only a feigned
obedience (Ps. lxvi. 3 ; cxliv. 7, 11).

Zech. xiv. 16-19 reveals a disinclination on the part
of some of the nations to make the long annual
pilgrimages to Jerusalem ; and Messiah's rule is with
"a rod of iron" and "in the midst among enemies"
(Ps. cx. 2).

When Satan shall be loosed they are at once, and
apparently, easily "deceived" and ready to believe his
lies, and to manifest the enmity of the natural heart by
fighting under him against God.

To bring out this awful fact, and exhibit the true
nature of man ; and to manifest the grace of God ; and
to show that, apart from Christ, nothing can exist, or
consist, or stand, Satan "MUST be loosed for a little

season." The great lesson of the ages will not be fully manifested or seen till then ; but even now it is being taught to angelic beings in heaven. The great object lesson can even now, but not till now, be taught them " by means of the church."

Now, saved sinners and rebels can be pointed to as " in Christ," and therefore for ever saved, safe, and secure. And all this is " according to the eternal purpose ("the purpose of the ages," RV. marg.) which He purposed in Christ Jesus our Lord" (Eph. iii. 11).

Now we see why Satan " must be loosed." Now we learn the secret of this mysterious necessity. It must be shown that time does not alter Satan's character ; and that the *goodness* of God has no more effect upon the old nature than the *judgments* of God.

J. (page 626), xx. 8. *The Nations deceived*

8. And will go out to deceive the Nations which are in the four corners of the earth, Gog and Magog, to gather them together to the (predicted) **war: the number of whom is as the sand of the sea.**] How, and with what lies, he will deceive them we are not told. But we are not without examples of how easily nations may be deceived by man, even in our own day. And Satan will find means to discredit God's dealings and misrepresent His words. As He deceived the angels, who, in consequence, "sinned," and shared his fall ; and lied to our first parents in the garden (Gen. iii.) ; and made the nations rebel (Gen. xi.), so again will he succeed in his final rebellion. It is idle to give reins to our imagination. For us the solemn fact must be sufficient.

" Gog and Magog " denote the nations as a whole.

Magog is mentioned as the first son of Japhet in Gen
x. 2. With him are associated his brethren, Gomer
(Kimmerians), Madai (Medians), Meshech (Muscovites),
etc. In Ezek. xxxviii. 5, are added Persians, and
Ethiopians, and Libyans. Josephus renders the word
Magog, Scythians (*Ant.* i. 6, 3). The two words com-
bine the nations North and East of Palestine.

Ezek. xxxviii. and xxxix. must be distinguished from
Rev. xx. Ezekiel records the war referred to in
Rev. xvi. 14; xvii. 14; xix. 17-21, which takes place
before the Millennium; while Rev. xx. takes place after
it. This is clear from the fact that Israel's restoration
is mentioned after the destruction of Gog and Magog.
See Ezek. xxxix. 25, "NOW will I bring again the captivity of Jacob, and have mercy upon the whole house
of Israel." This is conclusive, and should clear up
many doubts on this vexed question.

The word "Magog" is found only in Gen. x. 2 as a
son of Japhet; in Ezekiel, where it means a *land* or
country, of which Gog is the prince; and in Rev. xx. 8,
where "Gog and Magog" appears to be an inclusive
term for the Gentile *nations*.

It is absurd to talk about "John borrowing from
Ezekiel," as so many say. There is no "borrowing"
in the matter. Both prophecies are "given by inspiration of God," and refer to two distinct subjects. There
is no confusion between them if we rightly divide the
times to which they respectively belong.

J. (page 626), **xx. 9.** *The Nations Devoured*

9. **And they went up upon the breadth of the
Land, and encompassed the citadel of the saints,
and the beloved city: and there came down fire**

ouc of heaven,* and devoured them.] That the Land
is meant here, and not the earth, seems clear from
Isa. viii. 8, where we have the same expression. (So
Hab. i. 6.) It denotes the whole extent of the Land.

There are no contending armies here. The issue of
this invasion of the Land is speedily and finally termi-
nated by a special Divine judgment. Fire comes down
from Heaven and devours the mighty host. A special
judgment is reserved for Satan.

H. (page 626), xx. 10. *Satan Cast into the Lake of Fire*

**10. And the Devil that deceived them was cast into
a lake of fire and brimstone, where both † the Beast
and the False Prophet are, and they shall be tormented day and night for ever and ever]** Not now
is Satan merely to be " bound." At length he receives
his final doom.

This is the reason of Satan's hatred of this book of
the Revelation. It is the book which tells of his doom;
as Genesis foretells it (Gen. iii. 15). That lake of fire
was prepared for him and his angels (Matt. xxv. 41).
His dupes are devoured by fire from above; he is to be
tormented by fire from beneath.

THE FIFTH JUDGMENT

We now come to the last of these final five judgment
scenes — that of the Great White Throne. This
is not a "general judgment." The fact that there
are *five* judgments recorded in this last Vision on Earth
shows, not only that the expression "general" is foreign
to Scripture, but that such a judgment is unknown.

---

* G.L.T.Tr.A. WH. and RV. omit " from God."

† G.L.T.Tr.A. WH. and RV. add καὶ (*kai*) *both.*

As to the Church, if it can be called a "judgment" at all, the Church has already passed through hers as to service and works (not as to *standing*, of course), according to 2 Cor. v. 10, and Rom. xiv. 10, where wrong service will be "made manifest," and rewards will be "received" at the *Bēma* of Christ. The third of these five judgments is that of the Overcomers, who, like the Church, will be vindicated and rewarded.

This judgment is generally supposed to be identical with that of Matt. xxv: notwithstanding that the latter is not at all "general," but is confined to "living nations," and not one word is said of *resurrection*. Here, though only "the rest of the dead" are concerned, and there is not a word as to any except those who are raised from the dead, it is still taken to be "general," in spite of 1 Cor. xv., which speaks of the "order" of the resurrections; and Rev. xx. 4, 5, which speaks of two others.

This is sufficient to show the confusion which must necessarily ensue if we are not careful in "rightly dividing the Word of truth."

The passage (xx. 11-15) which records this last of the five judgments is seen, by the Structure, to consist of four pairs, as follows :

A³. (page 603), xx. 11-15.   *The Judgment of the Great White Throne.*

A₃ | K¹ | c¹ | 11-. The great white throne. " And I saw...
      | | d¹ | -11. The Judge who sat thereon
      | K² | c | 12-. The raised dead (from earth). "And I saw . . .
      | | d² | -12. Their judgment.
      | K³ | c³ | 13-. The raised dead (from the sea).
      | | d³ | -13. Their judgment.
      | K⁴ | c⁴ | 14. Death and the grave.
      | | d⁴ | 15. Their final judgment.

First we have the Throne itself :

c¹. (see above), **xx. 11-.**   *The Great White Throne*

11-. And I saw a great white throne,] "great," in distinction from the other thrones mentioned in this book, and that of chap. iv. 2-6.   That was set "in heaven.' This is seen in the last Vision "on earth"; as were also the thrones in the fourth verse.   It is not only "great," to indicate the greatness of the occasion, and of its power and authority : but "white," to indicate its purity, holiness, and righteousness.   There are no threatenings here.   No thunderings and lightnings : no voices.   Nothing " around " it : nothing " before " it. Only

d¹. (see above), **xx. -11.**   *The Judge who sat thereon*

-11. And him that sat thereon, from whose face the earth and the heaven fled away ; and no place was found for them.]   No name is given.   No form is described.   Only an awful, mysterious presence.

This is perhaps the moment of 2 Peter iii. 10-12. It is the " day of God," as distinct from " the day of Christ " (Phil. i. 6 ; ii. 16); and from "the day of the Lord."

It needs no human description nor interpretation. Heretics might say in Paul's day that "the resurrection is passed already" (2 Tim. ii. 18). Swedenborg may tell his followers that this judgment scene took place in 1757, and that *he saw it* with his own eyes.* We sweep aside all human assertions and opinions, and listen to the solemn and weighty words which tell us of the solemnity of this last judgment scene.

c⁹. (page 640), xx. 12-. *The Raised Dead (from the earth)*

12-. **And I saw the dead, the great and small, standing before the throne ;† and books were opened ; and another book was opened, which is the book of life :]** " The dead " are " the rest of the dead," who " lived not again " (*i.e.*, were not raised) till the thousand years were completed, as stated in verse 5.

This judgment is different from all the others. It differs from the first (xix. 11), in that that was a judicial act of summary retribution. And it differs from the others in that it is a deliberate session ; a formal process of judgment deciding according to the evidence produced.

Nothing is said as to the contents of these books. In iii. 5 ; xiii. 8 ; xvii. 8 ; xx. 12, 15 ; xxi. 27 we read that " the book of life " contains " *names*," and probably names also fill these " books." In the Old Testament also, it is mentioned (Ex. xxxii. 32. Ps. lxix. 28).

---

* *The Last Judgment*, page 40.

†G.L.T.Tr. WH. and RV. read θρόνου (*thronou*) *throne*, instead of θεοῦ (*theou*) *God*.

We need not speculate as to what is written in these books. Nor can we tell whether this other book—the book of life—is mentioned negatively, to exclude those not named in it; or positively, to embrace those who are. What we do know is that " the first resurrection " is specifically called " the resurrection of life "; and that those who have part in it will not be reckoned with " the rest of the dead which lived not again till the thousand years were finished." The words, " according to their works " looks as though there may be two classes of these " dead." But where the Word is silent, it is better for us to be silent also.

d². (page 640), xx. -12. *Their Judgment*

-12. **And the dead were judged out of the things written in the books, according to their works.**] These books, as Alford says, seem " the vouchers for the Book of Life." If so, they contain the evidence to show cause why the names are not written therein. There is no account of any name being found in the Book of Life. One thing, however, is clear, and that is, that the church of God cannot be here; for the standing of its members. is not of works at all; but is wholly of grace.

c³. (page 640), xx. 13-. *The Raised Dead (from the Sea)*

13-. **And the sea gave up the dead that were in it; and Death and the Grave** (Hades, i. 18; vi. 8) **gave up the dead that were in them** :] It is a question here of resurrection; and the language used is meant to include the unburied as well as the buried. There is nothing said about " souls," but only of persons *raised* from the dead.

d³. (page 640), xx. -13. *Their Judgment*

-13. **And they were judged, each one, according to their works.**] The Sinaitic MS. reads *condemned* instead of judged, but the latter word implies the former, if this is " the resurrection of condemnation " spoken of in other scriptures.

c⁴. (page 640), xx. 14. *Death and the Grave*

14. **And Death and the Grave were cast into the lake of fire. This is the second death,** even **the lake of fire.*** (15) **And whosoever was not found written in the Book of Life was cast into the lake of fire.**] The reference to the Book of Life in this connection seems to imply one of two things. (1) Either it is opened for condemnation, the name not being there ; or (2) it implies that the names have been " blotted out " (iii. 5).

In either case " the rest of the dead " would not include the Church, or Israel, or the Elect Remnant, nor the names of those who make up the super-human wild Beasts of Rev. xiii. and xvii.

No one can say which of these two views is correct. Nor can it be necessary for us to know.

Thus ends the description of these five judgments which conclude the last Vision of things " on earth ; " and which have to do with the earth " which now is."

The structure of this Seventh (and last) Vision " on Earth " has been given on page 603, and its members expanded, showing the five final judgments, as to their order.

But there is a further inter-relation between these five, if we look at them as a whole ; and have regard to

---

*L.T.Tr.A. WH. and RV. add " the lake of fire."

the events themselves, rather than their connection with " Men " and " Satan." The first and second judgments form one member, thus making four members in all, arranged as a simple alternation :—

The Seventh Vision "on Earth"

```
A'|  C | a | xix. 17-19. War. Before the Millennium
 &|      b | 20, 21. The lake of fire. Beast cast into it
B'|         D | c | xx. 1-3-. Satan bound
 |               d | -3. Nations not deceived for 1000
 |               | years
 |                   A²| e | 4. Thrones
 |                      f | 5-. Rest of dead
 |                         g | -5. First resurrection
 |                            h | 6. Its privileges
B²|         D | c | xx. 7. Satan loosed
 |               d | 8. Nations deceived
 |   C | a | 9. War. After the Millennium
 |       b | 10. The lake of fire. Satan cast into it
 |                   A³| e | 11. Great White Throne
 |                      f | 12-14-. Rest of dead
 |                         g | -14. Second death
 |                            h | 15. Its subjects
```

Thus we see one beautiful structure contained within the other ; both perfect ; showing how intimately these five members are related, and revealing a further hidden correspondence between them.

The next Vision introduces us to the eternal state of the New Heavens and the New Earth, and those who shall dwell therein.

20

THE PEOPLE ON THE NEW EARTH
(21:1—22:5)

This member corresponds with the member 𝕭 (chaps. ii. and iii.). Those chapters are occupied specially with the people who will be on the earth during the Day of the Lord and in the Great Tribulation—the concluding days of the old earth. These chaps. xxi. 1—xxii. 5, are occupied with the New Earth and the people who shall dwell therein, after all those judgments are ended.

This large member is divided into three parts:—

𝕭. (page 118), xxi. 1—xxii. 5. *The People of the New Earth*

𝕭 | A | xxi. 1, 2. Visions: (Heavens and Earth, etc.)

B | 3-8. Voices

A | xxi. 9—xxii. 5. Visions: (the Bride)

These again may be divided up and expanded. We will give each, in order :—

A. (see above), xxi. 1, 2. *Visions*
(*The New Heavens and Earth, and the New Jerusalem*)

A | a | b | xxi. 1-. Vision. "And I saw "

c | -1. The New Heavens and New Earth

a | *b* | 2-. Vision. "And I saw "

c | -2. The New Jerusalem

In this former Vision (A) two things are seen. (1) The New Heavens and Earth, and (2) the New Jerusalem.

In the latter Vision (*A*. xxi. 9—xxii. 5), we have the second Vision enlarged, extended, and more fully described. The two series of Visions are separated by the voices (B. xxi. 3-8).

Apart from what God is pleased to *show* us, and *tell* us, nothing could possibly be known by mortal man.

All imaginations, therefore, are worse than useless; they are misleading. Hence the importance of these significant expressions "And I saw," "And I heard," "And I saw."

The whole of this member (xxi. 1—xxii. 5) must be taken as coming after the judgment of the Great White Throne.

Some have looked on these two chapters as merely containing further details concerning the Millennium. But the fact of the New Heavens and the New Earth; and the passing away of the former heavens and earth; and of there being "no more sea," quite precludes the possibility of this being a mere recurrence to former things, and the filling in of further details.

This will be seen as we proceed.

a. (page 645), xxi. 1. *The New Heavens and Earth*

xxi. 1. **And I saw a new heaven and a new earth: for the former heaven and the former earth were passed away, and there was no more sea.**] Here again we have the same remarks to make as were made with reference to the "first" and "second" resurrections (pages 619-625). It is the former earth that had passed away, to give place to that which is not called the *second* but the "new." As we there said, the first heaven and earth

" which then was " (*i.e.* Gen. i. 1) " perished" (2 Pet. iii. 6), or passed away. The second heavens and earth " which are now," are kept in store, reserved unto fire (2 Pet. iii. 7). That fire is the means by which they shall " pass away " (2 Pet. iii. 10), and the New Heavens and the New Earth come into being. Both these passages are in agreement with Is. li. 6, 16 ; and lxv. 17.

Tradition talks about " the end of the world " ; and consequently errs, " not knowing the Scriptures nor the power of God." There will be an end of this age, but not of the world, as man thinks and speaks. There are other scriptures which speak of this *passing away* (see Matt. v. 18 ; xxiv. 34, 35. Mark xiii. 30, 31. Luke xvi. 17 ; xxi. 33).

All will be " new." The word rendered "new" (καινός, *kainos*) means *new*, not merely as to *time*, but as to *kind* and as to *quality*.

The heaven will be " new " ; the earth " new "; for there will be " no more curse," and therefore no more sin, or suffering, or sorrow.

Among these new things will be

a. (page 645), xxi. 2.   *The Holy City*

xxi. 2. **And I* saw the holy city, new Jerusalem, coming down out of heaven from God, prepared as a bride adorned for her husband.**] The name of the city is given in its Hebrew form ; not the Grecised name ; as though to mark it off from the earthly city. But it is none the less literal. The Heávens are literal. The Earth is literal. The Sea is literal. Why is not the City to be literal ? New, of course, it will be. New in its materials, size, shape, location, origin, and everything

---

* G.L.T.Tr.A. WH. and RV. omit " John."

connected with or relating to it. This city is further
described in the later vision, which is deferred so that we
may hear the heavenly voices which describe it and its
object.

B. (page 645), xxi. 3-8. *Voices*

```
B | d | e | 3-. A loud voice
  |   |                         ( Good bestowed, v. -3
  |   | f | -3, 4. Things uttered {
  |   |                         ( Evil removed, v. 4
  | d | e | 5-. He that sat on the throne.
  |   |                         ( Good bestowed, v. 5-7
  |   | f | -5-8. Things uttered {
  |   |                         ( Evil removed, v. 8
```

d. (above), xxi. 3. *The Loud Voice, and Things Uttered.*

xxi. 3. **And I heard a loud voice out of the throne***
saying, Behold, the Tabernacle of God is with men,
and He will dwell (or tabernacle) **with them, and they**
shall be His People, and God Himself shall be with
them,† and be **their God.**] No longer is this blessing to
be confined to Israel. All men on the new earth (for
these are the subjects of this section, 𝕭) are the
recipients of this wondrous blessing. Even with Israel,
this blessing was conditional (Lev. xxvi. 3, 11, 12.
1 Kings vi. 11-13; ix. 3-9). In the Millennium it will be
unconditional (Ezek. xx. 42-46; xxxvii. 23, 24, 26-28.
Ps. cxxxv. 21; lxviii. 16, 18. Zech. ii. 10; viii. 3, &c.),
but even then only of Israel. Here it is universal of
all earth's inhabitants. At length, as before the Fall,

---

* So L.T.A. WH. and RV. Tr. and Textus Receptus, B., &c., read
" heaven."

† T.Tr. WH. text, RV. marg., omit "and be their God." L.A.
and WH. marg. RV. agree with AV.

God dwells with men. These "men" are spoken of as "the nations" (ch. xxi. 24-26).

The blessed condition of the inhabitants of the New Earth is next further described.

4. **And God shall wipe away every tear from their eyes; and death shall be no more, neither sorrow, nor mourning, nor crying; neither shall there be any more pain: because the former things are passed away.**] Every tear, for there are many tears, and many causes for them. Death no longer, no more dying beds, funerals, or graves. Sorrow ceases. Mourning is at an end: and crying shall be hushed and pain unfelt (Isa. xxv. 7, 8 ; xxxv. 10. Jer. xxxi. 16).

We have further voices in the next verses, 5-8.

    d. (page 645), xxi. 5-8. *He that sat on the Throne, and Things Uttered*

xxi. 5. **And He that sitteth upon the throne said, "Behold, I make all Things new."
And He saith,***
    "Write: because these words are faithful and true."
(6) **And He said to me,**
    "They† are accomplished. I am the Alpha and the Omega, the beginning and the end. I will give unto him that thirsteth of the fountain of the water of life, freely. (7) **He that overcometh shall inherit these things‡; and I will**

---

  * L.T.Tr.b. A. WH. and RV. omit *to me.*

  † So L.T.Tr. Ab. WH. and RV.

  ‡ G.L.T.Tr.A. WH. and RV., read ταῦτα (*tauta*) *these things,* instead of πάντα (*panta*) *all things.*

> be his God, and 𝕳𝔢 shall be my son. (8)
> But the fearful, and unbelieving, and
> abominable, and murderers, and whore-
> mongers, and sorcerers, and idolators,
> and all liars, shall have their part in
> the lake which burneth with fire and
> brimstone : which is the second death."]

These are the words from the Throne. The command to write these things implies that the others had already been written.

Three times we have the expression " and He said ":

(1). All is to be made new ;

(2). All is faithful and true ; and

(3). All is accomplished which had been foretold and decreed.

John sees first the New Earth, then the Holy City ; then he hears of the blessings for the inhabitants of the city; and finally, the causes which shall have contributed to the exclusion of those who have no part in it.

The " fearful " are those who, through fear, *apostatise* : (the law provides for the cowardly, such as those in Gideon's army, Judges vii. 3). The "unbelieving " are like those of Titus i. 15. Matt. xi. 20-24. The " abominable " are like those in Lev. xviii. 22, 26, 27. And " murderers " and " sorcerers," *i.e.*, those that have commerce with unclean and lying spirits. These will abound in Antichrist's day; as will all the others here named.

We now come to the final two visions of the Bride and the City, described in xxi. 9—xxii. 5.

A. (page 645). xxi. 9—xxii. 5. *Vision.*
The Bride or the Holy City

A | *g* | xxi. 9-21.   Description   } The Holy City.
    | *h* | 22-27.   Privileges   }

  | *g* | xxii. 1, 2.   Description   } The Blessed Country.
    | *h* | 3-5.   Privileges   }

g. (see above), xxi. 9-21.   *Description. The Holy City*

xxi. 9. **And there came* one of the seven angels which had the seven vials full of the last seven plagues, and talked with me, saying,**

    "Come hither, I will show thee the Bride,
    the Lamb's wife."]

Here we are told exactly what was going to be shown to John. It was one of the Seven angels who had already shown John "great Babylon."

In order to see the harlot city (xvii. 1), John is taken into the wilderness (xvii. 3). To see the Holy City he is carried to a great mountain (xxi. 10).

It was the same with Ezekiel in chap. xl. 2.

We are not left to our own imagination as to what this Holy City is. We are distinctly told that it is *i.e.*, represents or contains "the Bride."

In chap. xix. we had the wife, γυνή (*gunē*). Here we have the Bride, νύμφη (*numphē*). The one was before the Millennium ; the other, the latter, is after it.

It does not say that the latter was then and there formed, but only that, at that point of the Vision, John saw it "coming down from heaven," where it had been ; but, for how long we are not told.

If the wife (chap. xix) was Israel; then this Bride is not Israel, but "of Israel."

---

* Omit πρός με (*pros me*) *to me*, G.L.T.Tr.A. WH. and RV.

We must remember the three distinct "callings" revealed in Scripture, and referred to on pages 589-593.

(1). We have the earthly calling of Israel, called out from all nations, for blessing in the Land. Israel was the "wife," and is so spoken of all through the Old Testament; and the marriage will be consummated when Rev. xix. 8 shall be fulfilled.

(2). We have "the heavenly calling," distinctly spoken of as such in Heb. iii. 1, of which a certain class of believing Israelites were "partakers." Among these we may put all those whom we speak of as "the Old Testament Saints."

In spite of the *earthly* promises to Israel, and in the midst of all those who cherished those *earthly* promises, there was an elect "heavenly calling" of those whose hopes were not earthly, but heavenly. They looked for no earthly portion, but they looked forward with a heavenly hope to a heavenly blessing. As it is written:

"These all died in faith, not having received the promises, but having seen them afar off, and were persuaded of them, and embraced them, and confessed that they were strangers and pilgrims (Gen. xxiii. 4. 1 Pet. ii. 11) on the earth. For they that say such things declare plainly that they seek a COUNTRY . . . a better country, that is, an HEAVENLY, wherefore God is not ashamed to be called their God: for he hath prepared for them a CITY" (Heb. xi. 13-16). And of Abraham it is said (*v.* 10): "He looked for THE CITY which hath FOUNDATIONS, whose builder and maker is God."

When the angel, therefore, says to John (Rev. xxi. 9), "Come hither, I will show thee the Bride, the Lamb's wife . . . and he showed me that great CITY, the holy

Jerusalem descending out of HEAVEN from God," what can we conclude but that here we have that "better country," and "the City" for which the Old Testament saints belonging to the "heavenly calling" looked ?

It will also be noted that the names "on the GATES" of the city are "the names of the twelve TRIBES of the children of Israel" (Rev. xxi. 12), while the names "in the FOUNDATIONS" are "the names of the TWELVE APOSTLES of the Lamb (*ver.* 14).

If this be not "the CITY" for which they and the Elect Remnant looked, then we ask, for what "City" did they look? Certainly not for an *earthly* city; but for this, of which we now see them, its blessed and happy inhabitants. No other city has these founda-tions; no other city has apostles and prophets to prophesy concerning God as its builder. God builds one City, His prophets and apostles are all concerned for the building of the City of the eternal ages. Their message concerning this city came from its builder and maker. The builder of it puts their names in the foundations of its walls; and the adornment of its foundations are the names of the twelve apostles. No other city could have such immortal, priceless foundations. Blessed foundations. This was the city; for this alone has foundations, all others will have vanished in *smoke*; this abides. This, then, is what Abraham, and his seed, by faith, looked for. This is the Holy City.

(3). Then, we have the other "calling," of which we read in Eph. i. 18, iv. 1. It is a "holy calling" (2 Tim. i. 9). It is a Divine calling.

If we identify the calling of the Church of God with the other callings we cannot but have confusion.

Here, in Rev. xxi., we have the New Heaven and the New Earth; we have the Twelve Tribes of Israel; and Twelve Apostles of the Lamb. We ask, What has all this to do with the Church—the Body of Christ? Has it not to do only and solely with the Holy City and with the Bride of the Lamb? The promise of Christ to the Twelve Apostles in Matt. xix. 28 (though that doubtless has its special fulfilment in the Millennium) has never been abrogated: but, we ask, what are we to do with it, if the Apostles form part of the Body of Christ? The Church is part of Christ, the Bridegroom; but the Apostles, here, form part of the Bride.*

In harmony also with this is the teaching of

EPHESIANS V. 25-33

Christians, in their selfishness, intrude themselves into the place of others as the Bride, and thus lose the blessed enjoyment of their own place which is theirs as part of the Bridegroom!

The Bride and the Bridegroom, though in a sense one, are yet distinct. And it is clear from all the scriptures relating to the Mystery, that the members of Christ's Body are part of the Bridegroom Himself. Whereas the elect Old Testament saints will form the Bride. See Isaiah xii. 6: "Cry out and shout, thou *Inhabitress* (marg.) of Zion: For great is the Holy One of Israel in the midst of thee." In Rev. xxii. 3, we read "The throne of God and of the Lamb shall be in it." Of

---

* This effectually disposes of the figment of "Apostolic Succession," which would never have been seriously entertained had not the truth connected with the Mystery been lost. And we ought to note that while the Twelve Apostles are thus separated off from the Church, the Apostle Paul was specially raised up to a different position altogether, and is identified with the Mystery.

the glory of this Holy City other scriptures speak. See Is. lx. 3, 14, 19, 20. Rev. xxi. 23, 24, 27. Is. liv. 11, 12.

True, the Apostle might address the saints concerning his desire to present them "as a chaste virgin to Christ" (2 Cor. xi. 2). But this no more declares that the Church *is* the Bride of Christ than that the Apostle himself was their father (1 Cor. iv. 15); or that he was their mother (Gal. iv. 19). In the one case he spoke of the painful anxiety of a mother; in another of the loving care of a father; while, in 2 Cor. xi. 2, he spoke of the jealousy of the friend of a bridegroom. The "Mystery" was a totally different thing.

So, in Eph. v. 28, 29, the argument is that husbands "ought to love their wives as their own bodies. He that loveth his wife loveth himself, for no man ever yet hated his own flesh; but nourisheth and cherisheth it, even as the Lord the Church, for we are members of His Body," *i.e.*, AS Christ loves HIS OWN BODY (Himself and the Church); so ought husbands to love their wives. Thus "the great secret" is employed as an argument as to the reciprocal duties of husbands and wives. In neither case is it said that the Church IS the wife, or that Christ IS the husband. But that AS Christ loves His Body (Himself and the Church), SO husbands ought to love their own bodies (*i.e.*, themselves and their wives).

The one thing that is clear, is that the Church is the Body of Christ; and that the *members* of that Body being "in Christ," are PART OF THE BRIDEGROOM. They cannot possibly, therefore, be the Bride herself as separate and distinct from the Bridegroom.

Another thing that is certain is that the mystery of the Church was not revealed in the Old Testament, but was "hid in God" (Eph. iii. 9) and "kept secret" (Rom. xvi. 25); "hid from ages and from generations" (Col. i. 26).

It is one thing to see an *illustration* of the Church in the Old Testament; but it is quite another thing to say that that is there *revealed*, which God distinctly declares *was not revealed !*

Gen. xxiv

has been, for example, widely taken as typical of Christ and the Church. Isaac is taken as the bridegroom, and Rebekah as the Church or the bride. True, the chapter *is illustrative*, but not of the Church. The bridegroom and the bride were both "ready' before either was called to the marriage. The bride was found in *the house of Abraham's brother*. Very special injunctions were given that she was not to be of "the Canaanites." "But," said Abraham to Eliezer, "thou shalt go unto *my country* and to *my kindred* and take a wife unto my son Isaac . . . thou shalt take a wife for my son *from thence*." Great emphasis is placed on this important condition in verses 3, 4, 7, 37, 38. Abraham and Nahor were brothers, and by Isaac's marriage with Rebekah, and Jacob's marriage with her brother Laban's daughters (Leah and Rachel), the *whole house of Nahor* was absorbed into the family of Abraham ! In direct contrast with this, it is again and again affirmed that the Church is composed of *both Jews and Gentiles*. These together make up, with Christ the Head, " one new man " (Eph. ii. 15). But *Gentiles* were expressly shut out when this typical wife was chosen; and Isaac, on receiving his bride, took her at once " into his mother Sarah's tent," thus forming the ground of the type as expounded in Gal. iv. 21-31.

Rebekah therefore represents, n >t the Mystery of Christ and the Church, but that great cloud of witnesses (the Old Testament saints), who, in the old dispensation, sacrificed, as she did, all wordly advantages for the Lord's sake. It is for these He is preparing that "city which hath foundations," and of which He Hinself is the Divine Architect. And truly, it is said of these, "if they had been mindful of that country from whence they came out (as Rebekah came), they might have had opportunity to return. But now they desire a better country, that is, an heavenly; wherefore God is not ashamed to be called their God: for He hath prepared for them a city" (Heb. xi. 15, 16).

It seems to us, therefore, quite clear that neither the "wife" in chap. xix. nor the Bride in chap. xxi. is the Church of God. The former is clearly referred to in the Parable of the "Ten Virgins" (Matt. xxv.), and in the prophecy of Psalm xlv. All these Scriptures are clear if we will only leave out the Church; but, all is confusion the moment we introduce it.

But, to return to this "Holy City," we repeat that all in this chapter (as in this whole Book) is intensely real.

It is a real city. Yet Barnes says, "No man can suppose that this is literally true." No! *We* do not "suppose" it, because we *believe* it to be true; and we find it easier to believe what God says, than to understand man's interpretation of it. It is strange that while materializing all really spiritual truths, interpreters should protest against the materialisation of those who would understand this of a literal city.

All other cities are shadows, if you like: for they all pass away; consequently, if this city be not real, then there never could have been the idea in God, of a city. We should have a *word* for which there would be no *thought*: a shadow without a substance!

Yes, this city is real, and its eternal duration is real also : for "there shall be no more curse" (xxii. 3).

This shows that it cannot refer to Millennial times, for the curse is seen in all its sin and wrath immediately on its close.

"Come and I will show thee the Bride," the angel says.

xxi. 10. **"And he carried me away by** (the) **spirit** (or in spirit) **to a mountain great and high, and showed me the holy * city Jerusalem, descending out of heaven from God, (11) having the glory of God : her radiance was like a stone most precious, even as a jasper stone, clear as crystal;]** Man says that "the idea of a city literally descending from heaven . . . . is absurd." † But we ask, Why ? True, it is contrary to our experience. But, are we to think everything absurd because we have heard nothing like it before ? We suppose it must ever be so with man. It was for this reason that travelling by railway was at first thought absurd ! To get from London to New York in a fortnight was once thought absurd ! For carriages to go without horses was an "idea" once thought to be absurd ! To telegraph without wires was once thought absurd !

For many generations no swans were known other than white ones ; and our experience would have led us to conclude that all swans were white. But now we know that in Australia there are *black* swans.

---

* G.L.T.Tr.A. WH. and RV. omit "the great."

† Barnes, *in loco.*

The experience of the savage is that wood will float, and iron will sink : hence, he will conclude an iron ship to be an impossiblity.

Many things we once thought, when measured by our experience, to be absurd have been proved to be the contrary.

And so it will be with this wondrous city. Absurd ! It would be absurd if God had no new and glorious things in store for man in a new Earth. Why is a new Earth less absurd than this Holy City ? With man it may be impossible ; and it may seem improbable. But " with God all things are possible." And he has prepared us for the revelation of it by saying to John " Write, for these words are faithful and true " (*v.* 5). In the face of this declaration, Who shall dare to question the reality of this description ? Man only exposes his folly and ignorance when he dares to question whether this is a literal city. Great Babylon was a literal city. Herodotus tells us that it was 120 furlongs on each side. Why should not this Holy City be 12000 ? Babylon had a wall 50 royal cubits wide and 200 in height. Why should not the wall of this Holy City be 144 cubits high ? Babylon had 100 gates of bronze. Why should not this have 12 gates of pearl ? In other words, why not believe what God says ? It is simpler, easier and happier.

There is a striking resemblance here to the earthly city described in Ezek. xl.—xlviii.

But the two cities are distinct in their origin and source ; and therefore not likely to be identical in their dimensions or character. Those who take the earthly city and the heavenly city to be the same, will necessarily be confused in their minds, and with their pens.

As to its light. There will be " no need of the sun." Its light is mysterious. Man once thought he knew all about "light," and raised objections against Gen. i. 3, because it was called into existence before the sun, moon, and stars. But since the discovery of the " X rays," man has found that he really knows very little about light; and Professor Röntgen has himself confessed as much when, asked what light is, he replied that *at present no one could venture to come to any conclusions.* So it is better to believe God, and to wait till man has discovered some more mistakes in things he once thought he knew.

Let us listen further to God's description of this Holy City :

xxi. 12. **And it had a wall great and high, and twelve gates, and at the gates twelve angels, and names written thereon, which are** (the names *) **of the twelve tribes of the sons of Israel: (**13**) On the east three gates; and † on the north three gates; and † on the south three gates; and † on the west three gates. (**14**) And the wall of the city had twelve foundations, and on ‡ them twelve § names of the twelve apostles of the Lamb.]** Twelve is the number that runs through all the measurements of this city. For twelve is the number of *governmental perfection* ; ‖ and here, God's government is supreme. All is in harmony, and the very numbers and measurements are used

---

* L.Tr^b.A^b. add " the names."

† L.T.Tr.A. WH. and RV. add " and."

‡ G.L.T.Tr.A. WH. and RV. read *on them.*

§ G.L.T.Tr.A. WH. and RV. add " twelve."

‖ *Three* is the number of *Divine* perfection ; *seven* of *spiritual* perfection ; *ten* of *ordinal* perfection ; and *twelve* of *governmental* perfection.

in absolute perfection. The order in the cardinal points
is E.N.S.W.; in Numbers it is E.S.W.N.; in Ezek. xlii.
16-19 it is the same as here; while in Ezek. xlviii. 16,
30-34 it is N.E.S.W.

The woman in chap. xii. had the changeful moon for
her foundation. Great Babylon had the Wild Beast.
But this city has twelve foundations.

The names inscribed thereon are the names of the
Twelve Apostles of the Lamb. The Twelve who followed
the Lord Jesus, the Lamb of God, when on earth.
These are separated from the other apostles, given after
the Ascension of Christ, to the Church of God (Eph. iv.
11-15).

All this shows that Israel is in question here, and not
the Church of God. The Church is part of the Bridegroom, and will then be " with Christ." This city is
separate from Christ, and occupies a distinct and
separate position as the Bride.

The Twelve Apostles are associated with the Twelve
Tribes, and not with the Church of God. Paul's
name is not here, nor are the other subsequent apostles
of the Church. Abraham "looked for a city which
hath foundations, whose builder and maker is God"
(Heb. xi. 10). Here is that city; and here are the
foundations. God is its maker and builder.

The Dimensions of the City

xxi. 15. **And he that talked with me had a measuring-rod of gold to measure the city, and the gates
thereof, and the wall thereof.** (16) **And the city
lieth four square, and its length is as great as its
breadth: and he measured the city with the reed,
12,000 stadia** (Eng., furlongs). **The length and the**

breadth, and the height of it are equal. (17) **And he measured the wall thereof, an hundred and forty and four cubits, according to the measure of a man, that is, of the angel.**] This means that, in the matter of measure, angels and men use the same.

In Ezek. xlviii. 16 we first have the measurement of each side 4,500. In verse 35 we have the total of the circumference 18,000.

When a square is given, it is usual to state the measure of one of the sides definitely, as in Ezek. xlv. 2; xlviii. 16-20, 30, 32-34.

In this case, the city will be 1,500 miles square. Otherwise the whole measure is first given, and then we have to divide it into four before we can have the measure of the sides, which is the point in question.

The " wall " is quite a different matter. That is 144 cubits high, equal all round.

We have the shadow of it in Exodus xxiv. Sinai, *changed in character* (because of the better blood than that of verse 6), to Sion. In Exodus we have Moses and Aaron, his two sons, and seventy Elders of Israel upon the Mount ; and we are told that they *saw* the God of Israel, that they ate and drank there, and that He laid not His hands on the nobles of Israel. We have in verse 4 the twelve pillars, which appear to answer to the Twelve Apostles. Now, all this was preliminary to the Lord dwelling in their midst. The time had not come for the people to dwell about and upon the Mount with God. The people were in a transition stage; therefore, a sanctuary was needful. But the heavenly Jerusalem is a magnificent mountain (Heb. xii. 22).

The inhabitants in this glorious dwelling dwell upon the Mount of God, and therefore the measurement belongs to its height, as well as to its length and breadth; and as Mount Sinai was once fenced off, so also is the New Jerusalem. At Sinai, Israel was outside the fence; but inasmuch as Moses, Joshua, and the Elders of Israel were admitted within the bounds, we see foreshadowed this city of the New Jerusalem. Under these conditions, therefore, the measure 12,000 refers to but one side; otherwise, the height of the city is not specified at all, which would be necessary if only the sum total of the four sides had been given.

Some have taken the measure 12,000 furlongs to be that of the circumference. But to this it may be answered that, as only one measurement is given, it must belong to one item of the city; because, otherwise, he gives a measurement which must first be divided by four before we know the length, breadth, and height; whereas, if he gives the measurement in one direction, and then tells us that all the other directions are equal to the one given, we have everything clear, without any roundabout way of getting at the thing intended. And, as we have to do with the Mount of God, which is the throne of God (Rev. xxii. 1)—Gen. xxii. 14 is fulfilled in Rev. v. 6; xxi. 22—where is there any difficulty in taking the one measurement as giving the length, breadth, or height? Is 375 miles high easier to believe than 1500?

The Materials of the City

xxi. 18. **And the building of the wall of it was of jasper: and the city was pure gold, like unto clear glass.** (19) **And the foundations of the wall of the city** were **adorned with every kind of precious stone. The first foundation** was **a jasper** (dark green, and transparent, with red veins): **the second, a sapphire** (**azure** blue, almost transparent) : **the third, a chalce-dony** (a kind of agate or onyx, probably bluish-white, and semi-transparent): **the fourth, an emerald** (a vivid green): (20) **the fifth, a sardonyx** (a mixture of chalce-dony and cornelian, a flesh colour) : **the sixth, a sardius** (probably the cornelian, the red being sometimes vivid) : **the seventh, a chrysolite** (yellow or gold in colour, and transparent): **the eighth, a beryl** (of a sea-green colour): **the ninth, a topaz** (to-day a yellow, but among the ancients it was a pale green): **the tenth, a chrysoprasus** (pale yellow and green, classed by moderns under topaz): **the eleventh, a jacinth** (a deep red flame colour or violet colour): **the twelfth, an amethyst** (a violet colour).] It is somewhat difficult to identify these stones with exactness, some of them being of various colours. But if we made a selection from the above, where we have a choice, they may be arranged thus :

X ⎧ Green (Jasper)
   ⎨   Blue (Sapphire)
   ⎪   Blue (Chalcedony)
   ⎩ Green (Emerald)

           Y ⎧ Red (Sardonyx)
              ⎩ Red (Sardine)

X ⎧ Yellow (Chrysolite)
   ⎨   Green (Beryl)
   ⎪ Yellow (Topaz)
   ⎩   Green (Chrysoprasus)

           Y ⎧ Violet (Jacinth)
             ⎩ Violet (Amethyst)

It will be observed that the twelve are arranged, according to colour, into sets of *four* alternating with

sets of *two* ; each pair of two differing from the pair of
fours by being similar (Red and Violet respectively).

The first pair of four is arranged as an introversion,
the second pair is arranged as an alternation.

xxi. 21. **And the twelve gates** were **twelve pearls ;
each one of the gates respectively was of one pearl :
and the street** (or street material) **of the city was
pure gold, as it were transparent glass**]   The word
" street " can scarcely mean that the city had only one
thoroughfare ; so that it seems better to take the word
generally, as denoting the street material of which all
the streets were made.

πλατεῖα (*plateia*), however, means any wide, open
space, such as the large, central square common to
most cities ; and this is included, if we take it of all the
space not built on ; or as the street material, which is
gold instead of mud.

The *Plateia* will doubtless be a broad open space.
A place for public gatherings. Not a street, as we
know it.   For this *Plateia* has the River of Life flowing
through it, and the Tree of Life growing in it. Thoroughfares there will of course be ; but there is a reason for
this wide, open space.   It reproduces Paradise.

The twelve gates imply the thoroughfares ; but the
gates are not for defence ; only for ornament : and
therefore constructed with that view.

h. (page 651), xxi. 22-27. *Privileges*

xxi. 22. **And I saw no temple therein : for the
Lord God the Almighty and the Lamb, are the
Temple of it.**]   No temple or " place of worship " is
needed ; for the whole city is hallowed and pervaded by
the presence of God.   This fact separates this part of
the book from the former part, where the temple is seen

(iii. 12 ; vii. 15 ; xi. 1, 16-19 ; xiv. 15, 17 ; xv. 5, 6, 8 ; xvi. 1, 17) ; and shows that we are here carried far beyond millennial times.

xxi. 23. **And the city hath no need of the sun, neither of the moon, that they should shine on her :* for the glory of God illumined her, and the Lamb is her light.**] The dwelling-place of God's glory in the Tabernacle and the Temple on Earth had no light of sun or moon ; for the Shechinah or glory of God was sufficient. This also marks off the period as being post-millennial ; for during the Millennium " the light of the moon shall be as the light of the sun, and the light of the sun shall be seven-fold " (Isa. xxx. 26). This refers to the Earth, though even then the Holy City in the Land will be independent of the sun and moon (see Isa. lx. 19, 20 ; and iv. 5).

24. **And the nations † shall walk** (or travel) **by means of her light : and the kings of the earth do bring their glory ‡ into her.** (25) **And her gates shall never be shut at all by day : for night shall not exist there** (it will be always day). (26) **And they shall bring the glory and honour of the nations unto it.**] So that nations will exist on the new Earth.

What is the origin of these Nations (Rev. xxi. 24)? Matt. xxv. 31-46 supplies the clue. When the Lord has put down all earthly oppositions, then those nations which remain are gathered together, and their status for the Millennium is determined : and it is determined by their conduct to the Jew, as shown by

---

* G.L.T.Tr.A. WH. and RV. read αὐτῇ (*autē*) *on her*, instead of ἐν αὐτῇ, *in her* or it.

† G.L.T.Tr.A. WH. and RV. omit " of the saved."

‡ L.T.Tr.A. WH. and RV. omit " and honour."

the term "My brethren." The result is, there are nations other than Israel, who enter into the earthly kingdom of the Son of man.

Now, as sin broke out in the garden, so also once more, sin breaks out among the nations under the Lord's Sovereignty after the Millennium.

The question is, do the terms "Gog and Magog" (xx. 8) include *every* nation (apart from Israel) at the end of the Millennium?   The terms Gog and Magog imply that only certain nations are concerned, and their locality also indicates the same thing—they dwell at the "four quarters of the earth."   They are those that are farthest away from the capital of the earth—the four corners· "The nations that are in the four corners of the earth." The devil's deceit includes the same idea that Jeroboam acted out I Kings xii. 27-33.   It is to be observed that the "four corners," are distinct from the "*breadth*" of the earth; that is, that the "four corners" lie *beyond the* "*breadth*."   These considerations localise Gog and Magog, and show that the rebellion is not universal.

The "four corners" then represent the extreme limits of the earth, which has Jerusalem for its centre; so that the points of the compass, N.S.E.W. are related to Jerusalem, and mean the farthest habitable parts of the earth in these directions.

Going up "upon the breadth of the earth" suggests a considerable width of territory, practically unoccupied; hence, that the people of Gog had purposely got as far away from the centre of government as they could.   As their hearts were far away, so they removed their persons; hence, Satan would easily find entrance to their foolish minds, to set up their own government, and then go *en masse* armed to throw off the yoke and get possession of the wonderful tree.

This leaves it open, that, at the end of the Millennium, the same experience will obtain as at the beginning: namely, that there will be " nations " for the Lord's right hand, or in other words, there will be nations to introduce to the New Kingdom upon the New Earth, and with this we may connect the Lord's promise to Abraham, Gen. xvii. 20, in connection with xxv. 1-4. Rom. iv. 16, 17 seems to include all who possess Abraham's faith—see 16, " us all." Now, if the same experience as to the nations, obtains at the end of the Millennium, as at the beginning, we see the " *Whence* " of the nations of Rev. xxi. 24. Those nations, during the Millennium, that walk in the Divine light of the earthly Jerusalem, are transferred to the new earth, to walk in the Heavenly light of the New Jerusalem.

We notice also, the same characteristic of the " goats " Matt. xxv.; they depart into an abiding fire, with Gog and Magog of Rev. xx. 9.

But only " kings " will " enter into " the city. This looks as if these " kings " were something more than individuals selected out of the nations to rule them.

The words, " of the saved," are spurious, being a later addition, arising from the traditional belief that there are only two classes—" saved and lost." But, as we have before observed, there are several classes of the saved, as there are several resurrections, differing in glory as star differs from star. Here, then, there are the nations with their kings; there are the citizens of this holy city; there is the Bride; there is the Church of God (occupying the highest place of all). The nations are not the Church; neither are the citizens of this holy city. But the mystery of Christ and the Church has its own peculiar privilege and destiny described in its

own Church Epistles.   Subordination is the Divine
plan of government, for eternity as well as for time.
Israel will be subordinate to the Twelve Apostles; the
overcomers will have precedence over the nations
(Rev. ii. 26; xii. 5); and the Church will rule angels
(1 Cor. vi. 3).   While the Holy City is independent of
created luminaries, the nations are not independent of
the light of the city.   They need no guide thither, for
her light is a constant pillar of cloud and of fire.

  xxi. 27.   **And there shall never enter into her anything unclean, or whosoever worketh abomination,
and a lie** (or a lying abomination): **but only** (*lit.*, except)
those who are written in the Lamb's book of life.]
This does not imply that there will then be any unclean
thing that could enter in to defile it.   It merely contrasts
this with all other cities which have ever existed.
It follows from this, that the nations then on the earth,
and their kings, are written in the book of life.   It also
follows that these, being among the saved, there must
be different parties of saved ones.   All saved *from* the
same eternal doom, but not all saved *for* the same state
in glory.   All will be in the eternal glory, but in different
positions.   The nations will occupy their own place;
while Israel and the Church will occupy theirs, respectively.

  The " working abomination " refers to idolatry :
either to the making of idols * or the worshipping of
them.†   The contrast is not between these and others
then on the earth ; but between these dwellers and all

---

 * See Isa. xliv. 9-18 ; xlv. 16 ; xlvi. 6.   Ezek. vii. 20 ; xxii. 3.
Deut. xxvii. 15.

 † Lev. xviii. 20-30.   Deut. xii. 31.   Jer. viii. 12 ; xi. 15.   Ezek.
xxxiii. 26.

former dwellers; between this city and all former cities.

The following first five verses of chap. xxii. form part of the last of these Visions. There ought never to have been a chapter division here. Chap. xxi. should end at xxii. 5; and chap. xxii. should commence at xxii. 6; containing, as it does, the Conclusion of the book, and corresponding exactly with the Introduction (page 129) in chap. i., as we shall see below.

It is the description of Paradise Regained which is the great subject of these five verses. It is not what man would have imagined, for he looks for an unsubstantial, spiritual existence. But here we have substance, and realities far grander than those in the book of Genesis. Here is the complement of Gen. i. and ii., where the beginnings and the endings meet and harmonise, and complete the whole. Gen. i., ii. is the " beginning." Rev. xxi. 1—xxii. 5 is the " end."

g. (page 651), xxii. 1, 2. *Description*

Paradise regained and Eden restored

xxii. 1. **And he showed me a** * **river of living water, clear as crystal, going forth out of the throne of God and of the Lamb.** (2) **In the midst of the street of it** (the city) **and of the river, on this side and on that side, was there the tree of life** (*i.e.,* trees of that kind), **producing twelve kinds of fruit, yielding its fruit according to each month: and the leaves of the tree were for the healing of the nations** (which are

---

* G.L.T.Tr.A. WH. and RV. omit " pure."

thus distinguished from the Citizens of the Holy City). **(3) And there shall be no longer any curse : and the throne of God and of the Lamb shall be in her : and His servants shall serve Him; (4) and they shall see His face : and His name shall be on their foreheads. (5) And there shall be no longer * any night : and they have no need of a lamp or (*lit.*, and) light of the sun; because the Lord God will give them light: and they shall reign for ever and ever.]** There is a similar provision for Millennial days (Ezek. xlvii. 12). But these final Visions of Paradise regained are as far beyond the Millennial City, as that will be beyond the past and present Jerusalem. All are literal and real.

We have the city and its light; and the river and trees; and the relations of the citizens and nations to all. It was promised to the overcomers in Rev. ii. 7, and the fulfilment is recorded in xxii. 14, 17. The overcomers are literal beings: so are the leaves of this tree for their use. Its healing leaves do not imply disease or suffering or pain, but clearly refer to the eating of the "tree of life" (Gen. ii. 9; iii. 22, 23, 24), and the prolongation of life "for ever."

That "tree of life" was intended to preserve Adam and Eve in life. But the fall entailed the loss of that wondrous gift. The man was driven out of the garden for the special reason that it should not be possible for him to eat of it : for the reason given is, "*lest he put forth his hand, and take also of the tree of life; and eat and live for ever.*"

It is clear from this that the "tree of life" was the means by which Adam would have lived on for ever.

---

* G.L.T.Tr. A.WH. and RV. read ἔτι (*eti*), *longer*, instead fo ἐκε (*ekei*), *there*.

Hence in the very day of his disobedience he was cut off from it, and his death was certain and sure.

So important was it that he should not " live for ever " in his sin and shame, that Cherubim and a flaming sword were placed to keep and preserve both it and him from this evil.

Eternal life was to be obtained and enjoyed henceforth only in and through Christ. " The Tree of life " was to be preserved; and here it is in Paradise, restored. No mere present " intermediate state " as Tradition teaches ; but a future glorious restoration of the Paradise lost. The tree of life will also be restored; and, by its leaves, life will be preserved and prolonged for ever and ever. No created being can stand apart from the Creator. The very mention of the Tree immediately brings to mind the curse, and we are told that it will then be no more.

The Bible begins with the description of man in Eden, the garden of the Lord, the Paradise of God. What God's counsels were with regard to that garden are not revealed ; for all was broken by the entrance of the old Serpent : and not until he shall have been cast into the lake of fire, will those counsels, for man. be renewed, restored, and carried out.

Elohim had created man ; and, as Jehovah Elohim, He visited man in that garden — revealing Himself and His wondrous works to man (Gen. ii. 19, 20). After the first sin, Adam and his wife heard the sound of the footsteps coming at the wonted hour of this Divine Communion (Gen. iii. 8). But Satan introduced himself, and insinuated doubts into the minds of our first parents as to the truth of God's words (Gen. iii. 1). He told them that the consequences of disobedience would not be as God had said. Eve had prepared the way for this by putting as a *contingency* ("lest ye die, " Gen. iii. 3), that which God had announced as a *certainty* ("Ye shall surely die," Gen. ii. 17). Satan at once seizes on this and assures them "Ye shall not surely die." They believed Satan's lie instead of God's truth. Here was their sin. They soon discovered which was truth, for the sentence was speedily executed; they were driven out from the Paradise of God; and, cut off from "the tree of life," they began to die the very day they ate of the tree of knowledge.

Students of God's Word have lost sight of all this foundation truth. It lies on the very threshold of the Scriptures, and is of infinite importance if we would understand all that is subsequently revealed.

The one question henceforth is, How shall man get back to that Paradise which he has lost ? The very next chapter tells us. In Gen. iv. we have, as the first step revealed, God's way, which Abel took; and man's way, which Cain invented. There never have been other than those two ways—"the way of God" on the one hand, and "the way of Cain" (Jude 11) on the other In the one way, the believing sinner is brought to the confession

"Nothing in my hand I bring."

In the other, independent, rebellious man says the opposite—"Something in my hand I bring." This is the one thing common to all systems of religion. They quarrel and fight to the death over the question as to what that "Something" is to be: but they are all at one in agreeing that it must be *something*. And so the weary conflict has gone on, and will continue to the end.

It is that end which we have before us here. And it is the object of the Apocalypse to tell us how that end will be reached.

" The Jew, and the Gentile, and the Church of God " (1 Cor. x. 32) each has its own destiny—

" The Church of God " will have been caught up to meet the Lord in the air, long before this, to enjoy its blessed portion for ever with the Lord.

"Israel" will have been "planted" in its own inheritance.

And now the Gentile, mankind as a whole, will regain the Paradise lost; and, in Eden restored, will have the glories and joys of God's manifested presence, as described in Rev. xxii. 1-5, 14, 17.

Tradition has made the Word of God of none effect Paradise is always used in Scripture of a definite place from Genesis to Revelation. It is described in Gen. ii. ; it is lost in Gen. iii. ; its restoration is spoken of in Luke xxiii. 43 ; it is seen in vision, in 2 Cor. xii. 2, 4 ; it is promised in Rev. ii. 7. And here (Rev. xxii. 1-5, 14, 17), we see the promise fulfilled, and the lost Paradise become Paradise regained. " The tree of life " and " the water of life " were, and will ever be, its chief distinguishing marks of blessedness.

Man ignores all this, and has turned Paradise into a present place, to which he has given his own name, and calls it " the Intermediate State "—a term unknown to Scripture ! There is no " tree of life " in it ; and no " water of life." It is man's *Tradition* pure and simple ; and is a poor substitute for the substantial glories of Divine revelation.

If Tradition be true, then Rev. xxii. is false, and there can be no " Paradise of God " at all.

The " Higher Critics " tell us that the Paradise of Gen. ii., iii. is a myth, and Christians generally treat the Paradise of Rev. ii. 7; xxii. 1-5, 14, 17 as a myth; for having substituted a present Paradise with Abraham's bosom " and "a great gulf" instead of "the tree of life " and " the water of life," they have no place left lor the Paradise of God, which is to be restored.

There are not two Paradises in the place of the one that was lost. Hence, by receiving and holding Tradition, they thus practically " take away from the words of this book " (xxii. 19) all that is said about it : for that solemn warning is given in immediate connection with this " water of life," (*v.* 17), and this " tree of life " (*v* 14).*

The word " servants " (verse 3) tells us that the church of God is not here (see pages 28-31). They shall " see His face " refers back to our first parents, who hid themselves among the trees of the garden. They shall reign in a higher sense than those in Rev. xx. 4-6 ; and that, not for a thousand years, but for ever and ever.

This is the brief summary of the New Heavens and the New Earth; of Paradise regained ; of the Holy City, and its inhabitants; and all the people of the New Earth. More is said below, page 684-6.

---

* See further on this subject, *Things to Come* (vol. viii.), May, 1902.

21

THE CONCLUSION
(22:6-21)

THE CONCLUSION OF THE WHOLE BOOK

This *Conclusion* is modelled precisely on the same lines, as to structure, as the *Introduction*. It is brief and very impressive. Its scope seems to be to anticipate the difficulties of the reader, by assuring him again and again as to the solemnity and truth of the words of this book.

Their absolute truth and certainty are pressed upon us. Thrice it is repeated in this Book that these say. ings are " faithful and true " : xix. 9 ; xxi. 5 ; xxii. 6. In the Introduction and Conclusion it is (three times) affirmed that these words came from God (and not, therefore, from John, though they came through John) : in i. 1 and xxii. 6, 16. In both also is a blessing pronounced on the readers and keepers of this book : i. 3 and xxii. 7.

This is what the Book claims to be. If these claims be not true, then the book is nothing better than a forgery ; and is unworthy of our attention or consideration.

It seems to be the one great purpose of this Conclusion to press these claims upon us in the strongest possible manner.

Four times we have the person testifying ; and four times the things testified. Four times we have the nearness of the Advent proclaimed ; and four times the blessing announced.

The following is the Structure, and when we compare it with the Introduction (page 129), we shall at once see that it is constructed on the same model :—

A. (page 118), xxii. 6-21.   CONCLUSION

A¹ | a¹ | **6-.** The Angel testifying
   | b¹ | -6. The things testified. "Which must speedily come to pass" (Compare i. -1)
   | B¹ | c¹ | 7-. Advent. " Behold, I come quickly "
   | | d¹ | -7. Benediction. " Blessed is he . . ." (See i. 3-)

A² | a² | 8, 9. The Angel testifying
   | b² | 10, 11. The things testified. "The prophecy of this book" (i. -3, " the time is at hand ")
   | B² | c² | 12, 13. Advent. " Behold, I come quickly . . . "
   | | d² | 14, 15. Benediction. " Right to the tree of life "

A³ | a³ | 16-. The Angel testifying. " I Jesus have sent mine angel " (i. -1-)
   | b³ | -16- The things testified. Jesus the hope of Israel (i. 4)
   | B³ | c³ | -16. Advent. The person of the coming one described as " the Morning Star "
   | | d³ | 17. Benediction. " Come " and take " the water of life "

A⁴ | a⁴ | 18-. Jesus Himself testifying. " I testify " (i. -17, 18)
   | b⁴ | -18, 19. The things testified. " If anyone . . . "
   | B⁴ | c⁴ | 20. Advent. " Surely I come quickly " (i. 7-). Promise and answering cry
   | | d⁴ | 21. Benediction. " The grace of our Lord " (i. -4-, 5-)

THE FIRST FOUR MEMBERS

a². (page 677), xxii. 6-.   *The Angel Testifying*

xxii. 6-. **And he said unto me,**] It is the angel of
i. 1, reassuring John as to the truth of what he had been
" sent " to show and to tell him.

b¹. (page 677), xxii. -6.   *The Things Testified*

-6. **" These words are faithful and true : and the
Lord God of the spirits* of the prophets sent his
angel to show unto His servants things which must
come to pass speedily.**] The reading "spirits of the
prophets " must be taken as the Figure *Metonymy*, by
which the word "spirits " is put for *the gifts of the Spirit*,
as in 1 Cor. xiv. 12, 32, &c. And the Figure is used
to emphasise the fact that the revelations made by
the prophets were given by the Holy Spirit of God;
and were not their own sending forth or of themselves.
Here, note also that it is still the "servants" of
God who are specially addressed as being concerned
in the interpretation of this book. (See page 28).

c¹. (page 677), xxii. 7-.   *The Advent*

7-. **And † behold, I come quickly :**] The words of the
Angel pass into the words of Christ, which he was commissioned to report. So in verse 12, and xi. 3. This
corresponds with chap. i. 7, as does xxii. 16.

d¹. (page 677), xxii. -7.   *The Benediction*

-7. **blessed is he that keepeth the words of the
prophecy of this book.**] Again the blessing of i. 3 is

---

*G.L.T.Tr.A. WH. and RV. read πνευμάτων τῶν (*pneumatōn
tōn*) *spirits of the*, instead of τῶν ἁγίων (*tōn hagiōn*) *the holy.*

† G.L.T.Tr.A. WH. and RV. add " and."

repeated, showing the importance of the study of this book. And it is "this book"; not merely certain parts of it, but the book as a whole. The Lord does not say who *understand it*, but who "keep its sayings" in their hearts, for the time is at hand; *i.e.*, the time next in order to the present.

No other dispensation is to intervene, and the sayings of this book are to be kept for the time that is at hand.

THE SECOND FOUR

a². (page 677), xxii. 8, 9. *The Angel Testifying*

8. **And ℥ John was he who heard and saw these things.* And when I heard and saw them I fell down to worship before the feet of the angel who was showing me these things. (9) And he saith to me "Beware; do it not: †I am a fellow-servant of thine, and of thy brethren the prophets, and of those who keep the words of this book: Worship God."]** Again John was about to make the same mistake. The double correction shows how firm is the decree that God alone is to receive worship; and that it may not be rendered to any created being. Observe, also, that the Angel is a "fellow-servant" with John (for all *serve* God). Brotherhood is not restricted to *flesh;* it is according to *nature.* "Fellow-servant" implies only common service according to station and position. (See page 28).

b². (page 677), xxii. 10, 11. *The Things Testified*

10. **And he saith unto me, "Seal not the words of the prophecy of this book: for the time is at**

---

* This is the order of the words according to G.L.Tr.A. WH. and RV.

† G.L.T.Tr.A. WH. and RV. omit γάρ (*gar*) *for*.

hand."] This command is in contrast with chap. x. 4, where it is a special prophecy in the midst of general prophecies, and is to be sealed up. It is in contrast also with Dan. xii. 4, 8, 9, where Daniel was to seal up the Vision, because another Dispensation was to intervene before that Vision could be fulfilled. That Dispensation concerned the mystery of Christ and the Church. That mystery will have been completed long before the Apocalypse opens, and therefore the command is given here " Seal not."

When the Angel commanded Daniel to seal up the Vision, he immediately added, " Many shall be purified, and made white, and tried ; but the wicked shall do wickedly : and none of the wicked shall understand " Dan xii. 10).

When the Angel, here, commands John not to seal up the prophecy, similar words are immediately added :

11. **He that is unjust** (pres. part. of condition), **let him act unjustly still** (aor., relating to acts, not to condition) : **and he that is defiled** (morally polluted), **let him defile himself still : and he that is righteous, let him work* righteousness still : and he that is holy, let him be holy still.**] These mysteriously solemn words have no reference to the Post-Millennial or Eternal state. They are given as a present statement, and as a reason for the injunction to " Seal not," which immediately precedes them.

(1) " Seal not the words." Proclaim them ; make them known ; even though evil men go on in their wickedness, and the righteous in their righteousness.

---

* L.T.Tr.A. WH. and RV. read δικαιοσύνην ποιησάτω (*dikaio sunēn poiēsatō*) *let him work righteousness*, instead of δικαιωθήτω (*dikaiōthētō*) *let him be righteous*.

Yea, though none heed them, and the wise reject them,
"Seal them not." The injunction is for those who
shall belong to the period when that which is now
called "the time at hand" shall have become time
present. In that case, they belong to the time of the
Apostasy.

(2) "The time is nigh." Let men go on their way;
the time is short. As though it said, in the spirit of
Matt. xxvi. 45, "Sleep on now, and take your rest; the
hour is at hand." Compare Ezek. iii. 27.

(3) A third reason follows. Let the wicked go on
with his wickedness, and the righteous in his righteousness. My advent is near; and my judgment and my
reward are with me.

c². (page 677), xxii. 12, 13. *The Advent*

12. * **Behold, I come quickly; and my reward is
with me, to give to every man as his work is.†
(13) I am the Alpha and the Omega, the First and
the Last, the Beginning and the End.]** This is the
great reason why the righteous are to persevere and
hold on their way. Their reward is certain, for the
Advent is sure. The Speaker is the Lord Jesus; and
that He is God is clear from the attributes used of
Him; for they belong only to God. (See Isa. xli. 4;
xliii. 10; xliv. 6; xlviii. 12.) Even though the Angel
be the speaker, he speaks in the name of Him who
commissions him. There are other places in this book
where fresh speakers are introduced without being
named.

---

* G.L.T.Tr.A. WII. and RV. omit "and."

† L.T.Tr.A. WH. and RV. read ἐστίν (*es'in*) *is*, instead of ἔσται
(*estai*) *shall be.*

682 / Conclusion

d². (page 677), xxii. 14, 15.   *The Benediction*

14. Blessed are they that do His commandments (or **wash their robes** *), that they may have right

* This is the reading of L.T.Tr. A. WH. and RV., instead of "keep His commandments," as in the AV. The MS. authorities are divided; the Vatican MS. (B) supporting the AV., and the Alex. (A) and Sinaitic (ℵ) supporting the RV. Thus both are ancient, and the reading of A and ℵ may have been originally a marginal gloss, finding its way later into the Text.

The Coptic Version also has the "*commandments*" reading as do the Fathers Tertullian, A.D. 200 ; Cyprian, Bishop of Carthage, 248-258 ; Tichonius, 390 ; Andreas, Bishop of Caesarea in Cappadocia, Cent. **vi.** ; and his successor, Arethas, Cent. **x.**

It is curious that, though the great Vatican MS. (B) supports the AV., the Vulgate does not follow it, but reads "that wash their robes," according to the Codex Amiatinus (A.D. 541) in Florence, and the Codex Fuldensis (Cent. vi.). Three Fathers also support the Vulgate reading, viz., Primasius (Cent. vi.) ; Fulgentius, Bishop in Africa (508-533) ; and Athanasius, Bishop of Alexandria (326-373).

The Clementine Vu'gate (Authorized by the Council of Trent) adds, "in the blood of the Lamb," though there is no Greek MS. authority for it whatsoever.

All the Romish Versions (including, of course, the English "Douai")' being made from the Clementine or Tridentine Vulgate, naturally have the full reading—"that wash their robes in the blood of the Lamb"— the latter part being *quite unauthorized by any Greek Text*, as we have said. They have this reading solely on textual grounds, and not because of any Romish or Protestant reasons.

The two readings are much alike,

ΟΙΠΛΥΝΟΝΤΕΣΤΑСΟΤΟΛΑСΑΥΤΩΝ

ΟΙΠΟΙΥΝΤΕΣΤΑСΕ̄ΤΟΑСΛΑΥΤΟΥ

The upper line is "that wash their robes." The lower line is "that do his commandments." The difference is exceedingly small, especially when we remember that ΟΙ was frequently written Υ. It looks as though the upper line was the original reading ; but many hold the opposite view.

In any case it is entirely a question of *reading* and not of *translation*.

to the tree of life, and may enter in through the
gates into the city.] It is to be noted that in the
passage which speaks of washing their robes (vii. 14), it
is the *past* tense, because the act is spoken of as having
been done in the past by those who have come out of
the great tribulation, But here, it is in the *present*
tense, because the words of the Angel contemplate, not
those now present in this dispensation of grace, or in the
next of judgment ; but in the yet future dispensation of
glory for the citizens of the holy city, distinguishing those
who had been on the former earth from the nations
of the new earth. The washing of robes has no reference to those in the previous dispensations.

15. **Without are dogs, and sorcerers, and whoremongers, and murderers, and idolators, and whosoever loveth and practiseth a lie]** These are not on
the new earth. They are " without," and, according
to xxi. 8, will have then been cast into the lake which
burneth with fire and brimstone. The expression
" dogs " is used in accordance with Eastern idiom of all
unclean, vile, and injurious persons.

THE THIRD FOUR

a³. (page 677), xxii. 16-. *Jesus Himself Testifying.*

xxii. 16-. ¶ **Jesus sent mine angel** (i. 1) **to testify
unto you]** It is the Lord Himself again, and the
pronoun is emphatic.

b. (page 677), xxii. -16-. *The Things Testified*

-16-. **these things in the assemblies.]** It is to
the assemblies of chaps. ii. and iii. that these things were
and will be specially testified. For them, this book will

have its special interpretation.   The *application* is for all
the servants of God (i. 1) now, and in all time ; but
the *interpretation* is specially for the *assemblies* who will
be on the earth during the fulfilment of " the prophecy
of this book."

c³.   (page 677), xxii. -16.   *The Advent*

-16. " **I am the Root and the Offspring of David,
the bright, the Morning Star.**"]   These titles are
essentially and exclusively Jewish : and proclaim their
owner as the coming one who shall confirm and fulfil all
the promises made unto David.   The Lord Jesus is
at once the " Root" whence David sprang, and the
"Offspring" which sprang from David.   (See Isa. xi. 1.
John viii. 55-59).   On this fact the Lord's question was
based in Matt. xxii. 41-46.

But there is a third title—" The Morning Star," which
ushers in the Eternal day.   The reference is to Num.
xxiv. 17.

d³.   (page 677), xxii. 17.   *Benediction*

17. **And the Spirit and the Bride say, Come thou,
And let him that heareth** (these things) **say, Come
thou.   And he that thirsteth, let him come.   And
he who willeth** (or desireth to enter), **let him take of
the living water freely.**]   This defines the Blessing,
and goes back to the very beginning, embracing the
enjoyment of all that was then lost.   In Gen. iii. 22-24,
the solemn sentence was pronounced and executed :—

" And now, lest he put forth his hand, and take also
of the tree of life, and eat, and live for ever ; therefore
the LORD God sent him forth from the Garden of Eden,
to till the ground from whence he was taken.   So he
drove out the man, and he placed (as in a Taber-

nacle) at the east of the Garden of Eden, Cherubim, and a flaming sword, which turned every way to keep (or preserve, Gen. ii. 15) the way of the tree of life."

In contrast with the *Expulsion* from " the tree of life we have here, at the close of the Apocalypse, " right to the tree of life " (*v.* 14) ; and the *Invitation* to "the water of life." The seed of the woman had been bruised in the heel ; the Serpent's head has been crushed. Hence the invitation " Come " can now be sent forth.

Man, who had been " sent forth " and " driven out," now at length sees Paradise restored, and hears the blessed invitation, " Come."

It is interesting to note how this invitation is given.

The Spirit first gives forth the welcome word, " Come "

The Bride who has been revealed from heaven repeats it.

Those who hear it take it up, and

Those who are athirst, and all who will are invited to come and " take the water of life freely."

Israel, who ought to have been the Bride, was blessed, and entrusted with the charge to " be a blessing " and to bring in full earthly blessing. Israel should have brought back Paradise again.

But Israel was unfaithful, and instead of being a Bride, became a harlot (Isa. i. 21). Hence, God removed Himself from them ; and, the Cherubim, the symbols of His presence, were taken away altogether.

Beautiful it is to see the recovered position of the Remnant, as the Bride, giving the invitation to " come " into Paradise restored.

The first Paradise was in the keeping of Adam and

his Bride. The man did not lose it for his race. He was "not in the transgression" (1 Tim. ii. 14). It was the woman, through Satan, who lost it.

But now, all is reversed. Satan is cast into the lake of fire; and it is the Bride who is privileged to say "Come!"

" The woman being deceived" was the cause of the sentence to go *forth;* but now, in this blessed time of reversal, she is the one to say "Come!"

The second man, the last Adam, has "restored all things" and " made all things new."

In this we see that Genesis is the book of the *beginnings;* and the Apocalypse is the book of the *endings,* the complement of Genesis (p. 57). Gen. i., ii. finds its correspondence in Rev. xxi., xxii.; and the last two chapters of the Bible refer back to the first two.

In the previous Benediction (*v.* 14), the blessing consisted in the right to eat of " the tree of life." In this it is the invitation to come and drink of " the water of life."

The first dread sentence is thus reversed, and the New Earth becomes Paradise restored. (See page 672-675).

" The Tree of Life," and " the Water of Life " are the great central subjects of the New Earth.

THE FOURTH (AND LAST) FOUR

a¹ (page 677), xxii. 18-. *The Lord Jesus Himself Testifying*

18-. 𝕴 *testify unto everyone that heareth the words of the prophecy of this book,]* The Lord Jesus Himself closes up the whole testimony. The pronoun " I " is very emphatic.

---

* G.L.T.Tr.A. WH. and RV. read μαρτυρῶ ἐγὼ (*marturō egō*) *I testify,* instead of συμμαρτυροῦμαι γὰρ (*summarturoumai gar*) *for I jointly testify.*

b⁴. (page 677), xxii. -18, 19. *The Things Testified*

-18. **If anyone add unto these things, God shall add unto him the plagues which are written in this book:** (19) **And if anyone take away from the words of** the **book of this prophecy, God shall take away his part from the tree* of life, and [out of] the holy city, which are written in this book.]** He who has given this book (i. 1) now closes it with this solemn warning. This warning, while it may refer especially to this book, yet, by a very true *application*, takes in the whole Scripture. But only the prophecy of this book comes within the true scope of this passage. The threat shows the extreme importance set by God upon this book. The adding of the "plagues" shows also the true character of the judgments recorded in the book; which are as real as those referred to in Deut. iv. 2; xii. 32.

There may be a still more literal interpretation which only those will understand whose lot will be cast in that dispensation of judgment.

c⁴. (page 677), xxii. 20. *The Advent*

20. **He who testifieth these things saith, "Surely I come quickly. Amen."]** So it will verily be.

This is the final announcement of the coming advent of the Lord Jesus. It is given by Himself. This is the one great subject of the whole book. It is all "prophecy," and this final promise is the key to its interpretation. To this, the Apostle, and all who hear, and read, and keep the words of the book of this prophecy, respond with holy, heart-felt desire.

---

* So G.L.T.Tr.A. WH. and RV.

Come, Lord Jesus| the use of the word "Lord"
characterises the utterance as John's : for none of His
people were ever so irreverent as to address Him merely
as Jesus. He Himself may do so, and say " I, Jesus."
The Holy inspiring Spirit may call Him " Jesus." But
it is irreverence of the grossest kind for His people ever to
address Him other than as Lord, Master, Saviour, or
Christ. John speaks of Him here, and also in the
Benediction that follows, as " Lord."

The Lord may condescend to call us "brethren " in
holy, infinite condescension ; but it is quite a different
thing for us to call Him "our elder brother." One
great lesson and effect of this book will be to inspire us
with greater reverence for Him who is at once the
author and subject of the Revelation.

Yea : in very deed and truth (He says) "I am
coming," and we reply, Amen, let it be verified :
Come, Lord Jesus ; let Thy parting promise be speedily
fulfilled.

d⁴. (page 677), xxii. 21. The Benediction

21. **The grace of* the Lord Jesus Christ† be with
all the Saints. Amen.‡**] This Benediction not only
completes the correspondence of the Structure, but
appropriately concludes the book, for, after all, there
was grace in giving Israel the Law, and there must be

---

* G.L.T.Tr.A. WH. and RV. omit " our."

† L.T. A. RV. (text, not margin), omit "Christ." WH. put it in
brackets.

‡ The Textual critics, as well as the oldest MSS., are much divided
as to these last four words. The weight of evidence is against " you,"
and in favour of " saints."

grace even in a dispensation of works. But "true" grace came by Jesus Christ. And now, in this dispen- sation, ALL is of grace. It is this that gives the Church its different standing and different destiny. May we, while we strive to rightly divide the word of truth, know, more and more fully, our own standing in grace; and thus be more and more qualified to understand the ways and words of God with reference to the coming dispensation of judgment, and the dispen- sation of glory which will follow it.

APPENDIX

On the Relation of Astrology to the Apocalypse

The Apocalypse has been branded by the enemies of revealed truth as a sacred fiction ; and the very early Christians had to bear the charge of Pagans that on account of there being such a resemblance between it and the worship of the SUN, as Tertullian says, they (the Christians) were only looked upon as another sect of sun worshippers, and that the construction of the book, and the symbols employed, are but borrowed ideas from Pagan Mysteries.

The conditions under which the apostle received these unfoldings as to himself, and the manner of presentation—by word and scenically portrayed—are said to be after the same order and with the same formula as that used by the hierophant in his dealings with the aspirant as he goes through the ordeal of initiation into those mysteries.

But this, instead of being a difficulty, is really a help to the understanding of the book, when we take into account the conditions of the period at which it was written, and the purpose God had in view in making this the closing book of Inspiration ; for it not only reflected upon the idolatry then prevailing, but looked onward to the great apostacy of the last days when that idolatry shall through Satanic energy again prevail and become the established religion of humanity.

There is such a thing as Divine irony. It is used with great effect when Elijah confronts the priests of Baal. So, here, the priests of Baal are once more to be met; and they are challenged with their own weapons.

When Jehovah was about to interfere on His people's behalf, and accomplish their deliverance from the tyranny of Pharaoh, He spake thus to Moses, that not only man and beast should suffer, but "against all the gods of Egypt I will execute judgment. I AM JEHOVAH" (Exodus xii. 12). It will be seen that every plague that was sent pointed to some characteristic quality or attribute supposed to belong to their gods, or to prove their impotence in what they professed to control.

This but foreshadows the days in which John was to *prophesy*. When established religion will be set up in a more blasphemous and defiant form, it will not only be the worship of demons—gods—and departed heroes; but also a living MAN who shall declare that he is GOD; at the same time blaspheming the God of Heaven. Then it is that we see the very weapons of their false philosophy turned against the foe to their eternal shame.

God graciously gave to Moses the evidence of the power He was about to delegate to him and also to Aaron in the first sign before they went into Pharaoh, when the rod which was cast on the ground became a serpent.

This is a well-recognised performance of all magicians to the present day. When they both went into Pharaoh with the magicians, every man's rod did the same, but Aaron's rod swallowed up their rods. To the King it was but the performance of another magician. This is an instance of the very weapons of the magicians' art being used against them. In the case of the sixth plague it is equally evident, for according to *Gleig* quoted in *The Philosophy of the Plan of Salvation*, "there were several altars upon which human sacrifices were occasionally offered when they desired to propitiate Typhon (the Serpent), the Evil Principle." The victims were burned, their ashes gathered, and the priests cast them into the air in order that evil might be averted from every place to which they were wafted. Moses does the same ; but affliction followed to King and people.

Then follows a blow against the worship of Osiris and Isis—the Sun and the Moon—who were supposed to control the elements. Jehovah strikes a blow against such wicked pretensions, and for three days the place is wrapped in "darkness that might be felt," and in this way God again asserted His supremacy.

The greatest blow of all was reserved for the last. The worship of the Sun-God was the prevailing worship of Egypt, and human sacrifice was followed in its ritual.

"The sacrifice of the *firstborn* in honour of the Sun-god (Osiris) was one of the most notorious rites of ancient Semitic worship. The first month of the year, and the first sign of the Zodiac referred to this sacrifice, called ' the *Sacrifice of Bel*.' It is to Accad, and not to Phœnicia, that we must look for the origin of human sacrifice in Western Asia. This inference is verified by two cuneiform texts in which mention is made of human sacrifice. We have clear indications in these of the sacrifice of children, such as took place in Carthage, in Phœnicia, and in Palestine—also in the British Isles " (*Trans. Bib. Arch.*, iv., p. 25, taken from *Trans. Victoria Inst.*, vol. xiv., p. 113).

This was the last and most staggering blow at their idolatry. This final plague brought down their whole system of religion at one blow, convincing both Pharaoh and the Egyptians that they had to deal with one who was above all gods, and declared his name, " I AM JEHOVAH."

This review of Israel's history in their beginnings prepares us to look for the same analogies in their future deliverance which the Book of Revelation records, the circumstances being in a very large measure parallel; Idolatry, as we have stated, being restored and established as the " religion of humanity." This shows why there is a very great similarity between the plagues of the one and the judgments of the other.

We have before us a book of 800 pages, in which the writer labours to prove that in this Revelation we have nothing more than an imitation of the mysteries or the revelations of Ceres. But as paganism will be again revived, and demon gods worshipped, and a greater than Pharaoh dispute God's title to deliver His people, the same procedure is adopted as when He first brought them out of Egypt, and blow follows blow, growing in intensity, and the very ceremonies observed common to initiation.

Yea, with greater blows, and with judgments of greater intensity, will Jehovah assert His glory and His power. See Ex. xxxiv. 10.

Extract from *The Origin of Pagan Idolatry*, by the Rev. George Stanley Faber, B.D., book vi., pp. 642 and 643 :—

" The whole machinery of the Apocalypse, from beginning to end, seems to me very plainly to have been borrowed from the machinery of the ancient

Mysteries: and this, if we consider the nature ot the subject, was done with the very strictest attention to poetical decorum.

"St. John himself is made to personate *an aspirant* about to be initiated: and, accordingly, the images presented to his mind's eye closely resemble the pageants of the Mysteries, both *in nature* and *in order of succession*.

"The prophet first beholds *a door opened* in the magnificent temple of heaven: and into this he is invited to enter by the voice of one, who plays *the hierophant*. Here he witnesses the unsealing of *a sacred book*: and forthwith he is appalled by a troop of *ghastly apparitions*, which flit in horrid succession before his eyes.

"Among these are pre-eminently conspicuous *a vast serpent*, the well-known symbol of the great father; and two portentous *wild beasts*, which severally come up out of the sea and out of the earth.

"Such hideous figures correspond with the canine phantoms of the Orgies which seemed to rise out of the ground, and with the polymorphic images of the principal hero-god who was universally deemed the offspring of the sea.

"Passing these terrific monsters in safety, the prophet, constantly attended by his *angel-heirophant* who acts the part of an interpreter, is conducted into the presence of *a female*, who is described as closely resembling the great mother of pagan theology.

"Like Isis, emerging from the sea and exhibiting herself to the eyes of the aspirant Apuleius, this female divinity, upborne upon the marine wild-beast, appears to float upon the surface of many waters. She is said to be *an open and systematical harlot*; just as the mother was the declared female principle of the fecundity, and she was also propitiated by literal fornication reduced to a religious system : and, as the initiated were made to drink a prepared liquor out of a sacred goblet ; so this harlot is represented as intoxicating the kings of the earth with *the golden cup* of her prostitution.

" On her forehead the very name of MYSTERY is inscribed : and the label teaches us that, in point of character, she is *the great universal mother* of idolatry.

" The nature of this Mystery *the officiating hiero-phant* undertakes to explain : and an important prophecy is most curiously and artfully veiled under the very language and imagery of the Orgies. To the sea-born great father was ascribed a three-fold state ; he lived, he died, and he revived : and these changes of condition were duly exhibited in the Mysteries.

" To the sea-born wild beast is similarly ascribed a three-fold state ; he lives, he dies, and he revives While dead, he lies floating on the mighty ocean, just like Horus or Osirus or Siva or Vishnou : when he revives, again like those kindred deities, he emerges from the waves : and, whether dead or alive, he bears seven heads and ten horns, corresponding in number with the seven ark-preserved Rishis and the ten aboriginal patriarchs.

" Nor is this all : as the worshippers of the great father bore his special mark or stigma, and were distinguished by his name ; so the worshippers of the maritime beast bear his mark, and are equally decorated by his appellation.

" At length, however, *the first* or *doleful part* of these sacred Mysteries draws to a close, and *the last* or *joyful part* is rapidly approaching. After the prophet has beheld the enemies of God plunged into a dreadful lake or inundation of liquid fire, which corresponds with the infernal lake or deluge of the Orgies, he is introduced into *a splendidly illuminated region*, expressly adorned with the characteristics of that *Paradise* which was the ultimate scope of the ancient aspirants : while, *without* the holy gate of admission, are the whole multitude of the profane, *dogs and sorcerers and whoremongers and murderers and idolators and whosoever loveth and maketh a lie.*

" The comparison might have been drawn out to a greater length ; but these hints may suffice."

He also remarks that :

" in the celebration of the mysteries, things were scenically and therefore literally exhibited " (Faber p. 149, vol. iii.).

One great fact is clearly established—for it was not many years after the writing of the Apocalypse, in the early centuries, that this book was discredited by the Fathers.

Jerome says that the Greek churches rejected it. When it first appeared it was not only attacked by the Eastern Christians, but, according to them, victoriously refuted : and it was looked upon by them as being at the best an obscure and bad poem on the SUN in spring. (*Epist.* cxxiii. *ad Dard,* quoted from *Mankind: their Origin and Destiny*, p. 511).

This is taken from a work, the purpose of which is to prove that the Apocalypse is *not a Divine Revelation* at all. Many have arrived at this conclusion besides this author; that not only this book, but that the whole Bible is written and constructed from the mysteries of Paganism. Even that excellent and reverent writer (Mr. Faber) asserts that the Apostle John used the ideas and phraseology of the mysteries, the basis of them being Serpent and SUN worship with the host of heaven.

" Occulus, who was a pupil of Pythagoras, says, ' The universe considered as a whole, displays nothing to us which betrays a commencement, or which foretells destruction; no one has seen it created, or increased, or improved, or deteriorated, or decreased; it is ever the same, existing in the same way, always equal, or similar to itself!'" (cap. i. § 6, *Origin and Destiny*, p. 394).

Further evidence is forthcoming to show that there was design in the figuration of the Constellations. This is from the Babylonian tablets known as the *Creation Legend*. It states that "some divine personage prepared the mansions ... He fixed the stars. Even the Lumâsi " (which word Prof. Sayce translates as meaning ' the Sheep of the Hero,' the *Hero* being the Sun). The conclusion arrived at is that the divine arranger fixed the constellations for each of the twelve months. (See *Primitive Constellations*, Robert Brown, Junr., vol. ii., p. 1, 1900).

An interesting account is also given of a recent scene on the Euphrates. It is called a prayer meeting of Star worshippers. The writer says that " to the number of about four thousand they still survive in their native land, principally along the banks of the Euphrates. They call themselves Mandaites, possessors of the ' Word,' the ' LIVING WORD.' "*

They erect their " MISHKNA " or tabernacle. " Towards midnight the Star worshippers, men and women, come slowly down to the Mishkna by the riverside . . . a signal is given, and a procession of priests moves to the Mishkna. One ' deacon' holds aloft the large wooden tau-cross . . . The sacred book SIDRA RABBA is laid upon the altar, folded back where the liturgy of the living is divided from the ritual of the dead. The high priest takes a live pigeon," extends his hands towards the polar star, upon which he fixes his eyes, and lets the bird fly, calling aloud, " In the name of the living one, blessed be the primitive light, the ancient light, the Divinity self-created " (Ibid., pp. 177-8).

" . . . Here, as so frequently, terrestrial ritual is based upon, and is a ' pattern ' of ' things in the heaven ' " (Ibid., p. 185).

" The stars near the *Centaur* permitted the introduction of a further figure, the Wild-beast, which, originally forming part of the constellation, showed the triumph of the Sun-god over the Beast of darkness, and over his own solar Lion " (p. 241).

" . . . Such then were the principles which obtained in the formation of the primitive constellations. Religious and mythological ideas, already *long current* and venerated, were stamped upon the sky as sacred and celestial forms."

" . . . The system so formulated in the Euphrates

* Our capitals.

valley was accepted and adopted in Western Asia. The constellations of Israelite and Phœnecian were those of Babylonian and Assyrian, even as Bêl reappeared as Baal, and Istar as Ashtoreth " (Ibid., pp. 240-2).

" The southern heavens are a reduplication of the northern, and regarded as the watery region. In this region is *Cetus*, which tries to devour the child of the woman " (R. Brown, Junr., *Law of Cosmic Order, Astrology in Apocalypse*, p. 81).

" He casts forth a river, it is there on the planisphere. It flows down below the horizon into the underworld. This Cetus is the beast rising out of the sea.

" The Beast upon whom sits the woman is Babylon."

" In the planisphere she sits upon Hydra, the seven or many headed dragon, which issues from the Crater or Chaos. All the fowls were filled with her flesh. This is the crow devouring the Hydra " (p. 91).

" The Tribes were considered parallel to the Zodiacal signs" (p. 113).

" The Apocalypse is a magnificent dream of the final triumph of Christ over Antichrist, a glorious vision of the moral cosmos of God's world, wrought out in conflict with Anarchy, and practically a warning and a consolation to the people of God in the time of their persecution " (p. 92).

Mr. Maunder refers to a great astronomical revolution that took place subsequent to the first naming of the signs. " Five thousand years ago, the Zodiac was planned, with the Bull of Taurus for its leader. Aries was then the last and least important of the twelve. The next view that we get of the state of Astronomy is some 2,000 years later. The Ram of Aries is now the prince of the Zodiac, Taurus has dropped to a second place, and the Zodiac itself has suffered an important change. . . How that revolution came about we have at present no means of knowing; but it has hitherto interposed a great barrier to our learning either from classical literature or from myths or monuments, anything trustworthy as to the true origin of the constellations, for the reason that the sources we have been consulting are, in consequence of that revolution, as ignorant of the matter as ourselves . . " (*XIX. Century*, Sep., 1900, No. 283, p. 459. Article, " The Oldest Picture Book of All ").

All this evidence goes to show that there is more than meets the eye in this wonderful Book.

To the unenlightened reader there is much that is meaningless. But when we consider the grand scope of the Apocalypse we can understand why it should look backward to the beginning and onward to the end; writing folly on man's perversion of primitive truth, smiting with judgment those who will attempt to revive it; and showing that the God of heaven is high over all the gods of the heathen. They will be unable to protect their worshippers when the living God shall arise to shake terribly the earth.

INDEX OF SUBJECTS

INDEX OF TEXTS

DANIEL

726 / Index of Texts

3:8	394
3:9	238
4:6	358
4:7	532
4:10	238
5:1	550
5:1-11	548, 549
6:12	394
6:13	613
8:3	648
9:9	52, 248
9:9, 10	598
9:19	254
10:3	254
10:10, 11	487
11:1-9	207
11:9	431
12:4-8	110
12:9, 10	54
12:10	146
12:11	489
12:14	630
13	634
13:7	237
14:1-4	110
14:9	617
14:14	310
14:16-19	635
14:20	240
14:20, 21	228

MALACHI

3:3	208
3:7	83
3:16	87
4:1	484
4:3	186
4:5	50, 51

MATTHEW

2:4-7	402
3:2	170, 268
3:11	22
4:1	337
4:6	403
4:8	133
4:17	170
4:23	450
4:29	463
5:10-12	377, 588
5:18	647
5:31	39
5:33-37	340
5:34-39	290
5:45	564
8:4	133
8:16	140
8:20	16
8:24	403
8:29	319
9:34	290
9:35	450
10:1-8	333
10:22	172
10:32	196
10:32, 33	96
10:39	616
10:41, 42	378
11:3	22
11:14	356
11:14, 15	51
11:15	50
11:17	458
11:20-24	650
11:27	133
12:28, 43-45	424
13:9, 43	50
13:10, 11, 34, 35	340
13:10-16	133
13:15	51
13:16	263
13:24	628
13:30-42	610
13:35	399
13:37	461
13:37-39	159
13:41	463
14:15	543

COMPARISONS

INDEX OF STRUCTURES

INDEX OF
GREEK WORDS EXPLAINED

INDEX OF
HEBREW WORDS EXPLAINED

OTHER TITLES BY E. W. BULLINGER

THE COMPANION BIBLE

The most complete and extensive one-volume study Bible available in the King James Version. *The Companion Bible* is a guide to the content and inter-related structure of God's Word for both pastor and layman alike.

ISBN 0-8254-2203-5   2141 pp.   hardcover

**GREAT CLOUD OF WITNESSES
IN HEBREWS ELEVEN**

A classic exposition including an examination of the great heroes of the faith. Full of rich, practical applications.

ISBN 0-8254-2247-7   462 pp.   paperback

NUMBER IN SCRIPTURE

A complete synopsis of the spiritual significance of numbers found in the Bible; a very famous reference book on biblical numerology.

ISBN 0-8254-2238-8   312 pp.   paperback

WITNESS OF THE STARS

An in-depth study of the constellations and principal stars as they pertain to prophetic truth. More than 40 charts and diagrams are included.

ISBN 0-8254-2245-0   212 pp.   paperback

WORD STUDIES ON THE HOLY SPIRIT
(Foreword by Warren W. Wiersbe)

An examination of each of the 385 occurrences of *pneuma* (spirit) in the New Testament by one of the greatest Greek and Hebrew scholars. Includes subject, text, and Greek word indexes.

ISBN 0-8254-2246-9   232 pp.   paperback

Available from your local Christian bookstore, or

P.O. Box 2607, Grand Rapids, MI 49501